Beginner's Guide to C# 2005

(With .NET 3.0)

First Edition

By

Gagan Sahoo

MCA

Khanna Book Publishing Co.(p) Ltd.

Delhi

Beginner's Guide to C# 2005 (With .NET 3.0)
by Gagan Sahoo

Published by Sheetal Khanna
For Khanna Book Publishing Co.(p) Ltd.
1694-95, Nai Sarak, Delhi - 110006
Ph No. : 011-23256658, 23283211
e-mail: contact@khannaedu.com

First Edition : October' 2007

Printed: Ziya Offset Works

Laser typesetting at : **Sharma Computers**, Sector – VII, Rohini, Delhi – 110085

PREFACE

The computers are becoming increasingly popular in day-to-day functioning in all kinds of work. At home and at work, small, compact electronic digital computers have moved more rapidly through the stages of development, deployment and social incorporation than any major technological innovation in history. That much is widely recognized.

.NET is the Microsoft Web services strategy to connect information, people, systems and devices through software. Integrated across the Microsoft platform, .NET technology provides the ability to quickly build, deploy, manage and use connected, security-enhanced solutions with Web services.

The Microsoft platform includes everything a business needs to develop and deploy a Web service-connected IT architecture: servers to host Web services, development tools to create them, applications to use them, and a worldwide network provide any help you need.

Microsoft C# as a simple, modern, object-oriented and type-safe programming language derived from C and C++. Most independent observers would probably change that to "derived from C, C++ and Java". Syntactically, C# is very similar to both C++ and Java, to such an extent that many keywords are the same and C# also shares the same block structure with braces ({ }) to mark blocks o code and semicolons to separate statements. C# language is designed from the start to work with .NET 3.0, however, means that its support for the features of .NET is both more complete and offered within the context of a more suitable syntax than for those other languages. While the C# language itself is very similar to Java, there are some improvements; in particular, Java is not designed to work with the .NET environment.

The 1st edition of this book is prepared for the students, developers, programmers and other audience like university students who studying BCA, MCA, MSc, BTech, MTech, etc can take as a prior text material for C# course with .NET 3.0. This book covers the basic concepts of C# technology with extensive practice exercises and solved examples inside chapter contents.

Author takes major efforts on examples on related topics. In each and every section of the book, the examples are given to step forward the concepts. Also, the beginners and expert developer can take help of the book for enhance their ability in C#.NET 3.0 technology. The authors try to implicit all types of questions in this material. Also, the free CD contains chapter-wise programs for quick reference. All the programs are executed under .NET 2005 environment with .NET 3.0.

Also, I would like to convey my sincere thanks to Mr. Puneet Khanna, **Khanna Book Publishing Co.(p) Ltd.** and his dedicated team for bringing out this book in an excellent form.

Valuable suggestions are comments for improvement are most welcome through Publishers.

Gagan Sahoo
Email : gbsahoo@yahoo.com

About The Author

Gagan Sahoo has more than 15 years of experience in the computer field working as a software developer, director of software development. He is a well-known author of various computer books including, VB, C++, Java. Since last 10 years, he has lots of experience in different computer project works. He has written number of project books including FoxPro, C, C++, VB, etc.

He has been programming in .NET since 2003 and tested so many code on Microsoft's .NET environment. His prime development of **Beginner's Guide to C# 2005 (With .NET 3.0)** book is one of the emerging .NET technology which was written to fullfil the need and development guide for the students and developers.

Contents

3. Variables and Data Types

.NET Framework 1

1.1 Introduction

Microsoft introduced its .NET technology in 2001. .NET (dot-net) is the name Microsoft gives to its general vision of the future of computing, the view being of a world in which many applications run in a distributed manner across the Internet. The languages (C++, Visual Basic 6.0, Java), frameworks (MFC, ATL, STL) and architectures COM, CORBA, EJB) that were touted as the silver bullets of software development eventually become overshadowed by something better or at the very least something new. The .NET Framework 3.0 platform is Microsoft's current offering within the land-scape of software engineering.

To the programmer's eye, the .NET Framework 3.0 platform consists of a runtime environment coupled with a base class library. If you are new to .NET, it is necessary to embrace some new ideas. .NET 3.0 changes the way you think of dealing with legacy code and version control; it changes the way program resources are disposed of; it permits code developed in one language to be used by another; it simplifies code deployment by eliminating a reliance on the system registry; and it creates a self-describing meta-language that can be used to determine program logic at runtime. A key component of the .NET 3.0 architecture is Web services, which are applications that can be used over the Internet. Clients and other applications can use these Web services as reusable building blocks.

1.2 Why .NET Framework ?

The Microsoft .NET Framework 3.0 is a platform for building, deploying, and running Web Services and applications. It provides a highly productive, standards-based, multi-language environment for integrating existing investments with next-generation applications and services as well as the agility to solve the challenges of deployment and operation of Internet-scale applications. The .NET Framework consists of three main parts: the common language runtime, a hierarchical set of unified class libraries, and a componentized version of Active Server Pages called ASP.NET.

The .NET Framework is one of the widest features for running applications on the Internet. To achieve these broad objectives, the .NET Framework designed settled on an architecture that separates the framework into two parts : the Common Language Runtime (CLR) and the Framework Class Library (FCL) as shown below :

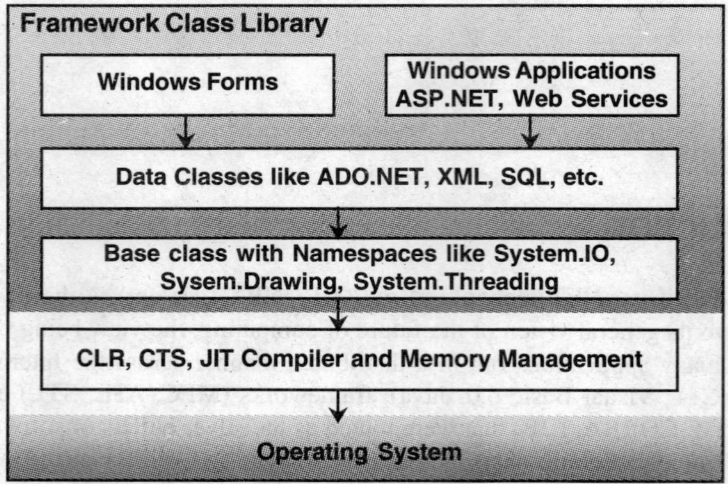

Fig. 1.1 .NET Framework class library.

The CLR – which is Microsoft's implementation of the CLI standard – handles code execution and all of the tasks associated with it: compilation, memory management, security, thread management and enforcement of type safety and use. Code that runs under CLR is referred to as managed code. This is to distinguish it from unmanaged code that does not implement the requirements to run in the CLR – such as COM or Windows API based components.

The other major component, the Framework Class Library, is a reusable code library of types (classes, structures and so on) available to applications running under .NET. As the above figure shows, these include classes for database access, graphics, inter-operating with unmanaged code, security and both Web and Windows forms. All languages that target the .NET Framework use this common class library. Thus, after you gain experience using these types, you can apply that knowledge to any .NET language you may choose to program in.

Firstly, distributed computing is rather like object oriented programming, in that it encourages specialized code to be collected in one place, rather than copied redundantly in lots of places. There are thus potential efficiency gains to be made in moving to the distributed model.

Secondly, by collecting specialized code in one place and opening up a generally accessible interface to it, different types of machines (phones, handhelds, desktops, etc.) can all be supported with the same code. Hence Microsoft's 'run-anywhere' aspiration.

Thirdly, by controlling real-time access to some of the distributed nodes (especially those concerning authentication), companies like Microsoft can control more easily the running of its applications. It moves applications further into the area of 'services provided' rather than 'objects owned'.

Interestingly, in taking on the .NET vision, Microsoft seems to have given up some of its proprietary tendencies (whereby all the technology it touched was warped towards its Windows operating system). Because it sees its future as providing software services in distributed applications, the .NET framework has been written so that applications on other platforms will be able to access these services. For example, .NET has been built upon open standard technologies like XML and SOAP.

At the development end of the .NET vision is the .NET Framework. This contains the Common Language Runtime, the .NET Framework Classes, and higher-level features like ASP.NET (the next generation of Active Server Pages technologies) and WinForms (for developing desktop applications).

The Common Language Runtime (CLR) manages the execution of code compiled for the .NET platform. The CLR has two interesting features. Firstly, its specification has been opened up so that it can be ported to non-Windows platforms. Secondly, any number of different languages can be used to manipulate the .NET framework classes, and the CLR will support them. This has led one commentator to claim that under .NET the language one uses is a 'lifestyle choice'.

Not all of the supported languages fit entirely neatly into the .NET framework, however (in some cases the fit has been somewhat Procrustean). But the one language that is guaranteed to fit in perfectly is C#. This new language, a successor to C++, has been released in conjunction with the .NET framework, and is likely to be the language of choice for many developers working on .NET applications.

As we kown Microsoft started development on the .NET Framework in the late 90s originally under the name of Next Generation Windows Services (NGWS). By late 2000 the first beta versions of .NET 1.0 were being released. Since then, the development reach to till .NET Framework 3.0 and 3.5 Beta 1.

1.3 .NET Framework 3.0

The Microsoft .NET Framework 3.0 (formerly WinFX) is the new managed code programming model for Windows. It combines the power of the .NET Framework version 2.0 with new technologies for building applications that have visually compelling user experiences, seamless communication across technology boundaries, and the ability to support a wide range of business processes. These new technologies are Windows Presentation Foundation (WPF), Windows Communication Foundation (WCF), Windows Workflow Foundation (WWF) and Windows CardSpace (WCS). The .NET Framework 3.0 is included as part of the Windows Vista™ operating system; you can install it or uninstall it using Windows Features Control Panel. This redistributable package is for Windows XP and Windows Server 2003.

Use the .NET Framework 3.0 today to build applications that have visually compelling user experiences, seamless communication across technology boundaries, the ability to support a wide range of business processes, and an easier way to manage your personal information online. This is the same great WinFX technology you know and love, now with a new name that identifies it for exactly what it is – the next version of Microsoft's development framework.

.NET 3 includes a new set of managed code APIs that are an integral part of Windows Vista and Windows Server 2008 operating systems. It is also available for Windows XP SP2 and Windows Server 2003 as a download. There are no major architectural changes included with this release; .NET Framework 3.0 includes version 2.0 of the Common Language Runtime.

.NET Framework 3.0 consists of four major new components:

- **Windows Presentation Foundation** (WPF), formerly code-named **Avalon**; a new user interface subsystem and API based on XML and vector graphics, which uses 3D computer graphics hardware and Direct3D technologies.
- **Windows Communication Foundation** (WCF), formerly code-named **Indigo**; a service-oriented messaging system which allows programs to interoperate locally or remotely similar to web services.
- **Windows Workflow Foundation** (WWF) allows for building of task automation and integrated transactions using workflows.
- **Windows CardSpace** (WCS), formerly code-named **InfoCard**; a software component which securely stores a person's digital identities and provides a unified interface for choosing the identity for a particular transaction, such as logging in to a website.

The following Fig. 1.2 shows the architecture of the .NET Framework 3.0.

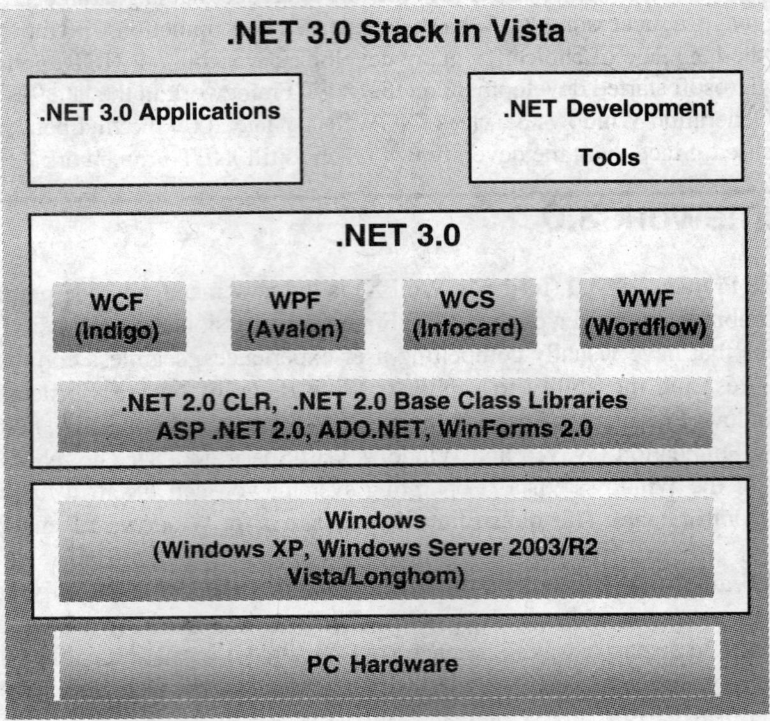

Fig. 1.2 architecture of the .NET Framework 3.0.

1.4 Features of .NET

.NET has a wide feature in software engineering. These are :

- **Full interoperability with existing code.** This is (of course) a good thing. Existing COM binaries can commingle (i.e., interop) with newer .NET binaries and vice versa. Also, Platform Invocation Service (Pinvoke) allows you to call C-based libraries (including the underlaying API of the operating system from .NET code. Programs written in different languages are all compiled into MSIL (Microsoft Intermediate Language)- the different parts can be combined to create a single, unified program. MSIL allows the .NET Framework to be language independent, because .NET programs are not tied to a particular programming language. Any language that can be compiled into MSIL is called a .NET-compliant language.
- **Complete and total language integration.** Unlike COM, .NET supports cross-language inheritance, cross-language exception handling and cross-language debugging.
- A common runtime engine shared by all .NET-aware languages. One aspect of this engine is a well-defined set of types that each .NET-aware language "understand".
- **A base class library.** This library provides shelter from the complexities of raw API calls and offers a consistent object model used by all .NET-aware languages. This library also called the Framework Class Library (FCL), can be used by any .NET language. The FCL contains a variety of reusable components, saving programmers that trouble of creating new components.
- **No more COM plumbing.** IClassFactory, IUnknown, IDispatch, IDL code and the evil VARIANT compliant data types (BSTR, SAFEARRAY, and so forth) have no place in the native .NET binary.
- **Execution Management.** The Common Language Runtime (CLR) is another central part of the .NET Framework – it executes C# programs. The CLR manages memory, security and other features, relieving the programmer of these responsibilities.
- **A truly simplified deployment mode.** Under .NET, there is no need to register a binary unit into the system registry. Furthermore, .NET allows multiple versions of the same *.dll to exist in harmony on a single machine.

1.5 Microsoft .NET and CLI Standards

The CLI defines a platform-independent virtual code execution environment. It specifies no operation system, so it could just as easily be Linux as Windows. The centerpiece of the standard is the definition of a Common Intermediate Language (CIL) that must be produced by CLI (Common Language Infrastructure) compliant compilers and a type system that defines the data types supported by any compliant language. That is, this intermediate code is compiled into the native language of its host operating system.

The CLI also includes the standards for the C# language, which was developed and promoted by Microsoft. As such it is the de facto standard language for .NET. However, other vendors have quickly adopted the CIL standard and produced – just a new a few – Python, Pascal, Fortran, Cobol and Eiffel .NET compilers.

As in Fig. 1.1, the .NET Framework is the Microsoft's implementation of the CLI standards. The most important thing to not about this implementation is that it contains a great deal more features that are specified by the CLI architecture which shown in Fig. 1.3.

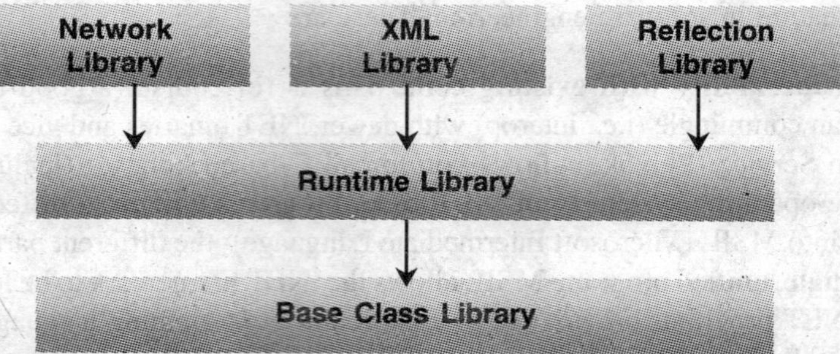

Fig. 1.3 CLI architecture.

The CLI implements in two aspects : the Kernel Profile and the Compact Profile. The Kernel Profile contains

- the types and classes. That is, the **Base Class Library** holds the basic data type classes as well as classes that provide simple file access, define security attributes and implement one-dimensional arrays.

The Compact Profile adds three class libraries :

- an XML library that defines simple XML parsing
- a Network library that provides HTTP support and access to ports
- and a Reflection library that supports reflection (a way for a program to examine itself through metacode)

1.5.1 CTS

Another building block of the .NET platform is the Common Type System (CTS). The common type system is a rich type system, built into the common language runtime, which supports the types and operations found in most programming languages. The common type system supports the complete implementation of a wide range of programming languages.

The CTS specification fully describes all possible data types and programming constructs supported by the runtime, specifies how these entities can interact with each other and detains how they represented in the .NET metadata format. Fig. 1.4 shows how .NET organize the CTS.

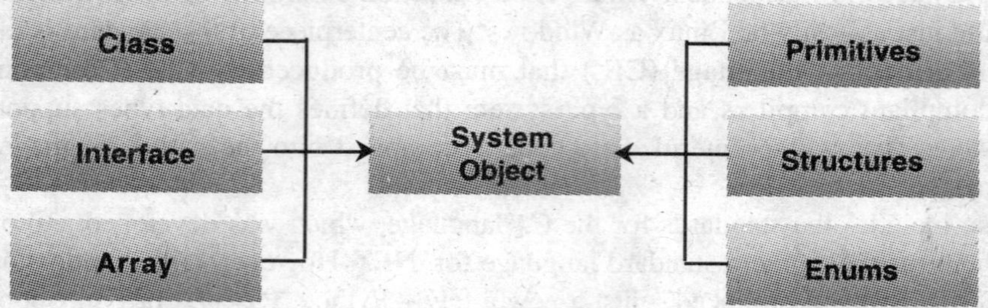

Fig. 1.4 Common Type System's base type.

From Fig. 1.4, it is obvious that the object has two categories : reference or value types. This taxonomy is based on how the types are stored and accessed in memory: reference types are accessed in s special memory area called a heap) via pointers, whereas value types are referenced directly in a program stack. The other things to note is that all types, both custom and .NET defined, must inherit from the predefined System.Object type. This ensures that all types support a basic set of inherited methods and properties.

That is the reference types are often referred to as classes and value types as structures (or just structs), mostly a byproduct of C#'s keyword class and struct used to declare them.
An instance of a reference type, called an object, is allocated and managed on the Garbage Collected (GC) heap and all read, write and sharing of it are performed through a reference (i.e., a pointer indirection).

A value type instance, called a value, on the other hand, is allocated inline as a sequence of bytes, the location of which based on the scope in which it is defined.

A compiler that is compliant with the CTS specifications is guaranteed that its types can be hosted by the Common Language Runtime. This alone does not guarantee that the language can communicate with other languages.

1.5.2 CLS

The Common Language Specification is a set of constructs and constraints that serves as a guide for library writers and compiler writers. It allows libraries to be fully usable from any language supporting the CLS, and for those languages to integrate with each other. The Common Language Specification is a subset of the common type system. The Common Language Specification is also important to application developers who are writing code that will be used by other developers. When developers design publicly accessible APIs following the rules of the CLS, those APIs are easily used from all other programming languages that target the common language runtime.

1.5.3 MSIL

MSIL (Microsoft Intermediate Language) is the CPU-independent instruction set into which .NET Framework programs are compiled. It contains instructions for loading, storing, initializing, and calling methods on objects.

Combined with metadata and the common type system, MSIL allows for true cross-language integration.

Prior to execution, MSIL is converted to machine code. It is not interpreted.

1.5.4 CLR

The Common Language Runtime manages the entire life cycle of an application. It locates code, compiles it, loads associated classes, manages its execution and ensures automatic memory management. Moreover, it supports cross-language integration to the permit code generated by different languages to interact seamlessly.

The common language runtime is the execution engine for .NET Framework applications. It provides a number of services, including the following:

- Code management (loading and execution)
- Application memory isolation
- Verification of type safety
- Conversion of IL to native code
- Access to metadata (enhanced type information)
- Managing memory for managed objects
- Enforcement of code access security
- Exception handling, including cross-language exceptions
- Interoperation between managed code, COM objects, and pre-existing DLLs (unmanaged code and data)
- Automation of object layout
- Support for developer services (profiling, debugging, and so on)

Thus, if you build .NET types that only expose CLS-compliant features, you can rest assured that all construct that is outside of the bounds of the CLS, you cannot guarantee that every .NET programming language can interact with your .NET code library.

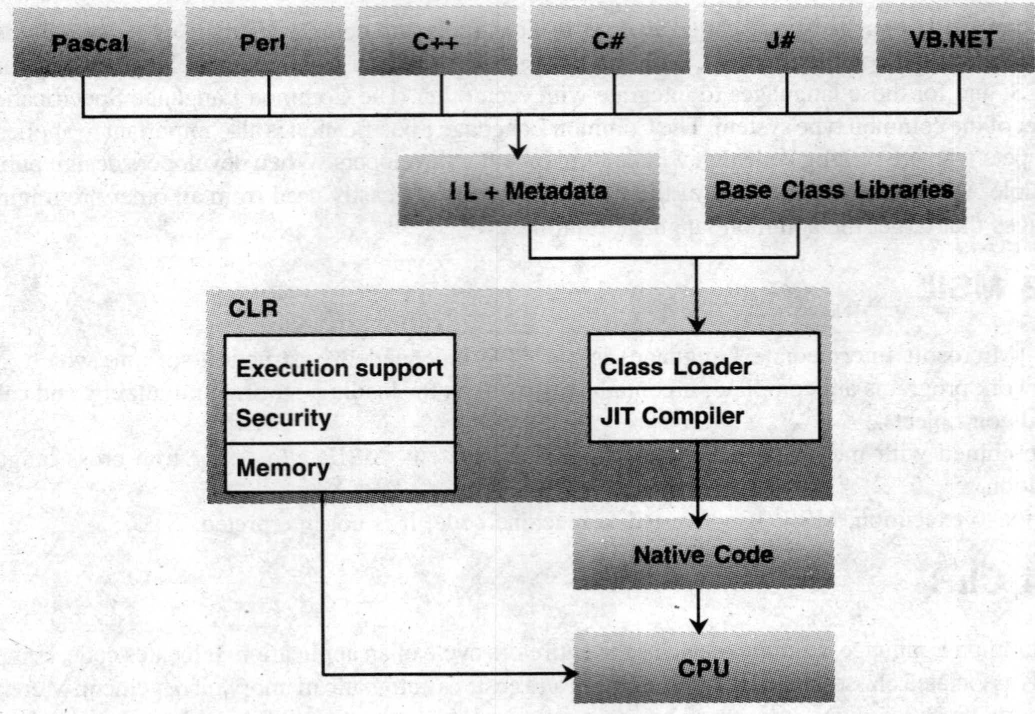

Fig. 1.5 CLR functions.

1.5.4.1 CLR Works

Compilers that are compliant with CLR generate code that is targeted for the runtime, as opposed to a specific to CPU. This code, known variously as Common Intermediate Language (CIL), Intermediate Language (IL), or Microsoft Intermediate Language (MSIL) is an assembler-type language that is packaged in an EXE or DLL file. Note that these are not standard executable files and require that the runtime's Just-in-Time (JIT) compiler convert the IL in term to a machine-specific code when an application actually runs. Because the CLR is responsible for managing this IL, the code is known as managed code.

Fig. 1.5 illustrates that the CLR neither knows – nor needs to know, which language an application is creates in. Its interaction is with the language independent IL. Because applications communicate through their IL (Intermediate Language), output from one compiler can be integrated with code produced by a different compiler. This means that IL produced on one platform can be run on any other platform that has its own framework and a JIT compiler that emits its own machine code. That is when a .NET program is executed; the CLR activates the JIT compiler. The JIT compiler converts MSIL into native code on a demand basis as each part of your program is needed. Thus, your C# program actually executes as native code even though it is initially compiled into MSIL. This means that your program run nearly as fast as it would if it had been compiled to native code in the first place, but it gains the portability benefits of MSIL.

In addition to MSIL, one other thing is output when you compile a C# program: metadata. The metadata is a set of tables that allows each code module to be self-descriptive. It describes the data used by your program and enables your code to interact with other code. The metadata is contained in the same file as the MSIL. Metadata has following uses :

- It uses by JIT compiler, which gathers all the type of information it needs for compiling directly from the metadata.
- It uses in Garbage collection process (memory management).
- .NET provides a set of classes that provide the functionality to read metadata from within a program. This functionality is known collectively as reflection.

1.5.5 Base Class Libraries

In addition to the CLR and CTS/CLS specification, the .NET platform provides a base class library that is available to all .NET programming languages. Not only does this base class library encapsulates various primitives such as threads, file input/output (I/O), graphical rendering and interaction with various external hardware devices, but it also provide support for a number of services required by most real-world application. For a high level, you can visualize the relationship between CLR, CTS, CLS and the base class library in Fig. 1.6.

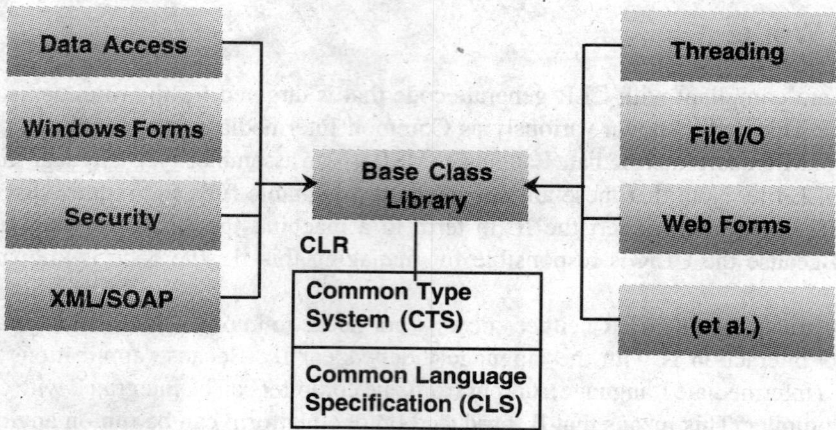

Fig. 1.6 Base class library with CLR.

1.5.6 Assemblies

An assembly is the primary building block of a .NET Framework application. It is a collection of functionality that is built, versioned, and deployed as a single implementation unit (as one or more files). All managed types and resources are marked either as accessible only within their implementation unit, or as accessible by code outside that unit.

Assemblies are self-describing by means of their manifest, which is an integral part of every assembly. The manifest:

- Establishes the assembly identity (in the form of a text name), version, culture, and digital signature (if the assembly is to be shared across applications).
- Defines what files (by name and file hash) make up the assembly implementation.
- Specifies the types and resources that make up the assembly, including which are exported from the assembly.
- Itemizes the compile-time dependencies on other assemblies.
- Specifies the set of permissions required for the assembly to run properly.

This information is used at run time to resolve references, enforce version binding policy, and validate the integrity of loaded assemblies. The runtime can determine and locate the assembly for any running object, since every type is loaded in the context of an assembly. Assemblies are also the unit at which code access security permissions are applied. The identity evidence for each assembly is considered separately when determining what permissions to grant the code it contains.

The self-describing nature of assemblies also helps makes zero-impact install and XCOPY deployment feasible.

All the managed code run in .NET must be contained in a assembly. Logically, the assembly is referenced as one EXE or DLL file. Physically, it may consist of a collection of one or more files that contain code or resources such as images or XML data.

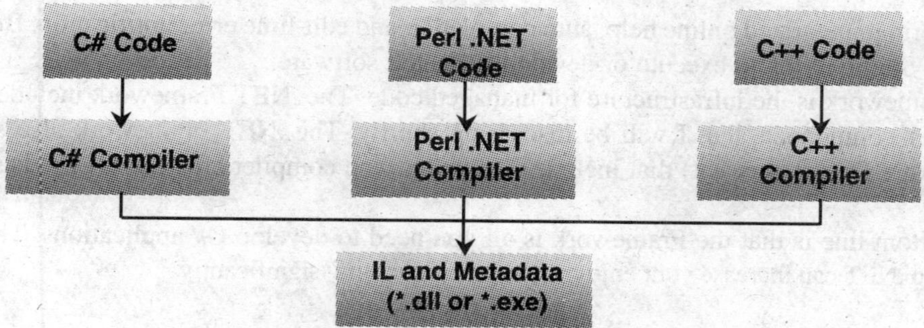

Fig. 1.7 Execution style of .NET assemblies.

As assembly is created which a .NET compatible compiler converts a file containing source code into a DLL or EXE file, but as shown in Fig. 1.7, an assembly contains a manifest, metadata and the compiler-generated Intermediate Language (IL).

- **Manifest.** Manifest is the part of metadata, describes the assembly with all the information needed about it.

  · Identity security
  · Assembly version
  · Scope of the assembly
  · Resolve references to classes and resources
  · Manifest can be store as .exe or .dll file with MSIL or separately as a PE file contains only the assembly manifest information.

- **Metadata.** Information produced by an application to describe the properties. The CLR uses metadata to load and run applications.
- **IL.** Intermediate Language (IL) is also known as Microsoft Intermediate Language (MSIL) or Common Intermediate Language (CIL). When we compile code that uses the .NET framework library we don't immediately create operating system specific code, we compile our code into IL. This IL is not specific to any O/S and also is not specific to any language supported by the .NET languages e.g. VB.NET, C#, J# VC++ etc. IL is also a language, which is converted into machine code JIT (just in time) compiler. IL is independent of the O/S machine.

1.6 Visual Studio .NET

Visual Studio .NET is not part of the .NET Framework. However, it deserves mention in an introduction of the .NET Framework. Visual Studio is an integrated development environment published by Microsoft for writing Windows programs. Visual Studio .NET can also be used to write managed applications in C#, C++, Visual Basic and any other language (such as Perl) that is integrated into the environment by a third-party.

Visual Studio .NET itself is a partially managed application and requires the .NET Framework to run. Visual Studio .NET is a very user-friendly and productive environment in which to write managed applications. It includes many helpful wizards for creating code, as well as useful features such as context coloring, integrated online help, auto completion and edit-time error notification. But, you do not need Visual Studio .NET to execute or develop managed software.

The Framework is the infrastructure for managed code. The .NET Framework includes the CLR as well as other components that I will be discussing shortly. The .NET Framework also ships with an SDK (Software Developers Kit) that includes command line compilers for C#, C++, Visual Basic, and IL.

The bottom line is that the Framework is all you need to develop C# applications. That being said Visual Studio .NET can increase your enjoyment and productivity significantly.

Exercise

1. What is .NET framework?
2. When was .NET framework announced?
3. What are the new features available in .NET 3.0?
4. Outline the features of .NET framework?
5. Define the following terms?
   - CTS
   - CLS
   - MSIL or IL
   - CLR
   - Base Class Libraries
   - CLI
6. What is Visual Studio .NET how it fits in the .NET framework?
7. What are the services provided by the CLR?

C# Basics 2

2.1 Introduction

In June 2000, Microsoft announced both the .NET platform and a new programming language called C#. C# is a strongly-typed object-oriented language designed to give the optimum blend of simplicity, expressiveness, and performance. The .NET platform is centered on a Common Language Runtime (similar to a JVM) and a set of libraries which can be exploited by a wide variety of languages which are able to work together by all compiling to an intermediate language (IL). C# and .NET are a little symbiotic: some features of C# are there to work well with .NET, and some features of .NET are there to work well with C# (though .NET aims to work well with many languages). This article is mostly concerned with C#, but sometimes it is useful to discuss .NET too. The C# language was built with the hindsight of many languages, but most notably Java and C++.

2.2 What is C#?

C# (pronounced "C sharp") is a new language designed by Microsoft to combine the power of C/C++ and the productivity of Visual Basic. This is a universal language that, although currently mostly used on the Microsoft Windows operating system, will be also used on other operating systems like Linux, BeOS, Macintosh, etc. C# is one of the languages used in the Microsoft .NET Framework. The Microsoft .NET Framework is a library of objects that create or draw things on the computer.

C# is Microsoft's new programming language for the .NET platform. It combines some of the best features of modern programming languages such as Java, C++ or Visual Basic. C# is an object-oriented language with single inheritance but multiple interfaces per class. It supports component-based programming by properties (smart fields), events and delegates (enhanced function pointers). C# is fully interoperable with other .NET languages such as VB.NET, Eiffel.NET or Oberon.NET.

Initial language specifications also reveal obvious similarities to Java, including syntax, strong web integration and automatic memory management. So, if you have programmed in either C++ or Java, adding C# to your ken of languages should be fairly straightforward.

The C# language is used to create applications that display on a black window referred to as the DOS prompt or DOS window.

2.3 C# Versus Java

Below is a list of features C# and Java share, which are intended to improve on C++.

- C# and Java are both new-generation languages descended from a line including C and C++. Each includes advanced features, like garbage collection, which remove some of the low level maintenance tasks from the programmer. In a lot of areas they are syntactically similar.
- Both C# and Java compile initially to an intermediate language: C# to Microsoft Intermediate Language (MSIL), and Java to Java bytecode. In each case the intermediate language can be run - by interpretation or just-in-time compilation - on an appropriate 'virtual machine'. In C#, however, more support is given for the further compilation of the intermediate language code into native code.
- C# contains more primitive data types than Java, and also allows more extension to the value types. For example, C# supports 'enumerations', type-safe value types which are limited to a defined set of constant variables and 'structs', which are user-defined value type.
- Unlike Java, C# has the useful feature that we can overload various operators.
- Like Java, C# gives up on multiple class inheritance in favor of a single inheritance model extended by the multiple inheritances of interfaces. However, polymorphism is handled in a more complicated fashion; with derived class methods either 'overriding' or 'hiding' super class methods.
- C# also uses 'delegates' - type-safe method pointers. These are used to implement event-handling.
- In Java, multi-dimensional arrays are implemented solely with single-dimensional arrays (where arrays can be members of other arrays. In addition to jagged arrays, however, C# also implements genuine rectangular arrays.

2.4 C# versus C++

Although it has some elements derived from Visual Basic and Java, C++ is C#'s closest relative.

- In an important change from C++, C# code does not require header files. All code is written inline.
- As touched on above, the .NET runtime in which C# runs performs memory management, taking care of tasks like garbage collection. Because of this, the use of pointers in C# is much less important than in C++. Pointers can be used in C#, where the code is marked as 'unsafe', but they are only really useful in situations where performance gains are at an absolute premium.

- Speaking generally, the 'plumbing' of C# types is different from that of C++ types, with all C# types being ultimately derived from the 'object' type. There are also specific differences in the way that certain common types can be used. For instance, C# arrays are bounds checked unlike in C++, and it is therefore not possible to write past the end of a C# array.
- C# statements are quite similar to C++ statements. To note just one example of a difference: the '**switch**' statement has been changed so that 'fall-through' behavior is disallowed.
- As mentioned above, C# gives up on the idea of multiple class inheritance. Other differences relating to the use of classes are: there is support for class 'properties' of the kind found in Visual Basic, and class methods are called using the . (dot) operator rather than the :: operator.

2.5 Why C#?

C# is directly related to C, C++ and Java. C# is someway correlated with Java. C# was originally designed by the great language expert Anders Hejlsberg in Microsoft Corporation. To developed an improved version which is more appropriate in cross-platform environment, Anders Hejlsberg and his team noted all the advanced features in C# comparing both C++ and Java. As it is parallel with Java, but take some more advancement in Windows operating system. This language takes the similar syntax of C, C++ and Java. It is fully object-oriented language. If you are little bit familiar with C/C++ syntax, then you will fill more comfortable in C#. Otherwise, this text book will guide you in depth for learning C# in .NET application.

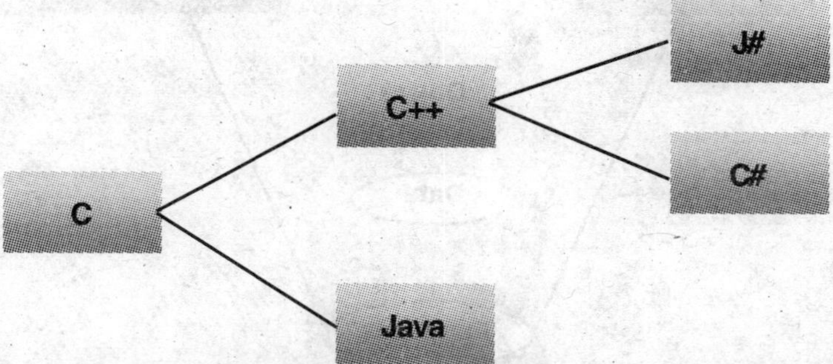

2.6 The Object-Oriented Programming (OOP) Paradigm

Object-oriented programming (OOP) is a different way of thinking about programming. In procedural programming, you think about functions and the execution through these functions. You think separately about data and how the functions interact with data. Object-oriented programming, however, forces you to think in terms of objects and the interaction between objects. An object is a self contained entity that describes not only certain data but the procedures to manipulate the data.

Object-oriented programming (OOP) deals with the overall program organization rather than the details of program operation. OOP has evolved to counter some of the drawbacks of procedural programming. Thus, OOP gives more emphasis on data, provides extensibility and models real world problems very well.

OOP treats data as an important and critical element in the program development. It ties data more closely to the functions that operate on it and thus avoids global access. OOP paradigm decomposes the problem into objects which model the real-world entities. It then builds data and functions around these objects. Thus, an object is a unit which encapsulates "data and the functions that operate on that data". This gives rise to the key term data encapsulation—which refers to the encapsulation of data and its function (also called member function in C#) into a single entity—the object. The data in an object cannot be accessed directly. It is hidden from accidental alteration. Data can be accessed only through the member functions in the object. This gives rise to the concept of data hiding. These two concepts of data encapsulation and data hiding simplify writing, debugging and maintaining programs.

Objects communicate or interact with one another through member functions. Thus, to summarize, data of an object can be accessed only by the member functions associated with that object. Functions of one object, however, can access functions of other objects. The following Fig. 2.1 represents the organization of data and functions in OOP.

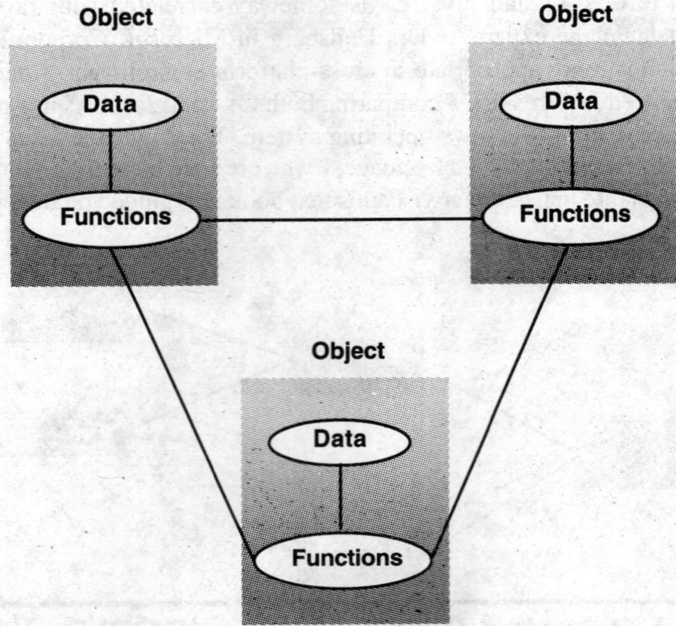

Fig. 2.1 Organization of data and functions in OOP.

Object-oriented programming is still a new concept of programming characterized by the following features :

- Emphasis on the data.
- Programs are made up of objects which model real-world entities.
- Data and functions are encapsulated.
- Data hiding protects data.
- Addition of new data and function is easy.

- Objects communicate through functions.
- Program design follows bottom-up approach.

Object-oriented programming has the following characteristics, which distributes it from conventional programming.

- **Object.** In object-oriented programming, you do not think of dividing the program into function, but into objects. Objects in the real-world can be represented by objects in the program. For example automobiles in a traffic-flow simulation problem, customers in a bank, student of a university, points in a plane, animals in an ecological simulation, positions in a game of chess, complex numbers, a linked list, a graphics object such as a circle, square, triangle, etc.—any of these real-world objects can be represented by an object in a program.
- **Classes.** A class in OOP is a template for objects. In other words a class is a specification of the data and the functions to be encapsulated with the data. A mere definition of a class does not create objects. It just gives the skeletal template. An analogy (to the relationship between classes and objects) would be the creation of variables of a particular type.
- **Data Abstraction.** As the word indicates, abstraction refers to the representation of only the essential features of the real-world object in the program object. This process does not include the background details and explanations. This concept of abstraction is used in classes. A class is thus defined as a list of abstract attributes and functions which operate on these attributes. The term Abstract Data Types (ADT) is used to refer to classes due to this reason.
- **Encapsulation.** Data encapsulation is the most significant characteristic of a class. By this term, we mean the wrapping up of data and functions which operate on the data into a single unit called the object. This encapsulation prevents free access to the data within an object. Access can only be done through the interface provided by the functions. Such insulation of data is referred to as data hiding.
- **Inheritance.** To understand the concept of sub-classes and inheritance and their roll in OOP, let us take an example. Consider the class of mammals. This class can be subdivided into sub-classes—dogs, cats, cows, whales, etc. as in Fig. 2.2 shown below :

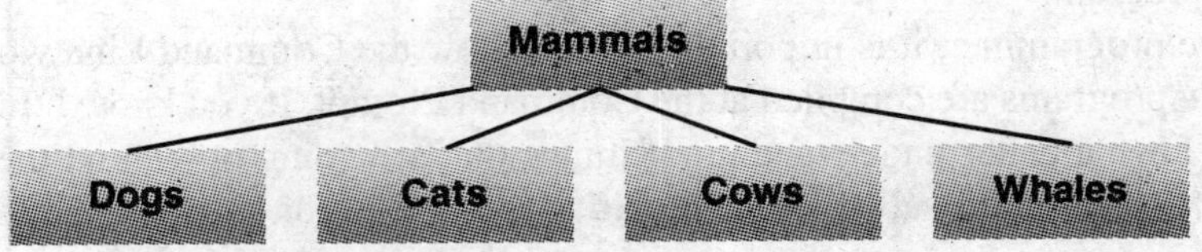

Fig. 2.2 A concept of class inheritance.

The idea behind this division is that each sub-class shares common characteristics with the class from which it is derived. Thus dogs, cats, cows, whales—all share the common characteristic of giving birth to young ones rather than laying eggs. Each sub-class or derived class has its own characteristics. For instance, dogs are carnivorous, while cows are herbivorous, and whales are aquatic in their habitat. Each derived class inherits some characteristics from the base class and adds new ones of its own. This is also known as inheritance.

- **Polymorphism.** Polymorphism is an important OOP concept used extensively in implementing inheritance. Polymorphism refers to the ability of one thing to take many (Poly) distinct forms (Morphism). In OOP, this one thing which may take several distinct forms may be an operator or a function. This provides the facility of sending the same message to objects of parent class and objects of the sub-classes. Each object may however respond to the message in its own way depending on the class/sub-class to which it belongs. This allows objects having different internal structures (of derived classes) to share the same external interface.

2.7 First C# Program

Let us look at the following program **HelloWorld** program :

```
// our first c# program
class HelloWorld
{
    static void Main()
    {
        System.Console.WriteLine("Hello World!");
    }
}
```

Primarily environment for a C# program is Microsoft's Visual Studio. In this text, we use Microsoft Visual Studio 2005, where we can edit, compile and execute our C# programs in two ways :

- Using csc.exe command line compiler.
- Using Visual Studio Integrated Development Environment (IDE).

2.7.1 Using csc.exe Command Line Compiler

A computer program is started in a regular computer file. A file for a C# program has the extension .cs. To make your programming fast, the C# language ships with many primary files that allow you to lay a foundation for your program.

To be an effective programmer, it is important to know how the Command Line works because, as mentioned already, C# programs are compiled at the Command Prompt. If you know how the Command Line works, you can have a better understanding of things that are going on behind the scenes.

Now to start our first program called **HelloWorld**, open any editor and type the following code :

```
// our first c# program
class HelloWorld
{
    static void Main()
    {
        System.Console.WriteLine("Hello World!");
    }
}
```

Now, save the file in a directory called **C:\TEMP** as **HelloWorld.cs** file.

There are various types of commands used on the command prompt. Some of them are as old as the operating system. Such is the case for commands used to create files or folders, copy files or folders, delete files or folders, format a drive, etc. Some other commands are created by a person like you who needs it for a particular application. For example, the C# language provides a command called csc to compile a program at the command line. In the same way, when you create a program, particularly when you create a source file, you can use some options that would be used at the command prompt.

Now at DOS prompt, go to the directory where you saved HellowWorld.cs (i.e., **C:\TEMP**). Here type,

C:\TEMP>csc HelloWorld.cs

Note

If you install Microsoft Visual Studio 2005, start your command prompt as :

- *Click Start*
- *Click Programs*
- *Click Visual C++ 2005 Express Edition*
- *Click Visual Studio Tools*
- *Click Visual Studio 2005 Command Prompt*

You will prompted as shown in Fig. 2.3.

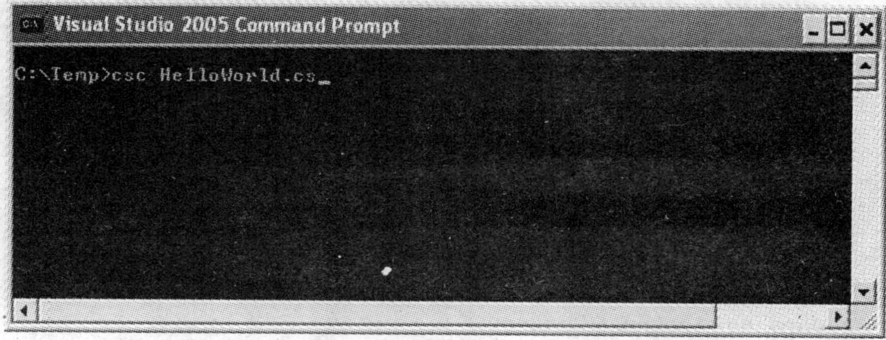

Fig. 2.3 Command prompt to compile C# program.

Now press Enter key to compile the first program. You will notice that the program is compiled with following messages as given in Fig. 2.4.

If you look the directory by typing :

C:\Temp>DIR

You will be notice that it creates another file called HelloWorld.exe as shown in Fig. 2.5.

```
Visual Studio 2005 Command Prompt

C:\Temp>csc HelloWorld.cs
Microsoft (R) Visual C# 2005 Compiler version 8.00.50727.42
for Microsoft (R) Windows (R) 2005 Framework version 2.0.50727
Copyright (C) Microsoft Corporation 2001-2005. All rights reserved.

C:\Temp>
```

Fig. 2.4 Compiled message of C# HelloWorld program.

```
Visual Studio 2005 Command Prompt

C:\Temp>csc HelloWorld.cs
Microsoft (R) Visual C# 2005 Compiler version 8.00.50727.42
for Microsoft (R) Windows (R) 2005 Framework version 2.0.50727
Copyright (C) Microsoft Corporation 2001-2005. All rights reserved.

C:\Temp>dir
 Volume in drive C has no label.
 Volume Serial Number is 8893-5511

 Directory of C:\Temp

10/18/2006  01:00 PM    <DIR>          .
10/18/2006  01:00 PM    <DIR>          ..
01/29/2007  08:11 PM               132 HelloWorld.cs
01/29/2007  08:32 PM             3,072 HelloWorld.exe
               2 File(s)          3,204 bytes
               2 Dir(s)   6,309,543,936 bytes free

C:\Temp>Hello_
```

Fig. 2.5 Program with .exe file.

This is the executable file that contains the MSIL version of the program. After creating the executable file, type the following at command prompt:

C:\Temp>HelloWorld

Where you will notice the output as shown in Fig. 2.6.

Although MSIL is not executable code, it is still contained in an exe file. The CLR automatically invokes the JIT compiler when you attempt to execute **HelloWorld.exe**.

The compiler that ships with the C# version we will use, that is, the compiler of the .NET Framework is a program called csc. Like most other programs, it has the extension .exe. This csc name is not standard. This means that another C# compiler may have another name; csc.exe is just the name of the compiler we will use.

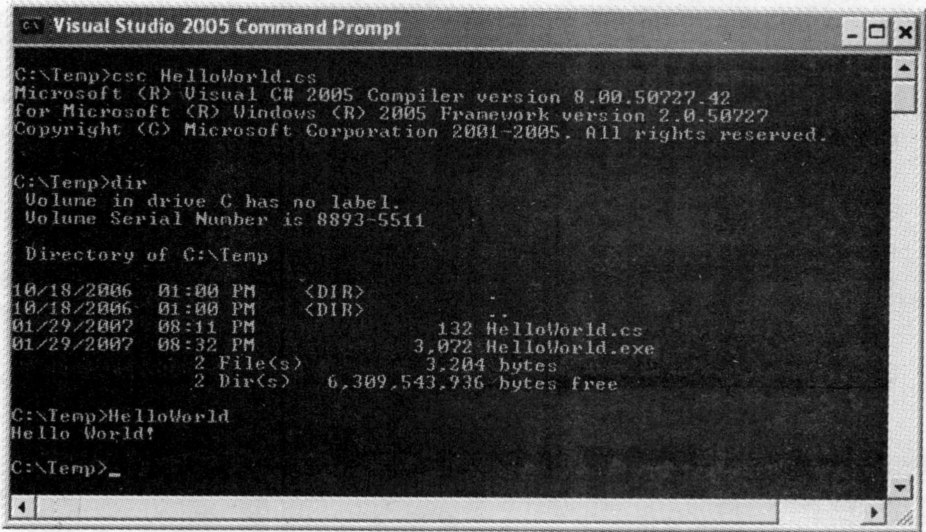

Fig. 2.6 Output of HelloWorld application

Let's break down this example.

1. The first line starts with '//' because it is a comment. Like C/C++ and Java '//' tells the compiler to ignore everything to the end of this line. The other type of commenting in C# is block commenting. Block comments start with "/*" and continue until "*/".

2. The next line starts with

   ```
   class HelloWorld
   {
   ```

   Or

   ```
   class HelloWorld {
   ```

   which uses the keyword class to declare that a new class is being defined. As mentioned the class is C#'s basic unit of encapsulation. HelloWorld is the name of the class. The class definition begins with the opening curly braces ({) and ends with the closing curly braces (}). The elements between the two braces are members of the class. The details of more on class will discussed in latter chapter.

3. The next important concept in this program is the declaration of the **Main()** method on the fourth line;

   ```
   static void Main()
   {
   ```

   Or

   ```
   static void Main() {
   ```

Note

Every C# program contains a Main() method where program execution begins and ends.

The next point to take note of is that the **Main()** method is defined as a static method within the class **HelloWorld**. There are three important concepts : **static**, **void** and **Main().**

4. Being a **static** method means an instance of the class containing **Main()** is not required to make a call to **Main()**. That is the **Main()** method is a global one and can be called without creating an instance of the class.
   - The keyword void tells the compiler that **Main()** method does not return any value.
   - In addition, the **Main()** method of a program is never global.
   - This means it must be contained within a class like in our example where **Main()** is within the class **HelloWorld** (**Main()** can be contained within a struct as well, but typically it's inside a class).
   - The empty parentheses {( )} that follow Main indicates that no information is passed to **Main()** method.

Also, the **Main()** method line can be written as :

```
// No return type, no arguments.
public static void Main() {
```

Or

```
// Integer return type, no arguments.
public static int Main() {
```

Or

```
// No return type, array of strings as arguments.
public static void Main(string[] args) {
```

Here,

- The **public** keyword is an access specifier.
- An access specifier determines how other part of a program can access a member of a class.
- When a class member is preceded by **public**, then that member can be accessed by code outside the class in which it is declared. More on access specifier will discuss in subsequent chapters.

5. The final key feature of this program is the line where we output text to the console with

```
System.Console.WriteLine("Hello World!");
```

Here,

- The line outputs the string **"Hello World!"** followed by a new line on the screen.
- The **WriteLine()** displays the string that is passed to it.
- **WriteLine()** is a method, defined in the class Console, that writes text to standard output followed by a new line.
- The class **Console** is contained in the namespace (grouping of classes) **System** that supports console I/O.
- Thus, the **WriteLine()** method is a console output. Note. More on the I/O operations in subsequent chapter.

- If you want to avoid having to fully qualify **Console** by writing **System.Console** you can put using System; at the beginning of the file. Now we can write

  Console.WriteLine("Hello World!");

- Also, notice that the **WriteLine()** statement ends with a semicolor, as does the using **System** statement.
- In general, statements in C# end with a semicolon (;) and the blocks are begin with a { and end with a }.

2.7.2 Using Visual Studio IDE

To start a C# Console application,

- Click Start
- Click Programs
- Click Visual C# 2005 Express Edition. It will show you the Visual Studio2005 first screen with all available products as shown in Fig. 2.7.

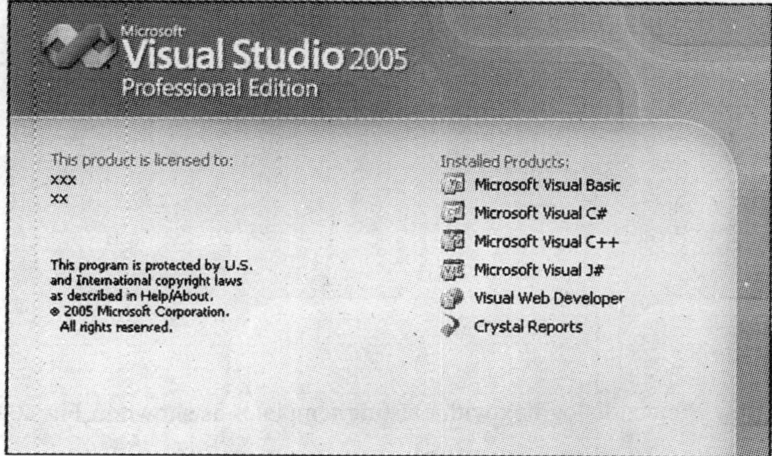

Fig. 2.7 First screen of Visual Studio 2005.

After few second, the screen will forward to the Start Page window as shown in 2.8.

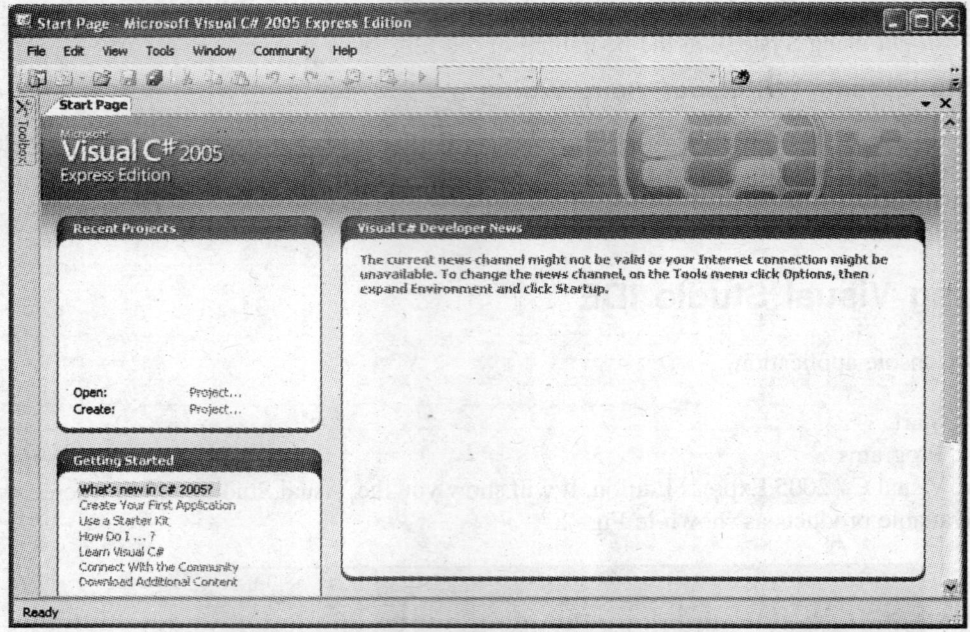

Fig. 2.8 Starting Visual C# 2005.

From Fig. 2.8,

- Click File >> New Project

  Or

- Press Ctrl+Shift+N

You will see the New Project dialog box with existing templates as shown in Fig. 2.9.

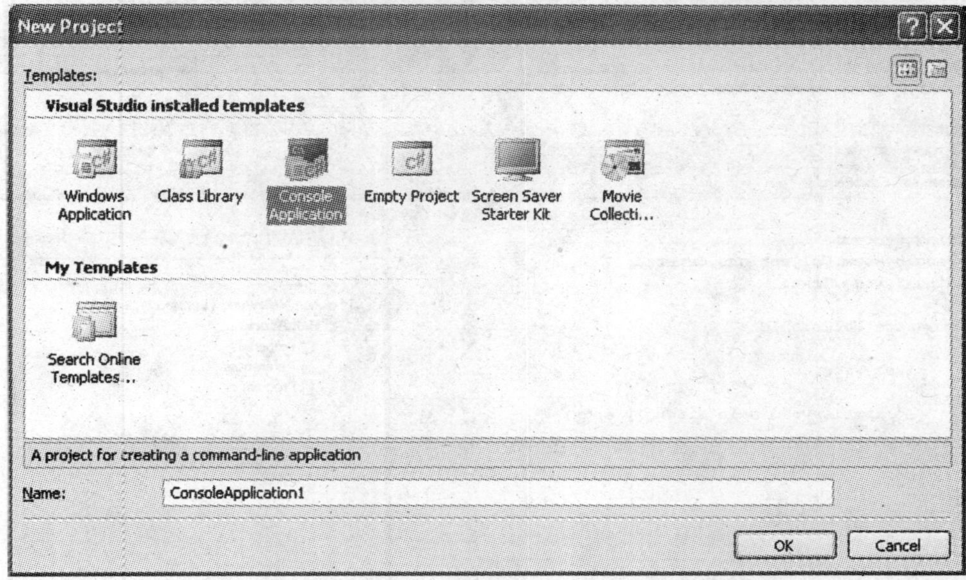

Fig. 2.9 New Project dialog box for starting a console application.

Here, click the Console Application button and type the project name as **HelloWorld** as shown in Fig. 2.10.

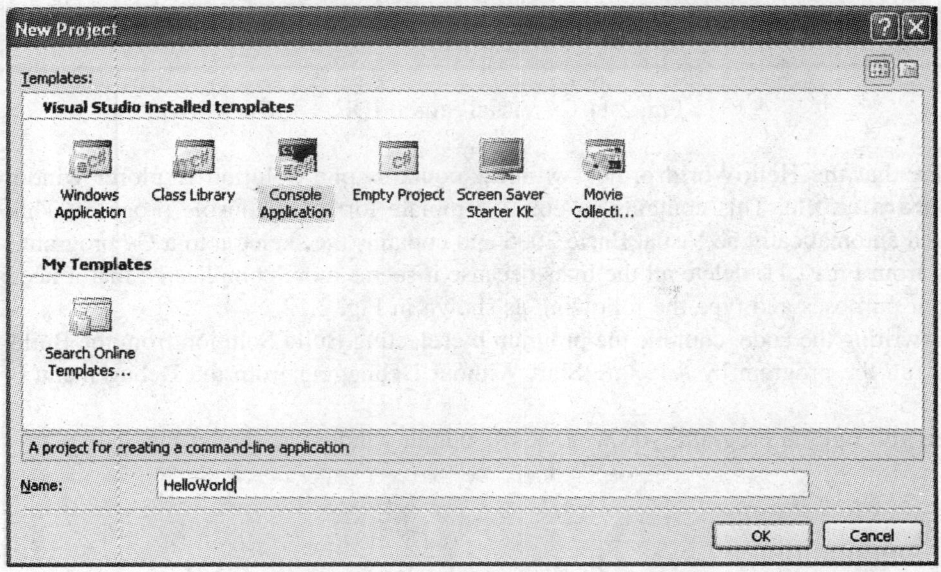

Fig. 2.10 Type the name and press OK button.

- Press OK button.

- Once the project is created, the Visual Studio IDE will look like as shown in Fig. 2.11.

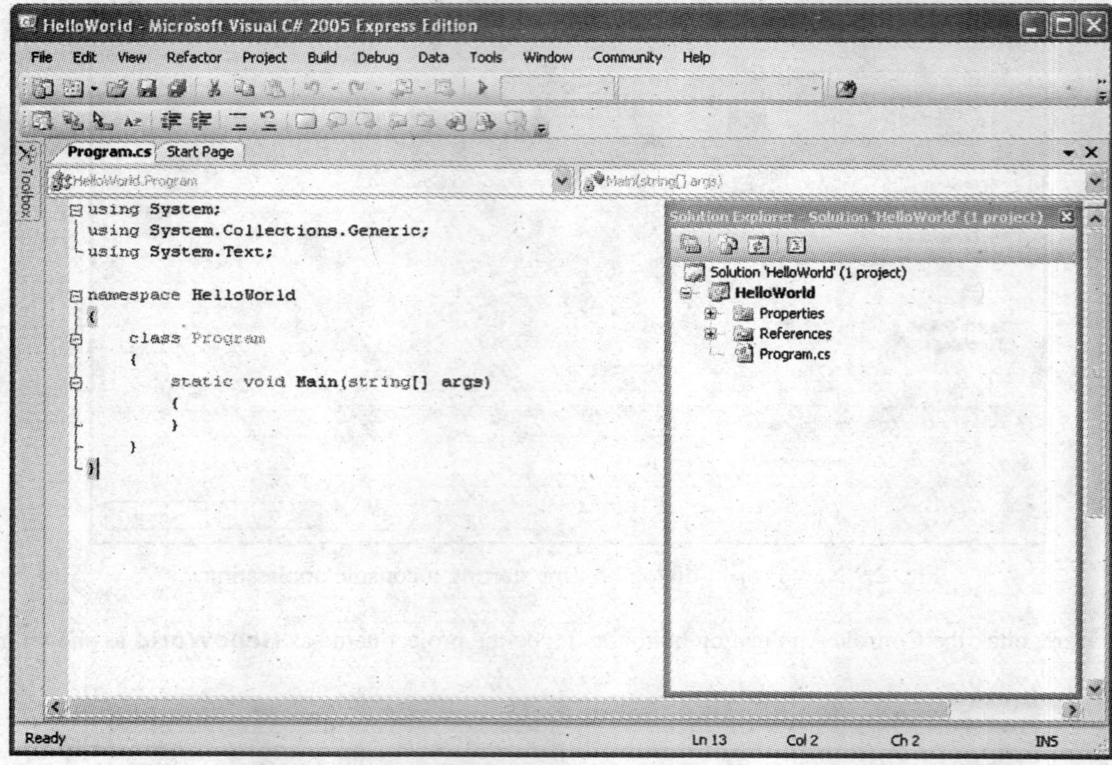

Fig. 2.11 C# Visual Studio IDE.

- Notice that the HelloWorld project window contains one Solution Explorer window with **Program.cs** file. This contains an empty template for a C# console program. This file is created automatically be Visual Basic 2005 and contains the skeleton to a C# program.
- Now from Fig. 2.11, delete all the lines because it seems more complicated that it needs to be for our purposes and type the following as shown in Fig. 2.12.
- After writing the code, compile the program by selecting Build Solution from the Build menu.
- Now run the program by selecting Start Without Debugging from the Debug menu or using Ctrl+F5.
- When you run the program, you will see the output window as shown Fig. 2.13.

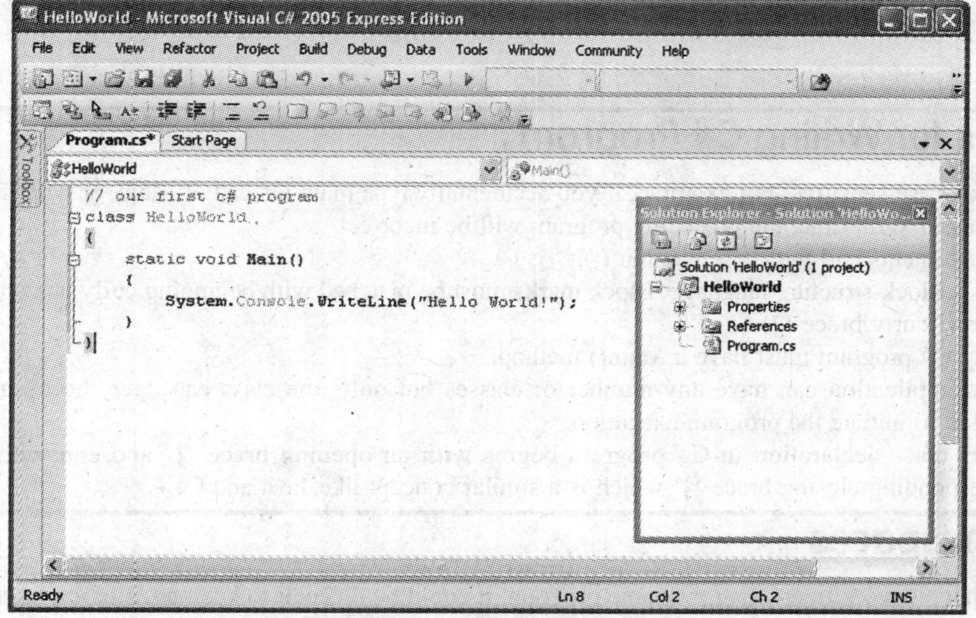

Fig. 2.12 HelloWorld program code.

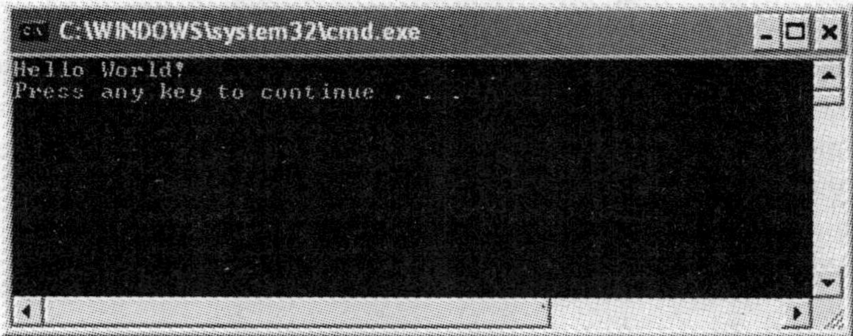

Fig. 2.13 HelloWorld program output.

- To save the file, on the main menu, click File -> Save
- Press Enter to close the DOS window and return to Visual C#.

As you saw in the first IDE screen, it contains several keywords like :

```
using System;
using System.Collections.Generic;
using System.Text;

namespace HelloWorld
{
    class Program
    {
        static void Main(string[] args)
        {
```

```
        }
    }
}
```

2.8 Rules for Writing C# Program

- C# is a case-sensitive. For example, if you accidentally type main instead of Main, or writeline instead of WriteLine, the preceding program will be incorrect.
- C# statements end with a semicolon (;).
- C# is a block-structure language. Block marks must be matched with beginning curly brace ({) and end curly brace (}).
- Every C# program must have a Main() method.
- A C# application can have any number of classes but only one class can have the Main() method to initiate the program execution.
- Every class declaration in C# program begins with an opening brace '{' and end with a corresponding closing brace '}' which is a similar concept like Java and C++.

2.9 Namespaces

When many people work in creating the same program, it could be difficult to keep track of the names of various classes. If more than one programmer creates a class with the same name in the same program, there would be conflict and the program would not work. The solution to avoid this situation is to delimit sections of code with names.

A **namespace** is a section of code that is identified by a specific name. That is name space contains group of code that can be called upon by C# program. The name could be anything such as somebody's name, the name of the company's department, or a city. To create a namespace, you start with the **namespace** keyword followed by the name of the section.

Like a class, the section that is part of a **namespace** starts with an opening curly bracket "{" and ends with a closing curly bracket "}".

For example;

```
namespace HelloWorld
{
    ...............
    ...............
}
```

Between the curly brackets, you can type anything that is part of the **namespace**. For example, you can create a class inside of a **namespace**. For example;

```
namespace HelloWorld
{
    class Program
    {
        ...............
        ...............
    }
}
```

For example, to create a **namespace**, change the file as follows:

```
namespace HelloWorld
{
    class Program
    {
        static void Main()
        {
        }
    }
}
```

2.9.1 The System Namespace

To make programming in C# a little easier, many classes have already been created and stored in various namespaces. Each namespace in C# is used to provide a specify set of classes. The most regularly used namespace in the C# language is called **System**. Inside of the **System** namespace is a class called **Console**. The **Console** class is used to display things on the console screen also called the DOS window.

The **Console** class contains assignments (called methods) to display information on the screen or to retrieve information from the user who types it in the DOS window. The method that is used to display text on the screen is called Write. To use the **Write()** method, inside of the parentheses, type the sentence between double-quotes. For example;

```
namespace HelloWorld
{
    class Program
    {
        static void Main()
        {
            System.Console.WriteLine("Hello World!");
        }
    }
}
```

Besides the **Write()** method, the **Console** class also provides a method called **WriteLine()**. The difference is that, after displaying something on the screen, the **Write()** method keeps the caret on the same line but **WriteLine()** transfers the caret the next line. We will see various examples of this behavior throughout our lessons.

2.9.2 Using Alias for Namespace

C# supports the aliases for their namespaces. We use the Console keyword for input/output operations. Instead of Console we can use user-defined names. These names are called the aliases. The format is:

```
using <user_defined_alial_name> = System.<class>;
```

For example,

```
using IO = System.Console; //Here, IO is the alias for System.Console
```

After declaring the alias, we can use the same alias name inside our program as :

```
IO.WriteLine("The C# .NET Programming");
```

2.9.3 The using Keyword

We saw that, to call an object or a method that is part of a namespace, you must "qualify" that method or object using the period operator. Instead of using this approach, if you already know the name of a namespace that exists or has been created in another file, you can use a special keyword to indicate that you are using a namespace that is defined somewhere. This is done with the **using** keyword. To do this, on top of the file (preferably), type **using** followed by the name of the namespace.

With the **using** keyword, you can include as many external namespaces as necessary. For example,

using System;

i.e., the program is using the **System** namespace.

```
using System;
namespace HelloWorld
{
    class Program
    {
        static void Main()
        {
            System.Console.WriteLine("Hello World!");
        }
    }
}
```

2.9.4 Passing Command Line Arguments

Many programs are written to accept command-line input. Collection of command-line input occurs in the **Main()** method.

..\CSharp_Book\Chap02\LineArg

```
// This program studies value incrementing and decrementing

// Namespace Declaration
using System;
// Program start class
class LineArg
{
    // Main begins program execution.
    public static void Main(string[] args)
    {
        // Write to console
        Console.WriteLine("Hello, {0}!", args[0]);
        Console.WriteLine("Welcome to the C# .NET Programming.");
    }
}
```

To run this program on-line right now, add your name (or any name) with the execution line as :
LineArg Friends

From the above program, you will notice an entry in the **Main()** method's parameter list. The parameter name is **args**. It is what you will use to refer to the parameter later in your program. The *string[]* expression defines the type of parameter that **args** is. The **string** type holds characters. These characters could form a single word, or multiple words. The "[ ]", square brackets denote an **Array**, which is like a list. Therefore, the type of the **args** parameter, is a list of words from the command-line.

You will also notice an additional **Console.WriteLine(...)** statement within the **Main()** method. The argument list within this statement is different than before. It has a formatted string with a "**{0}**" parameter embedded in it. The first parameter in a formatted string begins at number 0, the second is 1, and so on. The "**{0}**" parameter means that the next argument following the end quote will determine what goes in that position. Hold that thought, and now we will look at the next argument following the end quote.

This is the **args[0]** argument, which refers to the first string in the *args* array. The first element of an Array is number 0, the second is number 1, and so on. For example, if we wrote "**LineArg Friends**" on the command-line, the value of **args[0]** would be "Friends".

Now we will get back to the embedded "**{0}**" parameter in the formatted string. Since **args[0]** is the first argument, after the formatted string, of the **Console.WriteLine()** statement, its value will be placed into the first embedded parameter of the formatted string. When this command is executed, the value of **args[0]**, which is "Friends" will replace "**{0}**" in the formatted string. Upon execution of the command-line with "**LineArg Friends**", the output will be as follows :

```
Hello, Friends!
Welcome to the C# .NET Programming.
```

2.10 Using the C# Compiler

As we have noted earlier, C# classes are compiled in the first place to the Common Language Runtime Intermediate Language (IL). And as shown in our first example, one compiles these classes using the command-line command:

```
csc HelloWorld.cs
```

Where the required classes are held in more than one file, these should be listed, separated by spaces, as in:

```
csc HelloWorld.cs Hello.cs
```

Broadly speaking, one can compile C# classes into either executable files or dynamic link library - DLL - files (see the /t switch in the table below). An executable file is one that can contain a runnable program (note that in the classes compiled to an executable file, there should be only one 'Main' method). A .NET dynamic link library just collects together an assembly of classes, which can then be instantiated and utilised by programs in the course of their running.

If your classes reference external classes, the C# compiler must be able to locate them. By default, the compiler only looks within the 'mscorlib.dll' assembly, which supports the basic Common Language Runtime functions. To point the compiler in the direction of other classes, use the /r switch described in the table below (note that there is no equivalent to the Java approach of setting the environment variable CLASSPATH). To find the appropriate assembly for .NET framework classes, consult their documentation. The following gives a list of the compiler switches we have found useful, but we would advise you to look further at the .NET documentation to see which other ones are available.

Compiler Switch	Description
/r:dll or /reference:dll eg. /r:System.xml.dll, System.Net.dll	This tells the C# compiler to include one or more of the .NET framework DLLs. As the standard library namespaces are not automatically referenced by the compiler, it is necessary to tell it which ones are needed. This switch also allows you to include your own DLLs.
/out: file eg. /out:fred.dll	Specifies the filename to which the compiled code is to be written.
/doc: file eg. /doc:doc.xml	Requests the production of xml documentation into the specified file.
/t:type or /target:type eg. /t:exe - produce a console executable file (default) /t:library - produce a dll file /t:module - creates each file into its own dll, eg. fred.cs will be converted to fred.dll /t:winexe - produce a windows executable file	This is used to specify the type of output file produced.

If you are regularly compiling a program and using a lot of switches in your program, we have found it useful to put the compile command in a batch file rather than writing out the entire command each time.

2.11 C# Preprocessor Directives

Preprocessor directives tags included within class specifications; they are used to give the compiler additional information about regions of code. The following example shows that you can specify areas of code to be compiled or not, depending upon the presence of a tag:

```
/* Preprocessor Test */
#define MYVAR
public class PreTest
{
    public static void Main()
    {
        #if MYVAR
        print ("Hello");
        #endif
        print ("C# Programmers");
    }
}
```

In the above, the **#define** statement on line 5 acts as a boolean: it sets the variable **MYVAR** to be 'defined' rather than 'undefined'. Because it is defined, the code on line 16 gets compiled. If we were to remove the statement on line 5, the compiler would effectively treat the code on line 11 as commented out.

Note

In the previous version of this page we followed the MSDN documentation in using as our example the variable DEBUG. But it has been pointed out to us by a correspondent that the DEBUG variable is already defined by Visual Studio.NET when a project is compiled as 'debug' rather than 'release'. So if you're building from VS.NET you wouldn't want to explicitly redefine the variable DEBUG like this.

The following gives a list of some of the available preprocessor directives.

Directive	Action
#define symbol	Sets symbol to be 'defined' (true)
#undef symbol	Sets symbol to be 'undefined' (false)
#if symbol [operator symbol2]	The if statement evaluates the given expression. The possible operators can be ==, !=, &&, ||. If the expression evaluates to 'true', the code to the #else, #elif or #endif directive is compiled.
#else	Used in conjunction with the if statement.
#elif	Used in conjunction with the if statement as 'else-if'.
#endif	Ends the previous conditional directives
#warning text	The given text appears as a warning in the compiler output
#error text	The given text appears as an error in the compiler output
#line number[file]	Outputs a line number, and (optionally) a filename to the compiler output.
#region name	Marks the beginning of a region
#end region	Marks the ends of a region

2.12 Attributes

Attributes are used to give extra information to the .NET compiler. C# and the .NET framework have a few built-in attribute types, but it is also possible to create new ones by extending the System.Attribute class. Below we describe a few common uses of attributes.

It is possible to tell the compiler that a class is compliant with the .NET Common Language Specification (discussed in Chapter - 1) with code like the following:

```
using System;

[CLSCompliant(true)]
public class myClass
{
    // class code
}
```

Similar code can also be used to indicate that a class has been obsoleted.

Web services (mentioned in lesson 1) also make heavy use of attributes. Demonstrated by the example below, the attribute [WebMethod] is used to specify that a particular method is to be exposed as a web service.

```
[ WebMethod ]
public int Add(int num1, int num2)
{
    return num1+num2;
}
```

Exercise

1. What is C#?
2. How C# is related with the .NET framework?
3. Contrast between
   - C# and Java
   - C# and C++
   - C# and Visual Basic
4. C# is an object oriented programming language give reasons to support your answer?
5. What do you mean by strongly typed in oops?
6. What are the similarities between CLR and JVM?
7. Write a simple Hello World program in C#?
8. What is Command Line Compiler in C#?
9. Define the following:
   - Namespace
   - Preprocessor directives
   - Visual Studio IDE

Variables and Data Types 3

3.1 Introduction

A computer receives information from different applications in various forms. Sometimes a person types it using the keyboard. Sometimes the user clicks the mouse. Sometimes information comes from another, more complicated source. The idea is that the computer spends a great deal of its time with various pieces of information. Information provided to the computer through a program is called datum and the plural is data. Sometimes the word data is used both for singular and plural items. Data used by the computer comes and goes regularly as this information changes. For this reason, such information is called a variable.

When the user enters data in a program, the computer receives it and must store it somewhere to eventually make it available to the program as needed. For a program used to process employment applications, the types of information a user would enter into the program are the name, the residence, the desired salary, years of experience, education level, etc. Because there can be so much information for the same program, you must specify to the computer what information you are referring to and when. To do this, each category of piece of information must have a name.

3.2 Keywords

There are some reserved words in C#, which have predefined meaning to compiler. These reserved words are called Keywords. Some commonly used keywords are shown in listing 3.1.

To name the variables of your program, you must follow strict rules. In fact, everything else in your program must have a name. C# uses a series of words, called keywords, for its internal use. This means that you must avoid naming your objects using one of these keywords.

Listing 3.1 C# keywords.

```
abstract    const       extern      int         out         short
typeof      as          continue    false       interface   override
sizeof      uint        base        decimal     finally     internal
params      stackalloc  ulong       bool        default     fixed
is          private     static      unchecked   break       delegate
float       lock        protected   string      unsafe      byte
do          for         long        public      struct      ushort
case        double      foreach     namespace   readonly    switch
using       catch       else        goto        new         ref this
virtual     char        enum        if          null        return
throw       void        checked     event       implicit    object
sbyte       true        volatile    class       explicit    in
operator    sealed      try         while
```

Note. We can't use keywords as a variable name.

Once you avoid these words, there are rules you must follow when naming your objects.

3.3 Variables

A computer memory is divided into small blocks of space. Each of these blocks is large enough to hold one instance of a certain type of data. Each block of space is called a memory location. If the program specifies that location should be reserved to hold changing values.

A variable is the name given to these memory locations so that there is no need to remember the address of the location. Variables hold different kind of data and the same variable might hold different values during the execution of a program.

Definition

A variable is one that holds certain values. It is a sequence of alphabets and digits but the first character must be alphabet or underscore.

Each variable in C# language is associated with a specific type, which determines the size and layout its associated memory, the range of values that can be stored within the memory, and the set of operations that can be applied to it.

C# is a strongly "Typed" language. Thus all operations on variables are performed with consideration of what the variable's "Type" is.

Note

Contents of the variable may vary—hence the name variable.
A static variable is shared among all instances of a class. A static method can be called through the class in which it is defined.

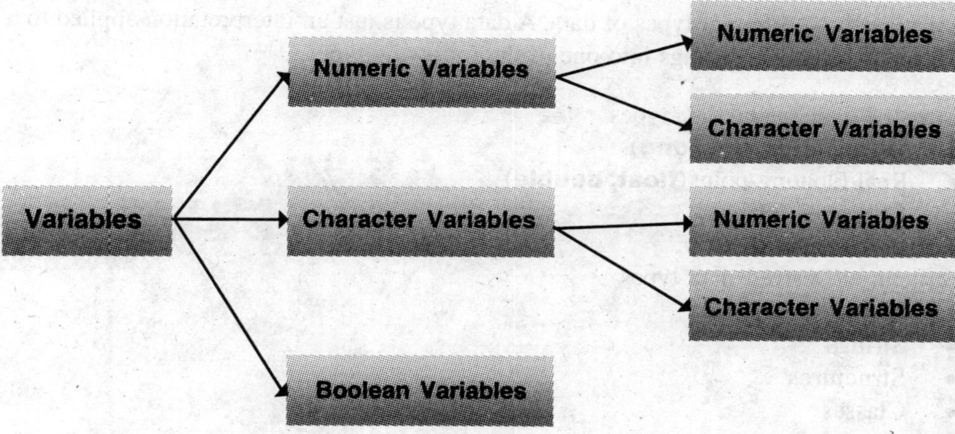

Fig. 3.1 Basic types of variables in C#.

3.3.1 Declaring Variables

Variables have characters. You declare all C# variables within whatever block of code needs them. To declare a variable,

- the variable name must start with a letter or an underscore (_).
- after the first letter or underscore, the name can have letters, digits, and/or underscores.
- the variable name must not have any special characters other than the underscore (_).
- the variable name cannot have a space.
- Variable name should not be reserved word. That is, variables cannot have the same name as a C# command or a library function.

Besides these rules, you can also create your own but that abide by the above. C# is case-sensitive. This means that the names Case, case, and CASE are completely different. For example, the main function is always written Main.

3.4 Concepts of Data Types

In order to use a variable in your program, the compiler must be aware of it. Once the compiler knows about a variable, it would reserve an amount of memory space for that variable.

A data type is an amount of space needed to store the information related to a particular variable.

The name of a variable allows you and the compiler to refer to a particular category of information in your program. The data type allows the compiler to reserve an adequate amount of memory space for a variable. Because you are the one who writes a program, you also tell the compiler the amount of memory space each particular variable will need. Based on this, the C# language provides categories of data types used to specify this amount of space needed for a variable.

Variables can hold different types of data. A data type is just an interpretation applied to a string of bytes. Data in C# language belongs into one of the following types.

1. Simple/Fundamental data types
   - Integer (**sint, int, long**)
   - Real/Floating-point (**float, double**)
   - Character (**char**)
   - Boolean (**bool**)
2. Structured/Derived data types
   - Arrays
   - Strings
   - Structures
   - Classes
3. Enumerated data type
4. Pointer data type
5. The void data type

Data types are the way to identify type of data and associated operations, which can perform on that data.

Out of all the listing basic four data types work lots in programming. These are: **char, int, float** and **string** types.

The variables are declared using following syntax :

```
type variable_name1, variable_name2, ......;
```

where type is one of the data type. The value variable can also be initialized during their declaration itself. For example, the following statement declares variable num of type integer and initializes it to a value 0.

```
int num = 0;
```

3.5 Integral Types

In C#, an integral is a category of types. They are whole numbers, either signed or unsigned, and the char type. The char type is a Unicode character, as defined by the Unicode Standard. Listing 3.2 shows the integral types, their size, and range

Listing 3.2. The size and range of C# integral data types.

C# Type	.Net Framework (System) type	Signed?	Bytes Occupied	Possible Values
int	System.Int32	Yes	4	-2147483648 to 2147483647
uint	System.UInt32	No	4	0 to 4294967295

byte	System.Byte	No	1	0 to 255
sbyte	System.Sbyte	Yes	1	-128 to 127
short	System.Int16	Yes	2	-32768 to 32767
ushort	System.Uint16	No	2	0 to 65535
long	System.Int64	Yes	8	-9223372036854775808 to 9223372036854775807
ulong	System.Uint64	No	8	0 to 18446744073709551615
float	System.Single	Yes	4	Approximately $\pm 1.5 \times 10^{-45}$ to $\pm 3.4 \times 10^{38}$ with 7 significant figures
double	System.Double	Yes	8	Approximately $\pm 5.0 \times 10^{-324}$ to $\pm 1.7 \times 10^{-308}$ with 15 or 16 significant figures
decimal	System.Decimal	Yes	12	Approximately $\pm 1.0 \times 10^{-28}$ to $\pm 7.9 \times 10^{28}$ with 28 or 29 significant figures
bool	System.Boolean	N/A	1 / 2	true or false
char	System.Char	N/A	2	Any Unicode character (16 bit)

Integral types are well suited for those operations involving whole number calculations.

3.5.1 Signed Integer

A double-word is large enough to contain double the amount of data that can be stored in a word. This is equivalent to 32 bits or 4 bytes or 4,294,967,295. Therefore, a double-word is used for large numbers that would not fit in a word.

To use a variable that would hold quite large numbers, declare it using the int keyword. A variable declared as **int** can store values between –2,147,483,648 and 2,147,484,647 negative or positive, that can fit in 32 bits.

For example;

..\CSharp_Book\Chap03\SignedInt

```
using System;
using System.Collections.Generic;
using System.Text;

namespace SignedInt
{
    class Program
    {
        static void Main()
        {
```

```
            // Declaring integer variables
            int X;
            int Y;

            // Assgning values
            X = 20;
            Y = -30;

            Console.WriteLine("The two numbers are : " + X + " " + Y);
            Console.WriteLine("The sum is : " + (X + Y));
        }
    }
}
```

As you will see the program window will look like as shown in Fig. 3.2.

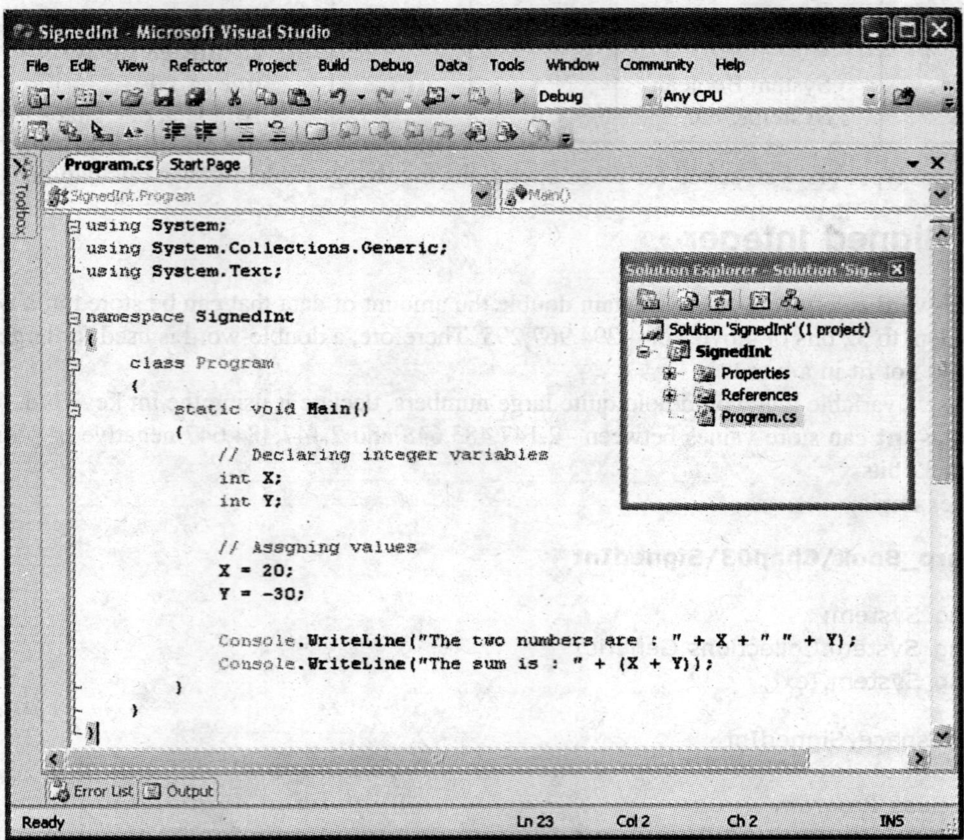

Fig. 3.2 Simple program window for declaring int variables.

When the above program executed, it will produce the following output as shown in Fig. 3.3.

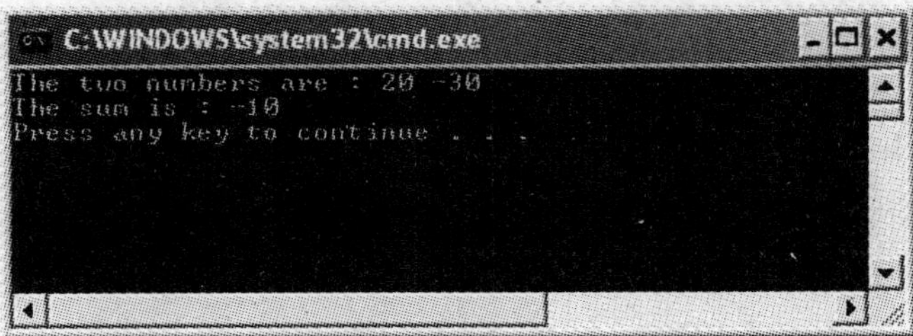

Fig. 3.3 Program output for int variables.

3.5.2 Unsigned Integer

If the variable must hold only positive natural numbers, you can declare it using the **uint** keyword. The **uint** keyword is used to identify a 32-bit positive integer whose value would range from 0 to 4,294,967,295. For example;

..\CSharp_Book\Chap03\UsignedInt

```
using System;

class UsignedInt
{
    static void Main()
    {
        // Declaring unsigned variables
        uint DayOfBirth;
        uint MonthOfBirth;
        uint YearOfBirth;

        // Assigning unsigned variables
        DayOfBirth   = 27;
        MonthOfBirth = 9;
        YearOfBirth  = 1997;

        Console.WriteLine("Mont Fort School");
        Console.Write("Student Date of Birth: ");
        Console.Write(MonthOfBirth);
        Console.Write("/");
        Console.Write(DayOfBirth);
        Console.Write("/");
        Console.Write(YearOfBirth);
        Console.WriteLine();
    }
}
```

When the above program executed, it will produce the following output as shown in Fig. 3.4.

Fig. 3.4 Program output for unsigned int variables.

3.5.3 Byte Data Type

A **byte** is an unsigned number whose value can range from 0 to 255 and therefore can be store in one byte. You can use it when you know a variable would hold a relatively small value such as people's age, the number of children of one mother, etc. To declare a variable that would hold a small natural number, use the **byte** keyword. For example;

```
byte Age;
```

You can initialize a **byte** variable when declaring it or afterwards. Here is an example that uses the **byte** data type:

..\CSharp_Book\Chap03\ByteVar

```
using System;
using System.Collections.Generic;
using System.Text;

namespace ByteVar
{
    class Program
    {

        static void Main()
        {
            // Declaring Byte variable
            Byte MyAge = 14;
            Byte FAge;

            Console.Write("My age is : ");
            Console.WriteLine(MyAge);
            FAge = 13;
            Console.Write("My friend's age is : ");
            Console.WriteLine(FAge);
```

```
        }
    }
}
```

When the above program executed, it will produce the following output as shown in Fig. 3.5.

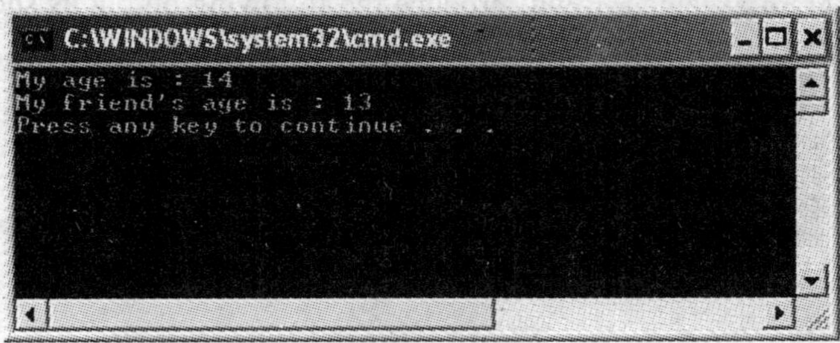

Fig. 3.5 Program output for Byte variables.

Make sure you do not use a value that is higher than 255 for a byte variable, you would receive an error. When in doubt, or when you think that there is a possibility a variable would hold a bigger value, don't use the **byte** data type as it doesn't like exceeding the 255 value limit.

3.5.4 Signed Byte

A **byte** number is referred to as signed if it can hold a negative or a positive value that ranges from -128 to 127, which can therefore fit in a **byte**. To declare a variable for that kind of value, use the **sbyte** keyword. For example;

..\CSharp_Book\Chap03\SignedByte

```
using System;
using System.Collections.Generic;
using System.Text;

namespace SignedByte
{
    class Program
    {
        static void Main()
        {
            // Declaring signed byte variable
            sbyte AreaTemp = -13;

            Console.Write("Area temperature ");
            Console.Write(AreaTemp);
            Console.Write(" Degree celsius");
```

```
            Console.WriteLine();
        }
    }
}
```

When the above program executed, it will produce the following output as shown in Fig. 3.6.

Fig. 3.6 Program output for Signed Byte variables.

3.5.5 Short Integers

A word, which is a group of 16 contiguous bits or 2 bytes, can be used to hold a natural number. As we have studied, the maximum numeric value that can fit in a word is 65535. Since the **byte** data type is used for very small numbers, whenever you plan to use a number in your program, the minimum representation you should use is a word.

The smallest integer you can store in a word is declared with the **short** keyword followed by a name. Because a **short** integer is signed by default, it can store a value that ranges from –32768 to 32767. Here is an example program that uses two short integers:

..\CSharp_Book\Chap03\ShortVar

```
using System;

class UsignedInt
{
    static void Main()
    {
        // Declaring unsigned variables
        uint DayOfBirth;
        uint MonthOfBirth;
        uint YearOfBirth;

        // Assigning unsigned variables
        DayOfBirth   = 27;
        MonthOfBirth = 9;
        YearOfBirth  = 1997;

        Console.WriteLine("Mont Fort School");
```

```
            Console.Write("Student Date of Birth: ");
            Console.Write(MonthOfBirth);
            Console.Write("/");
            Console.Write(DayOfBirth);
            Console.Write("/");
            Console.Write(YearOfBirth);
            Console.WriteLine();
        }
    }
```

When the above program executed, it will produce the following output as shown in Fig. 3.7.

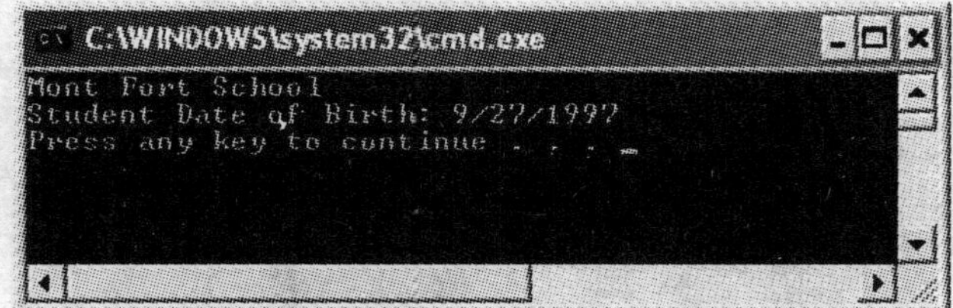

Fig. 3.7 Program output for short variables.

Because a **short** integer handles numbers that are larger than the signed **byte**, any variable you can declare for a signed **byte** can also be declared for a **short** variable.

3.5.6 Unsigned Short Integers

If a variable must hold positive and relatively small numbers, it is referred as an unsigned **short** integer. Such a variable can be declared using the **ushort** keyword. An unsigned short integer can hold numbers that range from 0 to 65535 and therefore can fit in 16 bits. For example;

..\CSharp_Book\Chap03\UnSShortVar

```
using System;
using System.Collections.Generic;
using System.Text;

namespace UnSShortVar
{
    class Program
    {
        static void Main()
        {
            // These variables must hold only positive integers

            ushort X;
```

```
            ushort Y;

            X = 16;
            Y = 2;

            Console.WriteLine("The two values are " + X + " and " + Y);
            Console.WriteLine("The sum is : " + (X + Y));
            Console.WriteLine();
        }
    }
}
```

When the above program executed, it will produce the following output as shown in Fig. 3.8.

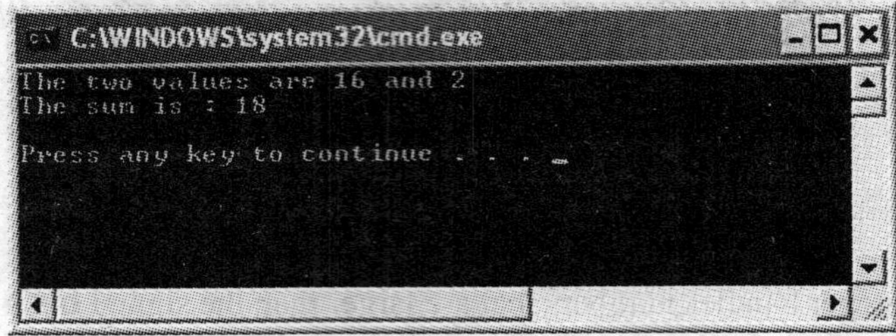

Fig. 3.8 Program output for unsigned short variables.

3.5.7 Long Integer

To use a variable that can hold very large numbers that would require up to 64 bits, declare it using the **long** keyword. This is for a number that can range between –9,223,372,036,854,775,808 and 9,223,372,036,854,775,807.

> **Note**
> *In C++, the long data type is 32 bits while in C#, the long data type is 64 bits.*

..\CSharp_Book\Chap03\LongVar

```
using System;
using System.Collections.Generic;
using System.Text;

namespace LongVar
{
    class Program
    {
        static void Main()
        {
```

```
            // Declaring int variable
            int l = 1780; // Length in meter
            int b = 450; // Breadth in meter

            // Declaring long variable
            long ParkArea;

            ParkArea = l * b;

            Console.Write("Park Area is : ");
            Console.Write(ParkArea / 1000);
            Console.Write(" square km.");
            Console.WriteLine();
        }
    }
}
```

When the above program executed, it will produce the following output as shown in Fig. 3.9.

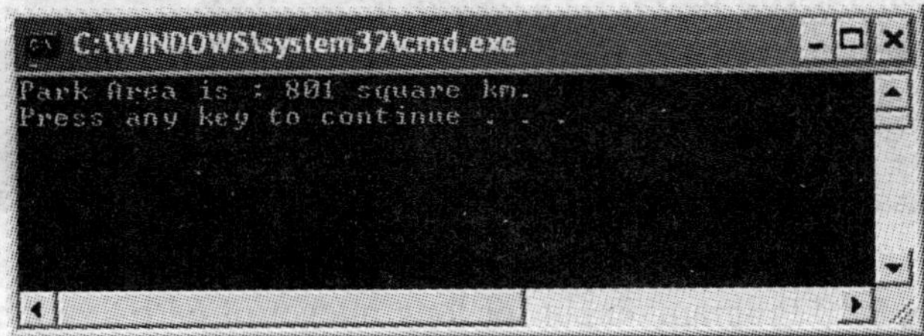

Fig. 3.9 Program output for long integer variable.

Although the **long** data type is used for large number, it mainly indicates the amount of space available but you don't have to use the whole space. For example, you can use the **long** keyword to declare a variable that would hold the same range of numbers as the **short**, the **int**, or the **unit** data types.

If you declare a variable as **long** but use it for small numbers that don't require 64 bits, the compiler would allocate the appropriate amount of space to accommodate the values of the variable. Consequently, the amount of space made available may not be as large as 64 bits. If you insist and want the compiler to reserve 64 bits, when assigning a value to the variable, add an **l** or an **L** suffix to it. For example,

..\CSharp_Book\Chap03\LongVar64

```
using System;
using System.Collections.Generic;
using System.Text;

namespace LongVar64
{
```

```
    class Program
    {
        static void Main()
        {
            // Declaring a long variable of 64 bit data
            long AnnualBudget;

            AnnualBudget = 678595436L;

            Console.Write("Annual budget for 2007-2008 is Rs. ");
            Console.Write(AnnualBudget + "/-");
            Console.WriteLine();
        }
    }
}
```

When the above program executed, it will produce the following output as shown in Fig. 3.10.

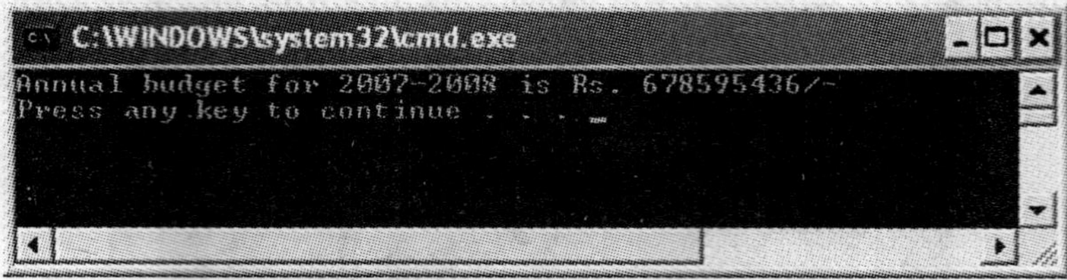

Fig. 3.10 Program output for long integer of 64 bit variable.

3.5.8 Unsigned Long Integer

You can use a combination of 64 bits to store positive or negative integers. In some cases, you will need a variable to hold only positive, though large, numbers. To declare such a variable, you can use the **ulong** data type. A variable declared as **ulong** can handle extremely positive numbers that range from 0 to 18,446,744,073,709,551,615 to fit in 64 bits.

3.5.9 Real Number or Floating Point and Decimal Types

A real number is a number that displays a decimal part. This means that the number can be made of two sections separated by a symbol that is referred to as the decimal separator or decimal symbol. This symbol is different by language, country, group of languages, or group of countries. In US English, this symbol is the period as can be verified from the Regional (and Language) Settings of the Control Panel as shown in Fig. 3.11.

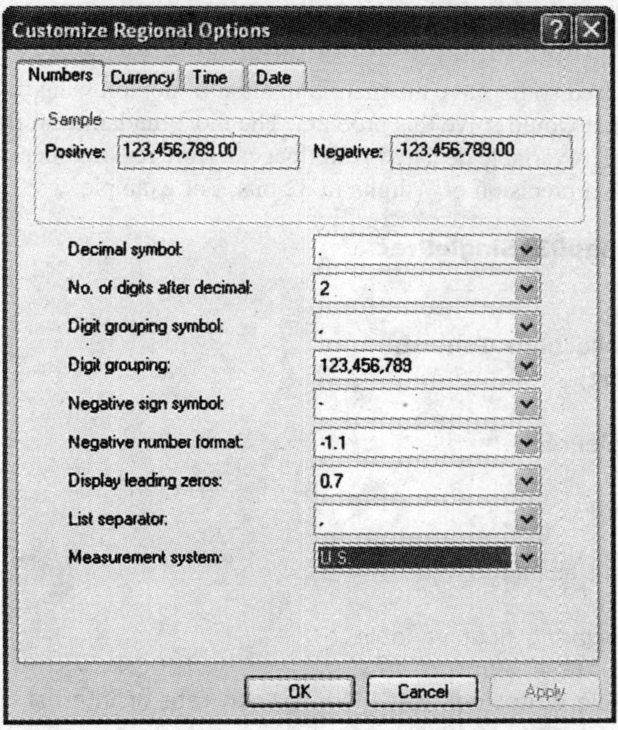

Fig. 3.11 Date setting.

On both sides of the Decimal Symbol, digits are used to specify the value of the number. The number of digits on the right side of the symbol determines how much precision the number offers.

A C# floating point type is either a **float** or **double**. They are used any time you need to represent a real number, as defined by IEEE 754. **decimal** types should be used when representing financial or money values. Listing 3.2 shows the floating point and decimal types, their size, precision and range.

Listing 3.3 The Floating Point and Decimal Types with Size, precision and Range.

Type	Size (in bits)	Precision	Range
float	32	7 digits	1.5 x 10-45 to 3.4 x 1038
double	64	15-16 digits	5.0 x 10-324 to 1.7 x 10308
decimal	128	28-29 decimal places	1.0 x 10-28 to 7.9 x 1028

Floating point types are used when you need to perform operations requiring fractional representations. However, for financial calculations, the decimal type is the best choice because you can avoid rounding errors.

3.5.10 Single-Precision Numbers

The integers we have used so far have the main limitation of not allowing decimal values. C# provides floating-point values that would solve this problem. The most fundamental floating variable is declared with the **float** keyword. A variable declared with float can store real numbers that range from ±1.5 × 10-45 to ±3.4 × 1038 with a precision of 7 digits in 32 bits. For example;

..\CSharp_Book\Chap03\SinglePrec

```
using System;
using System.Collections.Generic;
using System.Text;

namespace SinglePrec
{
    class Program
    {
        static void Main()
        {
            // Declaring float variable
            float rate = 8.5F;
            Console.WriteLine("ICICI Home Loan rate of interest : " + rate + "%");
            float IncrRate = (float) rate + 1;
            Console.WriteLine("Increased rate of interest in year 2007-2008 is : " +
                        IncrRate + "%");
        }
    }
}
```

When the above program executed, it will produce the following output as shown in Fig. 3.12.

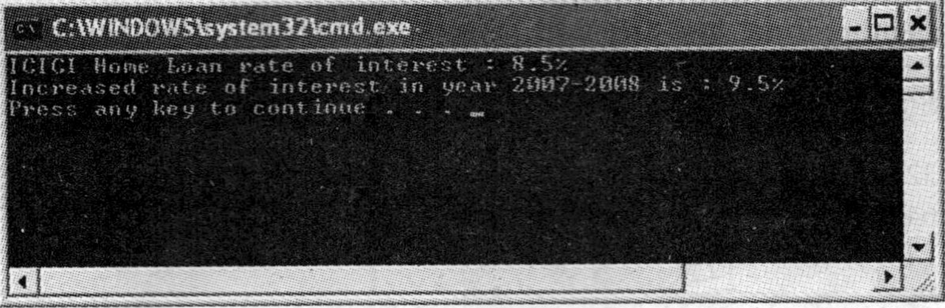

Fig. 3.12 Program output for float variable.

3.5.11 Double-Precision Numbers

When a variable is larger than the **float** can handle and requires more precision, you should declare it using the **double** keyword. A variable declared as **double** uses 64 bits to store very large numbers ranging from ±5.0 × 10-324 to ±1.7 × 10308 with a precision of 15 or 16 digits. For example;

..\CSharp_Book\Chap03\DoublePrec

```
using System;
using System.Collections.Generic;
using System.Text;

namespace DoublePrec
{
    class Program
    {
        static void Main()
        {
            // Declaring double variable
            double principal = 250000;
            int time = 5;
            float rate = 8.5F;

            double SI = (principal * time * rate) / 100;

            Console.WriteLine("Principal amount : " + principal);
            Console.WriteLine("Rate of interest : " + rate + "%");
            Console.WriteLine("Time period : " + time);
            Console.WriteLine("Interest is : " + SI);
        }
    }
}
```

When the above program executed, it will produce the following output as shown in Fig. 3.13.

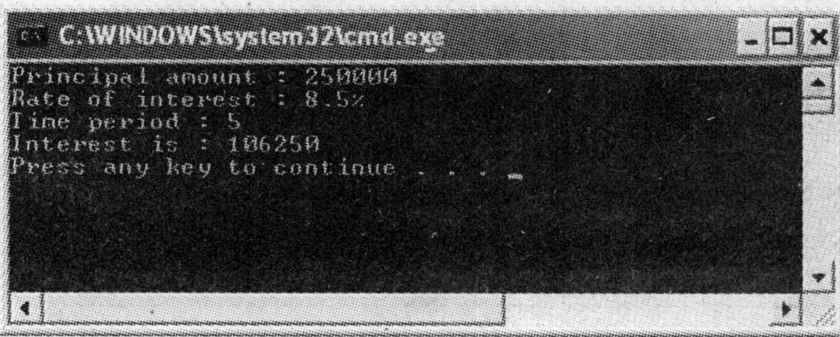

Fig. 3.13 Program output for double variable.

3.5.12 Decimal

The **decimal** data type can be used to declare a variable that would hold significantly large values that can be stored in a combination of 128 bits. You declare such a variable using the **decimal** keyword. The values stored in a **decimal** variable can range from ±1.0 × 10-28 to ±7.9 × 1028 with a precision of 28 to 29 digits. Because of this high level of precision, the **decimal** data type is suitable for currency values.

After declaring a **decimal** variable, you can initialize it with a natural number. For example;

..\CSharp_Book\Chap03\DecimalVar

```
using System;
using System.Collections.Generic;
using System.Text;

namespace DecimalVar
{
    class Program
    {
        static void Main()
        {
            // Declaring decimal variable
            decimal PerDay;

            float MonSalary = 15600;

            PerDay = (decimal) (MonSalary / 30);

            Console.WriteLine("Monthly Salary " + MonSalary);
            Console.WriteLine("Per day salary : " + PerDay);
        }
    }
}
```

When the above program executed, it will produce the following output as shown in Fig. 3.14.

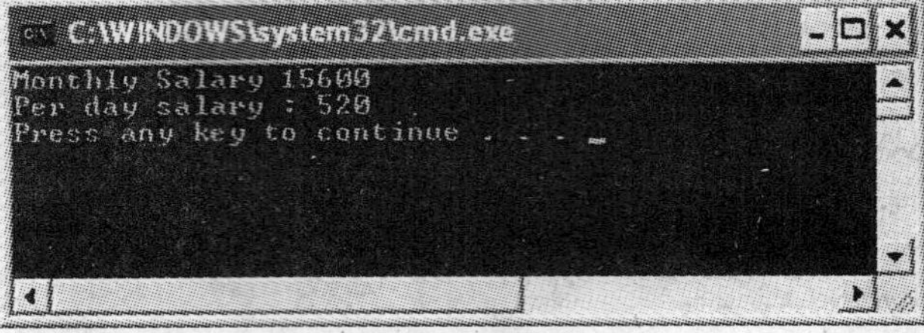

Fig. 3.14 Program output for decimal variable.

3.5.13 The Boolean Type

Boolean types are declared using the keyword, **bool**. They have two values: **true** or **false**. In other languages, such as C and C++, Boolean conditions can be satisfied where **0** means **false** and anything else means **true**. However, in C# the only values that satisfy a Boolean condition is **true** and **false**, which are official keywords.

Definition

A variable is referred to as Boolean if it is meant to carry only one of two logical values stated as true or false. For this reason, such a variable is used only when testing conditions or when dealing with conditional statements.

Here is an example shows one of many ways that Boolean types can be used in a program :

..\CSharp_Book\Chap03\BoolType

```
using System;
using System.Collections.Generic;
using System.Text;

namespace BoolType
{
    class Program
    {
        static void Main()
        {
            // Declaring Boolean variable
            bool AreYouOk = true;
            bool Text = false;

            Console.WriteLine("Are you ok! " + AreYouOk);
            Console.WriteLine("Text example " + Text);
        }
    }
}
```

From the above program, the Boolean values are written to the console as a part of a sentence. The only legal values for the **bool** type are either **true** or **false**, as shown by the assignment of true to **AreYouOK** and **false** to **Text**.

When the above program executed, it will produce the following output as shown in Fig. 3.15.

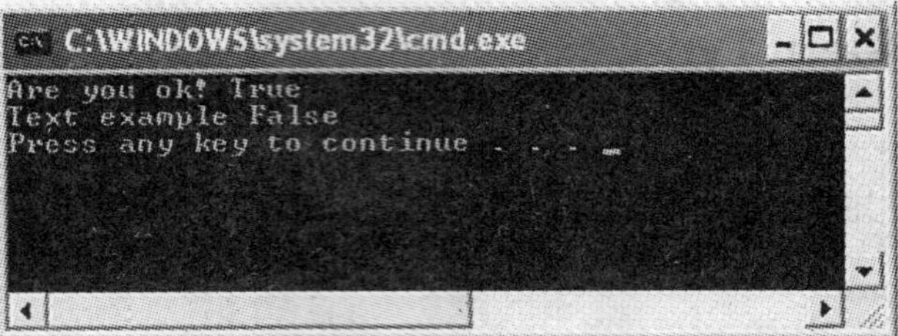

Fig. 3.15 Program output for Boolean variable.

3.5.14 Character Type

The character data type (char) consists of ASCII characters. The character type (**char**) occupies one byte of storage and can express a whole number in the range of –128 to 127 and 0 to 255, respectively. Unsigned characters have a range of 0 to 255. Typical declarations of character types are shown below:

```
char answer;        /* Declare a character variable answer */
char alpha = 'a';   /* Declare character variable alpha and initialize to it */
```

Note

ASCII code stores number codes for 256 characters.

When you declare a **char** data type, the respective character is represented in the memory as an integer code because it is easy to convert a number into binary equivalent. For example, if you are declaring

```
char ch = 'A';
```

then in memory it store as 65.

So, if you add 1 to ch, it will become 66, which is numeric code for 'B'.

..\CSharp_Book\Chap03\CharType

```
using System;
using System.Collections.Generic;
using System.Text;

namespace CharType
{
    class Program
    {
        static void Main()
        {
            // Declaring char variable
            char ch = 'Y';
            char opt = 'N';
```

```
            Console.WriteLine("The value of ch is : " + ch + " and its ASCII value is : "
                + (int)ch);
            Console.WriteLine("The value of opt is : " + opt + " and its ASCII value is : "
                + (int)opt);
        }
    }
}
```

When the above program executed, it will produce the following output as shown in Fig. 3.16.

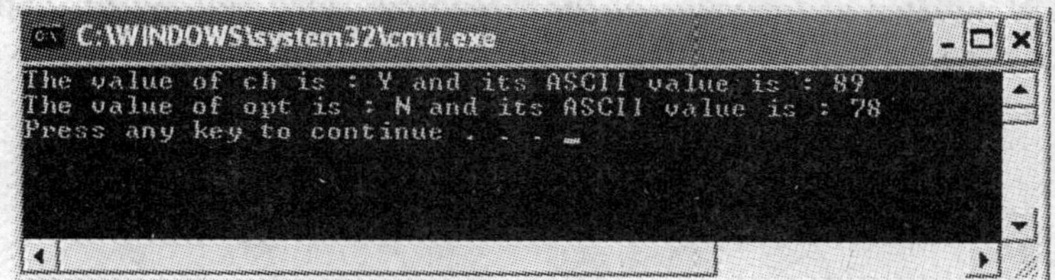

Fig. 3.16 Program output for char variable.

3.6 Reference Types

The pre-defined reference types are object and string, where object - as we have mentioned above - is the ultimate base class of all other types. New reference types can be defined using 'class', 'interface', and 'delegate' declarations which will be covered in subsequent chapter. Reference types actually hold the value of a memory address occupied by the object they reference. Consider the following piece of code, in which two variables are given a reference to the same object (for the sake of the example, this object is taken to contain the numeric property '**myValue**').

```
object x = new object();
x.myValue = 10;
object y = x;
y.myValue = 20;    // after this statement both x.myValue and y.myValue equal 20
```

This code illustrates how changing a property of an object using a particular reference to it is reflected in all other references to it. Note, however, that although strings are reference types, they work rather more like value types. When one string is set to the value of another, e.g.

```
string s1 = "hello";
string s2 = s1;
```

Then **s2** does at this point reference the same string object as **s1**. However, when the value of **s1** is changed, for instance with

```
s1 = "goodbye";
```

what happens is that a new string object is created for **s1** to point to. Hence, following this piece of code, **s1** equals "**goodbye**", whereas **s2** still equals "hello".

The reason for this behaviour is that string objects are 'immutable'. That is, the properties of these objects can't themselves change. So in order to change what a string variable references, a new string object must be created.

3.7 Boxing

C# allows you convert any value type to a corresponding reference type, and to convert the resultant 'boxed' type back again. The following piece of code demonstrates boxing. When the second line executes, an object is initiated as the value of 'box', and the value held by **i** is copied across to this object. It is interesting to note that the runtime type of box is returned as the boxed value type; the '**is**' operator thus returns the type of box below as '**int**'.

```
int i = 123;
object box = i;
if (box is int)
    {Console.Write("Box contains an int");}          // this line is printed
```

3.8 Structured/Derived Data Types

The data types, which is extracted/derived from fundamental data types are called derived data types. These data types can be derived by using the declaration operators or punctuators. For example, array, function, pointer, class, structure, enum, etc. That is :

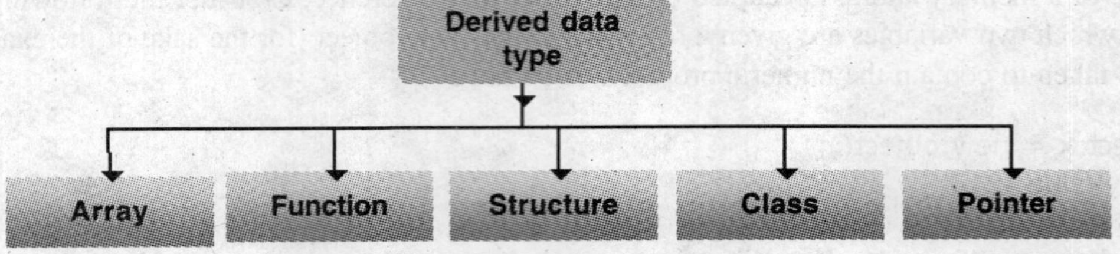

Fig. 3.17 Derived data types.

The details of these derived data types will be discussed in subsequent chapters.

3.8.1 const Keyword

C# allows us to declare the constants explicitly, much as we can declare variables. To declare a constant is just as declaring a variable except the value cannot be changed. The **const** keyword is used to declare constant. For example, the declaration,

```
const int x = 5;
```

or

```
int const x = 5;
```

will create an integer variable **x** with an initial value **5** that our program cannot change. The following are the important points about constant variables :

- A **const** variable gets its value either from explicit initialization (as in **const int x = 5**;) or it can get a default value (if, not initialized) by some hardware-dependent means.
- You can declare the **const** before or after the data type.
- You can declare to specify the size of an array. For example,

```
const int size = 10;
int a[size];
```

- We cannot assign the address of a **const** variable to a pointer. For example,

```
const int x = 5;
int *ptr = &x;        // Illegal, because ptr is not qualified as constant
```

..\CSharp_Book\Chap03\ConstType

```
using System;
using System.Collections.Generic;
using System.Text;

namespace ConstType
{
    class Program
    {
        static void Main()
        {
            // Declaring a constant
            const float PI = 3.14F;

            int radius = 5;
            double area = 0.0;
            area = PI * radius * radius;

            Console.WriteLine("Area of circle : " + area);
        }
    }
}
```

When the above program executed, it will produce the following output as shown in Fig. 3.18.

Fig. 3.18 Program output for char variable.

3.8.2 Enumerated Data Types

In C#, you can define your own data type and specify what values a variable of this type can take. The data type defined this way is known as *enumerated* (**enum**) data type. Enumerated data type helps in enhancing the readability of the code. That is this data type is used to give name to integer constants. By default, these numerical values are integers, but they can also be **long**s, **byte**s, etc. It is declared with keyword **enum**. For example,

```
enum color {Red, Yellow, Green, Brown}
enum months {January, February, March, April, May, June, July, August, September,
    October, November, December);
enum visible(On, Off);
enum doesit(Yes, No);
```

The above statement defines four integer constants. Enumerated values are by default starts with **0** and incremented by **1**. So, the above character is as :

```
const int Red = 0
const int Yellow = 1
const int Green = 2
const int Brown = 3
```

3.8.3 Pointer Notation

A pointer is a variable that holds the memory address of another type. In C#, pointers can only be declared to hold the memory addresses of value types (except in the case of arrays - see below). Pointers are declared implicitly, using the 'dereference' symbol *, as in the following example:

```
int *p;
```

Note that some coders place the dereferencer symbol immediately after the type name, eg.

```
int* p;
```

This variation appears to work just as well as the previous one.

This declaration sets up a pointer '**p**', which will point to the initial memory address of an integer (stored in four bytes).

The combined syntactical element ***p** ('p' prefixed by the dereferencer symbol '*') is used to refer to the type located at the memory location held by **p**. Hence given its declaration, ***p** can appear in integer assignments like the following:

```
*p = 5;
```

This code gives the value **5** to the integer that was initialized by the declaration. It is important, however, not to confuse such an assignment with one in which the derefencer symbol is absent, e.g.

```
p = 5;
```

The effect of this assignment is to change the memory location held by **p**. It doesn't change the value of the integer initialized by the original declaration; it just means that **p** no longer points to that integer. In fact, **p** will now point to the start of the four bytes present at memory location **5**.

Another important symbol for using pointers is the operator **&**, which in this context returns the memory address of the variable it prefixes. To give an example of this symbol, the following code sets up **p** to point to integer **i**'s memory location:

```
int i = 5;
int *p;
p = &i;
```

Given the above, the code

```
*p = 10;
```

changes the value of **i** to **10**, since '***p**' can be read as 'the integer located at the memory value held by **p**.

There is another important piece of notation for pointers. Pointers can be declared for structs, as in the following example (which uses the 'Coords' struct defined further below):

```
Coords x = new Coords();
Coords *y = &x;
```

One can then use the declared pointer **y** to access a public field of **x** (say **z**). This would be done using either the expression

```
(*y).z
```

or the equivalent expression, which uses the -> string:

```
y -> z
```

3.8.4 The void Data Type

The **void** data type, also known as empty data type, is useful in many situations. It is used to specify the return type of a function that is not supposed to return a value, empty argument list of a function and to declare generic pointer. We will discuss in length about *void* data type in **Functions** chapter.

Note

C# provides number of data types to utilize the memory in efficient manner.

3.9 Initializing Real Numbers

Because the double data type provides a better result with a better precision than the float, whenever you declare a variable as float and assign it a value as we did earlier, the compiler allocates 64 bits to store the values of the variable. If you insist on the variable being treated as float, when assigning it a value, add an **f** or an **F** suffix to the value. For example;

..\CSharp_Book\Chap03

```
using System;
using System.Collections.Generic;
using System.Text;

namespace RealNum
{
    class Program
    {
        static void Main()
        {
            double Rate;
            decimal IntRate;

            Rate = 8.5d; // Value treated as double
            IntRate = 8.5m; // Value treated as decimal

            Console.WriteLine("Interest rate is " + Rate);
            Console.WriteLine("Interest rate is " + IntRate);
        }
    }
}
```

When the above program executed, it will produce the following output :

```
Interest rate is 8.5
Interest rate is 8.5
```

From the code, when you declare a **double** variable, when initializing it, to make sure the value is treated as **double**, type the **d** or the **D** suffix to the right of the value.

Similarly, if you declare a variable using the **decimal** keyword, to indicate that the variable holds a **decimal** value, when initializing it, add an **m** or an **M** suffix to its value.

3.10 Literal Constants

A program must be able to store its input somewhere so that it can work with the data and process it into a form that is meaningful to the user. That is, a literal is a constant value which does not change its contents during the program execution.

When a value, such as 120, occurs in a program, it is referred to as a *literal constant*. That is,

- Literal because we can speak of it only in terms of its value, and
- Constant because its value cannot be changed.

Definition

A literal constant is a constant value which does changed during program execution.

Every literal constant has an associated data type. For example, 14 is of type **int**, 3.14142 is of type **double**, 'c' is of type **char**, etc.

Also, a literal constant as non-addressable through its value is stored somewhere in computer's memory; we have no means of accessing its address. Valid examples of integer constants of type *int* are:

```
120        -2312        0221        0x432        0xbc1
```

Valid examples of integer constants of type *long* are :

```
123456L    3442         0           0xffffffL    076549L
```

Valid examples of real constants of type *float* are :

```
123.45     12.543213    0.0         0.435E-12
```

Valid examples of real constants of type *double* are :

```
123.45     12.54E60     0.0         0.435E-55
```

3.11 Constants

Like literal constants, constants are also data values that never change their values during program execution. These are also called literals.

C# provides three types of constants. These are :

- Integer constants
- Character constants
- Boolean constants

Further the above constants are divided into sub-constants as shown in Fig. 3.19.

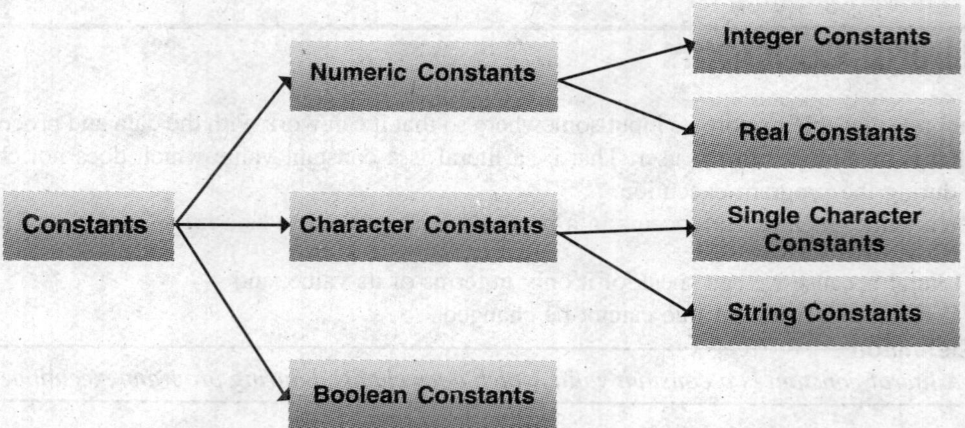

Fig. 3.19 Basic types of constants in C#.

3.11.1 Integer Constants

Integers are whole numbers without any fractional part. That is, an integer constant consists of sequence of digits preceded by an optional sign, plus (+) or minus (–). A decimal point and comma is not allowed in an integer constant. These are further divided into three types :

- Decimal (Base 10). An integer constant consisting of digits is taken as integer constant unless it begins with 0.
- Octal (Base 8). An integer constant beginning with 0 is taken as octal constant *e.g.* 010.
- Hexadecimal (Base 16). An integer constant beginning with 0X or 0x is called hexadecimal constant *e.g.* 0xc.

Definition

The constants, which has not fractional part is called integer constant.

The following are valid integer constants of type *int* :

```
123     +123     0       32765
3445    0x23b    7654    -3000
0200    -3523    0032    -0120
```

The following are invalid integer constants of type *int* :

.123 because decimal point is allowed.
3,2345 because comma not allowed.
45321 because value larger than permissible range of **int** type.

3.11.2 Character Constants

A character constant is an ASCII character enclosed by a pair of single quotation marks, *e.g.* 'c'. When C# compiler encounters such a character constant, it translates it into a corresponding ASCII code and stores that number in the program. "The constant 'a' appearing in the given code, for example, will be stored as 97.

Definition

The constants which is store in a variable within single quotation mark is called character constant.

Character variables can be assigned character constant as values. The following codes shows some examples of character constants and variables :

```
char var1 = 'A';      // Define character variable as character
char var2 = '\t';     // Define char variable as tag
var1 = 'B';           // Set char variable to char constant
```

3.11.3 Real/Floating-point Constants

Floating point are real numbers which has a fractional parts. These may be written in one of the two forms called fractional form or exponent form. The number **3.14159** is **AREA** is an example of a float-point constant. The decimal point signals that it is a floating-point constant, and not an integer. This number is written in normal decimal notation.

Definition

The constants, which is stored in a variable having fractional parts called real/floating-point constant.

You can also write floating-point constant using exponential notation. For example, the number **1234.56** would be written as **1.23456E3** in exponential notation. This is same as **1.23456** times **10**^{3}. The number following **E** is called exponent. It indicates how many places the decimal point must be moved to change the number to ordinary decimal notation.

The exponent can be positive or negative. The exponential number **6.35239E–5** is equivalent to **0.0000635239** in decimal notation. This is same as **6.35239** time **10**$^{-5}$.

The following are valid real constants of type **float**:

```
-123.456          +123.456          0.345
1234.             +1.24E12          0.0001E+2
1.E-2             1000.00E0         1.5E+10
```

The following are invalid real constants of type *float* :

```
15            because decimal point missing
12,34,33      because comma not allowed
```

```
+123.90E        because no digit specified for exponent
-123.56E+50     because exponent too large
45321           because value larger than permissible range of int type.
```

Note

A floating-point constant must have at least one digit before and after decimal point.

3.11.4 String Constants

Number of characters enclosed in double quotes is called string constants. String constant automatically end with a null character "**\0**" *e.g.* The string "john" will automatically represented as "**john\0**" in the memory and its size is not 4 but 5 characters. Valid examples of string constants are :

```
" " (null string) "a" "Hello Friends" "Hari's Mother"
```

Definition

The constants which is store in a variable within double quotation mark is called string constant.

Note

String is not a primitive data type in C, but it is internally handled as array of characters, where an array is a collection of similar values.
Assigning a value to a constant variable in an executable statement is a synt[illegible] error.

3.12 Punctuators

C# allows some of special characters in its coding called punctuators. These are :

[ ] { } ( ) , ; : * = #

- **Brackets [ ].** These two brackets are used for declaring single and multi-dimensional array subscripts. For example,

```
int[] num = new int[10];  // Declare as a single dimensional array with 10 elements.
```

- **Braces { }.** These two braces are used to indicate the start and end of a compound statement. That is a block of statements are enclosed within two braces to execute in one conditional loop. For example,

```
If <condition>
{  // Executing block of statements
   statement 1
   statement 2
   .
   statement n
}  // End of the block
```

- **Parentheses ( ).** These two are used in function calls and in function parameters. Also, it helps to group loop condition. For example;

```
if ((a > b) && (a > c)) // grouping a look condition
```

- **Comma ,.** It is used to separate two variable declarations in same line and to separate the function arguments. For example;

```
int a, b, c; // Declaring multiple variables in one line
```

- **Semicolon ;.** Like C++ language, semicolon (;) is used to terminate a C# program line. That is every executable statement in C# must be ended with semicolon (;). For example;

```
int a, b, c; // C# line ended with semicolon
```

- **Colon :.** It is used to labelled the statements which is transferred via a **goto** statement. Also it is used with **swtich case** statement to differentiate the **case** label. For example;

```
goto First;
.
.
First :  // Control transfer to a label.
```

- **Asterisk *.** It is used in pointer declaration. Also, it is used as a multiplication operator to multiply to operands, etc.For example;

```
salary = basic * DA; // Multiplying two operands
```

- **Equal sign =.** It is used to initialize value into a variable and an assignment operator in an expression. For example;

```
int a = 0;
sum = sum + total; // Assign value in an expression
```

- **Pound sign #.** It used to invoke the preprocessor directive like #define. For example

```
#define MYVAR
```

3.13 Strings

A string is a string of text characters. You typically create a string with a string literal, enclosed in quotes: "**This is an example of a string.**"

A string is an empty space, a character, a word, or a group of words that you want the compiler to consider "as is", that is, not to pay too much attention to what the string is made of, unless you explicitly ask it to. This means that, in the strict sense, you can put in a string anything you want.

Primarily, the value of a string starts with a double quote and ends with a double-quote. An example of a string is "**Welcome to C# .NET Programming!**". You can include such a string in the **Console.Write()** method to display it on the console. For example;

```
using System;

class BookClub
{
    static void Main()
    {
        Console.WriteLine("Welcome to C# .NET Programming (with .NET 3.0)!");
    }
}
```

When the above program executed, it will produce the following output :

```
Welcome to C# .NET Programming (with .NET 3.0)!
```

Sometimes, you will need to use a string whose value is not known in advance. Therefore, you can first declare a string variable. To do this, use the string keyword (in fact, it is a class) followed by a name for the variable. The name will follow the rules we defined above. An example of a string declaration is:

```
string Msg;
```

After declaring a string, you can give it a primary value by assigning it an empty space, a character, a symbol, a word, or a group of words. The value given to a string must be included in double-quotes. Here are examples of string variables declared and initialized:

```
string Empty  = " ";
string Gender = "F";
string FName  = "Nelson Mandela";
string Msg = "Welcome to C# .NET Programming (with .NET 3.0)!";
```

After initializing a string variable, you can use its name in any valid operation or expression. For example, you can display its value on the console using the **Console.Write()** or the **Console.WriteLine()** methods. For example;

```
using System;

class BookClub
{
    static void Main()
    {
        string Msg = "Welcome to C# .NET Programming (with .NET 3.0)!";
        Console.WriteLine(Msg);
    }
}
```

3.13.1 Escape Sequence

Some characters aren't printable, but you still need to use them in strings. Therefore, C# has a special syntax where characters can be escaped to represent non-printable characters. For example, it is common to use newlines in text, which is represented by the '**\n**' char. The backslash, '****', represents the escape. When preceded by the escape character, the '**n**' is no longer interpreted as an alphabetical character, but now represents a newline.

You may be now wondering how you could represent a backslash character in your code. We have to escape that too by typing two backslashes, as in '****'. Listing 3.3 shows a list of common escape sequences.

Listing 3.3 C# Character Escape Sequences.

Escape Sequence	Meaning
\'	Single Quote (')
\"	Double Quote (")
\\	Backslash (\)
\0 (zero)	Null, not the same as the C# null value
\a	Bell
\b	Backspace
\f	Form Feed
\n	New Line
\r	Carriage Return
\t	Horizontal Tab
\v	Vertical Tab
\u	A Unicode character specified by its number e.g. \u200
\x	A Unicode character specified by its hexadecimal code e.g. \xc8

Definition

Combination of characters preceded by a code-extension character (also called as escape character).

3.14 Comment

A comment is a sequence of characters, which improve the readability of a program. They can be inserted anywhere in the program.

Note

Compiler ignores the contents of a comment.

A comment can be inserted in a C# program in two different ways :

- **By using forward slash / asterisk combination** (/*) at beginning and asterisk slash at the end.

```
int a, b; /* Declares two integer variable */
```

Also, a comment can occupy more than one line but cannot be nested. To write more than one line comment,

```
/* Declares two integer variable
   for addition operation in C# */
```

Comments can appear on the same line like your previous example. Also like :

```
System.Console.WriteLine("Hello World!"); /* Comment can go here */
```

Definition

A comment started with / and ended with */ is called multiple line comment.*

- **By using double slash (//).** Whatever is written after double slash till the end of the line is treated as a comment and ignored by the compiler. For example,

```
// Declares two integer variable
int a, b;
  System.Console.WriteLine("Hello World!"); // Comment can go here
```

Definition

A comment with // is called single line comment.

Note

Since the compiler treats a comment as a single white-space character, you cannot include comments within tokens. The compiler ignores the characters in the comment.

3.15 Dates and Times

A date is a unit that measures the number of years, months, or days elapsed in a specific period. A time is a unit that counts the number of seconds that have elapsed since midnight of the day considered. Although dates and times are large subjects that would require a detailed study, at this time, we will consider them in simple terms.

To declare a variable that would hold date or time values, use the **DateTime** data type (like every data type we have used so far, except the string that is a class, DateTime is a structure).

..\CSharp_Book\Chap03

```
using System;
using System.Collections.Generic;
using System.Text;

namespace DateTimeObj
{
    class Program
    {
        static void Main()
        {
            // Storing current date and time
```

```
            DateTime curDt = DateTime.Now;       //Extracts current date

            Console.WriteLine("Current date and time is : " +  curDt);
        }
    }
}
```

When the above program executed, it will produce the following output :

```
Current date and time is : 3/2/2007 4:32:08 PM
```

The .NET Framework sets its starting periodic date to **January 1, 0001** at midnight (**12:00:00** or **0:00 AM**). If not assigned a specific value (in future lessons, we will learn that this is equivalent to declaring a variable using the default constructor), the variable is initialized to **1/1/0001** at midnight.

3.16 Objects

The **Object** data type (it is a class which will be discuss more in later chapter) is used to declare a variable whose type is not primarily defined and can be any of the other data types we have introduced. For example;

```
using System;

class Exercise
{
    static void Main()
    {
        object Whatever;
    }
}
```

3.17 .NET Support Data Types

All of the data types we have used so far are in fact complete classes. This means that they are equipped to handle their own assignments called functions as we will learn in subsequent lessons. When a data type (in this case a class) has to ability to perform assignments through its functions, it is able to better communicate with other variables, functions, or classes (the fact that the other languages, namely C/C++, Pascal, etc, use data types that are not considered classes doesn't mean they are less efficient or that they have an anomaly: it is simply the construct of the language!). These classes are defined in the **System** namespace. The classes of these data types are defined in the following listing 3.4.

Listing 3.4 .NET support data types.

Data Type	Class	Data Type	Class
bool	Boolean	char	Char
byte	Byte	sbyte	SByte
short	Int16	ushort	UInt16
int	Int32	uint	UInt32
long	Int64	ulong	UInt64
float	Single	double	Double
decimal	Decimal		

This means that, if you don't want to use the data types we have reviewed so far, you can use the class that is defined in the **System** namespace. To use one of these types, type the **System** namespace followed by a period. Then type the equivalent class you want to use. For example;

```
class Operations
{
    public double Addition()
    {
        System.Double a;
        System.Double b;
        System.Double c;

        a = 128.76;
        b = 5044.52;
        c = a + b;

        return c;
    }
}
```

Because the regular names of data types we introduced in the previous lesson are more known and familiar, we will mostly use them.

Because the data types are defined as classes, they are equipped with methods. One of the methods that each one of them has called **ToString**. As it s name implies, it is used to convert a value to a string.

Exercise

1. What are variables?
2. What is reserved?
3. What are the rules to define variables in C#?
4. How variables are declared in C#?
5. What are signed and unsigned integers?
6. How many data types are available in C#?

7. What is boxing?
8. Give an example to implement a Boolean type in C#?
9. What is constant and how it is declared in C#?
10. What are enum type, struct type and pointer type in C#?
11. What do you mean by void?
12. What are escape sequences in C#?
13. What are comments list out the types of comment available in C#?
14. What do you mean by the .NET support data types?
15. What are predefined data types?
16. What are structured data types?
17. Write some properties of constant in C#?
18. How many constants are provided by C#?
19. What are literals?
20. What are punctuators in C# list some of them?
21. What are single line comment and multiline comment in C#?
22. What are object data types in C#?
31. What are character constants ?
32. What are floating-point constants ?
33. What are string constants ?
34. Which of the following are invalid variables and why ?
    (a) PaidInterest
    (b) s-num
    (c) percent
    (d) 123
    (e) dit km
    (f) class
    (g) main
35. Some of the C# constants are written incorrectly. Identify the error and give the correct form.
    (a) 5,34
    (b) +345
    (c) 0.57–
    (d) 8.34E4
36. Following variables are written incorrectly. Identify the error and correct the variables.
    (a) 2Emp
    (b) EMP–
    (c) Stud name
    (d) A$
    (e) (roll)
    (f) S–Name
37. What will be the size of the following constant '\x', "\x" ?
38. Consider the following declaration :
    char ch = 97;
    char ch = 'a';
    Are they equal ?
39. Which punctuator is treated as an end of line marker ?

40. What will be the sizes of following constants ?
    (a) "PRITIMA\'S"
    (b) '\a'
41. Why Main() function is special ? Give two reasons.
42. Give the output of the following lines :
```
int j = 44;
Console.WriteLine("{0} \t {1} \t {2}", j++, j, ++j);
Console.WriteLine(j);
```
43. State True or False. (any four)
    (a) A variable of type char can hold value 310.
    (b) A short int and int variables may have equal sizes in C#.
    (c) The char is treated as one of the integer type.
    (d) An identifier declared as char type cannot hold numbers.
    (e) Data type long float is a valid data type.
44. Write the variable declaration whose name and data type are :

Variable	Data type
class1	character
status	character
rollno	integer
salary	floating point number
fact	double precision

Operators, Operands and Expressions

4

4.1 Introduction

Some confusion arises in the C# literature concerning the exact nature of an expression and operator. An expression in C# languages is nearly identical to the concept of expressions in other languages, such as BASIC, Pascal, C, C++, etc.

Variables and constants are the basic data objects manipulated in a program. Operators specify what is to be done to them. Expressions combine variables and constants to produce new values. The following section describes the details about operators, operands and expressions.

4.2 Operator

An operation is an action performed on one or more values either to modify the value held by one or both of the variables, or to produce a new value by combining existing values. Therefore, an operation is performed using at least one symbol and at least one value. The symbol used in an operation is called an operator. A value involved in an operation is called an operand.

A unary operator is an operator that performs its operation on only one operand. An operator is referred to as binary if it operates on two operands.

An operator is one, which works on data items and performs some mathematical calculation or change the data. C# provides six types of operators as shown in Fig. 4.1.

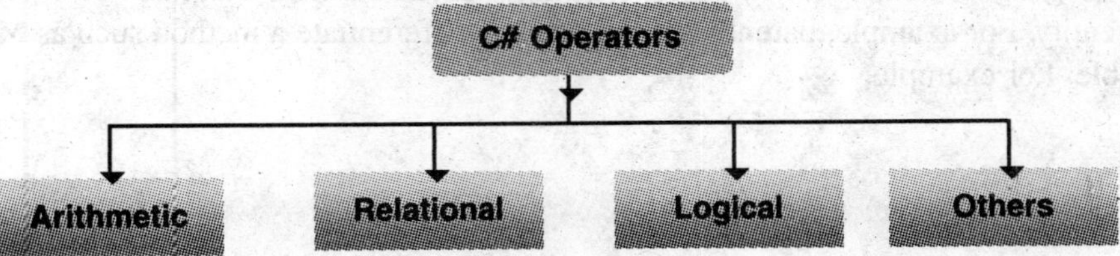

Fig. 4.1 C# operators.

Definition

Operators are the verbs of a language that let the user perform computations on values.

The operators includes : semicolon (;), curly brackets {}, parentheses (), comma (,), assignment (=), single-quote ('), double-quote ("), square brackets [ ], positive operator (+), negative operator (-), unary operator (the size operator) including arithmetical, relational and logical operators. Also, C# has other operators like increment (++), decrement (—). We are going to discuss these operators one by one in the coming section.

4.2.1 Semi-Colon (;)

The semi-colon is used to indicate the end of an expression or a declaration. For example;

```
using System;
```

As we will learn when studying the **for** conditional statement, there are other uses of the semi-colon.

4.2.2 Curly Brackets { }

Curly brackets are probably the most used and the most tolerant operators of C#. Fundamentally, curly brackets are used to create a section of code. As such they are required to delimit the bodies of namespaces, classes, structures, exceptions, etc. They are also optionally used in conditional statements. Curly brackets are also used to create variable scope. For example;

```
using System;

class Test
{               // Using curly bracket
    . . .
    . . .
}
```

4.2.3 Parentheses ( )

Like most computer languages, C# uses parentheses to isolate a group of items that must be considered as belonging to one entity. For example, parentheses are used to differentiate a method such as **Main()** from a regular variable. For example;

```
using System;

class Test
{
    static void Main()  // Using parentheses
    {
        . . .
```

```
        ...
    }
}
```

Parentheses can also be used to isolate an operation or an expression with regard to another operation or expression.

4.2.4 The Comma ,

The comma is used to separate variables used in a group. For example, a comma can be used to delimit the names of variables that are declared with the same data type. For example;
using System;

```
class Test
{
    static void Main()
    {
        string FirstName, LastName, FullName;    // Using comma
    }
}
```

The comma can also be used to separate the member of an enumerator or the arguments of a method.

4.2.5 The Assignment =

An assignment operator assigns the value of the right-hand operand to the storage location named by the left-hand operand. Therefore, the left-hand operand of an assignment operation must be a modifiable l-value. After the assignment, an assignment expression has the value of the left operand but is not a l-value. Thus, an assignment operator is used to assign the result of an expression to a variable. The usual assignment operator is '='.

In addition, C# has a set of compound assignment operator of the forms. Listing 4.1 shows the compound operators as :

Listing 4.1 The use of compound statements.

Operator	Example	Equivalent to
+=	x += 1	x = x + 1
–=	x –= 1	x = x – 1
*=	x *= 1	x = x * 1
/=	x /= 1	x = x / 1
%=	x %= 1	x = x % 1

4.2.5.1 Simple Assignment

When you declare a variable, a memory space is reserved for it. That memory space may be empty until you fill it with a value. To "put" a value in the memory space allocated to a variable, you can use the assignment operator represented as =. Based on this, the assignment operation gives a value to a variable. Its syntax is:

```
VariableName = Value
```

The **VariableName** factor must be a valid variable name. It cannot be a value such as a numeric value or a (double-quoted) string.

The simple-assignment operator assigns its right operand to its left operand. The value of the right operand is converted to the type of the assignment expression and replaces the value stored in the object designated by the left operand. For example,

```
class Test
{
    static void Main()
    {
        double x;
        int y;
        x = y;     // Simple assignment
    }
}
```

In this example, the value of **y** is converted to type **double** and assigned to **x**. For example, to assign a numeric value to a variable;

```
namespace Employee
{
    class Test
    {
        static void Main()
        {
            decimal Salary;

            // Using the assignment operator
            Salary = 12.55M;
        }
    }
}
```

Once a variable has been declared and assigned a value, you can call **Write()** or **WriteLine()** to display its value. For example;

```
namespace Employee
{
    class Test
```

```
    {
        static void Main()
        {
            decimal Salary;

            // Using the assignment operator
            Salary = 12.55M;
            System.Console.Write("Employee's Hourly Salary: ");
            System.Console.WriteLine(Salary);
        }
    }
}
```

When the above program executed, it will produce the following output

```
Employee's Hourly Salary: 12.55
Press any key to continue. . .
```

The above code declares a variable before assigning it a value. You will usually perform this assignment when you want to change the value held by a variable. Providing a starting value to a variable when the variable is declared is referred to as initializing the variable. For example;

```
namespace Operations
{
    class Test
    {
        static void Main()
        {
            // Using the assignment operator
            decimal Salary = 12.55M;

            System.Console.Write("Employee's Hourly Salary: ");
            System.Console.WriteLine(Salary);
        }
    }
}
```

When the above program executed, it will produce the following output

```
Employee's Hourly Salary: 12.55
Press any key to continue. . .
```

We saw that you can declare various variables at once by using the same data type but separating their names with commas. When doing this, you can also initialize each variable by assigning it the desired value before the comma or the semi-colon. For example;

```
namespace Employee
```

```
{
    class Test
    {
        static void Main()
        {
            // Initializing various variables when declaring them with the same data type
            double Num1 = 282.58, Num2 = 4548.46;

            System.Console.Write("Number 1 = ");
            System.Console.WriteLine(Num1);
            System.Console.Write("Number 2 = ");
            System.Console.WriteLine(Num2);
            System.Console.WriteLine();
        }
    }
}
```

When the above program executed, it will produce the following output

```
Number 1 = 282.58
Number 2 = 4548.46
Press any key to continue. . .
```

4.2.5.2 Compound Assignment

The compound-assignment operators combine the simple-assignment operator with another binary operator. Compound-assignment operators perform the operation specified by the additional operator, and then assign the result to the left operand. For example, a compound-assignment expression such as:

```
expression1 += expression2;
```

can be understood as :

```
expression1 = expression1 + expression2;
```

Example 11.8 Suppose that you have been storing your factory's production amount in a variable referred to as prod_amt, and your supervisor has just informed you of a new addition that needs to be applied to that production value. You can code this update in a statement that resembles the following :

```
prod_amt = prod_amt + 2.5;  // Add 2.5 to current production
```

Instead of this formula, you should use C#'s compound addition operator by coding the update in this way:

```
prod_amt += 2.5; // Add 2.5 to the current production
```

4.2.5.3 Multiple Assignments

If the same value is assigned to different variable of same type, the usual way is to used different assignment statement for each variable. However, C# permits use to assign the same value to more than one variable using multiple assignment statement. The syntax of a multiple assignment statement is :

```
varname1 = varname2 = varname3 = value;
```

where **varname1**, **varname2** and **varname3** are variables or array of element references of same type and value is a value to be assigned.

The order of assignment the value is from right to left. For example, the following statement assigns value **0** to variables **x**, **y** and **z**.

```
x = y = z = 0;
```

Note

In relational operator, = stands for assignment and == stands for exactly equal to.

4.2.6 Single Quote (')

The single quote (') is used to include one character to initialize, or assign a symbol to, a variable declared as **char**. A single is usually combined with another and a character is included between them. For example;

```
using System;

class Test
{
    static void Main()
    {
        char Gender;
        string FirstName, LastName, FullName;

        Gender = 'M';
    }
}
```

You can include only one character between single-quotes except if the combination of symbols can be evaluated to one character. This is the case for escape sequences. For example;

```
using System;

class Test
{
    static void Main()
    {
        Console.WriteLine('\n');
    }
}
```

4.2.7 Double Quote (")

The double-quote (") is used to delimit a string. Like the single-quote, the double-quote is usually combined with another. Between the combinations of double-quotes, you can include an empty space, a character, a word, or a group of words, making it a string. For example;

```
using System;
class Test
{
    static void Main()
    {
        Console.WriteLine("The C# .NET Programming");
    }
}
```

A double-quoted string can also be declared and then assigned to a variable.

4.2.8 Square Brackets [ ]

Square brackets are mostly used to control the dimension or index of an array. We will learn how to use them when we study arrays. For example;

```
using System;

namespace Brackets
{
    class Test
    {
        static void Main()
        {
            double[] number = new double[5];    // Declare as array type.

            // Array will be discussed more in Chapter - 7
            number[0] = 12.44;
            number[1] = 525.38;
            number[2] = 6.28;
            number[3] = 2448.32;
            number[4] = 632.04;
            Console.WriteLine();
        }
    }
}
```

4.2.9 Unary and Binary Operators

The operators we have discussed so far are all binary operators. C# provides two unary operators for which only one variable is required. You can use the addition and subtraction operators by themselves. When you do, they are called ***unary operators***.

4.2.9.1 The Positive Operator +

Algebra uses a type of ruler to classify numbers. This ruler has a middle position of zero. The numbers on the left side of the **0** are referred to as negative while the numbers on the right side of the rulers are considered positive:

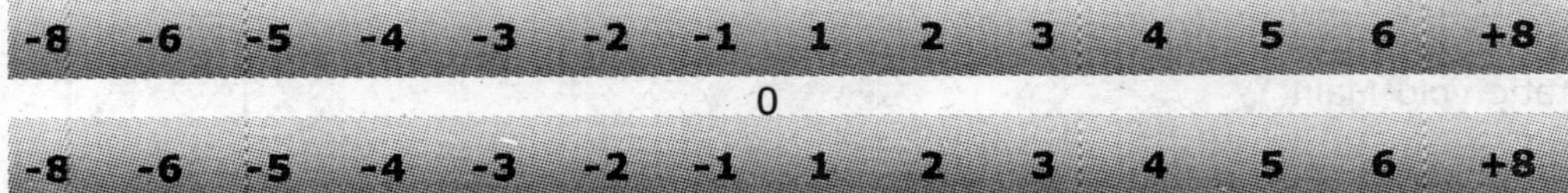

A value on the right side of 0 is considered positive. To express that a number is positive, you can write a + sign on its left. Examples are +4, +228, +90335. In this case the + symbol is called a unary operator because it acts on only one operand. The positive unary operator, when used, must be positioned on the left side of its operand, never on the right side.

As a mathematical convention, when a value is positive, you don't need to express it with the + operator. Just writing the number without any symbol signifies that the number is positive. Therefore, the numbers +4, +228, and +90335 can be, and are better, expressed as 4, 228, 90335. Because the value doesn't display a sign, it is referred as **unsigned.**

To express a variable as positive or **unsigned**, you can just type it. For example;

```
using System;

class Test
{
    static void Main()
    {
        // Displaying an unsigned number
        Console.Write("Number = ");
        Console.WriteLine(+802);
    }
}
```

When the above program executed, it will produce the following output :

```
Number = 802
Press any key to continue. . .
```

4.2.9.2 The Negative Operator –

As you can see on the above ruler, in order to express any number on the left side of 0, it must be appended with a sign, namely the - symbol. Examples are -12, -448, -32706. A value accompanied by -

is referred to as negative. The - sign must be typed on the left side of the number it is used to negate. Remember that if a number does not have a sign, it is considered positive. Therefore, whenever a number is negative, it MUST have a - sign. In the same way, if you want to change a value from positive to negative, you can just add a - sign to its left.

Here is an example that uses two variables. One has a positive value while the other has a negative value:

```
using System;

class Exercise
{
    static void Main()
    {
        // Displaying an unsigned number
        Console.Write("First Number  ");
        Console.WriteLine(+802);
        // Displaying a negative number
        Console.Write("Second Number ");
        Console.WriteLine(-802);
    }
}
```

When the above program executed, it will produce the following output :

```
First Number  802
Second Number -802
Press any key to continue. . .
```

The following section of code assigns four variables a positive or negative number. All the plus signs (+) and minus signs (–) are unary because they are not used between two variables.

```
The variable a becomes equal to negative 40.
The variable b becomes equal to positive 40.
The variable c becomes equal to negative a.
The variable d becomes equal to positive b.
a = –40;    // Assign 'a' a negative 40
b = +40;    // Assign 'b' a positive 40 (The plus sign is not needed)
c = –a;     // Assign 'c' the negative of 'a' (40)
d = +b;     // Assign 'd' the positive of 'b' (the plus sign is not needed)
```

The = and the preceding + operator are called *binary operators* because each have two *operands*. For example;

```
int val1 = 100, val2 = 200;
sum = val1 + val2;
```

In case of **+** operator, the two operands are **val1** and **val1**. In case of the preceding = operator, the two operands are **sum** and the value of the expression **val1 + val2.**

Definition
The operator which act on one operand is called unary operator and acts on two or more than two operands is called binary operator.

4.2.10 Unary Operator: The sizeof Operator

We have already seen that when declaring a variable, the compiler reserves a portion of space in the computer memory to hold that variable. We also illustrated how much space some data types need to store their variable. C# provides the unary **sizeof** operator that allows you to find out how much space a data type. You can use the **sizeof** operator as unsafe in your C# application.

To find out how much memory space a data type uses, type it between the parentheses of the **sizeof** operator. Remember that **sizeof** is unsafe. Therefore, a method that uses it must be preceded with the **unsafe** keyword. The **sizeof** operator has one of the following formats :

```
sizeof data
sizeof (data type)
```

The **sizeof** operator is a unary operator. The reason is that it operates on a single value. This operator produces a result that is the size, in bytes, of the data or data type specified. Most data types and variables require different amounts of internal storage on different computers. Therefore, the **sizeof** operator was provided to enable the same programs to be run on different kinds of computers. For example;

..\CSharp_Book\Chap05\SizeOf

```
using System;
using System.Collections.Generic;
using System.Text;

namespace SizeOf
{
    class Program
    {
        static void Main()
        {
            // The sizeof operator used to get the memory size used by

            // a variable declared with a certain a data type
            Console.WriteLine("The sizeof Operator");
            Console.WriteLine("===========================");
            Console.WriteLine("Data Type      Memory Size");
            Console.WriteLine("------------------------------------");
            Console.Write("char          ");
```

```
            Console.Write(sizeof(char));
            Console.WriteLine("   Bytes");
            Console.Write("bool          ");
            Console.Write(sizeof(bool));
            Console.WriteLine("   Bytes");
            Console.Write("int           ");
            Console.Write(sizeof(int));
            Console.WriteLine("   Bytes");
            Console.Write("uint          ");
            Console.Write(sizeof(uint));
            Console.WriteLine("   Bytes");
            Console.Write("short         ");
            Console.Write(sizeof(short));
            Console.WriteLine("   Bytes");
            Console.Write("ushort        ");
            Console.Write(sizeof(ushort));
            Console.WriteLine("   Bytes");
            Console.Write("byte          ");
            Console.Write(sizeof(byte));
            Console.WriteLine("   Bytes");
            Console.Write("sbyte         ");
            Console.Write(sizeof(sbyte));
            Console.WriteLine("   Bytes");
            Console.Write("float         ");
            Console.Write(sizeof(float));
            Console.WriteLine("   Bytes");
            Console.Write("double        ");
            Console.Write(sizeof(double));
            Console.WriteLine("   Bytes");
            Console.Write("decimal       ");
            Console.Write(sizeof(decimal));
            Console.WriteLine(" Bytes");
            Console.Write("long          ");
            Console.Write(sizeof(long));
            Console.WriteLine("   Bytes");
            Console.Write("ulong         ");
            Console.Write(sizeof(ulong));
            Console.WriteLine("   Bytes");
            Console.WriteLine("==============================");
            Console.WriteLine();
        }
    }
}
```

When the above program executed, it will produce the following output as shown in Fig. 4.2.

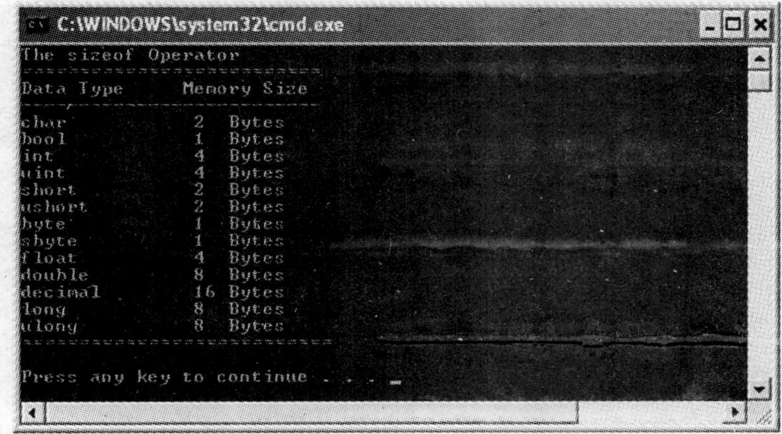

Fig. 4.2 Findig different sizes of data types.

4.2.11 The Minimum and Maximum Values of a Primitive Type

When you declare a variable, the compiler reserves an amount of memory space preparing to store its value. As different variables have different requirements, some of them use less or more memory than others. When you declare a variable, the data type you specify allows the compiler to know how mush space would be needed to store the value of that variable. There is a minimum and a maximum values that can be stored in the memory space reserved for a variable. Based on this, a value such as 224855 can be stored in space reserved for an int variable but it is beyond the space reserved for a Byte or a short.

To help you find out the minimum value that a data type can hold each structure of a primitive type is equipped with a constant member named **MinValue**. In the same way, the maximum value that a data type can support is represented by a constant field named **MaxValue**. You can check these minimum and maximum with the following program;

..\CSharp_Book\Chap04\PrimitiveType

```
..\CSharp_Book\Chap04\PrimitiveType
using System;
using System.Collections.Generic;
using System.Text;

namespace PrimitiveType
{
    class Program
    {
        static int Main()
```

```
{
    Console.WriteLine("====================================
            ========================================");
    Console.WriteLine("C# Type .NET Structure Minimum        Maximum");
    Console.WriteLine("====================================
            ========================================");
    Console.WriteLine("char    Char         {0}\t\t\t{1}", char.MinValue,
            char.MaxValue);
    Console.WriteLine("————————————————————————————————————
            ———————————");
    Console.WriteLine("byte    Byte         {0}\t\t\t{1}", byte.MinValue,
            byte.MaxValue);
    Console.WriteLine("————————————————————————————————————
            ———————————");
    Console.WriteLine("sbyte   SByte        {0}\t\t\t{1}", sbyte.MinValue,
            sbyte.MaxValue);
    Console.WriteLine("————————————————————————————————————
            ———————————");
    Console.WriteLine("short   Int16        {0}\t\t\t{1}", short.MinValue,
            short.MaxValue);
    Console.WriteLine("————————————————————————————————————
            ———————————");
    Console.WriteLine("ushort  UInt16       {0}\t\t\t{1}", UInt16.MinValue,
            UInt16.MaxValue);
    Console.WriteLine("————————————————————————————————————
            ———————————");
    Console.WriteLine("int     Int32        {0}\t\t{1}", int.MinValue, int.MaxValue);
    Console.WriteLine("————————————————————————————————————
            ———————————");
    Console.WriteLine("uint    UInt32       {0}\t\t\t{1}", UInt32.MinValue,
            UInt32.MaxValue);
    Console.WriteLine("————————————————————————————————————
            ———————————");
    Console.WriteLine("long    Int64        {0}\t{1}", long.MinValue, long.MaxValue);
    Console.WriteLine("————————————————————————————————————
            ———————————");
    Console.WriteLine("uint64  UInt64       {0}\t\t\t{1}", UInt64.MinValue,
            UInt64.MaxValue);
    Console.WriteLine("————————————————————————————————————
            ———————————");
    Console.WriteLine("float   Single       {0}\t\t{1}", float.MinValue,
```

```
                float.MaxValue);
        Console.WriteLine("--------------------------------
                -----------");
        Console.WriteLine("double  Double          {0}\t{1}", double.MinValue,
                double.MaxValue);
        Console.WriteLine("--------------------------------
                -----------");
        Console.WriteLine("decimal Decimal         {0} {1}", decimal.MinValue,
                decimal.MaxValue);
        Console.WriteLine("================================
                ==========================================");
        return 0;
    }
  }
}
```

When the above program executed, it will produce the following output as shown in Fig. 4.3.

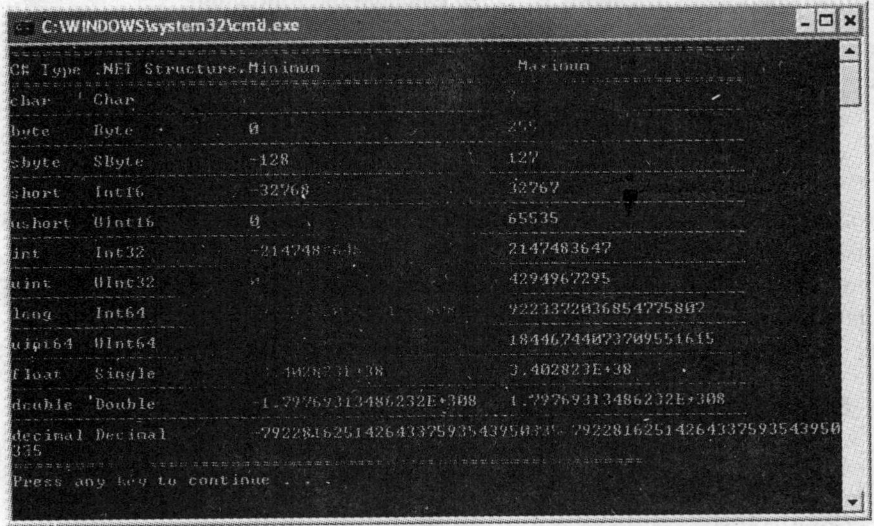

Fig. 4.3 Minimum and maximum values of C# .NET data type structure.

4.2.12 Arithmetical Operators

These are general mathematical operators, which works on more than one operands. For these operators always two or more than two operands are necessary that is why these operators are called binary operator. Listing 4.2 shows the arithmetic operator below :

Listing 4.2 Arithmetic operators.

Operators	Meaning	Example	Result
+	addition	9 + 4	13
–	subtraction	9 – 4	5
*	multiplication	9 * 4	36
/	division	9 / 4	2
%	modulus/remainder	9 % 4	1

Definition

There is no operator for exponentiation operation in C#. The % operator can only be used with integer type of data.

The difference between '**/**' and '**%**' operator is this '**/**' gives the quotient and '%' gives the remainder obtained during division. Most of these operators work in ways familiar to you. Multiplication and subtraction produce the same results (and the division operator usually does) that you get when you do these maths functions with a calculator.

For example; suppose, a = 5 and b = 2, then evaluate the following :

(*i*) a + b (*ii*) a – b (*iii*) a x b
(*iv*) a / b (*v*) a % b

Ans. (*i*) 5 + 2 = 7 (*ii*) 5 – 2 = 3 (*iii*) 5 x 2 = 10
(*iv*) 5 / 2 = 2 (*v*) 5 % 2 = 1

Now, from the above example, it is clear that '**/**' operator is used to find the quotient and the '**%**' operator is used to find the remainder.

In C#, you can also add string variables to add a new string. The operation is performed as if you were using numbers. For example, "**Hello**" + "**World**" would produce "**HelloWorld**". You can also add as many strings as possible by including the + operator between them. For example;

..\CSharp_Book\Chap05\NameAdd

```
using System;
using System.Collections.Generic;
using System.Text;

namespace NameAdd
{
    class Program
    {
        static void Main()
        {
            string FirstName = "Sidharth";
            string LastName  = "Sahoo";
            string FullName  = FirstName + " " + LastName;
            System.Console.Write("Full Name: ");
```

```
            System.Console.WriteLine(FullName);
        }
    }
}
```

When the above program executed, it will produce the following output :

```
Full Name: Sidharth Sahoo
Press any key to continue. . .
```

For example;

..\CSharp_Book\Chap05\Arithmetic

```
using System;
using System.Collections.Generic;
using System.Text;
// Use of Arighmetic operators
namespace Arithmetic
{
    class Program
    {
        static int Main()
        {
            // Initializing various variables when declaring them with the same data type
            double Value1 = 224.58, Value2 = 1548.26;
            double Result = Value1 * Value2;
            double Value3 = 224.58, Value4 = 1548.26;
            double Result1 = Value3 - Value4;
            double Value5 = 224.58, Value6 = 1548.26;
            double Result3 = Value1 / Value2;
            int Players = 26;

            System.Console.Write("244 + 835 = ");
            System.Console.WriteLine(244 + 835);
            System.Console.Write(Value1);
            System.Console.Write(" * ");
            System.Console.Write(Value2);
            System.Console.Write(" = ");
            System.Console.WriteLine(Result);
            System.Console.WriteLine();

            Console.Write(Value3);
            Console.Write(" - ");
```

```
            Console.Write(Value4);
            Console.Write(" = ");
            Console.WriteLine(Result1);

            System.Console.Write(Value5);
            System.Console.Write(" / ");
            System.Console.Write(Value6);
            System.Console.Write(" = ");
            System.Console.WriteLine(Result3);
            System.Console.WriteLine();

            // When the game starts, how many players will wait?
            Console.Write("Out of ");
            Console.Write(Players);
            Console.Write(" players, ");
            Console.Write(26 % 11);
            Console.WriteLine(" players will have to wait when the game starts.\n");
            return 0;
        }
    }
}
```

When the above program executed, it will produce the following output as shown in Fig. 4.4.

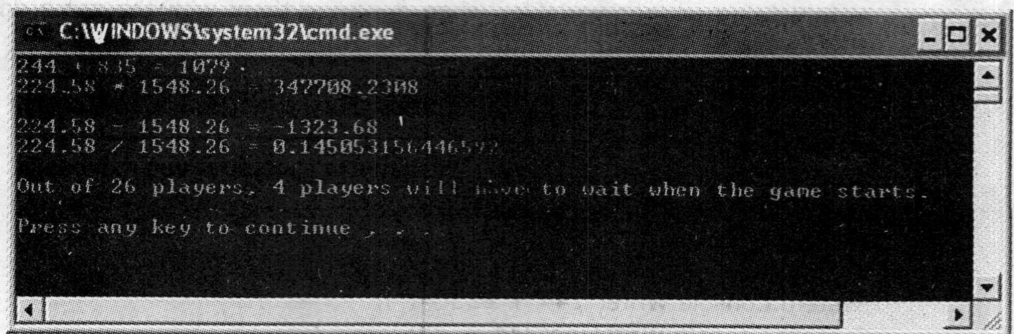

Fig. 4.4 Using arithmetic operators in C# program..

For example, write a program to calculate the torque.

..\CSharp_Book\Chap05\Torque

```
using System;
using System.Collections.Generic;
using System.Text;
```

```
// Program to calculate the torque
namespace Torque
{
    class Program
    {
        static int Main()
        {
            int t, m1, m2, g;
            Console.Write("Enter the value of m1=> ");
            m1 = int.Parse(Console.ReadLine()); // Data input
            Console.Write("Enter the value of m2=> ");
            m2 = int.Parse(Console.ReadLine());
            Console.Write("Enter the value of g => ");
            g = int.Parse(Console.ReadLine());

            t = ((2 * m1 * m2) / ( m1 + m2)) * g;
            Console.WriteLine("Torque is => {0} ", t);
            return 0;
        }
    }
}
```

When the above program executed, it will produce the following output as shown in Fig. 4.5.

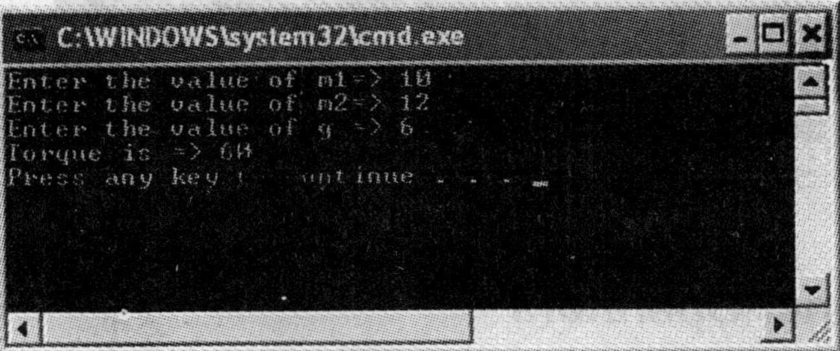

Fig. 4.5 Calculating the torque.

Example Write a program to convert the time given in minutes into hours and minutes.

..\CSharp_Book\Chap05\TimeToMin

```
using System;
using System.Collections.Generic;
using System.Text;

// Program to calculate the torque
namespace TimeToMin
```

```
{
    class Program
    {
        static int Main()
        {
            int t, hour, min;
            Console.Write("Enter the time in minutes => ");
            t = int.Parse(Console.ReadLine()); // Data input

            hour = t / 60;
            min = t % 60;

            Console.WriteLine("Hours are {0}", hour);
            Console.WriteLine("Munites are {0}", min);
            return 0;
        }
    }
}
```

When the above program executed, it will produce the following output as shown in Fig. 4.6.

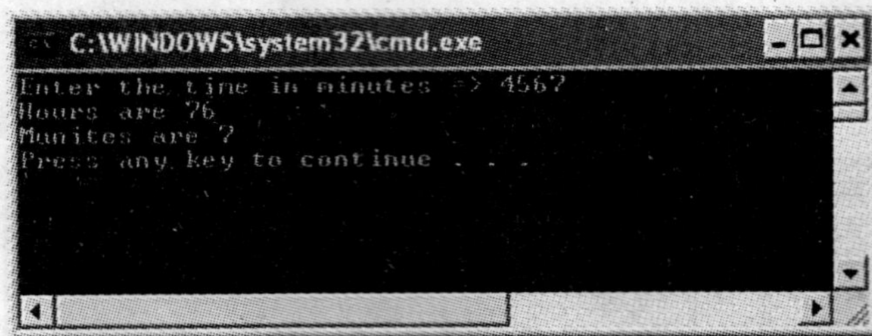

Fig. 4.6 Converting minutes into hours and minutes.

4.2.13 Relational Operators

The operators used to do comparison are called relational operators. In some expression it is required to compare the variables or constant. For example, first number is greater than second number etc. So, for doing comparison relational operators are required. The relational operators examine the constants and variable in the program, and operator based on what they find. The use of *relational operators* makes this possible. Listing 4.3 shows the relations operators below :

Definition

Relational operators are used to determine the relationship between different operands.

Listing 4.3 Relational operators.

Operators	Meaning	Example	Result
==	equal to	9 == 4	False
>	greater than	9 > 4	True
<	less than	9 < 4	False
>=	greater than equal to	9 >= 4	True
<=	less than equal to	9 <= 4	False
!=	not equal to	9 != 4	True

The six operators in the above table provide the foundation for comparing data in C#. Each operator always appears with two constants, variables, expression, or a mix of these—one on each side of the operators.

Note
In C#, the non-zero value is treated as true and zero value is treated as false.

The following Listing 4.4 will help you understanding the relational operators and their results :

Listing 4.4 Relational operators with example.

x	y	x > y	x < y	x >= y	x <= y	x == y	x != y
1	0	1	0	1	0	0	1
0	1	0	1	0	1	0	1
1	1	0	0	1	1	1	0
2	3	0	1	0	1	0	1

From the above table, the right part of table contains 0's and 1's. 0 means false and 1 means true.

Note
Relational operators are used in decision statements like if and while.

Assume that a program initializes four variables in this way :

```
int a = 10;
int b = 30;
int c = 35;
int d = 10;
```

The following statements are then true;

```
a is equal to d so a == d.
b is less than c so b < c.
c is greater than a so c > a;
b is greater than or equal to a so b >= a.
```

```
d is less than or equal to b so d <= b.
d is not equal to c so d != c.
```

These are not C# statements. However, they are statements of relational facts about the values in the variables.

..\CSharp_Book\Chap05\Relation

```
using System;
using System.Collections.Generic;
using System.Text;

namespace Relation
{
    class Program
    {
        static void Main()
        {
            int x = -5;
            uint y = 6;
            Console.WriteLine("The Relational result is {0} ", (x>y));
            if (x>y)
                Console.WriteLine("x is greater");
            else
                Console.WriteLine("y is greater");
        }
    }
}
```

When the above program executed, it will produce the following output :

```
The Relational result is False
y is greater
Press any key to continue. . .
```

From the above program, we compares one signed number and another unsigned number. But, C# compiler treats both the numbers are unsigned. Because, the comparison operator treats both are unsigned. So, the binary equivalent of –5 is 1101 becomes 13 and the binary equivalent of 6 is 101 because it is unsigned.

When the statement,

```
if (x>y)
```

read by compiler, it compare (1101 > 101), which produce a True result. That is,

```
x is greater
```

Note

Try to avoid the comparison between signed and unsigned values.

..\CSharp_Book\Chap05\Relational

```
// Demonstrating logical operators ==, !, !=, <, >
// operations using two variables
using System;
using System.Collections.Generic;
using System.Text;

namespace Relational
{
    class Program
    {
        static void Main()
        {
            int num1 = 15;
            int num2 = 24;
            bool HasTicketBooked = true;
            bool DoesIt;
            bool num3 = (num1 != num2);
            bool num4 = (num1 < 24);
            bool num5 = (num1 <= 24);

            Console.Write("Num 1 = ");
            Console.WriteLine(num1);
            Console.Write("Num 2 = ");
            Console.WriteLine(num2);
            Console.Write("Comparison of Num1 == 15 produces ");
            Console.WriteLine(num1 == 15);

            Console.Write("HasTicketBooked ? ");
            Console.WriteLine(HasTicketBooked);
            DoesIt = !HasTicketBooked;
            Console.Write("DoesIt          = ");
            Console.WriteLine(DoesIt);
            Console.Write("Num 3 = ");
            Console.WriteLine(num3);
            Console.Write("Num 4 = ");
            Console.WriteLine(num4);
            Console.Write("Num 5 = ");
            Console.WriteLine(num5);
        }
```

```
    }
}
```

When the above program executed, it will produce the following output as shown in Fig. 4.7.

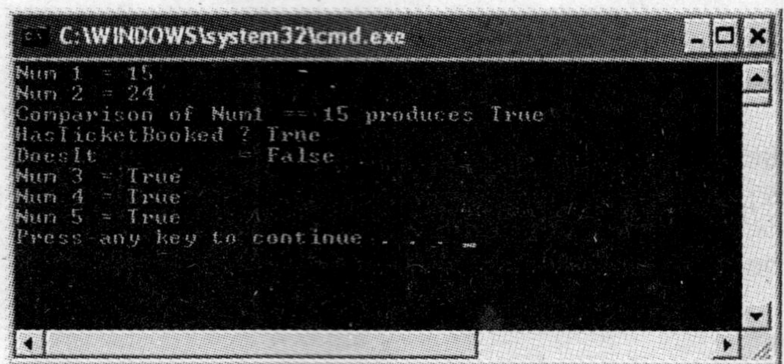

Fig. 4.7 Use of relational operators in C# program.

4.2.14 Logical Operators

These operators are used to combine one or more than one relational expression. By combining logical operators with relational operators, you can create more powerful data-testing statements. Listing 4.5 shows the logical operators below :

Listing 4.5 Logical Operators.

Operator	Meaning
||	OR
&&	AND
!	NOT

The True and False on each side of the operators represent a relational if test. For instance, the following tests are valid if tests that use logical operators (sometimes referred to as compound relational operators).

The following example tests the variables using **if** statement (which shall be discussed in succeeding chapters).

Note

If ((the variable a is less than the variable b) AND (the variable c is greater than the variable d)).print results are invalid to the screen.

```
if ((a < b) && (c > d))
    Console.Writeline("Result is invalid. ");
```

4.2.14.1 Logical AND Operators (&&)

Suppose we wish to ensure that two conditions are both **true** before we choose a certain path of execution. In this case, we can use the logical **&&** operator as follows :

```
if ((gender == 1) && (age >= 65))
    Console.Writeline("Senior Female");
```

This **if** statement contains two simple conditions. The condition **gender == 1** must be evaluated, for example, to determine if the person is a female. The condition **age >= 65** is evaluated to determine if a person is a senior citizen. The simple condition to the left of the **&&** operator is evaluated first because the preceding of the **&&** operator is evaluated next of **&&.** If necessary, the simple condition to the right of the **&&** operator is evaluated next because the preceding of **>=** is higher than the precedence of **&&.**

The **if** statement then considers the combined condition

```
(gender == 1) && (age >= 65)
```

This condition is **true** if and only if both of the simple conditions are **true.** Finally, if this combined condition is indeed **true**, then the statement **Console.Writeline("Senior Female");** is encountered. If either or both of the simple, conditions are **false**, then the program skips the statement and proceeds to the statement following the **if.**

Listing 4.6 Truth table for the && (logical AND) operator.

expression1	expression2	expression && expression2
false	false	false
false	true	false
true	false	false
true	true	true

The Table 11.5 summarizes the **&&** operator. The table shows all four possible combinations of **false** and **true** values for **expression1** and **expression2**. Such tables are often called *truth table*. C# evaluates to **false** or **true** all expressions that include relational operators, equality operators, and/or logical operators.

4.2.14.2 Logical OR Operator (||)

Now let us consider the || (logical OR) operator. Suppose we wish to ensure at some point in a program that either *or* both of two conditions are **true** before we choose a certain path of execution. In this case, we use the || operator as in the following program segment :

```
if (avgMark >= 90 || finalExam >= 90)
    Console.WriteLine("Student grade is A");
```

This preceding condition also contains two simple conditions. The simple condition **avgMark >= 90** is evaluated to determine if the student deserves an "A" in the course because of a solid performance throughout the semester. The simple condition **finalExam >= 90** is evaluated to determine if the student deserves an "A" in the course because of an outstanding performance on the final exam. The **if** statement then considers the combined condition

```
((avgMark >= 90) || (finalExam >= 90))
```

and awards the student an "A" if either or both of the simple conditions are **true**. Note that the message **"Student grade is A"** is not printed only when both of the simple conditions are **false**. Listing 4.7 is a truth table for the logical OR operator (||).

Listing 4.7 Truth table for the || (logical OR) operator.

expression1	expression2	expression && expression2
false	false	false
false	true	true
true	false	true
true	true	true

The **&&** operator has a higher precedence than the || operator. Both operators associ e from left to right. An expression containing **&&** or **||** operators is evaluated only until truth or falsehood is known.

4.2.14.3 Logical NOT Operator (!)

C# provides the **!** (logical negation) operator to enable a programmer to "reverse" the meaning of a condition. Unlike the **&&** and **||** operators, which combine two conditions (binary operators), the logical negation operator has only a single condition as an operand (unary operator). The logical negation operator is placed before a condition when we are interested in choosing a path of execution if the original condition (without the logical negation operator) is **false**, such as in the following program segment:

```
if ( !(grade == 'A'))
    Console.Write( "Poor performance");
```

The parentheses around the condition **grade == 'A'** are needed because the logical negation operator has a higher precedence than the equality operator. Listing 4.8 is a truth table for the logical negation operator.

Listing 4.8 Truth table for operator ! (logical negation).

expression	!expression
false	true
true	false

In most cases, the programmer can avoid using logical negation by expressing the condition differently with an appropriate relational or equality operator.

..\CSharp_Book\Chap05\Logical

```
// Demonstrating logical operators &&, ||
using System;
using System.Collections.Generic;
using System.Text;

namespace Logical
{
    class Program
    {
        static void Main()
        {
            int a = 4, b = 8, c = 6, d = 3;
            Console.WriteLine("a = {0}, b = {1}, c = {2}, d = {3}", a, b, c, d);
            Console.WriteLine();

            Console.WriteLine("(a>b) && (b>c) is {0}", ((a>b) && (b>c)));
            Console.WriteLine("(a>b) || (b>c) is {0}", ((a>b) || (b>c)));
            Console.WriteLine("(a>b) && (c==d) is {0}", ((a>b) && (c==d)));
            Console.WriteLine("(a>b) && (c<d) is {0}", ((a>b) && (c<d)));
            Console.WriteLine("(a>b) && (c>d) is {0}", ((a>b) && (c>d)));
            Console.WriteLine("(a<b) && (c<d) is {0}", ((a<b) && (c<d)));
            Console.WriteLine("(a<b) && (c>d) is {0}", ((a<b) && (c>d)));
            Console.WriteLine("(a==b) && (c==d) is {0}", ((a==b) && (c==d)));
            Console.WriteLine("(a>b) || (b>c) is {0}", ((a>b) || (b>c)));
            Console.WriteLine("(a>b) && (b>c) is {0}", ((a>b) && (b>c)));
            Console.WriteLine("(a>b) || (c==d) is {0}", ((a>b) || (c==d)));
            Console.WriteLine("(a>b) || (c<d) is {0}", ((a>b) || (c<d)));
            Console.WriteLine("(a>b) || (c>d) is {0}", ((a>b) || (c>d)));
            Console.WriteLine("(a<b) || (c<d) is {0}", ((a<b) || (c<d)));
            Console.WriteLine("(a<b) || (c>d) is {0}", ((a<b) || (c>d)));
            Console.WriteLine("(a==b) || (c==d) is {0}", ((a==b) || (c==d)));
        }
    }
}
```

When the above program executed, it will produce the following output as shown in Fig. 4.8.

```
C:\WINDOWS\system32\cmd.exe
a = 4, b = 8, c = 6, d = 3

(a>b) && (b>c) is False
(a>b) || (b>c) is True
(a>b) && (c==d) is False
(a>b) && (c<d) is False
(a>b) && (c>d) is False
(a<b) && (c<d) is False
(a<b) && (c>d) is True
(a==b) && (c==d) is False
(a>b) || (b>c) is True
(a>b) && (b>c) is False
(a>b) || (c==d) is False
(a>b) || (c<d) is False
(a>b) || (c>d) is True
(a<b) || (c<d) is True
(a<b) || (c>d) is True
(a==b) || (c==d) is False
Press any key to continue . . .
```

Fig. 4.8 Use of logical operators in C# program.

4.2.15 Increment and Decrement Operators (++, – –)

The increment (++) and decrement(– –) operator are used to increment or decrement the value of the variable by 1. These operators can be used before or after the variable. The unary operators (++ and – –) are called "prefix" increment or decrement operators when the increment or decrement operators appear before the operand and postfix if they appear after the variable.

Note

Postfix increment and decrement has higher precedence than prefix increment and decrement.

When the operator appears before its operand, the operand is incremented or decremented and its new value is the result of the expression. This is the most important feature C#. Let us illustrate it using an example :

```
a = 10
d = 12
b = a++   ...statement (1)
c = ++d   ...statement (2)
```

After the execution of above statements the value of **b** becomes **10** and value of **c** becomes **13**, because precedence of '=' is greater than the unary operator. So, in statement (1) a is assigned first than incremented. Whereas in statement (2) **d** is incremented first than assigned to **c**.

Note

The statement (1) is equivalent to the following statements :

b = a;

a = a + 1;

The statement (2) is equivalent to the following statements :

d = d + 1;

Note

> c = d;
>
> *After the execution of statement (1) and (2) the value of a and d are also incremented by 1. So value of a becomes 11 and value of d becomes 13.*

Also, from the above two statements :

```
a++ means a = a + 1 and
++d means d = d + 1
```

Similarly, if we consider the pre-decrement operator (– –), then the above statements can be rewritten as :

```
a = 10
d = 12
b = a--   ...statement (3)
c = --d   ...statement (4)
```

From the statement **3** and **4**,

```
a-- means a = a - 1 and
--d means d = d - 1
```

Let us consider the following cases :

- If we use the increment operator before the operand in an expression as :

```
sum = 0;
a = 10;
sum = sum + ++a; // Or sum = sum + (++a) is a pre-increment;
Console.WriteLine("The new value of a is : {0}", a);
Console.WriteLine("The sum is :  {0}", sum );
```

then the value of **a** and **sum** are changed in the following manner :

sum	a	sum
0	10	0
0	11 (after ++a)	11 [after sum + (++a) is a preincrement]

Here, the line,

sum = sum + ++a;

first increase the value of **a** as **a = a + 1** and then the new value of a (**11**) is added with the old value of sum. So, the execution of the equation becomes,

sum = 0 + 11;

i.e. the new sum's value become 11.

- If we use the increment operator after the operand in an expression as :

```
sum = 0;
a = 10;
sum = sum + a++; // Or sum = sum + (a++) is a post-increment;
Console.WriteLine("The new value of a is : {0}", a);
Console.WriteLine("The sum is : {0}", sum);
```

then the value of **a** and **sum** are changed in the following manner :

sum	a	sum
0	10	0
0	11 (after a++)	10 [after sum + (a++)]

Here, the line,

sum = sum + a++; // post-increment

first add the value **a** (**10**) with the old value of **sum** and the increase the value of **a** as **11**. That is, for the above line the increment value of **a** (**11**) does not affect the **sum** value. So, the execution of the equation becomes,

sum = 0 + 10;

i.e. the new **sum**'s value become **10**.

- If we use the decrement operator before the operand in an expression as :

```
sum = 0;
a = 10;
sum = sum + --a; // Or sum = sum + (--a) is a pre-decrement;
Console.WriteLine("The new value of a is : {0}", a);
Console.WriteLine("The sum is : {0}", sum);
```

then the value of **a** and **sum** are changed in the following manner :

sum	a	sum
0	10	0
0	9 (after --a)	9 [after sum + (--a) is a pre-decrement]

Here, the line,

sum = sum + --a; //Pre-decrement

first decrease the value of **a** as **a = a - 1** and then the new value of **a** (**9**) is added with the old value of **sum**. So, the execution of the equation becomes,

sum = 0 + 9;

i.e. the new **sum**'s value become **9**.

- If we use the decrement operator after the operand in an expression as :

```
sum = 0;
a = 10;
sum = sum + a--; // Or sum = sum + (a--) is a post-decrement;
Console.WriteLine("The new value of a is : {0}", a);
Console.WriteLine("The sum is : {0}", sum);
```

then the value of **a** and **sum** are changed in the following manner :

sum	a	sum
0	10	0
0	9 (after a--)	10 [after sum + (a--) is a post-decrement]

Here, the line,

sum = sum + a--; //Post-decrement

first add the value **a** (**10**) with the old value of **sum** and then decrease the value of **a** as **9**. That is, for the above line the decrement value of **a** (**9**) does not affect the **sum** value. So, the execution of the equation becomes,

sum = 0 + 10;

i.e. the new **sum**'s value become 10.

- If we use the increment and decrement operator with the WriteLine statement as cascading style as given below :

```
int a = 4;
int b = 8;
Console.WriteLine("{0}\t {1} \t {2}", a++, ++a, a++);
Console.WriteLine("{0}\t {1} \t {2}", b--, --b, b--);
```

then, the last two line will produce the following :

4 6 6
8 6 6

because, in a **WriteLine()** cascading line, the operations are occur from the last part of the statement. That is,

```
                        Execution sequence ——→ (1) ——→ (2) ——→ (3)
Console.WriteLine("{0}\t {1} \t {2}",a++,      ++a,      a++);
                                    Output ——→ (4) ——→ (6) ——→ (6)
```

The output of the above C# line, prints from right to left. Thus, in a cascading operation, the execution of expressions, are always from right to left.

Where the input, output and operations are :

Execution sequence	input	output	operation	New value
1	4	4	a++	5
2	5	6	++a	6
3	6	6	a++	7 (which is not printed)

Similarly, the next line has the following output execution style as :

```
                        Execution sequence ——→ (1) ——→ (2) ——→ (3)
Console.WriteLine("{0}\t {1} \t {2}", b--,     --b,      b--);
                                    Output ——→ (8) ——→ (6) ——→ (6)
```

Where the input, output and operations are :

Execution sequence	input	output	operation	New value
1	8	8	b--	7
2	7	6	--b	6
3	6	6	b--	5 (which is not printed)

It is not unusual to add or subtract a constant value to or from a variable. All you have to do is to declare another variable that would hold the new value. For example;

..\CSharp_Book\Chap05\IncDec

```
// This program studies value incrementing and decrementing
using System;
using System.Collections.Generic;
using System.Text;

namespace IncDec
{
    class Program
    {
        static void Main()
        {
            double Value = 12.75;
            double NewValue;
            Console.WriteLine("Techniques of incrementing and decrementing a value");
            Console.Write("Value = ");
            Console.WriteLine(Value);
            NewValue = Value + 2.42;
            Console.Write("Value = ");
            Console.WriteLine(NewValue);
        }
    }
}
```

When the above program executed, it will produce the following output :

```
Techniques of incrementing and decrementing a value
Value = 12.75
Value = 15.17
Press any key to continue. . .
```

The above technique requires that you use an extra variable in your application. The advantage is that each value can hold its own value although the value of the second variable depends on whatever would happen to the original or source variable.

Sometimes in your program you will not need to keep the original value of the source variable. You may want to permanently modify the value that a variable is holding. In this case you can perform the addition operation directly on the variable by adding the desired value to the variable. This operation modifies whatever value a variable is holding and does not need an additional variable.

To add a value to a variable and change the value that the variable is holding, you can combine the assignment "=" and the addition "+" operators to produce a new operator as +=. For example;

..\CSharp_Book\Chap05\PlusEqual

```
// This program studies value incrementing and decrementing
using System;
using System.Collections.Generic;
using System.Text;

namespace PlusEqual
{
    class Program
    {
        static void Main()
        {
            double Value = 12.75;

            Console.WriteLine("Techniques of incrementing and decrementing a value");
            Console.Write("Value = ");
            Console.WriteLine(Value);

            Value += 2.42;
            Console.Write("Value = ");
            Console.WriteLine(Value);
        }
    }
}
```

When the above program executed, it will produce the following output :

```
Techniques of incrementing and decrementing a value
Value = 12.75
Value = 15.17
Press any key to continue. . .
```

This program produces the same result as the previous. To decrement the value of a variable, instead of the addition, use the subtraction and apply the same technique. In the above program, the variable can have its value decremented by combining the assignment and the subtraction operations on the variable. This is done with the -= operator. For example;

..\CSharp_Book\Chap05\MinusEqual

```
// This program studies value incrementing and decrementing
using System;
using System.Collections.Generic;
using System.Text;

namespace MinusEqual
{
```

```
class Program
{
    static void Main()
    {
        double Value = 12.75;

        Console.WriteLine("Techniques of incrementing and decrementing a value");
        Console.Write("Value = ");
        Console.WriteLine(Value);

        Value -= 2.42;
        Console.Write("Value = ");
        Console.WriteLine(Value);
    }
  }
}
```

When the above program executed, it will produce the following output :

```
Techniques of incrementing and decrementing a value
Value = 12.75
Value = 10.33
Press any key to continue. . .
```

4.3 Expression

An operand or a combination of operands and operators that, when evaluated, yields a single value. Expressions are constructs denoting rules of computation of obtaining values of variables and generating new values by the application of operators. Expressions consist of operators and operands, *i.e.* variables, constants and functions.

Definition

An expression is a formula consisting of one or more operands and zero or more operators' link together to compute a value.

In the C# language, as in C, C++ and Pascal (and any other programming languages), expressions consists of the following :

- Single operands (constants, variables, or functions).
- Operands combined with operators and (typically) other operands (x + y).
- A function name (either build-in or user-defined).

There are four types of expression :

- **Arithmetic Expression.** For example, **sum = sum + num;**
- **Relational Expression.** For example, **Console.WriteLine(a > b);**
- **Logical Expression.** For example, **Console.WriteLine ((a > b)) && (c > d));**

- **Conditional Expression.** For example, **if ((x>y) && (x>=0))**

For example,

```
double principal, rate, interest;
double SI;                    // Simple interest
SI = (principal * rate * interest) / 100;          // Evaluated expression SI.
```

4.4 Operator Precedence and Direction

When combining operations in C#, there are two aspects involved: an operator's precedence and its direction. If you ask the compiler to add two numbers, for example 240 + 65, it will execute the operation by adding 240 to 65. In other words, it would read 240, then +, then 65, and evaluate the result. This is considered as operating from left to right: 240 -> + -> 65. This process is referred to as the direction of the operation.

As you will regularly combine operators on your various calculations, each operation is known for how much it "weighs" as compared to other operators. This is known as its precedence. This means that when a certain operator is combined with another, such as a + b * c, or x / y - z, some operators would execute before others, almost regardless of how you write the operation. That's why an operator could be categorized by its level of precedence.

One way you can avoid being concerned by the level of precedence of operator is by using parentheses to tell the compiler how to proceed with the operations, that is, what operation should (must) be performed first. Consider the following algebraic operation:

```
154 - 12 + 8
```

The question here is to know whether you want to subtract the addition of 12 and 8 from 154 or you want to add the difference between 154 and 12 to 8. Using parentheses, you can communicate your intentions to the compiler. This is illustrated in the following program:

..\CSharp_Book\Chap05\PreOperator

```
using System;
using System.Collections.Generic;
using System.Text;

namespace PreOperator
{
    class Program
    {
        static void Main()
        {
            int Operation1 = (154 - 12) + 8;
            int Operation2 = 154 - (12 + 8);
            Console.Write("Examining the effect of the parentheses in an operation");
            Console.Write("\n(154 - 12) + 8 = ");
```

```
                Console.Write(Operation1);
                Console.Write("\n154 - (12 + 8) = ");
                Console.Write(Operation2);
                Console.WriteLine();
            }
        }
    }
```

When the above program executed, it will produce the following output :

```
Examining the effect of the parentheses in an operation
(154 - 12) + 8 = 150
154 - (12 + 8) = 134
Press any key to continue. . .
```

As you can see, using the parentheses controls how the whole operation would proceed. This difference can be even more accentuated if your operation includes 3 or more operators and 4 or more operands.

C# always performs multiplication, division, and modulus first, and then computes addition and subtraction. Listing 4.9 shows the order of the operators you have seen so far. There are many more levels to C#'s precedence table of operators than those that Listing 4.9.

Listing 4.9 The order of precedence for the primary operators.

Order	Operators
=	Assignment
* / %	Arithmetic division, multiplication and modulus
– +	Arithmetic addition and subtraction
+=, –=, *=, /=, %=	Arithmetic assignment
,	Comma operator
++, – –	Increment / decrement Operator
&&, ||, !	Logical operator
==, !=, >=, <=, >, <	Comparison operator
sizeof	Compile time operator
? :	Conditional operator

Note

When more than one operators are involved in an expression, then the precedence determine the order in which the operands are evaluated.

The above expression is very simple. But problem arise when the expression is using more operators with same precedence. If operators in an expression are having the same precedence level, then associatively determines the direction of grouping of the operators. The C# operators are having two type operators :

- Left-associative *i.e.* operators group from left to right, which means that if there are two or more operators in the expression having the same precedence then they will be evaluated from left to right. Most of the operators in C# are left-associative.

For example, the expression

Sum = 2 * 3 / 2 will be treated as Sum = (2*3) / 2

- Right-associative : Only assignment, conditional and unary operators are right associative.

Note. When more than one operators having the same precedence are involved in an expression, then the associatively determine the order in which the operands are evaluated.

Listing 4.10 The operators and its execution associative.

Operators (precedence wise)	Associativity
! + – * & sizeof ++ – –	Right to left
* / %	Left to right
+ – (binary)	Left to right
< <= >= >	Left to right
== !=	Left to right
&&	Left to right
||	Left to right
?:	Right to left
= *= /= %= –+	Right to left
, (comma)	Left to right

So, the expression

a < b && c * d < e is interpreted as (a< b) && ((c * d) < e)

Following exmple shows C#'s order of operators is easy if you look at the intermediate results at a time. The three calculations in Fig. 11.2 show you how to do this.

8 + 4 * 6 – 8 / 4

8 + 24 – 8 / 4

8 + 24 – 2

32 – 2

30

3 * 4 / 2 + – 1

12 / 2 + 3 – . 1

6 + 3 – 1

9 – 1

8

21 / 3 + 6 % 2

7 + 6 % 2

7 + 0

7

4.4.1 Using Parentheses

If you want to override the order of precedence, put parentheses in your calculations. The parentheses actually reside on a level above the multiplication in parentheses, whether it is addition, subtraction, division, or something else—is always performed before the rest of the line. The other calculations are performed in their normal operator order. The first formula in this chapter, 2 + 3 + 2; produced an 8 because the multiplication performed before addition. In program however, adding parentheses around the addition as, in ((2+3)*2), the answer becomes 10.

The following calculations demonstrates how parentheses override the regular order of operators. These are the same three formulae that are calculated differently due to the use of parentheses.

6 + 2 * (3 – 4) / 2

6 + 2 * – 1 / 2

6 + –2 /2

6 + –1

5

3 + 4 / 2 + (3 – 1)

3 + 4 / 2 + 2

3 + 2 + 2

5 + 2

7

20 + (3 + 5) % 2

20 / 8 % 2

2 % 2

0

Exercise

1. Define operator and operand?
2. What are C# operators?
3. What is arithmetic operator?
4. What is relational operator?
5. What is logical operator?
6. What is difference between single assignment and compound assignment?
7. What is the purpose of Single Quotes (') in C# ?
8. What is unary operator what does it do?
9. What are binary operators?
10. Differentiate between unary and binary operator?
11. What are increment and decrement operators?
12. How many types of logical operators are there in C#?
13. What are primitive data types?
14. What is the difference between typeof and sizeof?
15. Give an example to get maximum or minimum values of primitive type?
16. What do you mean by post increment and pre increment?
17. What are the techniques available in C# for incrementing or decrementing a value?
18. What is the difference between pre decrement and post decrement?
19. What are expressions in C#?
20. What does an expression consist of?
21. How many types of expressions are there in C#?
22. Evaluate the following C++ expressions where a, b, c are integers and d, f are floating point numbers. The values are : a = 5, b = 3 and d = 1.5
    (a) c = a – (b++) *(– –d)
    (b) f = (++b)*b – a
23. What will be the value of the following if j = 5 initially :
    (a) (5 * ++j)% 6
    (b) *5 * j++) % 6
24. State why are following expressions invalid ?
    (a) asm = 5100 :: val < 35
    (b) age > 70 && < 90
25. What is the difference between num = 10 num = = 10 ?
26. Write the equivalent C++ statements for the following :
    (a) r1 = (–b + sqrt(b^2 – 4ac) / 2a
    (b) perimeter = 2*(l + b)
    (c) area = $3.14r^2$
    (d) s = 1/2 mv^2.
27. Write the corresponding C++ expressions for the following mathematical expressions :
    (a) $\sqrt{a^2 + b^2 + c^2}$
    (b) $e^x - x$
    (c) $(R + S)^4$

(d) $2 - 4y * (P + Q)^2$
(e) $A + B + e^y$
(f) $(A + B)^2 + (C + D)^4$

28. Given the value of a, b and c, evaluate the following expression :

    (a >= b) || (! c == b) && (c < a)

    a = 10, b = 5, c = 11

29. Write the corresponding C# expressions for the following mathematical expressions :

    (a) $f = \frac{a+b}{c} - d$

    (b) $z = x^3 + y^3 - \frac{\sqrt{xy}}{2}$

30. Write the equivalent C# statements for the following :

    (a) $r1 = (-b) + sqrt(b^2 - 4ac)/2a$

    (b) Perimeter = 2 Í(1 + b)

    (c) $S = ½ mv^2$

    (d) $Area = 3.14 r^2$

31. Write the equivalent C# expression for the following :

    (a) (x + 3)

    (b) $2(p/q/3)^2 / (r - 3)$

    (c) z = tan x

    (d) w = log(v);

32. What will be the output of the following expression ?

    y-x < 500 ? 150 : 50

    (a) x = 300 y = 700

    (b) x = 700 y = 800

33. What will be the output of following program segments ?

    (a)
```
static void Main()
{
    int x;
    x = 5;
    Console.WriteLine(x++);
    Console.WriteLine(x);
    Console.WriteLine(++x);
}
```
    (b)
```
static void Main()
{
    int r, x, y;
    x = 50;
    y = 10;
    r = (x > 45) ? x : y;
    Console.WriteLine(r);
}
```
    (c)
```
static void Main()
{
    int a;
```

```
        a = 25 + 4 - 4 ;
        Console.WriteLine(a);
    }
(d) static void Main()
    {
        int a = 1, b = 2, c = 4;
        a = +c + ++b / c;
        Console.WriteLine("a = " + a);
    }
(e) static void Main()
    {
        int a, b = 30;
        a = 30 / 2 * b;
        Console.WriteLine("a = " + a);
    }
(f) static void Main()
    {
        int x = 5, y = 5;
        Console.Write(x++);
        Console.Write(",");
        Console.Write(++x);
        Console.Write(",");
        Console.WriteLine(y++ + "," + ++y);
    }
(g) static void Main()
    {
        int x = 5, y = 5;
        Console.Write(x—);
        Console.Write(",");
        Console.Write(—x);
        Console.Write(",");
        Console.WriteLine(y— + "," + —y);
    }
```

Data Reading and Formatting

5

5.1 Introduction

In almost every computer program, the users have to input some data that will be stored in computer's memory and then subsequently processed. The input data may be from a keyboard, a disk file or from another computer via a communication channel. The intermediate and final results of the computations are also stored in computer's memory. And finally, there is need to output the results of the computations so that the user can use them in their day-to-day work. The output can be displayed on the computer screen, stored on a disk or transmitted via a communication channel to other computer.

C# contains no commands that perform input or output. To make up for this apparent oversight, C# compiler writers supply several useful input and output functions. The I/O statements in C# are both formatted and unformatted.

5.2 Understanding System.Console Class

As its name implies, the Console class encapsulates input, output and error stream manipulations for console-based applications. In previous chapter, we saw that the **Console** class allows using the **Write()** and the **WriteLine()** functions to display things on the screen. While the **Console.Write()** method is used to display something on the screen, the **Console** class provides the **Read()** method to get a value from the user. If you look the Console class as in your program, you will see its methods as shown in Fig. 5.1.

As you have seen, **WriteLine()** pumps a text string (including a carriage return) to the output stream. The **Write()** method pumps text to the output stream without a carriage return, while **Read()** is used to capture a single character from the input stream. To use it, the name of a variable can be assigned to it. The syntax used is:

```
VariableName = Console.Read();
```

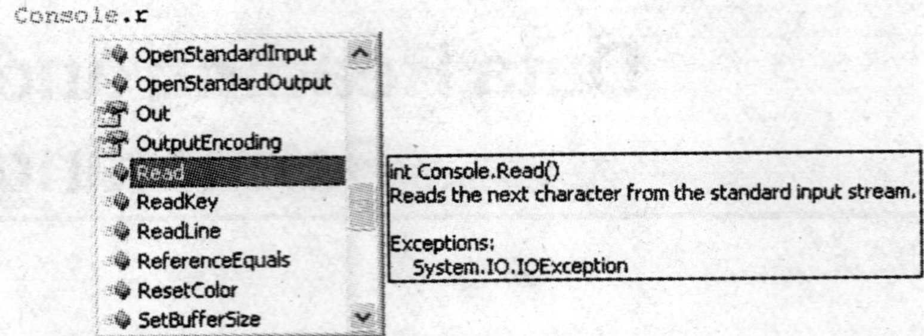

Fig. 5.1 Console Class method help.

For example,

```
char ch;
Console.WriteLine("Enter a character : ");
ch = (char) Console.Read();    // set for a char
Console.WriteLine("You enter a character as : " + ch);
```

This simply means that, when the user types something and presses Enter, what the user had typed would be given (the word is *assigned*) to the variable specified on the left side of the assignment operator.

Read() doesn't always have to assign its value to a variable. For example, it can be used on its own line, which simply means that the user is expected to type something but the value typed by the user would not be used for any significant purpose. For example some versions of C# (even including Microsoft's C# and Borland C#Builder) would display the DOS window briefly and disappear. You can use the **Read()** function to wait for the user to press any key in order to close the DOS window.

Besides **Read()**, the **Console** class also provides the **ReadLine()** method. Like the **WriteLine()** member function, after performing its assignment, the **ReadLine()** method sends the caret to the next line. Otherwise, it plays the same role as the **Read()** function. The syntax used is:

```
VariableName = Console.ReadLine();
```

For example,

```
string name;
Console.WriteLine("Enter your name : ");
name = Console.ReadLine();   // set for a string
Console.WriteLine("You enter your name as " + name);
```

Also, there is another method which is added by .NET Framework 2.0, i.e., **ReadKey()**. This method reads individual keystrokes directly from the keyboard, in a non-line-buffered manner. When this method called, it waits until a key is pressed by the user. When a key is pressed, **ReadKey()** returns the keystroke immediately. That is, the user does not need to press Enter key.

Remember that the **ReadKey()** returns information about the keypress in an object of type **ConsoleKeyInfo** which is a structure. It has the following properties :

- **char KeyChar.** It contains the char equivalent of the character that was pressed.
- **ConsoleKey Key.** The **Key** contains a value from the **ConsoleKey** enumeration, which is an enumeration of all the keys on the keyboards.
- **ConsoleModifiers Modifiers.** The **Modifiers** describes which, if any, of the keyboard modifiers ALT, CTRL or SHIFT were pressed when the keystroke was generated.

The syntax used is:

```
ConsoleKeyInfo keyHit;
...
...
Console.Write("Enter a character : ");
keyHit = Console.ReadKey();      // set for a char
```

The complete example is as :

..\CSharp_Book\Chap05\ReadKeyCh

```
using System;
using System.Collections.Generic;
using System.Text;

namespace ReadKeyCh
{
    class Program
    {
        static void Main()
        {
            char ch;          // For Read
            string name; // For ReadLine
            ConsoleKeyInfo keyHit; // For ReadKey

            Console.Write("Enter a character : ");
            ch = (char) Console.Read();    // set for a char

            Console.ReadLine();   // set for a string

            Console.Write("Enter your name : ");
            name = Console.ReadLine();  // set for a string

            Console.Write("Enter a character : ");
            keyHit = Console.ReadKey();  // set for a char
```

```
            Console.WriteLine();
            Console.WriteLine("You enter a character as : " + ch);
            Console.WriteLine("You enter your name as " + name);
            Console.WriteLine("You enter a character as : " + keyHit.KeyChar);

            Console.ReadLine();
        }
    }
}
```

When the above program executed, it will produce the following output as shown in Fig. 5.2.

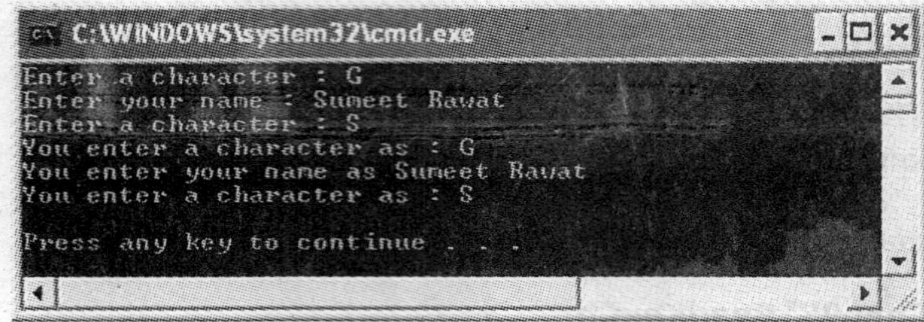

Fig. 5.2 Reading individual keystroke from keyboard.

5.3 Entering String Data

In most assignments of your programs, you will not know the value of a string when writing your application. For example, you may want the user to provide such a string. To request a string (or any of the variables we will see in this lesson), you can call the **Console.Read()** or the **Console.ReadLine()** function and assign it to the name of the variable whose value you want to retrieve. For example;

```
string EmpName;

Console.Write("Enter Employee Name: ");
FirstName = Console.ReadLine();
```

..\CSharp_Book\Chap05\StringRead

```
using System;
using System.Collections.Generic;
using System.Text;

namespace StringRead
{
    class Program
    {
        static void Main()
```

```
        {
            string EmpName, EmpAddress, EmpPhone;

            Console.WriteLine("-/- Pearl Software -/-");
            // Request Employee information from the user
            Console.Write("Enter Employee Name:  ");
            EmpName = Console.ReadLine();
            Console.Write("Enter Employee Address:  ");
            EmpAddress = Console.ReadLine();
            Console.Write("Enter Employee Phone: ");
            EmpPhone = Console.ReadLine();

            Console.WriteLine();
            // Display the details
            Console.WriteLine("========================================");
            Console.WriteLine("-/- Pearl Software -/-");
            Console.WriteLine("========================================");
            Console.Write("Employee:    ");
            Console.WriteLine(EmpName);
            Console.Write("Address:    ");
            Console.WriteLine(EmpAddress);

            Console.Write("Phone: ");
            Console.WriteLine(EmpPhone);
            Console.WriteLine("========================================\n");
        }
    }
}
```

When the above program executed, it will produce the following output as shown in Fig. 5.3.

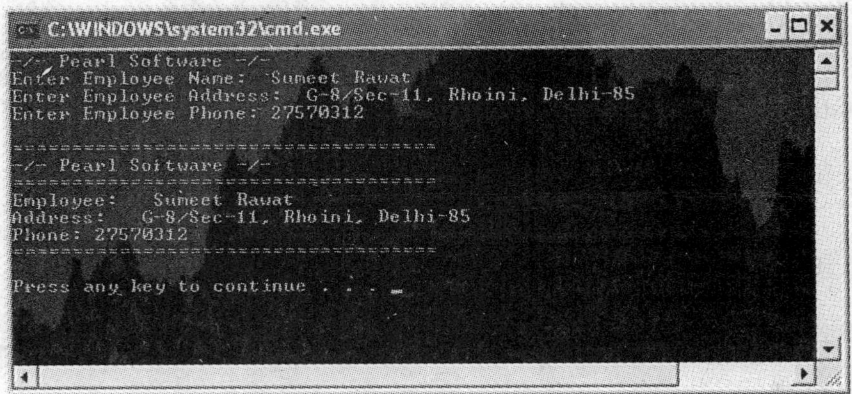

Fig. 5.3 Reading individual keystroke from keyboard.

5.4 Entering Numeric Data

In C#, everything the user types is a string and the compiler would hardly analyze it without your explicit asking it to do so. Therefore, if you want to get a number from the user, first request a string. For example;

```
using System;

namespace NumberRead
{
    class Program
    {
        static void Main()
        {
            int EmpNumber;
            string strNumber;

            strNumber = Console.ReadLine();
        }
    }
}
```

After getting the string, you must convert it to a number. To perform this conversion, each data type of the .NET Framework provides a mechanism called **Parse**. To use **Parse()**, type the data type, followed by a period, followed by **Parse**, and followed by parentheses. In the parentheses of **Parse**, type the string that you requested from the user. For example;

```
using System;

namespace NumberRead
{
    class Program
    {
        static void Main()
        {
            long Salary;
            string EmpSalary;

            EmpSalary = Console.ReadLine();
            Salary = long.Parse(EmpSalary);
        }
    }
}
```

An advanced but faster way to do this is to type **Console.ReadLine()** in the parentheses of Parse. This has the same effect. For example;

```
using System;

namespace NumberRead
{
    class Program
    {
        static void Main()
        {
            Long Salary;

            Salary = long.Parse(Console.ReadLine());
        }
    }
}
```

..\CSharp_Book\Chap05\NumberRead

```
using System;
using System.Collections.Generic;
using System.Text;

namespace NumberRead
{
    class Program
    {
        static void Main()
        {
            string EmpNo, EmpName, EmpAddress, EmpPhone, EmpSal;

            long Salary;    // Salary of employee

            Console.WriteLine("-/- Pearl Software -/-");
            // Request Employee information from the user
            Console.Write("Enter Employee No: ");
            EmpNo = Console.ReadLine();
            Console.Write("Enter Employee Name: ");
            EmpName = Console.ReadLine();
            Console.Write("Enter Employee Address: ");
            EmpAddress = Console.ReadLine();
            Console.Write("Enter Employee Phone: ");
            EmpPhone = Console.ReadLine();
            Console.Write("Enter Employee salary: ");
```

```
            EmpSal = Console.ReadLine();
            Salary = long.Parse(EmpSal);    // String converted into long type
            Console.WriteLine();

            // Display the contents
            Console.WriteLine("=======================================");
            Console.WriteLine("-/- Pearl Software -/-");
            Console.WriteLine("=======================================");
            Console.Write("Employee No.:   ");
            Console.WriteLine(EmpNo);
            Console.Write("Name:    ");
            Console.WriteLine(EmpName);
            Console.Write("Address:    ");
            Console.WriteLine(EmpAddress);

            Console.Write("Phone: ");
            Console.WriteLine(EmpPhone);
            Console.Write("Salary: ");
            Console.WriteLine(Salary);
        }
    }
}
```

When the above program executed, it will produce the following output as shown in Fig. 5.4.

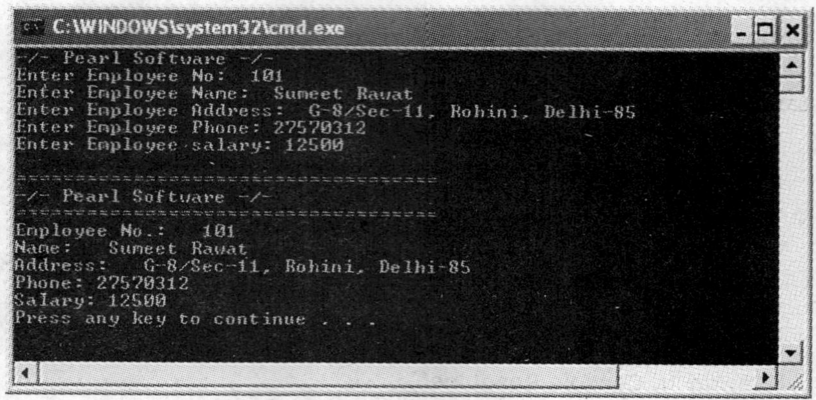

Fig. 5.4 Reading individual keystroke from keyboard.

Every numeric string has its corresponding internal representation. C# does not support to enter directly the the data type values like int, float, double, etc. from keyboard. C# has a method called **Parse()** to convert the numeric values into its corresponding data types. Microsoft explicitly states that the C# type and .NET structure type are indistinguishable. Because C#'s value types are supported by structures, the value types have method defined for them. As we discuss the datatypes in Chapter-3, each .NET structures are defined inside the **System** namespaace. That is, if you consider a .NET structure name called **Int16**, then its actual structure is **System.Int16**. The following Listing 5.1 shows you the .NET structure names, C# data type name and the equivalent Parse() method. Notice that each parse method take a string argument which is converting to its respective data type using the System namespace. The Parse() method returns a static value to corresponding data type.

Listing 5.1 .NET structure, C# data types and conversion method.

.NET Structure	Name C# data type name	Parse() method
Int16	short	static short Parse(string str)
Int32	int	static int Parse(string str)
Int64	long	static long Parse(string str)
Uint16	ushort	static ushort Parse(string str)
Uint32	uint	static uint Parse(string str)
Uint64	ulong	static ulong Parse(string str)
Single	float	static float Parse(string str)
Double	double	static double Parse(string str)
Decimal	decimal	static decimal Parse(string str)
Byte	byte	static byte Parse(string str)
Sbyte	sbyte	static sbyte Parse(string str)

For example, to enter different types of values into corresponding data types,

```
int num;
double salary;
float rate;
byte age;

Console.Write("Enter number : ");
num = int32.Prase(Console.ReadLine());  // Convert into C# int data type

Console.Write("Enter salary : ");
salary = Double.Prase(Console.ReadLine());       // Convert into C# double data type

Console.Write("Enter rate of interest : ");
salary = Single.Prase(Console.ReadLine());       // Convert into C# float data type

Console.Write("Enter age : ");
age = Byte.Prase(Console.ReadLine());  // Convert into C# byte data type
```

From, above all lines, the **ReadLine()** uses to read a string type data from keyboard and then it converts into corresponding data type using fully qualified names (**Int32, Double, Single, Byte**) of **System** namespace.

5.5 Entering Data and Time Data

As done with the regular numbers, you can request a date value from the user. This is also done by requesting a string from the user. For example;

```
using System;

namespace DateRead
{
    class Program
    {
        static void Main()
        {
            string strDateHired;
            strDateHired = Console.ReadLine();
        }
    }
}
```

After the user has entered the string you can then convert it to a **DateTime** value. Just like any value you request from the user, a date or time value that the user types must be valid, otherwise, the program would produce an error. Because dates and times follow some rules for their formats, you should strive to let the user know how you expect the value to be entered.

By default, if you request only a date from the user and the user enters a valid date, the compiler would add the midnight value to the date. If you request only the time from the user and the user enters a valid time, the compiler would add the current date to the value.

To deal with new dates and times, change the program as follows:

..\CSharp_Book\Chap05\DateRead

```
using System;
using System.Collections.Generic;
using System.Text;

namespace NumberRead
{
    class Program
    {
        static void Main()
        {
            string EmpNo, EmpName, EmpAddress, EmpPhone, EmpSal;
            DateTime EmpDOJ;    // Date of joining
            long Salary;    // Salary of employee
```

```
            Console.WriteLine("-/- Pearl Software -/-");
            // Request Employee information from the user
            Console.Write("Enter Employee No: ");
            EmpNo = Console.ReadLine();
            Console.Write("Enter Employee Name: ");
            EmpName = Console.ReadLine();
            Console.Write("Enter Employee Address: ");
            EmpAddress = Console.ReadLine();
            Console.Write("Enter Employee Phone: ");
            EmpPhone = Console.ReadLine();
            Console.WriteLine("Enter the joining date(mm/dd/yyyy hh:mm AM/PM)");
            EmpDOJ = DateTime.Parse(Console.ReadLine());
            Console.Write("Enter Employee salary: ");
            EmpSal = Console.ReadLine();
            Salary = long.Parse(EmpSal);    // String converted into long type
            Console.WriteLine();

            // Display the details
            Console.WriteLine("=====================================");
            Console.WriteLine("-/- Pearl Software -/-");
            Console.WriteLine("=====================================");
            Console.Write("Employee No.:    ");
            Console.WriteLine(EmpNo);
            Console.Write("Name:    ");
            Console.WriteLine(EmpName);
            Console.Write("Address:    ");
            Console.WriteLine(EmpAddress);

            Console.Write("Phone: ");
            Console.WriteLine(EmpPhone);
            Console.Write("Joining Date: ");
            Console.WriteLine(EmpDOJ);

            Console.Write("Salary: ");
            Console.WriteLine(Salary);
        }
    }
}
```

When the above program executed, it will produce the following output as shown in Fig. 5.5.

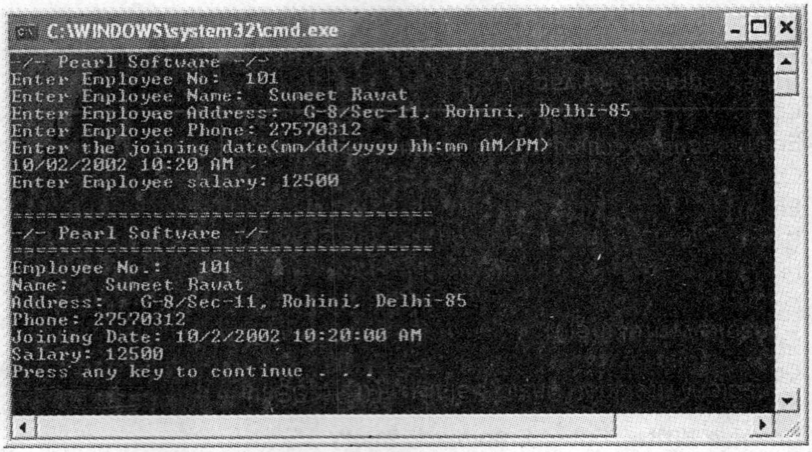

```
C:\WINDOWS\system32\cmd.exe
-/- Pearl Software -/-
Enter Employee No:  101
Enter Employee Name:  Sumeet Rawat
Enter Employee Address:  G-8/Sec-11, Rohini, Delhi-85
Enter Employee Phone: 27570312
Enter the joining date(mm/dd/yyyy hh:mm AM/PM)
10/02/2002 10:20 AM
Enter Employee salary: 12500

====================================
-/- Pearl Software -/-
====================================
Employee No.:   101
Name:   Sumeet Rawat
Address:   G-8/Sec-11, Rohini, Delhi-85
Phone: 27570312
Joining Date: 10/2/2002 10:20:00 AM
Salary: 12500
Press any key to continue . . .
```

Fig. 5.5 Reading individual keystroke from keyboard.

5.6 Data Formatting

Instead of using two **Write()** or a combination of **Write()** and **WriteLine()** to display data, you can convert a value to a string and display it directly. To do this, you can provide two strings to the **Write()** or **WriteLine()** and separate them with a comma:

1. The first part of the string provided to **Write()** or **WriteLine()** is the complete string that would display to the user. This first string itself can be made of different sections :

   (a) One section is a string in any way you want it to display
   (b) Another section is a number included between an opening curly bracket "{" and a closing curly bracket "}". This combination of "{" and "}" is referred to as a placeholder.

You can put the placeholder anywhere inside of the string. The first placeholder must have number 0. The second must have number 1, etc. With this technique, you can create the string anyway you like and use the placeholders anywhere inside of the string

2. The second part of the string provided to **Write()** or **WriteLine()** is the value that you want to display. It can be one value if you used only one placeholder with 0 in the first string. If you used different placeholders, you can then provide a different value for each one of them in this second part, separating the values with a comma.

For example;

..\CSharp_Book\Chap05\DataFormatA

```
using System;
using System.Collections.Generic;
```

```
using System.Text;

namespace DataFormatA
{
    class Program
    {
        static void Main()
        {
            String EmpName = "Sumeet Rawat";
            int Age = 32;
            double BSalary = 1250.00;

            Console.WriteLine("Employee Name: {0}", EmpName);
            Console.WriteLine("Age: {0}", Age);
            Console.WriteLine("Basic Salary: {0}", BSalary);

            Console.WriteLine();
        }
    }
}
```

When the above program executed, it will produce the following output :

```
Employee Name: Sumeet Rawat
Age: 32
Basic Salary: 12500
Press any key to continue. . .
```

5.7 Formatting Console Output

As mentioned already, the numeric value typed in the curly brackets of the first part is an ordered number. If you want to display more than one value, provide each incremental value in its curly brackets. The syntax used is:

```
Write("To Display {0} {1} {2} {n}", First, Second, Third, nth);
```

You can use the sections between a closing curly bracket and an opening curly bracket to create a meaningful sentence.

C# provides a flexible way to format data with **Write()** and **WriteLine()** methods embedded within a string literal. .NET introduces a new style of string formatting slightly indicative with C **printf()**function, but without the cryptic **%d**, **%s**, or **%c** flags. Consider the following example,

..\CSharp_Book\Chap05\ConOutput

```
using System;
using System.Collections.Generic;
using System.Text;

namespace ConOutput
{
    class Program
    {
        static void Main()
        {
            int value1 = 80;
            double value2 = 9.99;
            bool opt = true;

            // The '\n' token in a string literal inserts a newline.
            Console.WriteLine("Int is: {0}\nDouble is: {1}\nBool is: {2}",
                    value1, value2, opt);
        }
    }
}
```

When the above program executed, it will produce the following output :

```
Int is: 80
Double is: 9.99
Bool is: True
Press any key to continue. . .
```

From above code, the first parameter to **WriteLine()** method represents a string literal that contains optional placeholder designated by **{0}, {1}, {2}**, and so forth. The remaining parameters to **WriteLine()** are simply the values to be inserted into the respective placeholders (in this case, an int, a double and a bool).

Note

A curly bracket numbering always begins with zero.

Also, be aware that **WriteLine()** has been overloaded to allow you to specific placeholder values as an array of objects. Thus, you can represent any number of items to be plugged into the format string as follows :

```
// Fill placeholders using an array of objects.
object[] stuff = {"Hello", 20.9, 1, "three", "84", 99.99933};
Console.WriteLine("The Stuff: {0}, {1}, {2}, {3}, {4}, {5}", stuff);
```

It is also permissible for a given placeholder to repeat within a given string, For example, if you want to display:

```
5, Number 5, Number 9
```

then you have to place your **WriteLine()** method as :

```
Console.WriteLine("{0}, Number {0}, Number {0}", 9);
```

5.8 Data Conversion

We mentioned earlier that everything the user types using the keyboard is primarily a string and it's your job to convert it to the appropriate type. In reverse, if you have a value that is not a string, you can easily convert it to a string. To support this, each .NET Framework data type provides a mechanism called **ToString()**. Normally, in C#, as we mentioned with boxing, and as we have done so far, this conversion is automatically or transparently done by the compiler. In some cases, you will need to perform the conversion yourself.

To conversion a value of a primitive data type to a string, type the name of the variable, followed by a period, followed, followed by **ToString()**. For example;

..\CSharp_Book\Chap05\DataConvert

```
using System;
using System.Collections.Generic;
using System.Text;

namespace DataConvert
{
    class Program
    {
        static void Main()
        {
            String EmpName = "Sumeet Rawat";
            int Age = 32;
            double BSalary = 12500.00;

            Console.WriteLine("Full Name: {0}", EmpName);
            Console.WriteLine("Age: {0}", Age.ToString());
            Console.WriteLine("Basic Salary: {0}", BSalary.ToString());

            Console.WriteLine();
        }
    }
}
```

When the above program executed, it will produce the following output :

```
Employee Name: Sumeet Rawat
Age: 32
Basic Salary: 12500
Press any key to continue. . .
```

5.9 Number Formatting

To properly display data in a friendly and most familiar way, you can format it. Formatting tells the compiler what kind of data you are using and how you want the compiler to display it to the user. As it happens, you can display a natural number in a common value or, depending on the circumstance, you may prefer to show it as a hexadecimal value. When it comes to double-precision numbers, you may want to display a distance with three values on the right side of the decimal separator and in some cases, you may want to display a salary with only 2 decimal places.

The **System** namespace provides a specific letter that you can use in the **Write()** or **WriteLine()**'s placeholder for each category of data to display. To format a value, in the placeholder of the variable or value, after the number, type a colon and one of the appropriate letter from the following table. If you are using **ToString()**, then, in the parentheses of **ToString()**, you can include specific letter or combination inside of double-quotes. The letters and their meanings are shown in Listing 5.2.

Listing 5.2 Number formatting constants.

Character	Used For
c or C	Currency values. By default, the flag will prefix the local curtural symbol (a dollar sign ($) for US. English).
d or D	Decimal numbers. This flag may also specify the minimum number of digits used to pad the value.
e or E	Scientific numeric display such as $1.45e^5$
f or F	Fixed decimal numbers
g or G	General and most common type of numbers. This character can b used to format a number to fixed or exponential format.
n or N	Natural numbers i.e., used for basic numerical formatting (with commas).
r or R	Roundtrip formatting.
x or X	Hexadecimal formatting. If you use an uppercase X, your hex format will also contain uppercase character
p or P	Percentages

These format characters are suffixed to a given placeholder value using the color token (e.g., **{0:C}**, **{1:d}**, **{2:X)**, and so on). Let us consider the following code :

..\CSharp_Book\Chap05\StrFormat

```
using System;
using System.Collections.Generic;
using System.Text;

namespace strFormat
{
    class Program
    {
        static void Main()
        {
            Console.WriteLine("C format: {0:C}", 9989.987);
            Console.WriteLine("D9 format: {0:D9}", 9999);
            Console.WriteLine("E format: {0:E}", 9989.76543);
            Console.WriteLine("F3 format: {0:F3}", 9999.9999);
            Console.WriteLine("N format: {0:N}", 9999);
            Console.WriteLine("X format: {0:X}", 9999);
            Console.WriteLine("x format: {0:x}", 9999);
        }
    }
}
```

When the above program executed, it will produce the following output as shown in Fig. 5.6.

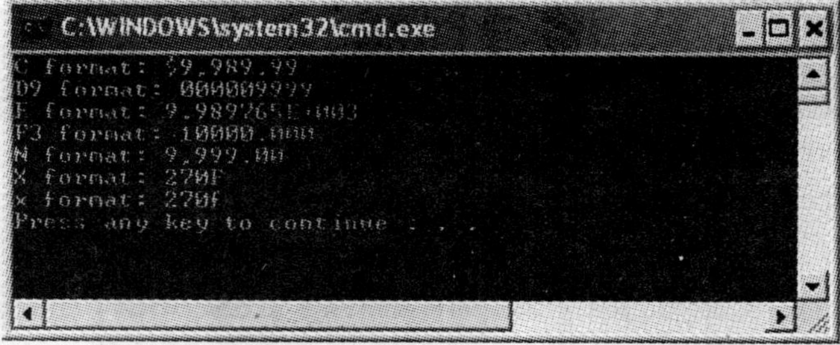

Fig. 5.6 Number formatting options.

..\CSharp_Book\Chap05\NumFormat

```
using System;
using System.Collections.Generic;
using System.Text;

namespace NumFormat
{
    class Program
```

```
    {
        static void Main()
        {
            String EmpName = "Sumeet Rawat";
            int Age = 32;
            const int hr = 8; // Working hour per day
            double BSalary = 12500.00;
            double DailySalary = BSalary / 30;
            double HourlySalary = DailySalary / hr;

            Console.WriteLine("Full Name: {0}", EmpName);
            Console.WriteLine("Age: {0}", Age.ToString());
            Console.WriteLine("Basic Salary: {0}", BSalary.ToString());
            Console.WriteLine("Daily Salary: {0} for {1} hours",
                        DailySalary.ToString(), hr.ToString());
            Console.WriteLine();
        }
    }
}
```

When the above program executed, it will produce the following output as shown in Fig. 5.7.

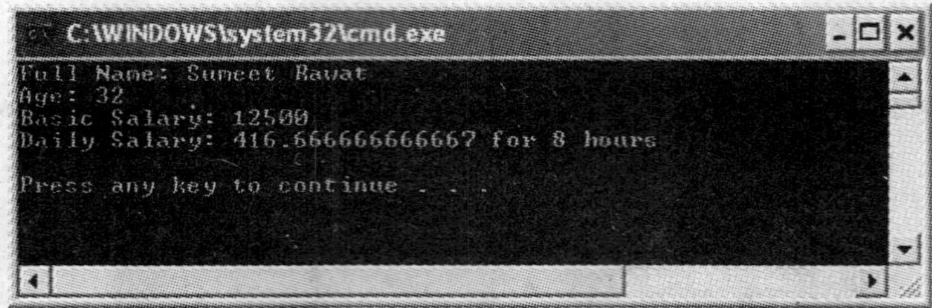

Fig. 5.7 Number formatting using ToString() method and number format options.

As you may have noticed, if you leave the parentheses of **ToString()** empty, the compiler would use a default formatting to display the value.

As opposed to calling **ToString()**, you can use the above letters in the curly brackets of the first part of **Write()** or **WriteLine()**. In this case, after the number in the curly brackets, type the colon operator followed by the letter.

..\CSharp_Book\Chap05\FormatD

```
using System;
using System.Collections.Generic;
using System.Text;
```

```
namespace NumberRead
{
    class Program
    {
        static void Main()
        {
            string EmpNo, EmpName, EmpAddress, EmpPhone, EmpSal;
            DateTime EmpDOJ;    // Date of joining
            Decimal Salary;    // Salary of employee
            Console.WriteLine("-/- Pearl Software -/-");
            // Request Employee information from the user
            Console.Write("Enter Employee No: ");
            EmpNo = Console.ReadLine();
            Console.Write("Enter Employee Name: ");
            EmpName = Console.ReadLine();
            Console.Write("Enter Employee Address: ");
            EmpAddress = Console.ReadLine();
            Console.Write("Enter Employee Phone: ");
            EmpPhone = Console.ReadLine();
            Console.WriteLine("Enter the joining date(mm/dd/yyyy hh:mm AM/PM)");
            EmpDOJ = DateTime.Parse(Console.ReadLine());
            Console.Write("Enter Employee salary: ");
            EmpSal = Console.ReadLine();
            Salary = long.Parse(EmpSal);    // String converted into long type
            Console.WriteLine();

            // Display the contents
            Console.WriteLine("========================================");
            Console.WriteLine("-/- Pearl Software -/-");
            Console.WriteLine("========================================");
            Console.Write("Employee No.:    ");
            Console.WriteLine(EmpNo);
            Console.Write("Name:    ");
            Console.WriteLine(EmpName);
            Console.Write("Address:    ");
            Console.WriteLine(EmpAddress);

            Console.Write("Phone: ");
            Console.WriteLine(EmpPhone);
            Console.Write("Joining Date: ");
            Console.WriteLine(EmpDOJ);

            Console.Write("Salary: {0:F}", Salary);
            Console.WriteLine();
```

```
        }
    }
}
```

When the above program executed, it will produce the following output as shown in Fig. 5.8.

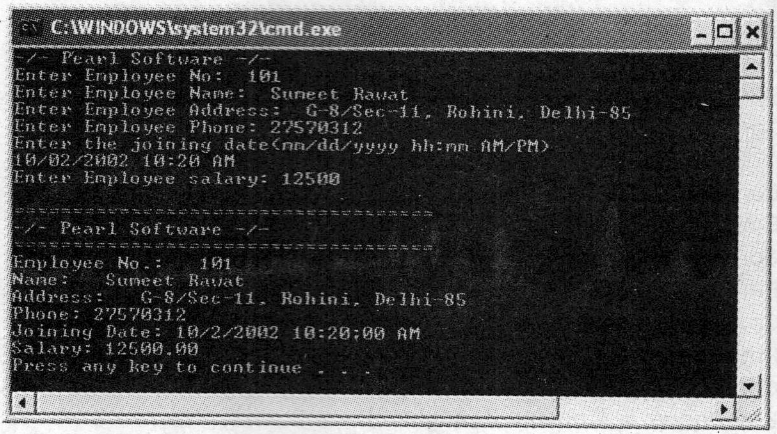

```
C:\WINDOWS\system32\cmd.exe
-/- Pearl Software -/-
Enter Employee No:  101
Enter Employee Name:  Sumeet Rawat
Enter Employee Address:  G-8/Sec-11, Rohini, Delhi-85
Enter Employee Phone: 27570312
Enter the joining date(mm/dd/yyyy hh:mm AM/PM)
10/02/2002 10:20 AM
Enter Employee salary: 12500

====================================
-/- Pearl Software -/-
====================================
Employee No.:   101
Name:   Sumeet Rawat
Address:   G-8/Sec-11, Rohini, Delhi-85
Phone: 27570312
Joining Date: 10/2/2002 10:20:00 AM
Salary: 12500.00
Press any key to continue . . .
```

Fig. 5.8 Number formatting numeric data using ToString() method.

5.10 Data Formatting using ToString()

This method is most commonly used with primitive types to convert numbers to a string format that can be displayed or printed. When used with objects, the default is to return the fully qualified name of the object : **<namespace>.<classname>**. It is common to override this and return a string containing selected values from members of the object.

For all the built-in numeric structure types, such as **Int32** or **Double**, you can use **ToString()** to obtain a formatted string representation of the value. The format for **ToString()** is :

```
Object.ToString();
Or
Object.ToString(string_format);
```

It returns the string representation of the invoking object as specified by the format specifier passed in **string_format**. For example,

```
String str = 289.98.ToString("C");
```

Notice how the format specifier is passed directly to **ToString()**. Unlike embedded format commands used by **WriteLine()** or **Format()**, which supply an argument-number and field-width component, **ToString()** requires only the format specifier, itself. The following Listing 5.3 shows the format values with **ToString()** method.

Listing 5.3 Formal values of ToString method.

Value	Format String	ToString() Implementation	Result
65894.98876	C	value.ToString("C")	$65,894.99
41	D5	value.ToString("D5");	00041
41	X	value.ToString("X");	29
0.25	p	value.ToString("p");	25.00%
65894.98876	r	value.ToString("r")	65894.99
65894.98876	e	value.ToString("e")	6.589499e+004
65894.98876	N5	value.ToString("N5")	65,894.98876
65894.98876	F2	value.ToString("F2")	65,894.99

The following examples shows all the above format into both double and int data type as :

..\CSharp_Book\Chap05\FmtToString

```
using System;
using System.Collections.Generic;
using System.Text;

//Demonstrating ToString() method for formatting data
namespace FmtToString
{
    class Program
    {
        static void Main()
        {
            double num1 = 65894.98876;
            double num2 = 0.25;
            int value1 = 41;

            string str = num1.ToString("C");
            Console.WriteLine("The currency format is : " + str);
            str = value1.ToString("D5");
            Console.WriteLine("The decimal format is : " + str);
            str = value1.ToString("X");
            Console.WriteLine("The hexadecimal conversions value is : " + str);
            str = num2.ToString("p");
            Console.WriteLine("The percentage format is : " + str);
            str = num1.ToString("r");
            Console.WriteLine("The rounded format value is : " + str);
            str = num1.ToString("e");
```

```
            Console.WriteLine("The scientific format value is : " + str);
            str = num1.ToString("N5");
            Console.WriteLine("The Number format value is : " + str);
            str = num1.ToString("F2");
            Console.WriteLine("The Fixed point format value is : " + str);
            Console.WriteLine();
        }
    }
}
```

When the above program executed, it will produce the following output as shown in Fig. 5.9.

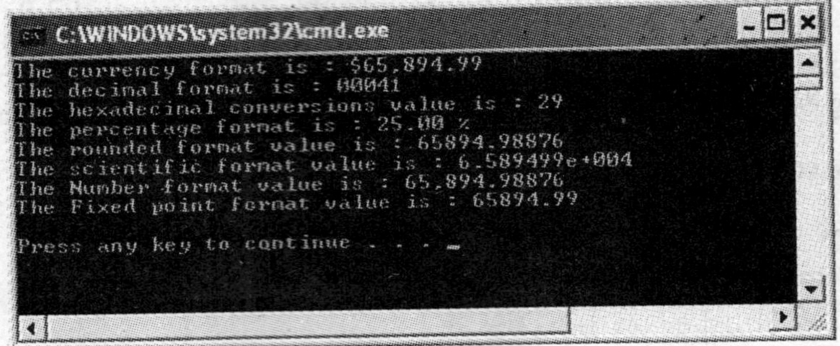

Fig. 5.9 Number formatting using ToString() method options.

.NET also provide special formatting characters that can be used to create custom numeric format. The nost useful characters are pound sign (#), zero (0), comma (,), perios (.), percent sign (%), and semi-color (;).

..\CSharp_Book\Chap05\ForCustom

```
using System;
using System.Collections.Generic;
using System.Text;
//Demonstrating ToString() using different characters
namespace ForCustom
{
    class Program
    {
        static void Main()
        {
            double num1 = 65894.98876;
            double num2 = 0.25;
            int value1 = 41;

            string str = num1.ToString("#######.##");
```

```
        Console.WriteLine("The value using pound (#) sign is : " + str);
        str = num1.ToString("##,##,###.00");
        Console.WriteLine("The value using pound (#) sign with comma (,) is : "
            + str);
        Console.WriteLine();
    }
  }
}
```

When the above program executed, it will produce the following output as shown in Fig. 5.10.

Fig. 5.10 Using custom format options.

5.11 Formatting DateTime Values

The **String.Format** method is the primary means of formatting date and numeric for display. It accepts a string composed of text and embedded format items followed by one or more data arguments. Date formatting requires a **DateTime** object. **DateTime** represents date and time. Also, the date and time representations can vary from country to country. For these reasons, C# provides an extensive formatting subsystems for time and date values. As with numbers, this object has its own set of standard format specifiers. The following Listing 5.4 shows different format specifiers for date and time (i.e., if current date is **2/12/2007**).

Listing 5.4 Formatting Dates with standard characters.

Format Specifier	Description	Example
d	Short date pattern	2/12/2007
D	Long date pattern	Monday, February 12, 2007
f	Full date/time pattern (short time)	Monday, February 12, 2007 1:20 PM
F	Full date/time pattern (full time)	Monday, February 12, 2007 1:20:25 PM
g	General date/time pattern (short time)	2/12/2007 1:20 PM

G	General date/time pattern (long time)	2/12/2007 1:20:25 PM
M, m	Month day pattern	February 12
Y, y	Year month pattern	February, 2007
t	Short time pattern	1:20 PM
T	Long time pattern	1:20:25 PM
s	Universal Shortable Date-Time pattern. Conforms to ISO 8601. Uses local time.	2007-02-12T1:20:25
u	Universal Shortable Date-Time pattern.	2007-02-12T1:20:25Z
U	Universal Shortable Date-Time pattern. Uses universal time.	Monday, February 12, 2007 1:20:25 PM

Here are some concrete examples that demonstrate date format. In each case, an instance of a **DateTime** object is passed as an argument to a format string.

..\CSharp_Book\Chap05\DateTimeFormat

```
using System;
using System.Collections.Generic;
using System.Text;
// Demonstrating DateTime data format
namespace DateTimeFormat
{
    class Program
    {
        static void Main()
        {

            DateTime curDt = DateTime.Now;        //Extracts current date

            Console.WriteLine("- - > d: Short date pattern {0:d}", curDt);
            Console.WriteLine("- - > D: Long date pattern {0:D}", curDt);

            Console.WriteLine("- - > f: Full date/time (short) pattern : {0:f}", curDt);
            Console.WriteLine("- - > F: Full date/time (long) pattern : {0:F}", curDt);
            Console.WriteLine("- - > g: General date/time (short time) pattern : {0:g}",
                    curDt);
```

```
            Console.WriteLine("- - > G: General date/time (long time) pattern : {0:G}",
                    curDt);
            Console.WriteLine("- - > M: Month day pattern : {0:M}", curDt);
            Console.WriteLine("- - > m: Month day pattern : {0:m}", curDt);
            Console.WriteLine("- - > Y: Year month pattern : {0:Y}", curDt);
            Console.WriteLine("- - > y: Year month pattern : {0:y}", curDt);
            Console.WriteLine("- - > t: Short time pattern : {0:t}", curDt);
            Console.WriteLine("- - > T: Long time pattern : {0:T}", curDt);
            Console.WriteLine("- - > s: Universal local Date-Time pattern : {0:s}", curDt);
            Console.WriteLine("- - > u: Universal Date-Time pattern : {0:u}", curDt);
            Console.WriteLine("- - > u: Universal Time pattern : {0:U}", curDt);
            Console.WriteLine();
        }
    }
}
```

When the above program executed, it will produce the following output as shown in Fig. 5.11.

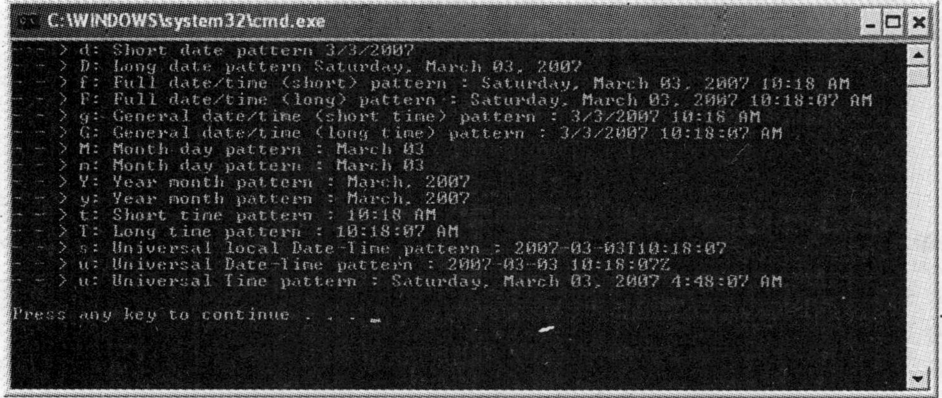

Fig. 5.11 Formatting date using standard characters.

You can also use the custom date formatting standards in your program. To create a custom date and time format, you will use one or more of the placeholders like **d**, **f**, **g**, **m**, **M**, **s** and **t** are the same as the date and time format specifiers in previous listing. Listing 5.5 lists some of the more useful ones for formatting dates and times.

Listing 5.5 Character patterns for custom date formatting.

Custom Format Specifier	Description	Example
d	Day of month. No leading zero.	6
dd	Day of month. Always have two digits.	06
ddd	Day of week with three-character abbreviation.	Tue
dddd	Day o week full name.	Tuesday
M	Month number. No leading zero.	2
MM	Month number with leading zero if needed.	02
MMM	Month name with three-character abbreviation.	Feb
MMMM	Full name of month.	February
y	Year. Last one or two digits.	7
yy	Year. Last one or two digits with leading zero if needed.	07
yyyy	Full-digit year	2007
H	Hours as a number between 0 and 23	6
HH	Hour in 24-hour format	18
mm	Minutes with leading zero if needed.	20
/	Separator for date component	2/12/2007

..\CSharp_Book\Chap05\DateTimeCustom

```
using System;
using System.Collections.Generic;
using System.Text;

// Demonstrating custom DateTime data format
namespace ArrayAsign
{
    class Program
    {
        static void Main()
        {
            DateTime curDt = DateTime.Now;      //Extracts current date
            string nDate, nDt;

            Console.WriteLine("Date is : {0:ddd MMM, yyyy}", curDt);
            Console.WriteLine("Time is : {0:hh:mm tt}", curDt);
            Console.WriteLine("New Date is : {0:dddd MMMM, yyyy}", curDt);
```

```
            nDate = String.Format("{0:dddd} {0:MM} {0:dd}", curDt);
            Console.WriteLine("Current date is : " + nDate);
            nDt = curDt.ToString("dd MM yyyy");
            Console.WriteLine("Current date is : " + nDt);
            // The standard short date format (d) is equivalent to this :
            Console.WriteLine(curDt.ToString("M/d/yyy"));
            Console.WriteLine(curDt.ToString("d"));
        }
    }
}
```

When the above program executed, it will produce the following output as shown in Fig. 5.12.

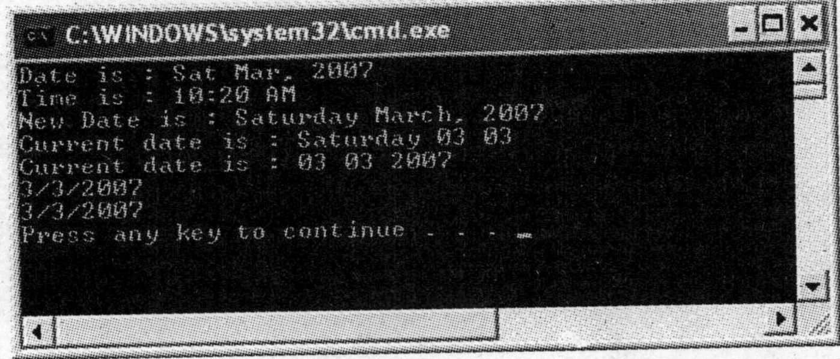

Fig. 5.12 Custome date time formatting options.

From the above program, the **ToString()** is recommended over **String.Format** for custom date formatting. It has more convenient syntax for embedding blanks and special separators between the date elements; in addition, its second parameter is a culture indicator that makes it easy to test different cultures.

Example. Write a program to display the system clock using DateTime object.

..\CSharp_Book\Chap05\SysClock

```
using System;
using System.Collections.Generic;
using System.Text;

// Demonstrating the system clock
namespace SysClock
{
    class Program
    {
        static void Main()
        {
```

```
            string curTime;
            int seconds;

            DateTime curDt = DateTime.Now;      //Extracts current date
            seconds = curDt.Second;

            for (; ; )
            {
                curDt = DateTime.Now;

                // Update time if seconds change
                if (seconds != curDt.Second)
                {
                    seconds = curDt.Second;
                    curTime = curDt.ToString("T");
                    if (curDt.Minute == 0 && curDt.Second == 0)
                        curTime = curTime + "\a"; // Rings alarm at top of hour
                    Console.WriteLine(curTime);
                }
            }
        }
    }
}
```

When the above program executed, it will produce the following output as shown in Fig. 5.13.

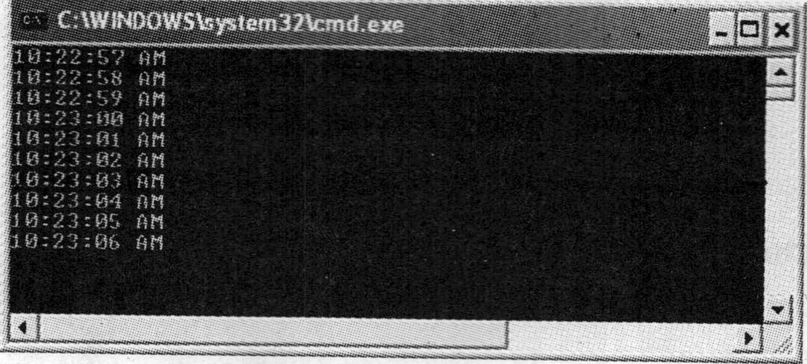

Fig. 5.13 Displaying system clock.

5.12 Line Formatting

In the above programs, to display a line of text, we easily used **Write()** or **WriteLine()**. To position text of different lengths one above the other, we had to "corrupt" a string by including extra-empty spaces. Such a technique is uncertain and less professional. Fortunately, you can highly format how a string or a line of text should display. The .NET Framework provides mechanisms to control the amount of space used to display a string of text and how to align that string on its line.

To specify the amount of space used to display a string, you can use its placeholder in **Write()** or **WriteLine()**. To do this, in the placeholder, type the 0 or the incrementing number of the placer and its formatting character if necessary and if any. Then, type a comma followed by the number of characters equivalent to the desired width. For example;

..\CSharp_Book\Chap05\FormatLin

```
using System;
using System.Collections.Generic;
using System.Text;

namespace FormatLin
{
    class Program
    {
        static void Main()
        {
            String EmpName = "Sumeet Rawat";
            int Age = 32;
            const int hr = 8; // Working hour per day
            double BSalary = 12600.00;
            double DailySalary = BSalary / 30;
            double HourlySalary = DailySalary / hr;

            Console.WriteLine("Full Name: {0, 15}", EmpName);
            Console.WriteLine("Age: {0, 15}", Age.ToString());
            Console.WriteLine("Basic Salary: {0:C, 10}", BSalary.ToString());
            Console.WriteLine("Daily Salary: {0:C, 10} for {1} hours",
                        DailySalary.ToString(), hr.ToString());
            Console.WriteLine();
        }
    }
}
```

When the above program executed, it will produce the following output as shown in Fig. 5.14.

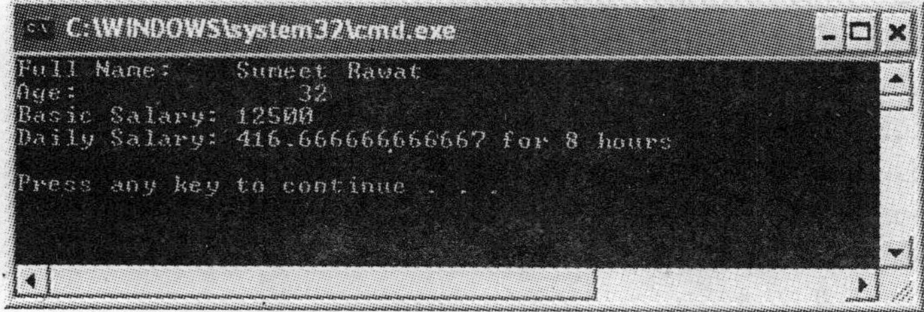

```
C:\WINDOWS\system32\cmd.exe
Full Name:     Sumeet Rawat
Age:                     32
Basic Salary: 12500
Daily Salary: 416.666666666667 for 8 hours

Press any key to continue . . .
```

Fig. 5.14 Line formatting with format options.

The sign you provide for the width is very important. If it is positive, the line of text is aligned to the right. This should be your preferred alignment for numeric values. If the number is negative, then the text is aligned to the left.

5.13 Date and Time Formatting

As mentioned earlier, when the user enters a date value for a **DateTime** variable, the compiler adds a time part to the value. Fortunately, if you want to consider only the date or only the time part, you can specify this to the compiler. To support this, the **DateTime** data type provides a series of letters you can use to format how its value should be displayed to the user. The character is entered in the placeholder of the **DateTime** variable after the 0 or the incremental numeric value. For example;

..\CSharp_Book\Chap05\FormatDT

```
using System;
using System.Collections.Generic;
using System.Text;

namespace FormatDT
{
    class Program
    {
        static void Main()
        {
            string EmpNo, EmpName, EmpAddress, EmpPhone, EmpSal;
            DateTime EmpDOJ, EmpTOJ;    // Date of joining and Time of joining

            Decimal Salary;    // Salary of employee
            Console.WriteLine("-/- Pearl Software -/-");
            // Request Employee information from the user
            Console.Write("Enter Employee No: ");
            EmpNo = Console.ReadLine();
            Console.Write("Enter Employee Name: ");
            EmpName = Console.ReadLine();
            Console.Write("Enter Employee Address: ");
            EmpAddress = Console.ReadLine();
            Console.Write("Enter Employee Phone: ");
            EmpPhone = Console.ReadLine();
            Console.WriteLine("Enter the joining date(mm/dd/yyyy)");
            EmpDOJ = DateTime.Parse(Console.ReadLine());
            Console.WriteLine("Enter the joining time(hh:mm AM/PM)");
            EmpTOJ = DateTime.Parse(Console.ReadLine());

            Console.Write("Enter Employee salary: ");
```

```
            EmpSal = Console.ReadLine();
            Salary = long.Parse(EmpSal);    // String converted into long type
            Console.WriteLine();

            // Display the details
            Console.WriteLine("====================================");
            Console.WriteLine("-/- Pearl Software -/-");
            Console.WriteLine("====================================");
            Console.Write("Employee No.:    ");
            Console.WriteLine(EmpNo);
            Console.Write("Name:    ");
            Console.WriteLine(EmpName);
            Console.Write("Address:    ");
            Console.WriteLine(EmpAddress);

            Console.Write("Phone: ");
            Console.WriteLine(EmpPhone);
            Console.WriteLine("Joining Date: {0:D}", EmpDOJ);
            Console.WriteLine("Joining Time: {0:t}", EmpTOJ);
            Console.WriteLine();
            Console.Write("Salary: {0:F}", Salary);
            Console.WriteLine();
        }
    }
}
```

When the above program executed, it will produce the following output as shown in Fig. 5.15.

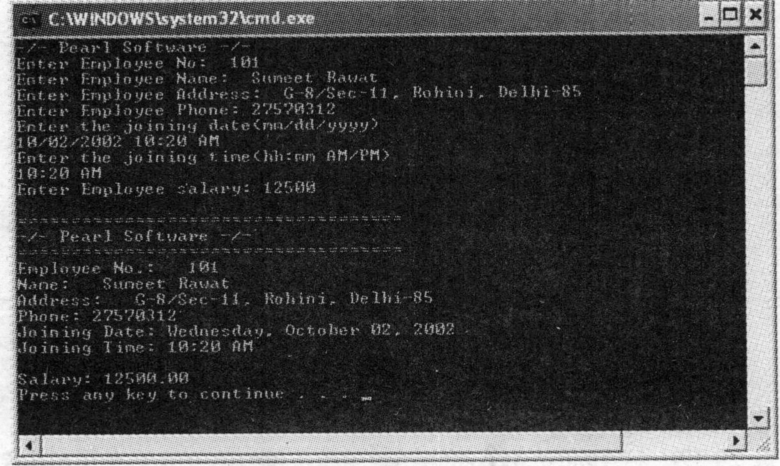

```
C:\WINDOWS\system32\cmd.exe
-/- Pearl Software -/-
Enter Employee No:  101
Enter Employee Name:  Suneet Rawat
Enter Employee Address:  G-8/Sec-11, Rohini, Delhi-85
Enter Employee Phone: 27570312
Enter the joining date(mm/dd/yyyy)
10/02/2002 10:20 AM
Enter the joining time(hh:mm AM/PM)
10:20 AM
Enter Employee salary: 12500

====================================
-/- Pearl Software -/-
====================================
Employee No.:    101
Name:    Suneet Rawat
Address:    G-8/Sec-11, Rohini, Delhi-85
Phone: 27570312
Joining Date: Wednesday, October 02, 2002
Joining Time: 10:20 AM

Salary: 12500.00
Press any key to continue . . . _
```

Fig. 5.15 Date and time formatting.

5.14 Working with Math Class Library

Math class defines number of standard mathematical operations in its inbuilt methods. This class helps us to solve common mathematical calculations. The Math is a sealed class, which cannot be inherited. Each method of the Math class contains an argument and use with the Math keyword. For example, suppose you want to find the square root of a number 400.0, then you must write as :

```
Console.WriteLine("The square root of 400 is ", Math.Sqrt(400.0));
```

Here, 400.0 is an argument for Sqrt method of Math class. It takes an argument as double type and also returns a double type value. Note that when us use Math class method, all Math class methods must be invoked by preceding the method name with the class name Math and a dot (.) operator.

The Math class contains several methods as listed in Listing 5.6.

Listing 5.6 Math class methods.

Method	Description
Abs(x)	Returns absolute value of x. x is double, float, decimal int, sort, long or sbyte type.
Acos(x)	Returns the arc cosine of x. The value of x must be between -1 and 1.
Ceiling(x)	Returns the smallest integer (represented as a floating-point value) not less than x. That is, it rounds x to the smallest integer not less than x.
Cos(x)	Returns the cosine value of x.
Exp(x)	Returns the natural logarithms base e raised to power x.
Floor(x)	Returns the largest integer (represented as a floating-point value) not greater than x. That is, it rounds x to the largest integer not greater than x. It is just opposite of **Ceiling(x)**.
Log(x)	Returns the natural logarithm for x.
Log10(x)	Returns the base 10 logarithm for x.
Max(x, y)	Returns the maximum value between x and y. Where x and y are same type like x is double, float, decimal int, sort, long or sbyte type.
Min(x, y)	Returns the minimum value between x and y. Where x and y are same type like x is double, float, decimal int, sort, long or sbyte type.
Pow(x, y)	Returns x raised to the power y value.
Round(x)	Returns x rounded to the nearest whole number. The Round method can take another parameter for the number of fractional digits as Round(x, y). x is the number and y is the number of fractional positions.
Sign(x)	Returns the sign of x. It returns -1 if x is less than zero, 0 if x is zero and 1 if x is greater than zero. Where as x can be double, float, decimal int, sort, long or sbyte type.

Sin(x)	Returns the size of x.
Sqrt(x)	Returns the square root of x.
Tan(x)	Returns the tangent of x.

Let us consider the following program which finds all the possible values of Math class methods.

..\CSharp_Book\Chap05\MathMethod

```
using System;
using System.Collections.Generic;
using System.Text;

namespace MathMethod
{
    class Program
    {
        static void Main()
        {
            int x = 10, y = 400;
            float a = 123.45F;
            float p = 12.5F, q = 12.1F;
            double b = 12.54E60;
            long c = 123456L;
            decimal d = 4576.56M;
            double angle = 45;

            Console.WriteLine("Abs({0:F2})        —> {1}", a, Math.Abs(a));
            Console.WriteLine("Acos({0})          —> {1}", 0, Math.Acos(0));
            Console.WriteLine("Ceiling({0:F3})    —> {1}", a, Math.Ceiling(a));
            Console.WriteLine("Cos({0})           —> {1}", angle, Math.Cos(angle));
            Console.WriteLine("Exp({0:F2})        —> {1}", x, Math.Exp(x));
            Console.WriteLine("Floor({0:F2})      —> {1}", a, Math.Floor(a));
            Console.WriteLine("Log({0})           —> {1}", x, Math.Log(x));
            Console.WriteLine("Log10({0})         —> {1}", x, Math.Log10(x));
            Console.WriteLine("Max({0}, {1})      —> {2}", p, q, Math.Max(p, q));
            Console.WriteLine("Min({0}, {1})      —> {2}", p, q; Math.Min(p, q));
            Console.WriteLine("Pow({0}, {1})      —> {2}", x, 2, Math.Pow(x, 2));
            Console.WriteLine("Round({0:F2})      —> {1}", a, Math.Round(a, 2));
            Console.WriteLine("Sign({0})          —> {1}", x, Math.Sign(x));
            Console.WriteLine("Sin({0})           —> {1}", angle, Math.Sin(angle));
            Console.WriteLine("Sqrt({0})          —> {1}", y, Math.Sqrt(y));
            Console.WriteLine("Tan({0})           —> {1}", angle, Math.Tan(angle));
        }
    }
}
```

When the above program executed, it will produce the following output as shown in Fig. 5.16.

```
C:\WINDOWS\system32\cmd.exe
Abs(123.45)              --> 123.45
Acos(0)                  --> 1.5707963267949
Ceiling(123.450)         --> 124
Cos(45)                  --> 0.52532198881773
Exp(10.00)               --> 22026.4657948067
Floor(123.45)            --> 123
Log(10)                  --> 2.30258509299405
Log10(10)                --> 1
Max(12.5, 12.1)          --> 12.5
Min(12.5, 12.1)          --> 12.1
Pow(10, 2)               --> 100
Round(123.45)            --> 123.45
Sign(10)                 --> 1
Sin(45)                  --> 0.850903524534118
Sqrt(400)                --> 20
Tan(45)                  --> 1.61977519054386

Press any key to continue . . .
```

Fig. 5.16 Use of Math class methods.

Exercise

1. Explain about the ReadLine and WriteLine methods of Console class.
2. What is KeyChar?
3. Name the .NET structure for int and double data type in Parse() method.
4. How can you enter date and time type data from keyboard. Explain its few formats.
5. What is the general format for Write/WriteLine method of Console class.
6. Explain any 5 format character constants.
7. What is ToString() method ?
8. How can you format lines in C# program?
9. Explain any five Math class methods.

Branching and Looping 6

6.1 Introduction

Control statements govern the flow of control in a program. A program written in the C# programming language takes the basic form of a sequence of command lines starting with a command verb and optionally including supporting clause. This implies that C# starts at the top of the list of commands and execute them one after the other until the list is exhausted. Although this model is basically accurate, the C# language provides several mechanisms for specifying branches, loops, and subroutines.

The capability to repeat tasks makes computer good tool for processing large amounts of information. Constructs are the control and looping command in programming languages. C# constructs include powerful as well as succinct and efficient looping commands similar to those of other programming languages with which you might already be familiar.

For example, the **while** loops let your programs repeat a series of statements, over and over, as long as a certain condition is met. The computers don't get bored when performing the same tasks repeatedly. That's one reason they are so important in the business data processing.

6.2 Structured Programming Technique

Structured programming techniques imply that the program development and coding must follow a top-down approach and structured programming constructs.

Top-down approach implies planning the program as a hierarchy of modules. Programming begins with top (main) module. When the main module is programmed, second level modules are then programmed. A program unit is coded only after the unit that calls for it to be performed has been coded.

In order to support the discipline of top-down programming, the following basic structured programming constructs are followed in programming :

- **Sequence.** The execution of instruction transfer in one way.
- **Selection.** This is called branching which executing one group of instructions depending on the outcome of a decision. In this category, C# language provides the following statements :
  - **if** statement
  - **if-else** statement
  - **else if** construct
  - **switch case** statement
- **Repetition.** This is called a looping structure, which executing a group of instructions repetitively either for a given number of times or until the required conditions are met. In this category, C# language provides the following statements :
  - **for** statement
  - **while** statement
  - **do-while** statement
- **Jumping.** This control statement is used to skip the further statements of an action on the spot and jump to the desired point of control. In this category, C# language provides the statements as :
  - **break** statement
  - **continue** statement
  - **goto** statement

6.2.1 Sequence

Sequence indicates that if there is no intervening control structure that flow of control normally passes from one instruction to the next in sequence. The sequence structure is built into C#. Unless directed otherwise, the computer executes C# statements one after the other in the order in which they are written. The flowchart segment of Fig. 6.1 illustrates a typical sequence structure in which two calculations are performed in order.

A *flowchart* is a graphical representation of an algorithm or of a portion of an algorithm. Flowcharts are drawn using certain special-purpose symbols such as rectangles, diamonds, ovals and small circles; these symbols are connected by arrow called *flowlines*.

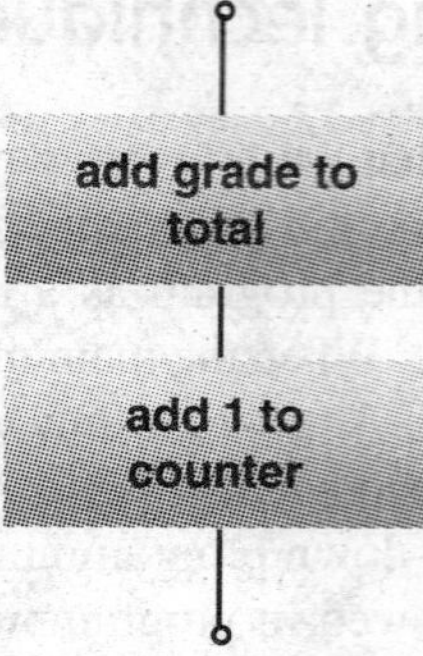

Fig. 6.1 Flowchart showing C# sequence structure.

Consider the flowchart segment for the sequence structure in above figure. We use the *rectangle symbol*, also called the *action symbol*, to indicate any type of action includes a calculation or an input/output operation. The flowlines in the figure indicate the order in which the actions are to be performed—first, **grade** is to be added to **total** then **1** is to be added to **counter**. C# allows us to have as many actions as we want in a sequence structure. As we will soon see, anywhere a single action may be placed, we may place several actions in sequence.

6.2.2 Selection

Selection indicates a decision. You may have one way, two way or multi-way selection that is to say that you may branch out to one, two or multiple locations within the program depending on the decision.

C# provides three types of selection structures. The **if** selection structure either performs (selects) an action if a condition is **true** or skips the action if the condition is **false**. The **if/else** selection structure performs an action if a condition is **true** and performs a different action if the condition is **false**. The **switch case...** selection structure performs one of many different actions depending on the value of an expression.

The **if** selection structure is called a *single-selection structure* because it selects or ignores a single action. The **if/else** selection structure is called a *double-selection structure* because it selects between two different actions. The **switch case...** selection structure is called a *multiple-selection structure* because it selects the action to perform from many different actions.

The flowchart of Fig. 6.2 illustrates the single-selection **if** structure.

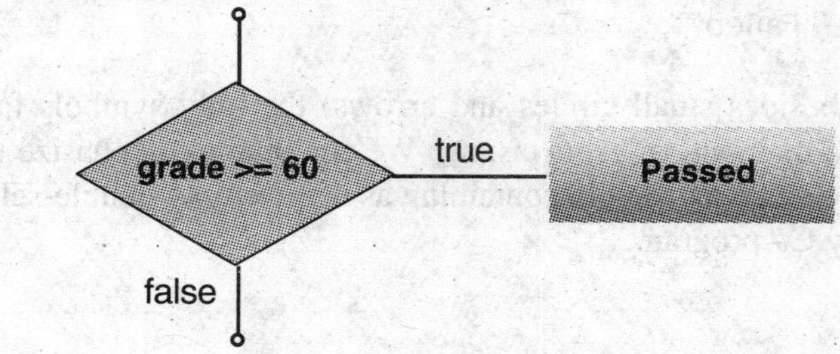

Fig. 6.2 Flowchart showing the single-selection if structure.

For example,

```
if (grade >= 60)
    Console.WriteLine("Passed");
```

This flowchart contains what is perhaps the most important flowchart showing symbol—the *diamond symbol*, also called the *decision symbol*, which indicates that a decision is to be made. The decision symbol contains an expression, such as a condition, that can be either **true** or **false**. The decision symbol has two flowlines emerging from it. One indicates the direction to be taken when the expression in the symbol is **true**; the other indicates the direction to be taken when the expression is **false**.

Actually, a decision can be made on any expression—if the expression evaluates to zero, it is treated as **false**, and if the expression evaluates to non-zero, it is treated as **true**.

Here, the flowchart of Fig 6.3 nicely illustrates the flow of control in the **if/else** structure.

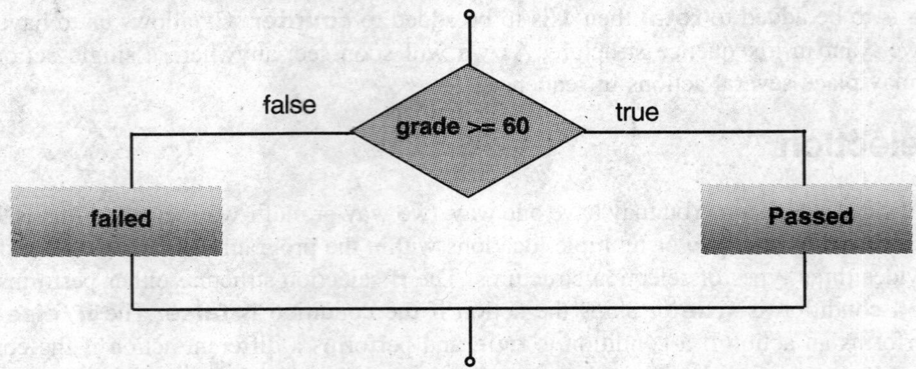

Fig. 6.3 Flowchart showing the double-selection if/else structure.

For example;

```
if (grade >= 60)
    Console.WriteLine("Passed");
else
    Console.WriteLine("Failed");
```

Once again, note that (besides small circles and arrows) the only symbols in the flowchart are rectangles (for actions) and a diamond (for a decision). We continue to emphasize this action/decision model of computing. Imagine again a deep bin containing as many empty double-selection structures as might be needed to build any C# program.

6.2.3 Repetition

If a statement has to be executed more than once the technique of repetition is applied. It saves the trouble of writing the same statement again and again.

As an example of an actual **while**, consider a program segment designed to find the first power of 2 larger than 1000. Suppose the integer (numeric) variable **product** has been initialized to 2. When the following **do while** repetition structure finishes executing, **product** will contain the desired answer :

```
product = 2
while (product <= 1000)
{
    product = product * 2
}
```

The flowchart of Fig. 6.4 illustrates the flow of control in the **while** structure that corresponds to the preceding **while** structure. The flowchart clearly shows the repetition. The flowline emerging from the rectangle wraps back to the decision that is tested each time through the loop until the decision becomes **false**. Then the **while** structure exits and control passes to the next statement in the program.

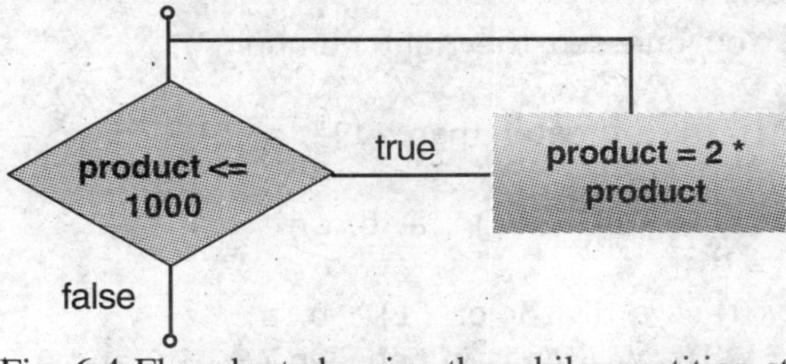

Fig. 6.4 Flowchart showing the while repetition structure.

When the **while** statement is entered, the value of **product** is 2. The variable **product** is repeatedly multiplied by 2, taking on the values 4, 8, 16, 32, 64, 128, 256, 512 and 1024 successively. When **product** becomes 1024, the **while** structure condition, **product <= 1000,** becomes **false**. This terminates the repetition —the final value of **product** is 1024. Program execution continues with the next statement after the **while**.

6.3 Selection (if Statement)

The **if** statement allows branching (decision making) depending upon the value or state of variables. In C# the **if** statement uses with relational operators. This statement is called decision statement because it tests a relationship, using the relational operator. Then it makes a decision about which statement to execute next, based on the result of that decision.

The **if** statement has the following format :

```
if (condition)
{
    A block of one or more C# statements
}
```

Note

*The **if** statement allows conditional execution. It tests a conditional expression enclosed within a pair of parenthesis and if that expression is evaluated as a nonzero value (i.e. any positive or negative value) then the statement(s) following **if** are executed.*

The condition includes any relational comparison and must be enclosed within parentheses. If the value of the condition is nonzero, then the body of **if** gets executed. The block of one or more C# statements can be any legal C# statement, such as an assignment or the **WriteLine()** statement, enclosed within braces. Some of valid **if** statements are :

- ```
  if (a > 0)
      Console.WriteLine("{0} is a positive number ", a);
  ```
- ```
  if (a)   // Same as : if (a != 0)
      Console.WriteLine("{0} is a nonzero number ", a);
  ```
- ```
  if (guess == num)
      Console.WriteLine("You guessed the right number ");
  ```
- ```
  if (a <= b)
      Console.WriteLine("{0} i is greater than {1}", a, b);
  ```
- ```
  if ((a < b) && (b > c))
      Console.WriteLine("{0} < {1} < {2}", a, b, c);
  ```
- ```
  if ((a % b == 0) && (b != 0))
      Console.WriteLine("{0} is a divisor or {1}", b, a);
  ```
- ```
  if ((ch >= '0') && (ch <= '9'))   // if ch is in between ASCII 0 and 9
      Console.WriteLine("{0} ", ch);
  ```

Note

If the block of if statement contains multiple statements, then enclose these statements inside a pair of braces ({ }).

The block of the **if**, sometimes called the body of the **if** statement, is usually indented a few spaces for readability. This lets you see at a glance exactly what executes if the condition is True.

Note

Note. *Do not put a semicolon after the parentheses of the relational test. The semicolons go after each statement inside the block.*

The following Fig. 6.5 shows the relational **True/False** operation of two variables a and b. If only one statement follows the **if**, the braces are not required, but they are helpful to include. The block executes only if the condition is **True**. If the condition is **False**, C# ignores the block, and simply executes the next statement in the program following the **if**.

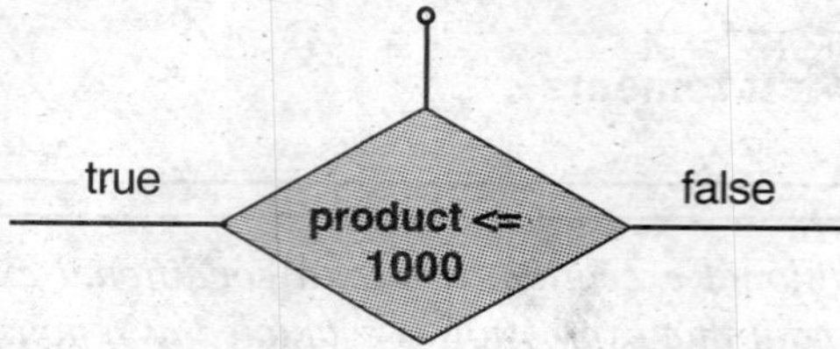

Fig. 6.5 Show the True/False operation of an if statement.

Although the (simple) **if** statement is used to check one condition, it can lead to executing multiple dependent statements. If that is the case, enclose the group of statements between an opening curly bracket "{" and a closing curly bracket "}".
  ```

For example;

```
if (age <= 21)
{
    Console.WriteLine("You are a minor.");
    Console.WriteLine("What is your grade ");
    grade = char.parse(Console.ReadLine());
}
```

If the value in **age** is less than or equal to 21, the lines of code in the block executes next. Otherwise, C# skips the entire block, and continues with the program.

Example Write a C# program to take a value from the user and print the square of it, unless it is more than 120. The message I cannot square numbers that appear if the user types too large a number.

..\CSharp_Book\Chap06\InSquare

```
using System;
using System.Collections.Generic;
using System.Text;

// Prints the square of the input value if the input value is less than 180
namespace InSquare
{
    class Program
    {
        static void Main()
        {
            int num, square;
            Console.WriteLine("What number do you want to see the square of? ");
            num = int.Parse(Console.ReadLine());
            if (num < 120)
            {
                square = num * num;
                Console.WriteLine("The square of {0} is {1}", num, square);
            }
            if (num >= 120)
            {
                Console.WriteLine("*** Square is not allowed for numbers over
                        120 *** ");
                Console.WriteLine("Run this program again and try a smaller value. ");
            }
            Console.WriteLine("\nThank you for requesting squares.");
        }
    }
}
```

When the above program executed, it will produce the following output as shown in Fig. 6.6.

```
C:\WINDOWS\system32\cmd.exe
What number do you want to see the square of? 10
The square of 10 is 100

Thank you for requesting squares.
Press any key to continue . . .
```

Fig. 6.6 Use simple if condition.

For example, Write a C# program to print the largest of 3 numbers using if statements. Also, check the nonzero value with proper message.

..\CSharp_Book\Chap06\Largest

```
using System;
using System.Collections.Generic;
using System.Text;

// Program to print the largest of 3 numbers
namespace Largest
{
    class Program
    {
        static void Main()
        {
            int a, b, c, d;
            Console.WriteLine("Enter any three numbers : ");
            a = int.Parse(Console.ReadLine());
            b = int.Parse(Console.ReadLine());
            c = int.Parse(Console.ReadLine());
            if ((a >= 0) && (b >= 0) && (c >= 0))   // only checks the nonzero value
            {
                d = a;
                if (b>d)
                    d = b;
                if (c>d)
                    d = c;
                Console.WriteLine("The largest is {0}", d);
            }
        }
    }
}
```

When the above program executed, it will produce the following output :

```
Enter any three numbers :
90
54
280
The largest is 280
Press any key to continue . . .
```

6.3.1 The else Statement

This statement also tests a conditional expression. The **else** statement never appears in a program without an **if** statement. This section introduces the **else** statement by showing you the popular **if-else** combination statement. The following illustrates its format :

```
if (condition)
{
    A block of 1 or more C# statements
}
else
{
    A block of 1 or more C# statements
}
```

If the condition evaluates to be nonzero, then the body of **if** is selected for action otherwise the body of **else** is selected for action.

The first part of the **if-else** is identical to the **if**-statement. If the second is **True**, the block of C# statements following the **if** executes. However, if the condition is **False**, the block of C# statements following the **else** executes. Although the simple **if**-statement determines only what happens if the condition is True, the **if-else** determines what happens if the condition is **False**. No matter what the outcome, the statement following the **if-else** executes next.

Some of valid **if-else** statements are :

- ```
  if (a > b)
      Console.WriteLine("{0} is greater than {1}", a, b);
  Else
      Console.WriteLine("{0} is greater than {1}", b a);
  ```
- ```
  if ((ch >= 'a') && (ch <= 'z'))
      Console.WriteLine("{0} is a lowercase letter");
  else
      Console.WriteLine("{0} is not a lowercase letter");
  ```
- ```
  if ((ch >= 'a') && (ch <= 'z')) ((ch >= 'A') && (ch <= 'Z'))
      Console.WriteLine("{0} is an alphabet");
  ```
  ```

```
else
    Console.WriteLine("{0} is not an alphabet");
```

- ```
  if ((sex == 'M') || (sex == 'm'))
      Console.WriteLine("You are a male");
  else
      Console.WriteLine("You are a female");
  ```
- ```
  if ((divisor != 0) && (num % divisor))
      Console.WriteLine("0} is not divisible by {1}", num, divisor);
  else
      Console.WriteLine("{0} is divisible by {1}", num, divisor);
  ```

Note

*If the condition is True, the entire block of statements following the **if** is performed. If the condition is False, the entire block of statements following the **else** is performed.*

For example, the following program asks the user for a number. The program then prints a line indicating that the number is greater than zero or that it is not, using the if-else statement.

..\CSharp_Book\Chap06\IfElse

```
using System;
using System.Collections.Generic;
using System.Text;

// Demonstrates if-else by printing whether an input value is greater than zero or not.
namespace IfElse
{
    class Program
    {
        static void Main()
        {
            int num;
            Console.WriteLine("What is your number? ");
            num = int.Parse(Console.ReadLine());
            if (num > 0)
            {
                Console.WriteLine("More than 0");
            }
            else
            {
                Console.WriteLine("Less or equal to 0");
            }
        }
    }
}
```

When the above program executed, it will produce the following output :

```
What is your number? 1208
More than 0
Press any key to continue . . .
```

6.3.2 Nested if

Nested **if/else** structures test for multiple causes by placing **if/else** selection structure inside **if/else** selection structure. The **if/else** selection structure uses the condition till three levels. The following illustrates its format :

```
if (condition)
{
    A block of 1 or more C# statements
}
else if (condition)
{
    A block of 1 or more C# statements
}
...
...
else
{
    A block of 1 or more C# statements
}
```

Example The following program finds the greatest among the three numbers.

..\CSharp_Book\Chap06\NestedIF

```
using System;
using System.Collections.Generic;
using System.Text;
namespace NestedIF
{
    class Program
    {
        static void Main()
        {
            int fn, sn, tn;    // Declare three different variable
            Console.Write("What is the first number? ");
```

```
            fn = int.Parse(Console.ReadLine());
            Console.Write("What is the second number? ");
            sn = int.Parse(Console.ReadLine());
            Console.Write("What is the third number? ");
            tn = int.Parse(Console.ReadLine());
            if ((fn > sn) && (fn > tn))
            {
                Console.WriteLine("The bigger value is {0}", fn);
            }
            else
                if ((sn > tn) && (sn > fn))
                {
                    Console.WriteLine("The bigger value is {0}", sn);
                }
                else
                {
                    Console.WriteLine("The bigger value is {0}", sn);
                }
        }
    }
}
```

When the above program executed, it will produce the following output :

```
What is the first number? 45
What is the second number? 63
What is the third number? 16
The bigger value is 63
Press any key to continue . . .
```

6.3.3 The if-else-if Ladder

When the programmer writes programs, the condition of the problem may increase its levels. On the same way, when the conditions are increased, the structure of **if/else** becomes extends its level higher into higher. That is, the structure becomes **if-else-if** form, which is called **if-else-if** ladder. The structure becomes :

```
if expression1
    statement1;
else
    if expression2
        statement2;
    else
```

```
if expression3
    statement3;
.... ...............
.... ...............
.... ...............
else
    statementN;
```

From the above structure, the execution counter always follows a top-down approach. It means, the execution counter will check the expression from top to bottom.

The compiler will check the first expression. If **expression1** is true, it will execute **statement1**. If **expression1** is false, then the compiler will check the second condition. If **expression2** is true, it will execute **statement2**. When the compiler finds a **expression-n** to be true, it will execute its corresponding statement. It that **expression-n** is false, the compiler will check the subsequent expression. This means that you can include as many conditions as you see fit using the **else if** statement. After examining all the known possible expresssions, if you still think that there might be an unexpected expression, you can use the optional single **else**.

The following example demonstrates a **if-else-if** ladder application program, i.e., a program to assign a grade as per a predefined condition.

..\CSharp_Book\Chap06\IfElseIf

```
using System;
using System.Collections.Generic;
using System.Text;

// Program to assign grade according to some initial condition
namespace IfElseIf
{
    class Program
    {
        static void Main()
        {
            int hardness, tensile, grade;
            float carbon;
            Console.Write("Enter the value of carbon ");
            carbon = float.Parse(Console.ReadLine());
            Console.Write("Enter the value of hardness ");
            hardness = int.Parse(Console.ReadLine());
            Console.Write("Enter the value of tensile ");
            tensile = int.Parse(Console.ReadLine());

            if ((hardness >= 50) && (carbon <= 0.7) && (tensile > 5600))
                grade = 10;
```

```
            else
                if ((hardness >= 50) && (carbon <= 0.7))
                    grade = 9;
                else
                    if ((carbon <= 0.7) && (tensile >= 5600))
                        grade = 8;
                    else
                        if ((hardness >= 50) && (tensile >= 5600))
                            grade = 7;
                        else
                            if ((hardness >= 50) || (carbon <= 0.7) || (tensile >= 5600))

                                grade = 6;
                            else
                                grade = 5;

            Console.WriteLine("The grade assign is : {0}", grade);
        }
    }
}
```

When the above program executed, it will produce the following output :

```
Enter the value of carbon 4
Enter the value of hardness 7
Enter the value of tensile 3
The grade assign is : 5
Press any key to continue . . .
```

Example Write a program to find the roots of a quadratic equation.

..\CSharp_Book\Chap06\RootQ

```
using System;
using System.Collections.Generic;
using System.Text;

// Program to calculate the roots of quadratic equation
namespace RootQ
{
    class Program
    {
        static void Main()
```

```
    {
        int a, b, c, d;
        double r1, r2; // Because the Math class returns only double type value

        Console.WriteLine("Enter the values of a, b and c ");
        a = int.Parse(Console.ReadLine());
        b = int.Parse(Console.ReadLine());
        c = int.Parse(Console.ReadLine());
        d = b * b - 4 * a * c;
        if (d < 0)
            Console.WriteLine("Roots are imaginary");
        if (d >= 0)
        {
            r1 = (-b + Math.Sqrt(d)) / (2 * a);
            r2 = (-b - Math.Sqrt(d)) / (2 * a);
            r1 = b + Math.Sqrt(d);
            if ( d == 0)
                Console.WriteLine("Roots are equal");
            Console.WriteLine("First root is {0:F}", r1);
            Console.WriteLine("Second root is {0:F}", r2);
        }
    }
  }
}
```

When the above program executed, it will produce the following output :

```
Enter the values of a, b and c
2
4
2
Roots are equal
First root is 4.00
Second root is -1.00
Press any key to continue . . .
```

6.3.4 The ? Alternative to if [The Ternary Operator (?:)]

The conditional operator, **?**: is C#'s only ternary operator. A ternary operator requires three operands (instead of the single and double operands of unary and binary operators). The conditional operator is used to replace **if-else** logic situations. The format of the conditional operator is :

conditional_expression ? expression1 : expression2;

Example Write a program to find maximum between three numbers.

..\CSharp_Book\Chap06\MaxThree

```
using System;
using System.Collections.Generic;
using System.Text;

// Program to find the maximum between two numbers
namespace MaxThree
{
    class Program
    {
        static void Main()
        {
            int a, b, c, max;

            Console.Write("Enter the value of a : ");
            a = int.Parse(Console.ReadLine());
            Console.Write("Enter the value of b : ");
            b = int.Parse(Console.ReadLine());
            Console.Write("Enter the value of c : ");
            c = int.Parse(Console.ReadLine());
            max = (a > b) ? (a > c ? a : c) : (b > c ? b : c);
            Console.WriteLine("Maximum number is {0}", max);
        }
    }
}
```

When the above program executed, it will produce the following output :

```
Enter the value of a : 254
Enter the value of b : 189
Enter the value of c : 196
Maximum number is 254
Press any key to continue . . .
```

6.4 The switch Statement

When defining an expression whose result would lead to a specific program execution, the **switch** statement considers that result and executes a statement based on the possible outcome of that expression, this possible outcome is called a **case**. The different outcomes are listed in the body of the **switch** statement and each case has its own execution, if necessary. The body of a **switch** statement is delimited from an opening to a closing curly brackets: "{" to "}". **switch** statement comes as a handy replacement of a long series of **if-else if** statement. Let us consider an example given below :

```
char ch;
int vowels = 0, consonants = 0;
Console.WriteLine("Enter  any character : ");
ch = int.Parse(Console.ReadLine());
if ((ch == 'A') || (ch == 'a'))
    vowels++;
else if ((ch == 'E') || (ch == 'e'))
    vowels++;
else if ((ch == 'I') || (ch == 'i'))
    vowels++;
else if ((ch == 'O') || (ch == 'o'))
    vowels++;
else if ((ch == 'U') || (ch == 'u'))
    vowels++;
else consonants++;
```

Now, if we write the above piece of code using **switch** statement, what we get is following piece of code :

```
switch (ch)
{
    case 'A' :
    case 'a' :
    case 'E' :
    case 'e' :
    case 'I' :
    case 'i' :
    case 'O' :
    case 'o' :
    case 'U' :
    case 'u' : vowels++; break;
    default : consonants++;
}
```

Thus, the **switch** statement has more flexibility and a clearer format than **else if** construct. The **switch** statement, sometimes referred to as the multiple-choice statement, lets your program choose from several alternatives. The format of the **switch** statement is a little longer that of other statements you have seen. The following presents its format :

```
switch (expression);
{
    case (expression1):
        [C# statements;
        break;]
```

```
    case (expression2):
        [C# statements;
        break;]
    case (expression3):
        [C# statements;
        break;]
    :
    :
    default:
        C# statements;
        break;
}
```

The expression can be any **int** or **char** expression, constant or variable. The subexpressions-expression1, expression2 and so on can be any other **int** or **char** constant. The number of **case** expressions following the **switch** line is determined by your application. The C# statements can be any block of C# code.

The **default** line is optional; not all **switch** statements include this line, although most do. It does not have to be the last line of the body of the **switch** statement.

Note

*In C#, you can omit the **break** keyword in a case. This creates the "fall through" effect as follows: after code executes in a case, if nothing "stops" it, the execution continues to the next case. This has caused problems and confusing execution in the past in some C# programs. To avoid it, C# requires code interruption at the end of every case. This interruption is done using the **break** keyword.*

Note

*In C#, the **default** section doesn't need a **break** keyword because it is the last. In C#, every case and the **default** section must have its own exit mechanism, which is taken care of by a **break** keyword.*

If the expression matches the first case, expression1, the statements that are usually under expression1 execute. If the expression matches the second case, expression2, the statements that are usually under expression2 execute. If none of the **case** expressions matches that of the **switch** expression, the **default** case block executes.

If this value matches with the item of any **case**, follow the action after the **case** until **break** statement is encountered.

The **case** expression value does not have to have parentheses around it. However, using them makes the value easier to find. Use a **break** statement after each **case** block to keep execution from "failing through" to the rest of the **case** statements.

Note

The expression of switch statement must be of type integer or character type. Floating-point constants are also not allowed as the value of expression. Variables or expressions with variables are not allowed. The default case need not be used as the last case. It can be placed at any place.

The examples of **switch** statements are :

- ```
  switch (grade)
  {
      case 'A' : Console.WriteLine("Secure more than 80%");
          break;
      case 'B' : Console.WriteLine("Secure more than 70% and less than 80");
          break;
      case 'C' : Console.WriteLine("Secure more than 60% and less than 70");
          break;
      case 'D' : Console.WriteLine("Secure more than 50% and less than 60");
          break;
      default : Console.WriteLine("Secure more than 50% and less than 60");
          break;
  }
  ```
- ```
  switch (opt)
  {
      case 'R' : Console.WriteLine("Rainy season");
          break;
      case 'S' : Console.WriteLine("Summer season");
          break;
      case 'W' : Console.WriteLine("Winter season");
          break;
      case 'P' : Console.WriteLine("Spring season");
          break;
      case 'A' : Console.WriteLine("Autumn season");
          break;
  }
  ```
- ```
  switch (draw)
  {
      case 'R' : Console.WriteLine("Draw rectangle");
          break;
      case 'C' : Console.WriteLine("Draw circle");
          break;
      case 'E' : Console.WriteLine("Draw ellipse");
          break;
  ```
  ```

```
    case 'P' : Console.WriteLine("Draw polygon");
         break;
    default : Console.WriteLine("Wrong choice");
         break;
}
```

A **break** statement in **switch** causes control to skip all the statements after it and jump to the next statement just after the **switch** block.

> **Note**
> *Forgetting a break statement when one is needed in a switch structure is a logical error. In a switch structure when the default clause is listed last, the break statement is not required.*

There is no need to **break** statement in default **case**, because **default** is the last **case** and so the **switch** has to terminate after it. The **break** is needed if you want to terminate the **switch** after execution of one choice. Otherwise the next **case** would get evaluated. We can also have **null** statements by just including a semicolon (;) or let the **switch** statement fall through by omitting any statements. The **default case** is optional and catches any other **case**s.

> **Note**
> *Omitting the space between the word case and integral value being tested in a switch structure can cause a logical error. For example, writing case3: instead of writing case 3: simply creates an unused label. The problem is that the switch structure will not perform the appropriate actions when the switch's controlling expression has value of 3.*

For example,

```
switch (ch)
{
    case 'A' :
    case 'a' :
    case 'E' :
    case 'e' :
    case 'I' :
    case 'i' :
    case 'O' :
    case 'o' :
    case 'U' :
    case 'u' : vowels++;
        break;
    case ' ' :
        spaces++;
        break;
    default : consonants++;
        break;
}
```

The **switch** statement can be used to combine cases executes as one. To do this, you can type two or more cases together.

In the above example, if the value of letter 'A', 'a', 'E', 'e', 'I', 'i', 'O', 'o', 'U' or 'u' then number of vowels is incremented. If the value of letter is ' ', then number of spaces is incremented. If none of these is **true** then the **default** condition is executed, that is, the number of consonants is incremented.

Example. Write a program to input two numbers and find their sum and difference using **switch** statement.

..\CSharp_Book\Chap06\Calculator

```
using System;
using System.Collections.Generic;
using System.Text;

// Demonstration of switch statement for finding sum and difference of
// any two numbers.
namespace Calculator
{
    class Program
    {
        static int Main()
        {
            int num1, num2, opt, sum, diff;
            sum = 0; // Assign the calculated variables
            diff = 0;
            Console.Write("Enter first number ");
            num1 = int.Parse(Console.ReadLine());
            Console.Write("Enter second number ");
            num2 = int.Parse(Console.ReadLine());
            Console.WriteLine("1 - > for addition ");
            Console.WriteLine("2 - > for difference ");
            Console.WriteLine("Enter your choice : ");
            opt = int.Parse(Console.ReadLine());

            switch (opt)
            {
                case 1:
                    sum = num1 + num2;
                    break;
                case 2:
                    if (num1 > num2)
                        diff = num1 - num2;
```

```
                else
                    diff = num2 - num1;
                break;
            default:
            {
                Console.WriteLine("\nInvalid option selected");
                break;
            }
        }
        if (opt == 1)
            Console.WriteLine("The sum of {0} and {1} is = {2:D}",
                    num1, num2, sum);
        else
            if (opt == 2)
            Console.WriteLine("The difference between {0} and {1} is = {2:D}",
                    num1, num2, diff);
        return 0;
    }
  }
}
```

When the above program executed, it will produce the following output as shown in Fig. 6.7.

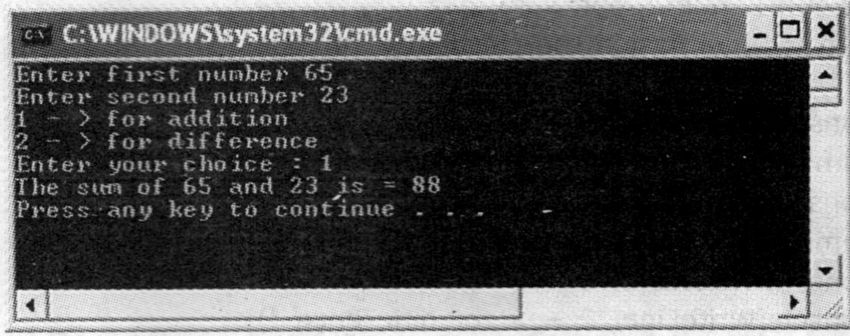

Fig. 6.8 Use of switch...case selection condition.

The program uses a **switch** statement to validate and select upon the users input choice, simulating a simple menu of choices.

Example Program to perform different tasks according to user choice

..\CSharp_Book\Chap06\DiffTask

```
using System;
using System.Collections.Generic;
using System.Text;
```

```
namespace DiffTask
{
    class Program
    {
        static int Main()
        {
            int r, l, b, ch;
            double a, c;

            Console.WriteLine("1. For area of circle");
            Console.WriteLine("2. For area of rectangle");
            Console.WriteLine("3. For circumference of circle");
            Console.WriteLine("4. For area of square");
            Console.Write("Enter your choice ");
            ch = int.Parse(Console.ReadLine());

            switch (ch)
            {
                case 1: Console.Write("Enter the radius of the circle ");
                    r = int.Parse(Console.ReadLine());
                    a = 3.14 * r * r;
                    Console.WriteLine("Area of circle is => {0}", a);
                    break;

                case 2: Console.Write("Enter the length ");
                    l = int.Parse(Console.ReadLine());
                    Console.Write("Enter the breadth ");
                    b = int.Parse(Console.ReadLine());
                    a = l * b;
                    Console.WriteLine("Area of rectangle is => {0}", a);
                    break;

                case 3: Console.Write("Enter the radius of the circle ");
                    r = int.Parse(Console.ReadLine());
                    c = 2 * 3.14 * r;
                    Console.WriteLine("Circumference of circle is => {0}", c);
                    break;

                case 4: Console.Write("Enter the side of square ");
                    l = int.Parse(Console.ReadLine());
                    a = l * l;
                    Console.WriteLine("Area of square is => {0}", a);
                    break;
```

```
            }
            return 0;
        }
    }
}
```

When the above program executed, it will produce the following output as shown in Fig. 6.8.

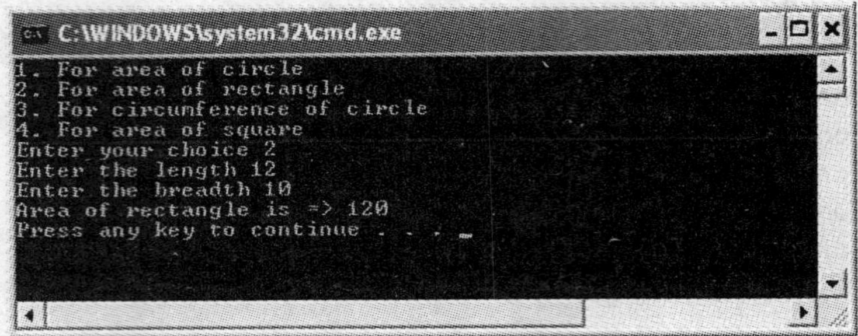

Fig. 6.8 Use of switch...case selection condition.

6.4.1 Nested Switch Statement

Like the **if** statement, the **switch** statement can be nested. The nested **switch** statement is always a part of the main **switch** block.

The program structure looks like :

```
switch (ctr)
{
    case 1 :
        switch (n)
        {
            case 0 :
                Console.WriteLine("Addition of numbers ");
                break;
            case 1 :
                Console.WriteLine("Subtraction of numbers ");
                break;
            case 2 :
                Console.WriteLine("Multiplication of numbers ");
                break;
        }
        break;
```

```
    case 2 :
        ...........
        ...........
        break;
}
```

6.5 The Concept of Loops

You use the loop concept on a daily basis. Whenever you have to repeat a certain procedure several times, you are performing a loop, just as your computer does with the **while** construct. Loops cause a section of your program to be repeated a certain number of times. The repetition continues while a condition is **true**. When the condition becomes **false**, the loop ends and control passes to the statements following the loop.

There are three kinds of loops in C# :

- the **for** loop,
- the **while** loop,
- the **do** loop and
- The **foreach** loop

6.5.1 Iteration, for Loops

The **for** statement encloses one or more C# statements that form the body of the loop, the statements in the loop repeat continuously a certain number of times. You, as a programmer, control the number of times the loop repeats.

The format of the **for** loop is :

```
for (start condition; continue condition; re-evaluation)
    program statements;
```

Where,

- **start condition.** This is an initialization expression. It initializes the variable(s) starting the loop (called loop variables) to initial value(s).
- **continue condition.** This is a conditional expression. It decides whether to enter the loop or to exit the loop based on some condition(s).
- **re-evaluation.** This is a modifier expression. It changes the value(s) of loop variable(s) after the action is performed each time.
- **program statements.** This is the statement block, that is to be repeatedly executed until *continue condition* is evaluated as nonzero (True).

C# evaluates the **start condition** before the loop begins. This **continue condition** is typically an assignment (such as **ctr = 1;**). However, it can be any legal expression you specify. C# evaluates the start expression only once, at the top of the loop. Then, C# never evaluates the start expression again.

Example Write a program to print first 10 natural numbers.

..\CSharp_Book\Chap06\NNum

```
using System;
using System.Collections.Generic;
using System.Text;

// Sample program using a for statement to display 10 natural numbers
// Program introduces the for statement, ctr to ten
namespace NNum
{
    class Program
    {
        static int Main()
        {
            int ctr;
            for (ctr = 1; ctr <= 10; ctr = ctr + 1)
            {
                Console.Write("{0} ", ctr);
            }
            Console.WriteLine();
            return 0;
        }
    }
}
```

When the above program executed, it will produce the following output :

```
1 2 3 4 5 6 7 8 9 10
Press any key to continue . . .
```

The above program declares an integer variable **ctr**. The first part of the **for** statement :

```
for (ctr = 1;
```

initializes the value of **ctr** to 1. This is the initialization expression (**ctr = 1**) gives the loop variable **ctr** the initial value 1. The **for** loop continues while the condition **ctr <= 10;** evaluates as **True**. As the variable **ctr** has just been initialized to 1, this condition is **True** and so the program statement :

```
Console.Write("{0} ", ctr);
```

is executed, which prints the value **ctr** to the screen, followed by a space character.

Next, the remaining statement of the **for** is executed.

```
ctr = ctr + 1;
```

which adds one to the current value of **ctr**. Then, the continue condition checks the condition (**ctr <= 10**). Control now passes back the conditional test,

```
ctr <= 10;
```

If this condition is true, the loop body (Console.Write("{0} ", ctr);) is executed, which evaluates as **true**, so the program statement

```
Console.Write("{0} ", ctr);
```

and then the re-evaluation expression (**ctr = ctr + 1**) changes the value of loop variable (incrementing it by 1) for next round of action (iteration). That is, **ctr** is incremented again, the condition reevaluated etc., until ctr reaches a value of 11.

When this occurs, the conditional test

```
ctr <= 10;
```

evaluates as **False**, and the **for** loop terminates, and program control passes to the statement return 0; which successfully returns to the end of program.

> **Note**
> *Do not put a semicolon after the right parenthesis. If you do, the **for** loop will think that there are no statements to execute. It will continue looping doing nothing each time, until the test expression becomes False.*

Example Write a program to print the mathematical table of number 1 to 10.

..\CSharp_Book\Chap06\MathTable

```
using System;
using System.Collections.Generic;
using System.Text;

// Program to print mathematical table
namespace MathTable
{
    class Program
    {
        static int Main()
        {
            int i, j, k;
            for (i = 1; i <= 10; i++)
            {
                for (j = 1; j <= 10; j++)
```

```
            {
                k = i * j;
                Console.WriteLine("{0} x {1} = {2} ", i, j, k);
            }
        }
        Console.WriteLine();
        return 0;
    }
  }
}
```

When the above program executed, it will produce the following output as shown in Fig. 6.9.

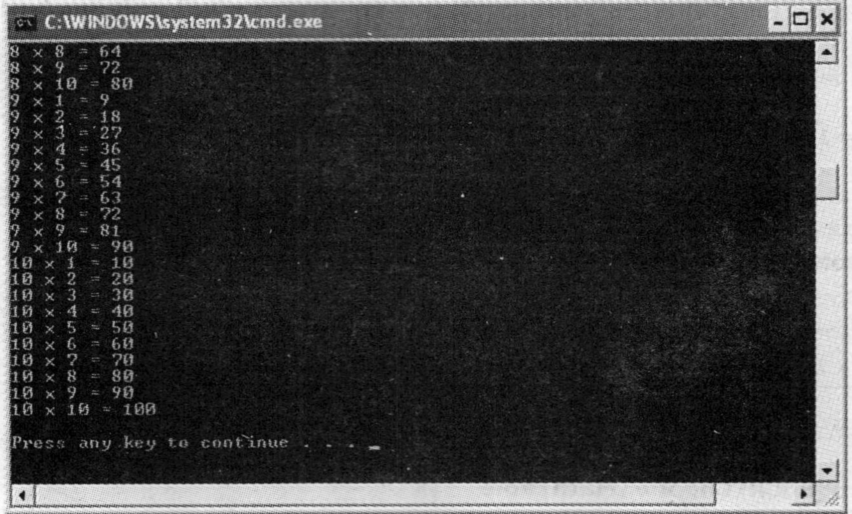

Fig. 6.9 Finding table using for loop

6.5.1.1 Use of comma (,) operator in for loop

We can combine two expression using a comma operator in a **for** loop. When two or more variables are used to control the loop, they are separated by *comma* operator. *Comma* operator allows more than one initialization in a **for** loops *start condition*, more than one tests in *continue condition* and more than one *re-evaluation*.

Example The following loop uses comma operator in each expression (*start condition*; *continue condition*; *re-evaluation*) :

```
for (i = 2, j = 10; i <= 10, j >= 1; i+=2, i-=2)
    Console.WriteLine(" {0}    {1} ", i, j);
```

will print,

```
2  10
4  8
6  6
8  4
10 2
```

Example The following loop uses comma operator in each expression (*start condition*; *continue condition*; *re-evaluation*) :

```
for (i = 1, j = 10; i <= j, i++, j = j - 2)
    Console.WriteLine(" {0}   {1} ", i, j);
```

will print,

```
1  10
2  8
3  6
4  4
```

Here,

- the initialization expression (i = 1, j = 10) gives the loop variables (i and j) the initial values (1 and 10 respectively).
- the the conditional expression checks the condition (i <= j).
- As far as this condition is true, action **Console.WriteLine(" {0}   {1} ", i, j);** is performed and then the *re-evaluation* expression (i++, j = j – 2) changes the value of loop variables (i is incremented by 1, j is decremented by 2 for the next iteration.
- When i and j each becomes 4, then *re-evaluation* expression (i++, j = j – 2) makes i = 5 and j = 2 for the next interaction.
- But before the action is taken for the next round, the condition i <= j is checked, which is false (as i = 5 and j = 2) and so the loop is terminated.

6.5.1.2 Variable declaration inside loop

We can declare variables inside a **for** loop. For example,

```
for (int i = 1, j = 15; i <= 10; i++)
    Console.WriteLine(" {0}  x  {1} = {2}", j, i, j*i);
```

From the above code, both **i** and **j** is declared as **int** type.

Example Write a program to print the table of a number using data type declaration inside a loop.

..\CSharp_Book\Chap06\VarInside

```
using System;
using System.Collections.Generic;
using System.Text;

// Demonstration of variable declaration inside a for loop.
namespace VarInside
{
    class Program
    {
        static int Main()
        {
            Console.WriteLine("The table of 15 is . . .");
            Console.WriteLine();
            for (int i = 1, j = 15; i <= 10; i++)
            {
                Console.WriteLine("{0} x {1} = {2}", j, i, j * i);
            }
            return 0;
        }
    }
}
```

When the above program executed, it will produce the following output as shown in Fig. 6.10.

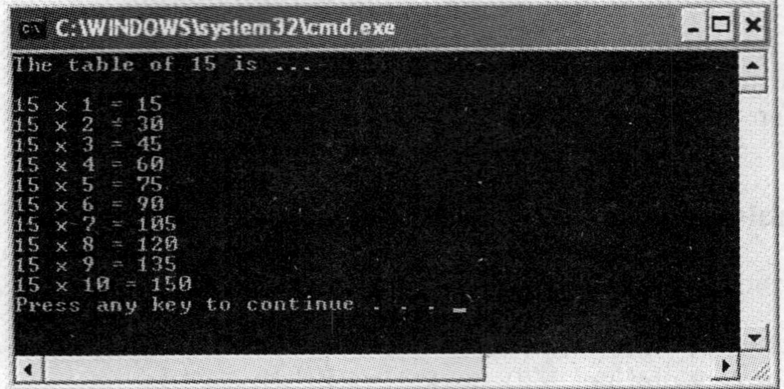

Fig. 6.10 Use of variable inside a loop

6.5.2 The while Statement

The **while** statement is one of several C# construct statements. A construct (from construction) is a programming language statement of a series of statements that controls looping. The **while** is a looping statement. Looping statements control execution of a series of other statements, causing parts of a program to execute repeatedly, as long as a certain statement is met.

The format of the **while** statement is :

```
while (test expression)
{
    program statements;
}
```

The parentheses around the test expression are required. As long as the test expression is **True** (non-zero), the block of one or more C# statements execute repeatedly until the test expression becomes **False** (evaluates to zero). If you want to execute just one statement in the body of the **while** loop, you do not have to enclose the statement in braces. Each statement within the body of the **while** loop requires semicolons at the end.

Definition

*A **while** loop is a pre-test loop. It first tests a specified conditional expression and as long as the conditional expression is evaluated to nonzero (true), action taken (i.e. statements or block after the loop is executed).*

The **while** loop can accept expression and not just conditions, the following are all legal expression:

- **while** (x = x + 1)
- **while** (n– –)
- **while** (count += i)

For these types of expression, when the result of x = x + 1, n– – or count += i, evaluates to 0, then only will the **while** condition fail and the loop will exited.

Some examples of **while** loop are :

- ```
  int num = 5;
  while (num != 0)
  {
      Console.WriteLine(num);
      num--;
  }
  ```

  this loop print a num starting from 5 and going down to 1, until the num becomes 0 which is the terminating condition of the loop.

- ```
  while (i++ < n);
  ```

  this loop counts i up to n.

```
r    int num = 5;
     while (num)
     {
         Console.WriteLine(num);
         num--;
     }
```

Here, the while (num) is same as saying while (num != 0). So, this example is same as :

```
int num = 5;
while (num != 0)
{
    Console.WriteLine(num);
    num--;
}
```

Example Write a program to find the factorial of any given number using **while** statement.

..\CSharp_Book\Chap06\Factorial

```
using System;
using System.Collections.Generic;
using System.Text;
// Demonstration of while statement to find the factorial of a number.
namespace Factorial
{
    class Program
    {
        static int Main()
        {
            int i;
            float N;
            double fact = 1;
            Console.Write("Enter any number to find factorial : ");
            N = int.Parse(Console.ReadLine());
            i = 1;
            while (i <= N)
            {
                fact = fact * i;
                i++;
            }
            Console.WriteLine("The factorial of {0} is {1:F2}", N, (double)fact);
            return 0;
```

```
        }
    }
}
```

When the above program executed, it will produce the following output :

```
Enter any number to find factorial : 5
The factorial of 5 is 120
Press any key to continue . . .
```

From the above program and flowchart the **counter i** increases till **N** and multiply with **fact** for finding the factorial of **N**.

Example Write a program to input any number and print them in reverse order using **while** statement. Whereas the number must be positive.

..\CSharp_Book\Chap06\Reverse

```
using System;
using System.Collections.Generic;
using System.Text;

// Demonstration of while statement to print any number in reverse order.
namespace Reverse
{
    class Program
    {
        static int Main()
        {
            long value, r_digit;
            value = 0;
            while (value <= 0)
            {
                Console.Write("Enter the number to be reversed. ");
                value = long.Parse(Console.ReadLine());
                if (value <= 0)
                {
                    Console.WriteLine("The number must be positive \n");
                    return 0;
                }
            }
            Console.Write("The reverse of number {0:D} is ", value);
            while (value != 0)
            {
                r_digit = value % 10;
                Console.Write(r_digit);
```

```
                value = value / 10;
            }
            Console.WriteLine();
            return 0;
        }
    }
}
```

When the above program executed, it will produce the following output as shown in Fig. 6.11.

Fig. 6.11 Reversing a number using while loop.

Suppose you are wrapping holiday gifts. The following include the looping steps, in a while-like format, that you go through to wrap them :

```
while (There are still unwrapped gifts)
{
    Get the next gift;
    Cut the wrapping paper;
    Wrap the gift;
    Put a bow on the gift;
    Fill out a name card for the gift;
    Put the wrapped gift with the others;
}
```

6.5.3 The do-while Statement

This loop is similar to the **while** loop, except that with **do-while**, the relational test occurs at the bottom of the loop. This ensures that the body of the loop executes at least once. The **do-while** loop tests for a positive relational test; as long as the test is **True**, the body of the loop continues to execute.

The format of the **do-while** loop is :

```
do
{
    program statements;
}
while (test expression);
```

As with the **while** statement, the test expression must have parentheses around it.

Definition

The do-while loop is a post-test or bottom-test loop. That is, it executes its body at least once without testing specified conditional expression and then makes test. The do-while loop terminates when the text expression is evaluated to be 0.

Note

Infinite loops are caused when the loop-continuation condition in a while, for or do-while structure never becomes false. To prevent this, make sure the value of the condition does change somewhere in the header or body of the loop so the condition can eventually become false.

Some examples of **do-while** loop are :

- ```
  int num = 5;
  do
  {
      Console.WriteLine(num);
      num--;
  } while (num != 0);
  ```

  this loop print a num starting from 5 and going down to 1, until the num becomes 0 which is the terminating condition of the loop.

- ```
  do
  {
      ....
  } while (i++ < n);
  ```

  this loop counts i up to n.

- ```
  int num = 5;
  do
  {
      Console.WriteLine(num);
      num--;
  } while (num);
  ```

  Here, the while (num) is same as saying while (num != 0). So, this example is same as :

  ```
  int num = 5;
  do
  {
      Console.WriteLine(num);
      num--;
  } while (num != 0);
  ```
  ```

Example Write a reverse a number using **do-while** loop to find any number in reverse order.

..\CSharp_Book\Chap06\RevDoWile

```
using System;
using System.Collections.Generic;
using System.Text;

// Demonstration of while statement to print any number in reverse order.
namespace RevDoWhile
{
    class Program
    {
        static int Main()
        {
            long value, r_digit;
            value = 0;
            do
            {
                Console.Write("Enter the number to be reversed. ");
                value = long.Parse(Console.ReadLine());
                if (value <= 0)
                {
                    Console.WriteLine("The number must be positive \n");
                    return 0;
                }
            } while (value <= 0);
            Console.Write("The reverse of number {0:D} is ", value);
            do
            {
                r_digit = value % 10;
                Console.Write(r_digit);
                value = value / 10;
            } while (value != 0);
            Console.WriteLine();
            return 0;
        }
    }
}
```

When the above program executed, it will produce the following output as shown in Fig. 6.12.

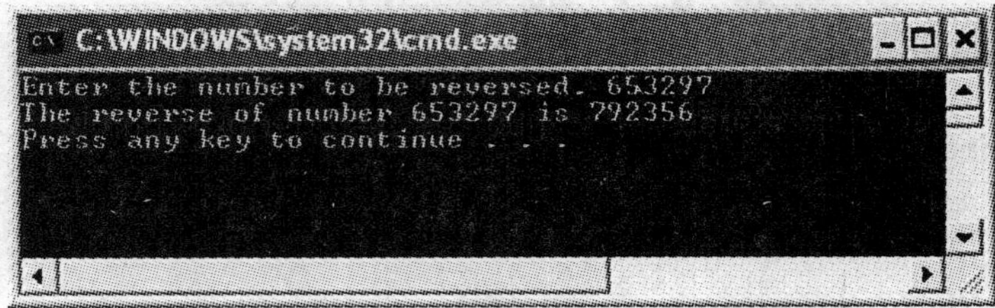

Fig. 6.12 Reversing a number using do...while loop.

6.5.4 The foreach Loop

A **foreach** loop is used to iterate through the items in a list. It operates on arrays or collections such as **ArrayList**, which can be found in the **System.Collections** namespace. The syntax of a foreach loop is:

foreach (<type> <item name> in <list>) { <statements> }

Here,

- The **type** is the type of item contained in the list. For example, if the type of the list was *int[]* then the type would be *int*.
- The **item name** is an identifier that you choose, which could be anything but should be meaningful. For example, if the list contained an array of people's ages, then a meaningful name for item name would be age.
- The **in** keyword is required.
- As mentioned earlier, the **list** could be either an array or a collection, as defined by types found in the System.Collections namespace.
- While iterating through the items of a list with a **foreach** loop, the list is read-only. This means that you cannot change the value of any items in the list within a foreach loop.

On each iteration through a *foreach* loop the list is queried for a new value. As long as the list can return a value, this value will be put into the read-only item name variable, causing the statements in the **foreach** block to be executed. When the collection has been fully traversed, control will transfer to the first executable statement following the end of the **foreach** block. The following program demonstrates how to use a **foreach** loop.

..\CSharp_Book\Chap06\ForEachLoop

```
using System;
using System.Collections.Generic;
using System.Text;

namespace ForEachLoop
{
```

```
    class Program
    {
        static int Main()
        {
            string[] names = { "Sumit", "Ashok", "Lokesh", "Fharuque" };

            foreach (string person in names)
            {
                Console.WriteLine("{0} ", person);
            }
            return 0;
        }
    }
}
```

When the above program executed, it will produce the following output :

```
Sumit
Ashok
Lokesh
Fharuque
Press any key to continue . . .
```

6.6 Conditional Nesting

A condition can be created inside of another to write a more effective statement. This is referred to as nesting one condition inside of another. Almost any condition can be part of another and multiple conditions can be included inside of others.

As we have learned, different conditional statements are applied in specific circumstances. In some situations, they are interchangeable or one can be applied just like another, which becomes a matter of choice. Statements can be combined to render a better result with each playing an appropriate role.

Here is an example of an **if** condition nested inside of a **do...while** loop:

D:\Olevel02\CSharp_Book\Chap06\CondNest

```
using System;

class CondNest
{
    static void Main()
    {
        char SittingDown;
        string SitDown;
        do {
```

```
            Console.Write("Are you sitting down now(y/n)? ");
            SitDown = Console.ReadLine();
            SittingDown = char.Parse(SitDown);

            if( SittingDown != 'y' )
                Console.WriteLine("Could you please sit down for the next exercise? ");
        } while( !(SittingDown == 'y') );

        Console.WriteLine();
    }
}
```

When the above program executed, it will produce the following output :

```
Are you sitting down now(y/n)? y
Press any key to continue . . .
```

6.7 Break Statement

As we already known about the **break** statement in **switch case** section, here is another review of **break** statement. The **break** statement is used to stop a loop for any reason or condition the programmer considers fit. The **break** statement can be used in a **while** condition to stop an ongoing action. The syntax of the **break** statement is simply:

```
break;
```

Although made of only one word, the **break** statement is a complete statement. Therefore, it can (and should always) stay on its own line (this makes the program easy to read). The **break** statement applies to the most previous conditional statement to it, provided that previous statement is applicable. The **break** statement is typically used to handle the cases in a **switch** statement as we saw it in the previous lesson.

Besides the **switch** statement, the **break** statement can also be used in other conditional statements. For example, you can use a **break** statement inside of a **for** loop to interrupt its count. The following program would display letter from d to n but it is interrupted by a **break** when it encounters k:

D:\Olevel02\CSharp_Book\Chap06\BreakProg

```
using System;

class BreakProg
{
    static void Main()
    {
        for (char c = 'd'; c <= 'n'; c++)
```

```
        {
            if (c == 'k')
                break;
            Console.WriteLine(c);
        }

        Console.WriteLine();
    }
}
```

When the above program executed, it will produce the following output as shown in Fig. 6.13.

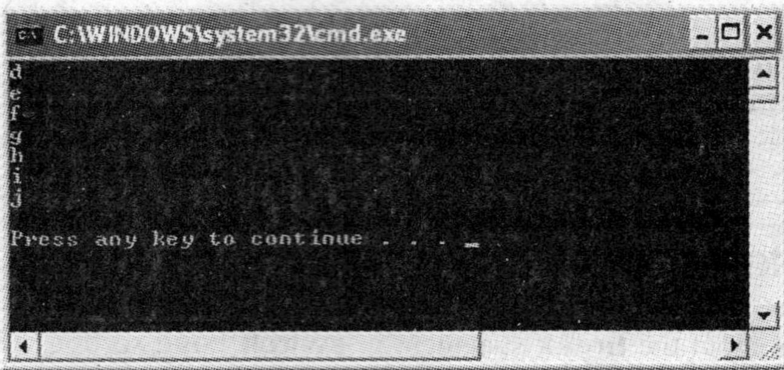

Fig. 6.13 Breaking a program execution in middle.

The **break** statement can also be used in a **do...while** or a **for** loop the same way.

6.8 The continue Statement

The **continue** statement does the opposite of the **break** statement; instead of existing a loop early, **continue** forces the computer to perform another iteration of the loop. If you put a **continue** statement in the body of a **for** or **while** loop, the computer ignores any statement in the loop that follows **continue**.

The format of **continue** statement is :

```
continue;
```

You use the **continue** statement when data is in the body of the loop is bad, out of bounds, or unexpected. Instead of acting on the bad data, you might want to read return to the top of the loop to get another data value. The following example helps to illustrate the use of **continue**.

> **Note**
> *The **continue** statement forces a new iteration of any of the three loop constructs: **for**, **while**, **do-while**.*

When processing a loop, if the statement finds a false value, you can use the continue statement inside of a **while**, **do...while** or a **for** conditional statements to ignore the subsequent statement or to jump from a false Boolean value to the subsequent valid value, unlike the **break** statement that would exit the loop. Like the **break** statement, the **continue** keyword applies to the most previous conditional statement and should stay on its own line.

The following programs asks the user to type 4 positive numbers and calculates the sum of the numbers by considering only the positive ones. If the user types a negative number, the program manages to ignore the numbers that do not fit in the specified category:

D:\Olevel02\CSharp_Book\Chap06\NumContinue

```
using System;
using System.Collections.Generic;
using System.Text;

namespace NumContinue
{
    class Prorgram
    {
        static void Main()
        {
            // Declare necessary variables
            double Number, Sum = 0;
            string Nbr;

            // Request 4 positive numbers from the user
            Console.WriteLine("Type 4 positive numbers.");
            // Make sure the user types 4 positive numbers
            for( int Count = 1; Count <= 4; Count++ )
            {
                Console.Write("Number: ");
                Nbr = Console.ReadLine();
                Number = double.Parse(Nbr);

                // If the number typed is not positive, ignore it
                if( Number < 0 )
                    continue;

                // Add each number to the sum
                Sum += Number;
            }

            // Display the sum
            Console.WriteLine("Sum of the numbers you entered = {0}\n", Sum);
            return 0;
        }
    }
}
```

When the above program executed, it will produce the following output as shown in Fig. 6.14.

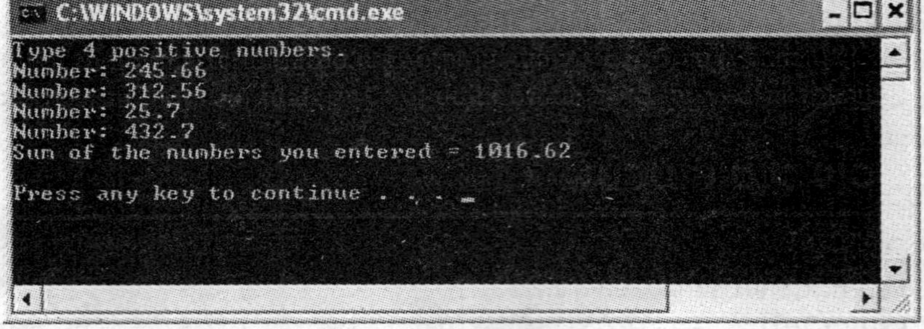

```
C:\WINDOWS\system32\cmd.exe
Type 4 positive numbers.
Number: 245.66
Number: 312.56
Number: 25.7
Number: 432.7
Sum of the numbers you entered = 1016.62

Press any key to continue . . .
```

Fig. 6.14 Continue a program execution.

Example The following program appears to print the numbers 1 through 10, each followed by C# programming. It doesn't. The **continue** in the body of the for loop clauses an early finish to the loop. The first **Console.WriteLine();** in the for loop executes. However, the second **Console.WriteLine();** does not execute because of the continue.

..\CSharp_Book\Chap06\Continue

```
using System;
using System.Collections.Generic;
using System.Text;

// Demonstrate use of continue statement
namespace Continue
{
    class Program
    {
        static int Main()
        {
            int ctr;
            for (ctr = 1; ctr <= 10; ctr++)  // Loop 10 times
            {
                Console.WriteLine(ctr);
                continue;   // Cause body to end early
                Console.WriteLine("C# .NET Programming \n");
            }
            Console.WriteLine();
            return 0;
        }
    }
}
```

When the above program executed, it will produce the following output as shown in Fig. 6.15.

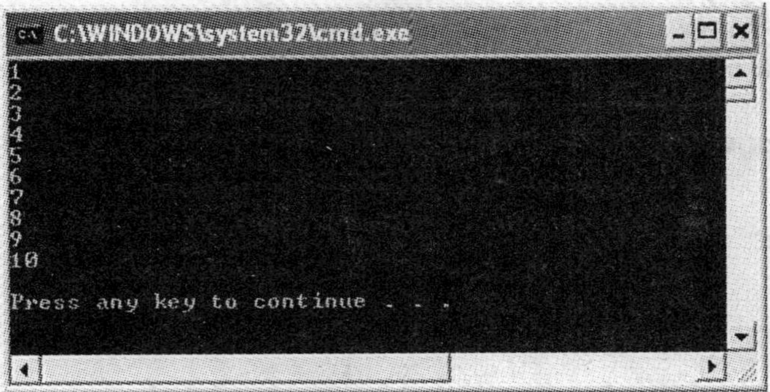

Fig. 6.15 Continue a program execution.

If you have such warnings enabled, C# gives you a warning message when you compile this type of program. The compiler recognizes that the second **WriteLine()** is unreachable code. The reason is that it will never execute because of the **continue**. Therefore, most programs do not use a **continue**, except after an **if** statement. This makes it a conditional **continue** statement, which is much more useful.

6.9 The goto Statement

The **goto** statement causes your program to jump to a different location, instead of executing the next statement in the sequence. The **goto** statement allows a program execution to jump to another section of the function in which it is being used. In order to use the **goto** statement, insert a name on a particular section of your function so you can refer to that name. The name, also called a label, is made of one word and follows the rules we have learned about C# names (the name can be anything), then followed by a colon. The format of the **goto** statement is :

```
goto statement label;
```

The statement label proceeds a line of code. Follow all such labels with a colon (:). C# then knows that they are labels, and does not confuse them with variables. For example, the following four lines of code have different statement label. These lines are not a program; they are individual lines that might be included in a program. Notice that each statement label appears to the left of its line :

```
pay:    Console.WriteLine("Please checks in the printer\n");
Again:  name = char.parse(Console.ReadLine());
Endit:  Console.WriteLine("That is all the processing.\n");
CALC:   percentage = (total / 5) * 100;
```

Such labels give **goto** statements a gets to which to go. When your program encounters a **goto** statement, it branches to the line beginning with the statement label indicated in the **goto** statement. The program then continues to execute sequentially until another **goto** changes the order again (or until the program ends).

The following program uses a **for** loop to count from 0 to 12, but when it encounters 5, it jumps to a designated section of the program:

..\CSharp_Book\Chap06\GoToFirst

```
using System;
using System.Collections.Generic;
using System.Text;

namespace GoToFirst
{
    class Program
    {
        static void Main()
        {
            for(int Count = 0; Count <= 12; ++Count)
            {
                Console.WriteLine("Count {0}", Count);

                if( Count == 5 )
                    goto MamaMia;
            }

        MamaMia:
            Console.WriteLine("\nStopped at 5");

            Console.WriteLine();
        }
    }
}
```

When the above program executed, it will produce the following output as shown in Fig. 6.16.

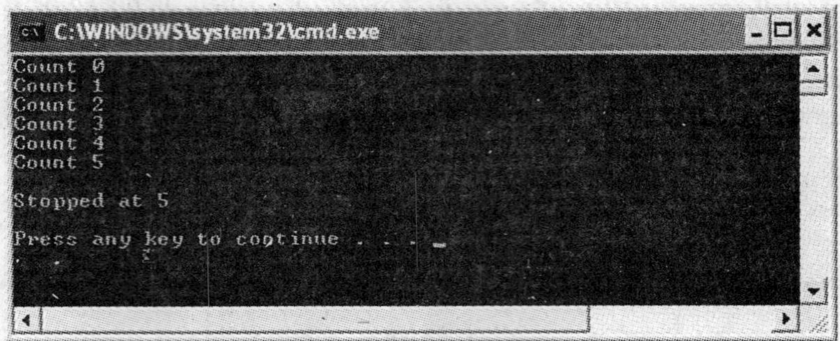

Fig. 6.16 Using conditional jumping.

Example 12.24 Write a program to find the factorial of any number using **goto** statement.

..\CSharp_Book\Chap06\GoTo

```
using System;
using System.Collections.Generic;
using System.Text;

// Demonstration of goto statement to find the factorial of any number.
namespace GoTo
{
    class Program
    {
        static int Main()
        {
            long i, N;
            float fact;
            Console.WriteLine("Enter any number ");
            N = long.Parse(Console.ReadLine());
            i = 1;
            fact = 1;
        FACT:
            if (i <= N)
            {
                fact = fact * i;
                i = i + 1;
                goto FACT;
            }
            if (N > 0)
                Console.WriteLine("Factorial is {0}", fact);
            return 0;
        }
    }
}
```

When the above program executed, it will produce the following output as shown in Fig. 6.17.

Fig. 6.17 Using conditional jumping.

Exercise

1. What is sequence construct?
2. What is selection construct?
3. What is iteration construct?
4. What is body of the loop?
5. What is exit condition?
6. What is the purpose of for loop?
7. What is the difference between while() and do while() loop?
8. What is the effect of absence of break in switch-case statement?
9. Differentiate between break and continue statements.
10. What is normal exit?
11. Write two different forms of if statement.
12. Construct logical expressions to represent the following conditions :
    (a) Weight is greater than or equal to 115 but less than 125.
    (b) x is even.
    (c) Donation is in the range 4000–5000 or guest is 1.
    (d) Ch is an uppercase letter.
13. What is the purpose of break statement ?
14. The use of goto statement is avoided in the structured programming. Why?
15. Which conditional operators are used to replace 'if ….. else' statements ? Give two examples.
16. What is the difference between 'return' and 'break' statement?
17. What is the difference between return() and exit() statement?
18. Write an appropriate for or while loop for the following situations described below :
    (i) A loop is to be repeated 200 times.
    (ii) A loop is to be repeated 200 times, except the loop is to be terminated if the value of the variable X become 175.
    (iii) A loop is to be repeated 75 times by incrementing the counter by 3 each time.
18. What is the effect of absence of break in switch-case statement ?
19. Find the output of the following code :

(a)
```
static void Main()
{
    int a = 1;
    int b = 5;
    b++;
    if (b == 5)
        Console.WriteLine("value is five ");
    else
        Console.WriteLine("value is not five ");
}
```

(b)
```
static void Main()
{
    int i = 1;
    while (i < 5)
```

(c)
```
static void Main()
{
    int total = 0, sum = 0;
    for (int i = -5; i < -8; i—)
        Console.WriteLine(i + 1);
}
```

(d)
```
static void Main()
{
    int i;
    for (i = 0; i < 10; i++) {
        if (i == 5) break;
        Console.WriteLine(i);
    }
}
```

```
        {
            Console.WriteLine(i);
            i = i*2;
        }
    }
```

(e)
```
static void Main()
{
    int total =0;
    int sum = 0;
    for (int i = 0; i <= 10; i++)
        sum = sum + i;
    Console.WriteLine(total);
}
```

(f)
```
static void Main()
{
    int i, j, x = 0;
    for(i = 0; i < 5; ++i)
        for(j = 0; j < i; j++)
        {
            switch (i + j - 1)
            {
                case -1 :
                case  0 :
                    x += 1;
                    break;
                case 1 :
                case 2 :
                case 3 :
                    x += 3;
                    break;
                default :
                    x += 3;
                    break;
            }
            Console.WriteLine(x);
        }
    Console.WriteLine(x);
}
```

20. Rewrite the below given program using for ( ) loop

```
#include <iostream.h>
void main()
{
    int i, sum = 0;
    i = 1;
    while (i <= 10)
    {
        sum = sum + i;
        i++;
    }
    Console.WriteLine(sum);
}
```

Programming

1. Write a program to find the minimum of three numbers.
2. Write a program to find the greatest common divisor of two numbers.
3. Write a program to convert decimal number into binary number.
4. Write a program to find the sum of series :
   $1 + x^1/2! + x^2/3! + \ldots\ldots\ldots\ldots + x^n/(n+1)!$
5. Write a program to implement Fibonacci series (,i.e. sum of previous two numbers is the next number).
   e.g.; 1 1 2 3 5 8 13
6. Write a program to swap two numbers without using third variable.
7. Write a program to check whether the number is prime or not.
8. Write a program to check whether the number is perfect or not.
9. Write a program to find number of 500, 100, 50, 20, 10, 5, 2 and 1 Re. notes in a given money.
10. Write a program to print the message for season.
11. Write a program to find maximum and minimum number between n numbers.
12. Write a program to find the sum of geometric series
    $s = a + ar + ar^2 + ar^3 + ar^4$

13. Write a program to find out Armstrong numbers
    e.g. $153 = 1^3 + 5^3 + 3^3$
14. Write a for loop which will produce the following output (hint: use two nested for loops)
    1
    22
    333
    4444
    55555
15. Write a C++ program to print the values of two integers before and after swapping.
16. Write a C++ program to find the largest number among the three numbers.
17. Write a program to find the sum of the following series taking only first 5 terms.
18. Write a program to find whether the given number is even or odd.
19. Write a program in C++ to accept monthly salary from the user, find and display income tax with the help of following rules :

MONTHLY SALARY	INCOME TAX
9000 or more	40% of monthly salary
7500 – 8999	30% of monthly salary
7499 or Less	20% of monthly salary

20. An electricity board charges according to the following rules :
    For the first 100 units – 40 P per unit (P – Paise)
    For the next 200 units – 50 P per unit
    Beyond 300 units – 60 P per unit
    All users have to pay meter charge also, which is Rs. 50/-
    Write a program to read the number of units consumed and print out the charges.

Arrays 7

7.1 Introduction

Arrays are data structure, which hold multiple variables of the same data type. An array is a sequence of objects all of which have the same type. The objects are called elements of the array and are numbered consecutively 0, 1, 2, ... These numbers are called index values or subscripts of the array. The term "subscript" is used because as a mathematical sequence, an array would be written with subscripts: n_0, n_1, n_2 .... These numbers locate the element's position within the array, thereby giving direct access into the array.

For example, suppose you want to store 5 different integer values into memory, and find the sum of the values. So, your program becomes :

..\CSharp_Book\Chap07\AddFiveNum

```
namespace AddFiveNum
{
    class Program
    {
        static void Main()
        {
            int num1, num2, num3, num4, num5, sum;
            Console.WriteLine("Enter any five numbers:");

            num1 = int.Parse(Console.ReadLine());
            num2 = int.Parse(Console.ReadLine());
            num3 = int.Parse(Console.ReadLine());
            num4 = int.Parse(Console.ReadLine());
            num5 = int.Parse(Console.ReadLine());

            sum = num1 + num2 + num3 + num4 + num5;
```

```
            Console.WriteLine("Total is: {0:F}", sum);
        }
    }
}
```

When the above program executed, it will produce the following output as shown in Fig. 7.1.

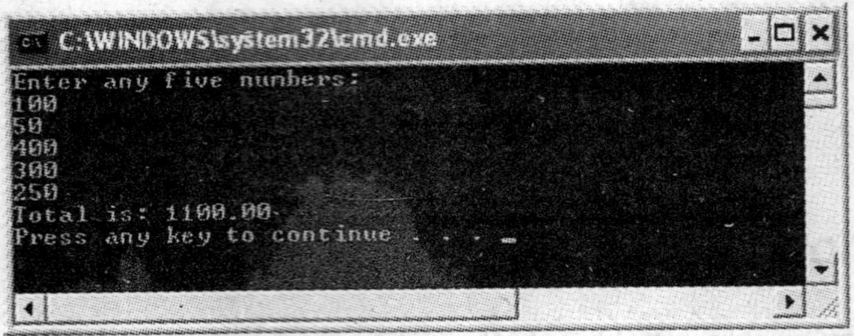

Fig. 7.1 Addition of five numbers.

From the above program declaration, all the time the memory of computer declares five different locations, and consumes extra memory for processing five integer values. But the same program can be modified by using the array method using a single name with subscript. A subscript is a number, within brackets, that differentiates one element of an array from another. The elements are the individual variables in an array. An array has the following syntax, using square brackets to access each indexed value (called an element).

data_type[] num;

where **data_type** is any C# data type declaration and *num* is the name of the array, and subscript range is the length of the array. Fig. 7.2 shows the diagrammatic representation of an array.

num - Name of the array

100

50

400

300

250

Fig. 7.2 Diagrammatical representation of an array num.

From the Fig. 7.2 the variable **num** declares five different locations (subscripts) starting from 0 (zeroth) place. So, it takes only one variable and holds all the five elements with same name. The example given below shows the modified declaration of C# source codes. Also the above figure shows that an array named **num** with 5 elements: **num[0]** contains 100, **num[1]** contains 50, **num[2]** contains 400, **num[3]** contains 300, and **num[4]** contains 250. The figure actually represents a region of the computer's memory because an array is always stored in this way with its elements in a contiguous sequence.

Definition

The variables which are declared using fundamental data types are called scalar variable or non-subscripted variable.

7.2 One-dimensional Array

As we have already discussed about array and the storing elements in an array, it refers to one-dimensional array. The elements of one-dimensional array store all the elements in a consecutive order of entry into an array name. The subscripts of an array are increased simultaneously one-by-one to input the values into array.

A one-dimensional array is a list of variables that are all of the same type and are referenced through a common name. An individual variable in the array is called an array element. Arrays form a convenient way to handle groups of related data.

Definition

An array is a collection of homogeneous data elements described by a single name, and each element is an array is refer by the array name with the subscript or index enclosed in square bracket [ ].

To declare a one-dimensional array, specify the type, name, dimensions, and size. That is, keep three things in mind :

- the declaration of the array
- assigning memory locations to the array
- initializing or putting values into the memory locations of the array

So, to declare an array, the syntax is :

```
data_type[] array_name; // declare int array reference
```

where **data_type** is a valid C# data type, **array_name** is the name of the array.

```
float[ ] salary; // declare float array reference
```

Note

The subscript of the array begin with zero and end with size-1.
The rules for naming an array are same as for other variables but the size of the array always be positive integer constant or an expression that evaluates a positive integer constant at compilation time.

To assigning memory locations to the array, the syntax is :

```
arrayname = new type[size];
```

Here,

- **arrayname** is the name of the array.
- The **type** of the array is integer.
- **size** is used to declare the length of array arrayname.
- **new** is used to create memory location.

For example,

```
num = new int[10]; // create a 10 elements int array
```

tell the compiler that

- **num** is the name of the array.
- its type is integer.
- it is one-dimensional (linear).
- the number of elements in the array are 10, *i.e.* its size is 10.
- each integer value requires 4 bytes of memory.
- array **num** allocates a contiguous block of 40 bytes.

The above array declaration can also be declared in different way. That is,

```
//The array num is declared with 10 element of int array in memory
int[ ] num = new int[10];
```

7.2.1 Accessing Elements of an Array

If the array declaration statement is

```
int[] a = new int[100];
```

the valid range of subscript is 0 to 99, *i.e.* lower bound is 0 and upper bound is the value one less that specified by the dimension specifier in the declaration statement.

To access an element of an array, the subscripted variables are used which are formed by affixing each subscript in brackets to the name of an array.

The first element of array named **a** is accessed as **a[0]**, third as **a[2]**, ... , and the last element as **a[99]**. In general the *i*th element as **a[i-1]**.

7.2.2 Initializing an Array

When the array is declared, the individual elements of array will get values according to the storage class of the array. In the declaration statement,

```
int[] b = new int[10];
```

Individual elements of the array will get garbage values, as the storage class is auto by default. However, in C#, it is possible to initialize the elements of the array at the compilation time, by specifying the values of the individual elements in the array declaration itself.

> **Note**
>
> *If, instead of initializing an array with execution time assignment statements, you initialize the arrays at compile time with an array initializer list, your program will execute faster.*

Using braces, you can initialize any type of array. The syntax is,

```
datatype[] arrayname = {List of values};
```

For example, if you want to initialize an integer array that holds five student's **age**, you can use the following declaration :

```
int[] stud_age = {14, 15, 12, 13, 16};
```

Otherwise, you can declare the above as :

int[] stud_age = new int [5] {14, 15, 12, 13, 16};

This combines all the three steps : declaration, memory declaration and array initialization. The values stored in array **stud_age** is :

```
stud_age[0] = 14
stud_age[1] = 15
stud_age[2] = 16
stud_age[3] = 17
stud_age[4] = 18
```

initializes 5 different **age**s into **stud_age** array as shown in Fig. 7.3.

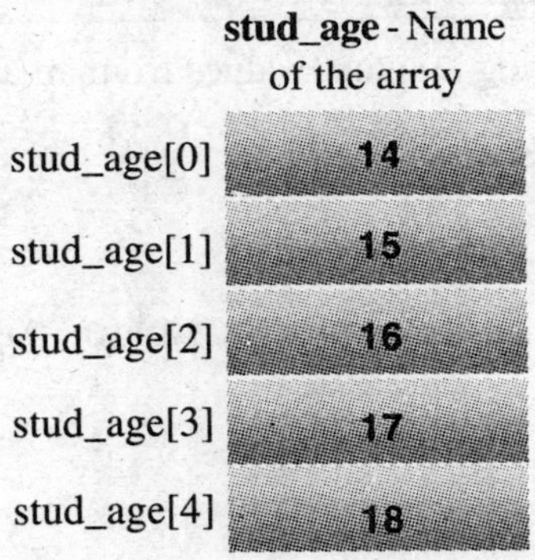

stud_age - Name of the array

stud_age[0] 14

stud_age[1] 15

stud_age[2] 16

stud_age[3] 17

stud_age[4] 18

Fig. 7.3 Diagrammatical representation of an array num.

..\CSharp_Book\Chap07\ArrayAsign

```
using System;
using System.Collections.Generic;
using System.Text;

namespace ArrayAsign
{
    class Program
    {
        static void Main()
        {
            Console.WriteLine("The five age's are : ");
            int[] stud_age = new int[5] { 14, 15, 12, 13, 16 };
            Console.WriteLine(stud_age[0]);
            Console.WriteLine(stud_age[1]);
            Console.WriteLine(stud_age[2]);
            Console.WriteLine(stud_age[3]);
            Console.WriteLine(stud_age[4]);
        }
    }
}
```

When the above program executed, it will produce the following output as shown in Fig. 7.4.

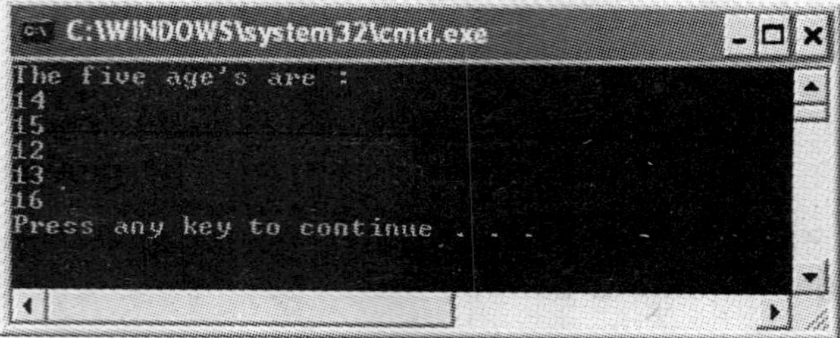

Fig.7.4 Displaying assigned values from an array.

Let us consider some other declaration types :

- Look at the following declaration statement :

  ```
  Int[] b = new int [10] {18, 0, 11, -14, 17, 22, 14, 10, 19, 25};
  ```

  initializes elements

  ```
  b[0] to 18,
  b[1] to 0,
  ```

```
b[2] to 11,
b[3] to -14,
b[4] to 17,
b[5] to 22,
b[6] to 14,
b[7] to 10,
b[8] to 19, and
b[9] to 25,
```

which declares total 10 integer spaces in array *b* and stored 10 different values.

- Look at the following declaration :

  ```
  int[ ] b = new int[10] {18, 0, 11, -14, 17};
  ```

  Here, the first five elements gets values 18, 0, 11, –14 and 17 respectively; the rest gets value 0 as the elements of the partially initialized array initialized to 0, by default.

- Look at the following declaration :

  ```
  int[ ] b = new int[ ] {18, 0, 11, -14, 17};
  ```

  In this declaration statement, number is supplied for the size of the array. In this case, the compiler counts the number of elements in the initialization list and fixes that as the array size.

- Look at another type of declaration :

  ```
  int[ ] b = new int [6] {18, 0, 11, -14, 17, 22, 14, 10, 19, 25};
  ```

  Here, the C# compiler will flag an error message as the initialization list contains more elements than the declared size.

Note

When you use a loop for entering elements into an array, loop counter's value must be 1 less than the size of array.
For example,

```
int num[10];
while (i < 10)
{
    Colsone.WriteLinecin >> num[i];
    i++;
}   // The last value of i < 10.
```

Example Write a program to print the values of an initialized array or 10 elements.

..\CSharp_Book\Chap07\ArrayPos

```
using System;
using System.Collections.Generic;
using System.Text;

// Demonstration of a sample program to print initialized array elements
namespace ArrayPos
{
    class Program
    {
        static void Main()
        {
            int[ ] num = new int[10] {18, 0, 11, -14, 17, 22, 14, 10, 19, 25};

            for (int i = 0; i < 10; i++)
                Console.WriteLine("The element at {0:D} position is: {1:D}", i, num[i]);
        }
    }
}
```

When the above program executed, it will produce the following output as shown in Fig. 7.5.

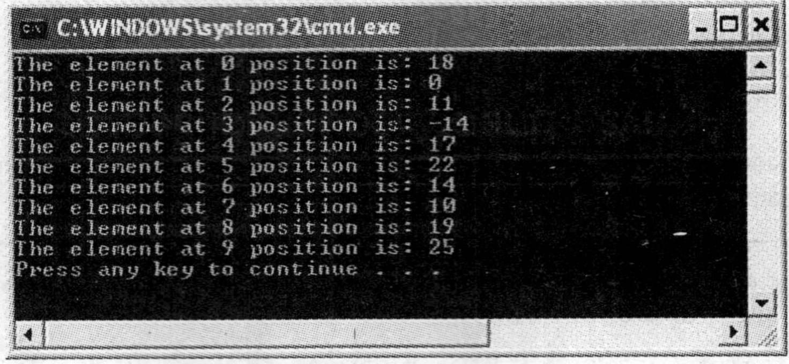

Fig. 7.5 Positional values of an arrray.

7.2.3 Entering Data into One-dimensional Array

Rarely will you know the contents of arrays when you declare them. Usually, you fill an array with user input or from a disk file's data. The **for** loop is a perfect tool for looping through arrays once you fill them with value. The following program segment shows the way data is entered into one-dimensional array.

```
int num[5];
for (int i = 0; i < 5; i++)
```

```
{
    num[i] = int.Parse(Console.ReadLine());
}
```

Here, the above code will input 5 integer values into the array num.

Note

The declaration statement int a[10], and even if we attempt to access the 16th element as a[15], which of course is not a valid array element, in our program, the C# system will not flag any error at any stage. It will just pick up a garbage value from the accessed memory location. Student must take care of this problem.

An array name cannot appear on the left side of an assignment statement.

Example Write a program to enter any five integer values and print their sum.

..\CSharp_Book\Chap07\ArraySum

```
using System;
using System.Collections.Generic;
using System.Text;

// Demonstration of a sample program for array handling
namespace ArraySum
{
    class Program
    {
        static void Main()
        {
            int[] num = new int[5];
            int i, sum = 0;

            for (i = 0; i < 5; i++)
            {
                Console.Write("Enter value {0:D} ->", i);
                num[i] = int.Parse(Console.ReadLine());
                sum = sum + num[i];
            }

            Console.WriteLine();
            Console.WriteLine("The sum of all the 5 elements are {0:D}", sum);
        }
    }
}
```

When the above program executed, it will produce the following output as shown in Fig. 7.6.

```
C:\WINDOWS\system32\cmd.exe
Enter value 0 ->100
Enter value 1 ->50
Enter value 2 ->400
Enter value 3 ->300
Enter value 4 ->250

The sum of all the 5 elements are 1100
Press any key to continue . . .
```

Fig. 7.6 Sum of 5 array elements.

Example Suppose in your class, all the students are securing different percentage of marks in 11th class, and you want to increase 15 percent marks of each student. If the class contains 10 students in computer science, write a C# program to solve the above problem.

..\CSharp_Book\Chap07\ArrayIncr

```
using System;
using System.Collections.Generic;
using System.Text;

// Demonstration of one-dimensional array
namespace ArrayIncr
{
    class Program
    {
        static void Main()
        {
            float[] per = new float[10];
            int i;

            Console.WriteLine("Enter student's percentage");
            for (i = 0; i < 10; i++)
                per[i] = float.Parse(Console.ReadLine());

            // increase by 15 marks to each student
            for (i = 0; i < 10; i++)
                per[i] = per[i] + 15;

            // Display the increased percentage of 20 students
            Console.WriteLine("Increased percentages are");
            for (i = 0; i < 10; i++)
                Console.WriteLine(per[i]);
```

```
        }
    }
}
```

When the above program executed, it will produce the following output as shown in Fig. 7.7.

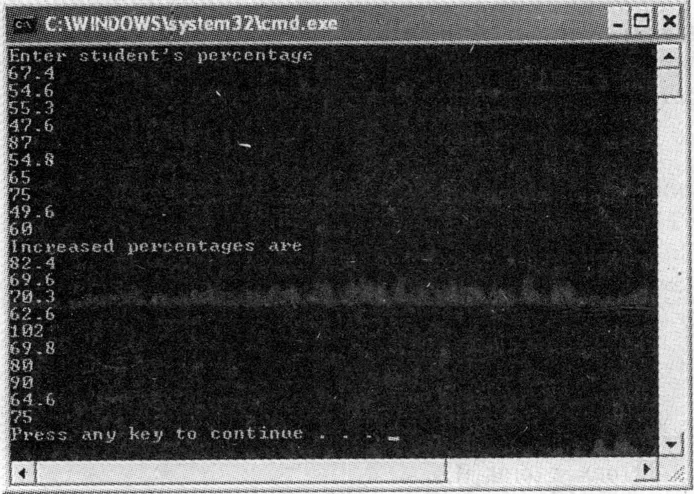

Fig. 7.7 Increasing the array positional value.

Example Write a program to read the noonday temperature for each day for a month and then report the month's average temperature, as well as its hottest and coolest days of the month.

..\CSharp_Book\Chap07\ArrayTemp

```
using System;
using System.Collections.Generic;
using System.Text;

// Program to find the hottest and coolest day in a month
namespace ArrayTemp
{
    class Program
    {
        static void Main()
        {
            int[] temp = new int[31];
            int days, i, max, min;
            float avg;

            Console.Write("How many days in the month? ");
            days = int.Parse(Console.ReadLine());
```

```
            for (i = 0; i < days; i++)
            {
                Console.Write("Enter noon day temperature for day {0:D} : ", i + 1);
                temp[i] = int.Parse(Console.ReadLine());
            }

            // Find average temperature
            avg = 0;
            for (i = 0; i < days; i++)
                avg = avg + (float)temp[i];

            Console.WriteLine("Average temperature : {0:F}", avg/days);
            // Find the minimum and maximum temperature in the month
            min = 100;
            max = 0;
            for (i = 0; i < days; i++)

            {
                if (min > temp[i])
                    min = temp[i];
                if (max < temp[i])
                    max = temp[i];
            }
            Console.WriteLine("Maximum temperature : {0:D}", max);
            Console.WriteLine("Minimum temperature : {0:D}", min);
        }
    }
}
```

When the above program executed, it will produce the following output as shown in Fig. 7.8.

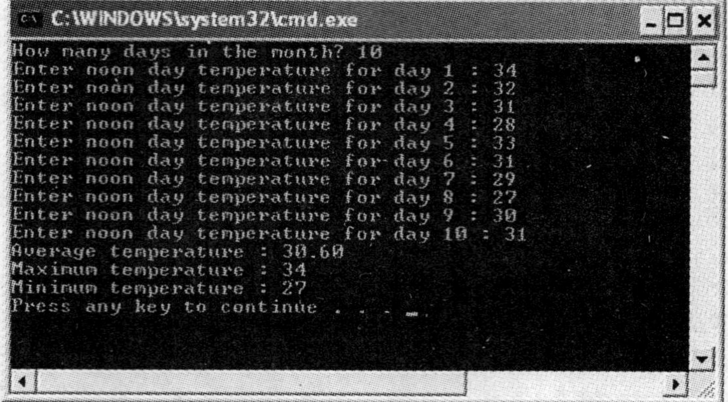

Fig. 7.8 Finding the maximum and minimum temperature.

7.3 Searching Arrays : Linear/Sequential Search

Often a programmer will be working with large amount of data stored in arrays. It may be necessary to determine whether an array contains a value that matches a certain key value. The process of finding a particular element of an array is called *searching*. In this section we discuss the simple *linear search* technique.

The linear search compares each element of the array with the *search key*. Since the array is not in any particular order, it is just as likely that the value will be found in the first element as the last. On average, therefore, the program must compare the search key with half the element of the array for a value in the array. To determine that a value is not in the array, the program must compare the search key to every element in the array.

Algorithm for linear search :

Steps :
1. Enter the boundaries for an array, N.
2. I = 1.
3. Enter the array element, range[I].
4. if I <= N then 6 else 5.
5. I = I + 1 Repeat step 3.
6. ctr = 0; pos = 0.
7. Enter the search value, search.
8. while (ctr <= N) repeat steps 9 and 10.
9. if (range[ctr] = search) then pos = ctr + 1.
10. ctr = ctr + 1.
11. print pos.
12. END.

Note

A linear search examines each value in turn until the target is found or the end of the list is reached.

The aforementioned algorithm describes that an element search is search in the array range to find the position. In the step 9 the statement **pos = ctr + 1** is written because, the array position started from **0**th place, but for the general user it will show as 1st if found.

The linear searching method works well for small arrays or for unsorted arrays. The following program shows the search array elements position in between 10 elements.

The pre-requisite for searching an array is to know the number of elements in the array to end the search operation. Consider the Fig. 7.9 of array with 10 elements.

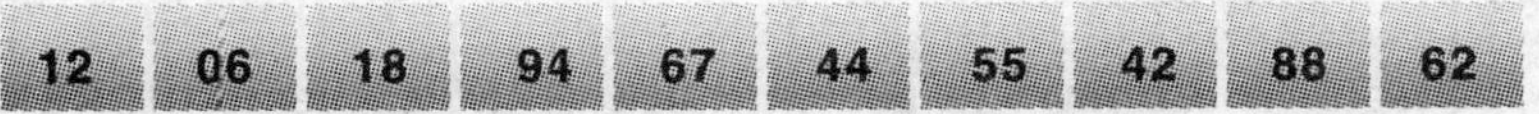

Fig. 7.9 Searching an element in sequential search method.

If we want to find the value 18, the search operation goes like this :

Start with the first element, search key compared the value of 18 with 12 for equality. Since they are not same, 18 is compared with the second element 06. This is also not equal. So, the search operation continues with the third element 18. Since it is the element we wanted, the search operation is completed successfully. Similarly, if we search for 62, which is the last element in the array, the entire set of elements are compared with search key, to reach the last one. The worst case is that the element we are searching is not in the array. In this case we will get the false statement for the search method, after having gone through the entire array.

The linear searching method works well for small arrays or for unsorted arrays. The following program shows the search array elements position in between 10 elements.

Example Write a program to input an array num with 10 different integer values and search a particular value and its position in array.

..\CSharp_Book\Chap07\ArraySearch

```
using System;
using System.Collections.Generic;
using System.Text;

// Search an element and its position in an array
namespace ArraySearch
{
    class Program
    {
        static void Main()
        {
            int[] num = new int[10];
            int i, pos = 0, value;

            Console.Write("Please enter the Values ... ");
            for (i = 0; i < 10; i++)
                num[i] = int.Parse(Console.ReadLine());

            Console.Write("Enter the search value ");
            value = int.Parse(Console.ReadLine());
            for (i = 0; i < 10; i++)
            {
                if (value == num[i])
                    pos = i + 1;
            }

            Console.WriteLine("The search value {0:D}'s position is {1:D}", value, pos);
        }
    }
}
```

When the above program executed, it will produce the following output as shown in Fig. 7.10.

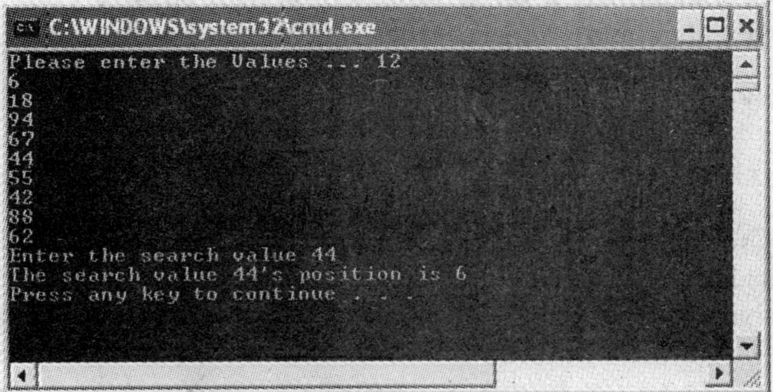

Fig. 7.10 Searching an element using sequential search method.

7.3.1 Binary Search

The binary search uses the "divide and conquer" method. It repeatedly divides the array into two pieces and refocuses on the piece that could contain the target value.

Note

The binary search algorithm requires that the list is sorted, but provides significant improvements in efficiency over a linear search.

The binary search is far more efficient than the linear/sequential search because each iteration reduces the search by a factor of two. For example, if the array has 1,000 elements, the linear search could require 1,000 iteration, while the binary search would require more than 10.

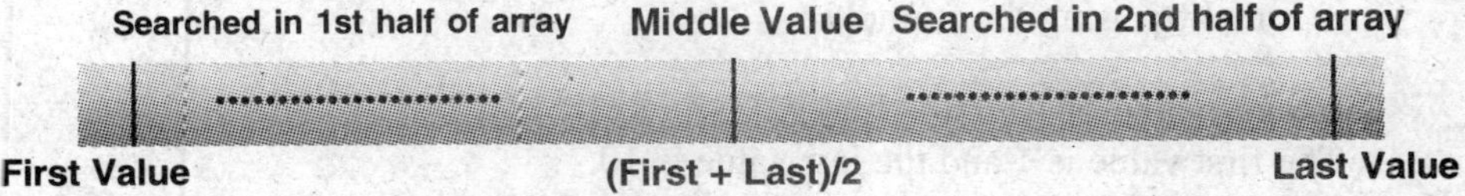

Fig. 7.11 Binary search sketch diagram for middle value.

Using the binary search method, we can dramatically increase the efficiency of the search operation. This method requires the array to be in a sorted form (sorting of array logic will be explained in next section).

Algorithm of binary search :

Steps : 1. Arrange your range values
2. Input the search number
3. first = 1; last = NUM; find = 0; mid = 0
4. while (first <= last) and opt = 0) repeat 5 to 7

```
5. mid = (first + last) / 2
6. if (range[mid] = search) then pos = mid; opt = 1
7. if (range[mid] < search) then first = mid + 1
       else last = mid - 1
8. if (opt = 1) then print pos
       else print "Search not success"
9. END.
```

The logic is very simple. The search operation starts with the middle element, by dividing the array into two halves. If middle element is equal to the search element, the search ends successfully. If the middle element is larger than the search element, the search continues with the left half, otherwise, it continues with right half.

Note

Each comparison in a binary search eliminates half of the remaining values under consideration.

We will use this method with a set of 10 elements arranged in an ascending order (05, 10, 12, 24, 46, 56, 66, 67, 86, 98). Let us assume that we want to search for the number 66.

In the given Fig. 7.12, first and last value represents the first and last element positions in the array.

Fig. 7.12 Sorted elements in an array for binary search.

The steps are as follows :

Step 1 : Find the middle value by dividing this array into two halves. The middle element is found by using the formula :

Integer value of [(First + Last)/2]
The first value is 1 and the last value is 10.
Therefore, the middle value = (1 + 10)/2 = 5.5

We can either round off this value or truncate it. By rounding off we will start at the 6th element and by truncating, at the 5th. We choose the latter.

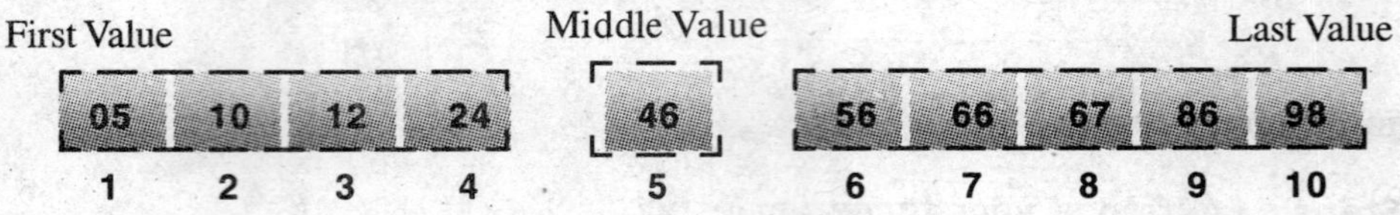

Fig. 7.13 Search step after first operation.

The 5th element is the middle value *i.e.* value 46. Although 46 is not equal to 66 and it is smaller than 66. So, we conclude that the search element should be in the right half, *i.e.* between the 6th and 10th element. (Remember, the array is sorted).

Step 2 : We mark the 6th element as a first element and thereby reducing the scope of the search operation again the array elements get into two halves. Look at the Fig. 7.14 given below:

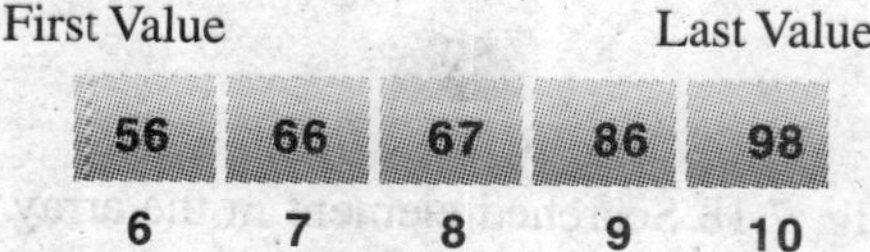

Fig. 7.14 Right half of the array after second operation.

Step 3 : Repeat step 1 again.
Find the middle element using the formula = Integer value of [(First+Last)/2]
Now, First = 6 and Last = 10
Therefore, middle value = (6 + 10)/2 = 8
This time the middle element in the partial array is 8th element.
The value is shown in Fig. 7.15 as 67.

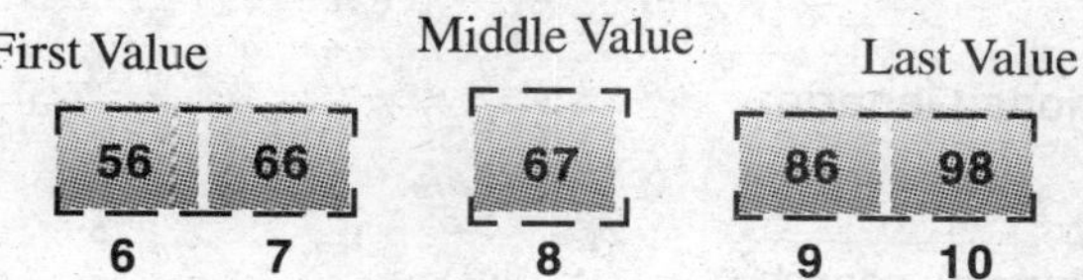

Fig. 7.15 Search operation to the right half after third operation.

The value 67 is not equal to 66, but greater than 66. So, it is concluded that the search element should be in the left hand, *i.e.* between 6th and 7th element.

Now again, the search scope is reduced to another half. Look at the reduced size of array is given in Fig. 7.16. In this part of array, the last element is 7th element and it is marked as Last.

Fig. 7.16 Search operation the left half after fourth operation.

Step 4 : Repeat step 1 again.
Middle value = (6 + 7)/2 = 6.5
And the middle value is placed as shown in Fig. 7.17.

First Value Middle Value Last Value

56 66

6 7

Fig. 7.17 Search operation after final step.

The value of 6th element is 56 which is less than 66. So, it is clear that the element should be on the right of this array. Since the 7the element is the only element on the right half, it becomes low and high for the next search as shown in Fig. 7.18.

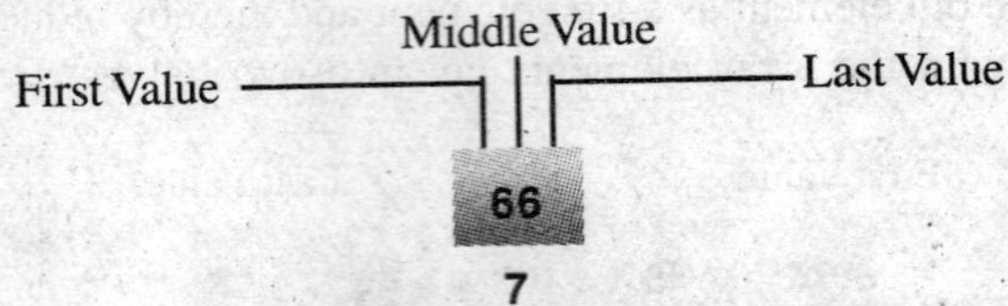

Fig. 7.18 Searched element in the array.

Step 5 : Since this time the middle element is 7 itself, it is compared with 66. They are equal and search ends successfully.

Example Write a program to search an element and its position in an input array using binary search method.

D:\Olevel02\CSharp_Book\Chap07\BinarySearch

```
using System;
using System.Collections.Generic;
using System.Text;

// Demonstration of binary search.
namespace BinarySearch
{
    class Program
    {
        static void Main()
        {
            int[] range = new int[101];
            int tn, T, i, j, first = 0, last, find, mid = 0, search, N;

            Console.Write("Enter the total numbers in the array : ");
            N = int.Parse(Console.ReadLine());
            for (i = 0; i < N; i++)
            {
                Console.Write("Enter the number {0} : ", (i + 1));
                range[i] = int.Parse(Console.ReadLine());
            }

            // Sorting procedures before binary search.
            for (i = 0; i < N - 1; i++)
            {
                for (j = i + 1; j < N; j++)
```

```
            {
                if (range[i] > range[j])
                {
                    T = range[i];
                    range[i] = range[j];
                    range[j] = T;
                }
            }
        }

        first = 0;
        find = 0;
        last = N - 1;

        Console.WriteLine("The sorted elements are : ");
        for (i = 0; i < N; i++)
            Console.Write("{0:D}   ", range[i]);
        Console.WriteLine();

        // Binary search procedure.
        Console.WriteLine("Enter the element to search : ");
        search = int.Parse(Console.ReadLine());
        while ((first <= last) && (find == 0))
        {
            mid = (first + last) / 2;
            if (range[mid] == search)
                find = mid;
            else
                if (range[mid] < search)
                    first = mid + 1;
                else
                    last = mid - 1;
        }

        if (find > 0)
            Console.WriteLine("The position of the array element is : " + ++find);
        else
            Console.WriteLine("Search not perfect");

    }
  }
}
```

When the previous program executed, it will produce the following output as shown in Fig. 7.19.

```
C:\WINDOWS\system32\cmd.exe
Enter the total numbers in the array : 10
Enter the number 1 : 5
Enter the number 2 : 10
Enter the number 3 : 12
Enter the number 4 : 24
Enter the number 5 : 46
Enter the number 6 : 56
Enter the number 7 : 66
Enter the number 8 : 67
Enter the number 9 : 86
Enter the number 10 : 98
The sorted elements are :
5  10  12  24  46  56  66  67  86  98
Enter the element to search :
66
The position of the array element is : 7
Press any key to continue . . .
```

Fig. 7.19 Searching an element using binary search method.

7.4 Insertion and Deletion

The insertion operation is happened when a new element is inserted into an existing array. It is very easy to add an element at the end of the array, but to add in between the array (at **loc** place), all the elements from the inserted place will shift one step forward to place the new element. For example;

Suppose the array **range** has the values 100, 200, 500, 300, and 600, and the value **num** *i.e.*; 400 has to be inserted in the array **range**.

Fig. 7.20 Inserting an integer type data value in an array range.

If you decided to insert the element 400 at 4th location in array range then all the elements from 4th location will be shifted towards right. The final inserted array will be :

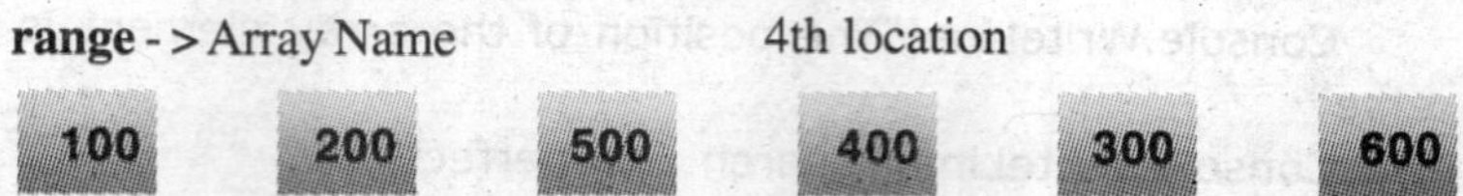

Fig. 7.21 Inserted the integer value 400 in an array range.

Example Write a program to insert an integer value in an array named **range** in a particular location. Suppose the element **range** of int type will be inserted into the array **range** of **loc** place in N numbers.

Thus, the algorithm of Element insert is :

Steps : 1. Input the data values into the range
2. Input the location loc, and the value num
3. if (loc < N) then prev = loc + 1 else STOP
4. while (prev > 1) repeat steps 5 and 6
5. range[prev] = range[prev−1]
6. prev = prev − 1
7. range[prev] = num
8. END.

D:\Olevel02\CSharp_Book\Chap07\InsertArr

```
using System;
using System.Collections.Generic;
using System.Text;

// A value num is inserted in an array range at loc place.
namespace InsertArr
{
    class Program
    {
        static void Main()
        {
            int[] range = new int[101];
            int N, num, loc, prev, i;

            Console.Write("Enter the total numbers in the array : ");
            N = int.Parse(Console.ReadLine());
            for (i = 0; i < N; i++)
            {
                Console.Write("Enter the number {0} : ", (i + 1));
                range[i] = int.Parse(Console.ReadLine());
            }

            Console.WriteLine();
            Console.Write("Enter the inserted value : ");
            num = int.Parse(Console.ReadLine());
            Console.Write("Enter the location to insert in array :  ");
            loc = int.Parse(Console.ReadLine());
            Console.WriteLine();

            if (loc <= N)
            {
```

```
                prev = N;
                while (prev >= loc)
                {
                    range[prev] = range[prev - 1];
                    prev = prev - 1;
                }
                range[prev] = num;
                N = N + 1;
                Console.WriteLine("The resulted output is :\n");
                for (i = 0; i < N; i++)
                    Console.WriteLine(range[i]);
            }
            else
                Console.WriteLine("Your location is not in the array range");
        }
    }
}
```

When the above program executed, it will produce the following output as shown in Fig. 7.22.

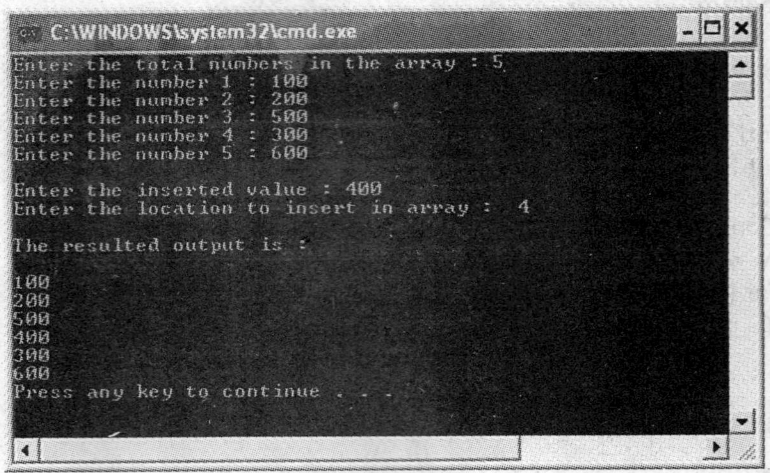

Fig. 7.22 Inserting elements into an array.

From the above program execution, the value 170 is inserted in array **range** at 2nd location. The program has input 6 integer values as 120, 320, 140, 250, 105 and 230 respectively. The actual size of array becomes N (*i.e.* total length 6) value of prev (as 5). Because, the input value in the array starts from 0th place onwards and the 6th value is stored at 5th place.

Here, we choose 2nd location for storing the value 170 so the statement,

range[prev] = range[prev-1]

becomes insert of the value 170 at the 2nd place from downwards by the condition has while (**prev >= loc**). Thus, the total length of the array becomes 6 (*i.e.* **N = 6**).

Deletion From Array. The deletion operation of an element forms an array is used to delete an element from any location (loc place). While deleting an element from loc place all the elements will shift one step towards left position. Thus the (**loc + 1**)th element shifted the loc place and so on. For example;

Suppose the array **range** has the values 123, 219, 233, 312, 265 and 300, and the value **num** *i.e.* 219 have to be deleted in the array **range**.

range - > Array Name

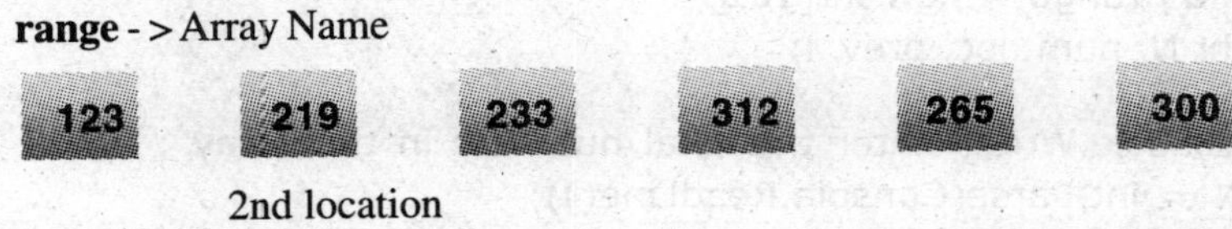

2nd location

Fig. 7.23 Deleting an integer type data value from an array range.

If you decided to delete the element 219 at 2nd location in array **range** then all the elements from 3rd location will be shifted towards left. The final deleted array will be :

range - > Array Name

2nd location

Fig. 7.24 Array after deleting an element at 2nd location.

Example Write a program to delete an integer value from an array named **range** of a particular location. Suppose the element **num** of **int** type will be deleted from the array **range** of **loc** place in N numbers.

Thus, the algorithm for deletion operation is :

```
Steps : 1. Input the data values into the range
        2. Input the location loc, and the value num
        3. prev = 1
        4. while (prev > loc) repeat steps 5 and 6
        5. range[prev] = range[prev + 1]
        6. prev = prev + 1
        7. loc = loc – 1
        8. END.
```

D:\Olevel02\CSharp_Book\Chap07\DeleteArr

```
using System;
using System.Collections.Generic;
```

```
using System.Text;

// A value num is deleted from an array range at loc place.
namespace DeleteArr
{
    class Program
    {
        static void Main()
        {
            int[] range = new int[101];
            int N, num, loc, prev, i;

            Console.Write("Enter the total numbers in the array : ");
            N = int.Parse(Console.ReadLine());
            for (i = 0; i < N; i++)
            {
                Console.Write("Enter the number {0} : ", (i + 1));
                range[i] = int.Parse(Console.ReadLine());
            }

            Console.WriteLine();
            Console.Write("Enter the location to delete the array element : ");
            loc = int.Parse(Console.ReadLine());
            loc = loc - 1;
            Console.WriteLine();

            if (loc < N)
            {
                num = range[loc];
                prev = loc;
                while (prev < N)
                {
                    range[prev] = range[prev + 1];
                    prev = prev + 1;
                }

                N = N - 1; // Decrease the length of array by 1.
                Console.WriteLine("The resulted output is :\n");
                for (i = 0; i < N; i++)
                    Console.WriteLine(range[i]);
                Console.WriteLine("The deleted value is : " + num);
            }
            else
                Console.WriteLine("Your location is not in the array range to delete.");
```

```
        }
    }
}
```

When the above program executed, it will produce the following output as shown in Fig. 7.25.

```
C:\WINDOWS\system32\cmd.exe
Enter the total numbers in the array : 6
Enter the number 1 : 123
Enter the number 2 : 219
Enter the number 3 : 233
Enter the number 4 : 312
Enter the number 5 : 265
Enter the number 6 : 300

Enter the location to delete the array element : 2

The resulted output is :

123
233
312
265
300
The deleted value is : 219
Press any key to continue . . .
```

Fig. 7.25 Deleting elements from an array.

From the above program execution, the value 219 is deleted from the array **range** of 2nd location. The program input 6 integer values as 123, 219, 233, 312, 265 and 300 respectively. So, for deleting the value 219 at 2nd location, the array becomes reduced to 1 length from its original length. Now actual size of array N is 5 (From 1 to 5) but for internal storage the **range** is from 0 to 4. Because, the input value in the array starts from 0th place onwards, and the 2nd value is deleted for 1st position from array. So, if the length of the array is 6 then, one int value can easily be deleted from the array range and the actual length will be 5. Here, we choose 2nd location for deleting the value 219, so the statement,

```
range[prev] = range[prev + 1]
```

becomes adjusting the value one step down from the loc place onwards.

Thus, the total length of the array becomes 5 (*i.e.* **N = 5**).

7.5 Sorting Arrays

Suppose, for instance that high school uses C# programs for its grade reports, and the principal wants to see the top 10 grade-point averages. You cannot print the first 10 grade-point averages in the list of student averages because the top 10 grade points may not (and probably do not) appear as the first 10 array elements. Because the grade points are not in any sequence, the program would have to sort the array elements into numeric order (from high to low grade points), or search the array for the 10 highest grade points.

You need a method for putting arrays in a specific order. This is called sorting of an array. When you sort an array, you put that array's elements in a specific order, such as alphabetic order or numeric order. A dictionary is in alphabetic order, and so to a phone book.

You can also reverse the order of a sort, called a descending sort. For instance, if you wanted to look at a list of all employees in descending salary order, the names of the highest-paid employees would be printed first.

Fig. 7.26 shows a list of eight numbers in an array called *Range* in unsorted order. The middle list of numbers is an ascending sorted order of unsorted. The third list of numbers is a descending sorted order of unsorted.

Unsorted array Range	**Ascending Order**	**Descending Order**
21	4	54
13	8	27
17	11	21
8	13	17
11	17	13
27	21	11
54	27	8
4	54	4

Fig. 7.26 A list of unsorted numbers sorted in both ascending and descending order.

7.5.1 Linear Sort

This sorting method is based on comparing and exchanging the top element with least value, until all elements in an array are stored.

The algorithm begins by comparing the top-most element with the remaining elements. An exchange of two elements takes place only then if top-most element is smaller than the element with which it is being compared. After $n-1$ comparison, the smallest among the total of n elements ascends to the top of the array, *i.e.* to the 1st location.

One round of scanning through the set of elements of an array is called a 'pass'. Now, leaving the 1st element, the remaining $n-1$ elements are scanned to find the next smallest element. This continues till the array is sorted.

As an example, let us take six elements : 71, 16, 12, 84, 96, 20 in Fig 7.27.

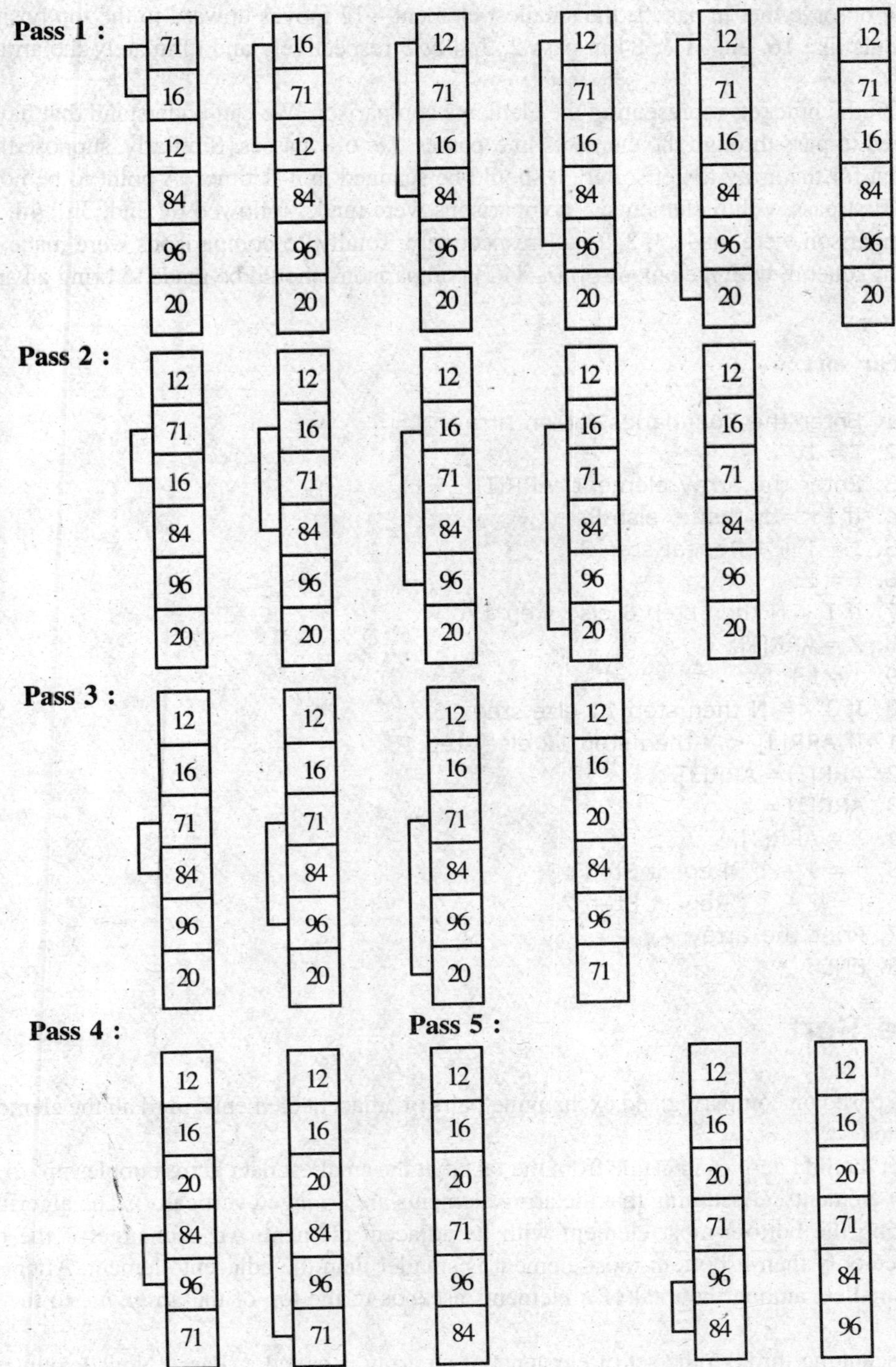

Fig. 7.27 Linear sort steps.

You can easily observe that in pass 1, the smallest element—12 moves upward to the top position followed by elements like 16, 20, 71 & 84 in pass 2, 3, 4 & 5 respectively and ultimately the array is sorted.

In the Fig. 15.5, the brackets representing the elements comparison. We can understand that having 6 elements, we need to pass through the elements in 5 passes, *i.e.* 6–1 passes. Similarly, suppose there are *n* elements, then for the array to get sorted, it should be scanned in *n*–1 times. A point to be noted, here is that in the first pass with 6 elements, 5 comparisons were made, followed by 2nd, 3rd, 4th and 5th passes the comparison were made 4, 3, 2 & 1 respectively. Totally 15 comparisons were made, *i.e.* 6 * (6–1)/2 = 15. In general, with *n* elements, [*n*(*n*–1)/2] comparisons should be made to bring an array in a sorted form.

Algorithm of linear sort :

Steps :
1. Enter the boundaries for an array, N.
2. I = 1.
3. Enter the array element, ARR[I].
4. If I <= N then 6 else 5.
5. I = I + 1 Repeat step 3.
6. I = 1.
7. If I < N then step 8 else step 17.
8. X = ARR[I].
9. J = I + 1.
10. If J <= N then step 11 else step 16.
11. If ARR[J] < X then step 12 else step 15.
12. ARR[I] = ARR[J].
13. ARR[J] = X.
14. X = ARR[J].
15. J = J + 1 : Repeat Step 10.
16. I = I + 1 : Repeat Step 7.
17. Print the array.
18. END.

7.5.2 Bubble Sort

This sort method is based on comparing and exchanging pairs of adjacent elements, until all the elements in an array are sorted.

The bubble sort method derives its name from the fact that the smallest data item 'bubbles up' to the top of an array of *n* elements. (Assuming that the array elements are arranged vertically). The algorithm begins by comparing the bottom-most element with its adjacent element. An exchange of the two elements takes place only then if bottom-most element is smaller than the adjacent element. After *n*–1 comparisons, the smallest among the total of *n* elements ascends to the top of the array, *i.e.* to the 1st location.

One round of scanning through the set of elements of an array is called a 'Pass'. Now, leaving the

1st element, the remaining n–1 elements are scanned to find the next smallest element. This continues till the array is sorted. As an exercise, let us take five elements : 44, 34, 23, 22, 05 (note that these are in descending order).

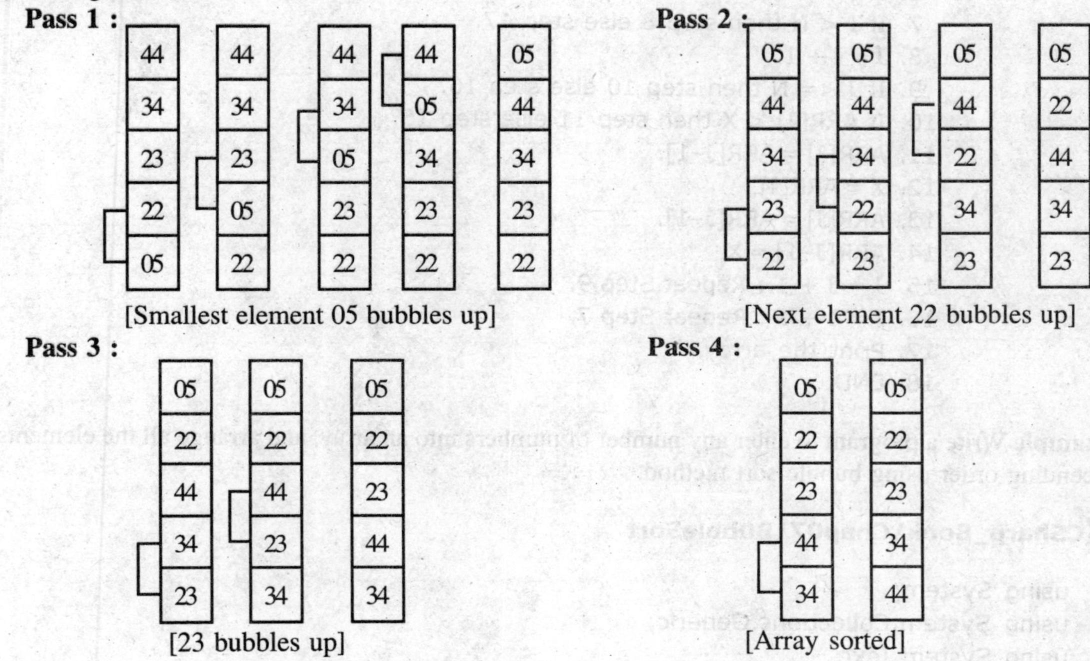

Fig. 7.28 Bubble sort steps.

You can easily observe that in pass 1, the smallest element 05 pops up to the top position. In the second pass, next smallest element 22 pops up followed by 23 & 34 in the passes 3 & 4 respectively and ultimately the array is sorted.

In Fig. 7.28, the brackets represent the elements comparison. We can understand that having 5 elements, we need to pass through the elements in 4 passes, *i.e.* 5–1 passes. Similarly, suppose there are n elements, then for the array to get sorted, it should be scanned n–1 times *i.e.* an array of n elements needs n–1 passes to get sorted an array using the bubble sort method.

A point to be noted, here is that in the first pass with 5 elements, 4 comparisons were made, followed by 2nd, 3rd & 4th passes where comparisons were made 3, 2 & 1 respectively. Totally 10 comparisons were made, *i.e.* 5 * (5 – 1)/2 = 10. In general, with n elements, $n(n - 1)/2$ comparisons should be made to bring an array in a sorted form.

Algorithm of bubble sort :

Steps : 1. Enter the boundaries for an array, N.
2. I = 1.
3. Enter the array element, ARR[I].

4. If I <= N then 6 else 5.
5. I = I + 1 Repeat step 3.
6. I = 1.
7. If I < N then step 8 else step 17.
8. J = I + 1.
9. If J <= N then step 10 else step 16.
10. If ARR[J] < X then step 11 else step 15.
11. ARR[J] = ARR[J-1].
12. X = ARR[J].
13. ARR[J] = ARR[J-1].
14. ARR[J-1] = X.
15. J = J + 1 : Repeat Step 9.
16. I = I + 1 : Repeat Step 7.
17. Print the array.
18. END.

Example Write a program to enter any number of numbers into an array, and arrange all the elements in ascending order using bubble sort method.

..\CSharp_Book\Chap07\BubbleSort

```
using System;
using System.Collections.Generic;
using System.Text;
// Demonstration of sorting an array using bubble sort method.

namespace BubbleSort
{
    class Program
    {
        static void Main()
        {
            int[] item = new int[100];
            int num, i, j, temp;

            Console.Write("How many numbers you want to sort? ");
            num = int.Parse(Console.ReadLine());

            Console.WriteLine("Enter the element into array : ");
            for (i = 0; i < num; i++)
                item[i] = int.Parse(Console.ReadLine());

            for (i = 0; i < num-1; i++)
                for (j = i + 1; j < num; j++)
```

```
                if (item[i] > item[j])
                {
                    temp = item[i];
                    item[i] = item[j];
                    item[j] = temp;
                }
            Console.WriteLine("The sorted elements are :");
            for (i = 0; i < num; i++)
                Console.WriteLine(item[i]);
        }
    }
}
```

When the above program executed, it will produce the following output as shown in Fig. 7.29.

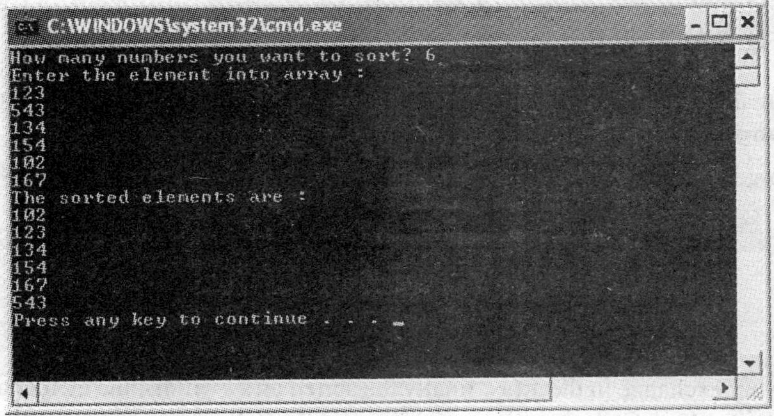

Fig. 7.29 Sorting array elements using bubble sort method.

7.5.3 Selection Sort

A selection sort is one in which successive elements are selected in an order and placed into their proper sorted positions. The elements of the input may have to be preprocessed to make the ordered selection possible.

Any selection sort can be conceptualized as the following general algorithm that uses a descending priority queue.

> **Note**
> *Selection sort works by putting each value into its final position. One at a time*

When the elements are stored in one-dimensional array, from all the elements the sort procedure searches the smallest element and that element is exchanged with the first element of the array. Next, the second smallest element is searched and exchanged with the second element of the existing array and so on.

For example, suppose the array list **range[]** contains the following in Fig. 7.30 elements as :

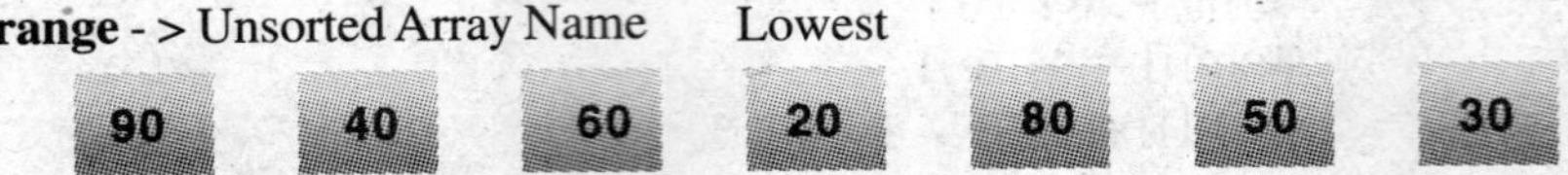

Fig. 7.30 Unsorted array range with lowest value 20.

From the above array the smallest element is 20 and exchanged with the first element 90. So, after the first exchange the array **range** will be in Fig. 7.31 as :

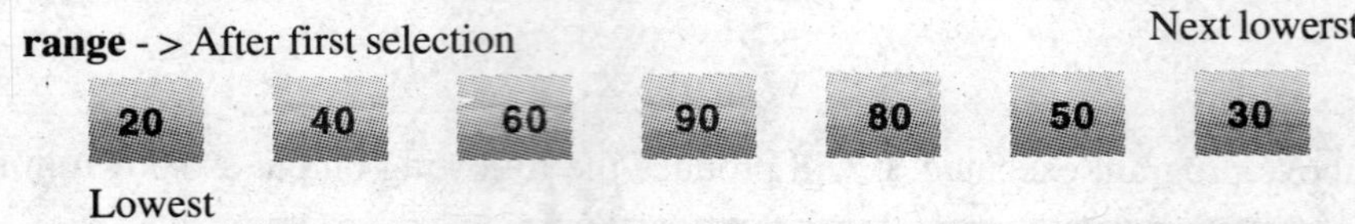

Fig. 7.31 After first selection of 20 with the exchange of first place.

The second smallest value in the array is 30 and will be exchanged with the second element 40. Thus, the array **range** will be in Fig. 7.32 as :

Fig. 7.32 After second selection of 30 with the exchange of second place.

and so on. After every exchange in the array, finally the sorted array will list the elements as in Fig. 7.33:

range - > After first selection

Fig. 7.33 After every selection the sorted array of range.

Algorithm for selection sort. Suppose, the array list range stores 7 elements, and are sorted into ascending order. The variable **loc** and lowest checks position and the lowest element in the unsorted array list **range**. N is declared to store the total number of elements in the array.

```
Steps : 1. Input the total element for array (i.e., N)
        2. Input the elements into array range[]
        3. for i = 0 to N - 1 repeat 4 to 9
        4. lowest = list[i]; loc = i;
        5. for j = i + 1 to N repeat 6
        6. if range[j] > lowest then
                lowest = range[j];
                loc = j;
```

7. T = range[i];
8. range[i] = range[loc];
9. range[loc] = T;
10. END.

From the above example, the outer loop continues N–1 times from 0th position and the inner loop continues N times from (i + 1)th position. So, each element of the outer loop searches its smallest element in the inner loop and interchanges with the subsequent position of array range.

Thus, the steps of interchange values are :

90 40 60 20 80 50 30	Initial array of unsorted elements
20 40 60 90 80 50 30	First interchange
20 30 60 90 80 50 40	Second interchange
20 30 40 90 80 50 60	Third interchange
20 30 40 50 80 90 60	Fourth interchange
20 30 40 50 60 90 80	Fifth interchange
20 30 40 50 60 80 90	Last interchange

Example Write a program to perform the selection sort.

D:\Olevel02\CSharp_Book\Chap07\SeleSort

```
using System;
using System.Collections.Generic;
using System.Text;
// Demonstration of the program for selection sort.

namespace SeleSort
{
    class Program
    {
        static void Main()
        {
            int loc, lowest, T, N, i, j, x;
            int[] range = new int[101];

            Console.Write("Enter the number of elements in your array : ");
            N = int.Parse(Console.ReadLine());

            Console.WriteLine("Enter the element into array :");
            for (i = 0; i < N; i++)
            {
                Console.Write("Location {0}. value : {1}: ", i, i + 1);
```

```
                range[i] = int.Parse(Console.ReadLine());
            }

            for (i = 0; i < N - 1; i++)
            {
                lowest = range[i];
                loc = i;
                for (j = i + 1; j < N; j++)
                {
                    if (lowest > range[j])
                    {
                        loc = j;
                        lowest = range[j];
                    }
                }
                T = range[i];
                range[i] = range[loc];
                range[loc] = T;
            }

            Console.WriteLine("The sorted list is ....");
            for (i = 0; i < N; i++)
                Console.WriteLine(range[i]);
        }
    }
}
```

When the above program executed, it will produce the following output as shown in Fig. 7.34.

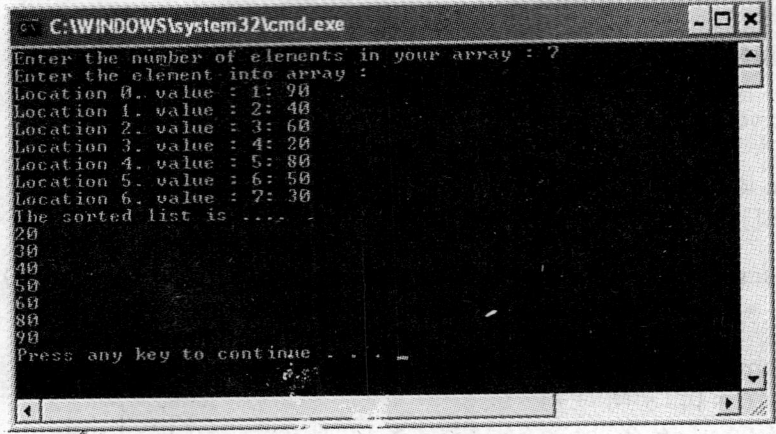

Fig. 7.34 Sorting array elements using selection sort method.

7.5.4 Insertion Sort

An insertion sort is one that sorts a set of records by inserting elements into an existing sorted list. When the number of values is stored in any array, they are treated as either sorted elements or unsorted elements, but as insertion sort, consider any one of the element is picked and placed in the sorted part of the array. The process continues till all the elements are arranged in an order.

> **Note**
> *Insertion sort works by inserting each value into a previously sorted subset of the list.*

From the previous selection sort, suppose the same unsorted elements are considered as in Fig. 7.35 :

range - > Unsorted array name

90 40 60 20 80 50 30

Fig. 7.35 Unsorted array elements in array range.

From the above elements suppose, 90 is the sorted part and remaining elements are the unsorted part and 40 is the first element of the unsorted part. When you will insert the element in the sorted part, the sorted element will check with the unsorted element and exchange their position as in Fig 7.36 :

range - > After first exchange

Fig. 7.36 After first exchange in array range.

After the second moment, the next element of the unsorted part (*i.e.* 60) will be inserted in the sorted part, and the array range will be in Fig. 7.37.

range - > After second exchange

Fig. 7.37 After second exchange in array range.

Like this the remaining sorted elements after every insertion will be :

```
20  40  60  90  80  50  30
20  40  60  80  90  50  30
20  40  50  60  80  90  30
20  30  40  50  60  80  90
```

Algorithm of Insertion sort :

Steps : 1. Input the array list range[N]

2. T = 0, j = 0

3. for i = 2 to N repeat steps 4 to 9

4. T = range[i]
5. j = i–1
6. while (T <= range[j] and j >= 0) repeat steps 7 and 8
7. range[j + 1] = range[j]
8. j = j – 1
9. range[j + 1] = T
10. print the array range
11. END

Example Write a program to perform the insertion sort.

D:\Olevel02\CSharp_Book\Chap07\InsrtSort

```
using System;
using System.Collections.Generic;
using System.Text;

// Demonstration of the program for insertion sort.
namespace InsrtSort
{
    class Program
    {
        static void Main()
        {
            int[] numbers = { 90, 40, 60, 20, 80, 50, 30 };

            for (int index = 1; index < numbers.Length; index++)
            {
                int key = numbers[index];
                int position = index;

                // Shift larger values to the right
                while (position > 0 && numbers[position - 1] > key)
                {
                    numbers[position] = numbers[position - 1];
                    position—;
                }
                numbers[position] = key;
            }

            Console.WriteLine("Sorted numbers are :");
            for (int index = 0; index < numbers.Length; index++)
                Console.WriteLine(numbers[index]);
        }
    }
}
```

When the above program executed, it will produce the following output as shown in Fig. 7.38.

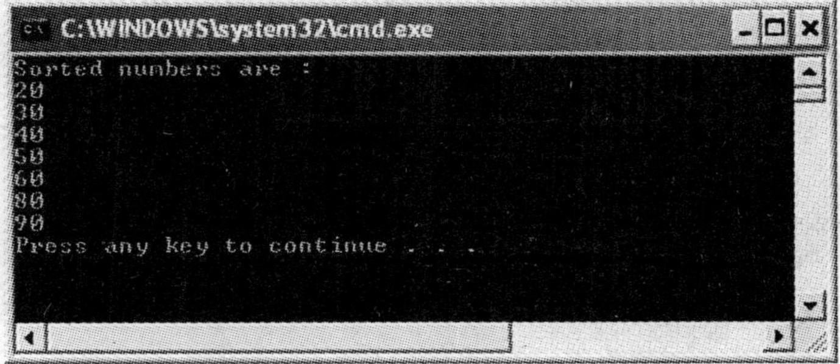

Fig. 7.38 Sorting array elements using insertion sort method.

7.6 Merging of Two Sorted Array

Merging is the process of combining two or more sorted files into a third sorted file. Otherwise in arrays, two or more arrays are sorted into a third array. We can use this technique to sort an array in the following ways.

Divide the array into n sub arrays of size 1 and merge adjacent (disjoint) pairs of files. We then have approximately n/2 arrays of size 2. Repeat this process until there is only one file of remaining size n. The figure given below illustrates how this process operates on a sample array. Each individual array is contained in brackets.

For example, suppose two sorted array lists **rang1** and **rang2** are given in Fig. 7.39. Then select the smaller elements from the two arrays, and sort both the elements. After sorting them store these elements in the third array **rang3**.

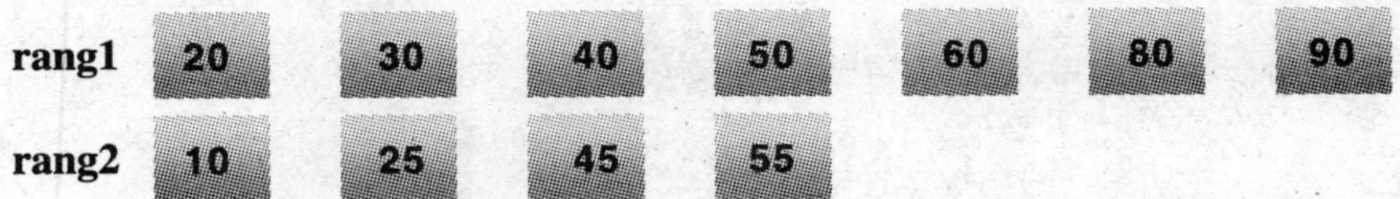

Fig. 7.39 Two array rang1 and rang2 for merge sort.

From the two arrays, 20 and 10 are the two first smaller elements in both the array **rang1** and **rang2** respectively. When both the elements are compared, it produces 10 as the lowest element in the third array **rang3**. Thus, the final array rang3 will be :

```
rang3[i] = rang2[i];     // i is the position of array.
```

i.e.;

```
rang3  10
```

Similarly, if the merging procedure continue and the second array (**rang2**) element stored in the third array (**rang3**), then the remaining values of second array will be shifted to next location of array.

So, the above process will continue till all the array elements of **rang1** and **rang2** array are shifting to the third array.

If the elements of any given array are all smaller elements than next array, then all the elements of that array are stored in the final array, which is a copy of elements to final array. Like this, on next step the resulted array will be in Fig. 7.40 :

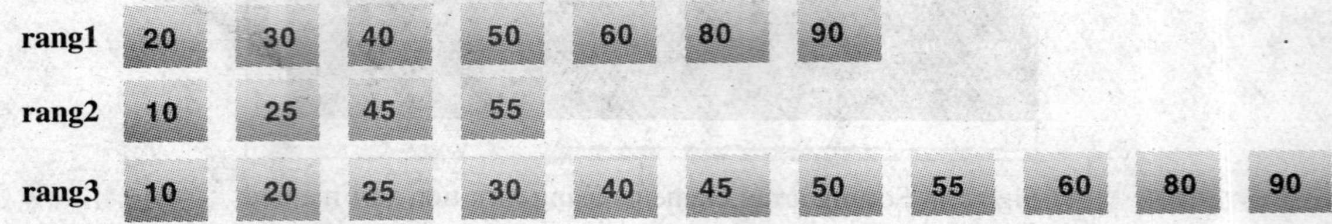

Fig. 7.40 The resulted array rang3 after merging rang1 and rang2.

Algorithm of Insertion sort :

Steps :
```
 1. START
 2. i = 0; j = 0; k = 0  // Positions of three array
 3. Input the length of your two arrays as M and N
 4. Arrange your array rang1 and rang2
 5. while (i <= M) and (j <= N) repeat 6
 6. if rang1[i] < rang2[j] then
         rang3[k] = rang1[i]
         i = i + 1;
         k = k + 1;
    else
         rang3[k] = rang2[j]
         j = j + 1;
         k = k + 1;
    (end of the while loop)
 7. while (i <= M)
         rang3[k] = rang1[i]
         k = k + 1
         i = i + 1
    (end of the while loop)
 8. while (j <= N)
         rang3[k] = rang2[j]
         k = k + 1
         j = j + 1
    (end of the while loop)
 9. T = M + N;
10. for (k = 0; i < T; k++)
         print rang3[k]
11. END.
```

From the above algorithm, **rang1**, **rang2** and **rang3** are two arrays. **rang1** and **rang2** are sorted their M and N elements. The variables j, k, and i are declared as subscripts for using in the three **rang1**, **rang2** and **rang3** respectively. The array **rang1** and **rang2** elements are compared and stored in **rang3** array till **rang3[M + N]**.

D:\Olevel02\CSharp_Book\Chap07\MergeSort

```
using System;
using System.Collections.Generic;
using System.Text;

// Demonstration for MERGE sort operation by using two sorted arrays.
// Note: Input only sorted elements in the array rang1 and rang2.
namespace MergeSort
{
    class Program
    {
        static void Main()
        {
            int M, N, i, j, k, T;
            int[] range1 = new int[100];
            int[] range2 = new int[100];
            int[] range3 = new int[201];

            Console.Write("Enter your first array length : ");
            M = int.Parse(Console.ReadLine());
            Console.WriteLine("Enter sorted elements of range1 : ");
            for (i = 0; i < M; i++)
            {
                range1[i] = int.Parse(Console.ReadLine());
            }

            Console.Write("Enter your second array length : ");
            N = int.Parse(Console.ReadLine());
            Console.WriteLine("Enter sorted elements of range1 : ");
            for (i = 0; i < N; i++)
            {
                range2[i] = int.Parse(Console.ReadLine());
            }

            i = 0;   // Assign to start from 0th position in array.
            j = 0;
            k = 0;
```

```
            while ((i < M) && (j < N))
            {
                if (range1[i] < range2[j])
                {
                    range3[k] = range1[i];
                    k = k + 1;
                    i = i + 1;
                }
                else
                {
                    range3[k] = range2[j];
                    k = k + 1;
                    j = j + 1;
                }
            }
            while (i <= M)
            {
                range3[k] = range1[i];
                k = k + 1;
                i = i + 1;
            }
            while (j <= N)
            {
                range3[k] = range2[j];
                k = k + 1;
                j = j + 1;
            }

            Console.WriteLine("The resulted output is as :");
            T = M + N;
            for (k = 0; k < T; k++)
                Console.WriteLine(range3[k]);
        }
    }
}
```

When the above program executed, it will produce the following output as shown in Fig. 7.41.

```
C:\WINDOWS\system32\cmd.exe
Enter your first array length : 7
Enter sorted elements of range1 :
20
30
40
50
60
80
90
Enter your second array length : 4
Enter sorted elements of range1 :
10
25
45
55
The resulted output is as :
10
20
25
30
40
45
50
55
60
80
90
Press any key to continue . . .
```

Fig. 7.41 Merging two sorted array elements using merge sort method.

7.7 Finding Maximum and Minimum in an Array

We know that an array stores values in a sequence from its starting index 0th place onwards. It is easy to find the maximum and minimum value in an array. There are two methods to find the maximum and minimum value in an array—with sorted array and from unsorted array. In this section we will discuss about on unsorted array.

To find the maximum and minimum value each element of the array will be checked with a variable and if the value is less than the array value then it will be assumed that the array value is minimum otherwise maximum. The program given below demonstrates the maximum and minimum value in an array.

Let us consider the Fig. 7.42 of unsorted array **ARR** with 6 values.

Fig. 7.42 Unsorted array to find maximum and minimum.

The steps are as follows :

Step 1 : Let us consider the array index 1 value 65 as maximum and minimum.
i.e. max = 65 and min = 65

Step 2 : The array index position 1 value will check with the array index position 2. *i.e.*

```
if max > ARR[2]
```

```
        max = max;
    else
        min = ARR[2];
```

Here, the index position 2 contains a number 17, which is less than the previous max 65 and greater than the previous min 65. So, the new max is 65 and new min is 17.

Step 3 : Repeat step 2 with next index position 3, *i.e.* the array value 19. When it will compare with the previous max and min, the new max remain 65 and the new min remain 17.

```
if max > ARR[2]
```

Finally, you will notice that all remaining array values will be checked with previous max and min and produce the final maximum and minimum value as 96 and 17 respectively. The Fig. 7.43 shows the maximum and minimum values in an unsorted array.

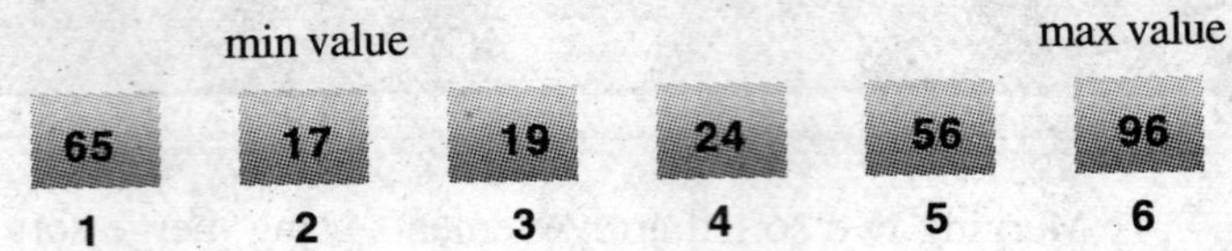

Fig. 7.43 Unsorted array for finding maximum and minimum.

If we consider about a sorted array, then it is very easy to find its maximum and minimum value. If the array is sorted in ascending order, then the lower index positional value is the minimum and upper index positional value is the maximum. If the array is sorted in descending order, then the lower index positional value is the maximum and upper index positional value is the minimum.

Let us consider the Fig. 7.44 of sorted array **ARR** (with ascending order) with 6 values.

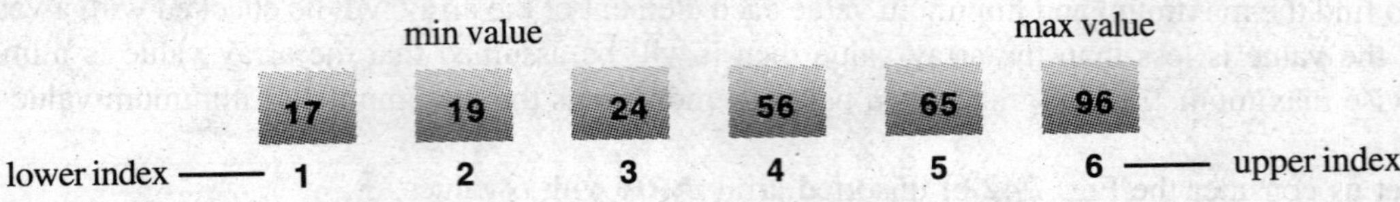

Fig. 7.44 Sorted array for finding maximum and minimum.

From the Fig. 7.28, the array index position 1 has the number 17, which is the minimum value, and array index position 6 has the number 96 which is the maximum value.

Algorithm of minimum and maximum :

Steps : 1. Enter the boundaries for an array, N.
2. I = 1.
3. Enter the array element, ARR[I].
4. If I <= N then 6 else 5.

5. I = I + 1 Repeat step 3.
6. I = 1.
7. max = ARR[1].
8. max = ARR[1].
9. If I < N then step 8 else step 13.
10. If (ARR[I] > max) then max = ARR[I] else step 11.
11. If (ARR[I] < max) then min = ARR[I] else step 12.
12. I = I + 1 Repeat step 9.
13. Print max and min.
14. END.

Example Write a program to find the maximum and minimum value in an array.

..\CSharp_Book\Chap07\FindMaxMin

```
using System;
using System.Collections.Generic;
using System.Text;

// Program to find minimum and maximum value of a given array
namespace FindMaxMin
{
    class Program
    {
        static void Main()
        {
            int[] num = new int[100];
            int min, max, i, size;

            Console.Write("Enter the size of your array ... ");
            size = int.Parse(Console.ReadLine());

            Console.WriteLine("Please enter the Values ... ");
            for (i = 0; i < size; i++)
                num[i] = int.Parse(Console.ReadLine());

            max = num[0]; // Initialize the default value to max and min
            min = num[0];

            for (i = 0; i < size; i++)
            {
                if (num[i] > max)
                    max = num[i];
                if (num[i] < min)
                    min = num[i];
            }
```

```
            Console.WriteLine("The maximum value in the list is {0}", max);
            Console.WriteLine("The minimum value in the list is {0}", min);
        }
    }
}
```

When the above program executed, it will produce the following output as shown in Fig. 7.45.

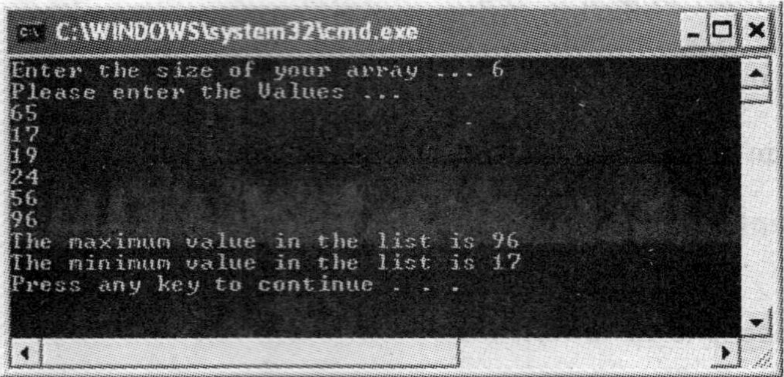

Fig. 7.45 Finding maximum and minimum element in an array.

7.8 Multidimensional Arrays

A multidimensional array is an array with more than one subscript. A single-dimensional array is a list of values, but a multidimensional array simulates a table of values, or even multiple tables of values. The most commonly used table is a two-dimensional table (an array with two subscripts).

C# supports two types of multidimensional arrays: rectangular and jagged. A rectangular array is a single array with more than one dimension, with the dimensions' sizes fixed in the array's declaration. The following code creates a 2 by 3 multi-dimensional array:

```
int[,] squareArray = new int[2,3];
```

As with single-dimensional arrays, rectangular arrays can be filled at the time they are declared. For instance, the code;

```
int[,] squareArray = {{1, 2, 3}, {4, 5, 6}};
```

creates a 2 by 3 array with the given values. It is, of course, important that the given values do fill out exactly a rectangular array.

To declare a two-dimensional array, use the general form :

```
data_type[ , ] array_name = new int[row][col];
```

where **data_type** is a valid C# data type, **array_name** is the name of the array (i.e. a rectangular array). **row** and **col** specifies the dimensions of array.

You can create arrays of two or more dimensions, for example, to create a 10×12 two-dimensional integer array called arr, you would use this statement :

```
int [,] arr = new int[10][12];
```

declare the integer array table with 10 rows and 12 columns.

Here, the array tell the compiler that,

- **arr** is the name of the array,
- its type is integer,
- it is two-dimensional,
- the number of the elements in the array are 120, *i.e.* equal to the product of the two dimension specifiers,
- since each integer value requires 4 bytes of memory, therefore for arr, compiler allocates a contiguous block of 480 bytes.

For example, if there are three students, and each having 5 different marks then, matrix array contains 3 rows and 5 columns. That is in Fig. 7.46 :

	Mark0	**Mark1**	**Mark2**	**Mark3**	**Mark4**
Row 0 for first student	56	43	43	65	54
Row 1 for first student	65	54	76	34	54
Row 2 for first student	48	67	54	56	31

Fig. 7.46 The row and column value in a two dimensional array.

Otherwise, the same matrix array can arrange like this in Fig. 7.47 :

56	43	43	65	54
65	54	76	34	54
48	67	54	56	31

Fig. 7.47 The 3×4 matrix array in two dimensional form.

7.8.1 Initializing Two-dimensional Array

To make a multidimensional array initialization match the array's subscripts, some programmers like to visualize how arrays are filled. C# does not mind if you initialize a multidimensional array as if it were a single-dimensional array. But you have to make sure that you keep track of the row order if you initialize this way. For instance, the following two definitions reserve storage and initialize **array1** and **array2** as:

```
int[,] squareArray = {{1, 2, 3}, {4, 5, 6}};
```

```
int[,] array1 = int [2][4]
        {  12, 34, 54, 55,
           32, 10, 43, 87};

int[,] array2 = int [4][4]
        {  1,  2,  3,  4,
           5,  6,  7,  8,
           9,  10, 11, 12,
           13, 14, 15, 16};
```

Fig. 7.48 shows the multidimensional array.

Array1 — Columns

Rows	0	1	2	3
0	12	34	54	55
0	32	10	43	87

Array2 — Columns

Rows	0	1	2	3
0	1	2	3	4
1	5	6	7	8
2	9	10	11	12
3	13	14	15	16

Fig. 7.48 Table contents two multidimensional arrays after initialization.

Initializing **array1** and **array2** with or without the nested braces is no different. The nested braces seem to show the dimensions and how C# fills them a little better, but the choice of using nested braces is yours.

> **Note**
> *The two-dimensional array can be treated as array of arrays where its each element of the array will be a one-dimensional array.*
> *Character array (array of strings) will be discussed in next chapter.*

Example Write a program to display a 4×4 array with row and column format.

..\CSharp_Book\Chap07\TwoDArray

```
using System;
using System.Collections.Generic;
using System.Text;

// Demonstration of multidimensional array
namespace TwoDArray
{
    class Program
    {
        static void Main()
        {
            int[,] array =   {{ 1,  2,   3,  4},
                              { 5,  6,   7,  8},
                              { 9,  10, 11, 12},
                              {  13, 14, 15, 16}};
            int i, j;

            // Displaying the array in row, and column
            for (i = 0; i < 4; i++)
            {
                for (j = 0; j < 4; j++)
                    Console.Write("    {0:D2}", array[i,j]);
                Console.WriteLine();
            }
        }
    }
}
```

When the above program executed, it will produce the following output as shown in Fig. 7.49.

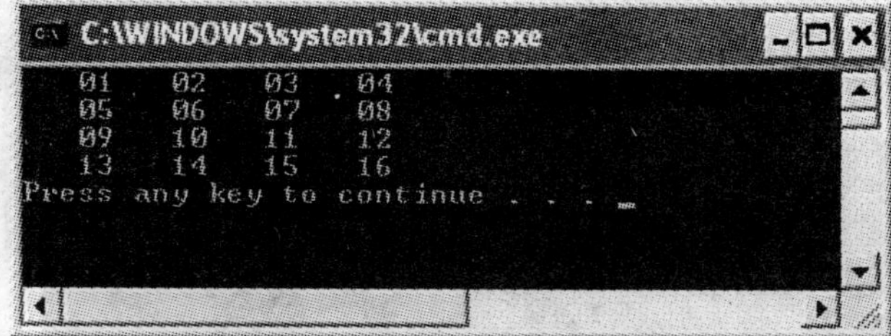

Fig. 7.49 Displaying a two-dimensional array elements.

Example Write a program to declare a 4Í4 array with the products of the indices, and then display the array in row, column format.

..\CSharp_Book\Chap07\ArrayProduct

```
using System;
using System.Collections.Generic;
using System.Text;

// Demonstration of multidimensional array
// with the products of the indices
namespace ArrayProduct
{
    class Program
    {
        static void Main()
        {
            int[,] array = new int [4, 4];
            int i, j;

            // Calculating the product of indices
            for (i = 0; i < 4; i++)
                for (j = 0; j < 4; j++)
                    array[i,j] = i * j;

            // Displaying the array in row, and column
            for (i = 0; i < 4; i++)
            {
                for (j = 0; j < 4; j++)
                    Console.Write("    {0:D}", array[i, j]);
                Console.WriteLine();
            }
        }
    }
}
```

When the above program executed, it will produce the following output as shown in Fig. 7.50.

Fig. 7.50 Finding the sequential-product of an array.

7.8.2 Entering Data into Two-dimensional Array

The following program segment is used to enter the data into a two-dimensional array :

```
int[,] num = new int [3, 3];
int i, j;
for (int i = 0; i < 3; i++)
    for (int j = 0; j < 3; j++)
        cin >> num[i, j];
```

Here, the above code will input 3 integer values into the array num.

Example Write a program to input data into a 3×3 array and display the array elements with row and column format.

..\CSharp_Book\Chap07\ArrayInput

```
using System;
using System.Collections.Generic;
using System.Text;

// Demonstration of multidimensional array with input values
namespace ArrayInput
{
    class Program
    {
        static void Main()
        {
            int[,] num = new int[4, 4];
            int i, j;

            // Input data into array
            Console.WriteLine("Enter the num values : ");
            for (i = 0; i < 3; i++)
            {
                for (j = 0; j < 3; j++)
                    num[i, j] = int.Parse(Console.ReadLine());
            }

            // Displaying num values
            Console.WriteLine("The array is : ");
            for (i = 0; i < 3; i++)
            {
                for (j = 0; j < 3; j++)
```

```
                Console.Write("    {0:D2}", num[i, j]);
            Console.WriteLine();
        }
      }
    }
}
```

When the above program executed, it will produce the following output as shown in Fig. 5.51.

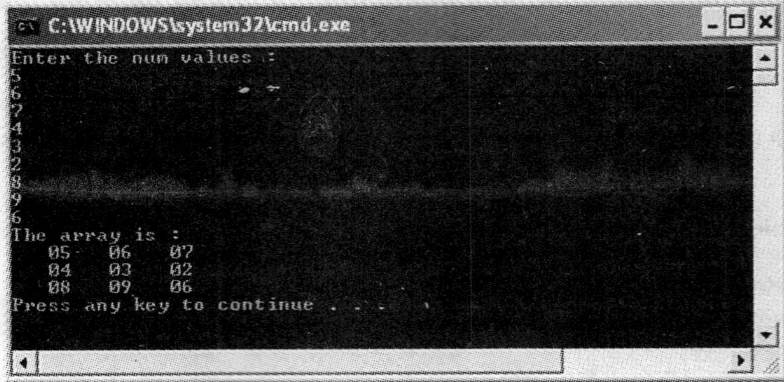

Fig. 7.51 Displaying a two-dimensional array elements.

Example Write a program to find the sum of two 3×3 matrices.

..\CSharp_Book\Chap07\ArraySumInd

```
using System;
using System.Collections.Generic;
using System.Text;

// Demonstration of multidimensional array with input values
namespace ArraySumInd
{
    class Program
    {
        static void Main()
        {
            int[,] a = new int[3, 3];
            int[,] b = new int[3, 3];
            int[,] c = new int[3, 3];
            int i, j;

            // Input data into array
            Console.WriteLine("Enter elements of Ist array :");
            for (i = 0; i < 3; i++)
```

```
        {
            for (j = 0; j < 3; j++)
                a[i, j] = int.Parse(Console.ReadLine());
        }

        Console.WriteLine("Enter elements of IInd array :");
        for (i = 0; i < 3; i++)
        {
            for (j = 0; j < 3; j++)
            b[i, j] = int.Parse(Console.ReadLine());
        }

        // Steps to add two matrices
        for (i = 0; i < 3; i++)
        {
            for (j = 0; j < 3; j++)
                c[i,j] = a[i,j] + b[i,j];
        }

        Console.WriteLine("First matrix is :");
        for (i = 0; i < 3; i++)
        {
            for (j = 0; j < 3; j++)
                Console.Write("   {0:D2}", a[i, j]);
            Console.WriteLine();
        }

        Console.WriteLine("Second matrix is :");
        for (i = 0; i < 3; i++)
        {
            for (j = 0; j < 3; j++)
                Console.Write("   {0:D2}", b[i, j]);
            Console.WriteLine();
        }

        Console.WriteLine("Sum of two matrices is :");
        for (i = 0; i < 3; i++)
        {
            for (j = 0; j < 3; j++)
                Console.Write("   {0:D2}", c[i, j]);
            Console.WriteLine();
        }
    }
  }
}
```

When the above program executed, it will produce the following output as shown in Fig. 7.52.

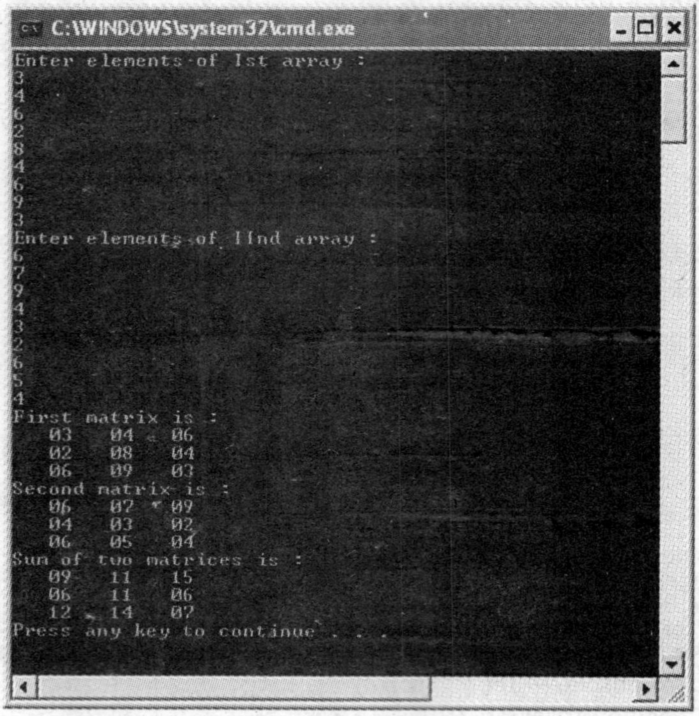

```
C:\WINDOWS\system32\cmd.exe
Enter elements of Ist array :
3
4
6
2
8
4
6
9
3
Enter elements of IInd array :
6
7
9
4
3
2
6
5
4
First matrix is :
   03   04   06
   02   08   04
   06   09   03
Second matrix is :
   06   07   09
   04   03   02
   06   05   04
Sum of two matrices is :
   09   11   15
   06   11   06
   12   14   07
Press any key to continue . . .
```

Fig. 7.52 Finding the sum of two matrixes.

Example Write a program to create two matrixes 3×3 and find the product of two matrixes. For example, if the two matrices are :

Matrix - M

$$\begin{bmatrix} M_{11} & M_{12} & M_{13} \\ M_{21} & M_{22} & M_{23} \\ M_{31} & M_{32} & M_{33} \end{bmatrix}$$

Matrix - N

$$\begin{bmatrix} N_{11} & N_{12} & N_{13} \\ N_{21} & N_{22} & N_{23} \\ N_{31} & N_{32} & N_{33} \end{bmatrix}$$

then the product will be :

Matrix - M×N

$$M \times N = \begin{bmatrix} M_{11}\times N_{11} + M_{12}\times N_{21} + M_{13}\times N_{31} & M_{11}\times N_{12} + M_{12}\times N_{22} + M_{13}\times N_{32} & M_{11}\times N_{13} + M_{12}\times N_{23} + M_{13}\times N_{33} \\ M_{21}\times N_{11} + M_{22}\times N_{21} + M_{23}\times N_{31} & M_{21}\times N_{12} + M_{22}\times N_{22} + M_{23}\times N_{32} & M_{21}\times N_{13} + M_{22}\times N_{23} + M_{23}\times N_{33} \\ M_{31}\times N_{11} + M_{32}\times N_{21} + M_{33}\times N_{31} & M_{31}\times N_{12} + M_{32}\times N_{22} + M_{33}\times N_{32} & M_{31}\times N_{13} + M_{32}\times N_{23} + M_{33}\times N_{33} \end{bmatrix}$$

So, as we want to multiply two matrices M and N, where the matrix M is of order $m \times n$ and the matrix N is of order $p \times q$, the product of matrix, say matrix $M \times N$, then will be of order map with entry $(M \times N)ij$, which appears in the *i*th row and *j*th column is given as :

(M×N)*ij* = the sum of the products of the entries in the *i*th row of matrix M with corresponding entries in the *j*th column of matrix N

$$= a_{i0}\times b_{0j} + a_{i1}\times b_{1j} + a_{i2}\times b_{2j} + \ldots + a_{i(n-1)}\times b_{(n-1)j} = \sum_{k=0}^{n-1} a_{ik}\times b_{kj}$$

..\CSharp_Book\Chap07\MatrixProd

```
using System;
using System.Collections.Generic;
using System.Text;

// Program to find the product of two matrices.
namespace MatrixProd
{
    class Program
    {
        static void Main()
        {
            int[,] mat1 = new int[3,3];
            int[,] mat2 = new int[3,3];
            int[,] mat3 = new int[3,3];
            int ROW, COL, i, j, k;

            // Input data into first matrix
            Console.WriteLine("Enter first matrix elements :");
            for (i = 0; i < 3; i++)
            {
                for (j = 0; j < 3; j++)
                    mat1[i, j] = int.Parse(Console.ReadLine());
            }

            // Input data into second matrix
            Console.WriteLine("Enter second matrix elements :");
            for (i = 0; i < 3; i++)
            {
                for (j = 0; j < 3; j++)
                    mat2[i, j] = int.Parse(Console.ReadLine());
            }

            // Initializing the third matrix
            for (i = 0; i < 3; i++)
            {
                for (j = 0; j < 3; j++)
                {
```

```
                mat3[i,j] = 0;
            }
        }

        // Doing product of two matrices
        for (i = 0; i < 3; i++)
        {
            for (j = 0; j < 3; j++)
            {
                for (k = 0; k < 3; k++)
                {
                    mat3[i,j] += mat1[i,k] * mat2[k,j];
                }
            }
        }

        Console.WriteLine("First matrix is :");
        for (i = 0; i < 3; i++)
        {
            for (j = 0; j < 3; j++)
                Console.Write("    {0:D2}", mat1[i, j]);
            Console.WriteLine();
        }

        Console.WriteLine("Second matrix is :");
        for (i = 0; i < 3; i++)
        {
            for (j = 0; j < 3; j++)
                Console.Write("    {0:D2}", mat2[i, j]);
            Console.WriteLine();
        }

        Console.WriteLine("Product of the matrix is :");
        for (i = 0; i < 3; i++)
        {
            for (j = 0; j < 3; j++)
                Console.Write("    {0:D2}", mat3[i, j]);
            Console.WriteLine();
        }
    }
  }
}
```

When the above program executed, it will produce the following output as shown in Fig. 7.53.

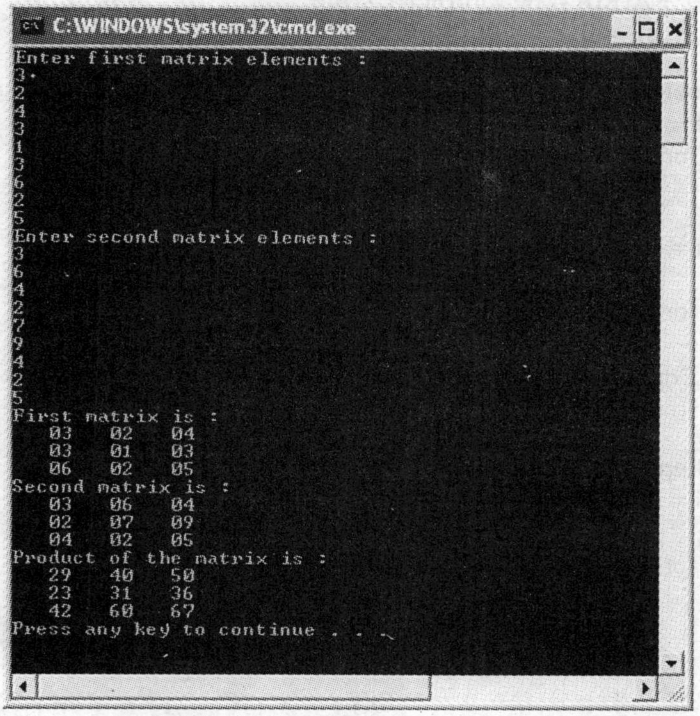

```
C:\WINDOWS\system32\cmd.exe
Enter first matrix elements :
3
2
4
3
1
3
6
2
5
Enter second matrix elements :
3
6
4
2
7
9
4
2
5
First matrix is :
   03   02   04
   03   01   03
   06   02   05
Second matrix is :
   03   06   04
   02   07   09
   04   02   05
Product of the matrix is :
   29   40   50
   23   31   36
   42   60   67
Press any key to continue . . .
```

Fig. 7.53 Finding the product of two matrixes

Example Write a program in C# to find and display the sum of both the diagonal elements of a two dimensional array MATRIX[4,4] containing integers.

..\CSharp_Book\Chap07\SumDiagonal

```
using System;
using System.Collections.Generic;
using System.Text;

// Program to find the sum of diagonals of a matrix
namespace SumDiagonal
{
    class Program
    {
        static void Main()
        {
            const int M = 4;
            const int N = 4;
```

```
int[,] MATRIX = new int[M,N];
int i, j, s1 = 0, s2 = 0;

Console.WriteLine("Enter the element in the array :");
for(i = 0; i < M; i++)
     for(j = 0; j < N; j++)
          MATRIX[i, j] = int.Parse(Console.ReadLine());

for(i = 0; i < M; i++)
{
     for(j = 0; j < N; j++)
          Console.Write("   {0:D2}", MATRIX[i, j]);
     Console.WriteLine();
}

// Steps to find the sum of left to right diagonal
for(i = 0; i < M; i++)
{
     for(j = 0; j < N; j++)
     {
          s1 = s1 + MATRIX[i,j];
          i++;
     }
}

// Steps to find the sum of right to left diagonal
Console.WriteLine("Matrix with diagonal sum is :");
for (i = 0; i <= M; i++)
{
     for (j = N - 1; j >= 0; j—)
     {
          s2 = s2 + MATRIX[i,j];
          i++;
     }
}
Console.WriteLine("————————————");
Console.WriteLine("{0:D}              {1:D}", s2, s1);
   }
  }
}
```

When the above program executed, it will produce the following output as shown in Fig. 7.54.

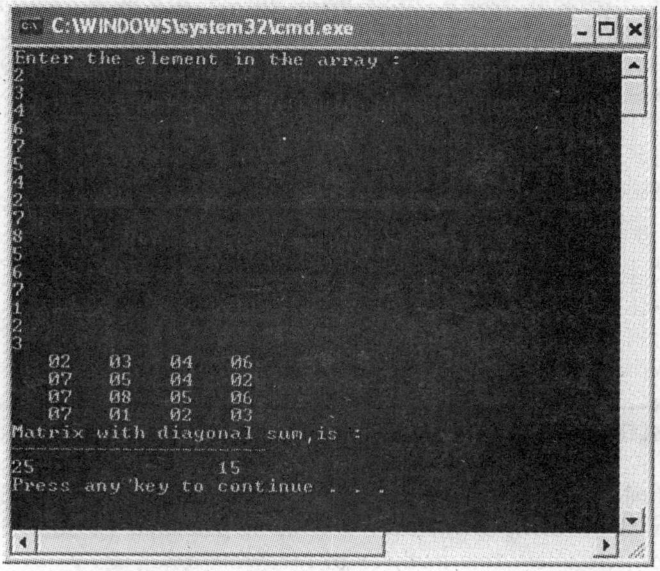

```
C:\WINDOWS\system32\cmd.exe
Enter the element in the array :
2
3
4
6
7
5
4
2
7
8
5
6
7
1
2
3
     02     03     04     06
     07     05     04     02
     07     08     05     06
     07     01     02     03
Matrix with diagonal sum,is :

25                 15
Press any key to continue . . .
```

Fig. 7.54 Finding the sum of diagonals of a matrix.

7.9 Jagged Arrays

A rectangular array is a two-dimensional array in which the length of each row is the same for the entire array. However, C# also allows you to create a special type of two-dimensional array called a jagged array. A jagged array is an array of arrays in which the length of each array can differ. Thus, a jagged array can be used to create a table in which the lengths of the rows are not the same.

Using jagged arrays, one can create multidimensional arrays with irregular dimensions. This flexibility derives from the fact that multidimensional arrays are implemented as arrays of arrays. The following piece of code demonstrates how one might declare an array made up of a group of 4 and a group of 6 elements:

```
int[][] jag = new int[2][];
jag[0] = new int [4];
jag[1] = new int [6];
```

The code reveals that each of **jag[0]** and **jag[1]** holds a reference to a single-dimensional int array. To illustrate how one accesses the integer elements: the term **jag[0][1]** provides access to the second element of the first group.

To initialize a jagged array whilst assigning values to its elements, one can use code like the following:

```
int[][] jag = new int[][] {new int[] {1, 2, 3, 4}, new int[] {5, 6, 7, 8, 9, 10}};
```

Be careful using methods like **GetLowerBound**, **GetUpperBound**, **GetLength**, etc. with jagged arrays. Since jagged arrays are constructed out of single-dimensional arrays, they shouldn't be treated as having multiple dimensions in the same way that rectangular arrays do.

To loop through all the elements of a jagged array one can use code like the following :

```
for (int i = 0; i < jag.GetLength(0); i++)
    for (int j = 0; j < jag[i].GetLength(0); j++)
        Console.WriteLine(jag[i][j]);
```

Or

```
for (int i = 0; i < jag.Length; i++)
    for (int j = 0; j < jag[i].Length; j++)
        Console.WriteLine(jag[i][j]);
```

7.10 Using System.Array Class

Every .NET array you create is automatically derived from **System.Array**. This class defines a number of helpful methods that make working with arrays much more palatable. Listing 7.1 gives a rundown of some (but not all) of the more interesting methods of Array class.

Listing 7.1 Select Methods of System.Array

Method	Meaning of Method
BinarySearch()	This static method searches a (previously sorted) array for a given item. This method receives the sorted array in which to search and the key for which to search. The method returns the index in the array at which it finds the key (but a negative number if the key was not found).
Clear()	This static method sets a range of elements in the array to empty value (0 for value types; null for reference types).
CopyTo()	This method is used to copy elements from the source array into the destination array.
Length	This read-only property is used to determine the number of elements in an array.
Rank	This property returns the number of dimensions of the current array.
Reverse()	This static method returns the number of contents of a one-dimensional array.
Sort()	This method sorts a one-dimensional array of intrinsic types. When this method returns, the array contains its original elements sorted in ascending order.

The following code makes use of the static **Reverse()** and **Clear()** method (and the Length property) to pump out some information about an array of string name Names to the console.

..\CSharp_Book\Chap07\StudName

```
using System;
using System.Collections.Generic;
using System.Text;
namespace StudName
{
    class Program
    {
        static void Main()
        {
            // Array of strings.
            string[] Names = { "Sumit", "Rakesh", "Amar", "Karthik", "Prakash" };
            //Print name as declared
            Console.WriteLine("Here is the array");

            // Use of Length property
            for (int i = 0; i < Names.Length; i++)
                Console.WriteLine("Name : {0}\t", Names[i]);
            Console.WriteLine("\n");

            //Reverse array and print
            Array.Reverse(Names);
            Console.WriteLine("Here is the array once reversed:");
            for (int i = 0; i < Names.Length; i++)
                Console.WriteLine("Name : {0}\t", Names[i]);
            Console.WriteLine("\n");

            //Clear out all
            Console.WriteLine("Clear out some elements...");
            Array.Clear(Names, 1, 3); // Clear elements for 1 to 3 position
            for (int i = 0; i < Names.Length; i++)
                Console.WriteLine("Name : {0}\t", Names[i]);
            Console.ReadLine();
        }
    }
}
```

When the above program executed, it will produce the following output as shown in Fig. 7.55.

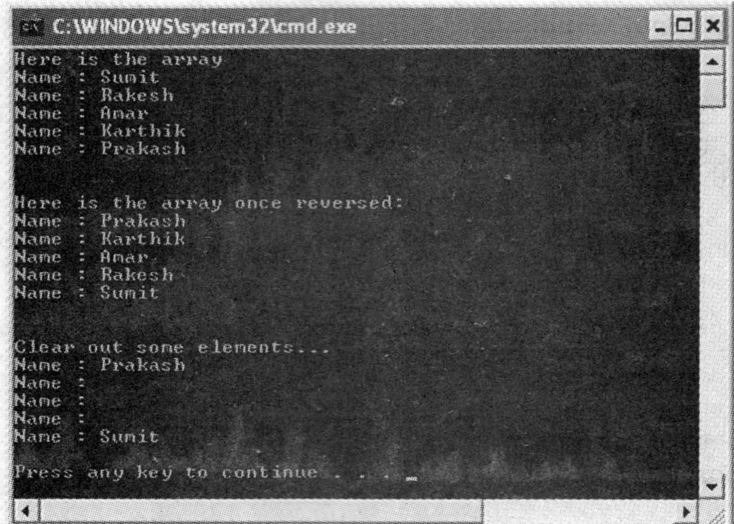

Fig. 7.55 Use of System.Array methods.

7.11 Using ArrayList Class

In most programming languages, conventional arrays have a fixed size – they cannot be changed dynamically to conform to an application's execution-time memory requirement. In C#, the **ArrayList** class supports dynamic arrays, which can grow or shrink as needed. An **ArrayList** is a variable-length array of object references that can dynamically increase or decrease in size.

An **ArrayList** is created with an initial size. When this size is exceeded, the collection is automatically enlarged. When objects are removed the array can be shrunk. **ArrayList** defines several methods of its own. Listing 7.2 gives some of the methods of **ArrayList** class.

Listing 7.1 Methods of ArrayList class.

Method	Meaning of Method
Add()	Add an object to the ArrayList. Returns an int specifying the index in which the object was added.
Capacity()	Gets of sets the number of elements in the list.
Clear()	Removes all the elements fro the ArrayList.
CopyTo()	Copy one list to another ArrayList.
Contains()	Returns true of an ArrayList has a specified element.
Count()	Gets total number of elements in ArrayList.
IndexOf()	Returns the index of the first occurrence of the specified object in the ArrayList.

Insert()	Insert a value at a specific index position.
Remove()	Remove the first occurrence of an item having the specified value.
RemoveAt()	Delete the value at a specific index.
RemoveRange()	Removes a specified number of elements starting at a specified index in the ArrayList.
Sort()	Sorts the ArrayList.

The following program demonstrates some of **ArrayList** methods.

..\CSharp_Book\Chap07\NameArray

```
using System;
using System.Collections;
using System.Text;

namespace NameArray
{
    class Program
    {
        static void Main()
        {
            // Declaing an ArrayList
            ArrayList Names = new ArrayList();
            string search;
            Console.WriteLine("Current number of elements in ArrayList Names : "
                    + Names.Count);

            Console.WriteLine("Adding Elements to ArrayList");
            Names.Add("Sumit");
            Names.Add("Rakesh");
            Names.Add("Amar");
            Names.Add("Karthik");
            Names.Add("Prakash");
            Console.WriteLine("Current number of elements in ArrayList Names : "
                    + Names.Count);

            // Displaying the names of ArrayList
            Console.WriteLine("Names are ...\n");
            for (int i = 0; i < Names.Count; i++)
                Console.WriteLine("{0}\t", Names[i]);

            Console.WriteLine("Removing 2 names from list:");
            // Remove elements from the array list.
```

```
            Names.Remove("Rakesh");
            Names.Remove("Karthik");
            Console.WriteLine("Current number of elements in ArrayList Names : "
                    + Names.Count);
            // Displaying the names of ArrayList
            Console.WriteLine("Presently names are ...\n");
            for (int i = 0; i < Names.Count; i++)
                Console.WriteLine("{0}\t", Names[i]);

            // Adding 4 more names into ArrayList
            Names.Add("Harish");
            Names.Add("Ekta");
            Names.Add("Payal");
            Names.Add("Vivek");
            Console.WriteLine("The current capacity of ArrayList Names : "
                    + Names.Capacity);
            Console.WriteLine("Current number of elements in ArrayList Names : "
                    + Names.Count);
            Console.WriteLine("Presently names are ...\n");
            for (int i = 0; i < Names.Count; i++)
                Console.WriteLine("{0}\t", Names[i]);

            // Sorting the names in ArrayList
            Names.Sort();
            Console.WriteLine("Sorted names are ...\n");
            for (int i = 0; i < Names.Count; i++)
                Console.WriteLine("{0}\t", Names[i]);

            Console.WriteLine("Searching a name using binary search method\n");
            Console.Write("Enter the name : ");
            search = Console.ReadLine(); //Enter name for binary search
            Console.WriteLine("Index of Ekta is : " + Names.BinarySearch(search));
            Console.ReadLine();
        }
    }
}
```

When the above program executed, it will produce the following output as shown in Fig. 7.56.

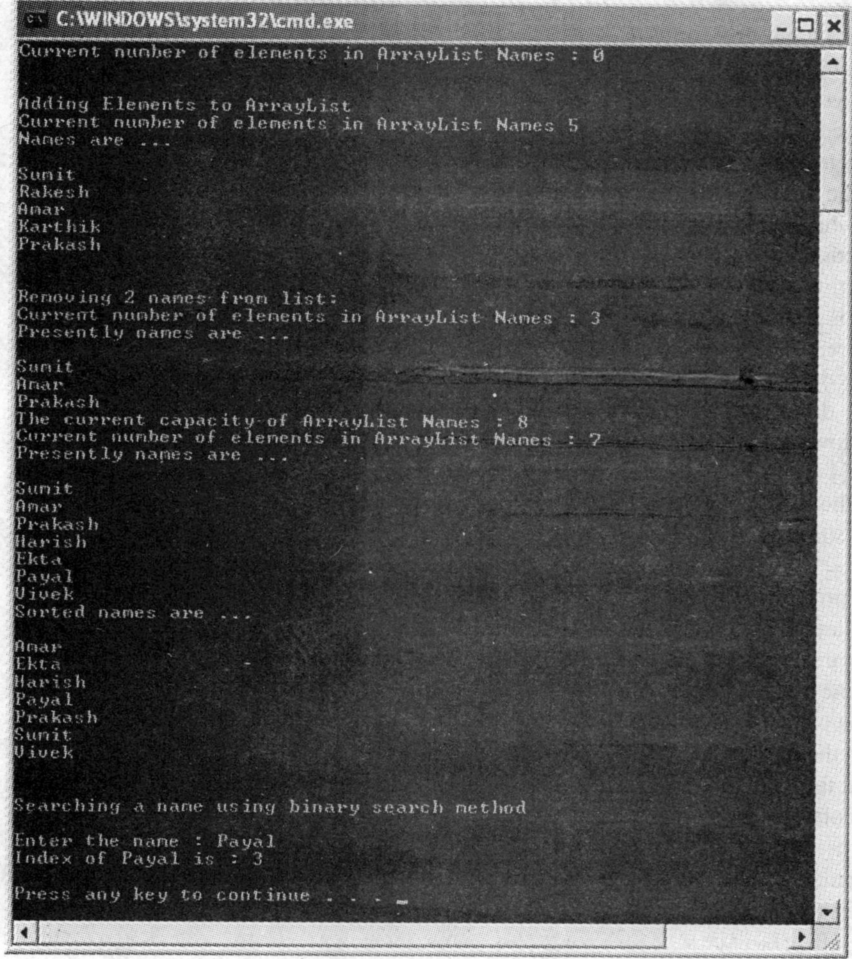

Fig. 7.56 Use of ArrayList class methods.

Exercise

1. Define an array how it is different from other variables ?
2. What are the different types of arrays ?
3. What do you mean by subscript in an array ?
4. What are the benefits of using arrays ?
5. What do you mean by rank of an array ?
6. How will you declare an array ?
7. How multidimensional arrays are implemented in C# ?
8. What is variable size array ?
9. What is the difference between Array and ArrayList.

10. How arrays are useful for us ?
11. What is jagged array ?
12. How will you implement a jagged array ?
13. How jagged array is useful for us ?
14. What is System.Array class ?
15. What is the difference between one dimensional array and two dimensional array ?
16. Explain what happens when multiple values occur in the list to be sorted using:
    (a) selection sort.
    (b) insertion sort.
17. An array is a collection of
    (a) different data type
    (b) same data type
    (c) same data type placed next to each other in memory
18. Is the following declaration correct ? If not why ?
    float[] sum[20];
19. What is the difference between these two statements ?
    (a) int[] sum = new int[10];
    (b) m[1] = 10;
20. Give the proper array declaration for the following :
    (a) Declare an integer array which can hold 25 values.
    (b) Declare a one dimensional array of four character called letters.
    (c) Define a two dimensional array called max 3 * 4 of integer.
21. Write one or more statements to carry out each of the following operations :
    (a) Sum the first 100 elements of the numeric list T.
    (b) Print the even elements of the numeric list T for values of the subscript ranging from 0 to 100.
    (c) Calculate the sum of all elements of the numeric table P. Let M represent the number of rows and N represent the number of columns.
    (d) Calculate the elements of the numeric table H which has 8 rows and 12 columns. Each element of H is determined by the formula :
        Hij = 1+i *j;
    (e) Print the value of each subscript and each corresponding element for those elements whose value does not exceed 15.
    (f) Print the elements of the fourth column of the array A[5][9].
22. Write the statements for the following :
    (a) Assign the value 9 to the second element of the array A[7].
    (b) Assign the value 7 to the element stored at location 5 row and 3 column of A[6][5].
23. Write the value of individual array element :
    (a) int c[8] = { 2,7,9,6,1,4,3,8}
    (b) int p[2][4] = { 1,1,3,3,5,5,7,7}
24. Give the contents of the array A[4][2], if the entered data is 12, 17, 6, 11, 20, 19, 21, 3.
25. How is an array of objects created ?
26. How are multidimensional array implemented in C#?
27. Which element is num[9] of the array num ?
28. Trace the steps when sorting the following list: 23, 48, 49, 69, 12, 85, 20, 37, 51, 69, 23 using:
    (a) selection sort.

(b) insertion sort.

29. Trace the steps when sorting the following list: 11, 22, 33, 44, 55, 66, 77, 88, 99 using:
    (a) selection sort.
    (b) insertion sort.
30. Compare the different executions of each sort with the lists in Exercise 28 and Exercise 29. How many comparisons are made in each ?
31. What optimization can be performed during a linear search if the data is sorted ?
32. What would happen if the list used in a binary search was not sorted ?
33. Why are three assignment statements necessary to exchange two values, as seen in the selection sort ? What is the role of the Temp or T variable in the selection sort example?
34. Sort the following list of numbers usin selection sort shoing the list at intermediate stages:
    9 5 4 2 1 6
35. Repeat Exercise 34 using the insertion sort.
36. Explain why a binary search algorithm is efficient. What assumption is being made?
37. What will be the output of the following program segment ?

(a)
```
static void Main()
{
    int[] a = {6, 5, 4, 3, 2, 1};
    int i;
    for ( i = 5; i>=0; i—)
    {
        Console.WriteLine(a[i]);
    }
}
```

(b)
```
static void Main()
{
    int[] a = new int[5];
    int i;
    for ( i = 0; i < 5; i++)
        a[i] = 5 * i;
    for ( i= 0; i < 5; i++)
        Console.WriteLine(a[i]);
}
```

(c)
```
static void Main()
{
    int a, b = 0;
    int[] c = { 1, 2, 3, 4, 5, 6, 7, 8, 9, 0};
    for(a = 0; a< 10; ++a)
        if (( a % 2) == 0) b += c[a];
            Console.WriteLine(b);
}
```

Programming

1. Write a program to perform the following tasks :
   - Read an array of 10 integers.
   - Multiply each element of array by 5.
   - Display the new array.
2. Write a program to print the array in reverse order.
3. Write a program to find the product of two matrices.
4. Write a program to find the sum of row and column of a matrix.
5. Write a program to delete an element in an integer array.
6. Write a program to print all the prime numbers in a 4×4 matrix and if there is no prime number, then print a message.
7. Write a program to print the upper and lower diagonal values of a 3×3 matrix.
8. Write a program to read and then to check the equality of two matrix.
9. Write an interactive C++ program to accept an integer and convert it into an equivalent hexadecimal number.
10. Write a program to find the sum of array elements.
11. Write a program to find the transpose of a matrix.
12. Write a program to calculate the function :

$$f = 2x^2 + 3x + 4 \quad , x < 2$$
$$= 0 \quad , x = 2$$
$$= -(2x^2 + 3x + 4) \quad , x > 2$$

13. Write an interactive C# program to accept an integer and reverse the integer. Display both the numbers on your screen.
14. Write a program to accept a date (dd/mm/yyyy) and check for the validity of the date.
15. Write a program to find second maximum element of a matrix.
16. Write a program in C# to print first 10 multiples of an integer N, where N is to be entered by user.
17. Write a program to accept the total sales of three products by three salesman in a double dimensional array. Calculate the total sales of each salesman and total sales of each product.
18. Write an interactive of C# program to accept an integer and convert it into an equivalent binary.
19. Write a function to find the sum of odd numbers in a matrix.
20. Write a program to arrange any 10-element using exchange sort method.
21. Write a program to initialize an array of 5 names and initialize another array with their respective telephone numbers. Search for a name input by the user, in the list. If found, display "Search Successful" and print the name along with the telephone number, otherwise display "Search unsuccessful. Name not enlisted".
22. Modify the algorithm for the selection sort and the insertion sort to count the:
    (a) number of comparisons.
    (b) number of exchanges.
    (c) number of times each loop is executed.
23. Each of the sorting algorithms presented in this chapter arranges lists of numbers in ascending order. Rewrite the sort algorithms to arrange a list in descending order.
24. Modify the linear search method to optimize the search if you assume the list is softed. In other words, do not examine any more values that you need to in order to assert that the target value is not present.

String Handling 8

8.1 Introduction

In the previous chapter we discuss one-dimensional and two-dimensional arrays. Each of the arrays illustrated so far contained numeric elements. We can also have array of character. Using array of characters, we can store string data. But do remember that as such strings are not directly supported, through sometimes loosely we refer to array of characters as strings. Array of characters or the programming languages to manipulate text such as words and sentences use strings. As with other data types, strings can be constants or variables.

8.2 Strings

A string constant is a sequence of characters enclosed by double quotes. The following are examples of some string constants :

```
"Programming in C#"
"Hari\'s friend is Ram"
```

Notice that the embedded spaces are significant. And if quotes, single (') or double ("), are part of the string, they must be used with the escape sequence.

The way a group of integers can be stored in an integer array, similarly a group of characters can be stored in a character array. Character arrays are many a times also called as 'strings'. Character arrays or strings are the data types used by programming languages to manipulate text such as words and sentences.

Definition

Group of characters or words is called as a string.

8.3 String as Array

In C#, a string is an array of characters with the following exceptional features :

- An extra component is appended to the end of the array and its value is set to the **NULL** character [\0]. This means that the total number of characters in the array is always 1 more than the string length.
- The string may be initialized with a string literal as follows :

```
char[] str = "Sharma";
```

Note that this array has 7 elements: 'S', 'h', 'a', 'r', 'm', 'a', and '\0'.

str - A character array name

Fig. 8.1 A character array declaration with null position.

- The entire string may be sent as an output as a single object as follows :

```
Console.WriteLine(str);
```

The system would copy characters from string to System.out.println until the **NULL** character '\0' is encountered.

- The entire string may be input as a single object as follows :

```
str =  Console.ReadLine();
```

The system would copy characters from **ReadLine()** into space until a white space character is encountered. The user must ensure that space is defined to be a character string that must be long enough to hold the input.

We might wonder how more than one variable could have the same name; that seems to violate the rules of variables. If two variables have the same name, how would Java know which we you want when we use the name? Array variables are distinguished from each other by a subscript.

Suppose we want to store our name in a character array called name. We can use either of the following definitions:

```
char[] name = "Mr. Rabin Singh";
char[] name =  new char[16] {"Mr. Rabin Singh"};
```

Because Java knows to reserve an extra element for the null zero at the end of every string, we do not have to specify the 16 as long as we initialize the array with a value. You know that the variable name is an array because brackets follow its name. The array has a single name called name, which contains

16 elements. The array is stored in memory (refer Fig. 8.2). Each element is a character. We can manipulate individual elements in the array by using their subscripts:

For instance, the following System.out.println function prints name array :

```
Console.WriteLine((name);
```

When the **NULL** character is sent to **Console.WriteLine()**, nothing is printed-not even a blank. This is evident by printing one apostrophe immediately before the character and another apostrophe immediately after the characters.

Of course, you can have arrays of strings, just like you can have arrays of any other type of object. For example,

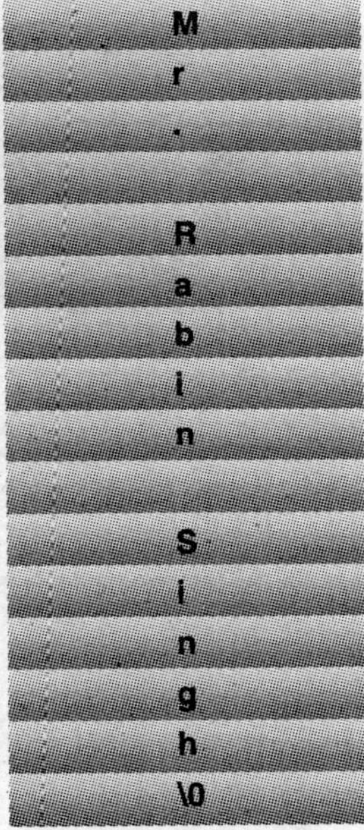

Fig. 8.2 Storing a character array in memory.

Example Write a program to demonstrate string array.

D:\Olevel02\CSharp_Book\Chap08\CharClass

```
using System;
using System.Collections.Generic;
using System.Text;

namespace CharString
{
    class Program
    {
```

```
        static void Main(string[] args)
        {
            string[] str = {"one apple", "two bananas", "three oranges", "four guavas"};

            for (int i = 0; i < str.Length; i++)
                Console.WriteLine ("str[" + i + "] : " + str[i]);
        }
    }
}
```

When the above program executed, it will produce the following output as shown in Fig. 8.3.

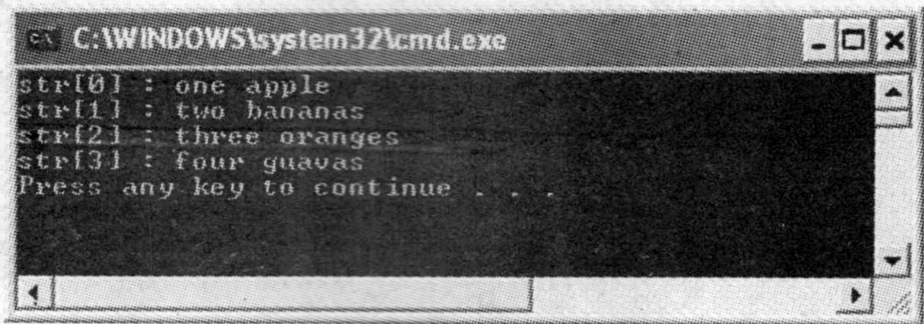

Fig. 8.3 String array.

8.4 String Variables

A string variable is actually an array of characters. String variables are declared as shown in the following statement :

```
string str; // Declaring a string object
```

Here,

- **str** is a string variable.
- its type is character.

A string constants is a sequence of characters enclosed by double quotes. In C#, a string is an array of characters with the following exceptional features :

- The entire string may be input as a single object, like this :

```
str = Console.ReadLine();
```

8.4.1 Initializing Elements at Declaration Time

You already know how to initialize character arrays that hold strings when you define the arrays. You simply assign the array a string. For example,

```
string str = "Sharma"; // Declaring and assigning a value to a string variable
```

If you also want to initialize state with a value, you can use the following code :

```
string[] state = "Delhi";    // Reserve space and initialize state as first string
```

Example This little demo program handles strings.

..\CSharp_Book\Chap08\strState

```
using System;
using System.Collections.Generic;
using System.Text;

// Demonstrating Stings
namespace strState
{
    class Program
    {
        static void Main()
        {
            // Array of strings assigns 5 strings.
            string[] Names = { "Delhi", "Mumbai", "Kolkata", "Chennai", "Bangalore" };

            Console.WriteLine("Metros are ....");
            Console.WriteLine("\n");
            for (int i = 0; i < Names.Length; i++)
                Console.WriteLine("{0}\t", Names[i]);
            Console.WriteLine("\n");
        }
    }
}
```

When the above program executed, it will produce the following output as shown in Fig. 8.4.

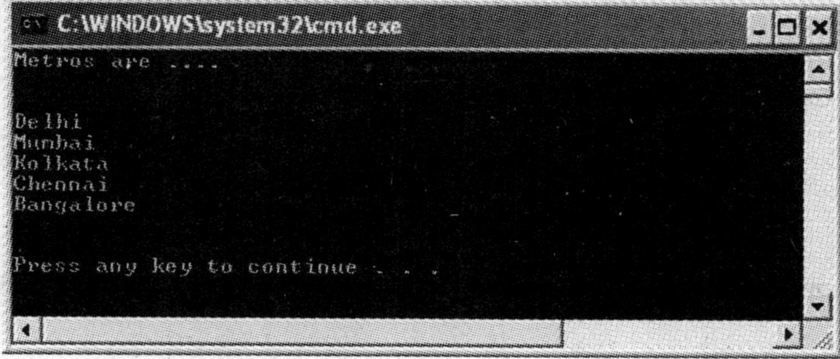

Fig. 8.4 Array of string.

8.4.2 Input/Output of String Data

The input/output of string data can be performed using **ReadLine()** and **WriteLine()** methods as illustrated in the following program :

Example Write a program to enter cities and print them.

..\CSharp_Book\Chap08\strInOut

```
using System;
using System.Collections.Generic;
using System.Text;

// Demonstrating input/output of string data
// Input data will be terminated by Enter key.
namespace strInOut
{
    class Program
    {
        static void Main()
        {
            string[] Cities = new string[15];
            int n;

            Console.Write("How many Metro city names to enter ? ");
            n = int.Parse(Console.ReadLine());

            Console.WriteLine("\n");
            Console.WriteLine("Enter the metro city names...");

            for (int i = 0; i < n; i++)
                Cities[i] = Console.ReadLine();
            Console.WriteLine("\n");
            Console.WriteLine("The Cities are :");
            for (int i = 0; i < n; i++)
                Console.WriteLine("{0}\t", Cities[i]);
        }
    }
}
```

When the above program executed, it will produce the following output as shown in Fig. 8.5.

```
C:\WINDOWS\system32\cmd.exe
How many Metro city names to enter ? 5


Enter the metro city names...
Delhi
Mumbai
Kolkata
Chennai
Bangalore


The Cities are :
Delhi
Mumbai
Kolkata
Chennai
Bangalore
Press any key to continue . . .
```

Fig. 8.5 Array of string.

8.5 Using System.String Class

A string is a series of characters treated as a single unit. These characters can be uppercase letters, lowercase letters, digits and various special chracters such as +, -, *, /, $ and others. A string is an object of class String in the System namespace. The String class contains several methods that operate on string. The following Listing 1.1 shows some of usable listings in C#.

Listing 1.1 C# String class methods.

Method	Description
Compare()	Simply compares to strings.
CompareTo()	This method compares two string. It returns 0 if the strings are equal, a negative number of the string that invokes CompareTo is less than the string passed as an argument, a positive number if the string that invokes CompareTo is greater than the string passed as an argument.
Concat()	This is a static method which concatenates two strings and returns a new string contains the characters from both the original strings.
Contains()	This method is used to determine if the current string object contains a specified string.
Copy()	Creates a new string by copying into another string.
CopyTo()	Copies a specified number of characters from a string into a char array.
EndsWith()	Determines whether a substring exists at the end of the string.
Equals()	Determines if two strings are equal or not.

Format()	This static method is used to format a string literal using other primitives (i.e., numerical data and other strings) and the {0} notation.
IndexOf()	This method located the first occurrence of a character or a substring in a string.
Insert()	This method is used to receive a copy of the current string that contains newly inserted string data.
Join()	Joins an array of strings together.
Length	It will return the length of a string.
LastIndexOf()	This method locates the last occurrence of a character or a substring in a string.
PadLeft()	This method returns copies of the current string that has been padded with specific data from left.
PadRight()	This method returns copies of the current string that has been padded with specific data from right.
Remove()	Removes characters from a string.
Replace()	Replaces all the occurrence of a character with a new character in a string.
Split()	Creates an array of strings by splitting the string.
StartsWith()	Determines whether a substring exists at the beginning of the string.
Substring()	This method returns a string that represents a substring of the current string.
ToCharArray()	This method returns a character array representing the current string.
ToLower()	This method creates a copy of a given string in lowercase.
ToUpper()	This method creates a copy of a given string in uppercase.
Trim()	This method removes white space from the string.
TrimEnd()	This method removes white space from the end of the string.
Start()	This method removes white space from the beginning of the string.

Here are some string methods that test the string operations :

Example Write a program to create a duplicate copy of your name and print it using **CopyTo()** method.

..\CSharp_Book\Chap08\strCopy

```
using System;
using System.Collections.Generic;
using System.Text;

// Demonstrating Sting method CopyTo()
namespace strCopy
```

```
{
    class Program
    {
        static void Main()
        {
            String str1;
            char[] str2;
            str2 = new char[30];

            Console.Write("What is your name ? ");
            str1 = Console.ReadLine();
            Console.WriteLine("The length of your name is : " + str1.Length);

            str1.CopyTo(0, str2, 0, str1.Length);
            Console.Write("Copied string is : ");
            for (int i = 0; i < str2.Length; i++)
                Console.Write(str2[i]);
            Console.WriteLine("\n");
        }
    }
}
```

When the above program executed, it will produce the following output as shown in Fig. 8.6.

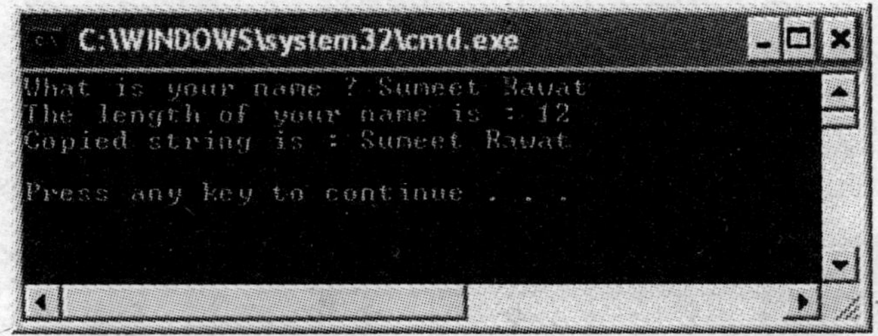

Fig. 8.6 Using String class method, copying string into an array.

When you wish to concatenate existing strings into a new string that is the sum of all its parts, C# provides the + operator as well as the static **String.Concat()** method. The following program illustrates a **Concat()** method.

Example Write a program to enter your first and last name and make a single string as name which will print your complete name.

..\CSharp_Book\Chap08\strCat

```
using System;
using System.Collections.Generic;
```

```
using System.Text;

// Demonstrating Sting method Concat()
namespace strCopy
{
    class Program
    {
        static void Main()
        {
            String str1, str2, str3;

            Console.Write("What is your first name ? ");
            str1 = Console.ReadLine();

            Console.Write("What is your last name ? ");
            str2 = Console.ReadLine();

            // Concatenating names
            str3 = String.Concat(str1, " ");  // Concatenate first name with space
            str3 = String.Concat(str3, str2); // Concatenate last name with str3

            Console.WriteLine("Full Name is : " + str3);
            Console.ReadLine();
        }
    }
}
```

When the above program executed, it will produce the following output as shown in Fig. 8.7.

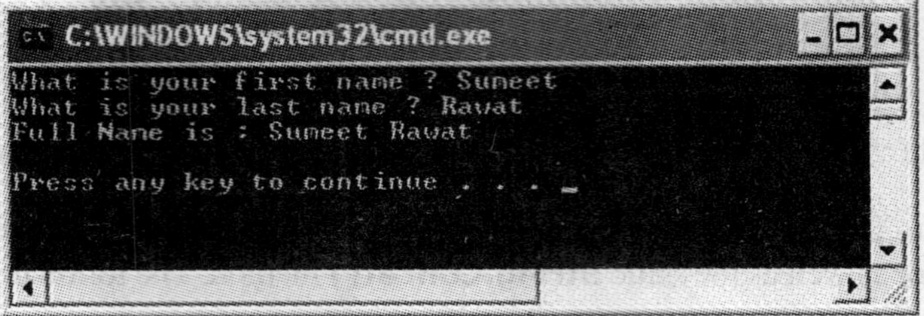

Fig. 8.7 Concatenating two strings.

8.5.1 Comparing Strings

CompareTo() method compares the string s1 with s2 on an alphabetic, element-by-element basis. If s1 alphabetizes before s2, **CompareTo()** returns a negative value. If s1 and s2 are exactly same, **CompareTo()** returns a 0. If s1 alphabetizes after s2, **CompareTo()** returns a positive value. The following example gives usage of **CompareTo()** method.

Example Write a program to compare two strings.

..\CSharp_Book\Chap08\strCompare

```
using System;
using System.Collections.Generic;
using System.Text;

// Demonstrating Sting method CompareTo()
namespace strCompare
{
    class Program
    {
        static void Main()
        {
            String str1, str2, str3;
            int opt = 0;

            Console.Write("What is your first string ? ");
            str1 = Console.ReadLine();
            Console.Write("What is your second string ? ");
            str2 = Console.ReadLine();

            // Comparing strings
            opt = str1.CompareTo(str2);
            if (opt == 0)
                Console.Write("String are exactly equal");
            else
                if (opt < 0)
                    Console.Write("String " + str1 + " less than " + str2);
                else
                    if (opt > 0)
                        Console.Write("String " + str1 + " more than " + str2);
            Console.ReadLine();
        }
    }
}
```

When the above program executed, it will produce the following output as shown in Fig. 8.8.

Fig. 8.6 Comparing two strings.

8.5.2 Basic String Operations

As we saw different string methods in previous section, here we concern about some of usable string methods like **Contains(), Replace(), Insert(), ToUpper(), ToLower(), IndexOf(), LastIndexOf()**, etc.

D:\Olevel02\CSharp_Book\Chap08\OtherStr

```
using System;
using System.Collections.Generic;
using System.Text;
// Other string methods

namespace OtherStr
{
    class Program
    {
        static void Main()
        {
            String str1 = "C# .NET Programming for beginners and programmers.";

            Console.WriteLine(" - - > str1 contains 'ing'? {0}", str1.Contains("ing"));
            Console.WriteLine(" - - > str1 contains 'pro'? {0}", str1.Contains(“pro”));
            Console.WriteLine(str1.Replace('.', '!'));
            Console.WriteLine(str1.Insert(0, "Welcome to"));
            Console.WriteLine("Uppercase string is : {0}", str1.ToUpper());
            Console.WriteLine("Lowercase string is : {0}", str1.ToLower());
            Console.WriteLine("Index of first occurrence of Pro: {0}", str1.IndexOf("Pro"));
            Console.WriteLine("Index of last occurrence of Pro: {0}",
                    str1.LastIndexOf("pro"));
            Console.ReadLine();
        }
    }
}
```

When the above program executed, it will produce the following output as shown in Fig. 8.9.

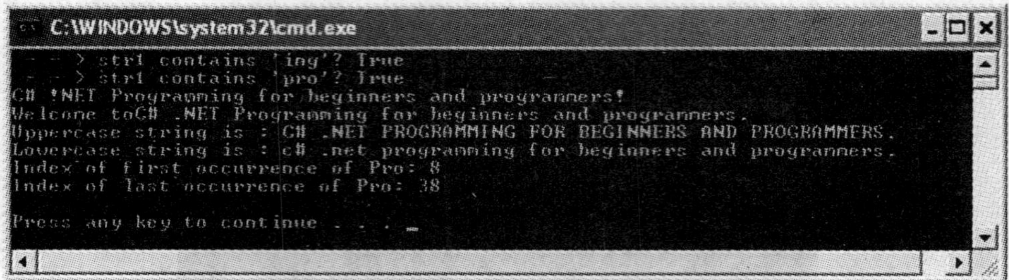

Fig. 8.9 Demonstrating other string methods.

Example Write a program to input any given string to calculate the total number of characters and vowels present in the string and also reverse the string :

Example : INPUT

Enter string	:	SNOWY
OUTPUT :		
Total number of characters		: 05
Number of Vowels		: 01
Reverse string		: YWONS

D:\Olevel02\CSharp_Book\Chap08\CountVowel

```
using System;
using System.Collections.Generic;
using System.Text;
// Calculating total number of characters and vowels present in the string
// and also reverse the string.

namespace CountVowel
{
    class Program
    {
        static void Main()
        {
            char[] str1;
            str1 = new char[50];
            Console.Write("Enter any string : ");
            String str = Console.ReadLine();

            String strn;

            // Calculate Total no. of characters
            int l = str.Length;
            // Copy the string into a char array
            str.CopyTo(0, str1, 0, str.Length);
            int c = 0;
            char ch;

            for (int i = 0; i <= l - 1; i++)
            {
                // Extracting character at each index
                ch = str1[i];
                switch (ch)
                {
                    case 'A':
                    case 'a':
```

```
                    case 'E':
                    case 'e':
                    case 'I':
                    case 'i':
                    case 'O':
                    case 'o':
                    case 'U':
                    case 'u': c = c + 1;
                        break;
                }
            }

            Console.WriteLine("Total number of characters : " + l);
            Console.WriteLine("Number of vowels : " + c);
            Console.Write("Reverse string : ");

            char ch1;
            // Extracting characters in reverse order
            for (int j = l - 1; j>=0; j—)
            {
                ch1 = str1[j];
                Console.Write(ch1);
            }
            Console.ReadLine();
            Console.WriteLine();
        }
    }
}
```

When the above program executed, it will produce the following output as shown in Fig. 8.10.

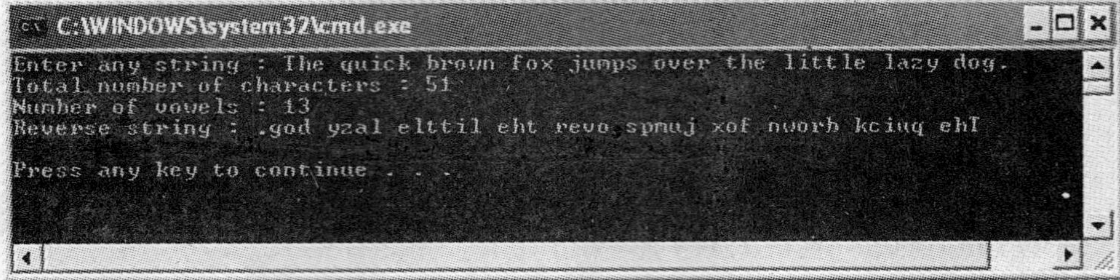

Fig. 8.10 Counting vowels in a string.

8.6 Using Format() Method

The **String.Format** method is the primary means of formatting date and numeric data for display. It accepts a string composed of text and embedded format items followed by one or more data arguments.

Each format item references a data argument and specifies how it is to be formatted. The CLR creates the output string by converting each data value to a string (using **ToString**), formatting it according to its corresponding format item, and then replacing the formatting item with the formatted data value. For example,

```
String str1 = String.Format("The square root of {0} is {1}.", 100, 10);
Console.WriteLine(str1);
```

When the above two linesexecuted, it will produce the following output

```
The square root of 100 is 10.
```

The above example contains three parameters. So, according to the example, the syntax of **Format()** method is :

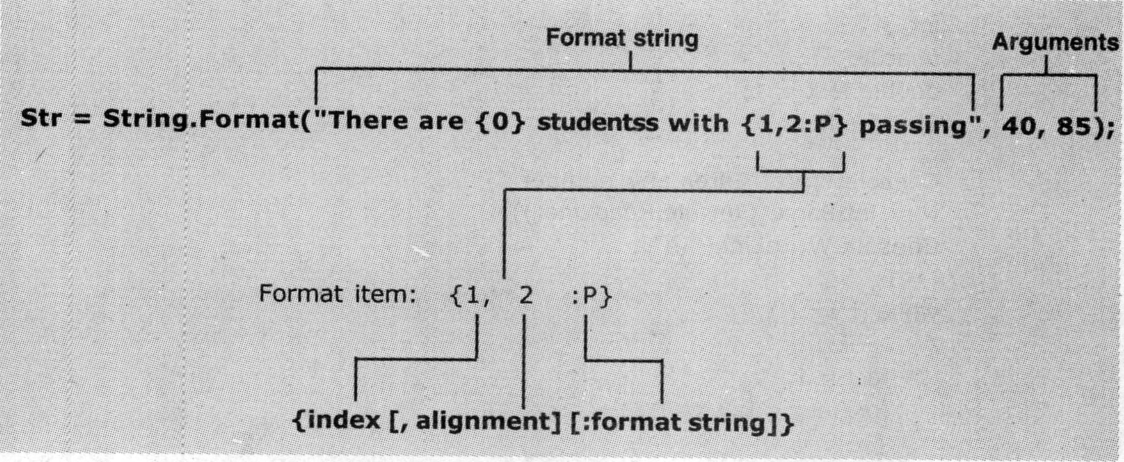

Fig. 8.11 String.Format example with its parameters.

From Fig. 8.11, each format item consists of three things :

- an **index.** It is a zero-based integer that indicates the argument to which is to be applied. The index can be repeated to refer to the same argument more than once.
- an **optional alignment.** It is an integer that indicates the minimum width of the area that contains the formatted value. If the alignment value is positive, the argument value is right justified, if the value is negative, it is left justified.
- and **format string.** It contains the formattingg codes to be applied to the argument value. If it is not speciied, the output of the argument's **ToString** method is used. .NET provides several standard formatting codes to be used with numbers and dates as well as codes that are used to create custom formatting strings.

Let consider the following program Factorial program for formatting:

..\CSharp_Book\Chap08\FormatFact

```
using System;
using System.Collections.Generic;
using System.Text;

// Demonstration the Format() method in Factorial program
namespace FormatFact
{
    class Program
    {
        static int Main()
        {
            int i;
            float N;
            double fact = 1;
            String str;

            Console.Write("Enter any number ");
            N = int.Parse(Console.ReadLine());
            Console.WriteLine("\n");
            i = 1;
            while (i <= N)
            {
                fact = 1;
                for (int j = 1; j <= i; j++)
                {
                    fact = fact * j;
                }
                str = String.Format("Factorial of: {0,3:D} is: {1,8:D}", i,
                        fact.ToString("########"));
                Console.WriteLine(str);
                i++;
            }
            return 0;
        }
    }
}
```

When the above program executed, it will produce the following output as shown in Fig. 8.12.

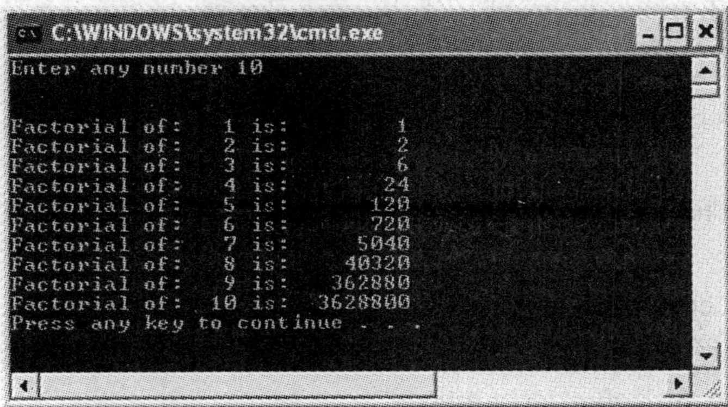

Fig. 8.12 Formatting using Format method.

From above program, the **Format()** contains two format specifiers, one for i and one for fact. Notice that the argument numbers are speciried just as they are when using **WriteLine()**. Also, notice that regular text, such as **"Factorial of:"** is included. This text is passed through and becomes part of the output string.

8.7 Using System.StringBuilder Class

The primary drawback of strings is that memory must be allocated each time the contents of a string variable are changed. Suppose we create a loop that iterates 100 tmes and concatenates one character to a string during each iteration. We could end up with a hundred strings in memory, each differing from its preceding one by a single character.

The **StringBuilder** class addreesses this problem by allocating a work area (buffer) where its method can be applied to the string. Unlike **System.String**, **StringBuilder** provided numerous members that allow you to append, insert, delete, remove and replace characters from the object. After the operations are complete, the **ToString** method is called to convert the buffer to a string that can be assigned to a string variable. The following Listing 1.1 shows some of usable **StringBuilder** methods in C#.

Listing 1.1 C# StringBuilder class methods.

Method	Description
Append()	It allows adding values to the end of the StringBuilder object.
Insert()	It allows various datatype values to be inserted at any position in StringBuilder object
Remove()	It allows for deleting any portion of a StringBuilder object.
Replace()	It searchs for a specified string or character and substitutes another stting or character in its place.
Length	It returns the number of characters currently in a StringBuilder.

Capacity()	It returns the number of characters that can be stored in a StringBuilder without allocating more memory.

The following program introduces some of the **StringBuilder** method in an example that creates a comma delimited list.

..\CSharp_Book\Chap08\StrAppend

```
using System;
using System.Collections.Generic;
using System.Text;

//Demonstrating StringBuilder methods
namespace StrAppend
{
    class Program
    {
        static void Main()
        {
            // Create comma delimited string with quotes around names
            string fname = "Gagan Arvind ";
            string lname = "Sahoo Kumar";
            Console.WriteLine("First name : " + fname);
            Console.WriteLine("Last name : " + lname);

            StringBuilder nName = new StringBuilder();
            nName.Append(fname).Append(lname);
            nName.Replace(" ", "','");
            //Insert quote at beginning and end of string
            nName.Insert(0, " "'").Append(" ");
            Console.WriteLine("The names are : " + nName);
        }
    }
}
```

When the above program executed, it will produce the following output as shown in Fig. 8.13.

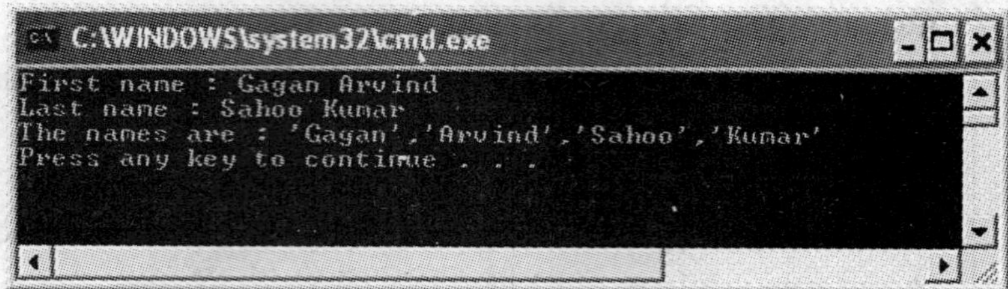

Fig. 8.13 Use of StringBuffer methods.

Here, all operations occur in a single buffer and require no memory allocation until the final assingment to nName.

When you create a **StringBuilder** object, you may specify (via a constructor argument) the intial number of characters the object can contain. If you do not do so, the default capacity of a **StringBuilder** is 16. In either case, if you add more character data to a **StringBuilder** than it is able to hold, the buffer is resized on the fly. The following example demonstrates the an automatic resize of buffer.

..\CSharp_Book\Chap08\BufResize

```
using System;
using System.Collections.Generic;
using System.Text;

//Demonstrating StringBuilder for resizing buffer
namespace BufResize
{
    class Program
    {
        static void Main()
        {
            StringBuilder myBuffer = new StringBuilder("C# .NET Programming Example");
            Console.WriteLine("Capacity of this StringBuffer: {0}", myBuffer.Capacity);
            myBuffer.Append(" contains total : ");
            myBuffer.AppendFormat("{0}, {1}.", 140, 640);
            Console.WriteLine("Capacity of this StringBuffer: {0}", myBuffer.Capacity);
            Console.WriteLine(myBuffer);
        }
    }
}
```

When the above program executed, it will produce the following output as shown in Fig. 8.14.

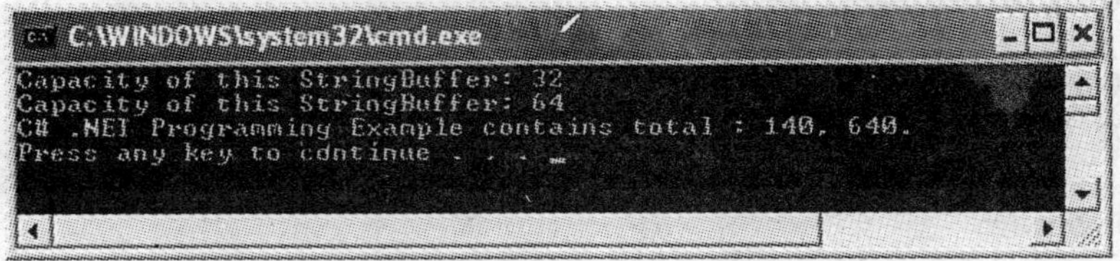

Fig. 8.14 Use of StringBuffer methods to resize buffer.

8.8 Using System.Char Class

C# textual data is represented by the intrinsic C# string and char data types. All .NET-aware languages map textual data to same underlying types (**System.String** and **System.Char**), both of which are Unicode under the hood.

The **System.Char** type provides you with a great deal of functionality beyond the ability to hold a single pointer of character data (which must be placed between sintle quote). Using the static methods of **System.Char**, you are able to determine if a given char is numerical, alphabetical a point of puncutation or whatnot. The following Listing 1.1 shows some of usable **Char** methods in C#.

Listing 1.1 C# char class methods.

Method	Description
Parse()	Converts data into a character.
IsDigit()	Determines whether a character is a defined Unicode digit..
IsLetter()	Determines whether a character is a letter.
IsLetterOrDigit()	Determines whether a character is a letter or a digit.
IsLower()	Determines whether a character is a lowercase letter.
IsUpper()	Determines whether a character is an uppercase letter.
ToUpper()	Converts a character to its uppercase equivalent.
ToLower()	Converts a character to its lowercase equivalent.
IsPunctuation()	Determines whether a character is a punctuation mark.
IsSymbol()	Determines whether a character is a symbol.
IsWhiteSpace()	Determines whether a character is a whitespace character.
CompareTo()	Compares two character values.

The following program checks out the **Char** class method as given :

..\CSharp_Book\Chap08\CharClass

```
using System;
using System.Collections.Generic;
using System.Text;

//Demonstrating Char class methods
namespace CharClass
{
    class Program
    {
        static void Main()
        {
            StringBuilder myBuffer = new StringBuilder("C# .NET Programming Example");
            Console.WriteLine("—> char.IsDigit('A'): {0}", char.IsDigit('A'));
            Console.WriteLine("—> char.IsDigit('5'): {0}", char.IsDigit('5'));
            Console.WriteLine("—> char.IsLetter('L'): {0}", char.IsLetter('L'));
            Console.WriteLine("—> char.IsDigit('15'): {0}", char.IsLetter("15", 1));
```

```
        Console.WriteLine("—> char.IsLetterOrDigit('!'): {0}", char.IsLetterOrDigit('!'));
        Console.WriteLine("—> char.ToLower('A'): {0}", char.ToLower('A'));
        Console.WriteLine("—> char.IsLower('A'): {0}", char.IsLower('A'));
        Console.WriteLine("—> char.ToUpper('b'): {0}", char.ToUpper('b'));
        Console.WriteLine("—> char.IsUpper('A'): {0}", char.IsUpper('A'));
        Console.WriteLine("—> char.IsWhiteSpace('C# Programming , 2'): {0}",
               char.IsWhiteSpace("C# Programming", 2));
        Console.WriteLine("—> char.IsWhiteSpace('C# Programming , 2'): {0}",
               char.IsWhiteSpace("C# Programming", 3));
        Console.WriteLine("—> char.IsPunctuation('!'): {0}", char.IsPunctuation('!'));
        Console.WriteLine("—> char.IsPunctuation('>'): {0}", char.IsPunctuation('>'));
        Console.WriteLine("—> char.IsPunctuation(','): {0}", char.IsPunctuation(','));
    }
  }
}
```

When the above program executed, it will produce the following output as shown in Fig. 8.15.

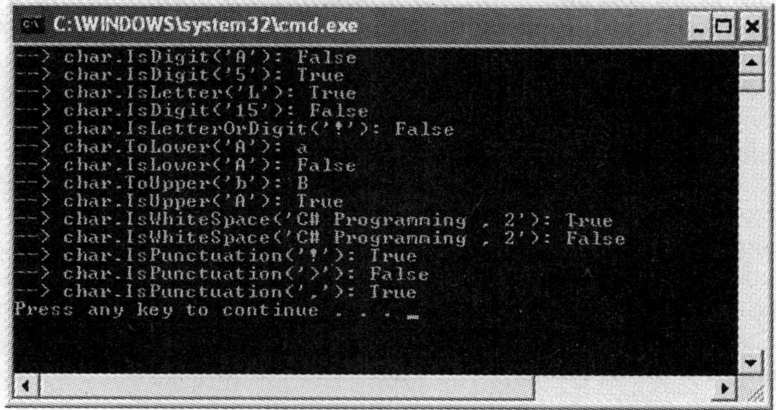

Fig. 8.14 Use of Char class methods.

Exercise

1. What is the difference between System.String and System.StringBuilder classes?
2. Consider the following string :
   String hannah = "Did Hannah see bees ? Hannah did.";
   (*a*) What is the value displayed by the expression hannah.Length?
   (*b*) What is the value returned by at 12 position of the string.?
   (*c*) Write an expression that refers to the letter b in the string referred to by hannah.
3. How long is the string returned by the following expression? What is the string?
   "Was it a car or a cat I saw?".substring(9, 12)

5. Show two ways to concatenate the following two strings together to get the string "Hi, mom.":
   String hi = "Hi, ";
   String mom = "mom.";

Programming

1. Write a program that computes your initials from your full name and displays them.
2. An anagram is a word or a phrase made by transposing the letters of another word or phrase; for example, "parliament" is an anagram of "partial men," and "software" is an anagram of "swearoft." Write a program that figures out whether one string is an anagram of another string. The program should ignore white space and punctuation.
3. Write an application that inputs text and outputs the text in uppercase and lowercase letters.
4. Write an application that inputs several lines of text and a search character, and uses method String method indexOf to determine the number of occurrences of the character in the text.
5. Write an application on the above program that input several lines of text and uses String method indexOf to determine the total number of occurrences of each letter of the alphabet in the text. Uppercase and lowercase letters should be counted together. Store the totals for each letter in an array, and print the values in tabular format after the totals have been determined.
6. Write an application that reads a series of strings and outputs only those strings beginning with the letter "a". The results should be output to a text area.
7. Write an application that reads a series of strings and prints only those strings ending with the letter "ED". The results should be output to a text area.
8. Write your won versions of the String methods for searching strings.
9. Write an application that inputs an integer code for a character and displays the corresponding character. Modify this program so that is generates all possible three-digit codes in the range 000 to 255 and attempts to print the corresponding characters. Display the results in a text area.
10. The StringBuffer class can be used to simulate what occurs when using the + operator on strings. Write the calls to the methods of a StringBuffer object to implement the following use of the + operator :
    line = "The " + "cat" + "in " + "the " + "hat "
11. How is String used in C# ? Explain any three string methods by example.

Methods in C# 9

9.1 Introduction

One of the purposes of writing a program is to perform assignments. An assignment can also be called a function. The C# doesn't have the same notion of a function as did traditional and previous languages like C/C++, Pascal, etc. Instead, in C#, a function must belong to a class. Therefore, in C#, a function is a section whose job is to take care of an operation that would complement a class. Because a function in this case belongs to a particular class, the function is also called a method. From now on, the name method will be used for a function.

> **Note**
> *In C++, a function can be declared anywhere, making it distinct from a method. In C#, a function can be declared only inside of, or as a member of, a class*

A method helps you separate your code into modules that perform a given task.

9.2 Method Structure

Methods are extremely useful because they allow you to separate your logic into different units. You can pass information to methods, have it perform one or more statements, and retrieve a return value. The capability to pass parameters and return values is optional and depends on what you want the method to do. Here's a description of the syntax required for creating a method:

```
attributes modifiers return-type method-name(parameters )
{
    statements
}
```

Here,

- The **return-type** can be any C# type. It can be assigned to a variable for use later in the program.
- The method name is a unique identifier for what you wish to call a method. To distinguish a method from a variable, it is always followed by parentheses, sometimes empty.
- Parameters allow you to pass information to and from a method. They are surrounded by parenthesis.
- Statements within the curly braces carry out the functionality of the method. Since a method is used to perform an assignment, its job is included between an opening curly bracket "{" and a closing curly bracket "}".

For example, suppose you want to print a new line method for displaying different messages at different rows of your screen.

```
// Called method
void print_message()
{
    Console.WriteLine("This is a module called print_message method.");
}
```

From the above method, the called function **print_message()** displays the output in a new line on the screen, and the shape of the **Main()** function is as :

..\CSharp_Book\Chap09\StartMethod

```
using System;

class StartMethod
{
    // Called method
    void print_message()
    {
        Console.WriteLine("This is a module called print_message method.");
    }

    static void Main()
    {
        StartMethod st = new StartMethod();
        st.print_message();
    }
}
```

When the above program executed, it will produce the following output :

```
This is a module called print_message method.
Press any key to continue . . .
```

To call a method, it is only necessary to write its name inside the **Main()** function. The code associated with the method name is executed at that point in the program. When the method terminates, execution begins with the statement which follows the method name.

In the above program,

- the function **print_message()** is invoked from **Main()** function.
- the control passes to **print_message()** method.
- inside the body of the method **print_message()**, the C# line executed.
- simultaneously the execution control returned back to **Main()** function to execute the remaining statements if it is there.
- As there are no further statements inside the **Main()** body, the program terminates by returning to the operating system.

From above program, when a method is declared without static, it should be invoke each method using dot (.) operator. That is, create an instance of the class and invoke the method as :

```
StartMethod st = new StartMethod();
st.print_message();
```

9.3 Static Methods

Unlike some other languages like C/C++, Pascal, Visual Basic, etc, but like Java, C# doesn't have the notion of global function: every method must belong to a class. For this reason, every program uses at least one class and we call this primary class, the main class. Because of this feature of the language, it imposes some rules on the way methods can be called. If you create a method in the main class of your project, you should indicate that the method will always belong to this main class. The method must be created as static.

The 'static' modifier declares a method to be a class method. The methods (as well as the enumerations, properties and variables) specified in a class can be associated either with the class's instances (ie. the reference types it specifies) or with the class itself. These methods are called, respectively, 'instance methods' and 'class methods'. Class methods, declared with the 'static' modifier, can be called even when there exists no current instances of the class.

There is no equivalent modifier for instance methods, since methods are instance methods just in case their declaration does not include the word 'static'.

To define a method as static, type the **static** keyword to its left. For example;

..\CSharp_Book\Chap09\StaticMethod

```
using System;

class StaticMethod
{
    // Called method
    static void print_message()
```

```
    {
        Console.WriteLine("This is a module called print_message method.");
    }

    static void Main()
    {
        print_message();
    }
}
```

When the above program executed, it will produce the following output :

```
This is a module called print_message method.
Press any key to continue . . .
```

As we have used the **Main()** function so far, the behavior of a method is defined between its delimiting curly brackets. The section inside the curly brackets is called the body of a method. In the body of the method **print_message()**, a message is written using **WriteLine()** console. The method is declared as static inside **StartMethod** class. To call it, we type its name followed by parentheses and ending with a semi-colon inside **Main()** function.

9.4 Method that Returns a Value

Methods can either return a type or not. A method that doesn't return a type must give its return type as 'void'. A method that does return a type must name the type returned. To declare a method that returns a value, provide its return type to the left of its name.

After a method has performed its assignment, it must clearly demonstrate that it is returning a value. To do this, you use the **return** keyword followed by the value that the method is returning. The value returned must be of the same type specified as the return type of the method. The syntax is :

return [(value/variable/expression)];

A method can also return an expression, provided the expression produces a value that is conform to the return type.

A method will stop and return a value if it reaches a '**return**' statement at any point in its execution. The type returned is given at the end of such a **return** statement; its type must correspond with that specified in the method declaration. The following piece of code illustrates this point.

```
public static int examplemethod()
{
    int i = 0;
    // process i
    Return i;
}
```

When a method returns a value, the compiler considers such a method as if it were a regular value. This means that you can use the **Console.Write()** or the **Console.WriteLine()** method to display its value. To do this, simply type the name of the method and its parentheses in the **Console.Write()** of the **Console.WriteLine()** methods' parentheses.

The following program asks the user for a temperature in Celsius and then converts that temperature to Fahrenheit. The parameter and the return type are both floating-point values. You know the return type is a floating-point value because of the word float before the function **convert()**'s definition. See if you can follow this program. Except for the Celsius calculation, the program is similar to those you have seen.

Example Write another program to convert the Celsius to Fahrenheit using method declaration.

..\CSharp_Book\Chap09\CelsToFahren

```
using System;

class CelsToFahren
{
    static float convert()
    {
        float f_temp;
        float result = 0;
        Console.Write("Enter the Celsius value : ");
        f_temp = float.Parse(Console.ReadLine());
        result = (float)(f_temp * (9.0 / 5.0) + 32.0);
        return (result);
    }

    static void Main()
    {
        Console.WriteLine("The Fahrenheit equivalent is : {0:F}", convert());
    }
}
```

When the above program executed, it will produce the following output :

```
Enter the Celsius value : 36
The Fahrenheit equivalent is : 96.80
Press any key to continue . . .
```

9.5 Access Modifiers

Before we go in depth, it is important to know the access modifiers or member visibility. Members (methods, fields, constructor and so on) of a given class or structure must specify their visibility level.

If you define a member without specifying an accessibility keyword, it automatically defaults to private. C# offers the method access modifiers shown in Listing 9.1

Listing 9.1 C# accessibility keywords.

Access Modifier	Description
public	Marks a member as accessible from an object variable as well as any derived classes.
private	Marks a method as accessible only by the class that has defined the method. In C#, all members are private by default.
protected	Marks a method as usable by the defining class, aw well as any derived classes. Protected methods, however, are not accessible from an object variable.
internal	Defines a method that is accessible by any type in the same assembly, but not outside the assembly.
protected internal	Defines a method whose access is limited to the current assembly or types derived from the defining class in the current assembly.

As we already know, members that are declared public are directly accessible from an object reference via the dot (.) operator. Private members cannot be accessed by an object reference, but instead are called internally by the object to help the instance get its work done (i.e., private helper functions).

Protected members are only truly useful when you create class hierarchies. As far as internal or internal protected members are concerned, they are only truly useful when you are creating .NET code libraries (such as a managed *.dll)

To illustrate the implications of these keywords, assume you have created a class (**StartMethod**) using each of the possible member access modifiers :

```
// Member visibility options.
class StartMethod
{
    // Accessible anywhere.
    public void PublicMethod(){ }

    // Accessible only from StartMethod types.
    private void PrivateMethod(){ }

    // Accessible from StartMethod and any descendent.
    protected void ProtectedMethod(){ }

    // Accessible from within the same assembly.
    Internal void InternalMethod(){ }
```

```
    // Assembly-rrotected access.
    Protected internal void ProtectedInternalMethod(){ }

    // Unmarked members are private by default in C#.
    Void SomeMethod(){ }
}
```

Now assume we have to created an instance of **StartMethod** and attempt to invoke each method using the dot operator.

```
static void Main()
{
    // Make an object and attempt to call members.
    StartMethod St = new StartMethod();
    St.PublicMethod();
    St.InternalMethod();
    St.ProtectedInternalMethod();
    St.PrivateMethod();          //Error
    St.ProtecteedMethod();       //Error
    St.SomeMethod();             //Error
}
```

If you compile this program, you will find that the protected and private members are not accessible from an object.

9.5.1 Local Variables

In the body of a method, we can also declare variables that would be used internally. A variable declared in the body is referred to as a local variable. It cannot be accessed outside of the method it belongs to. After declaring a local variable, it is made available to the method and you can use it as you see fit, for example, you can assign it a value prior to using it. The variable is said to be accessible or visible within the function only and has a local scope.

Following are some of features of local variables :

- They can be used only the statements that are inside the same block in which local variables are declared. That is, the local variables are not known outside of their own code block. For example,

```
static void fun1()
{
    int a; a = 5;
}
static void fun2()
{
    int a; a = 10;
}
```

Here, the integer variable a is declared twice, once in **fun1()** and once in **fun2()**, but the a in **fun1()** has no effect to the a in **fun2()**. This is because a is known only to the code within the block in which it is declared.

- We can also declare local variables inside any code block that is nested inside another code block. For example, consider the following function :

..\CSharp_Book\Chap09\LocalVar

```
static void fun()
{
    int guess;
    Console.WriteLine("Think a number : ");
    guess = int.Parse(Console.ReadLine());

    if (guess == 18)
    {
        int age;
        Console.WriteLine("What is your age : ");
        age = int.Parse(Console.ReadLine()); ;
        Console.WriteLine("Your age is accurate for voting : ");
    }
}
```

When the above program executed, it will produce the following output :

```
Think a number :
18
What is your age : 20
Your age is accurate for voting :
Press any key to continue . . .
```

Here, the local variable guess is created at the entry of the function **fun()** and so its scope remains until the terminating curly brace of the function **fun()** is encountered. However, the local variable **age** is created upon entry into the **if** code block and destroyed upon the exit from the if block. That is, **age** is known only within the **if** block and cannot be referenced else-where within the outer block (i.e. of the **fun()**).

9.5.2 Global Variables

As mentioned with functions, C# doesn't have the notion of global variables (in C/C++, Visual Basic, Pascal, etc, a global variable is one that is declared outside of any class; such a variable is made available to any function, or even file, of the same program without being declared again where needed). Still, if you want to use the same variable in various methods of the main class, you can declare it outside of any method. The variable must be declared as static. That is, you must type the static keyword to its left when declaring it. For example;

..\CSharp_Book\Chap09\GlobalVar

```
using System;

class Global_Var
{
    static float f_temp; // Global variable, it should not private
    static float convert()
    {
        float result = 0;
        Console.Write("Enter the Celsius value : ");
        f_temp = float.Parse(Console.ReadLine());
        result = (float)(f_temp * (9.0 / 5.0) + 32.0);
        return (result);
    }
    static void Main()
    {
        Console.WriteLine("The Fahrenheit equivalent is : {0:F}", convert());
    }
}
```

When the above program executed, it will produce the following output :

```
Enter the Celsius value : 36
The Fahrenheit equivalent is : 96.80
Press any key to continue . . .
```

After declaring such a variable, you can access from any method that belongs to the same class.

9.5.3 Arguments

Like a variable, an argument is represented by its type of value. For example, one method may need a character while another would need a string. Yet another method may require a decimal number. This means that the method or class that calls a method is responsible for supplying the right value, even though a method may have an internal mechanism of checking the validity of such a value.

The value supplied to a method is typed in the parentheses of the method and it's called an argument. In order to declare a method that takes an argument, you must specify its name and the argument between its parentheses. Because a method must specify the type of value it would need, the argument is represented by its data type and a name. If the method would not return a value, it can be declared as **void**.

Suppose you want to define a method that displays the side length of a square. Since you would have to supply the length, you can define such a method as follows:

```
using System;

public class SquareProgram
{
    void DisplaySide(double Length)
    {
        ...
        ...
    }

    static void Main()
    {
        ...
        ...
    }
}
```

In the body of the method, you may or may not use the value of the argument. Otherwise, you can manipulate the supplied value as you see fit. In this example, you can display the value of the argument as follows:

```
using System;

public class SquareProgram
{
    void DisplaySide(double Length)
    {
        Console.Write("Length: ");
        Console.WriteLine(Length);
    }

    static void Main()
    {
        ...
        ...
    }
}
```

In this case, remember to define the method as **static** if you plan to access it from **Main()**. In order to call a method that takes an argument, you must supply a value for the argument when calling the method; otherwise you would receive an error. Also, you should/must supply the right value; otherwise, the method may not work as expected and produce an unreliable result. For example;

```
using System;

public class SquareProgram
{
```

```
    static void DisplaySide(double Length)
    {
        Console.Write("Length: ");
        Console.WriteLine(Length);
    }

    static void Main()
    {
        DisplaySide(35.55);
        Console.WriteLine();
    }
}
```

As mentioned already, a method that takes an argument can also declared its own variable. Such variables are referred to as local.

A method can take more than one argument. When defining such a method, provide each argument with its data type and a name. The arguments are separated by a comma.

..\CSharp_Book\Chap09\PassingArg

```
using System;

class Cylinder
{
    static double GetTheRadius()
    {
        double rad;

        do
        {
            Console.Write("Radius: ");
            rad = double.Parse(Console.ReadLine());
            if (rad < 0)
                Console.WriteLine("Please enter a positive number");
        } while (rad < 0);
        return rad;
    }

    static double GetTheHeight()
    {
        double h;

        do
        {
            Console.Write("Height: ");
```

```
            h = double.Parse(Console.ReadLine());
            if (h < 0)

                Console.WriteLine("Please enter a positive number");
        } while (h < 0);
        return h;
    }

    static double CalculateBaseArea(double rad)
    {
        return rad * rad * Math.PI;
    }

    static double CalculateLateralArea(double rad, double hgt)
    {
        return 2 * Math.PI * rad * hgt;
    }

    static double CalculateTotalArea(double rad, double hgt)
    {
        return 2 * Math.PI * rad * (hgt + rad);
    }

    static double CalculateVolume(double rad, double hgt)
    {
        return Math.PI * rad * rad * hgt;
    }

    static void ProcessCylinder()
    {
        double Radius;
        double Height;
        double BaseArea;
        double LateralArea;
        double TotalArea;
        double Volume;

        Console.WriteLine("Enter the dimensions of the cylinder");
        Radius = GetTheRadius();
        Height = GetTheHeight();

        BaseArea = CalculateBaseArea(Radius);
        LateralArea = CalculateLateralArea(Radius, Height);
        TotalArea = CalculateTotalArea(Radius, Height);
        Volume = CalculateVolume(Radius, Height);
```

```
        Console.WriteLine("\nCylinder Characteristics");
        Console.WriteLine("Radius:   {0}", Radius);
        Console.WriteLine("Height:   {0}", Height);
        Console.WriteLine("Base:     {0:F}", BaseArea);
        Console.WriteLine("Lateral: {0:F}", LateralArea);
        Console.WriteLine("Total:    {0:F}", TotalArea);
        Console.WriteLine("Volume:   {0:F}", Volume);
    }

    static void Main()
    {
        ProcessCylinder();

        Console.WriteLine();
    }
}
```

When the above program executed, it will produce the following output as shown in Fig. 9.1.

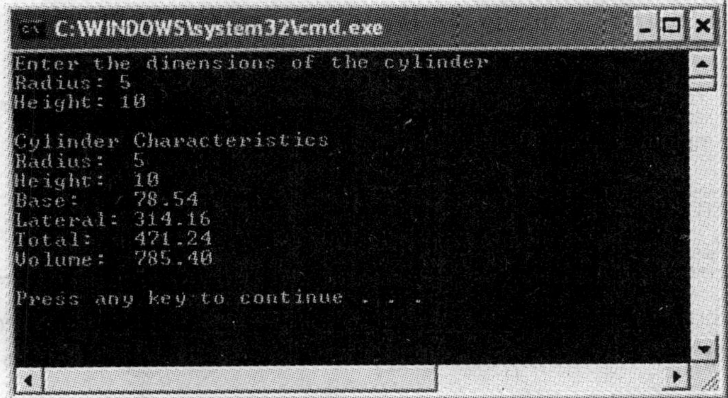

Fig. 9.1 Arguments in C# method.

9.5.4 Formal Variables/Parameters

The variables (or parameters), which accept the actual variables inside the method are called formal variables. Each method definition contains an argument list called the formal argument list. Items in the list are optional, so the actual list may be empty or it may contain any combination of data types, such as int, float and char.

Formal variables is a list of variables that will accept different types of values being supplied to the method by the calling program. Formal parameters are declared after the method name and inside parenthesis.

Let us consider another example,

..\CSharp_Book\Chap09\FormalPara

```
using System;

// Demonstrating Formal parameter
class Formal_Parameter
{
    static float MAX(float a, float b)
    {
        if (a > b)
            return a;
        else
            return b;
    }

    static void Main()
    {
        int x = 20, y = 30;
        Console.WriteLine("Maximum is : {0:F}", MAX(x, y));
    }
}
```

When the above program executed, it will produce the following output :

```
Maximum is : 30.00
Press any key to continue . . .
```

In the above method, a and b are formal parameters. They are called formal because actual parameter values are supplied to the method by the calling program and formal parameters use the copy of those actual parameters.

9.5.5 Actual Variables/Parameters

The variables, which are associated with function name during function call, are called actual variables. When the program calls the function, an argument list is also passed to the function. This list is called the actual argument list. For example,

```
static void Main()
{
    .
    .
    sum_twonum(20, 60.5, 80);   // Passing actual arguments into the function
    .
    .
}
```

Here, 20, 60.5 and 80 are the actual arguments, which are passed into the **sum_twonum()** methods variable list a, b and c respectively.

Let us consider the MAX() method of formal variable section. If we write its code for actual variables, then the **Main()** function block is :

..\CSharp_Book\Chap09\ActualPara

```
using System;

// Demonstrating Actual parameter
class Actual_Parameter
{
    static float MAX(float a, float b)

    {
        if (a > b)
            return a;
        else
            return b;
    }

    static void Main()
    {
        float x, y;
        Console.Write("Enter first no. ");
        x = float.Parse(Console.ReadLine());
        Console.Write("Enter second no. ");
        y = float.Parse(Console.ReadLine());
        Console.WriteLine("Maximum is : {0:F}", MAX(x, y));
    }
}
```

When the above program executed, it will produce the following output :

```
Enter first no. 30
Enter second no. 33
Maximum is : 33.00
Press any key to continue . . .
```

In the above calling program (which is **Main()**, because it is calling the method **MAX()**), **x** and **y** are the actual parameters.

9.6 Passing Argument to Method

C# provides two methods for passing variables between functions, e.g.,

- Passing variables by value
- Passing variables by address (ref)
- Output Parameter
- Params Modifier

Other than these four, a method argument can be :

- Type void as an argument
- Characters as arguments
- Integers as arguments
- Floats as arguments
- Doubles as arguments
- Arrays as arguments

9.6.1 Passing by Value

When calling the methods that take one or more arguments, we made sure we provided the needed argument. This is because an argument is always required and the calling function or class must provided a valid value when calling such a method.

The phrases "passing by value" and "passing by copy" mean the same thing in computer terms. Some textbooks and C# programmers say that the arguments are passed by value, and some say that they are passed by copy. Both describe one of the two methods by which arguments are passed to receiving functions.

Figure 9.2 shows the action of passing an argument by value. The actual variable i is not passed, but the value of i (which is 10) is passed to the receiving method. There is not just one variable called i, but actually two variables. The first is local to **Main()**, and the second is local to **print_it(int i)**. Both the variables have the same name, but because they are local to their respective methods, no conflict exists. The variable does not have to be called i in both the methods; the value of i is sent to the receiving method, so it does not matter what the receiving method called the variable that receives the value.

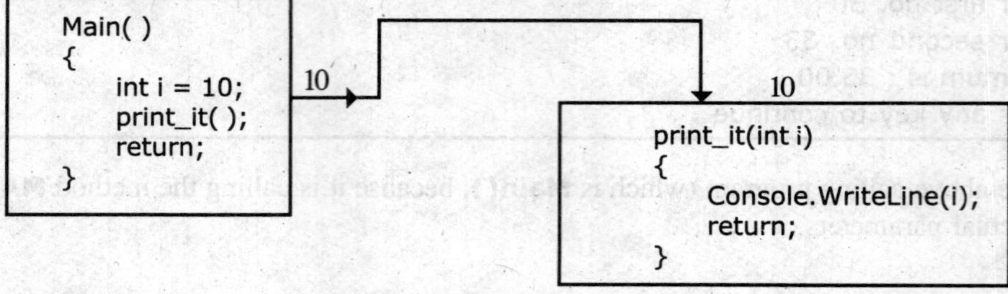

Fig. 9.2 Passing the variable i by value.

In this case, when passing and receiving variables among the methods, you should retain the same names. Even though they are not the same variables, they hold the same value. In this example, the value of 10 is passed from **Main()**'s i to **print_it()**'s i.

Because a copy of i's value is passed to the receiving method (and not the actual variable). With this technique, you can pass a copy of a variable to a receiving method, but the receiving method cannot modify the calling method's variable. Thus, you have true separation of methods and variables.

All of the C# no array variables that you have seen so far are passed by value. You do not have to do anything special to pass variables by value except to pass them in the calling method's argument list. And receive them in the receiving method's parameter list.

When an argument (local variable) is passed by value, a copy of the variable's value is assigned to the receiving method's parameter. If more than one variable is passed by value, a copy of each variable's value is assigned to the receiving method's parameters.

..\CSharp_Book\Chap09\PassByValue

```
using System;
using System.Collections.Generic;
using System.Text;

// Passing by value
namespace PassByValue
{
    class Pass_by_Value
    {
        static void calc_fact(long n)
        {
            long fact = 1;
            int i;
            for (i = 1; i <=n; ++i)
                fact *= i;
            Console.WriteLine("The factorial of {0} is {1:F}", n, fact);
        }

        static void Main()
        {
            long number;

            Console.Write("Enter a number ");
            number = long.Parse(Console.ReadLine());
            calc_fact(number);
        }
    }
}
```

When the above program executed, it will produce the following output :

```
Enter a number 10
The factorial of 10 is 3628800.00
Press any key to continue . . .
```

Lets look at the function **calc_fact()**. The declaration of the function :

```
static void calc_fact(long n)
```

indicates there is no return data type and a single integer is accepted, known inside the body of the function as **n**. Next comes the declaration of local variables.

```
long fact = 1;
```

Then, the program works by accepting a variable from the keyboard, which is then passed to the function. In other words, the variable number inside the main body is then copied to the variable **n** in the function, which then calculates the correct answer.

9.6.2 Passing by Address

The phrases "passing by address" and "passing by reference" mean the very same thing. Some textbooks and C# programmers say that arguments are passed by address, and some say that they are passed by reference. When you pass an argument (local variable) by address, the variable's address is assigned to the receiving function's parameter. (If you pass more than one variable by address, each of their addresses is assigned to the receiving function's parameters).

In C# we can pass variables into methods 'by reference'. Where a variable is passed by reference, the 'ref' modifier must be used both in the method head and the method invocation.

Passing by reference is most obviously useful in cases where we want to treat a value type like a reference type. For instance, the method call in the following code does change the value of the variable a passed into the '**change()**' method.

```
public static void Main()
{
    int a = 0;
    change(ref a);  // Following this method invocation, a == 5
}

public static void change(ref int b)
{
    b = 5;
}
```

Let us consider the following program:

..\CSharp_Book\Chap09\PassByRef

```
using System;

public class Payroll
{
    static void Earnings(double ThisWeek, double Salary)
    {
        ThisWeek = 42.50;

        Console.WriteLine("\nIn the Earnings() function, ");
        Console.Write("Weekly Hours   = ");
        Console.WriteLine(ThisWeek);
        Console.Write("Salary         = ");
        Console.WriteLine(Salary);
        Console.Write("Weekly Salary:  = ");
        Console.WriteLine(ThisWeek * Salary);
    }

    static void Main()
    {
        double Hours, Rate;

        Rate = 15.58;
        Hours = 26.00;

        Console.WriteLine("In the Main() function, ");
        Console.Write("\nWeekly Hours    = ");
        Console.Write(Hours);
        Console.Write("\nSalary          = ");
        Console.WriteLine(Rate);
        Console.Write("Weekly Salary     = ");
        Console.WriteLine(Hours * Rate);

        Console.WriteLine("\nCalling the Earnings() function");

        Earnings(Hours, Rate);

        Console.Write("\nAfter calling the Earnings() function, ");
        Console.WriteLine("\nin the Main() function,");
        Console.Write("\nWeekly Hours    = ");
        Console.Write(Hours);
        Console.Write("\nSalary          = ");
        Console.WriteLine(Rate);
        Console.Write("Weekly Salary     = ");
        Console.WriteLine(Hours * Rate);
```

```
        Console.Write("\n");
    }
}
```

When the above program executed, it will produce the following output as shown in Fig. 9.3.

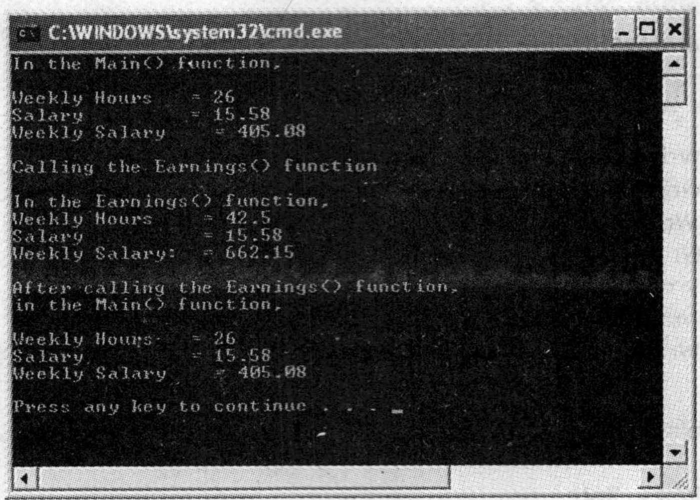
```
In the Main() function.

Weekly Hours     = 26
Salary           = 15.58
Weekly Salary     = 405.08

Calling the Earnings() function

In the Earnings() function.
Weekly Hours      = 42.5
Salary            = 15.58
Weekly Salary:    = 662.15

After calling the Earnings() function,
in the Main() function.

Weekly Hours     = 26
Salary           = 15.58
Weekly Salary     = 405.08

Press any key to continue . . .
```

Fig. 9.3 Artument as pass by value.

Notice that the weekly hours and salary values are the same before and after calling the Earnings() method.

When you declare a variable in a program, the compiler reserves an amount of space for that variable. If you need to use that variable somewhere in your program, you call it and make use of its value. There are two major issues related to a variable: its value and its location in the memory.

The location of a variable in memory is referred to as its address.

If you supply the argument using its name, the compiler only makes a copy of the argument's value and gives it to the calling method. Although the calling method receives the argument's value and can use in any way, it cannot (permanently) alter it. C# allows a calling method to modify the value of a passed argument if you find it necessary. If you want the calling method to modify the value of a supplied argument and return the modified value, you should pass the argument using its reference.

To pass an argument as a reference, when defining and when calling the method, precede the argument's data type with the **ref** keyword. You can pass 0, one, or more arguments as reference in the program or pass all arguments as reference. The decision as to which argument(s) should be passed by value or by reference is based on whether or not you want the called method to modify the argument and permanently change its value.

Here are examples of passing some arguments by reference:

```
void Area(ref double Side); // The argument is passed by reference
bool Decision(ref char Answer, int Age); // One argument is passed by reference
```

```
// All arguments are passed by reference
float Purchase(ref float DiscountPrice, ref float NewDiscount, ref char Commission);
```

You add the ampersand when defining when calling the method. The above would be called with:

```
Area(ref Side);
Decision(ref Answer, Age);
Purchase(ref DiscountPrice, ref NewDiscount, ref Commission);
```

If you want a calling function to modify the value of an argument, you should supply its reference and not its value, using the **ref** keyword.

Another option consists of passing an argument using the **out** keyword. For example;

..\CSharp_Book\Chap09\UsingOut

```
using System;

class Exercise
{
    static void Initializer(out double n)
    {
        n = 128.44;
    }

    public static void Main()
    {
        double Number = 15.25;

        Console.WriteLine("Number = {0}", Number);
    }
}
```

When the above program executed, it will produce the following output :

```
Number = 15.25
Press any key to continue . . .
```

9.6.3 Output Parameter

If you pass an argument with **out**, any modification made on the argument would be kept when the method ends. When calling a method that takes an out argument, precede the argument with the out keyword.

Where a method parameter is defined (and invoked) using the '**out**' modifier, it is passed by reference. The difference between the '**out**' and the '**ref**' modifier is this: a parameter modified by the 'out' keyword need not be assigned a value before being passed into the method, but must be assigned a value in the method.

The reason that one might use output parameters is to return multiple values from a method. For instance, in the following code an integer and a boolean is passed to the '**change()**' method. This method sets the boolean to indicate whether or not the integer is greater than 0, and returns the value of the integer doubled.

```
public static void Main()
{
    bool b;
    int c = change(5, out b);
}
public static void change(int a, out bool b)
{
    b = false;
    if (a > 0)
        b = true;
    return (2 * a);
}
```

For example;

..\CSharp_Book\Chap09\OutArg

```
using System;

class Exercise
{
    static void Initializer(out double n)
    {
        n = 128.44;
    }

    public static void Main()
    {
        double Number = 15.25;

        Console.WriteLine("Number = {0}", Number);
        Initializer(out Number);
        Console.WriteLine("Number = {0}", Number);
    }
}
```

When the above program executed, it will produce the following output :

```
Number = 15.25
Number = 128.44
Press any key to continue . . .
```

Also, the arguments can be passed by reference. The following program demonstrates the passing arguments by reference.

..\CSharp_Book\Chap09\PassByRef

```
using System;

class Cylinder
{
    static void GetTheRadius(ref double rad)
    {
        do
        {
            Console.Write("Radius: ");
            rad = double.Parse(Console.ReadLine());
            if (rad < 0)
                Console.WriteLine("Please enter a positive number");
        } while (rad < 0);
    }

    static void GetTheHeight(out double h)
    {
        do
        {
            Console.Write("Height: ");
            h = double.Parse(Console.ReadLine());
            if (h < 0)
                Console.WriteLine("Please enter a positive number");
        } while (h < 0);
    }

    static double CalculateBaseArea(double rad)
    {
        return rad * rad * Math.PI;
    }

    static double CalculateLateralArea(double rad, double hgt)
    {
        return 2 * Math.PI * rad * hgt;
    }

    static double CalculateTotalArea(double rad, double hgt)
    {
        return 2 * Math.PI * rad * (hgt + rad);
    }
```

```
    static double CalculateVolume(double rad, double hgt)
    {
        return Math.PI * rad * rad * hgt;
    }

    static void ProcessCylinder()
    {
        double Radius = 0.00;
        double Height = 0.00;
        double BaseArea;
        double LateralArea;
        double TotalArea;
        double Volume;

        Console.WriteLine("Enter the dimensions of the cylinder");
        GetTheRadius(ref Radius);
        GetTheHeight(out Height);

        BaseArea = CalculateBaseArea(Radius);
        LateralArea = CalculateLateralArea(Radius, Height);
        TotalArea = CalculateTotalArea(Radius, Height);
        Volume = CalculateVolume(Radius, Height);

        ShowCylinder(Radius, Height, BaseArea, LateralArea, TotalArea, Volume);
    }

    static void ShowCylinder(double rad, double hgt, double BArea,
            double Lateral, double Total, double vol)
    {
        Console.WriteLine("\nCylinder Characteristics");
        Console.WriteLine("Radius:   {0}", rad);
        Console.WriteLine("Height:   {0}", hgt);
        Console.WriteLine("Base:     {0:F}", BArea);
        Console.WriteLine("Lateral:  {0:F}", Lateral);
        Console.WriteLine("Total:    {0:F}", Total);
        Console.WriteLine("Volume:   {0:F}", vol);
    }

    static void Main()
    {
        ProcessCylinder();

        Console.WriteLine();
    }
}
```

When the above program executed, it will produce the following output as shown in Fig. 9.4.

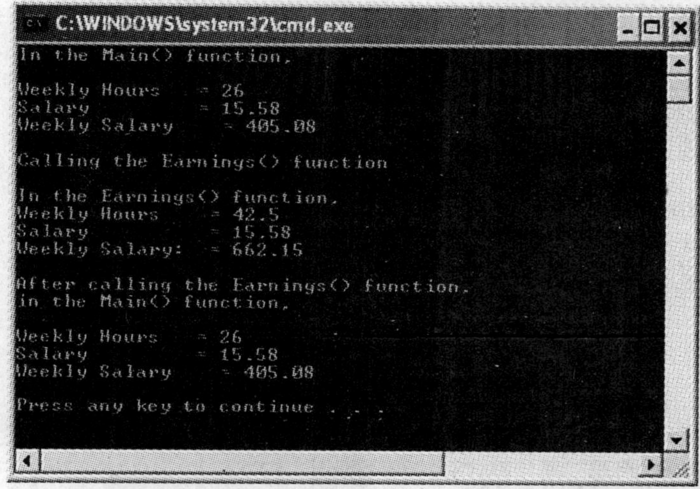

Fig. 9.4 Artument as pass by reference.

Note that the distinction between output and reference parameters are :

- Output parameters do not need to be initialized before they passed to the method. The reason for this ? The method must assign output parameters before exiting.
- Reference parameters must be initialize before they are passed to the method. The reason for this ? You are passing a reference to an existing variable. If you do not assign it to an initial value, that would be the equivalent of operating on an unassigned local variable.

Example. Write a program to swap two strings using reference method.

..\CSharp_Book\Chap09\SwapString

```
using System;
using System.Collections.Generic;
using System.Text;

// Demonstrating reference parameter as string
namespace SwapString
{
    class Program
    {
        static void Main()
        {
            string str1 = "C# Programming";
            string str2 = "Console Application";
```

```
            Console.WriteLine("Before swap : {0}, {1} ", str1, str2);
            SwapStrings(ref str1, ref str2);
            Console.WriteLine("After swap : {0}, {1} ", str1, str2);
        }

        // Reference parameter
        public static void SwapStrings(ref string s1, ref string s2)
        {
            string strTemp = s1;
            s1 = s2;
            s2 = strTemp;
        }
    }
}
```

When the above program executed, it will produce the following output as shown in Fig. 9.5.

Fig. 9.5 String artument as pass by reference.

From the above code, the caller has assigned an initial value to local string data (str1 and str2). once the call to **SwapStrings()** returns, s1 new contains the value "**Console Application**", while s2 reports the value "C# Programming".

9.6.4 Params Modifier

One can pass an arbitrary number of types to a method by declaring a parameter array with the '**params**' modifier. Note, though, that it is not necessary to place these additional types into an array before calling the method - they can simply be listed in the method invocation (see the next code block for an example). Types passed as '**params**' are all passed by value. The following code gives an example of the use of the '**params**' modifier; the method called ignores the first type passed to it (a double) and returns the sum of all (an arbitrary number of) the integer values passed to it.

```
public static void Main()
{
    double a = 1;
    int b = 2;
    int c = 3;
    ind d = totalIgnoreFirst(a, b, c);
}
```

```
public static int totalIgnoreFirst(double a, params int[] intArr)
{
    int sum = 0;
    for (int i=0; i < intArr.Length; i++)
        sum += intArr[i];
    return sum;
}
```

Let us consider the following example :

..\CSharp_Book\Chap09\ParamMod

```
using System;
using System.Collections.Generic;
using System.Text;

namespace ParamMod
{
    class Param_Para
    {
        // Returns average of some number of doubles.
        static double CalculateAverage(params double[] values)
        {
            double sum = 0;
            for (int i = 0; i < values.Length; i++)
                sum += values[i];
            return (sum / values.Length);
        }

        static void Main()
        {
            // Pass in a comma-delimited list of doubles....
            double average;
            average = CalculateAverage(4.0, 3.2, 5.7);
            Console.WriteLine("Average of 4.0, 3.2, 5.7 is : {0}", average);
            // ..or pass an array of doubles.
            double[] data = { 4.0, 3.2, 5.7 };
            average = CalculateAverage(data);
            Console.WriteLine("Average of data is : {0}", average);
            Console.ReadLine();
        }
    }
}
```

When the above program executed, it will produce the following output :

```
Average of 4.0, 3.2, 5.7 is : 4.3
Average of data is 4.3
Press any key to continue . . .
```

9.6.5 Method without an Argument

In C#, the use of void is not yet required, but its use is considered wisely. The following program has a simple function to calculate the sum of first 10 natural numbers that receives no arguments and does not return a value. The main functions calls the function **sum_num()**. When the **sum_num()** function is finished, control is returned to the **Main()** function. This is one of the simplest types of functions you can write.

Example 17.19 Write a program to demonstrate without an argument.

..\CSharp_Book\Chap09\VoidArgument

```
using System;
using System.Collections.Generic;
using System.Text;

// Program illustrate without an argument
namespace VoidArgument
{
    class Program
    {
        //
        static void sum_num()
        {
            int i, sum = 0;
            for (i = 1; i <= 10; i++)
                sum+=i;
            Console.WriteLine(sum);
        }

        static void Main(string[] args)
        {
            Console.Write("Sum of first 10 natural numbers is : ");
            sum_num();
        }
    }
}
```

When the above program executed, it will produce the following output :

```
Sum of first 10 natural numbers is : 55
Press any key to continue . . .
```

9.6.6 Characters as Arguments

Character information can also be passed to a method. In the next example, a single character is intercepted from the keyboard, in the function **Main()** and passed to the method **char_out()**.

Example 17.20 Write a program to demonstrate character type argument into a method.

..\CSharp_Book\Chap09\CharArgument

```
using System;
using System.Collections.Generic;
using System.Text;

// Program to demonstrate char type parameter
namespace CharArgument
{
    class Program
    {
        static void char_out(char ch)
        {
            int j, k;
            Console.WriteLine("You enter an character : " + ch);

            k = ((int)ch) + 1;
            Console.WriteLine();

            for (j = 1; j < 6; j++)
            {
                Console.WriteLine("The ASCII value of next character is : {0}", k);
                k = k + 1;
            }
        }
        static void Main()
        {
            char inchar;

            Console.Write("Enter one character from keyboard : ");

            inchar = char.Parse(Console.ReadLine());

            char_out(inchar);
            Console.WriteLine();
```

```
        }
    }
}
```

When the above program executed, it will produce the following output as shown in Fig. 9.6.

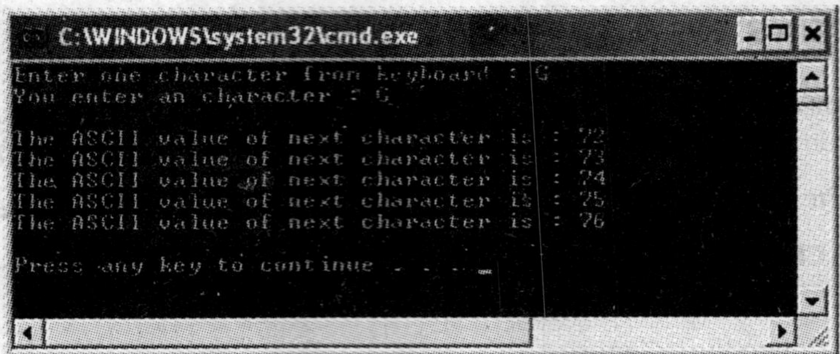

Fig. 9.6 Character argument in method call.

From the output, we notice that a single character is displayed its next ASCII values.

9.6.7 Integers as Arguments

In our previous sections, we study number of examples by passing integer type (**int**) of values into different method. Here, is a simple example to pass as an integer argument and calculate the area, volume and cube of a side.

Example 17.21 Write a program to input a side and find the area, volume and cube.

..\CSharp_Book\Chap09\IntArgument

```
using System;
using System.Collections.Generic;
using System.Text;
// Program to demonstrate int type parameter
namespace IntArgument
{
    class Program
    {
        static void Main(string[] args)
        {
            int length;
            Console.Write("Enter the length : ");
            length = int.Parse(Console.ReadLine());
            cal_side(length);
        }
```

```
        static void cal_side(int side)
        {
            int area, volume, cube;

            area = side * side;
            volume = side * side * side;
            cube = 6 * area;
            Console.WriteLine("The side is : {0}", side);
            Console.WriteLine("The area is : {0}", area);
            Console.WriteLine("The volume is : {0}", volume);
            Console.WriteLine("The cube is : {0}", cube);
        }
    }
}
```

When the above program executed, it will produce the following output as shown in Fig. 9.7.

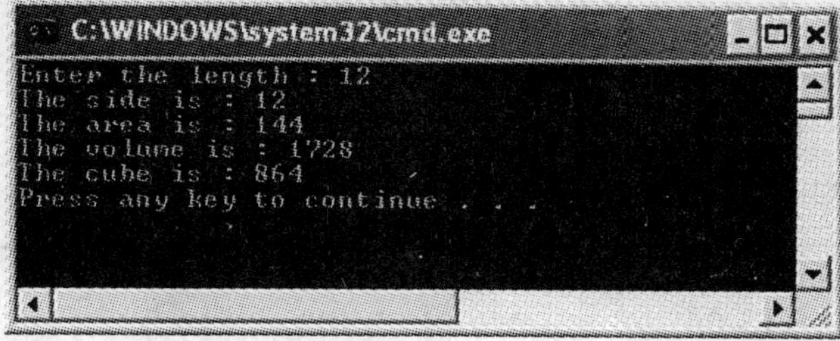

Fig. 9.7 Integer argument in method call.

From the output, notice that the **side** and all calculated values are integer. The method **cal_side()** receives an integer type of value and calculate the respective measure.

9.6.8 Floats as Arguments

Floats are just as easy to pass as arguments to a method as are integer values. The following example will calculate the area of a circle. In this, the radius of circle will be as **float** type argument.

Example 17.22 Write a program to calculate the area of a circle.

..\CSharp_Book\Chap09\FloatArgument

```
using System;
using System.Collections.Generic;
using System.Text;

// Program to demonstrate float type parameter
namespace FloatArgument
```

```
{
    class Program
    {
        static void Main(string[] args)
        {
            float r;
            Console.Write("Enter the radius of circle : ");
            r = float.Parse(Console.ReadLine());
            area_circle(r);
        }

        static void area_circle(float radius)
        {
            float area = 0;
            area = (float)(3.14 * radius * radius);
            Console.WriteLine("The area of circle is : {0:F2}", area);
        }
    }
}
```

When the above program executed, it will produce the following output

```
Enter the radius of circle : 6
The area of circle is : 113.04
Press any key to continue . . .
```

From the above output, notice that the **radius** is passed as a float type argument.

9.6.9 Doubles as arguments

The **double** type is a very precise **float** value. The following program accepts two **double** values from the keyboard. The function **cal_power()** will raise the first number to the power specified by the second number.

..\CSharp_Book\Chap09\DoubleArgument

```
using System;
using System.Collections.Generic;
using System.Text;

// Program to demonstrate float type parameter
namespace DoubleArgument
{
    class Program
```

```
{
    static void Main(string[] args)
    {
        double db, dp;

        Console.Write("Enter the base number : ");
        db = double.Parse(Console.ReadLine());;
        Console.Write("Enter the power : ");
        dp = double.Parse(Console.ReadLine());;
        cal_power(db, dp);
    }

    static void cal_power(double baseValue, double power)
    {
        double dans;
        dans = 0;
        dans = Math.Pow(baseValue, power);
        Console.WriteLine("The result is : {0:F}", dans);
    }
  }
}
```

```
Enter the base number : 10
Enter the power : 5
The result is : 100000.00
Press any key to continue . . .
```

9.6.10 Arrays as arguments

An array can be passed to a function either as pass-by-address or call-by-reference. We already use the pass-by-address concept in previous section.

To pass an array argument to a method, specify the name of the array without any brackets. For example, if an array **hourlyTemp** has been declared as :

```
int[] hourlyTemp;
```

the method call statement :

```
modifyArray(hourlyTemp, 24);
```

passes array **hourlyTemp** and its size to method **modifyArray()**. While passing an array to a method, the array size is normally passed as well so that the method processes the specific number of elements in the array (otherwise, we would need to build this knowledge into the called method itself or place the array size in a global variable). When we pass an array object into a method we no longer would have to pass the size of the array as an argument.

C# automatically passes arrays to methods using simulated call-by-reference the called methods can modify the element values in the callers, the originally arrays. The values of the name of the array are the address of the first element of the array. Because the starting address of the array is passed, the called method knows precisely where the array is stored. Therefore, when the called method modifies array elements in its method body, it is modifying the actual elements of the array in their original memory locations.

Passing arrays simulated call-by-reference makes sense for performance reasons. If arrays were passed call-by-value, a copy of each element would be passed. For large and frequently passed arrays, this would be time consuming and would consume considerable storage space for the copies of the arrays.

Although entire arrays are passed simulated call-by-reference yet the individual array elements are passed call-by-value, exactly as simple variables are. Such simple single pieces of data are called scalar or scalar quantities. To pass an element of an array to a method, use the subscripted name of the array element as an argument in the method call.

For a method to receive an array through a method call, the method's parameter list must specify that an array would be received. For example, the method header for method **modifyArray()** might be written as :

```
void modifyArray(int b[], int arraySize)
```

indicating that **modifyArray()** accepts to receive an array of integers in parameter b and the number of array elements in parameter arraySize. The size of the array is not required between the array brackets. If it is included, the compiler would ignore it. Because arrays are passed simulated call-by-reference, when the called method uses the array name b, it would, in fact, be referring to the actual array in the caller (array **hourlyTemp** in the preceding call).

Note the strange appearance of the method prototype for modifyArray :

```
void modifyArray(int [], int);
```

This prototype could have been written as follows :

```
void modifyArray(int ArrayName[], int varName)
```

Remember that the prototype tells the compiler the number of arguments and the types of each argument (in the order in which the arguments are expected to appear).

The program given below demonstrates the difference between passing an entire array and passing an array element. The program first prints the five elements of integer array a. Next, a and its size are passed to method modifyArray where each of a's elements is multiplied by 4. Then a is reprinted in **Main()**. As the output shows, the elements of a are indeed modified by modifyArray. Now, the program prints the value of **a[3]** and passes it on to method **modifyElement**. Method **modifyElement** multiplies its argument by 4 and prints the new value. Note that when **a[3]** is reprinted in **Main()**, it has not been modified because individual array elements are passed call-by-value.

Example 12.23 Write a program to pass an entire array and an individual array element into a method.

..\CSharp_Book\Chap09\ArrayArg

```
using System;
using System.Collections.Generic;
using System.Text;

// Program to demonstrate Array as arugemnt
namespace ArrayArg
{
    class Program
    {
        static void Main(string[] args)
        {
            int i;
            int[] num = {20, 18, 13, 24, 9, 5};
            int Ln1 = num.Length; // Find the length of array num[]
            Console.WriteLine("Effects of passing entire array call-by-reference ");
            Console.WriteLine("The values of the original array are : ");
            for (i = 0; i < Ln1; i++)
                Console.WriteLine(num[i]);
            Console.WriteLine("The values of the modified array are : ");
            // Passes the array its length for further modification
            modifyArray(num, Ln1);
        }

        static void modifyArray(int[] b, int sizeOfArray) {
            for (int j = 0; j < sizeOfArray; j++)
                // Array is modified after multiplying by 4 with each element
                b[j] *= 4;
                for (int j = 0; j < sizeOfArray; j++)
                    Console.WriteLine(b[j]); // Prints the modified array
        }
    }
}
```

When the above program executed, it will produce the following output as shown in Fig. 9.8.

```
C:\WINDOWS\system32\cmd.exe
Effects of passing entire array call-by-reference
The values of the original array are :
20
18
13
24
9
5
The values of the modified array are :
80
72
52
96
36
20
Press any key to continue . . .
```

Fig. 9.8 Array argument as coll-by-reference.

Example 17.24 Write a program to pass an initialized array as an argument to a method and print the average or the array elements.

..\CSharp_Book\Chap09\ArrayArgument

```
using System;
using System.Collections.Generic;
using System.Text;

// Program that passes by address
// Program to demonstrate array type parameter
namespace ArrayArgument
{
    class Program
    {
        static void Main()
        {
            float[] arr = new float[10] {12.3F, 25.7F, 70.3F, 16.5F, 80.5F, 7.3F, 61.5F,
                                        10.5F, 20.5F, 120.5F};
            array_avg(arr);
        }

        static void array_avg(float[] fnum)
        {
            int i;
            float avg;
            avg = 0;
            Console.WriteLine("The array elements are : ");
            for (i = 0; i < 10; i++)
```

```
            {
                Console.Write("{0:F2}    ", fnum[i]);
                avg += fnum[i];
            }

            Console.WriteLine("The average is : {0:F2}", avg/10);
        }
    }
}
```

When the above program executed, it will produce the following output as shown in Fig. 9.9.

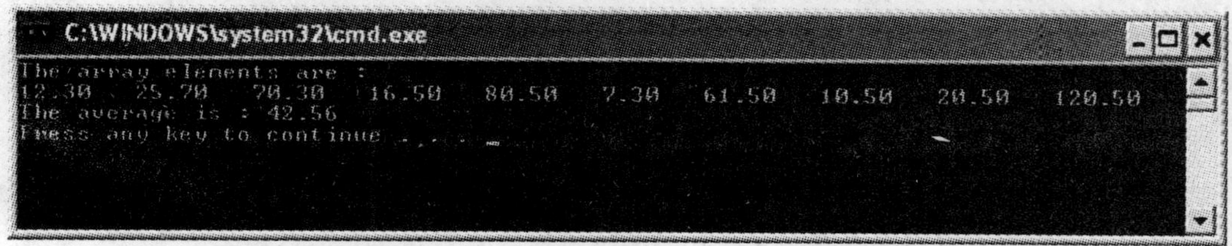

Fig. 9.9 Calculate average of an array argument as coll-by-reference.

The average is determined by summing each of the terms together and dividing by the total number of terms.

Example 17.25 Write a program using method to sort an array using exchange sort of ten elements and its algorithm.

The following steps define an algorithm for sorting an array :

```
Steps.  1. Set i to 0.
        2. Set j to i+1.
        3. If a[i] > a[j], exchange their values.
        4. Set j to j+1. If j < n goto step 3.
        5. Set i to i+1. If i < n-1 goto step 2.
        6. a is new sorted in ascending order.
```

n is the number of elements in the array

The implementation of the above algorithm as a method in C#, accepting the array and its size, returning the sorted array in ascending order so it can be printed out by calling module. The array should consist of ten elements.

..\CSharp_Book\Chap09\ExchangeSort

```
using System;
using System.Collections.Generic;
```

```
using System.Text;

// Demonstration of exchange sort of ten numbers.
namespace ExchangeSort
{
    class Program
    {
        static void Main()
        {
            int[] numbers = new int[] {10, 9, 8, 23, 19, 11, 2, 7, 1, 13, 12};
            int loop;
            Console.WriteLine("Before the sort, the array was : \n");
            for (loop = 0; loop < 11; loop++)
                Console.Write("{0} ", numbers[loop]);
            Console.WriteLine("\n");
            sort(numbers, 11);
            Console.WriteLine("After the sort, the array is :  \n");
            for (loop = 0; loop < 11; loop++)
                Console.Write("{0} ", numbers[loop]);
            Console.WriteLine("\n");
        }

        static void sort(int[] a, int elements)
        {
            int i = 0, j, temp;
            while (i < (elements - 1))
            {
                j = i + 1;
                while (j < elements)
                {
                    if (a[i] > a[j])
                    {
                        temp = a[i];
                        a[i] = a[j];
                        a[j] = temp;
                    }
                    j++;
                }
                i++;
            }
        }
    }
}
```

When the above program executed, it will produce the following output as shown in Fig. 9.10.

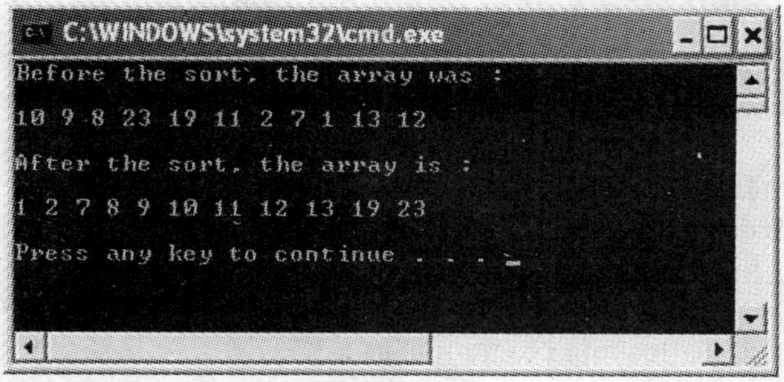

```
C:\WINDOWS\system32\cmd.exe
Before the sort, the array was :
10 9 8 23 19 11 2 7 1 13 12
After the sort, the array is :
1 2 7 8 9 10 11 12 13 19 23
Press any key to continue . . .
```

Fig. 9.10 Exchange short of an array argument as coll-by-reference.

9.7 Method Overloading

A typical program involves a great deal of names that represent variables and methods of various kinds. The compiler does not allow two variables to have the same name in the same function. Although two methods should have unique names in the same program, C# allows you to use the same name for different functions of the same program following certain rules. The ability to have various methods with the same name in the same program is referred to as overloading. The most important rule about function overloading is to make sure that each one of these methods has a different number or different type(s) of arguments.

> **Note**
> *The different versions of an overloaded method are distinguished by their signature, which is the number, type and order of the parameters.*

Each method has a signature. This comprises the method's name and its parameters (excepting their names), but not the method's return type. In the following method header, the elements making up the method's signature are emphasised - note also that the 'params' keyword is not included in the signature.

```
public static int myMethod(int a, ref double b, out bool c, params int[] d)
```

The importance of the signature is that no class is allowed to contain two methods with the same signature. Since the signature takes in more than the method name, however, it is possible for one class to have methods sharing a name. For example, a class with the method whose header is given above might also contain a method with the header:

```
public static int myMethod(int a, ref double b)
```

Note, however, that since neither its return type nor the params keyword are part of a method's signature this class could not also contain a method with the header:

```
public static void myMethod(int e, ref double f, out bool g, int[] h)
```

Let us consider the following example, which used the sum of two number with different parameters. Notice that the method name is same for all three methods, but the return type, and method parameters are different :

```
public static int myMethod(int a, int b)
public static double myMethod(float a, float b)
public static long myMethod(float a, float b)
```

and the complete method overloading program is as :

..\CSharp_Book\Chap09\MethodOv

```
using System;
using System.Collections.Generic;
using System.Text;

// Demonstration method overloading.
namespace MethodOv
{
    class Program
    {

        public static int myMethod(int a, int b)
        {
            int sum = 0;
            sum = a + b;
            return sum;
        }
        public static double myMethod(float a, float b)
        {
            double sum = 0;
            sum = a + b;
            return sum;
        }

        public static long myMethod(long a, long b)
        {
            long sum = 0;
            sum = a + b;
            return sum;
        }
```

```
        static void Main()
        {
            int p = 10, q = 20;
            float l = 35.6F, m = 12.60F;
            long x = 2350, y = 4560;
            Console.WriteLine("Sum of two integer numbers is : {0}", myMethod(p, q));
            Console.WriteLine("Sum of two real numbers is : {0:F2}", myMethod(l, m));
            Console.WriteLine("Sum of two long numbers is : {0:F2}", myMethod(x, y));

        }
    }
}
```

When the above program executed, it will produce the following output as shown in Fig. 9.11.

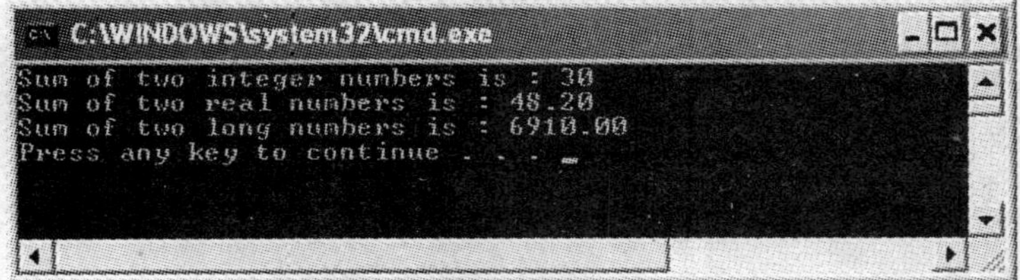

Fig. 9.11 Method overloading.

9.8 Recursion Method

This is where a function repeatedly calls itself to perform calculations. When a loop repetitively calls, a function is called as recursion. For example the factorial of an integer n can be calculated as the following algorithm :

Consider the calculation of n factorial (n! = 6!)

i.e., $6! = 6\times5\times4\times3\times2\times1$

$6! = 6\times5!$

$6! = 6\times(6-1)!$

$n! = n\times(n-1)!$

Example Write a program to find the factorial of any number using recursion method.

..\CSharp_Book\Chap09\FactRecur

```
using System;
using System.Collections.Generic;
using System.Text;

// Demonstration of recursion method on factorial
```

```
namespace FactRecur
{
    public class Fact_num
    {
        int factorial(int n)
        {
            if (n == 1)
                return (1);
            else
                return (n * factorial(n - 1));
        }
        static void Main()
        {
            Fact_num FCT = new Fact_num();
            Console.WriteLine("Factorial of 3 is: " + FCT.factorial(3));
            Console.WriteLine("Factorial of 4 is: " + FCT.factorial(4));
            Console.WriteLine("Factorial of 5 is: " + FCT.factorial(5));
            Console.WriteLine("Factorial of 6 is: " + FCT.factorial(6));
        }
    }
}
```

When the above program executed, it will produce the following output as shown in Fig. 9.12.

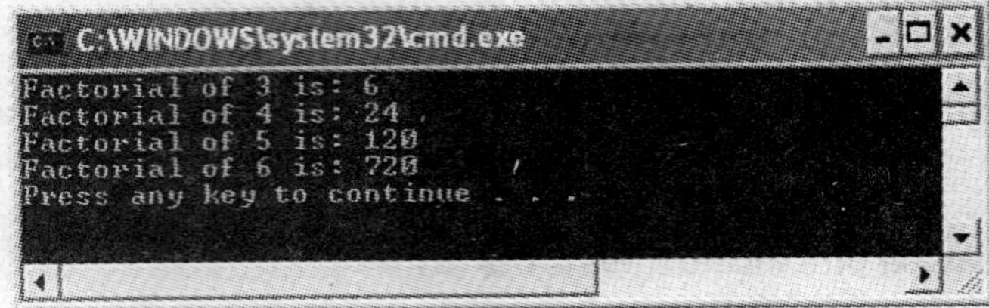

Fig. 9.12 Factorial using recursion method.

Example 9.13 Write a program to find the x^n using recursion function.

..\CSharp_Book\Chap09\xtonRecur

```
using System;
using System.Collections.Generic;
using System.Text;

// Demonstration of recursion function of x to the power n.
namespace xtonRecur
{
    public class powerN
    {
```

```
        int x_powern(int x, int n)
        {
            if (n == 0)
                return (1);
            else
                return (x * x_powern(x, n - 1));
        }
        static void Main()
        {
            powerN Pr = new powerN();
            int x, n;
            Console.Write("Enter the value of x : ");
            x = int.Parse(Console.ReadLine());
            Console.Write("Enter the value of n : ");
            n = int.Parse(Console.ReadLine());
            Console.WriteLine("The value of x^n is : " + Pr.x_powern(x, n));
        }
    }
}
```

When the above program executed, it will produce the following output as shown in Fig. 9.13.

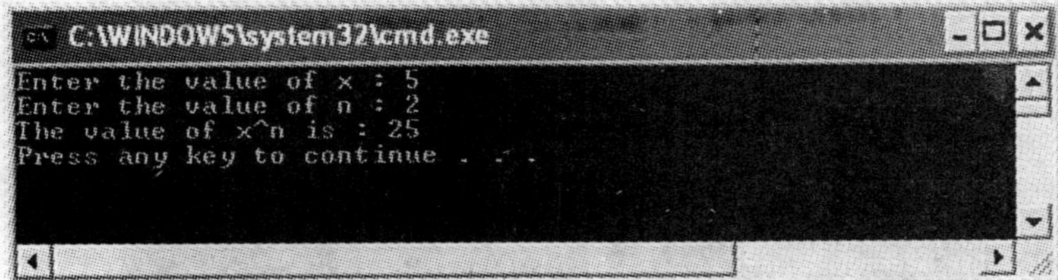

Fig. 9.13 X^n using recursion method.

Example Write a program to find the sum of 'n' natural numbers using recursion function.

..\CSharp_Book\Chap09\sumnRecur

```
using System;
using System.Collections.Generic;
using System.Text;
// Sum of natural numbers using recursion function.
namespace sumnRecur
{
    public class SumN
    {
        long sum_n(long sum, long num)
        {
```

```
            return sum + num;
        }
        static void Main()
        {
            SumN Sm = new SumN();
            int n, ctr = 1, num;
            long sum = 0;

            Console.Write("Enter the value of n : ");
            n = int.Parse(Console.ReadLine());

            while (ctr<=n)
            {
                Console.Write("Enter the value for  : {0} :", ctr);
                num = int.Parse(Console.ReadLine());
                sum = Sm.sum_n(sum, num);
                ctr++;
            }

            Console.WriteLine("The sum is : {0:F2}", sum);
        }
    }
}
```

When the above program executed, it will produce the following output as shown in Fig. 9.14.

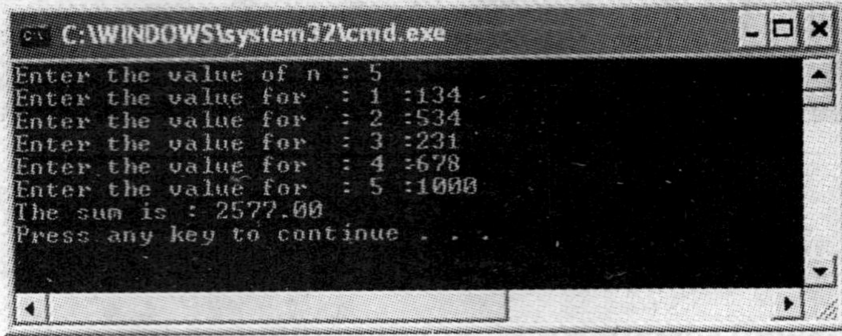

Fig. 9.14 Sum of n using recursion method.

Example Write a program to find the Fibonacci number using recursion function.

..\CSharp_Book\Chap09\FibRecur

```
using System;
using System.Collections.Generic;
using System.Text;

// Demonstration of recursion function to find Fibonacci number.
namespace FibRecur
{
```

```
    public class Fib
    {
        int fib_series(int a, int b)
        {
            return a + b;
        }

        static void Main()
        {
            Fib Fb = new Fib();
            int a = 1, b = 1, c = 0, i = 0, n;

            Console.Write("Enter the value of n : ");
            n = int.Parse(Console.ReadLine());

            Console.WriteLine();
            Console.WriteLine("The series is...");
            Console.WriteLine(a);
            Console.WriteLine(b);

            while (i < n - 2)
            {
                c = Fb.fib_series(a, b);

                Console.WriteLine(c);
                a = b;
                b = c;
                i++;
            }
        }
    }
}
```

When the above program executed, it will produce the following output as shown in Fig. 9.15.

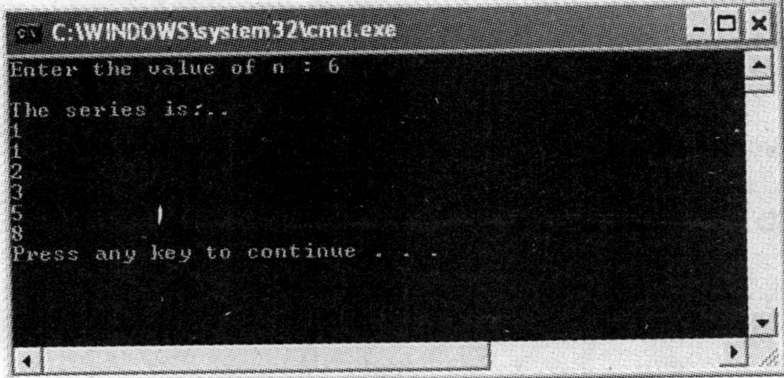

Fig. 9.15 Fibonnacci series using recursion method.

Example 7.20 Write a program to calculate GCD of two numbers using recursive function.

..\CSharp_Book\Chap09\gcd

```
using System;
using System.Collections.Generic;
using System.Text;

// Demonstration of recursion function to find the GCD.
namespace gcd
{
    public class GCD
    {
        int r, r1;
        int gcd_recur(int x, int y)
        {
            while (r == 0)
            {
                if (x < y)
                {
                    r = x % y;
                    r1 = y / x;
                }
                else
                {
                    r = y % x;
                    r1 = x / y;
                }
                y = x;
                x = r;
                r = gcd_recur(x, y);
            }
            return (r);
        }

        static void Main(string[] args)
        {
            GCD gd = new GCD();
            int a, b;

            Console.WriteLine("Enter first number to find the GCD : ");
            a = int.Parse(Console.ReadLine());
            Console.WriteLine("Enter second number to find the GCD : ");
            b = int.Parse(Console.ReadLine());
```

```
            Console.WriteLine("The greatest common divisor is : " + gd.gcd_recur(a, b));
        }
    }
}
```

When the above program executed, it will produce the following output as shown in Fig. 9.16.

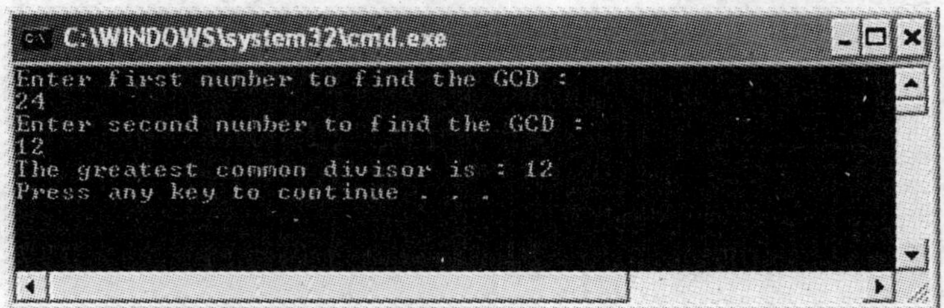

Fig. 9.16 GCD using recursion method.

Example 7.21 Write a function that interchanges the value of two integers A and B without using any extra variable.

..\CSharp_Book\Chap09\swapNumber

```
using System;
using System.Collections.Generic;
using System.Text;

// Swapping two numbers without third variable
namespace swapNumber
{
    class Change_num
    {
        void SWAP(int A, int B)
        {
            A = A + B;
            B = A - B;
            A = A - B;
            Console.WriteLine("After swapping x is - > " + A);
            Console.WriteLine("After swapping y is - > " + B);
        }

        static void Main(string[] args)
        {
            Change_num CH = new Change_num();
            int x, y;
```

```
            Console.Write("Enter first number (x) : ");
            x = int.Parse(Console.ReadLine());
            Console.Write("Enter second number (y) : ");
            y = int.Parse(Console.ReadLine());
            Console.WriteLine();

            Console.WriteLine("The two numbers are : {0} and {1}", x, y);
            Console.WriteLine();

            CH.SWAP(x, y);
        }
    }
}
```

When the above program executed, it will produce the following output as shown in Fig. 9.17.

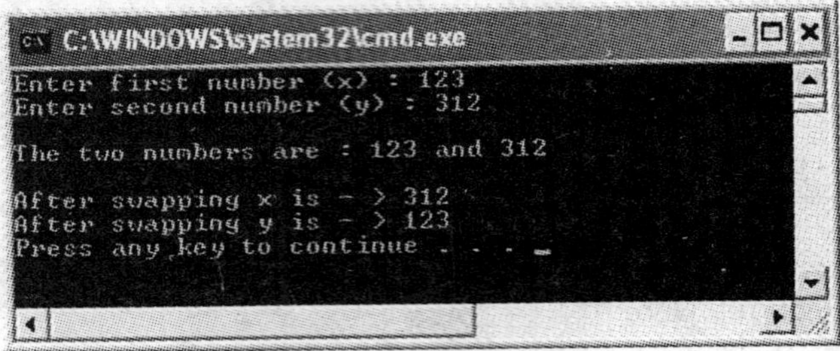

Fig. 9.17 Swapping of two numbers.

Exercise

1. What is a method ?
2. How will you use the library method ?
3. Write some advantages of using method.
4. Why are we using return statement ?
5. What are the three basic components of a method definition ?
6. How will you write the first line of method definition ?
7. What do you mean by the scope of the variable ?
8. Differentiate between value type and reference type?
9. Contrast between local variable and global variable ?
10. What is static variable ?
11. Suppose method M1 calls method M2 within a program. Does the order of method definition make any difference? Explain.
12. What is the purpose of void in a method definition ?
13. When a method is accessed, must the data type of the actual parameter agree with the data type as the parameter in the corresponding method declaration ?

14. Differentiate between the privately and publicly derived visibility modes.
15. What is a recursion ? What is the advantage of using recursive method ?
16. Is it necessary that the name of actual parameter should be the same as that of the formal parameter ?
17. What is the meaning of following ?
    (a) void fab(int n);
    (b) int binary(int n);
    (c) float sum(int a, float b, int c);
    (d) char ch(char choice);
18. Write the first line of the method definition for each of the following :
    (a) A method called area that accepts two floating point variables a and b and returns floating point quantity.
    (b) A method called Display that is not accepting any variable and not returning anything.
19. What is the meaning of the following method definition ?
    (a) void binary(int n);
    (b) long float fact(float n);
20. Are the private data members of a class accessible outside of the class ?
21. What is the difference between private and public member of a class ?
22. In an overloaded function, how is matching done ?
23. What is function overloading ?
24. What will be the output of the following program ?
    (a)
```
class Program
{
    // Called method
    static int sum_array(int[] num, int ctr)
    {
        int sum = 0;
        for (int i = 0; i < ctr; ++i)
            sum += num[i];
        return sum;
    }
    static void Main()
    {
        int[] arr = {10, 23, 43, 55, 32, 14, 87, 56, 65, 34};
        Console.WriteLine("Sum is : " + sum_array(arr, 10));
        Console.WriteLine("Sum is : " + sum_array(arr, 5));
        Console.WriteLine("Sum is : " + sum_array(arr, 0));
    }
}
```
    (b)
```
class Program
{
    static void change(int[] x, int i)
    {
        x[i] = x[i] * i;
    }
```

```
        static void Main()
        {
            int[] x = {11, 21, 31, 41};
            for(int i = 0; i<4; i++)
            {
                change(x, i);
                Console.WriteLine(x[i]);
            }
        }
    }
(c) class Program
    {
        static void display(double d)
        {
            Console.WriteLine("Real : " + d);
        }
        static void display(int i)
        {
            Console.WriteLine("Integer : " + i);
        }
        static void display(char Ch)
        {
            Console.WriteLine("Character : " + Ch);
        }
        static void display(string Ch)
        {
            Console.WriteLine("String : " + Ch);
        }
        static void Main()
        {
            double F = 3.1416;
            display('A');
            display(F);
            display("String");
        display(45);
        }
    }
(d) class Program
    {
        static int add(int j)
        {
            if (j >= 4)
                j = j * j;
            else
```

```
            j = j * 2;
        return (j);
    }
    static void Main()
    {
        int i = 4;
        int a;
        a = add(i);
        Console.WriteLine(a);
    }
}
```

(e)
```
class Program
{
    static void square(int i, int j)
    {
        i = i * j;
        j = j * j;
    }
    static void Main()
    {
        int i = 4, j = 10;
        square(i, j);
        Console.WriteLine(i);
        Console.WriteLine(j);
    }
}
```

Programming

1. Write the method definition for the following :
   (a) A method called root accepts three integers and returns floating point quantity.
   (b) A method called perimeter accepts two integers and returns an integer.
   (c) A method called check accepts one integer and one character and returns nothing.
   (d) A method called calculates accepts nothing and returns nothing.
2. Write a program to calculate the root of quadratic equation using a method.
3. Write a method that accepts two parameters A and B and interchange their values.
4. Any year is entered through the keyboard. Write a method to determine whether the year is leap or not.
5. Write a method pow(a, b) to calculate the value of a raised to the power b.
6. Write a menu driven program-using method to do the following tasks :
   (a) To check whether the number is even or odd.
   (b) To find the sum of even numbers.
   (ci) To find the sum of odd numbers.
   (d) exit

7. Write a menu driven program to calculate :
   (a) Area of rectangle.
   (b) Area of circle.
   (c) Area of cube.
8. Write a recursive method to calculate the factorial of a number.
9. Write a recursive method to generate the fibonacci series.
10. Write a recursive method to calculate a to the power b.
11. Write a method to calculate $x^i / x!$.
12. Use the concept of function overloading to compute the area of rectangle with Hero's formula and also, the area of circle.
13. Use the concept of function overloading to convert a character from lowercase to uppercase [or uppercase to lowercase] and also, to increment an integer.
14. Write a program to calculate the volume of cube ($side^3$), volume of cylinder($3.14 * r^2 * h$) and volume of rectangle(l * b * h).
15. Suppose an array P containing float is arranged in ascending order. Write a user defined method in C# to search for one float from P with the help of binary search method. The method should return an integer 0 to show absence of the number and integer 1 to show the presence of the number in the array. The method should have the parameters as (1) an array P (2) the number DATA to be searched (3) number of elements N.
16. Write a program to calculate the sum and average of odd, even and natural numbers using methods.
17. Write a method SUM() in C++ with two arguments, double x and int n. The method should return a value of type double and it should find the sum of the following series :
    $1 + x^2/1! + x^4/2! + x^6/3! + x^8/4! + x^{10}/5! + \ldots\ldots + x^{2n}/n!$ up to N terms
18. Write a program that inputs a series of integers and passes them one at a time to function called even(), which uses the modulus operator to determine if an integer is even. The method should take an integer argument and return true if an integer is even otherwise false.
19. A large chemical company pays its salespeople on a commission basis. The salespeople receive Rs. 200 per week plus 9 % of their gross sales for that week. For example, a salesperson who sells Rs. 5000/- worth of chemicals in a week receives Rs. 200/- plus 9% of Rs. 5000/-, or a total of Rs. 650/-. Develop a C# program that will input each salesperson's gross sales for last week and calculate and display that salesperson's earnings.
20. Write a method to find the sum of series :
    $$\frac{1}{1^2} + \frac{1}{2^2} + \frac{1}{3^2} + \frac{1}{4^2} + \frac{1}{5^2} + \ldots\ldots \text{ up to N terms.}$$
21. Write a method to find the sum of series :
    $$1 + \frac{1}{2!} + \frac{1}{3!} + \frac{1}{4!} + \frac{1}{5!} + \frac{1}{6!} + \ldots\ldots \text{ up to N terms.}$$
22. Write a method to find the sum of series :
    $$1 + \frac{1}{x} + \frac{1}{x^2} + \frac{1}{x^3} + \frac{1}{x^4} + \ldots\ldots \text{ up to N terms.}$$

Structure and Enumeration 10

10.1 Introduction

In many data processing applications, individual pieces of data need to be *grouped together* to form a complete description of some item. For example, a book can have its author, title, price, and publisher . When we group all these information together we define a complete *record* of the book.

Note that each individual piece of information (i.e title, author etc. usually called "fields" or "members") might be of a different *type*. So, we can't group these fields together as elements in an array because all the elements of arrays must be of the same type.

Definition

A structure provides a means of grouping variables of different data type under a single name.

The first structure gives you the ability to group data together and work with that data as a whole. Being able to manipulate several values of different data types in a single variable makes programs easier to write and maintain.

10.2 Understanding Structure Variables

A structure is a collection of one or more values, each potentially of a different data type. As you know, the elements in an array must be the same data type, and you must refer to the entire array by its name. Each element (called a member) in a structure can be a different data type.

Suppose that you want to use a structure Employee to keep track of employee information. You might want to track the following pieces of information about an employee :

empcode
empname

empdesig
empsalary

This **Employee** structure would have four members.

After deciding on the members, you must decide what data types to use for the members. Here, empcode can be integer, the empname and the empdesig can be character arrays, the empsalary can be floating-point value. This information is represented in Listing 10.1 here :

Listing 10.1 For sample structure data types

Member Name	Data type
empcode	Integer
empname	string
empdesig	string
empsalary	Floating-point

Each structure you define can have an associated structure name, called *structure tag*. Structure tags are not required in most cases, but defining one for each structure in your program is generally a good idea. The structure tag is not a variable name. Unlike array names that reference arrays as variables, a structure tag is just a label for the structure's format.

Note

The structure tag provides a shorthand way of declaring structures.

You name structure tags yourself, using the name rules of variables. If you give the Employee structure a structure tag named emp, you are telling C# that the tag called emp contains one integer followed by two character arrays and a floating-point value.

A structure tag is actually a new data type that you, the programmer, define. When you want to store an integer, you do not have to define to C# what an integer is C# already knows. When you want to store a Employee information, however (using the example described here) that you need a new data type. That data type is your structure tag called *emp* and it looks like the structure just described (one integer, two character arrays, an a floating-point value).

Note

No memory is reserved for structure tags. A structure tag is your own data type (user defined data type). C# does not reserve memory for the integer data type until you declare an integer variable. C# does not reserve memory for a structure until you declare a structure variable.

A structure is an enhanced version of the primitive data types we have used in previous lessons. The difference is that, like a class, a structure is created from one primitive type or by combining various primitive types, resulting in an advanced data type that is not inherently built in the C# language.

10.3 Defining a Structure

To define a structure, you use the **struct** statement. **struct** defines a new data type for your program. The format of the structure statement is :

```
struct [struct tag]
{
    Data member;
    Data member;
        :
    Data member;
    ..
    ..
}
```

The variables or members of the structure are declared within the body.

> **Note**
> *The struct declaration is a user defined data type.*

As mentioned earlier, the structure tag is optional hence, the brackets in the format. Each member definition is a normal variable definition, such as **int i**; or **float sales**; or any other valid variable definition, including variable pointers if the structure requires a pointer as a member. At the end of the structure's definition and before the final semicolon, you can specify one or more structure variables.

> **Note**
> *Any variable you declare within the body of the structure is referred to as a member of that structure.*

To create a structure, you use the same formula as a class but with the **struct** keyword. Here is an example of a structure:

```
struct Employee
{
    public int empcode;
    public string empname;
    public string empdesig;
    public float empsalary;
    .
    .
}
```

Like a class, a structure can have fields. They are listed in the body of the structure.

..\CSharp_Book\Chap10\StructDisp

```
using System;
using System.Collections.Generic;
using System.Text;

namespace StructDisp
{
    public struct Employee
    {
        public int empcode;
        public string empname;
        public string empdesig;
        public float empsalary;
        public void display()
        {
            Console.WriteLine("An Employee details");
            for (int i = 1; i <= 35; i++)
                Console.Write("=");

            Console.WriteLine();
            Console.WriteLine("Employee code : " + empcode);
            Console.WriteLine("Employee name : " + empname);
            Console.WriteLine("Employee designation : " + empdesig);
            Console.WriteLine("Employee salary : " + empsalary);
        }
    }

    public class Program
    {
        static void Main()
        {
            Employee emp;
            // Assigning static field
            emp.empcode = 100;
            emp.empname = "Mr. Santosh Rana";
            emp.empdesig = "Manager";
            emp.empsalary = 11600;
            emp.display();
        }
    }
}
```

When the above program executed, it will produce the following output as shown in Fig. 10.1.

```
C:\WINDOWS\system32\cmd.exe
Enter first number (x) : 123
Enter second number (y) : 312

The two numbers are : 123 and 312

After swapping x is - > 312
After swapping y is - > 123
Press any key to continue . . .
```

Fig. 10.1 Displaying structure information.

10.4 Enum

Enums are strongly typed constants. They are essentially unique types that allow you to assign symbolic names to integral values. In the C# tradition, they are strongly typed, meaning that an enum of one type may not be implicitly assigned to an enum of another type even though the underlying value of their members are the same. Along the same lines, integral types and enums are not implicitly interchangable. All assignments between different enum types and integral types require an explicit cast.
Enums lend themselves to more maintainable code because they are symbolic, allowing you to work with integral values, but using a meaningful name to do so. For example, what type of code would you rather work with - a set of values named North, South, East, and West or the set of integers 0, 1, 2, and 3 that mapped to the same values, respectively. Enums make working with strongly typed constants via symbolic names easy.

Enums are value types, which means they contain their own value, can't inherit or be inherited from, and assignment copies the value of one enum to another. You will see in this lesson and elsewhere that enums are used and referred to with both lower case, **enum**, and upper case, **enum**. Strangely enough, the relationship between the two is that the C# type, **enum**, inherits the **Base Class Library** (BCL) type, **enum**. Use the C# type, **enum**, to define new enums and use the BCL type, **enum**, to implement static enum methods.

10.5 Declaring Enum

In C#, you can define your own data type and specify what values a variable of this type can take. The data type defined this way is known as *enumerated* (**enum**) data type. Enumerated data type helps in enhancing the readability of the code. That is this data type is used to give name to integer constants. By default, these numerical values are integers, but they can also be longs, bytes, etc. It is declared with keyword *enum*. For example,

```
enum color {Red, Yellow, Green, Brown}
enum months {January, February, March, April, May, June, July, August, September, October,
        November, December);
enum visible(On, Off);
enum doesit(Yes, No);
```

The above statement defines four integer constants. Enumerated values are by default starts with 0 and incremented by 1. So, the above character is as :

```
const int Red = 0
const int Yellow = 1
const int Green = 2
const int Brown = 3
```

The following program contains an **enum** definition and code that uses that **enum** in a **switch** statement. Instead of using the numbers 0, 1, and 2 in the **switch** statement, the code is more meaningful through the use of the **Volume enum**.

..\CSharp_Book\Chap10\EnumData

```
using System;
using System.Collections.Generic;
using System.Text;

namespace EnumData
{
    // declares the enum
    public enum Volume
    {
        Low,
        Medium,
        High
    }

    // demonstrates how to use the enum
    class EnumSwitch
    {
        static void Main()
        {
            // create and initialize
            // instance of enum type
            Volume myVolume = Volume.Medium;
            // make decision based
            // on enum value

            switch (myVolume)
            {
                case Volume.Low:
                    Console.WriteLine("The volume has been turned Down.");
                    break;
```

```
                case Volume.Medium:
                    Console.WriteLine("The volume is in the middle.");
                    break;
                case Volume.High:
                    Console.WriteLine("The volume has been turned up.");
                    break;
            }
            Console.ReadLine();
        }
    }
}
```

When the above program executed, it will produce the following output :

```
The volume is in the middle.
Press any key to continue . . .
```

You can also override the default numerical values of any and all of the enumeration elements. In the following example, the first literal is set to value 1. The other literals are then set up according to the second rule given above, so **DAYS.Sunday** will end up equal to 7.

```
public enum DAYS
{
    Monday=1,
    Tuesday
    Wednesday,
    Thursday,
    Friday,
    Saturday,
    Sunday
}
```

In the two examples given, the values of each literal has been unique within the enumeration. This is usually how you will want things to be, but in fact the values need not be unique. In the following case, the value of **DAYS**.Thursday is also set to equal 1. The values assigned to the other literals will follow the rules given previously, so both **DAYS.Tuesday** and **DAYS.Friday** will equal 2, etc.

```
public enum DAYS
{
    Monday=1,
    Tuesday
    Wednesday,
    Thursday=1,
    Friday,
```

```
    Saturday,
    Sunday
}
```

In C# enumerations are type-safe, by which we mean that the compiler will do its best to stop you assigning illicit values to enumeration typed variables. For instance, the following code should not compile:

```
int i = DAYS.Monday;
```

In order to get this code to compile, you would have to make explicit casts both ways (even converting from **DAYS** to **int**), ie:

```
int i = (ind)DAYS.Monday;
DAYS d = (DAYS)i;
```

At this point you may be wondering what happens if you cast an int to an enumeration value where that same value is defined for two elements within the enumeration. And the answer is this: one of the elements is given 'primary' status, so it gets picked ahead of the other.

A useful feature of enumerations is that one can retrieve the literal as a string from the numeric constant with which it is associated. In fact, this is given by the default **ToString()** method, so the following expression comes out as true:

```
DAYS.Monday.ToString()=="Monday"
```

The following code prints out both the literal and its constant value for the specified enumeration.

..\CSharp_Book\Chap10\EnumOver

```
using System;
using System.Collections.Generic;
using System.Text;

namespace EnumOver
{
    public class EnumTest
    {
        public enum DAYS : byte
            { Monday, Tuesday, Wednesday, Thursday, Friday, Saturday, Sunday }

        public static void Main()
        {
            Array dayArray = Enum.GetValues(typeof(EnumTest.DAYS));
            foreach (DAYS day in dayArray)
                Console.WriteLine("Number {1} of EnumTest.DAYS is {0}",
```

```
                        day, day.ToString("d"));
        }
    }
}
```

When the above program executed, it will produce the following output as shown in Fig. 10.2.

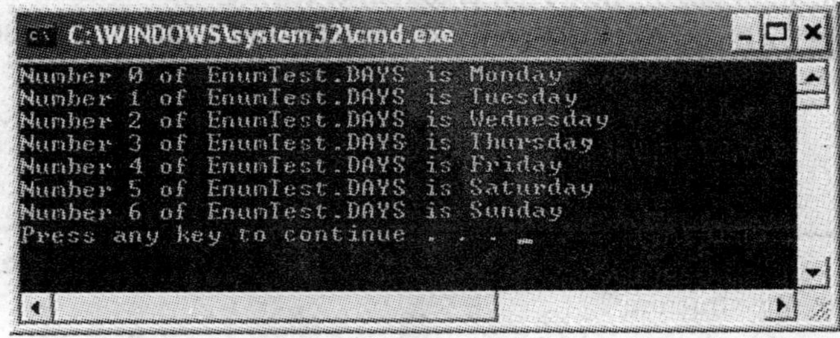

Fig. 10.2 Literal and constant value of enum.

Since it's not immediately obvious what's going on in the main method here, let's take the time to go through it.

On line,

```
Array dayArray = Enum.GetValues(typeof(EnumTest.DAYS));
```

we use the static **GetValues** method of the **Enum** class. When you pass this class an enumeration type - in this case, the type corresponding to **EnumTest.DAYS** - it returns an array of all the values of the elements within that enumeration. Note that the Enum class also has the GetNames method, which returns the literal strings.

On line,

```
foreach (DAYS day in dayArray)
```

we set up a foreach loop, pulling out, into day, each value in the dayArray in turn. Note that this value is of type **DAYS**.

On line 11 we use string interpolation as part of the Console.WriteLine method. This method makes use of the **String.Format** method, so is equivalent to:

```
Console.WriteLine(String.Format("Number {1} of EnumTest.DAYS is {0}",
        day, day.ToString("d")));
```

And what the **String.Format** method does is to take 'textual representations' of the objects it is passed as parameters, and slots them into the appropriate places within the 'format string' it is passed. So this line of code is basically equivalent to:

```
Console.WriteLine("Number " + day.ToString("d").ToString() + " of EnumTest.DAYS is "
        + day.ToString());
```

Now, we've already noted that **day.ToString()** will return a literal string, but what about the method **day.ToString("d")**? Well, we had a stab at explaining this a while ago, but did very badly. In fact, we just made an error. So hopefully the following will be better.

The **ToString** method can take a single **IFormatProvider** parameter which indicates how the string conversion should be conducted. Values for this parameter can include things like "g", "d", "x", "f", etc. The stated implication of "d", however, is to render in 'Decimal format'. And when we use this on an enumeration member, it provides a string representation of the *numerical value* of the enumeration member.

Exercise

1. What do you mean by the structure ?
2. What are structure variables ?
3. Structures are value type or reference type ?
4. What is structure tag ?
5. What are enums ?
6. How will you define a structure in your program ?
7. Is structure declaration is user defined type ?
8. What do you mean by the member of a structure ?
9. Write the syntax of enum declaration ?
10. Enums are value type or reference type ?
11. Are enumerations type safe in C# ?
12. What is the difference between structure and class ?
13. What is the difference between an array and structures ?
14. What are the similarities between a class and a structure ?
15. What is the default accessibility for members of a struct ?
16. What are the individual elements of a structure called ?
17. What are the two ways to initialize members of a structure ?
18. Do you pass structures by copy or by address ?
19. How many members does the following structure declaration contain ?

```
struct student
{
    int rollno;
    struct subjectmarks;
    long int total;
    float per;
    char grade;
}
```

20. What is the advantage of creating an array of structures instead of using individual variable names for each structure variable ?
21. Declare a structure having following fields :
    (a) an integer quantity won
    (b) an integer quantity lost

(c) a floating-point quantity result.

21. Declare a enumerated data type code with the following values :
    D, R, W, C
23. Describe with examples the use of enumerated data type.
24. Why are enumerations often termed as symbolic constants ?
25. Write a structure specification that includes three variables called hours, minutes and seconds. Call this structure time (all are int type).
26. Differentiate between structure variable declarations and structure type declaration.
27. Define a structure consisting of two integer members called hra and da.
28. What is the advantage of creating an array of structures instead of using individual variable names for each structure variable ?

Programming

1. Write a structure that a video store can use in a program to track the video tape inventory. Make sure that the structure includes the tape's title, the length of the tape (in minutes), the cost of the tape, the rental price of the tape, and the date of the movie's release.
2. Declare two structure one is called employee : Name, address, phone number, salary and second is called perks : da = 20 % of salary, hra = 25 % of salary, Net = salary + da + hra. Write a program to calculate the net salary of an employee.
3. Declare a structure having following members : Customer no., name, Number of units consumed and bill. The bill is to be calculated according to the following conditions:

Units consumed	**Tariff**
For the first 100 units	Rs. 0.40 per unit
For the next 200 units	Rs. 0.50 per unit
For the next 300 units	Rs. 0.75 per unit
For the next 400 units	Rs. 1.00 per unit
Beyond 1000 units	Rs. 1.50 per unit

   Write a program to calculate the bill and displaying the information of all the customers in the sorted order of customer no.
4. Declare the structure accounts of 10 customers with the following fields : Name of the depositor, Account number, Type of account (s for saving and c for current) , balance amount. Write a menu driven program to perform the following operations :
   (a) To initialize the structure members.
   (b) To deposit money.
   (c) For withdrawal of money after checking minimum balance (minimum balance is Rs. 500).
   (d) To display the information of particular customer according to account number.
   (e) To display the status of all customers.
5. Write a program to accept the name and total marks of 20 students in an array. Display the names of the students (including marks) securing highest and lowest marks using structure.
6. Develop a structure to store information about employees of an organization consisting of following data elements :

Data item	Type	Width
Code	Integer	
Name	String	50
Dept	String	15
Join_date	Date	8

7. Declare a structure to represent a complex number (a number having real part and an imaginary part). Write a program to add, subtract, multiply and divide two complex numbers.
8. A blood bank maintains the record of donor : name, date of birth, address and blood group. Write a program to enter the data of donor and display list of donor.
9. Write a program in C# to store the information of country, its capital and per capita income, and perform the following operation :
   (a) display country and per capita income, given its capital
   (b) display capital and per capita income, given its country
   (c) display country and capital, given its per capita income.

Object-Oriented Programming 11

11.1 Introduction

For many years (roughly 1970 to 1990), *structured programming* was the most common way to organize a program. This is characterized by a functional-decomposition style - breaking the algorithms into every smaller function. However, as programs became larger, the programming become complex.

There have been several post-structured programming attempts to control complexity. One of these is to use software *components*—pre-constructed software "parts" to avoid programming. And when you have to program, use *object-oriented programming* (OOP)

11.2 Object-Oriented Programming

Object-oriented programming (OOP) is a programming language model organized around "objects" rather than "actions" and data rather than logic. Historically, a program has been viewed as a logical procedure that takes input data, processes it, and produces output data. The programming challenge was seen as how to write the logic, not how to define the data. Object-oriented programming takes the view that what we really care about are the objects we want to manipulate rather than the logic required to manipulate them. Examples of objects range from human beings (described by name, address, and so forth) to buildings and floors (whose properties can be described and managed) down to the little widgets on your computer desktop (such as buttons and scroll bars). OOP is often said to incorporate these techniques :

- **Inheritance.** The concept of a data class makes it possible to define subclasses of data objects that share some or all of the main class characteristics. Called inheritance, this property of OOP forces a more thorough data analysis, reduces development time, and ensures more accurate coding.

- **Encapsulation.** *Encapsulation* is grouping data and functions together and keeping their implementation details private.
- **Data hiding.** Since a class defines only the data it needs to be concerned with, when an instance of that class (an object) is run, the code will not be able to accidentally access other program data. This characteristic of data hiding provides greater system security and avoids unintended data corruption.
- **Polymorphism.** *Polymorphism* is the ability of different functions to be invoked with the same name.

Definition

Object-oriented programming is not just another way of programming; it is a new way of organizing programs.

11.3 The Object-Oriented Programming (OOP) Paradigm

Object-oriented programming (OOP) deals with the overall program organization rather than the details of program operation. OOP have evolved to counter some of the drawbacks of procedural programming. Thus, OOP gives more emphasis on data, provides extensibility and models real world problems very well.

OOP treats data as an important and critical element in the program development. It ties data more closely to the functions that operate on it and thus avoids global access. OOP paradigm decomposes the problem into objects which model the real-world entities. It then builds data and functions around these objects. Thus, an object is a unit which encapsulates "data and the functions that operate on that data". This gives rise to the key term *data encapsulation*—which refers to the encapsulation of data and its function (also called member method in C#) into a single entity—the object. The data in an object cannot be accessed directly. It is hidden from accidental alteration. Data can be accessed only through the member functions in the object. This gives rise to the concept of *data hiding*. These two concepts of data encapsulation and data hiding simplify writing, debugging and maintaining programs.

Objects communicate or interact with one another through member functions. Thus, to summarize, data of an object can be accessed only by the member functions associated with that object. Functions of one object, however, can access functions of other objects. The following Fig. 11.1 represents the organization of data and functions in OOP.

In a procedural programming, a given problem is divided into small sized sub problems, each sub problem represents a specific task that can be handled efficiently and effectively. Then to solve each sub problem, a function/procedure is written. In this approach, there is no mention of data as shown in Fig. 11.2.

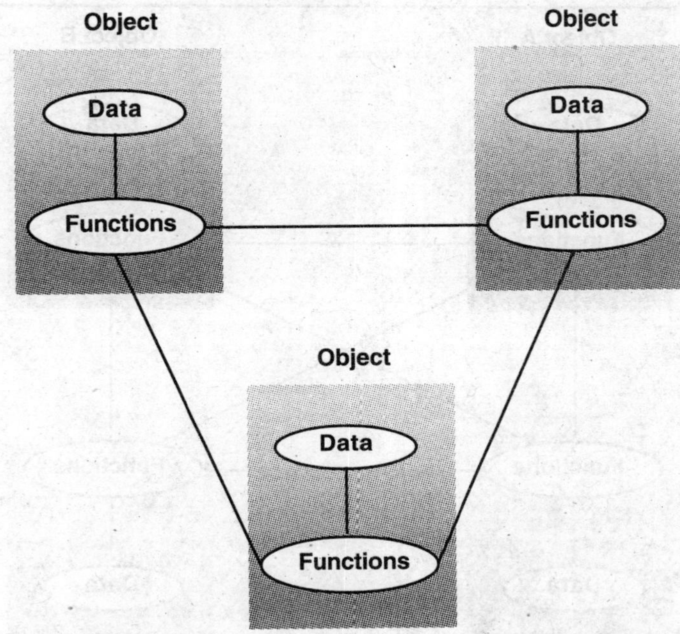

Fig. 11.1 Organization of data and functions in OOP.

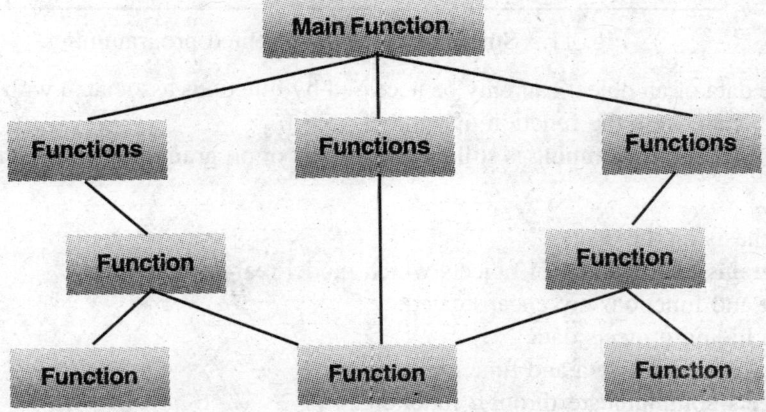

Fig. 11.2 Structural of procedural programming.

The object-oriented programming treats the data as a most critical element in the program design and does not allow it to be scattered around the program. It ties the data and functions that operate on it and protects it from the other functions as shown in Fig. 11.3.

Object oriented programming allows decomposition of a problem into a number of entities called objects and then builds data and functions around these objects.

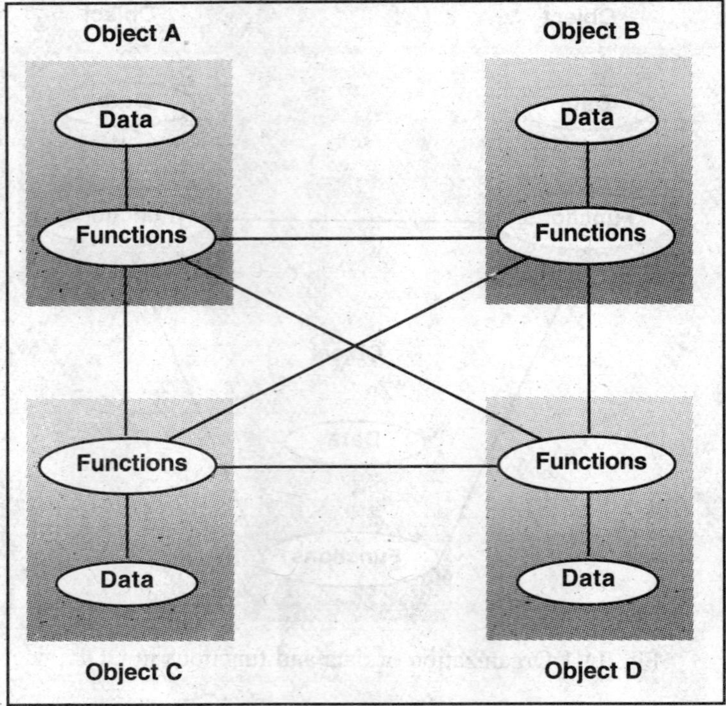

Fig. 11.3 Structure of object-oriented programming.

Here, the data of an object can only be accessed by functions associated with it. However, function of one object can access the function of another object.

Object-oriented programming is still a new concept of programming characterized by the following features :

- Emphasis on the data.
- Programs are made up of objects which model real-world entities.
- Data and functions are encapsulated.
- Data hiding protects data.
- Addition of new data and function is easy.
- Objects communicate through functions.
- Program design follows bottom-up approach.

11.4 Some Basic Concepts of OOP

Object-oriented programming (OOP) models real-world objects with software counterparts. It takes advantages of *class* relationships where objects of a certain class—such as a class of vehicles—have the same characteristics. It takes advantages of *inheritance* relationships and even *multiple inheritance* relationships where newly created classes of objects are derived by inheriting characteristics of existing classes, yet contain unique characteristics of their own. An object of class convertible certainly has the characteristics of class automobile, but a convertible's roof goes up and down.

Definition

The object-oriented programming use objects as basic building blocks, where each object is an instance of some class and classes are related to each other through inheritance. As the name implies, a fundamental concept behind OOP is the use of objects.

Some of the basic concepts are :

- Object
- Classes

Let us discuss briefly some of the concepts used extensively in object-oriented programming.

11.4.1 Objects

An object is an entity that has state, behaviour and identity, *i.e.* an object is defined by a class. The structure and behaviour of similar objects are defined in their common class. The term instance and object are interchangeable. Each object has following characteristics :

- **State.** The state of an object encompasses all of the (usually static) property of the object plus the current (usually dynamic) values of each of these properties.
- **Behaviour.** The behaviour of an object tells how it acts and reacts to the outside world in terms of its state changes and message passing.
- **Identity.** The identity of an object is the property which distinguishes it from all other objects.

Definition

An object is a software bundle of variables and related methods. In object-oriented terminology, a particular object is called an instances.

For example automobiles in a traffic-flow simulation problem, customers in a bank, student of a university, points in a plane, animals in an ecological simulation, positions in a game of chess, complex numbers, a linked list, a graphics object such as a circle, square, triangle, etc.—any of these real-world objects can be represented by an object in a program.

Definition

An object is a programming structure that groups related to methods and the data those methods use.

The object which a message is sent to is called the **receiver** of the message. Messages define the *interface* to the object. Everything an object can do is represented by its message interface. So you shouldn't have to know anything about what is in the black box in order to use it. Providing access to an object only through its messages, while keeping the details private is called *information hiding.* An equivalent buzzword is *encapsulation.*

11.4.2 Classes

An object is defined via its **class,** which determines everything about an object. Objects are individual *instances* of a class. For example, you may create an object call Dog from class Animal. All object-oriented languages have some means, usually called a *factory,* to "manufacture" object instances from a class definition.

Bjarne Stroustrup of Bell Labs extended the C language to be capable of Object-Oriented Programming (OOP), and it became popular in the 1990's as C++. There were several enhancements, but the central change was extending struct to allow it to contain functions and use inheritance. These extended structs were later renamed *classes*.

A *class* is a user-defined data type used to implement an abstract object, giving you the capability to use object-oriented programming with C#. A class includes members. A *member* can be either data, known as a data member or a function known as a *member function* as shown in Fig. 11.4.

For example, a particular can be taught of as an object, while the concept of all cars can be taught of as a class. Fig. 11.5 graphically depicts three specific objects : My Car, Sumit's car and Brother's car. The car class represents the idea of a car and the three objects represent actual cars.

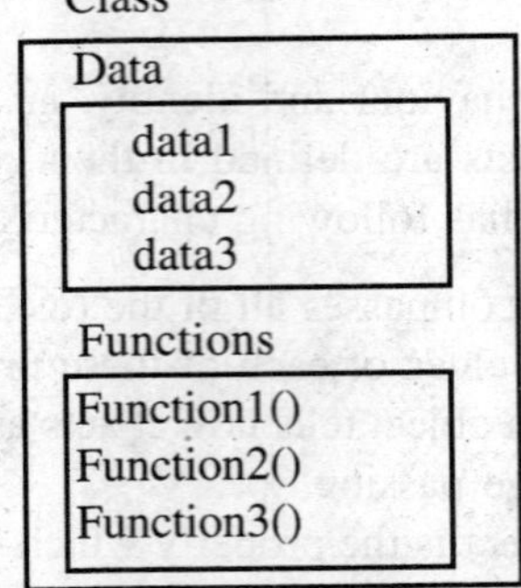

Fig. 11.4 Class contains data members and member functions.

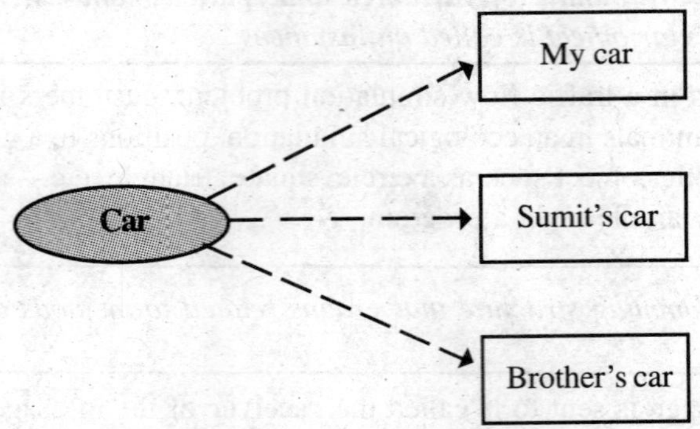

Fig. 11.5 A car class and three car objects.

Classes can be used to define other classes. For example, suppose we had a class that represents all vehicles, including cars, airplanes and trains. It would contain the characteristics common to all vehicles, such as how fast they move. We can then use the vehicle class to create or derive our car class. It would contain all of the characteristics of a generic vehicle and we could then add the specific details that make a car unique among other vehicle types. A class representing each specific vehicle type that can be derived from the generic vehicle class.

Definition

A class is a blueprint that defines the variables and the methods common to all objects of a certain kind.

Public and Private parts. All member fields in a class are *private* by default (no code outside the class can reference them), whereas fields of a struct are *public*, meaning that anyone can use them. For example,

```
public struct Employee
{
        public int empcode; // Structure data member
        public  string empname;
        public string empdesig;
        public float empsalary;
};
```

could be rewritten as a class like this :

```
public class Employee
{
    public int empcode;     // Data member
    public string empname;     //..........
    public string empdesig;    //..........
    private float empsalary;   //..........
    public void display()
    {
    }  // Member method
};
```

The public and private keywords may be written before any declarations, but it is common to group all public members, then all private members. For example,

```
class Point
{
    public int getX();
    public int getY();
    public int setX();
    public int setY();
    public int x;
    public int y;
};
```

11.4.3 Message

A single object alone is generally not very useful. Instead, an object usually appears as a component of a larger program or application that contains many other objects. Through the interaction of these objects, programmers achieve higher-order functionality and more complex behaviour. Your bicycle hanging from a hook in the garage is just a bunch of metal and rubber; by itself, the bicycle is incapable of any activity. The bicycle is useful only when another object (you) interacts with it (pedal). Software objects interact and communicate with each other by sending *messages* to each other.

11.4.4 Abstraction

As the word indicates, abstraction refers to the representation of only the essential features of the real-world object in the program object. This process does not include the background details and explanations. This concept of abstraction is used in classes. A class is thus defined as a list of abstract attributes and functions which operate on these attributes. The term Abstract Data Types (ADT) is used to refer to classes due to this reason.

11.4.5 Encapsulation

Data encapsulation is the most significant characteristic of a class. By this term, we mean the wrapping up of data and functions which operate on the data into a single unit called the object. This encapsulation prevents free access to the data within an object. Access can only be done through the interface provided by the functions. Such insulation of data is referred to as *data hiding*.

Encapsulating related variables and methods into a neat software bundle is a simple yet powerful idea that provides two primary benefits to software developers :

- **Modularity.** The source code for an object can be written and maintained independently of the source code for other objects. Also, an object can be easily passed around in the system. You can give your bicycle to someone else, and it will still work.
- **Information hiding:** An object has a public interface that other objects can use to communicate with it. The object can maintain private information and methods that can be changed at any time without affecting the other objects that depend on it. You don't need to understand the gear mechanism on your bike to use it.

11.4.6 Sub-classes and Inheritance

Just as in our daily lives, the concept of hierarchical classification helps in establishing relationships among program elements. This also serves another purpose. It shortens an object oriented program. This is writing a function for code which is repetitively used and reused many times. This is better than repeating the code in the program at different points where it is required. Such an approach is used quite often in procedural programming to shorten program length and improve program organization.

To understand the concept of sub-classes and inheritance and their roll in OOP, let us take an example. Consider the class of mammals. This class can be subdivided into sub-classes—Dogs, Cats, Cows, Whales, *etc.* as in Fig. 11.6 shown below :

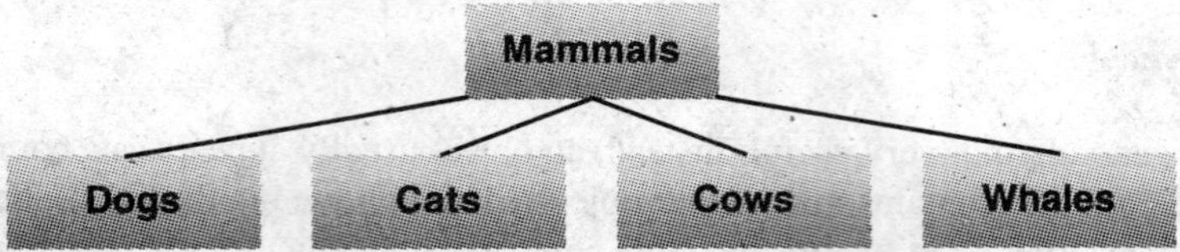

Fig. 11.6 A concept of class inheritance.

The idea behind this division is that each sub-class shares common characteristics with the class from which it is derived. Thus dogs, cats, cows, whales—all share the common characteristic of giving birth to young ones rather than laying eggs. Each sub-class or derived class has its own characteristics.

For instance, dogs are carnivorous, while cows are herbivorous, and whales are aquatic in their habitat. Each derived class inherits some characteristics from the base class and adds new ones of its own. This is also known as inheritance. The advantage of inheritance is two-fold. Through inheritance, we can add additional features to a new class from an existing one. The new class will have the combined features of both the classes. And, existing classes can be reused and we need not start from scratch. Without inheritance, the class *cows* from the class *mammals*, only those features that are unique to *cows* need to be defined in the class defined for cows.

The concept of deriving one class from another is called inheritance. By using one class to form the basis of another class definition, inheritance promotes reuse. Fig. 11.7 shows an inheritance derivation in a class diagram. By convention, the arrows point from the new class to the class from which it was derived.

Definition

New classes can be derived from previously created classes. This derivation is called inheritance.

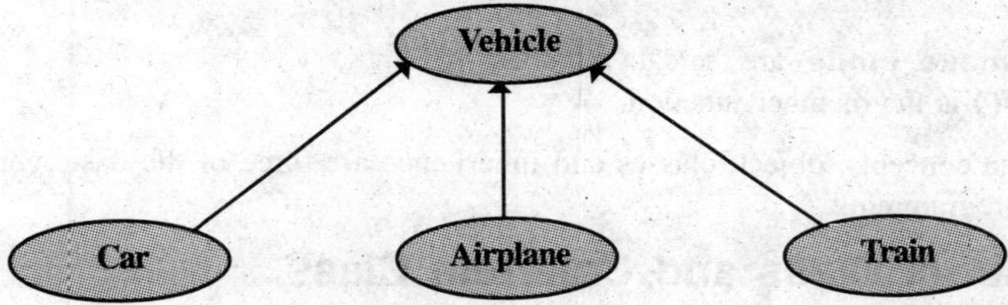

Fig. 11.7 A class diagram, showing three new classes derived from an existing class.

Inheritance offers the following benefits :

- Subclasses provide specialized behaviours from the basis of common elements provided by the superclass. Through the use of inheritance, programmers can reuse the code in the superclass many times.
- Programmers can implement superclasses called *abstract classes* that define common behaviours. The abstract superclass defines and may partially implement the behavior, but much of the class is undefined and unimplemented. Other programmers fill in the details with specialized subclasses.

11.4.7 Class Attributes

In C# program every class contains certain information. This information are called the attributes. These are the data attributes which are different from one program to another. It describes the qualities of the objects that belong to the same class. The class attributes are defined by variables.

Definition

The variables which are declared in a class are called attributes.

These attributes are also called data members. A class has one or more variable types, called members. The two kinds of members : data members and member functions.

- data members of a class are simple variables.
- member functions are functions defined within a class that act on the data members in the class.

Let us consider a simple example;

```
public class car
{
    // Data members
    public string carno;
    public int make;
    public string model;
    ............
    public void display();   //  Member function
}
```

Here,

- **carno**, **make**, **model** are the data members
- **display()** is the member function.

Above all the concepts, object, classes and inheritance are three of the basic concepts used on object oriented programming.

11.4.8 Abstract Class and Concrete Class

An abstract class, or abstract base class (ABC), is one that is designed only as a parent class and from which child classes may be derived, and which is not itself suitable for instantiation. Abstract classes are often used to represent abstract concepts or entities. The incomplete features of the abstract class are then shared by a group of sibling sub-classes which add different variations of the missing pieces. In C#, an abstract class is defined as a class having at least one pure virtual method, i.e., an abstract method, which may or may not possess an implementation.

Abstract classes are superclasses which contain abstract methods and are defined such that concrete subclasses are to extend them by implementing the methods. The behaviours defined by such a class are "generic" and much of the class will be undefined and unimplemented. Before a class derived from an abstract class can be instantiated, it must implement particular methods for all the abstract methods of its parent classes.

In computing, when specifying an abstract class, the programmer is referring to a class which has elements that are meant to be implemented by inheritance. The abstraction of the class methods to be implemented by the sub-classes is meant to simplify software development.

A concrete class, however, is a class for which entities (instances) may be created. This contrasts with abstract classes which cannot be instantiated because it defeats its purpose of being an 'abstract'. Most object oriented programming languages allow the programmer to specify which classes are considered abstract and will not allow these to be instantiated (in C#, for example, the keyword abstract is used). This also enables the programmer to focus on planning and design. The actual implementation of course is to be done in the derived classes.

In C#, an abstract class is a class having at least one pure virtual function. They cannot be instantiated and will generate an error if an attempt is made. They are meant to function as stubs, allowing the programmer to identify what modules of functions (behaviour or methods) are needed without having to actually implement them. This is in line with OOP's philosophy of allowing the programmer to concentrate on how an object should behave without going into the actual detail.

11.4.9 Polymorphism

Polymorphism is an important OOP concept used extensively in implementing inheritance. Polymorphism refers to the ability of one thing to take many (Poly) distinct forms (Morphism). In OOP, this one thing which may take several distinct forms may be an operator or a function. This provides the facility of sending the same message to objects of parent class and objects of the sub-classes. Each object may however respond to the message in its own way depending on the class/sub-class to which it belongs. This allows objects having different internal structures (of derived classes) to share the same external interface.

11.5 Function Overloading

It is often the case that in C you need to develop a set of functions, which perform similar actions for different data types. For example, if you want to sort arrays of objects into a given order, you need to write a function that compares two elements for every data type. It is a natural requirement to use the same name for the whole set of these functions. Unfortunately, you can't do this in C because all your functions must have distinct names. As you would have come to expect by now, C# is more flexible to do the overloading operations to your function.

When the programmers write functions, all programmers face the demandingly creative job of thinking up new function names. Sure, you can invent any old name for a function and the compiler gets a queue to all the functions for compiling. So, to avoid the compilation error and better speed the overloading of function concepts comes into track.

In C# it is possible to define several functions with the same name, performing different actions. The functions must only differ in their argument lists. This technique is known as ***function overloading***. The polymorphism word also does the same technique like function overloading. Function overloading can be done for functions :

- having different number of arguments
- having different types of arguments

Example The program given below use same function with different arguments.

..\CSharp_Book\Chap11\MethodOver

```
using System;

public class NewProject
{
    // Show methow with int parameter
    static void show(int roll)
    {
```

```
        Console.WriteLine("Your class roll no. is {0}", roll);
    }
    // Show methow with double parameter
    static void show(double fees)
    {
        Console.WriteLine("Your admission fees was {0:F2}", fees);
    }
    // Show methow with string parameter
    static void show(string name)
    {
        Console.WriteLine("Your name is " + name);
    }
    static void Main()
    {
        // Main method calling all overloaded functions
        NewProject.show(100);
        NewProject.show(5450.00);
        NewProject.show("Mr. Sidharth Sahoo");
        Console.WriteLine();
    }
}
```

```
Your class roll no. is 100
Your admission fees was 11200.33
Your name is Mr. Sidharth.
Press any key to continue . . .
```

In the above program, three methods **show()** are defined, which only differ in their argument lists: **int, double, string**. The methods have the same name. The definition of several functions with the same name is called 'method *overloading*'.

It is interesting that the way in which C# compiler implements function overloading is quite simple. Although the functions share the same name in the source text (in this example **show()**), the compiler and hence the linker use quite different names. The conversion of a name in the source file to an internally used name is called 'name mangling', e.g., the C# compiler might convert the name **static void show (int)** to the internal name Vshowl, while an analogous function with a char argument might be called VshowC. The actual names, which are internally used, depend on the compiler and are not relevant for the programmer, except where these names show up in e.g., a listing of contents of a library.

On the other way, the example given below also use a function overloading with prototyped to function main as :

Example Write a program for method overloading using different types of arguments.

..\CSharp_Book\Chap11\OverSquare

```
using System;

// Demonstrates the overloading function having types of arguments
public class NewProject
{
    static int square(int a)
    {
        return a * a;
    }
    static float square(double a)
    {
        return (float)(a * a);
    }
    static double square(long a)
    {
        return (double)(a * a);
    }
    static void Main()
    {
        int p = 12;
        float q = 25.5F;
        double r = 30.70;

        Console.WriteLine("The square of {0:D} is : ", NewProject.square(p));
        Console.WriteLine("The square of {0:F2} is : ", NewProject.square(q));
        Console.WriteLine("The square of {0:F2} is : ", NewProject.square(r));
    }
}
```

After running the above program displays the square of three different types of variables, producing on screen these lines :

```
The square of 12 is : 144
The square of 25.5 is : 650.25
The square of 30.70 is : 942.49
Press any key to continue . . .
```

Three overloaded square functions are prototyped above function main. Each function has the same name, but is considered distinct because each differs in at least one parameter. The program implements each function separately, just as each would be if their names were not the same.

Overloaded function can clarify a program's meaning. Despite the different data types involved, it's obvious that each output statement in **Main()** displays the square of an argument. This is much nearer than having separate **squareInt**, **squareDouble**, and **squareLongDouble** function names. Of course, it's up to you to overload functions that perform more or less the same jobs. If you name every function in your program the same (provided each differs by at least one argument), your code might be as incomprehensible as a novel written using only one word.

11.5.1 Finding the Best Match

A function call first matches the prototype having the same number and type of arguments and then calls the appropriate function for execution. A best match must be unique. The function selection involves the following steps :

- The compiler first tries to find an exact match in which the types of actual arguments are the same and use that function.
- If an exact match is not found, the compiler uses the integer promotions to the actual arguments, such as,

  char to **int**
  float to **double**

  to find a match.

- When wither of them fails, the compiler tries to use the built-in conversions (the implicit assignment conversions) to the actual arguments and then uses the function whose match is unique. If the conversion is possible to have multiple matches, then the compiler will generate an error message. Suppose we use the following two functions :

  long square(long n)
  double square (double x)

  A function call such as

  square(10)

  will cause an error because **int** argument can be converted to either **long** or **double**, thereby creating an ambiguous situation as to which version of **square()** should be used.

- If all of the steps fail, then the compiler will try the user-defined conversions in combination with integral promotions and built-in conversions to find a unique match. User-defined conversions are often used in handling class object. For example,

..\CSharp_Book\Chap11\OverVolume

```
using System;

// Demonstrates the overloading function having types of arguments
public class NewProject
{
    static void Main()
    {
        int p = 12;
        float q = 25.5F;
```

```
        double r = 30.70;

        Console.WriteLine("Volume of cube is : {0:D}", NewProject.volume(8));
        Console.WriteLine("Volume of cylinder is : {0:F2}", NewProject.volume(2.5, 6));
        Console.WriteLine("Volume of rectangular box is : {0:F2}",
            NewProject.volume(100L, 50, 5));
    }
    static int volume(int s)      // Cube
    {
        return (s * s * s);
    }
    static double volume(double r, int h)   // Cylinder
    {
        return (3.4519 * r * r * h);
    }
    static long volume(long l, int b, int h)  // Rectangular box
    {
        return (l * b * h);
    }
}
```

Overloading of the functions should be done with caution. We should not overload unrelated functions and should reserve function overloading for functions that perform closely related tasks. Sometimes, the default arguments may be used instead of overloading. This may reduce the number of functions to be defined. Overloading functions are extensively used for handling class objects.

11.6 What are the Benefits of Object-Orientation ?

Reuse, quality, an emphasis on modeling the real world (or a "stronger equivalence" with the RW than other methodologies), a consistent and seamless OOA/OOD/OOP package, naturalness (our "object concept"), resistance to change, encapsulation and abstraction (higher cohesion/lower coupling), and etc.

On resistance to change, system objects change infrequently while processes and procedures (top-down) are frequently changed, providing object-oriented systems with more resilient system organization.

- Faster development
- Increased Quality
- Easier maintenance
- Enhanced modifiability
- Exploit power of OOPs
- Reuse of software and designs, frameworks
- Systems more change resilient, evolvable
- Reduced development risks for complex systems, integration spread out
- Appeals to human cognition, naturalness

Exercise

1. Give some characteristics or features of object-oriented programming.
2. What is class ?
3. What is abstraction ?
4. Define Inheritance.
5. What is an object ?
6. What is an attribute ?
7. What do you understand by Polymorphism ? Give a suitable example of the same.
8. Give two examples of Object-Oriented Language.
9. What is the fundamental idea of Object-Oriented Programming ?
10. What do you understand by programming paradigm ?
11. What is procedural programming paradigm ?
12. What is Object-Oriented Programming ? How is it different from Procedural Programming ?
13. How does function overloading implement polymorphism ?
14. Distinguish between an object and class.
15. Differentiate between Data hiding and Encapsulation.
16. How are abstraction and encapsulation inter-related ?
17. What is the significance of classes in OOP ?
18. What is the key to reusability in OOP ?
19. What two features of an object are linked together by encapsulation ?

Programming

1. Write the the overloaded function called sum() that add two integer and return integer; that add two double precision quantity and return double precision quantity; that add one float and one integer and return floating point quantity.
2. Give an example illustrating function overloading in a C# program.
3. Use the concept of function overloading to compute the area of rectangle.
4. Use the concept of function overloading to convert a character from lowercase to uppercase [or uppercase to lowercase] and to increment an integer.
5. Create a function sroot() that returns the square root of its argument. Overload sroot() three way : have it returned the square root of an integer, a long integer and a double.
6. Create a function called min() that returns the smaller of the two numeric arguments used to call the function. Overload min() so that it accepts characters, integers, and double as arguments.
7. Write a program using overloaded function to compute the area of rectangle and area of triangle using hero's formula.
8. Use the concept of function overloading to compute the volume of rectangle, volume of triangle and perimeter of circle.

Classes and Objects 12

12.1 Introduction

C# is a bunch of small additions to C, C++ and Java, with a few major additions. One major addition is the object-oriented approach. As the name object-oriented programming suggests, this approach deals with objects. Classes are collections of data related to a single object type. Classes not only include information regarding the real world object, but also functions to access the data, and classes possess the ability to inherit from other classes.

If a class is a house, then the functions will be the doors and the variables will be the items inside the house. The functions usually will be the only way to modify the variables in this structure, and they are usually the only way even to access the variables in this structure. The key idea is that the outside world doesn't need to know exactly what data is stored inside the class—it just needs to know which functions it can use to access that data. This allows the implementation to change more easily because nobody should have to rely on it except the class itself.

12.2 Classes

A *class* is user-defined data type used to implement an abstract object, giving you the capability to use object-oriented programming with C#. A class includes members. A *member* can be either data, known as a data member or a method known as a *member method*.

Data members can be of any type, including C# defined types such as **int** and **double** or user-defined types, including other classes. Member functions manipulate the data members, create and destroy class variables, and even redefine C# operators to act on the class objects.

A class is a technique of creating one or a group of variables to be used as a foundation for a more detailed variable. A class must be created in a computer file. You can create such a file with only one class or you can create many classes inside of one file.

12.3 Class Declaration

As you know that, all members of a structure are public by default. You may feel that this is not typical of OOP. With member functions, it would not be reasonable to explicitly forbid access to some members, but rather to permit access to some functions from the public interface of the structure, keeping all other members private by default. In this respect, the C# classes are an improvement on structures.

Definition

A class is a representation of some entity with a collection of data and operations necessary for the manipulation of the data.

A simple class is declared in C# in the same way as a struct, except that it also contains method declarations and uses the class keyword in place of struct. Such functions may either be declared in full or as prototypes. It is normal to only give prototypes in the class declaration and to provide their implementation separately.

Note

Structure and classes are known as the user defined data types.

class is a C# keyword and all the normal keyword restrictions apply. One way of thinking about a C# class is to note that they resemble structures. You simply use the keyword class instead of struct, and the members of the structure become private by default. Everything else is exactly same as with structures. The format of the class declaration is as under :

```
public/private/protected class class_name
{
    private data_members;
    private member_functions;
    public data_members;
    public member-functions;
    protected data_members;
    protected member-functions;
    ...
    ...
}
```

The above declaration shows the class_name is the class tag and used different access specifier like private, public and protected to their respective data_members and member_methods. The section between the curly brackets, { and }, of a class is referred to as its body. In the body of a class, you can create a list of the parts that make up the class. Each of these parts must be a complete variable with a name and a data type.

Thus, a class declaration looks similar to a structure declaration, except that it has both function and data as members, instead of just data. By default all the class members are private.

This class declaration is roughly equivalent to the combination of an ordinary structure declaration plus a set of function prototypes. It declares the following :

- The contents of each instance of class_name : the data_members and member_functions.
- The members are of private, protected, or public specifier.

Example Consider how you might store the date and time in a class and take advantage of OOP's benefit. A class is a kind of structure that encapsulates data and functions into a handy package.

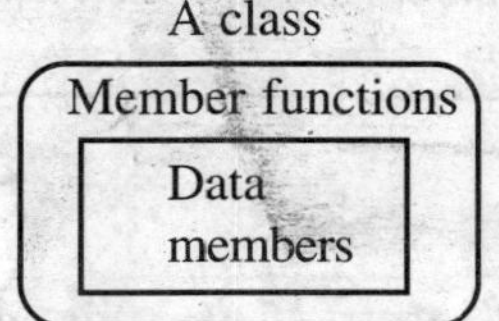

Fig. 12.1 A class encapsulates data and functions.

```
public class Employee
{
    int empcode;   // Data member
    string empname;   //..........
    string empdesig;   //..........
    float empsalary;   //..........
    void display()  // Member method
    {
        ...
        ...
    }
}
```

For example, here are the characteristics that make up an employee, declared as the parts of the above Employee class and each declared as a variable. The variables declared in the body of a class are referred to as its member variables and each member variable is referred to as a field. The fields can be any type

Here the class Employee looks very much like a structure, except that it begins with the class keyword. Technically, a class is a struct with added capabilities. Braces enclosed the four members of the class, which are preceded by **public**, one of three *access specifiers* define the ways statements may use members of a class. Later, you will examine two other access specifiers, **private** and **protected**. The public access specifier makes the members available to all users of the class. Access specifier ends with a colon.

Classes, fundamental elements of C#, are collections variables and functions operate on those variables. Together these variables and functions describe the qualities of an object.

12.3.1 Members

Like a structure, a class has one or more variable types, called members. The two kinds of members are data members and member functions (discussed in previous section). Members have a new attribute:

visibility. Just as global variables are visible to all functions and local variables are not, individual members of a class can be made visible everywhere or not. A member's visibility is determined by the visibility label, which will be discussed fully in the forthcoming sections.

Definition

A class of nothing but data members, all of which are visible outside the class, has another name : a structure.

12.3.2 Data Members

Data members of a class are exactly like the variables in a structure. The previous example describes a class Employee and the class describes five data members and one member function. The variables in a class definition are called data members and a class's functions are called member functions. For example, in previous class declaration of **Employee**, the following are the data members :

```
int empcode;
string empname;
string empdesig;
float empsalary;
```

A class's variables and functions can have one of 3 basic accessibility types :

- **public** members are visible directly through an object,
- **private** members are completely hidden, only accessible within the class's member functions,
- **protected** members behave like **private** members, except that subclasses have direct access to them.

12.3.3 Class Member Methods

Member methods are method defined within a class that acts on the data members in the class. The use of member methods distinguishes a class from a struct.

Definition

A method is a group of programming language statements that are given a name. A method is associated with a particular class. Each method has a method definition that specifies the code that gets executed when the method is invoked. Member methods are methods defined within a class that act on the data members in the class.

When a method is called, the flow of control transfers to that method. One by one, the statements of that method are executed. When that method is done, control returns to the location where the call was made and execution continues. This process is pictured in Fig. 12.2.

The following is the member methods of the **Employee** class, which includes some extra member methods than the previous example :

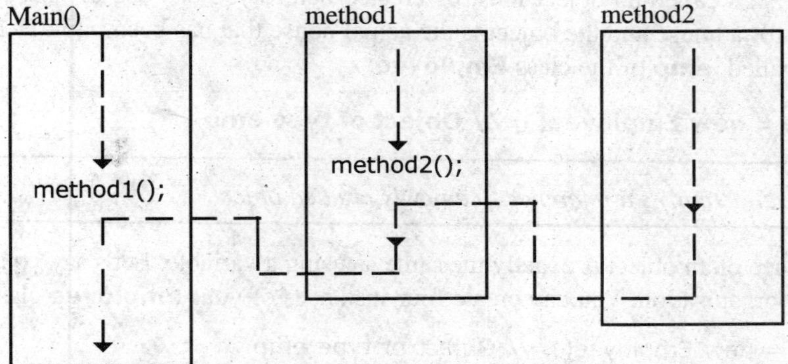

Fig. 12.2 The flow of control following method invocations.

```
public class Employee
{
    int empcode;   // Data member
    string empname;   //..........
    string empdesig;   //..........
    float empsalary;   //..........
    void display()  // Member method
    {
        ...
        ...
    }
}
```

The above example of **Employee** class uses a member method **display()**. The class is definitely not a struct anymore.

12.3.4 Objects

An *object* is a self-contained abstraction of an item. The item could be a student record, employee and customer record or any screen window. An object includes all the data necessary to represent the item and the functions, or method that manipulate this data. The perfect object knows everything about itself, including how to input, output, and manipulate its data. Otherwise, an object is an instance of a class. It can be uniquely identified by its name and it defines a state, which is represented by the values of its attributes at a particular time.

Definition

A class is a blueprint of an object; it reserves no memory space to data. Each object has its own data space; an object is an instance of a class.

An object contains variables and methods. The values of the variables define the state of the object and the methods define the behaviors of the object.

An instance of a class called an object must be created before you can use it. This is because the class is like the plans for a house and the object is the actual house that has been built. Here is how you instantiate an object called **emp** of the class **Employee**;

```
Employee emp = new Employee(); // Object of type emp
```

> **Note**
> *The new operator returns a reference to a newly created object.*

Creating an instance of an object is exactly the same as using a variable. Let's say you want to have four employees in an organisation. You can create four instances of your **Employee** class, like this :

```
Employee emp = new Employee(); // Object of type emp
Employee emp1 = new Employee(); // Object of type emp1
Employee emp2 = new Employee(); // Object of type emp2
Employee emp3 = new Employee(); // Object of type emp3
```

The syntax for accessing a class member is similar to that of accessing a member of a structure, *i.e.*, using dot operator (.) as shown below :

```
objectName.publicDataMemberName;
objectName.publicFunctionMemberName(actualArguments);
```

Note that only **public** members can be accessed outside the class specification. The **private** and **protected** class members can only be accessed by member functions that can be **private** or **public**.

After declaring a member of a class, to access it from another class, first declare a variable from its class as we saw earlier. To actually access the member, use the period operator "." as follows:

```
using System;

public class Employee
{
    int empcode;        // Data member
    public string empname;
    string empdesig;
    private float empsalary;
    void display()  // Member method
    {
        ...
        ...
    }
}
```

12.3.5 Accessing Class Data Members

The parts of an object fall into two main categories: those you can touch and those you don't have access to. For example, for a car parked at the mall, you can see or touch its doors and its tires but you don't see its engine or its spare tire, you don't even know if it has one. The parts of an object that you have access to are referred to as public. Those you can't see or touch are referred to as private.

A C# class also recognizes that some parts of a class can be made available to other classes and some other parts can be hidden from other classes. A part that must be hidden from other classes is private and it can be declared starting with the **private** keyword. If you declare a member variable and want to make it available to other classes, you must start its name with the **public** keyword. The **public** and **private** keywords are referred to as access level.

By default, if you declare a member variable (or anything else) in a class but don't specify its access level, the member is considered private and cannot be accessed from outside, that is by a non-member, of that class. Therefore, to make a member accessible by other classes, you must declare it as **public**. You can use a mix of **public** and **private** members in a class and there is no rule on which access level should be listed first or last. For example;

```
public class Employee
{
    int empcode;  // Data member
    public string empname;
    string empdesig;
    private float empsalary;    //..........
    void display()  // Member method
    {
        ...
        ...
    }
}
```

Just keep in mind that if you omit or forget the access level of a member of a class, the member is automatically made **private**.

```
class Program
{
    static void Main()
    {
        Employee emp = new Employee(); // Object of type emp
        emp.empcode = 100; // Use of period operator for accessing data member
        emp.empname = "Ms. Sujata";
        emp.empdesig = "PGT Computer";
        emp.empsalary = 12500;
        ...
        ...
        ...
    }
}
```

The above code with the dot operators (.) in **empcode**, **empdesig** and **empsalary** produce errors as inaccessible due to its protection level.

So, to reduce confusion as to what member is public or private, we will always specify the access level of a member variable.

```
public class Employee
{
    public int empcode;     // Data member
    public string empname;  // . . . . . . . . . .
    public string empdesig;  // . . . . . . . . . .
    private float empsalary; // . . . . . . . . . .
    public void display()
    {
        . . .
        . . .
    }   // Member method
}
```

Thus the complete program is as :

..\CSharp_Book\Chap12\ClassStart

```
using System;
using System.Collections.Generic;
using System.Text;

namespace ClassStart
{
    public class Employee
    {
        public int empcode;     // Data member
        public string empname;
        public string empdesig;
        public float empsalary;
        void display()  // Member method
        {
        }
    }

    class Program
    {
        static void Main()
        {
            Employee emp = new Employee(); // Object of type emp
```

```
            emp.empcode = 100;
            emp.empname = "Ms. Sujata";
            emp.empdesig = "PGT Computer";
            emp.empsalary = 12500;
            Console.WriteLine("An Employee details");
            Console.WriteLine("Employee code : " + emp.empcode);
            Console.WriteLine("Employee name : " + emp.empname);
            Console.WriteLine("Employee designation : " + emp.empdesig);
            Console.WriteLine("Employee salary : " + emp.empsalary);
        }
    }
}
```

When the above program executed, it will produce the following output as shown in Fig. 12.3.

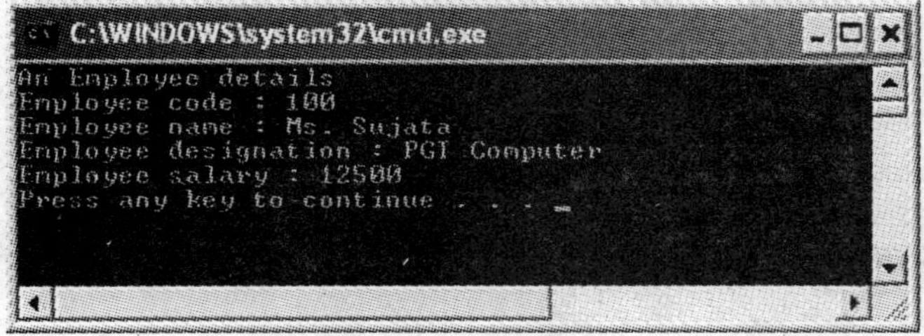

Fig. 12.3 Displaying class information.

12.3.6 Accessing Class Member Methods

Look at the class declaration given below :

```
public class Employee
{
    int empcode;   // Data member
    public string empname;
    string empdesig;
    private float empsalary;
    void display() // Member method
    {
        ...
        ...
    }
}
```

Just keep in mind that if you omit or forget the access level of a member of a class, the member is automatically made private.

A method's job is to carry a specific assignment within a program. As such, it could provide a value once the assignment has been carried. In some cases, a method must produce a result. If it doesn't, then it is considered **void**. The type of value that a method can provide (or return) is written on the left side of the method name. If the method doesn't produce a result, type **void** to its left. The assignment that a method carries is included between an opening curly bracket "{" and a closing curly bracket "}". For example;

```
public class Employee
{
    ....
    ....
    public void display()    // Member method
    {
        ...
        ...
    }
}
```

The most regularly used method of a C# program is called **Main**.

```
public class Employee
{
    ....
    ....
    public void display()
    {
        ...


        ...
    }  // Member method
    public assign_emp()
    {
        ...
        ...
    }
}
```

After creating a method, in its body delimited by its curly brackets, you can define the desired behavior. For example, you can write the member variables in the parentheses of **Console.Write()** or **Console.WriteLine()**. For example;

```
public class Employee
{
    public int empcode;     // Data member
```

```
public string empname;      //..........
public string empdesig;     //..........
private float empsalary;    //..........
public void display()
{
    Console.WriteLine("An Employee details");
    Console.WriteLine("Employee code : " + empcode);
    Console.WriteLine("Employee name : " + empname);
    Console.WriteLine("Employee designation : " + empdesig);
    Console.WriteLine("Employee salary : " + empsalary);
}
}
```

Let us try the complete program to assign employee and display employee using **Employee** class.

..\CSharp_Book\Chap12\ClassMemb

```
using System;
using System.Collections.Generic;
using System.Text;

// Demonstrating Class member methods to display member data values
namespace ClassMemb
{
    public class Employee

    {
        public int empcode;     // Data member
        public string empname;    //..........
        public string empdesig;   //..........
        private float empsalary;  //..........
        public void display()
        {
            Console.WriteLine("An Employee details");
            Console.WriteLine("Employee code : " + empcode);
            Console.WriteLine("Employee name : " + empname);
            Console.WriteLine("Employee designation : " + empdesig);
            Console.WriteLine("Employee salary : " + empsalary);
        }

        public void assign_emp()
        {
            empcode = 100;
```

```
            empname = "Ms. Sujata";
            empdesig = "PGT Computer";
            empsalary = 12500;
        }
    }

    class Program
    {
        static void Main()
        {
            Employee emp = new Employee(); // Object of type emp
            emp.assign_emp();// Accessing method
            emp.display();
        }
    }
}
```

When the above program executed, it will produce the following output as shown in Fig. 12.4.

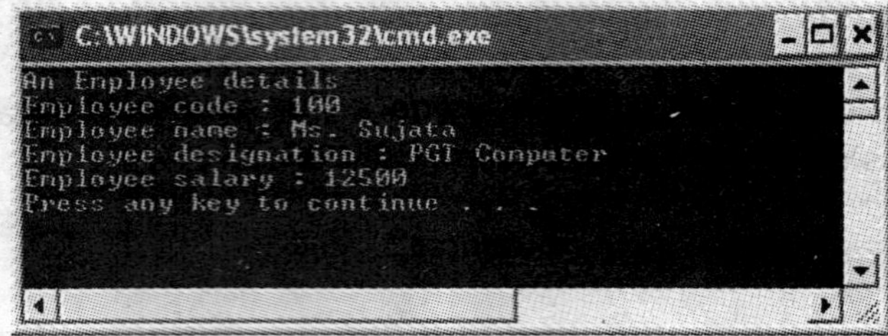

Fig. 12.4 Displaying class data members values using member method.

12.4 Static Fields

Imagine you create a class called **Employee**. To access it in the **Main()** function, you can declare its variable, as we have done so far. A variable you have declared of a class is also called an instance of the class. In the same way, you can declare various instances of the same class as necessary:

```
using System;

public class Employee
{
    public int empcode;      // Data member
    public string empname;    //. . . . . . . . . .
    public string empdesig;   //. . . . . . . . . .
    private float empsalary;  //. . . . . . . . . .
}
```

```
public class NewEmployee
{
    static void Main()
    {
        Employee emp1 = new Employee();
        Employee emp2 = new Employee();
    }
}
```

Each one of these instances gives you access to the members of the class but each instance holds the particular values of the members of its instance. Consider the results of the following program:

..\CSharp_Book\Chap12\StaticFields

```
using System;
using System.Collections.Generic;
using System.Text;

// Demonstrating static fields
namespace StaticFields
{
    public class Employee
    {
        public int empcode;    // Data member
        public string empname;
        public string empdesig;
        public float empsalary;
    }

    public class Program
    {
        static void Main()
        {
            Employee emp1 = new Employee();

            // Initialize class data members
            emp1.empcode = 100;
            emp1.empname = "Ms. Sujata";

            emp1.empdesig = "PGT Computer";
            emp1.empsalary = 12500;

            Console.WriteLine("First employee details");
            Console.WriteLine();
            Console.WriteLine("Employee code : " + emp1.empcode);
```

```
            Console.WriteLine("Employee name : " + emp1.empname);
            Console.WriteLine("Employee designation : " + emp1.empdesig);
            Console.WriteLine("Employee salary : " + emp1.empsalary);
            Console.WriteLine();

            Employee emp2 = new Employee();

            // Initialize class data members
            emp2.empcode = 101;
            emp2.empname = "Ms. Jyoti";
            emp2.empdesig = "PGT Economics";
            emp2.empsalary = 12500;
            Console.WriteLine("Second employee details");
            Console.WriteLine();
            Console.WriteLine("Employee code : " + emp2.empcode);
            Console.WriteLine("Employee name : " + emp2.empname);
            Console.WriteLine("Employee designation : " + emp2.empdesig);
            Console.WriteLine("Employee salary : " + emp2.empsalary);
        }
    }
}
```

When the above program executed, it will produce the following output as shown in Fig. 12.5.

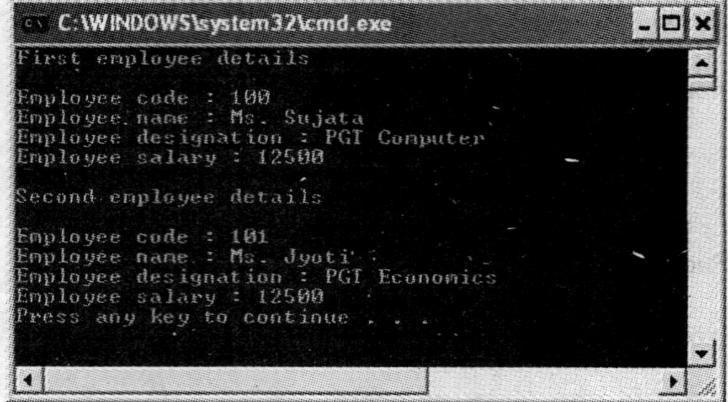

Fig. 12.5 Accessing simple data members in Main() method.

All of the member variables and methods of classes we have used so far are referred to as *instance members* because, in order to access them, you must have an instance of a class declared in another class in which you want to access them.

C# allows you to declare a class member and refer to it regardless of which instance of an object you are using. Such a member variable is called static. To declare a member variable of a class as static, type the **static** keyword on its left. Whenever you have a static member, in order to refer to it, you must "qualify" it in the class in which you want to call it. Qualifying a member means you must give its complete location, including the name of its class and the namespace (if any) in which its class was created. For example;

..\CSharp_Book\Chap12\StaticFld

```
using System;
using System.Collections.Generic;
using System.Text;

// Demonstrating static fields
namespace StaticFld
{
    public class Employee
    {
        public static int empcode; // Data member
        public static string empname;
        public string empdesig;
        public float empsalary;
    }

    public class Program
    {
        static void Main()
        {
            Employee emp1 = new Employee();

            // Assigning static field
            Employee.empcode = 100;
            Employee.empname = "Ms. Sujata";

            emp1.empdesig = "PGT Computer";
            emp1.empsalary = 12500;

            Console.WriteLine("First employee details");
            Console.WriteLine();
            Console.WriteLine("Employee code : " + Employee.empcode);
            Console.WriteLine("Employee name : " + Employee.empname);

            Console.WriteLine("Employee designation : " + emp1.empdesig);
            Console.WriteLine("Employee salary : " + emp1.empsalary);
            Console.WriteLine();

            Employee emp2 = new Employee();
```

```
            // Initialize class data members
            Employee.empcode = 101;
            Employee.empname = "Ms. Jyoti";
            emp2.empdesig = "PGT Economics";
            emp2.empsalary = 12500;
            Console.WriteLine("Second employee details");

            Console.WriteLine();
            Console.WriteLine("Employee code : " + Employee.empcode);
            Console.WriteLine("Employee name : " + Employee.empname);
            Console.WriteLine("Employee designation : " + emp2.empdesig);
            Console.WriteLine("Employee salary : " + emp2.empsalary);
            Console.ReadLine();
        }
    }
}
```

When the above program executed, it will produce the following output as shown in Fig. 12.6.

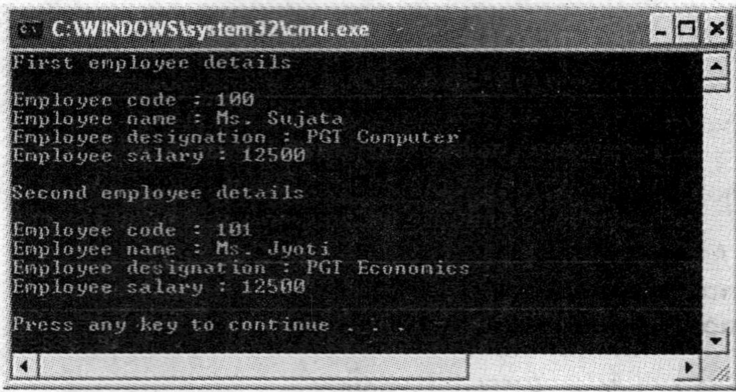

Fig. 12.6 Accessing static field in Main() method.

Notice that when a member variable has been declared as static, you don't need an instance of the class to access that member variable outside of the class. Based on this, if you declare all members of a class as static, you don't need to declare a variable of their class in order to access them.

12.5 Class Static Methods

Like a member variable, a method of a class can be defined as static. This means that this particular method can access any member of the class regardless of the instance if there are many instances of the class declared.

To define a method as static, type the **static** keyword to its left. For example;

..\CSharp_Book\Chap12\StaticMemb

```
using System;
using System.Collections.Generic;
using System.Text;

namespace StaticMemb
{
    public class Employee
    {
        static int empcode;     // Data member
        static string empname;
        static string empdesig;
        static private float empsalary;

        static public void display()
        {
            Console.WriteLine("An Employee details");
            Console.WriteLine("Employee code : " + empcode);
            Console.WriteLine("Employee name : " + empname);
            Console.WriteLine("Employee designation : " + empdesig);
            Console.WriteLine("Employee salary : " + empsalary);
        }

        static public void assign_emp()
        {
            empcode = 100;
            empname = "Ms. Sujata";
            empdesig = "PGT Computer";
            empsalary = 12500;
        }
    }

    class Program
    {
        static void Main()
        {
            Employee.assign_emp();  // Accessing method
            Employee.display();
        }
    }
}
```

When the above program executed, it will produce the following output as shown in Fig. 12.7.

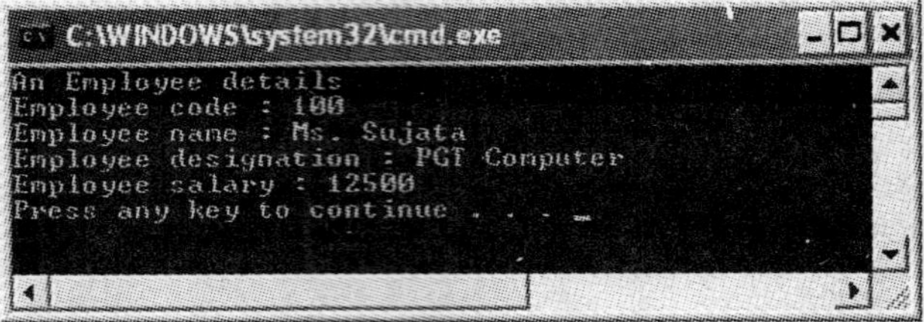

Fig. 12.7 Accessing static method in Main() method.

The **ReadLine()**, the **Write()**, and the **WriteLine()** methods of the **Console** class that we have used so far are examples of static methods.

A static class:

1. Is a class whose members must be accessed without an instance of the class. In other words, the members of a static class must be accessed directly from (using the name of) the class, using the period operator.
2. Is a class whose members must be created as **static**. In other words, you cannot add a non-static member to a **static** class: all members, except for constants, must be **static**.

To create a static class, precede the **class** keyword with the **static** keyword. Based on the above two rules. For example;

..\CSharp_Book\Chap12\UsingStatic

```
using System;
using System.Collections.Generic;
using System.Text;

namespace Staticity
{
    public static class Square
    {
        public static double Side;

        public static double Perimeter()
        {
            return Side * 4;
        }

        public static double Area()
        {
            return Side * Side;
        }
    }
```

```
class Program
{
    static void Main(string[] args)
    {
        Square.Side = 36.84;
        Console.WriteLine("Square Characteristics");
        Console.Write("Side:       ");
        Console.WriteLine(Square.Side);
        Console.Write("Perimeter: ");
        Console.WriteLine(Square.Perimeter());
        Console.Write("Area:       ");
        Console.WriteLine(Square.Area());
    }
  }
}
```

When the above program executed, it will produce the following output as shown in Fig. 12.8.

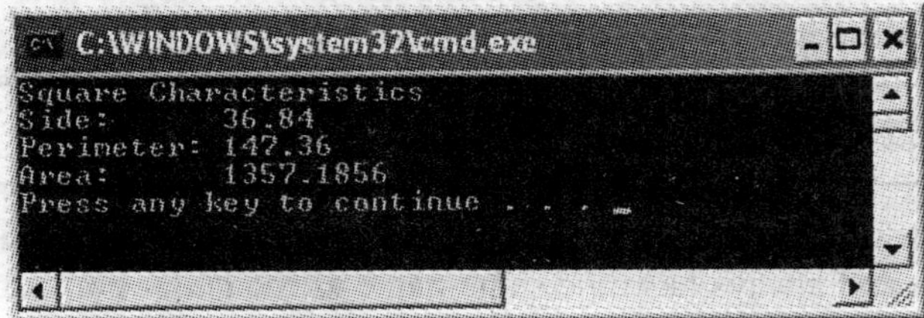

Fig. 12.8 Accessing static data and method in Main() method.

12.6 Class Constructor

A constructor is a special method that is created when the object comes to life. This particular method holds the same name as the class and it initializes the object whenever that object is created. When you create a class, if you don't declare a constructor, the compiler creates one for you; this is useful because it lets all other objects of the program know that the object exists. This compiler-created constructor is called the default constructor. If you want, you can create your own constructor.

The constructor's job is to set up the object so that it can be used. A constructor is similar to a general method, but with the following differences.

- No return type.
- No **return** statement.

Constructors have one purpose—to allow you to guarantee that objects are correctly initialized. The compiler will guarantee that your constructors are called, inserting constructor calls as necessary.

Definition

The constructor is a special class member method that enables an object to initialize itself when it is created.

The following are some special characteristics of a constructor :

- They are generally declared in public section.
- They are invoked automatically when the objects of a given class is created.
- They do not have any return type.
- They cannot be inherited. However, the derived class can invoke the base class constructor.
- Like other member methods, they can be overloaded.
- They can have default arguments.
- We cannot refer to their address.
- An object with a constructor cannot be used as a member of union.

Every *class* has a constructor, which is called automatically any time an instance of a *class* is created. Constructors are declared as member functions with the same name as the class. Constructors may also have arguments. If a constructor has arguments, then the arguments should be added to the declaration of any object of that class and when the new operator is used.

Note

Remember that the method must not return any value.

The purpose of constructors is to initialize *class* members when the *class* is created. Constructors do not have return values and always have the same name as the *class*. For example,

```
public class Employee
{
    ....
    ....

    // Class constructor method
    public Employee()
    {
        // Body of the constructor like a member method body
    }
    static public void display()
    {
        Console.WriteLine("An Employee details");
        Console.WriteLine("Employee code : " + empcode);
        Console.WriteLine("Employee name : " + empname);
        Console.WriteLine("Employee designation : " + empdesig);
        Console.WriteLine("Employee salary : " + empsalary);
    }
}
```

Note

If we use a member method to initialize the data members of an object after an object is created, we need invoke it on that object with initial values for the data members as parameters. If large numbers of objects of a class are to be created, then we have to invoke member method on every occurrence of the object

12.6.1 Default Constructors

When you declare a variable of a class, a special method must be called to initialize the members of that class. This method is automatically provided for every class and it is called a constructor. Whenever you create a new class, a constructor is automatically provided to it. This particular constructor is called the default constructor. You have the option of creating it or not. Although a constructor is created for your class, you can customize its behavior or change it tremendously.

The above example declares a constructor method **public Employee()** as public access specifier, the class declares a default Employee constructor. It's a default constructor because it declares no parameters.

A constructor holds the same name as its class and doesn't return any value, not even **void**. For example;

```
public class Employee
{
    ....
    ....
    // Default class constructor method
    public Employee()
    {
        // Body of the constructor like a member method body
    }
}
```

12.6.2 The Constructor Initializer

A constructor can be used to initialize the member variables of a class. As such, a constructor provides a valuable alternative to a method initializer, the type of method we saw earlier. To use a constructor to initialize the member variables of a class, provide as arguments the necessary variables that you intend to initialize. You don't have to initialize all member variables in the constructor, only those that need to be initialized. In fact, you should initialize only those members that you think the other objects would need when using this object. This means that your object may have fields that, either the external objects don't need to modify (or access) or the member variable(s) will be initialized later when called from the needed object(s).

To implement a default constructor, you can just initialize the desired members of the class. For a member variable of a numeric type, you can just assign the desired constant to each. If the variable is a character, assign a single-quoted symbol to it. If the variable is a string, then assign a double-quoted value to the variable.

For example;

..\CSharp_Book\Chap12\ClassConst

```
using System;
using System.Collections.Generic;
using System.Text;

namespace ClassConst
{
    public class Employee
    {
        static int empcode;     // Data member
        public string empname;
        public string empdesig;
        static private float empsalary;

        // Class constructor method
        public Employee()
        {
            // Initialize class data members
            empcode = 100;
            empname = "Ms. Sujata";
            empdesig = "PGT Computer";
            empsalary = 12500;
        }

        public void display()
        {
            Console.WriteLine("An Employee details");
            Console.WriteLine("Employee code : " + empcode);
            Console.WriteLine("Employee name : " + empname);
            Console.WriteLine("Employee designation : " + empdesig);
            Console.WriteLine("Employee salary : {0:F2}", empsalary);
        }
    }

    class Program
    {
        static void Main()
        {
            Employee emp = new Employee(); // Object of type emp
            emp.display();
        }
    }
}
```

When the above program executed, it will produce the following output as shown in Fig. 12.9.

```
C:\WINDOWS\system32\cmd.exe
An Employee details
Employee code : 100
Employee name : Ms. Sujata
Employee designation : PGT Computer
Employee salary : 12500.00
Press any key to continue . . .
```

Fig. 12.9 Class constructor to assign data member.

When an object of a class is created, C# calls the *constructor* for that class. If no constructor is defined, C# invokes a *default constructor*, which allocates memory for the object, but *doesn't initialize it*.

Like every method, a constructor can be equipped with a body. In this body, you can access any of the member variables (or method(s)) of the same class. When introducing classes other than the main class, we saw that, to use such a class, you can declare its variable and allocate memory using the new operator. You can notice that we always included the parentheses when declaring such a variable. For example;

```
static void Main()
{
    Employee emp = new Employee(); // Object of type emp
    emp.display();
}
```

12.6.3 Parameterized Constructors

In the previous section, we saw that there is always a default constructor for a new class that you create; you just the option of explicitly creating one or not. The default constructor as we saw it doesn't take arguments: this is not a rule, it is simply assumed. Instead of a default constructor, you may want to create a constructor that takes an argument.

The parameterized constructors can pass value into the constructors who have different parameters in the constructor functions. The value will be transferred from the Main() function to the constructor either with direct values or through variables.

The parameterized constructors always pass initial values or stored variables, as arguments into the constructor object, otherwise there will be an error at the constructor object. For example, if the constructor declared as :

```
public Employee(int, string, string, float)
{
    . . .
    . . .
}
```

means that the **Employee** constructor has four parameters in its body. There will be four values or five variable values will be passed to the parameterized constructor.

With this type of constructor, when you declare an instance of the class, you can use this new constructor to initialize the class. For example;

```
using system

public class Employee
{
    ...
    ...
    // Parameterized class constructor method
    public Employee(int ecode, string ename, string edesig, float esalary)
    {
        // Initialize class data members
        empcode = ecode;
        empname = ename;
        string empdesig = edesig;
        empsalary = esalary;
    }

    class Program
    {
        static void Main()
        {
            // Object of type emp, default constructor invoked
            Employee emp = new Employee();
            Console.WriteLine("Here is the employee information :
            ...
            Employee emp1 = new Employee(100, "Ms. Sujata", "PGT Computer", 12500);
            ...
        }
    }
```

..\CSharp_Book\Chap12\ParaConst

```
using System;
using System.Collections.Generic;
using System.Text;

namespace ParaConst
```

```
{
    public class Employee
    {
        static int empcode;    // Data member
        public string empname;
        public string empdesig;
        static private float empsalary;

        // Default class constructor method
        public Employee()
        {
            // Initialize class data members
            empcode = 100;
            empname = "Ms. Sujata";
            string empdesig = "PGT Computer";
            empsalary = 12500;
        }

        // Parameterized class constructor method
        public Employee(int ecode, string ename, string edesig, float esalary)
        {
            // Initialize class data members
            empcode = ecode;
            empname = ename;
            string empdesig = edesig;
            empsalary = esalary;
        }

        public void display()
        {
            Console.WriteLine("Employee code : " + empcode);
            Console.WriteLine("Employee name : " + empname);
            Console.WriteLine("Employee designation : " + empdesig);
            Console.WriteLine("Employee salary : " + empsalary);
        }

        class Program
        {
            static void Main()
            {
                // Object of type emp, default constructor invoked
                Employee emp = new Employee();

                Console.WriteLine("Here is the employee information : ");
```

```
            for (int i = 1; i <= 35; i++)
                Console.Write("=");
            Console.WriteLine();
            emp.display(); // Display the default constructor value.
            Console.WriteLine();

            Employee emp1 = new Employee(100, "Ms. Sujata",
                                "PGT Computer", 12500);
            Console.WriteLine("Here is the same employee information : ");
            for (int i = 1; i <= 40; i++)
                Console.Write("=");
            Console.WriteLine();

            emp1.display(); // Display the parameterized constructor value.
            Console.WriteLine();
        }
    }
  }
}
```

When the above program executed, it will produce the following output as shown in Fig. 12.10.

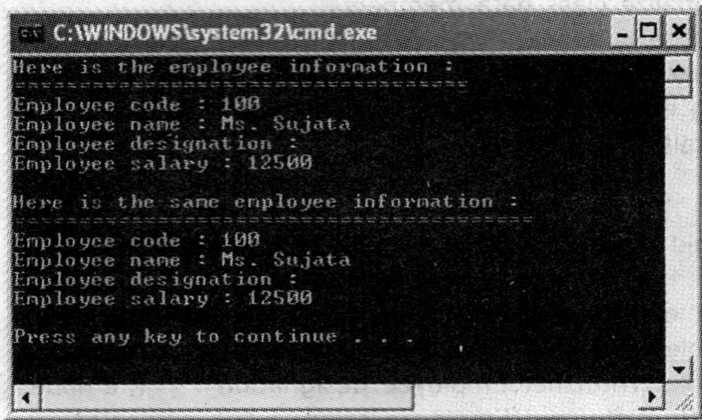

Fig. 12.10 Parameterized class constructor to assign data member.

12.6.4 Static Constructor

You are always free to establish the initial value of static data using the member initialization sysntax, what if the value for your static data needed to be obtained from a database or external file? To perform such task requires a method scope of static constructor. For example,

```
class Employee
{
    ...
    ...

    public Employee()
    {
        // Initialize class data members

        empcode = 100;
        empname = "Ms. Sujata";
        string empdesig = "PGT Computer";
        empsalary = 12500;
    }
    ...
    ...
}
```

Here are a few points of interest regarding static constructors:

- A given class (or structore) may define only a single static constructor.
- A static constructor executes exactly one time, regardless of how may objects of the type are created.
- A static constructor does not take an access modifier and cannot take any parameters.
- The runtime invokes the static constructor when it creates an instance of the class or before accessing the first static member invoked by the caller.
- The static constructor executes before any instance-level constructors.

12.6.5 Constructor Overloading

Constructors are a primary candidate for overloading. By provoding multiple versions of a constructor, you have a variety of ways to create and initialize an object.

The default constructor is the favorite place to provide default values to the members of a class. Besides the default constructor, you can add as many constructors as you judge necessary. This feature of C# allows you to create various constructors for different reasons. This also means that the methods or constructors of a class can be overloaded.

One of the rules of method overloading consists of having methods with different types of arguments. The most basic constructor you would create can use a single argument. When implementing a constructor that takes one argument, you should initialize the member that corresponds to the unique argument and initialize the other members with default values.

Like any other method, a constructor can be overloaded. In other words, you can create a class and give it more than one constructor. The same rules used on overloading regular methods also apply to constructors: the different constructors must have different number of arguments or a different number of arguments.

For example;

..\CSharp_Book\Chap12\ConOverload

```
using System;
using System.Collections.Generic;
using System.Text;

namespace ConOverload
{
    public class Employee
    {
        static int empcode;     // Data member
        public string empname;
        public string empdesig;
        static private float empsalary;

        // Default class constructor method
        public Employee()
        {
            // Initialize class data members
            empcode = 100;
            empname = "Ms. Sujata";
            empdesig = "PGT Computer";
            empsalary = 12500;
        }
        // Parameterized class constructor method 1
        public Employee(int ecode, string ename, string edesig, float esalary)
        {
            // Initialize class data members
            empcode = ecode;
            empname = ename;
            string empdesig = edesig;
            empsalary = esalary;
        }
        // Parameterized class constructor method 2
        public Employee(int ecode, string ename, string edesig)
        {
            // Initialize class data members
            empcode = ecode;
            empname = ename;
            empdesig = edesig;
        }
        // Parameterized class constructor method 3
```

```
        public Employee(int ecode, string ename)
        {
            // Initialize class data members
            empcode = ecode;
            empname = ename;
        }
        public void display()
        {
            Console.WriteLine("Employee code : " + empcode);
            Console.WriteLine("Employee name : " + empname);
            Console.WriteLine("Employee designation : " + empdesig);
            Console.WriteLine("Employee salary : " + empsalary);
        }
    }
    class Program
    {
        static void Main()
        {
            // Object of type emp, default constructor invoked
            Employee emp = new Employee();
            Console.WriteLine ("Here is the default constructor employee
                        information : ");
            for (int i = 1; i <= 35; i++)
                Console.Write("=");
            Console.WriteLine();

            emp.display(); // Display the default constructor value.

            Employee emp1 = new Employee(101, "Ms. Jyoti", "PGT Computer", 12500);
            Console.WriteLine("Here is the parameterized constructor
                        employee information : ");
            for (int i = 1; i <= 38; i++)
                Console.Write("=");

            Console.WriteLine();
            emp1.display(); // Display the default constructor value.
            Console.WriteLine();
            Console.WriteLine("First constructor overload method ");
            for (int i = 1; i <= 32; i++)
                Console.Write("=");
            Console.WriteLine();

            Employee emp2 = new Employee(102, "Ms. Sangeeta", "PGT Economics");
            emp2.display();// Display first consructor overloaded method value.
```

```
            Console.WriteLine();
            Console.WriteLine("Second constructor overload method ");
            for (int i = 1; i <= 32; i++)
                Console.Write("=");
            Console.WriteLine();

            Employee emp3 = new Employee(103, "Mr. Raman", "PGT Maths.");
            emp3.display(); // Display second consructor overloaded method value.

            Console.WriteLine();
            Console.WriteLine("Third constructor overload method ");
            for (int i = 1; i <= 32; i++)
            Console.Write("=");
            Console.WriteLine();

            Employee emp4 = new Employee(104, "Mr. Akash");
            emp4.display(); // Display second consructor overloaded method value.
        }
    }
}
```

When the above program executed, it will produce the following output as shown in Fig. 12.11.

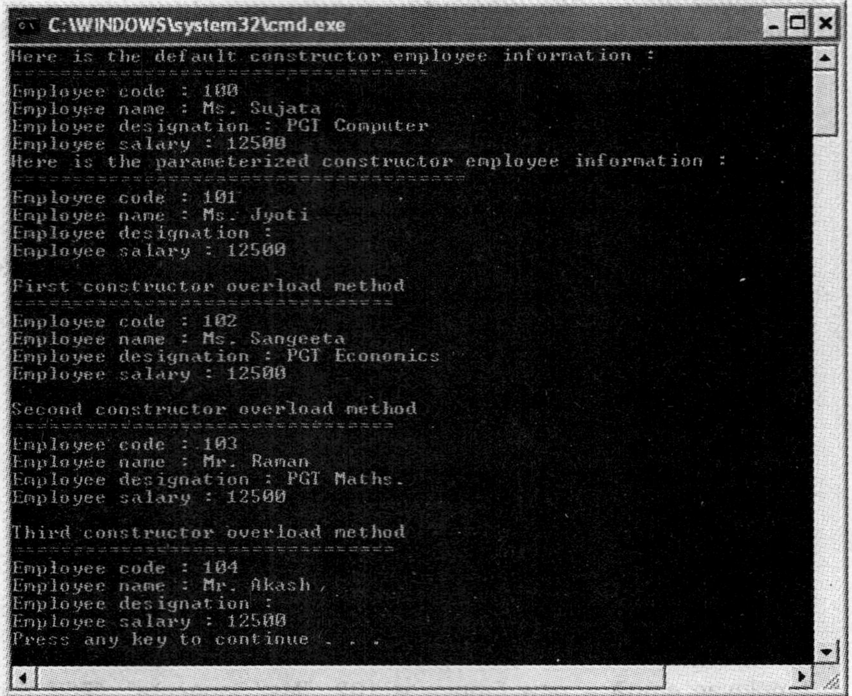

Fig. 12.11 Class constructor overloading data.

12.7 The Destructors

The destructor is the counterpart of the constructor. It is a member function that called automatically when a class object goes out of scope. Its purpose is to perform any cleanup work necessary before an object is destroyed.

As opposed to a constructor, a destructor is called when a program has finished using an object. A destructor does the cleaning behind the scenes. Like the default constructor, the compiler always creates a default destructor if you don't create one. Unlike the constructor, the destructor cannot be overloaded. This means that, if you decide to create a destructor, you can have only one. Like the default constructor, a destructor also has the same name as its class. While a constructor is a method used to initialize an instance of a class, a destructor is used to destruct an instance of class when that variable is not used anymore. Like the constructor, the destructor has the same name as the class. This time, the name of the destructor starts with a tilde "~".

> **Definition**
>
> *The destructor is a special member function that destroys the object when it goes out of scope.*

Like constructors, destructors also have some special characteristics that are listed below :

- They are declared in public section.
- They are invoked automatically when the objects go out of scope.
- They do not have any return type.
- They cannot be inherited. However, the derived class can invoke the base class destructor.
- They do not have any argument.
- They cannot be overloaded.
- We cannot refer to their address.
- An object with a destructor cannot be used as a member of a union.
- A destructor can call other member functions.

The destructor for the class Employee from the previous examples could be declared as follows :

..\CSharp_Book\Chap12\ClassDestructor

```
using System;
using System.Collections.Generic;
using System.Text;

// Demonstrates the destructor method
namespace ClassDestructor
{
    public class Employee
    {
        static int empcode;     // Data member
        public string empname;
```

```
        public string empdesig;
        static private float empsalary;
        // Default class constructor method
        public Employee()
        {
            // Initialize class data members
            empcode = 100;
            empname = "Ms. Sujata";
            string empdesig = "PGT Computer";
            empsalary = 12500;
        }
        ~Employee() // No argument
        {
            Console.WriteLine("Employee destructor!!!");
        }
        public void display()
        {
            Console.WriteLine("An Employee details");
            Console.WriteLine("Employee code : " + empcode);
            Console.WriteLine("Employee name : " + empname);
            Console.WriteLine("Employee designation : " + empdesig);
            Console.WriteLine("Employee salary : " + empsalary);
        }
    }
    class Program
    {
        static void Main()
        {
            // Object of type emp, default constructor invoked
            Employee emp = new Employee();
            Console.WriteLine ("Here is the employee information : ");

            for (int i = 1; i <= 32; i++)
                Console.Write("=");
            Console.WriteLine();
            Console.WriteLine();
            emp.display(); // Display the default constructor value.
            Console.WriteLine();
        }
    }
}
```

When the above program executed, it will produce the following output as shown in Fig. 12.12.

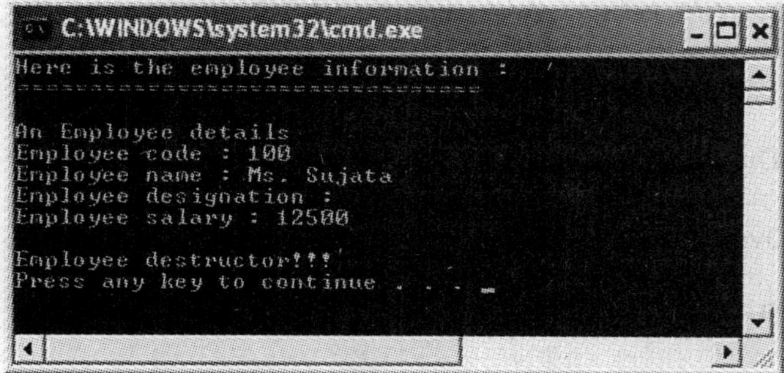

Fig. 12.12 Class destructor to clear class object.

12.8 Overloaded Class Member Methods

In the previous example, you learned how constructor overload method by declaring multiple methods of the same names that differs in at least one parameter. You may use a similar technique for overload class's member functions.

Overloaded member methods are particularly useful when some (but not all) of a member method's parameters are needed. For example, as in your **Employee** class of previous section has **display()** method does not have method arguments.

Simply put, when a class has a set of identically named members that differ by the number (or type) of parameters, the member in question is said to be overloaded. In the Employee class, we have overloaded the class cons3tructor, given that we have provided two definitions that differ only by the parameter set:

```
pubic class Emploee
{
    // Overloaded constructors
   public Employee()
   {
   }
   // Parameterized class constructor method 1
   public Employee(int ecode, string ename, string edesig, float esalary)
   {
      ...
      ...
   }
      ...
      ...
}
```

Constructors, however, are not the only members that may be overloaded for a type. By way of example, assume you have the same **Employee** class with different arguments in **empOver** method. By doing so, we allow the object of various different input parameters :

```
// The overload empOver() method.
public void empOver(int ecode, string ename, string edesig,
float esalary)
{. . .}

 public void empOver(int ecode, string ename, string edesig)
{. . .}
 public void empOver(int ecode, string ename) {. . .}
```

and the **Main()** function as :

```
class Program
{
    static void Main()
    {
        . . .
        . . .
        Employee emp1 = new Employee(100, "Ms. Sujata", "PGT Computer", 12500);
        . . .
        . . .
    }
}
```

Suppose, you want to set only the empcode, empname and empdesig, letting the class default to the empsalary. Currently, there is no easy way to initialize overloading **Employee** constructor with differing number of parameters makes it possible for the program to pass zero or more arguments, as in the statement:

```
Employee Emp1 = new Employee(100, "Ms. Sujata", "PGT Computer");
```

For example;

..\CSharp_Book\Chap12\ClassMethodOverload

```
using System;
using System.Collections.Generic;
using System.Text;

namespace ClassMethodOverload
{
    public class Employee
    {
        static int empcode;     // Data member
        public string empname;
        public string empdesig;
        static private float empsalary;
```

```
// Default class constructor method
public Employee()
{
    // Initialize class data members
    empcode = 100;
    empname = "Ms. Sujata";
    string empdesig = "PGT Computer";
    empsalary = 12500;
}
// Parameterized class constructor method
public Employee(int ecode, string ename, string edesig, float esalary)
{
    // Initialize class data members
    empcode = ecode;
    empname = ename;
    empdesig = edesig;
    empsalary = esalary;
}
// Overloaded class method 1
public void empOver(int ecode, string ename, string edesig, float esalary)
{
    // Initialize class data members
    empcode = ecode;
    empname = ename;
    empdesig = edesig;
    empsalary = esalary;
}
// Overloaded class method 2
public void empOver(int ecode, string ename, string edesig)
{
    // Initialize class data members
    empcode = ecode;
    empname = ename;
    empdesig = edesig;
}
// Overloaded class method 3
public void empOver(int ecode, string ename)
{
    // Initialize class data members
    empcode = ecode;
    empname = ename;
}
```

```
        public void display()
        {
            Console.WriteLine("Employee code : " + empcode);
            Console.WriteLine("Employee name : " + empname);
            Console.WriteLine("Employee designation : " + empdesig);
            Console.WriteLine("Employee salary : " + empsalary);
        }
    }

    class Program
    {
        static void Main()
        {
            // Object of type emp, default constructor invoked
            Employee emp = new Employee();
            Console.WriteLine("Here is the employee information : ");
            for (int i = 1; i <= 35; i++)
                Console.Write("=");
            Console.WriteLine();
            emp.display(); // Display the default constructor value.
            Employee emp1 = new Employee(101, "Ms. Jyoti", "PGT Computer", 12500);
            Console.WriteLine("Here is the same employee information : ");
            for (int i = 1; i <= 38; i++)
                Console.Write("=");
            Console.WriteLine();

            emp1.display(); // Display the parameterized constructor value.
            Console.WriteLine();
            Console.WriteLine("First overload method ");
            for (int i = 1; i <= 32; i++)
                Console.Write("=");
            Console.WriteLine();
            emp1.empOver(102, "Ms. Sangeeta", "PGT Economics", 12500);
            emp1.display();// Display the overloaded class member method  value.
            Console.WriteLine();
            Console.WriteLine("Second overload method ");
            for (int i = 1; i <= 32; i++)
                Console.Write("=");
            Console.WriteLine();

            emp1.empOver(103, "Mr. Raman", "PGT Maths.");
            emp1.display(); // Display the overloaded class member method  value.
            Console.WriteLine();
```

```
            Console.WriteLine("Third overload method ");
            for (int i = 1; i <= 32; i++)
                Console.Write("=");
            Console.WriteLine();
            emp1.empOver(104, "Mr. Akash");
            emp1.display();// Display the overloaded class member method value.
            Console.WriteLine();
        }
    }
}
```

When the above program executed, it will produce the following output as shown in Fig. 12.13.

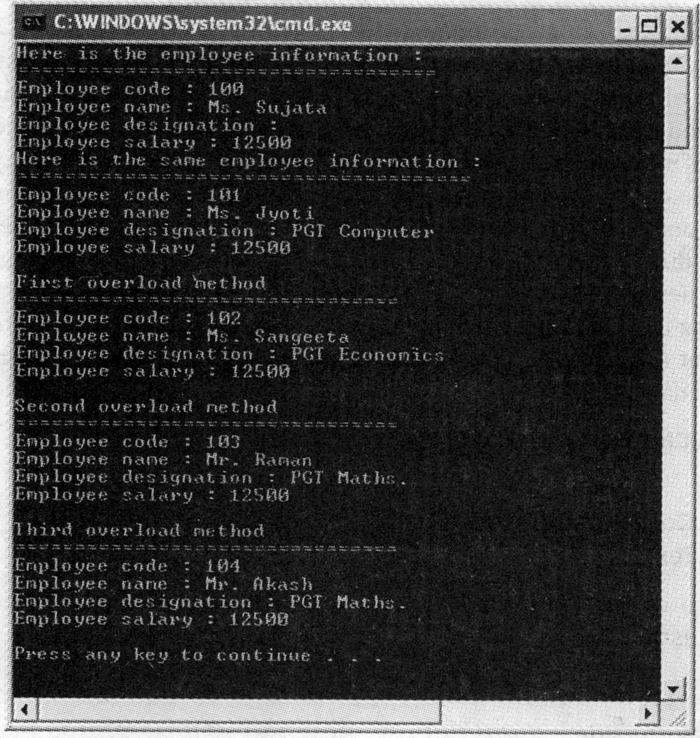

Fig. 12.13 Overloading class member method with variety of data.

The above example uses six member method, by which two is constructor methods. After compiling the program, the compiler executes all the three **empOver()** method and the **display()** method every time with the each **empOver()** method and some of the employee data member always has the previous value of **empOver()**.

12.8.1 Nesting Class

A class can be created inside of another class. A class created inside of another is referred to as nested. To nest a class, simply create it as you would any other. Here is an example of a **class** called **Inside** that is nested in a **class** called **Outside**:

```
public class Outside
{
    public class Inside
    {
        . . .
        . . .
    }
}
```

In the same way, you can nest as many classes as you wish in another class and you can nest as many classes inside of other nested classes if you judge it necessary. Just as you would manage any other class so can you exercise control on a nested class. For example, you can declare all necessary fields, properties, or methods in the nested class or in the nesting class. When you create one class inside of another, there is no special programmatic relationship between both classes: just because a class is nested does not mean that the nested class has immediate access to the members of the nesting class. They are two different classes and they can be used separately as you judge it necessary.

The name of a nested class is not "visible" outside of the nesting class. To access a nested class outside of the nesting class, you must qualify the name of the nested anywhere you want to use it. For example, if you want to declare an Inside variable somewhere in the program but outside of Outside, you must qualify its name. For example;

..\CSharp_Book\Chap12\NestingClass

```
using System;
using System.Collections.Generic;
using System.Text;

// Simple demo of nesting class
namespace NestingClass
{
    // Main class
    public class Outside
    {

        // Inner class, i.e., nesting class
        public class Inside
        {
            public Inside()
            {
                Console.WriteLine();
                Console.WriteLine("Inside class contents");
```

```
                Console.WriteLine("Use the inside class data memmbers if require");
            }
        }

        public Outside()
        {
            Console.WriteLine("Outside class contents");
            Console.WriteLine("Use the outside class data memmbers if require");
        }
    }
    class Program
    {
        static void Main()
        {
            // Declaring outside class object.
            Outside Recto = new Outside();

            // Declaring inside class object.
            Outside.Inside Ins = new Outside.Inside();
        }
    }
}
```

When the above program executed, it will produce the following output as shown in Fig. 12.14.

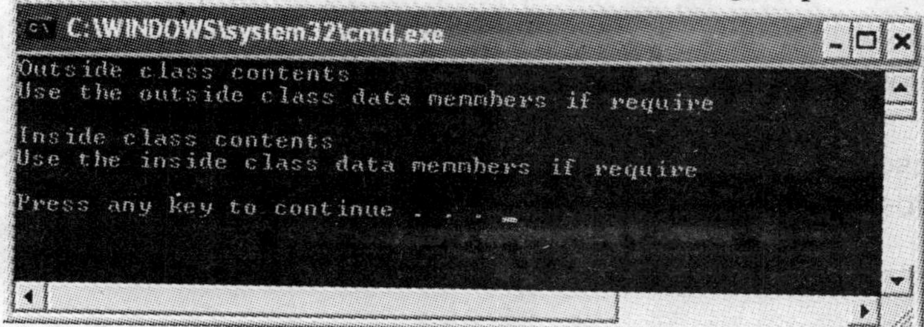

Fig. 12.14 Nesting class.

Because there is no programmatically privileged relationship between a nested class and its "container" class, if you want to access the nested class in the nesting class, you can use its static members. In other words, if you want, you can declare static all members of the nested class that you want to access in the nesting class. For example;

..\CSharp_Book\Chap12\NestClStatic

```
using System;
using System.Collections.Generic;
using System.Text;

namespace NestClStatic
```

```
{
   public class Outside
   {
      public class Inside
      {
         public static string InMessage;
         public Inside()
         {
            Console.WriteLine();
            Console.WriteLine("Inside class contents");
            Console.WriteLine("Use the inside class data memmbers if require");

            InMessage = "Sitting inside while it's raining";
         }

         public static void Show()
         {
            Console.WriteLine("C# Programming .NET Programming ");
         }
      }

      public Outside()
      {
         Console.WriteLine("Outside class contents");
         Console.WriteLine("Use the outside class data memmbers if require");
      }

      public void Display()
      {
         Console.WriteLine(Inside.InMessage);
         Inside.Show();
      }
   }

   class Program
   {
      static void Main()
      {
         Outside Recto = new Outside();
         Outside.Inside Ins = new Outside.Inside();

         Recto.Display();
      }
   }
}
```

When the above program executed, it will produce the following output as shown in Fig. 12.15.

```
C:\WINDOWS\system32\cmd.exe
Outside class contents
Use the outside class data memmbers if require

Inside class contents
Use the inside class data memmbers if require
Sitting inside while it's raining
C# Programming .NET Programming
Press any key to continue . . .
```

Fig. 12.15 Nesting class with static data.

In the same way, if you want to access the nesting class in the nested class, you can go through the static members of the nesting class. To do this, you can declare static all members of the nesting class that you want to access in the nested class. For example;

..\CSharp_Book\Chap12\StaticAllNest

```
using System;
using System.Collections.Generic;
using System.Text;

namespace StaticAllNest
{
    public class Outside
    {
        public class Inside
        {
            public static string InMessage;

            public Inside()
            {
                Console.WriteLine();
                Console.WriteLine("Inside class contents");
                Console.WriteLine("Use the inside class data memmbers if require");

                InMessage = "Sitting inside while it's raining";
            }

            public static void Show()
            {
                Console.WriteLine("C# Programming .NET Programming");
            }
            public void FieldFromOutside()
            {
                Console.WriteLine(Outside.OutMessage);
```

```
            }
        }

        private static string OutMessage;

        public Outside()
        {
            Console.WriteLine("Outside class contents");
            Console.WriteLine("Use the outside class data memmbers if require");

            OutMessage = "Standing outside! It's cold and raining!!";
        }

        public void Display()
        {
            Console.WriteLine(Inside.InMessage);
            Inside.Show();
        }
    }

    class Public
    {
        static void Main()
        {
            Outside Recto = new Outside();
            Outside.Inside Ins = new Outside.Inside();

            Recto.Display();
            Console.WriteLine();
            Ins.FieldFromOutside();
        }
    }
}
```

When the above program executed, it will produce the following output as shown in Fig. 12.16.

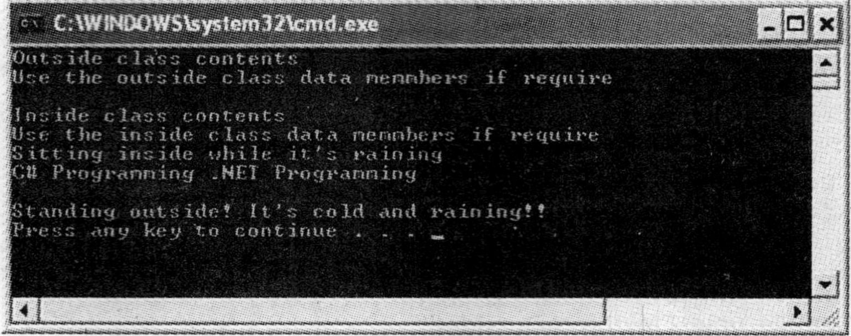

Fig. 12.16 Nesting class accessing nesting data.

Instead of static members, if you want to access members of a nested class in the nesting class, you can first declare a variable of the nested class in the nesting class. In the same way, if you want to access members of a nesting class in the nested class, you can first declare a variable of the nesting class in the nested class. For example;

..\CSharp_Book\Chap12\NestInNest

```
using System;
using System.Collections.Generic;
using System.Text;

namespace NestInNest
{
    public class Outside
    {
        // A member of the nesting class
        private string OutMessage;

        // The nested class
        public class Inside
        {
            // A field in the nested class
            public string InMessage;

            // A constructor of the nested class
            public Inside()
            {
                Console.WriteLine();
                Console.WriteLine("Inside class contents");
                Console.WriteLine("Use the inside class data memmbers if require");

                this.InMessage = "Sitting inside while it's raining";
            }

            // A method of the nested class
            public void Show()
            {
                // Declare a variable to access the nesting class
                Outside outsider = new Outside();
                Console.WriteLine(outsider.OutMessage);
            }

        } // End of the nested class

        // A constructor of the nesting class
        public Outside()
        {
```

```
            Console.WriteLine("Outside class contents");
            Console.WriteLine("Use the outside class data memmbers if require");

            this.OutMessage = "Standing outside! It's cold and raining!!";
        }

        // A method of the nesting class
        public void Display()
        {
            Console.WriteLine(insider.InMessage);
        }

         // Declare a variable to access the nested class
        Inside insider = new Inside();
    }

    class Program
    {
        static void Main()
        {
            Outside Recto = new Outside();
            Outside.Inside Ins = new Outside.Inside();

            Ins.Show();
            Recto.Display();
        }
    }
}
```

When the above program executed, it will produce the following output as shown in Fig. 12.17.

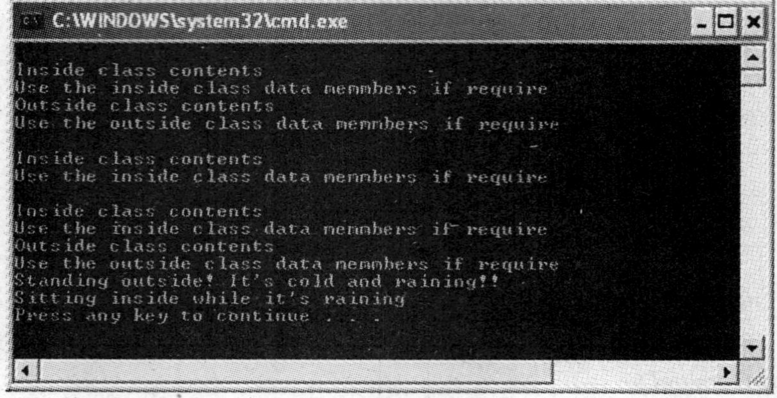

Fig. 12.17 Accessing members in nesting class.

12.8.2 A Class as a Field

Just like any of the variables we have used so far, you can make a class or a structure a member variable of another class. To use a class in your own class, of course you must have that class. You can use one of the classes already available in C# or you can first create your own class. Here is an example of a class:

```
class Point
{
    public short x;
    public short y;
}
```

A field is a member variable created from another class instead of a primitive type. To use one class as a member variable of another class, simply declare its variable as you would proceed with any of the member variables we have declared so far. For example;

```
public class Point
{
    public short x;
    public short y;
}
```

```
ublic class CoordinateSystem
{
    public Point Start;
}
```

After a class has been declared as a member variable of another class, it can be used regularly. Because the member is a class, declared as a reference, there are some rules you must follow to use it. After declaring the member variable, you must make sure you have allocated memory for it. You must also make sure that the variable is initialized appropriately before it can be used; otherwise you would receive an error when compiling the program.

12.8.3 Returning a Class From a Method

Like a value from a regular type, you can return a class value from a method of a class. To do this, you can first declare the method and specify the class as the return type. For example;

```
public class Point
{
    public short x;
    public short y;
}
```

```
public class CoordinateSystem
{
    private Point Start;
    private Point End;
    public Point GetThePoint()
    {
    }
}
```

After implementing the method, you must return a value that is conform to the class, otherwise you would receive an error when compiling the application. You can proceed by declaring a variable of the class in the body of the method, initializing the variable, and then returning it. For example;

..\CSharp_Book\Chap12\ReturnClass

```
using System;
using System.Collections.Generic;
using System.Text;

namespace ReturnClass
{
    public class Point
    {
        public short x;
        public short y;
    }

    public class CoordinateSystem
    {
        private Point Start;
        private Point End;

        public Point GetThePoint()
        {
            Point pt = new Point();

            Console.Write("Enter the x coordinate of the point: ");
            pt.x = short.Parse(Console.ReadLine());
            Console.Write("Enter the y coordinate of the point: ");
            pt.y = short.Parse(Console.ReadLine());
            return pt;
        }
    }
}
```

Once a method has returned a value of a class, the value can be used as normally as possible.

12.8.4 Passing a Class as Argument

Once a class has been created, it can be used like any other variable. For example, its variable can be passed as argument to a method of another class. When a class is passed as argument, its public members are available to the method that uses it. As done for the arguments of primitive types, you can pass more than one class as argument to a method. For example;

..\CSharp_Book\Chap12\PassClass

```
using System;
using System.Collections.Generic;
using System.Text;

namespace PassClass
{
    public class Point
    {
        public short x;
        public short y;
    }

    public class CoordinateSystem
    {
        // Declaring class as a variable
        public Point Start;
        public Point End;

        public Point GetThePoint()
        {
            Point pt = new Point();

            Console.Write("Enter the x coordinate of the point: ");
            pt.x = short.Parse(Console.ReadLine());
            Console.Write("Enter the y coordinate of the point: ");
            pt.y = short.Parse(Console.ReadLine());
            return pt; // Returning class object
        }

        public double DistanceFromOrigin(Point pt)
        {
            double sqr1 = Math.Pow(pt.x, 2);
            double sqr2 = Math.Pow(pt.y, 2);
            double distance = Math.Sqrt(sqr1 + sqr2);
            return distance;
        }
```

```
        public double DistanceBetween2Points(Point pt1, Point pt2)
        {
            double sqr1 = Math.Pow(pt2.x - pt1.x, 2);
            double sqr2 = Math.Pow(pt2.y - pt1.y, 2);
            double distance = Math.Sqrt(sqr1 + sqr2);
            return distance;
        }
    }

    class Program
    {
        private static CoordinateSystem IdentifyCoordinates()
        {
            CoordinateSystem coord = new CoordinateSystem();

            Console.WriteLine("Start Point");
            coord.Start = coord.GetThePoint();
            Console.WriteLine("End Point");
            coord.End = coord.GetThePoint();

            return coord;
        }

        private static void Show(CoordinateSystem c)
        {
            Console.WriteLine("Coordinate System");
            Console.WriteLine("Starting Point: P({0}, {1})", c.Start.x, c.Start.y);
            Console.WriteLine("Ending Point:   Q({0}, {1})", c.End.x, c.End.y);
            Console.WriteLine("Distance Between Both Points: {0:F}",
            c.DistanceBetween2Points(c.Start, c.End));
        }

        static void Main(string[] args)
        {
            CoordinateSystem coord = IdentifyCoordinates();

            Console.WriteLine();
            Show(coord);
        }
    }
}
```

When the above program executed, it will produce the following output as shown in Fig. 12.18.

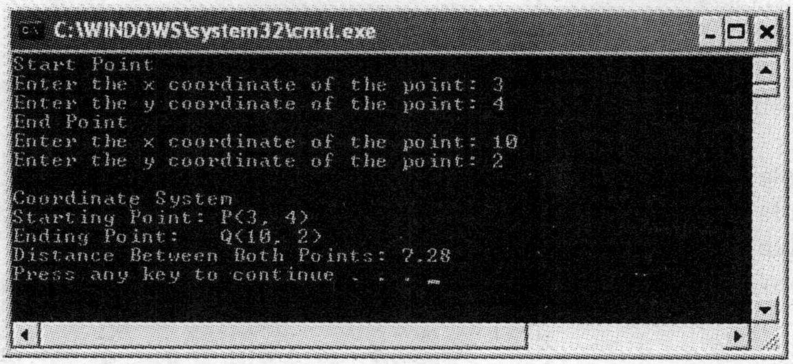

```
C:\WINDOWS\system32\cmd.exe
Start Point
Enter the x coordinate of the point: 3
Enter the y coordinate of the point: 4
End Point
Enter the x coordinate of the point: 10
Enter the y coordinate of the point: 2

Coordinate System
Starting Point: P(3, 4)
Ending Point:   Q(10, 2)
Distance Between Both Points: 7.28
Press any key to continue . . .
```

Fig. 12.18 Passing class as argument.

Because classes are always used as references, when passing a class as argument, it is implied to be passed by reference. To reinforce this, you can type the **ref** keyword to the left of the argument. For example;

..\CSharp_Book\Chap12\PassClassRef

```
using System;
using System.Collections.Generic;
using System.Text;

namespace PassClassRef
{
    public class Point
    {
        public short x;
        public short y;
    }

    public class CoordinateSystem
    {
        public Point Start;
        public Point End;

        public Point GetThePoint()
        {
            Point pt = new Point();

            Console.Write("Enter the x coordinate of the point: ");
            pt.x = short.Parse(Console.ReadLine());
            Console.Write("Enter the y coordinate of the point: ");
```

```
            pt.y = short.Parse(Console.ReadLine());
            return pt;
        }

        public double DistanceFromOrigin(ref Point pt)
        {
            double sqr1 = Math.Pow(pt.x, 2);
            double sqr2 = Math.Pow(pt.y, 2);
            double distance = Math.Sqrt(sqr1 + sqr2);
            return distance;
        }

        public double DistanceBetween2Points(ref Point pt1, ref Point pt2)
        {
            double sqr1 = Math.Pow(pt2.x - pt1.x, 2);
            double sqr2 = Math.Pow(pt2.y - pt1.y, 2);
            double distance = Math.Sqrt(sqr1 + sqr2);
            return distance;
        }
    }

    class Program
    {
        private static CoordinateSystem IdentifyCoordinates()
        {
            CoordinateSystem coord = new CoordinateSystem();

            Console.WriteLine("Start Point");
            coord.Start = coord.GetThePoint();
            Console.WriteLine("End Point");
            coord.End = coord.GetThePoint();

            return coord;
        }

        private static void Show(CoordinateSystem c)
        {
            Console.WriteLine("Coordinate System");
            Console.WriteLine("Starting Point: P({0}, {1})", c.Start.x, c.Start.y);
            Console.WriteLine("Ending Point:   Q({0}, {1})", c.End.x, c.End.y);
            Console.WriteLine("Distance Between Both Points: {0:F}",
            c.DistanceBetween2Points(ref c.Start, ref c.End));
        }
```

```
        static void Main(string[] args)
        {
            CoordinateSystem coord = IdentifyCoordinates();

            Console.WriteLine();
            Show(coord);
        }
    }
}
```

When the above program executed, it will produce the following output as shown in Fig. 12.19.

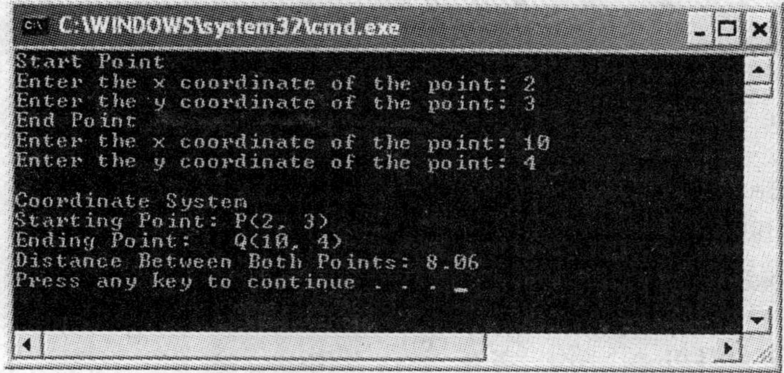

Fig. 12.19 Passing class as reference.

12.9 Self-Reference in C# Using this

We have mentioned two techniques of accessing the members of a class, one consisted of declaring a variable of the class, the other had to do with static members. None of these techniques is important if you want to access a field or method of a class from another method of the same class. We know already that the members of a class are made available to all other members of the same class without being declared or qualified. Consider the following class:

```
class Triangle
{
    double Base;
    double Height;
    double Area;

    void Show()
    {
        double Area;

        Area = Base * Height / 2;
    }
}
```

When the Area variable is used in the **Show()** method, there are two variables available and named Area. It makes it confusing to know what particular variable is being accessed. C#, like many other languages, provides a special member of a class that allows you to specify the member of a class when accessing it. This member is called **this**.

When using the **this** member variable (in C/C++, it is a pointer), you can access any member of a class within any method of the same class. For example;

..\CSharp_Book\Chap12\UsingThis

```
using System;
using System.Collections.Generic;
using System.Text;

namespace UsintThis
{
    class Triangle
    {
        double Base;
        double Height;

        public void Show()
        {
            double Area;

            // Using "this" to access the members of this class
            this.Base = 24.55;
            this.Height = 20.75;

            // You cannot use this to access Area because Area
            // is not a member of this class
            Area = this.Base * this.Height / 2;
            Console.WriteLine("Triangle Characteristics");
            Console.WriteLine("Base:   {0}", this.Base);
            Console.WriteLine("Height: {0}", this.Height);
            Console.WriteLine("Area:   {0}", Area);
        }
    }

    class Program
    {
        static void Main(string[] args)
        {
            Triangle tri = new Triangle();
            tri.Show();
        }
    }
}
```

When the above program executed, it will produce the following output as shown in Fig. 12.20.

```
C:\WINDOWS\system32\cmd.exe
Triangle Characteristics
Base:    24.55
Height: 20.75
Area:     254.70625
Press any key to continue . . .
```

Fig. 12.20 Using self-reference this in C#.

There are exceptions when using **this**:

- The **this** member can never be declared: it is automatically implied when you create a class
- **this** cannot be used in a class A to access a member of class B. The following will cause an error:

```
class Triangle
{
    static void Main()
    {
        Triangle tri = new Triangle();
        this.tri.Show();
    }
}
```

this cannot be used in a **static** method. The following program will not compile because **this** is used in the **Show()** method declared as a **static** method:

```
using System;

class Triangle
{
    static double Base;
    static double Height;

    static public void Show()
    {
        double Area;

        // Using "this" to access the members of this class
        this.Base = 24.55;
        this.Height = 20.75;

        // You cannot use this to access Area because Area
```

```
        // is not a member of this class
        Area = this.Base * this.Height / 2;

        Console.WriteLine("Triangle Characteristics");
        Console.WriteLine("Base:    {0}", this.Base);
        Console.WriteLine("Height: {0}", this.Height);
        Console.WriteLine("Area:    {0}", this.Area);
    }
}

class Program
{
    static void Main()
    {
        Triangle.Show();
    }
}
```

Exercise

1. What is the default accessibility for a class ?
2. Can you use access modifiers with destructors ?
3. What is an abstract class ?
4. Give an example that implements an abstract class ?
5. When do you absolutely have to declare a class as abstract ?
6. What is the difference an abstract class and a sealed class ?
7. What is the difference between structure and a class ?
8. Differentiate between a data type struct and a data type class in C#.
9. Can base constructors can be private ?
10. Is there any difference between constructor overloading and function overloading ?
11. C# provides a default constructor for us. You write a constructor that takes a string as a parameter, but want to keep the no parameter one. How many constructors should you write ?
12. Declare a class that reads the height of a person in inches and converts the height in feet and inches.
13. Declare a class that accepts two integers and swaps the two integers.
14. Declare a class employee having following members:

    Data member:

    employee number, employee name, employee address, employee department

    Member method:

    to read data member

    to display
15. What is a copy constructor ? What do you understand by constructor overloading ?
16. What is the output of following program:

    (a) public class sum

```
{
    int x, y, total;
    public sum(int a, int b)
    {
        x = a;
        y = b * 2;
    }
    public void display()
    {
        total = x + y;
        Console.WriteLine(total);
    }
}
class Program
{
    static void Main()
    {
        sum s = new sum(9, 5);
        s.display();
    }
}
```

(b)

```
public class adam
{
    public void print(double d)
    {
        Console.WriteLine("Double ");
    }
    public void  print(int i)
    {
        Console.WriteLine("int");
    }
}
class Program
{
    static void Main()
    {
        adam eve =  new adam();
        char  ch = 'A';
        int number = 66;
        double  pi = 3.14;
        string st = "AString ";
        eve.print(ch);
        eve.print(pi);
        eve.print(number);
    }
```

```
    }
(c) public class item
    {
        static int count;  // count is STATIC
        static int number;
        public void getdata(int a)
        {
            number = a;
            count++;
        }
        public void getcount()
        {
            Console.WriteLine("count : " + count);
        }
    };
    class Program
    {
        static void Main()
        {
            item a = new item();
            item b = new item();
            item c = new item();
            a.getcount( );// display count
            b.getcount( );
            c.getcount( );
            a.getdata(100);    // getting data into object a
            b.getdata(200);    // getting data into object b
            c.getdata(300);    // getting data into object c
            Console.WriteLine("After reading data ");
            a.getcount( );// display count
            b.getcount( );
            c.getcount( );
        }
    }
```

Programming

1. Write a program to calculate factorial of a given number .Use constructor to initialize data members.
2. Write a program to find the sum of odd and even numbers and use a constructor to initialize data member and destructor to release memory.
3. Write a program to generate Fibonacci series by using a constructor to initialize the data members.
4. Enter any two variables through constructor parameters and write a program to swap and print the values.

5. Write a class with name employee and basic as its data members, to find the gross pay of any employee for the following allowances and deduction, Use meaningful variables.

    Dearness Allowance = 25% of Basic Pay
    House Rent Allowance = 15% of Basic Pay
    Provident Fund = 8.3% of Basic Pay
    Net Pay = Basic Pay + Dearness Allowance + House Rent Allowance
    Gross Pay = Net Pay – Provident Fund.

6. Write a program using a function called area() to compute the area of a :

    (*a*) circle (pr^2) where p = 3.14
    (*b*) square (side * side)
    (*c*) rectangle (length * breadth)

    Display the menu to output the area as per User's choice.

7. Declare a library class having :

    Data member

    Member code, Member name, Date of joining, Address, Phone number
    Game [Game which is played by the member]
    Code [P for permanent member and T for temporary member]
    Fee

    Member method

    to read the data member
    to calculate fee
    if member is temporary its fee is double
    Fee for different Games

Cricket	Rs. 1000
Tennis	Rs. 2000
Badminton	Rs. 2500
Table Tennis	Rs. 500

    to display the record for all members.

    Write a program to use the aforementioned class.

8. Write a program in C# to generate single calculator using classes and accepting the two integers and operators from Main() program.

9. Write a program to implement a class STUDENT having following members :

    Data member

    Name of the student
    Marks of the student

    Member method

    to assign initial values
    to compute total and average
    to display the data

10. Define a class student with the following specification :

    Data members

admno	integer
sname	20 chracters
eng, math , science	float
total	float

Member methods

ctotal()	A function to calculate eng + math + science
takedata()	function to accept values for admno, sname, eng, math, science and invoke ctotal() to calculate total
showdata()	function to display all the data members on the screen.

11. Define a class employee with the following specifications :

Data members

empno	integer
ename	20 characters
basic, hra, da	float
netpay	float

Member methods

Public member function of class employee

havedata()	function to accept values for empno, sname, basic, hra, da and invoke calculate() to calculate netpay.
calculate()	A function to calculate basic + hra + da with float return type
dispdata()	function to display all the data members on the screen.

12. Define a class worker with the following specifications :

Data members

roll_no	integer
wno	integer
wname	25 characters
hrwrk, wgrate	float (hour worked and wage rate per hour)
totwage	float (hrwrk * wgrate)

Member methods

in_data( )	a function to accept values for wno, wname, hrwrk, wgrate and invoke calcwg( ) to calculate totpay.
calcwg( )	A function to find hrwrk * wgrate with float return type
out_data( )	a function to display all the data members on the screen you should give definitions of functions.

13. Define a class report with the following specifications :

Data members

adno	4 digit admission number
name	20 characters
marks	an array of 5 floating point values
average	average marks obtained

Member methods

getavg()	to compute the average obtained in five subjects
readinfo()	function to accept values for adno, name, marks, and invoke the function getavg().
displayinfo()	function to display all data members on the screen you should give function definitions.

14. Define a class batsman with the following specifications :

Data members

bcode	(4 digit code number)
bname	(20 characters)

innings, notout, runs integer type
batavg it is calculated according to the formula : batavg = **runs/(innings-notout)**

Member methods

readdata() function to accept values for bcode, name, innings, notout and invoke the function calcavg()

calcavg() function to compute batavg

displaydata() function to display the data members on the screen.

15. Define a class BOOK with the following specifications :

Data members

BOOK_NO	integer type
BOOK_TITLE	20 characters
PRICE	float (price per copy)

Member methods

INPUT()	Function to read BOOK_NO, BOOK_TITLE, PRICE
TOTAL_COST()	A function to calculate the total cost for N number of copies, where N is passed to the function as argument.
PURCHASE()	Function to ask the user to input the number of copies to be purchased. It invokes TOTAL_COST() and prints the total cost to be paid by the user.

16. Declare a class Directory with the following specifications :

Data members

Docunames	–	an array of strings of size [10][25] (to represent all the names of Documents inside Directory)
Occupied, Freespace	–	long (to represent total number of bytes available in Directory)

Member methods

Newdocuentry()	–	A function to accept values of Docunames, Freespace and Occupied from user
Retfreespace()	–	A function that returns the value of total Kilobytes available (1 Kilobyte = 1024 bytes)
Showfiles()	–	A function that displays the names of all the Documents in Directory.

17. Define a class with complete function definitions COMPETITION in C++ with following specifications:

Data members

event_no	–	integer
description	–	char(30)
score	–	integer
qualified	–	char

Member methods

input()	–	To take input for event_no, description and score
Award ( )	–	To award qualified as 'y' if score is more than the cut off score passed as int to the function else award 'N'
show()	–	To display all details

18. Declare a class called MOVIE with the following members :

Data members :

Name of the movie
Name of the director
Name of the producer

Grading

Member Functions :

To initialize the data members

To display the movie details

Write a program to perform the above member functions.

19. Declare a class having following :

Data member

Name of society

House number

Number of members

Flat type

Income

Member function

to read data member

to allocate flat according to income

Income >= 10,000 Flat type = HIG

Income >= 5000 and Income < 10,000 Flat type = MIG

Income < 5000 Flat type = LIG

Write a program to perform the above member functions.

Inheritances and Polymorphism 13

13.1 Introduction

People usually think of inheritance as a child receiving certain traits from his parents. This is true whether we are talking about people or about C# class objects. C# enables us to define *parent* or *base* or *derived* classes. The derived class inherits all the public data members and public member functions from the base class. This, in effect, makes them a part of the derived class's public interface.

Inheritance is one of the primary concepts of object-oriented programming. It allows you to reuse existing code. Through effective employment of reuse, you can save time in your programming.

13.2 Concept of Inheritance

One advantage of object-oriented programming is the re-usage of code. The capability to define custom data types using classes enables us to reuse the code that we develop. This works well if we always need exactly the same object. In real world, however, we may need an object that is almost similar to an already developed object but not exactly similar. *Inheritance* enables us to reuse an object more quickly; thus making slight adjustments where necessary.

Definition

Inheritance is the act of deriving a new class from an existing one. It is analogous to creating a new house blueprint from an existing blueprint that has similar characteristics

13.3 Base Class With Single Inheritance

When a class is defined in normal class declaration, it is called a *base class*. Otherwise, the class at the top of the hierarchy is the base class and the other class is the derived class. That is a child class of one parent can itself be the parent of another derived class. Furthermore, multiple classes can be derived from a single parent. Therefore, inheritance relationships often develop into class hierarchies. Figure 13.1 shows the base class and the derived class :

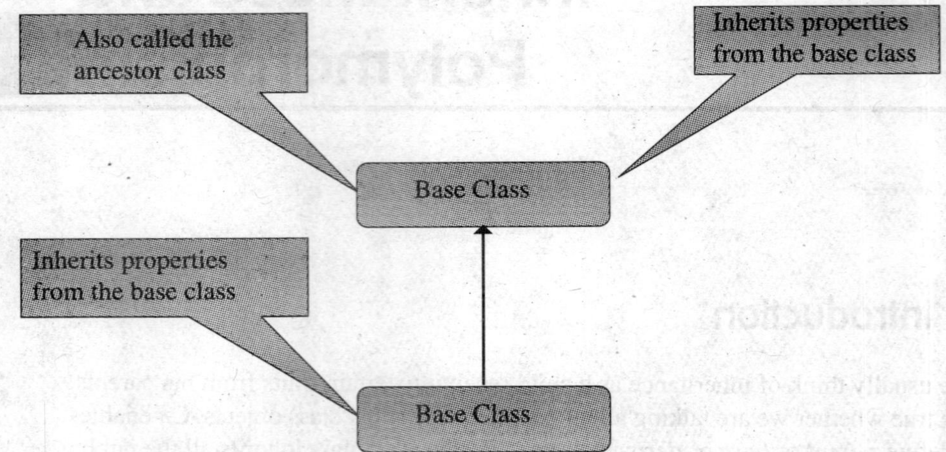

Fig. 13.1 A single inheritance of class.

When a derived class is declared with only one base, then the class is called single inheritance.

Note

The child of one class can be parent of one or more other classes, creating a class hierarchy. A primary purpose of inheritance is to reuse existing software.

Classes in C# can only inherit from one class at a time (single inheritance). Some languages (such as C++) allow a class to inherit from several classes at once (multiple inheritance) but this is not the case in C#. A class can only extend one class at a time. Although, there is no restriction on how many times you can use inheritance to extend the hierarchy, you must do so one extension at a time. Multiple inheritances are a nice feature, but it leads to very complex object hierarchies. C# has a mechanism that provides many of the same benefits, without so much complexity, called interfaces (covered in an upcoming section).

13.4 Declaring Derived classes

A derived class inherits data members and member functions from its base class. However, a derived class does not inherit any constructor and destructor. A derived class may itself be a base class from which, additional classes could be derived. In Fig. 13.2, for instance, derived class A inherits properties from the base class at the top level. Derived class B inherits those properties plus any new ones in class A. Derived class C inherits properties from the top base class and from derived classes A and B, in general, though, a derived class begins its existence with a copy of its base class's members, including any members inherited from more distantly related classes:

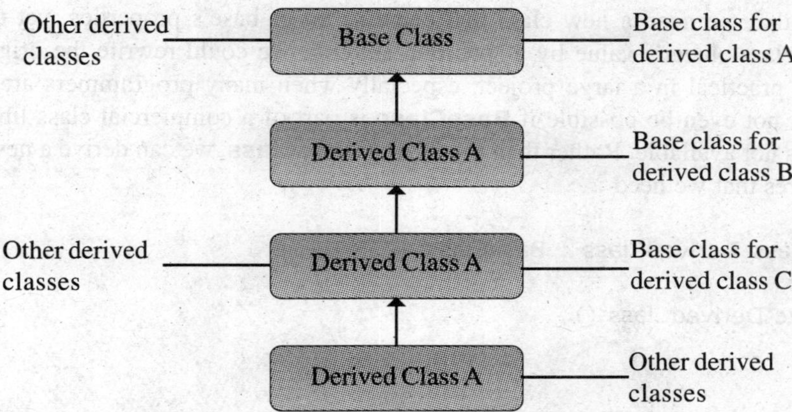

Fig. 13.2 A derived class may be a base class for other derivations.

The example given below demonstrates the mechanism of inheritance. Consider a base class **BaseClass,** declared as:

```
public class BaseClass
{
    public int counter;
    public BaseClass()
    {
        counter = 0;
    }
    public void newset(int n)
    {
        counter = n;
    }
    public void factorial()
    {
        .
        .
        .
    }
}
```

From the aforementioned declaration, base's member function resembles those typically found in C# classes from which, new classes might be derived. Member *counter* represents the class's private data. Only **BaseClass** member functions may refer directly to *counter*. The default constructor, base(), initializes the counter to zero. Two member functions **newset(int n)** and **void factorial()** are used to assign counter a new value and calculates the factorial value.

Suppose that we need a new class that contains all of base's properties, yet can increment and decrement a class object's value by a specified amount. We could rewrite the original class but that might not be practical in a large project, especially when many programmers are involved. Such a change might not even be possible if **BaseClass** is part of a commercial class library to which, the source code is not available. Rather than modifying **BaseClass**, we can derive a new class from it and add the features that we need :

```
public class DerivedClass : BaseClass
{
   public DerivedClass ()
   {
   }

   // Assigning the new value to counter
   public void changeVal(int n)
   {
      // Counter is again assigned as counter is public
      counter = n;
   }
}
```

> **Note**
> *Inherited variables and methods can be used in the derived class as if they had been declared locally.*

The derived class is named **DerivedClass**. Immediately following the derived class name and incorporate the definition of one class into another by using the colon (**:**) symbol. After those elements, comes the name of a base class (**BaseClass**) from which, **DerivedClass** receives its inheritance. Figure 13.3 illustrates the parts of derived and its constructor. The above declaration creates a superclass called **BaseClass** and a subclass called **DerivedClass**. Notice how the symbol colon (**:**)is used to create a subclass of **BaseClass**.

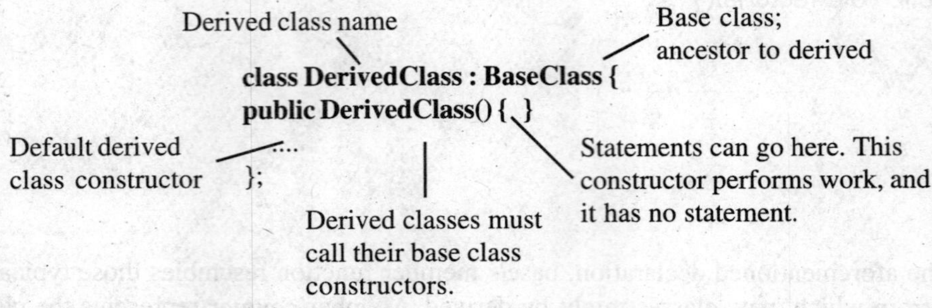

Fig. 13.3 Some parts of a derived class.

The public members of a public class remain public in the derived class. In a derived class, the declaration that begins as follows :

```
class DerivedClass : baseClass
{
    ...
    ...
}
```

all of public members of **BaseClass** become public members in **DerivedClass**. Any private members in **BaseClass** remain private to their original declaring class and **DerivedClass** may not access those members in **BaseClass**.

Inheritance in C# is handled through the colon symbol (**:**). When one class inherits from another class, the child class extends the parent class.

When a class is based on another class, all public (we will also introduce another inheritance-oriented keyword for this issue) members of the parent class are made available to the derived class that can use them as easily. While other methods and classes can also use the public members of a class, the difference is that the derived class can call the public members of the parent as if they belonged to the derived class. That is, the child class doesn't have to "qualify" the public members of the parent class when these public members are used in the body of the derived class.

Example Write a program to demonstrate inheritance in C#.

..\CSharp_Book\Chap13\ClassInher

```
using System;
using System.Collections.Generic;
using System.Text;

// Demonstrating the inheritance in C#
// Demonstrates a sample example on class inheritance
// with a factorial
namespace ClassInher
{
    public class BaseClass
    {
        public int counter;
        public BaseClass ()
        {
            counter = 0;
        }

        public void newset(int n)
        {
            counter = n;
        }
```

```
        public void factorial()
        {
            int i;
            double fact = 1.0;
            for (i = 1; i <= counter; i++)
                fact = fact * i;
            Console.WriteLine("The factorial of {0} is : {1:F2}", counter, fact);
        }
    }
    public class DerivedClass : BaseClass
    {
        // Assigning the new value to counter
        public void changeVal(int n)
        {
            // Counter is again assigned as counter is public
            counter = n;
        }
    }
    class Program
    {
        static void Main()
        {
            BaseClass b = new BaseClass ();
            DerivedClass d = new DerivedClass ();

            // The base class may be used by itself.
            b.newset(5);
            b.factorial();

            // The derived class access to all public member of its base class
            d.changeVal(6);
            d.factorial();
        }
    }
}
```

When the above program executed, it will produce the following output as shown in Fig. 13.4.

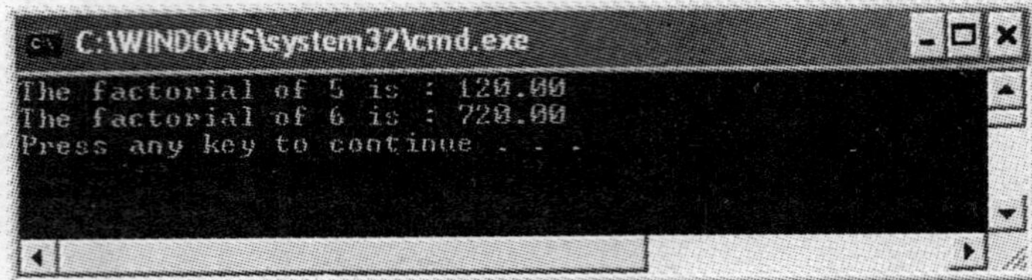

Fig. 13.4 Demonstrating a simple class inheritance.

Example Demonstrates a sample example on class inheritance for finding the area of triangle and rectangle.

..\CSharp_Book\Chap13\InhrArea

```
using System;
using System.Collections.Generic;
using System.Text;

// Demonstrating the inheritance in C#
namespace InhrArea
{
    class CPolygon
    {
        protected int width, height;
        public void set_values (int a, int b)
        {
            width = a; height = b;
        }
    }

    class CRectangle : CPolygon
    {
        public int area()
        {
            return (width * height);
        }
    }
    class CTriangle : CPolygon
    {
        public int area()
        {
            return (width * height / 2);
        }
    }

    class Program
    {
        static void Main()
        {
            CRectangle rect = new CRectangle();
            CTriangle trgl = new CTriangle();

            rect.set_values (4, 5);
            trgl.set_values (4, 5);
```

```
            Console.WriteLine("The area of rectangle : {0}", rect.area());
            Console.WriteLine("The area of triangle : {0}", trgl.area());
        }
    }
}
```

When the above program executed, it will produce the following output :

```
The area of rectangle : 20
The area of triangle : 10
Press any key to continue . . .
```

The objects of the classes **CRectangle** and **CTriangle** each contain members inherited from **CPolygon**. These are: width, height and **set_values()**. If we see the concept graphically, then we conclude that the **CRectangle** and **CTriangle** inherits the properties from **CPolygon** class as shown in Fig. 13.5.

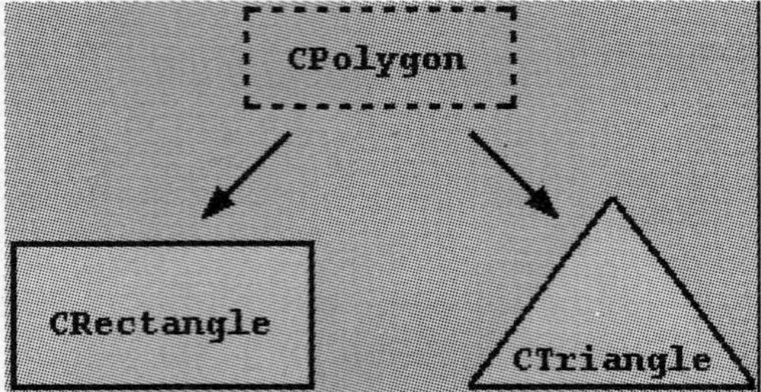

Fig. 13.5 Inheriting class example.

Note

The protected access specifier is similar to private. Its only difference occurs in fact with inheritance. When a class inherits from another one, the members of the derived class can access the protected members inherited from the base class, but not its private members.

Since we wanted width and height to be accessible from members of the derived classes **CRectangle** and **CTriangle** and not only by members of **CPolygon**, we have used protected access instead of private.

We can summarize the different access types according to who can access them in the following listing 13.1.

Listing 13.1 Different access types in inheritance.

Access	public	protected	private
members of the same class	Yes	Yes	Yes
members of derived classes	Yes	Yes	No
not members	Yes	No	No

In our example, the members inherited by **CRectangle** and **CTriangle** have the same access permissions as they had in their base class **CPolygon** :

```
CPolygon.width              // protected access
CRectangle.width            // protected access
CPolygon.set_values()       // public access
CRectangle.set_values()     // public access
```

This is because we have used the public keyword to define the inheritance relationship on each of the derived classes :

```
class CRectangle : CPolygon { ... }
```

This public keyword after the colon (**:**) denotes the minimum access level for all the members inherited from the class that follows it (in this case **CPolygon**). Since public is the most accessible level, by specifying this keyword the derived class will inherit all the members with the same levels they had in the base class.

If we specify a more restrictive access level like protected, all public members of the base class are inherited as protected in the derived class. Whereas if we specify the most restricting of all access levels: private, all the base class members are inherited as private.

13.5 Member Visibility Mode

So far, we have discussed about the private and public access specifiers in the preceding chapters and the new specifiers **protected**, **internal** and **protected internal** has been discussed in this section. The private and public specifiers are related only to single class, not like class inheritance. This chapter discusses these specifiers in other manners, as they are inherited.

Note

Visibility modifiers determine which variables and methods are inherited.

- **public.** A derived class cal access the public, protected and internal members of its base class if the derived class is in the same assembly as the base class. A base class's public members are accessible anywhere that the program has a reference to object of that base class or to an object of one of that base class's derived classes.
- **private.** A derived class cannot access private members of its base clad directly. A base class's private members are accessible only within the definition of that base class only.
- **protected.** A base class's protected members have an intermediate level of protection between public and private access. A base class's protected members can be accessed only in that base class or in any classes derived from that base class.
- **internal.** A base class's internal members can be accessed only by object in the same assembly. Note that an internal member is accessible in any part of the assembly in which that internal member is declared.

- **protected internal.** The permissions allowed by this access level are those allowed by the 'protected' level plus those allowed by the 'internal' level. The access level is thus more liberal than its parts taken individually. This modifier should only be used for internal classes (ie. classes declared within other classes).

13.5.1 Access Modifiers

Another aspect of classes in C# is the accessibility of the members (both variables and methods) in the class. There are several options in Java to allow you to closely tailor how accessible you want these members to be.

As a general rule of thumb, you want to limit the scope of program elements (and this includes class members) as much as possible-the fewer places something is accessible, the fewer places it can be accessed incorrectly.

There are four different access modifiers for class members in Java: private, protected, public, and default (or the absence of any modifier). This is slightly complicated by the fact that classes within the same package have different access than classes outside the package. Thus, here are two listings, which show both the accessibility and inheritability of classes and member variables from within the same package and from outside the package (packages are discussed in a later section):

Listing 13.2 Access within the class's package.

Access Modifier	Inherited	Accessible
Default (no modifier)	Y	Y
Public	Y	Y
Protected	Y	Y
Internal	Y	Y
Internal protected	Y	Y
Private	N	N

This Listing 13.2 shows how class members are accessed and inherited from, with respect to other members in the same package. For example, a member that is declared to be private cannot be accessed by, or inherited from, other members of the same package. On the other hand, members, declared using the other modifiers, could be accessed by and inherited from all other members of that package.

Listing 13.3 Access outside of a class's package.

Access Modifier	Inherited	Accessible
default (no modifier)	N	N
Public	Y	Y
Protected	Y	Y

Internal	Y	Y
Internal protected	Y	Y
Private	N	N

For example, this table shows that a protected member could be inherited from, but not accessed, by classes outside its package.

The main item to note in the above charts is that public members are available to anyone, who wants to access them, (notice that constructors are always public) whereas, private members are never accessible nor inheritable outside the class. So, any member variable or method that is to be kept strictly internal to the class, should be private.

It is common in object-oriented languages to support the idea of information hiding within the class by making all the member variables of the class private and accessing them through methods that are in a specific format called, Accessor methods.

13.5.2 Class Modifier

There are seven different - optional - class modifiers. Four of these - '**public**', '**internal**', '**protected**' and '**private**' - are used to specify the access levels of the types defined by the classes. The following five different access levels can be specified with these four modifiers:

- **public.** The 'public' keyword identifies a type as fully accessible to all other types. This is the implicit accessibility of enumeration members and interface members.
- **Internal.** If a class is declared as 'internal', the type it defines is accessible only to types within the same assembly (a self-contained 'unit of packaging' containing code, metadata etc.). This is the default access level of non-nested classes.
- **Protected.** If a class is declared as 'protected', its type is accessible by a containing type and any type that inherits from this containing type. This modifier should only be used for internal classes (ie. classes declared within other classes).
- **protected internal.** The permissions allowed by this access level are those allowed by the 'protected' level plus those allowed by the 'internal' level. The access level is thus more liberal than its parts taken individually. This modifier should only be used for internal classes (ie. classes declared within other classes).
- **Private.** Where a class is declared as 'private', access to the type it defines is limited to a containing type only. This modifier should only be used for internal classes (ie. classes declared within other classes). We now turn to the final three class modifiers:
- **New.** The 'new' keyword can be used for 'nested' classes. A nested class is one that is defined in the body of another class; it is in most ways identical to a class defined in the normal way, but its access level cannot be more liberal than that of the class in which it is defined. A nested class should be declared using the 'new' keyword just in case it has the same name as (and thus overrides) an inherited type.

- **Abstract.** A class declared as 'abstract' cannot itself be instanced - it is designed only to be a base class for inheritance.
- **Sealed.** A class declared as 'sealed' cannot be inherited from.

13.6 Inheritance Types

C# supports three types of inheritances. These are :

- Single Inheritance
- Heirarchical Inheritance
- Multilevel Inheritance

13.6.1 Single Inheritance

A derived class with only one base class is called single inheritance. Let us consider a simple example to illustrate single inheritance. Figure 13.6 shows a base class baseemp and a derived class derivedemp. The class baseemp contains four private data members and two public member functions. The class derivedemp contains four data members and six member functions.

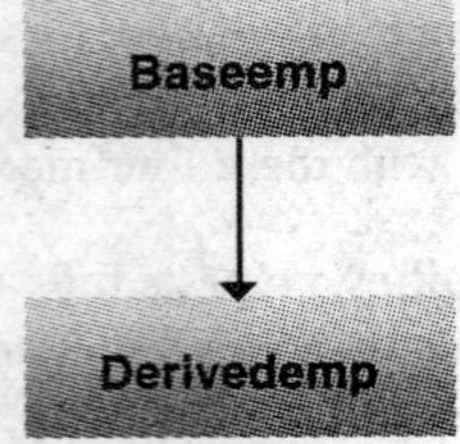

Fig. 13.6 Single inheritance.

The base class **baseemp** is as :

```
public class baseemp  // Base class or super class of employee
{
    private int empcode;
    private string empname;
    private string empdesig;

    public void input_data()
    {
        Console.Write("Enter employee code : ");
        empcode = int.Parse(Console.ReadLine());
        Console.Write("Enter employee name : ");
        empname = Console.ReadLine();
        Console.Write("Enter employee designation : ");
        empdesig = Console.ReadLine();
    }
```

```
    public void display()
    {
        Console.WriteLine("Employee code : " + empcode);
        Console.WriteLine("Employee name : " + empname);
        Console.WriteLine("Employee designation : " + empdesig);
    }
};
```

and the derived class **derivedemp** is as :

```
// Derived class or subclass for baseemp
public class derivedemp: baseemp
{
    double salary, gross;
    float da, hra;

    public void input_salary()
    {
        input_data();  // Read the address from base class
        Console.Write("Enter salary : ");
        salary = double.Parse(Console.ReadLine());
        da = (float)cal_da();
        hra = (float)cal_hra();
        gross = (double)cal_gross();
    }

    public double cal_da()
    {
        return (1.20 * salary);
    }

    public double cal_hra()
    {
        return (0.15 * salary);
    }

    public double cal_gross()
    {
        return (salary + da + hra + salary);
    }

    public void print_salary()
    {
        display(); // Print the address from base class
```

```
            Console.WriteLine("Basic salary : {0:F2}", salary);
            Console.WriteLine("Dearness allowance : {0:F2}", da);
            Console.WriteLine("House rent allowance : {0:F2}", hra);
            Console.WriteLine("Gross : {0:F2}", gross);
        }
    };
```

Example The example given below uses for single inheritance to employee class with the address part and the calculation part.

..\CSharp_Book\Chap13\EmpDerived

```
using System;
using System.Collections.Generic;
using System.Text;

namespace EmpDerived
{
    public class baseemp  // Base class or super class of employee
    {
        private int empcode;
        private string empname;
        private string empdesig;

        public void input_data()
        {
            Console.Write("Enter employee code : ");
            empcode = int.Parse(Console.ReadLine());
            Console.Write("Enter employee name : ");
            empname = Console.ReadLine();
            Console.Write("Enter employee designation : ");
            empdesig = Console.ReadLine();
        }

        public void display()
        {
            Console.WriteLine("Employee code : " + empcode);
            Console.WriteLine("Employee name : " + empname);
            Console.WriteLine("Employee designation : " + empdesig);
        }
    };

    // Derived class or subclass for baseemp
    public class derivedemp: baseemp
    {
        double salary, gross;
```

```
        float da, hra;

        public void input_salary()
        {
            input_data();   // Read the address from base class
            Console.Write("Enter salary : ");
            salary = double.Parse(Console.ReadLine());
            da = (float)cal_da();
            hra = (float)cal_hra();
            gross = (double)cal_gross();
        }

        public double cal_da()
        {
            return (0.30 * salary);
        }

        public double cal_hra()
        {
            return (0.15 * salary);
        }

        public double cal_gross()
        {
            return (salary + da + hra + salary);
        }

        public void print_salary()
        {
            display(); // Print the address from base class
            Console.WriteLine("Basic salary : {0:F2}", salary);
            Console.WriteLine("Dearness allowance : {0:F2}", da);
            Console.WriteLine("House rent allowance : {0:F2}", hra);
            Console.WriteLine("Gross : {0:F2}", gross);
        }
    };

    class Program
    {
        static void Main()
        {
            // Declares Object of type employee
            derivedemp emp = new derivedemp();

            emp.input_salary();
```

```
            Console.WriteLine("Here is the employee information : ");
            for (int i = 1; i <= 40; i++)
                Console.Write("=");

            Console.WriteLine();
            emp.print_salary();
        }
    }
}
```

When the above program executed, it will produce the following output as shown in Fig. 13.7.

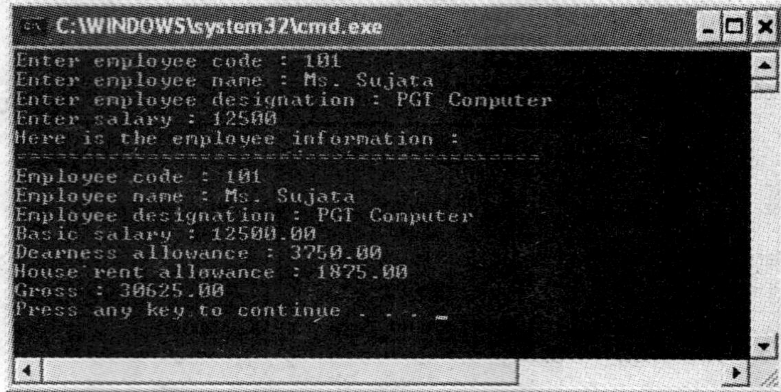

Fig. 13.7 Demonstrating the single inheritance on employee.

The above example derived from class specifies the keyword **public** in front of the base class's name. This specifies **public** derivation, which means that the public members of the base class are public members of the derived class, and protected members (if) of the base class are protected members of the derived class.

You can also specify the keyword **private** in front of the base class's name. This specifies private derivation, which means that both the public and protected members of the base class are private members of the derived class. Those members are accessible to the derived class's member functions, but not to anyone using the derived class. Whereas the private derivation is rarely used.

13.6.2 A Sample Review Test

Like your previous examples about employee class and the methods like:

```
public class baseemp  // Base class or super class of employee
{
    // Data members- Employee full name
    private String emp_name;
    private String address;// Employee address
    private String city; // Employee city
```

```
    private String state;    // Employee state
    public double salary;   // Employee salary

    // Class constructor
    public void input_data(String a, String b, String c, String d, double val)
    {
        emp_name = a;
        address = b;
        city = c;
        state = d;
        salary = val;
    }

    public void print_data()
    {
        Console.WriteLine("________________________________________________");
        Console.WriteLine("Employee name -> " + emp_name);
        Console.WriteLine("Address ->  " + address);
        Console.WriteLine("City -> " + city);
        Console.WriteLine("State -> " + state);
        Console.WriteLine("Basic Salary -> " + salary);
    }
};

// Derived class or subclass for baseemp
public class derivedemp : baseemp
{
    double gross;
    double da, hra;

    public void cal_da() // Receiving the emp reference
    {
        da = 0.3 * salary;  // Calculates 120% DA
        Console.WriteLine("Da is -> {0:F2}", da);
    }

    public void cal_hra()  // Receiving the emp reference
    {
        hra = 0.15 * salary;    // 15% as hra
        Console.WriteLine("House rent allowance is -> {0:F2}", hra);
    }

    public void cal_gross() // Receiving the emp reference
    {
```

```
        gross = salary + hra + da;
        Console.WriteLine("Gross salary is: {0:F2}", gross);
    }
};
```

By the class inheritance, the **baseemp** and **derivedemp** class can be programmed as :

Example Write a program to demonstrate the class concept in regard with base and derived class as mentioned above.

..\CSharp_Book\Chap13\EmpObject

```
class Program
{
    static void Main()
    {
        // Declared the derived class object
        derivedemp emp = new derivedemp();
        emp.input_data("Sangram Singh",  "F-25/28, Sector-7, Rohini",
                       "Delhi", "DL", 5000);

        // Method object with pass-by-reference
        emp.print_data();
        emp.cal_da(); // Passes the reference of emp object
        emp.cal_hra();
        emp.cal_gross();
    }
}
```

When the above program executed, it will produce the following output as shown in Fig. 13.8.

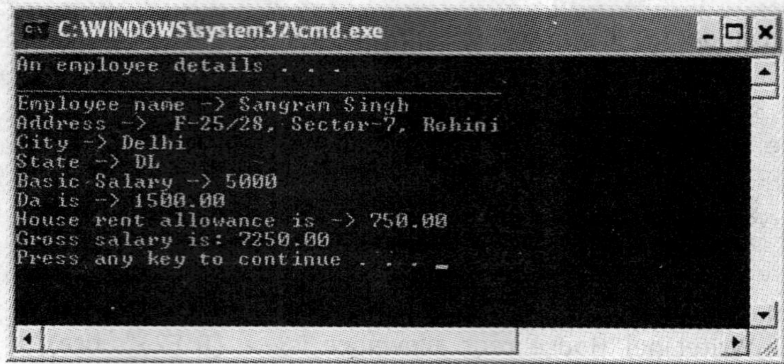

Fig. 13.8 Using base class data members in derived class.

The aforementioned example derived from class specifies the keyword **extends** in front of the base class's name. This specifies a **public** derivation, which means that the public members of the base class are public members of the derived class and protected members if the base classes are the protected members of the derived class.

We can also specify the keyword **private** in front of the base class's name. This specifies private derivation, which means that both the public and protected members of the base class are private members of the derived class. Those members are accessible to the derived class's member functions but not to anyone using the derived class whereas the private derivation is rarely used.

13.6.3 Hierarchical Inheritance

In the pervious example you have seen that we are deriving one class from one base class. It is possible to derive more than one derived class from a single class. This type of inheritance is known as hierarchical. As an example, Fig. 13.9 shows a hierarchical classification of students in a college. All the students have certain things in common features from the base class **Students**.

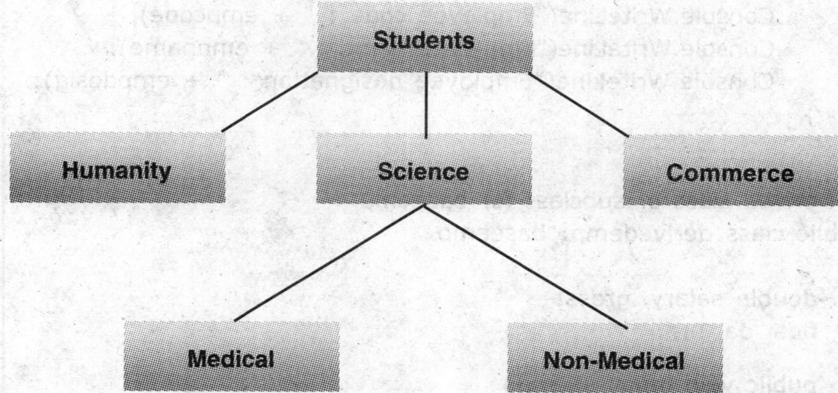

Fig. 13.9 Hierarchical classification of students.

If you consider our previous example of classes **baseemp** and **derivedemp**, then we can join another class **derivedcust** which follows the same feature of **baseemp** class. The example is given as:

..\CSharp_Book\Chap13\EmpCust

```
using System;
using System.Collections.Generic;
using System.Text;

namespace EmpCust
{
    public class baseemp  // Base class or super class of employee
    {
```

```
        private int empcode;
        private string empname;
        private string empdesig;

        public void input_data()
        {
            Console.Write("Enter employee code : ");
            empcode = int.Parse(Console.ReadLine());
            Console.Write("Enter employee name : ");
            empname = Console.ReadLine();
            Console.Write("Enter employee designation : ");
            empdesig = Console.ReadLine();
        }

        public void display()
        {
            Console.WriteLine("Employee code : " + empcode);
            Console.WriteLine("Employee name : " + empname);
            Console.WriteLine("Employee designation : " + empdesig);
        }
    };

    // Derived class or subclass for baseemp
    public class derivedemp: baseemp
    {
        double salary, gross;
        float da, hra;

        public void input_salary()
        {
            input_data();  // Read the address from base class
            Console.Write("Enter salary : ");
            salary = double.Parse(Console.ReadLine());
            da = (float)cal_da();
            hra = (float)cal_hra();
            gross = (double)cal_gross();
        }

        public double cal_da()
        {
            return (1.20 * salary);
        }

        public double cal_hra()
        {
```

```
        return (0.15 * salary);
    }

    public double cal_gross()
    {
        return (salary + da + hra + salary);
    }

    public void print_salary()
    {
        display(); // Print the address from base class
        Console.WriteLine("Basic salary : {0:F2}", salary);
        Console.WriteLine("Dearness allowance : {0:F2}", da);
        Console.WriteLine("House rent allowance : {0:F2}", hra);
        Console.WriteLine("Gross : {0:F2}", gross);
    }
};

// Derived class or subclass for baseemp
public class derivedcust : baseemp
{
    public int acc_no;
    public float balance;

    public void read_cust()
    {
        Console.WriteLine("Enter information for customer : ");
        input_data();
        Console.Write("Enter the account number : ");
        acc_no = int.Parse(Console.ReadLine());
        Console.Write("Enter the balance amount : ");
        balance = float.Parse(Console.ReadLine());
    }

    public void show_cust()
    {
        display();
        Console.WriteLine("Customer Account Number  : {0}", acc_no);
        Console.WriteLine("Customer Balance  : {0:F2}", balance);
    }
};

class Program
{
```

```
        static void Main()
        {
            derivedemp emp = new derivedemp();    // Declares Object of type employee
            derivedcust cust = new derivedcust();
            emp.input_salary();
            cust.read_cust();

            Console.WriteLine("Here is the employee information : ");
            for (int i = 1; i <= 32; i++)
                Console.Write("=");
            Console.WriteLine();
            emp.print_salary();

            Console.WriteLine("Here is the customer information : ");
            for (int i = 1; i <= 32; i++)
                Console.Write("=");
            Console.WriteLine();
            cust.show_cust();
        }
    }
}
```

When the above program executed, it will produce the following output as shown in Fig. 13.10.

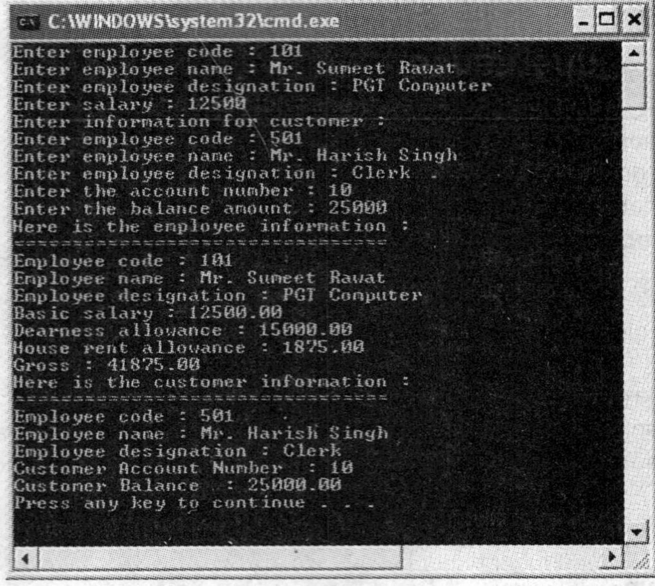

Fig. 13.10 Demonstrating the hierarchical inheritance.

13.6.4 Multilevel Inheritance

In single inheritance we have seen that we can derive a class from single base class. Sometimes it is possible that the derived class is also the base class for another class. This type of inheritance is known as multilevel inheritance. Figure 13.11 shows a multilevel inheritance between three classes **A, B** and **C**. The class **A** serves as a base class for the derived class **B** which in turn serves as a base class for the derived class **C**. The class **B** is known as *intermediate base class* since it provides a link for the inheritance between **A** and **C**.

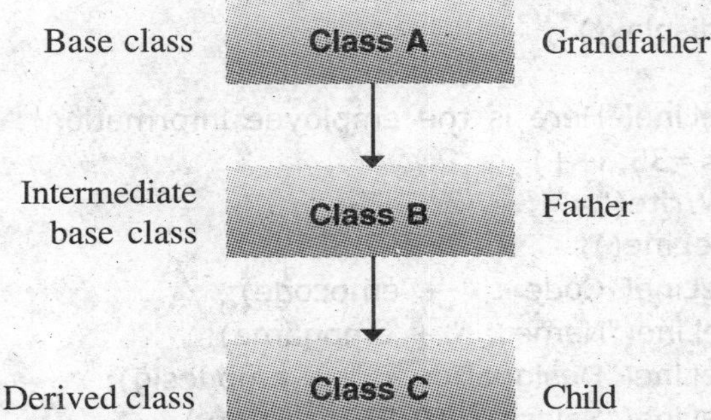

Fig. 13.11 Multilevel inheritance.

Let us consider an example of three classes **Employee**, **Customer** and **Emp_Cust**. Here, the class **Employee** serves as a base class for the derived class **Customer** which in turn serves as a base class for the derived class **Emp_Cust**.

Example The example given below uses for multilevel inheritance to **Employee** and **Customer** classes with the address part and the calculation part.

..\CSharp_Book\Chap13\MultiLevel

```
using System;
using System.Collections.Generic;
using System.Text;
namespace MultiLevel
{
    public class Employee // Base class or super class of employee
    {
        private int empcode;
        private string empname;
        private string empdesig;
        public double salary;

        public void empinput_data()
        {
            Console.WriteLine("Enter employee information : ");
            Console.Write("Enter code : ");
```

```
            empcode = int.Parse(Console.ReadLine());
            Console.Write("Enter name : ");
            empname = Console.ReadLine();
            Console.Write("Enter designation : ");
            empdesig = Console.ReadLine();
            Console.Write("Enter salary : ");
            salary = double.Parse(Console.ReadLine());
        }

        public void empdisplay()
        {
            Console.WriteLine("Here is the employee information : ");
            for (int i=0; i<=35; i++)
                Console.Write("=");
            Console.WriteLine();
            Console.WriteLine("Code : " + empcode);
            Console.WriteLine("Name : " + empname);
            Console.WriteLine("Designation : " + empdesig);
            Console.WriteLine("Salary : {0:F2}", salary);
        }
    };

    // Derived class or subclass for baseemp
    public class Customer : Employee
    {
        int custcode;
        string custname;
        string custdesig;
        double  balance;

        public void custinput_data()
        {
            Console.WriteLine("Enter customer information : ");
            Console.Write("Enter code : ");
            custcode = int.Parse(Console.ReadLine());
            Console.Write("Enter name : ");
            custname = Console.ReadLine();
            Console.Write("Enter designation : ");
            custdesig = Console.ReadLine();
            Console.Write("Enter balance : ");
            balance = double.Parse(Console.ReadLine());
        }

        public void custdisplay()
        {
```

```
        Console.WriteLine("Here is the customer information : ");
        for (int i=0; i<=35; i++)
            Console.Write("=");

        Console.WriteLine();
        Console.WriteLine("Code : {0}", custcode);
        Console.WriteLine("Name : " + custname);
        Console.WriteLine("Designation : " + custdesig);
        Console.WriteLine("Balance : {0:F2}", balance);
    }
};

// derived class of derived class as multilevel class hierarcy
public class Emp_Cust : Customer
{
    public void get_data()
    {
        // Input employee information
        empinput_data();
        Console.WriteLine();
        // Input customer information
        custinput_data();
    }

    public void show_data()
    {
        // Display employee information
        empdisplay();
        Console.WriteLine();
        // Display customer information
        custdisplay();
    }
};

class Program
{
    static void Main()
    {
        // Declares Object of type Employee and Customer
        Emp_Cust empcust = new Emp_Cust();
        empcust.get_data();
        empcust.show_data();
    }
}
}
```

When the above program executed, it will produce the following output as shown in Fig. 13.12.

```
C:\WINDOWS\system32\cmd.exe
Enter employee information :
Enter code : 101
Enter name : Ms. Sujata
Enter designation : PGT Computer
Enter salary : 12500

Enter customer information :
Enter code : 501
Enter name : Mr. Harish Singh
Enter designation : Clerk
Enter balance : 25000
Here is the employee information :
=====================================
Code : 101
Name : Ms. Sujata
Designation : PGT Computer
Salary : 12500.00

Here is the customer information :
=====================================
Code : 501
Name : Mr. Harish Singh
Designation : Clerk
Balance : 25000.00
Press any key to continue . . .
```

Fig. 13.12 Demonstrating the multilevel inheritance.

13.7 Polymorphism

Polymorphism is an important OOP concept used extensively in implementing inheritance. Polymorphism refers to the ability of one thing to take many (Poly) distinct forms (Morphism). In OOP, this one thing which may take several distinct forms may be an operator or a function. This provides the facility of sending the same message to objects of parent class and objects of the sub-classes. Each object may however respond to the message in its own way depending on the class/sub-class to which it belongs. This allows objects having different internal structures (of derived classes) to share the same external interface.

13.7.1 The new Modifier

Imagine you create a class used to process a circle as we saw earlier. You can use this as the base class for a cube. Both the square and the cube have an area but their values are different. This means that, as mentioned in our introduction to inheritance, when deriving the cube class, you would have to calculate a new area for the cube.

If you create or declare a new member in a derived class and that member has the same name as a member of the base class, when creating the new member, you may want to indicate to the compiler that, instead of overriding that same method that was defined in the base class, you want to create a brand new and independent version of that method. When doing this, you would be asking the compiler to hide the member of the base class that has the same name, when the member of the current class is invoked. To do this, type the **new** keyword to its left. For example;

..\CSharp_Book\Chap13\NewType

```
using System;

namespace NewType
{
    class Circle
    {
        private double _radius;

        public double Radius
        {
            get { return (_radius < 0) ? 0.00 : _radius; }
            set { _radius = value; }
        }

        public double Diameter
        {
            get { return Radius * 2; }
        }

        public double Circumference
        {
            get { return Diameter * 3.14159; }
        }

        public double Area
        {
            get { return Radius * Radius * 3.14159; }
        }
    }

    class Sphere : Circle
    {
        new public double Area
        {
            get { return 4 * Radius * Radius * 3.14159; }
        }

        public double Volume
        {
            get { return 4 * 3.14159 * Radius * Radius * Radius / 3; }
        }
    }

    class Program
    {
```

```
        public static int Main()
        {
            Circle c = new Circle();
            c.Radius = 25.55;

            Console.WriteLine("Circle Characteristics");
            Console.WriteLine("========================");
            Console.WriteLine("Side:        {0:F2}", c.Radius);
            Console.WriteLine("Diameter: {0:F2}", c.Diameter);
            Console.WriteLine("Circumference: {0:F2}", c.Circumference);
            Console.WriteLine("Area:        {0:F2}", c.Area);

            Sphere s = new Sphere();
            s.Radius = 25.55;
            Console.WriteLine("--------------------------");
            Console.WriteLine("Sphere Characteristics");
            Console.WriteLine("========================");
            Console.WriteLine("Side:        {0:F2}", s.Radius);
            Console.WriteLine("Diameter: {0:F2}", s.Diameter);
            Console.WriteLine("Circumference: {0:F2}", s.Circumference);
            Console.WriteLine("Area:        {0:F2}", s.Area);
            Console.WriteLine("Volume: {0:F2}", s.Volume);
            Console.WriteLine();
            return 0;
        }
    }
}
```

When the above program executed, it will produce the following output as shown in Fig. 13.13.

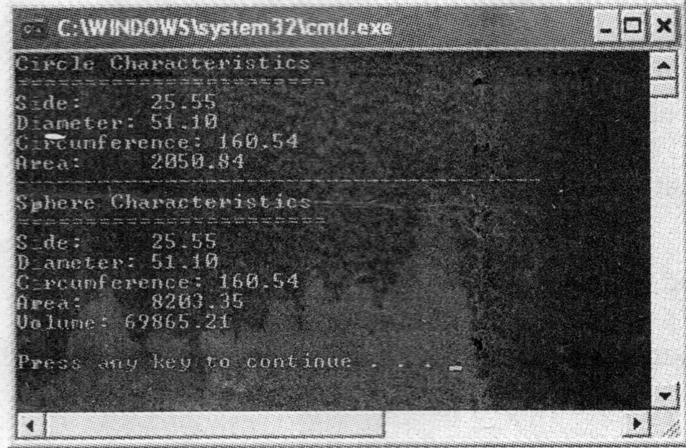

Fig. 13.13 Use of new modifier in inheritance.

13.7.2 Protected Members

To maintain a privileged relationship with its children, a parent class can make a set list of members available only to classes derived from it. With this relationship, some members of a parent class have a protected access level. Of course, as the class creator, it is your job to specify this relationship.

To create a member that derived classes only can access, type the **protected** keyword to its left. Here are examples:

..\CSharp_Book\Chap13\ProtectedMemb

```
using System;
using System.Collections.Generic;
using System.Text;

namespace People
{
    public class Person
    {
        private string _name;
        private string _gdr;

        public Person()
        {
            this._name = "Not Available";
            this._gdr    = "Unknown";
        }

        public Person(string name, string gender)
        {
            this._name = name;
            this._gdr  = gender;
        }

        protected string FullName
        {
            get { return _name; }
            set { _name = value; }
        }

        protected string Gender
        {
            get { return _gdr; }
            set { _gdr = value; }
        }
```

```
        public void Show()
        {
            Console.WriteLine("Name:       {0}", this.FullName);
            Console.WriteLine("Gender:     {0}", this.Gender);
        }
    }

    class Programs
    {
        static void Main()
        {
            People.Person man = new People.Person("Sumeet Rawat", "Male");

            Console.WriteLine("Computer Professional");
            Console.WriteLine("----------------------");
            man.Show();

            Console.WriteLine();
        }
    }
}
```

When the above program executed, it will produce the following output as shown in Fig. 13.14.

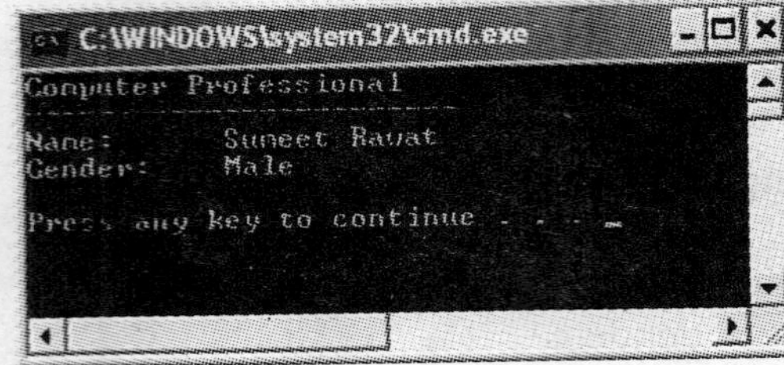

Fig. 13.14 Use of protected access in class inheritance.

You can access protected members only in derived classes. Therefore, if you instantiate a cla outside, you can call only public members:

13.7.3 Virtual and Override Members

We have just mentioned that you can create a new version of a member in a derived class for a memb that already exists in the parent class. After doing this, when you call that member in your program, y need to make sure that the right member gets called, the member in the base class or the equivale member in the derived class.

Polymorphism provides a way for a subclass to customize how it implements a method defined its base class. When you create a base class, if you anticipate that a certain property or method wou need to be redefined in the derived class, you can indicate this to the compiler. On the other hand, wh creating your classes, if you find out that you are customizing a property of method that already existed in the base class, you should let the compiler know that you are providing a new version. In both cases, the common member should be created as virtual.

If a base class wishes to define a method that may be overridden by a sub-class, it must specify the method as virtual.

To create a **virtual** member, in the base class, type the **virtual** keyword to the left of the property or method. For example, based on this, the Area property of our **Circle** class can be created as follows:

```
class Circle
{
    public virtual double Area
    {
        get
        {
            return Radius * Radius * 3.14159;
        }
    }
}
```

In fact, in C#, unlike C++, if you omit the **virtual** keyword, the compiler would display a warning. When you derive a class from an abstract, since the methods (if any) of the abstract class were not implemented, you must implement each one of them in the derived class. When customizing virtual members in a derived class, to indicate that a member is already virtual in the base class and that you are defining a new version, type the **override** keyword to the left of its declaration. For example, the Area property in our Sphere class can be created as follows:

```
class Sphere : Circle
{
    public override double  Area
    {
        get
        {
            return 4 * Radius * Radius * 3.14159;
        }
    }

    public double Volume
    {
        get
        {
            return 4 * 3.14159 * Radius * Radius * Radius;
        }
    }
}
```

13.7.4 Hiding Methods

Where one method 'hides' another, the hidden method does not need to be declared with any special keyword. Instead, the hiding method just declares itself as 'new'. So, where the Square class hides the Rectangle class' getArea method, the two methods might just be written thus:

```
public double getArea() // in Rectangle
{
    return length * width;
}

public new double getArea() // in Square
{
    return length * length;
}
```

Note that a method can 'hide' another one without the access modifiers of these methods being the same. So, for instance, the Square's getArea method could be declared as private, i.e.,

```
private new double getArea()
{
    return length * length;
}
```

This leads us to an important point. A 'new' method only hides a super-class method with a scope defined by its access modifier. Specifically, where the access level of the hiding method is 'private', as in the method just described, this method only hides the super-class method for the particular class in which it is defined.

To make this point more concrete, suppose that we introduced a further class, **SpecialSquare**, which inherits from **Square**. Suppose further that **SpecialSquare** does not overwrite the **getArea** method. In this case, because **Square**'s **getArea** method is defined as private, **SpecialSquare** inherits its **getArea** method directly from the **Rectangle** class (where the **getArea** method is public).

The final point to note about method hiding is that method calls do not always 'slide through' in the way that they do with virtual methods. So, if we declare two variables thus:

```
Square sq = new Square(4);
Rectangle r = sq;
```

then run the code

```
double area = r.getArea();
```

the **getArea** method run will be that defined in the **Rectangle** class, not the **Square** class.

13.7.5 Method Overriding

Suppose that we define a **Square** class which inherits from a **Rectangle** class (a square being a special case of a rectangle). Each of these classes also specifies a 'getArea' instance method, returning the area of the given instance.

For the **Square** class to '**override**' the **Rectangle** class' **getArea** method, the **Rectangle** class' method must have first declared that it is happy to be overridden. One way in which it can do this is with the '**virtual**' keyword. So, for instance, the **Rectangle** class' **getArea** method might be specified like this:

```
public virtual double getArea()
{
    return length * width;
}
```

To override this method the **Square** class would then specify the overriding method with the '**override**' keyword. For example:

```
public override double getArea()
{
    return length * length;
}
```

Note that for one method to override another, the overridden method must not be static, and it must be declared as either '**virtual**', '**abstract**' or '**override**'. Furthermore, the access modifiers for each method must be the same.

The major implication of the specifications above is that if we construct a new **Square** instance and then call its '**getArea**' method, the method actually called will be the **Square** instance's **getArea** method. So, for instance, if we run the following code:

```
Square sq = new Square(5);
double area = sq.getArea();
```

then the **getArea** method called on the second line will be the method defined in the **Square** class.

There is, however, a more subtle point. To show this, suppose that we declare two variables in the following way:

```
Square sq = new Square(4);
Rectangle r = sq;
```

Here variable r refers to sq as a **Rectangle** instance (possible because the **Square** class derives from the **Rectangle** class). We can now raise the question: if we run the following code

```
double area = r.getArea();
```

then which getArea method is actually called - the **Square** class method or the **Rectangle** class method?

The answer in this case is that the **Square** class method would still be called. Because the **Square** class' **getArea** method '**overrides**' the corresponding method in the **Rectangle** class, calls to this method on a **Square** instance always 'slide through' to the overriding method.

13.7.6 Abstract Classes

In a program, you can create a class whose role is only meant to provide fundamental characteristics for other classes. This type of class cannot be used to declare a variable. Such a class is referred to as abstract. Therefore, an abstract class can be created only to serve as a parent class for other classes. To create an abstract class, type the **abstract** keyword to the left of its name. For example;

```
abstract class Ball
{
    protected int TypeOfSport;
    protected string Dimensions;
```

13.7.7 Abstract Properties and Methods

When a class has been defined as an abstract base class, it may define any number of abstract members (which is analogous to a C++ pure virtual function). When creating a class that would mainly be used as a base for future inheritance, you can create one or more properties and make them abstract. To do this, when creating the property, type the **abstract** keyword to its left. Because you would not define the property, you can simply type the get keyword and its semi-colon in the body of the property.

A method of a class also can be made abstract. An abstract method can be a member of only an abstract class. Abstract method can be used whenever you wish to define a method that does not supply a default implementation. By doing so, you enforce a polymorphic trait or each descendent, leaving them to contend with the task of providing the details behind your abstract method. If you make a method abstract in a class, you must not implement the method. To create an abstract method, when creating its class, type the **abstract** keyword to the left of the method's name. End the declaration with a semi-colon and no body for the method since you cannot implement it. For example;

```
public abstract class Ball
{
    protected int TypeOfSport;
    protected string Dimensions;

    public abstract CalculateArea();
}
```

In the same way, you can create as many properties and methods as you see fit. You can choose what properties and methods to make abstract. This is important for inheritance.

..\CSharp_Book\Chap13\AbstractClass

```
using System;
using System.Collections.Generic;
using System.Text;
```

```
namespace AbstractClass
{
    public abstract class ShapeDescription
    {
        public abstract string Name { get; }
        public virtual string Description()
        {
            string Msg = "A quadrilateral is a geometric figure " +
                        "that has four sides and four angles.";
            return Msg;
        }
    }
    public class Square : ShapeDescription
    {
        private double _side;
        public Square()
        {
            _side = 0.00;
        }
        public Square(double s)
        {
            _side = s;
        }
        public override string Name
        {
            get { return "Square"; }
        }
        public override string Description()
        {
            // Get the introduction from the parent
            string Introduction = base.Description() +
                "\nA square is a quadrilateral that has four " +
                "equal sides and four right angles.";
            return Introduction;
        }
    }
    public class Rectangle : ShapeDescription
    {
        double _length;
        double _height;
```

```
        public Rectangle()
        {
            _length = 0.00;
            _height = 0.00;
        }

        public Rectangle(double L, double H)
        {
            _length = L;
            _height = H;
        }

        public override string Name
        {
            get { return "Rectangle"; }
        }

        public override string Description()
        {
            // Get the introduction from the parent
            string Introduction = base.Description();

            string Msg = Introduction +
                    "\nA rectangle is a quadrilateral that has adjacent " +
                    "perpendicular sides. This implies that its four " +
                    "angles are right.";
            return Msg;
        }
    }

    public class Program
    {
        static void DisplaySquare(Square S)
        {
            Console.WriteLine("Square Characteristics");
            Console.WriteLine("Name:        {0}", S.Name);
            Console.WriteLine("Description: {0}", S.Description());
        }
        static void DisplayRectangle(Rectangle R)
        {
            Console.WriteLine("Rectangle Characteristics");
            Console.WriteLine("Name:        {0}", R.Name);
            Console.WriteLine("Description: {0}", R.Description());
        }
```

```
        static void Main()
        {
            Square Sq = new Square();
            Rectangle Rect = new Rectangle();
            Console.WriteLine("===========================================");
            DisplaySquare(Sq);
            Console.WriteLine("===========================================");
            DisplayRectangle(Rect);
            Console.WriteLine("===========================================");

            Console.WriteLine();
        }
    }
}
```

When the above program executed, it will produce the following output as shown in Fig. 13.15.

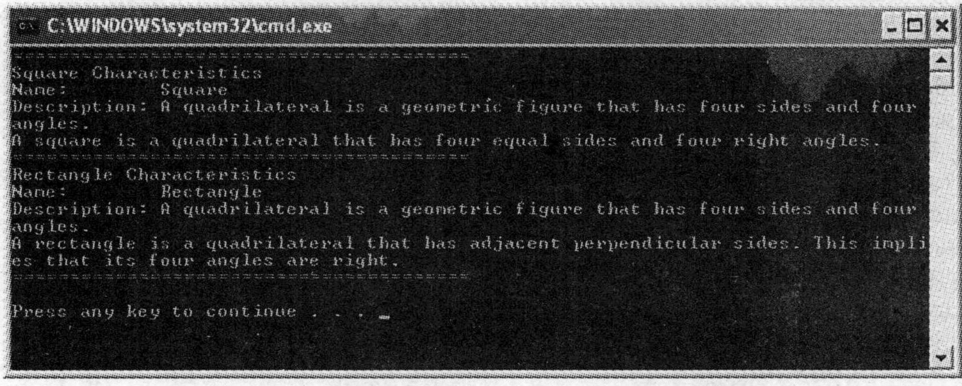

Fig. 13.15 Use of abstract method in polymorphism.

13.7.8 Sealed Classes

Any of the classes we have used so far in our lessons can be inherited from. If you create a certain class and don't want anybody to derive another class from it, you can mark it as sealed. In other words, a sealed class is one that cannot serve as base for another class.

To mark a class as sealed, type the **sealed** keyword to the left of the **class** keyword. For example;

```
public sealed class Ball
{
    public int TypeOfSport;
    public string Dimensions;
}
```

Exercise

1. Explain inheritance with a suitable example?
2. What are visibility modifier in C#?
3. What is new keyword in C#?
4. How many different class modifiers are there in C#?
5. What are the types of inheritance in C#?
6. What is multilevel inheritance?
7. What do you mean by hierarchical inheritance?
8. What is polymorphism?
9. How polymorphism is useful?
10. Does C# support multiple-inheritance?
11. Can you prevent your class from being inherited and becoming a base?
12. Can you allow class to be inherited, but prevent the method from being over-ridden?
13. Can you override private virtual methods?
14. What is virtual method?
15. When you inherit a protected class-level variable, who is it available to?
16. Are private class-level variables inherited?
17. What do you mean by reusability of code in C#?
18. How will you implement single inheritance in C#?
19. What do mean by sealed class?
20. How can you prevent a class to be inherited?
21. What are abstract classes?
22. List out the properties of an abstract class?
23. What is method overriding?
24. How method overriding is different from method overloading?
25. What is an abstraction?
26. What is virtual keyword?
27. Describe the relationship between a parent class and a child class.
28. How does inheritance support software reuse?
29. Why would a child class override one or more of the methods of its parent class?
30. What is the defining characteristic of a class hierarcy?
31. How constructor and destructor work in inheritance?
32. Consider the following declarations and answer the questions given below :

```
class living_being
{
    char name[20];
    protected int jaws;
    public void inputdata(char, int){ }
    void outputdata( ) { }
};
class animal : living_being
{
    int tail;
```

```
    protected int legs;
    public void readdata(int, int) {}
    public void writedata( ) {}
};
class cow : animal
{
    int horn_size;
    public void fetchdata(int) {}
    public void displaydata( ) {}
};
```

(a) Name the base class and derived class of the class animal.
(b) Name the data member(s) that can be accessed from function displaydata().
(c) Name the member function(s), which can be accessed by an object of cow class.
(d) Is the member function outputdata() accessible to the objects of animal class ?

33. Consider the following and answer the questions given below :

```
class School
{
    int A;
    protected int B,C;
    public void INPUT(int) {}
    public void OUTPUT( ) {}
};
class Dept : School
{
    int X, Y;
    protected void IN (int,int) {}
    public void OUT( ) {}
};
class Teacher : Dept
{
    int P;
    void DISPLAY (void) {}
    public void ENTER( ) {}
};
```

(a) Name the base class and derived class of the class Dept.
(b) Name the data member(s) that can be accessed from function OUT( ).
(c) Name the private member function(s) of class Teacher.
(d) Is the member function OUT( ) accessible by the objects of Dept. ?

34. Consider the following and answer the questions given below :

```
class A
{
    void anyval( );
    protected int x, y;
    public void getvalA( ) {};
    public void putvalA( ) {};
```

```
};
class B : A
{
    int a, b;
    protected int c, d;
    void getvalB{};
    public void putvalB( ) {}
};
class C public B
{
    int P;
    protected int q;
    void getval( ) {}
    public void showval( ) {}
};
```

(a) Name all the member functions, which are accessible by the objects of class C.
(b) Name all the protected members of class B.
(c) Name the base class and derived class of class B.
(d) Name the data members, which are accessible from member functions of class C.

35. Given the following class definitions answer the questions that follows :

```
class Book
{
    char Title[20];
    char Author[20];
    int No_of_pages;
    public void read() {};
    public void show() {};
};
class Textbook : Book
{
    int no_of_chapters, no_of_assignments;
    protected int standard;
    public void readtextbook() {};
    public void showtextbook() {};
};
class Physicsbook : Textbook
{
    char Topic[20];
    public void readphysicsbook() {};
    public void showphysicsbook() {};
};
```

(a) Name the members, which can be accessed from the member functions of class Physicsbook.
(b) Name the members, which can be accessed by an object of class Textbook.
(c) Name the members, which can be accessed by an object of class Physicsbook.
(d) What will be the size of an object (in bytes) of class Physicsbook ?

36. Consider the following and answer the questions given below :

```
class PUBLISHER
{
    char Pub[12];
    double Turnover;
    protected void Register() {}
    public PUBLISHER() {}
    public void Enter() {}
    public void Display() {}
};
class BRANCH
{
    char CITY[20];
    protected float Employees;
    public BRANCH() {}
    public void Haveit() {}
    public void Giveit() {}
};
class AUTHOR : BRANCH, PUBLISHER
{
    int Acode;
    char aname[20] ;
    float Amount;
    public AUTHOR() {}
    public Void Start() {}
    public Void Show() {}
};
```

(a) Write the names of data members, which are accessible from object belongs to class AUTHOR.
(b) Write the names of all the member functions which are accessible from objects belonging to class BRANCH.
(c) Write the names of all the members which are accessible from member functions of class AUTHOR.
(d) How many bytes will be required by an object belonging to class AUTHOR ?

37. Consider the following and answer the questions given below :

```
class Medicines
{
    char Category[10];
    char Date_of_manufacture[10];
    char Company[20];
    public Medicines() {}
    public void entermedicinedetails() {}
    public void showmedicinedetails() {}
};
class Capsules : Medicines
{
    protected char capsule_name[30];
```

```
    char Volume_label[20];
    public float Price;
    public Capsules() {}
    public entercapsuledetails() {};
    public void showcapsuledetails() {}
};
class Antibiotics : Capsule
{
    int Dosage_units;
    char Side_effects[20];
    int Use_within_days;
    public Antibiotics() {};
    public void enterdetails() {}
    public void showdetails() {}
};
```

(a) How many bytes will be required by an object of class Medicines and an object of class Antibiotics respectively ?
(b) Write names of all the member functions accessible from the object of class Antibiotics.
(c) Write names of all the members accessible from member functions of class Capsules.
(d) Write names of all the data members which are accessible from objects of class Antibiotics.

Interfaces and Properties 14

14.1 Introduction

In the last two chapters, we studied number of different mechanism on class and class methods. Imagine you start creating a class and, while implementing or testing it, you find out that this particular class can be used instead as a general base that other classes can be derived from. An interface is a special class whose purpose is to serve as a template that actual classes can be based on.

14.2 Defining an Interface

An *interface* looks like a class, but has no implementation. The only thing it contains are definitions of **events**, **indexers**, **methods** and/or **properties**. The reason *interfaces* only provide definitions is because they are inherited by *classes* and *structs*, which must provide an implementation for each interface member defined.

An interface is primarily created like a class: it has a name, a body and can have members.

To create an interface, instead of the **class** keyword, you use the **interface** keyword. By convention, the name of an interface starts with **I**. For example;

```
interface InterfaceName
{
    member declarations;
}
```

Here,

- **InterfaceName** is an user-define name
- **member declarations** contains the name of the members of the interface.

The syntax of the **interface** declaration is identical to that of a class except that the keyword interface replaces **class**. This should not be surprising, because in interface is basically a class that declared, but does not implement, its members. An instance of it cannot be created, and classes that inherit from it must implement all of its method.

This sounds similar to an abstract class, which also cannot be instantiated and requires derived classes to implement its abstract methods. The difference is that an abstract class has many more capabilities. It may be inherited by subclasses, and it may contain state data and concrete method.

Aside from their differing roles, there are numerous implementation and usage difference between a class and an interface:

- An interface cannot inherit from a class.
- An interface can inherit from multiple interfaces.
- A class can inherit from multiple interfaces, but only one class.
- Interface members must be methods, properties, events or indexers.
- All interface members must have public access (the default).
- By convention, in interface name should begin with an uppercase I.

14.3 Creating an Interface

Let us consider the following example for an interface:

```
public interface IShapeFunction
{
    double GetArea();        // public abstract method
}
```

14.3.1 An Interface as a Base Class

After creating an interface, you can derive other interfaces or other classes from it. An **interface** is used to lay a foundation for other classes. For this reason, it is the prime candidate for class derivation. To derive from an interface, use the same technique we have applied in inheritance so far. Here is an example of a class named **Circle** that derives from an interface named **IShapeFunction**:

```
class Circle : IShapeFunction // Inherit Interface as a base class
{
    private double radius;
    public Circle(double rad)
    {
        radius = rad;
    }

    public double GetArea()
    {
        return (Math.PI*radius * radius);
    }
    public string ShowMe()
```

```
        {
            return ("Circle");
        }
    }

    class Rectangle : IShapeFunction // Inherit interfaces
    {
        private double width, height;

        public Rectangle(double myWidth, double myHeight)
        {
            width = myWidth;
            height = myHeight;
        }

        public double GetArea()
        {
            return (width * height);
        }
    }
```

From the above two inherited classes **Circle** and **Rectangle**, it inherits the interface **IShapeFunction** and implement its GetArea method.

Conceptually, it is useful to think of a class that implements one or more interfaces as having multiple types. It has its own innate type, but is also can be viewed as having the type of each interface it implements.

14.3.2 Creating Interface Object

Let us consider the following code :

```
Circle myCircle = new Circle(4);
IShapeFunction myICircle = myCircle;
```

So, the complete code is :

..\CSharp_Book\Chap14\InterDemo

```
class Program
{
    static void Main()
    {
        Circle myCircle = new Circle(4);
        // Interface variable that reference to circle object.
        IShapeFunction myICircle = myCircle;
```

```
            Rectangle myRectangle = new Rectangle(4, 8);

            // Place shape instances in an array
            IShapeFunction[] myShapes = {myCircle, myRectangle};

            // The next two statements print the same results
            Console.WriteLine(myCircle.GetArea().ToString());
            Console.WriteLine(myShapes[0].GetArea().ToString());
            Console.WriteLine(myCircle.ShowMe()); //Class method
            Console.WriteLine(myCircle.GetArea().ToString());

            // The following will not compile because myICircle can access
            // only numbers of the IShapeFunction interface.
            Console.WriteLine(myCircle.ShowMe());
        }
    }
```

When the above program executed, it will produce the following output as shown in Fig. 14.1.

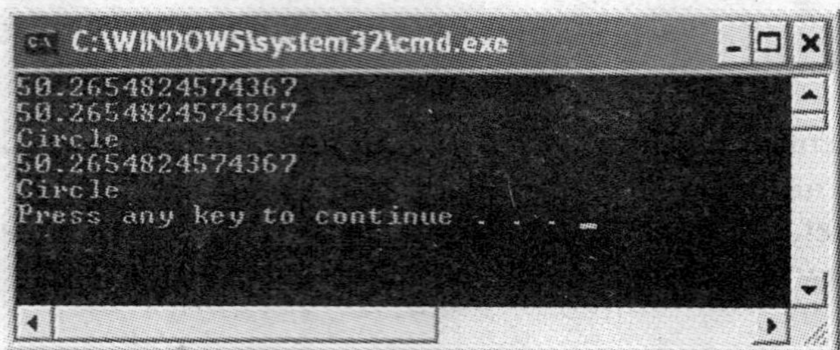

Fig. 14.1 Simple interface using circle example.

Here, the first statement creates an instance of the **Circle** class. The second statement creates a variable that refers to this circle object. However, because it is specified as an **IShapeFunction** type, it can only access members of that interface. This is why an attempt to reference the **ShowMe** method fails. By using the interface type, you effectively create a filter that restricts access to members of the interface only.

One of the most valuable aspects of working with interfaces is that a programmer can treat disparate classes in a similar manner as long as they implement the same interface.

```
IShapeFunction[] myShapes = {myCircle, myRectangle};
Console.WriteLine(myShapes[0].GetArea().ToString()));
```

This code creates an array that can contain any class that implements the **IShapeFunction** interface. Its only interest is in using the **GetArea** method, and it nei3ther has nor requires any knowledge of other class members. We can easily extend this example to create a class to work with this array that has no knowledge of a **Circle** or **Rectangle** class.

So, to access the shapes, implement another class as :

..\CSharp_Book\Chap14\ShapeDm

```
public class ShapeUtil
{
    public static double SumAreas(IShapeFunction[] funArray)
    {
        double tot = 0.0;
        for (int i = 0; i < funArray.Length; i++)
        {
            tot += funArray[i].GetArea();
        }
        return tot;
    }
}
```

So, to access the method, implement the class as :

```
shapeUtil.SumArea(myShapes);
```

This code in this class can be used with any concrete class that implements the **IShapeFunction** interface.

In previous program, we create an instance of each class using the **new** operator. Then, we declare in object of type **IShapeFunction** interface. Now, we cast the **Circle** object.

14.4 Working with Interfaces

You may not always know at compile time whether a class implements a specific interface. This is often the case when working with a collection that contains a number of types. To perform this check at runtime, use the as or is keyword in your code. That is,

```
// (1) as keyword to determine if interface is implemented
Circle myCircle = new Circle(5,0);
IShapeFunction myICircle
myICircle = myCircle as IShapeFunction;
if (myICircle != (null) // interface is implemented
```

If the object can be treated as the specified interface, you are returned a reference to the interface in question. If not, you receive a null reference.

Notice that when you make use of the as keyword, you have no need to make use of try/catch logic, given that if the reference is not null, you know you are calling on a valid interference reference.

But on the case of is, if the object in question is not compatible with the spcified interface, you are returned the value false. On the other hand, if the type is compatible with the interface in ques3tion, you can safely call the memebrs of without needing to make use of try/catch logic.

```
// (2) is keyword to determine if interface is implemented
Circle myCircle = new Circle(5,0);
if (myICircle is IShapeFunction) // True if interface implemented
```

14.5 Implementation of Interfaces

As we know that the interfaces are used as the superclasses whose properties are inherited by classes. So, it is necessary to create a class which inherits the properties of an interface. That is, consider our previous interface,

```
public interface IShapeFunction
{
    double GetArea(); // public abstract method
}

class Circle : IShapeFunction // Inherit Interface as a base class
{
    private double radius;
    public Circle(double rad)
    . . .
    . . .
}
```

Here, the class **Circle** implements the interface **IShapeFunction**. Also, we can inherit more than one interfaces in same class. That is,

```
class ClassName : SuperClass, Interface1, Interface2, ...
{
    . . .
    . . .
}
```

For example,

```
class Circle : Area, IshapeFunction, Draw3D
{
    . . .
    . . .
}
```

Here, Area is a base class and **IshapeFunction**, **Draw3D** are two interfaces. Let us consider the following example,

..\CSharp_Book\Chap14\MultInter

```
using System;
using System.Collections.Generic;
```

```
using System.Text;

namespace MultInter
{
    interface Area
    {
        int square();
    }

    interface Perimeter
    {
        float Perim();
    }

    class Shape : Area, Perimeter
    {
        int l, b;

        public Shape(int l, int b)
        {
            this.l = l;
            this.b = b;
            Console.WriteLine("Length is : " + l);
            Console.WriteLine("Breadth is : " + b);
        }

        public int square() // Implement square(), method of interface
        {
            return (l * b);
        }

        public float Perim() // Implement square(), method of interface
        {
            return (2 * (l + b));
        }
    }

    class Program
    {
        static void Main(string[] args)
        {
            Shape Sh = new Shape(5, 6);
            Area Ar = (Area)Sh; //Casting
            Console.WriteLine();
            Console.WriteLine("Area of rectangle = " + Ar.square());
```

```
            Perimeter Pr = (Perimeter)Sh;
            Console.WriteLine("Perimeter of rectangle = " + Pr.Perim());
        }
    }
}
```

When the above program executed, it will produce the following output as shown in Fig. 14.2.

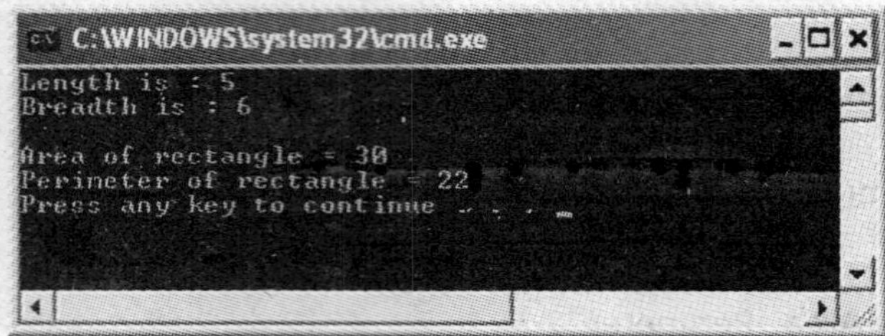

Fig. 14.2 Working with multiple interface.

Here, notice that we cannot use an interface directly. That is, we cannot write,

```
Area Ar = Area();
```

We should always create an instance of the implementing class and the cast the object to the interface type. That is,

```
Area Ar = (Area)Sh; //Casting
```

Also, the C# language doesn't allow multiple inheritance which is the ability to create a class based on more than one class. Multiple inheritance is allowed only if the bases are interfaces. To create multiple inheritance, separate the names of interface with a comma. For example;

```
class Shape : Area, Perimeter
{
    int l, b;
    . . .
    . . .
}
```

14.6 Interface Properties

Like methods, properties are specified in an interface without any body. The properties is declared inside interface as :

```
Property_type property_name {
    get;
    set;
}
```

For example,

```
public interface Area
{
    int square
    {
        get;
        set;
    }
}
```

The get or set will be present for read-only and write-only properties, respectively. To implement the interface properties, let us consider the following example,

..\CSharp_Book\Chap14\IntProper

```
using System;
using System.Collections.Generic;
using System.Text;

namespace IntProper
{
    public interface Area
    {
        int square
        {
            get;
            set;
        }
    }

    class Shape : Area
    {
        int l, b;

        public Shape()
        {
            l = 0;
            b = 0;
        }

        public int square
        {
            get
            {
```

```
                l = 5;
                b = 6;
                return (l * b);
            }

            set
            {
                l = value;
                b = value;
            }
        }
    }

    class Program
    {
        static void Main(string[] args)
        {
            Shape Sh = new Shape();
            Console.WriteLine();
            Console.WriteLine("Area of rectangle = " + Sh.square);
        }
    }
}
```

When the above program executed, it will produce the following output :

```
Area of rectangle = 30
Press any key to continue . . .
```

14.7 Interface Indexers

An interface can also specifies as an indexer. It can be declare as on one-dimensional array. The general form is :

```
Property_type this[int index] {
    get;
    set;
}
```

Here is an example to display the new area of rectangle as :

..\CSharp_Book\Chap14\InterIndex

```
using System;
using System.Collections.Generic;
using System.Text;
```

```
namespace IntIndex
{
    public interface Area
    {
        // Interface property
        int square
        {
            get;
            set;
        }

        // Interface property
        int this[int index]
        {
            get;
        }
    }

    class Shape : Area
    {
        int l, b;

        public Shape()
        {
            l = 0;
            b = 0;
        }

        public int square
        {
            get
            {
                l = 5;
                b = 6;
                return (l * b);
            }

            set
            {
                l = value;
                b = value;
            }
        }
```

```
        // get a return value using an index
        public int this[int index]
        {
            get
            {
                l = 10;
                b = 15;
                return (l * b);
            }
        }
    }

    class Program
    {
        static void Main(string[] args)
        {
            Shape Sh = new Shape();
            Console.WriteLine();
            Console.WriteLine("Area of rectangle = " + Sh.square);

            Sh.square = 0;
            Console.WriteLine("New area of rectangle = " + Sh[0]);
        }
    }
}
```

When the above program executed, it will produce the following output :

```
Area of rectangle = 30
New area of rectangle = 150
Press any key to continue . . .
```

14.8 Inheriting Interface

As like inheriting a class, an interface can inherit another interface. Just as a class can serve as a base class to other classes (which can in turn function as base class to yet another class), it is possible to build inheritance relationships among interfaces. As you might expect, the topmost interface defines a general behavior, while the most derived interface defines more specific behaviors. Inheriting interface concepts applies same syntax notation as for inheriting classes. For example,

..\CSharp_Book\Chap14\InterInhr

```
using System;
using System.Collections.Generic;
using System.Text;
```

```
// Inheriting interface
namespace InterInhr
{
    public interface First
    {
        void first_interface();
    }

    // Second now includes First_interface()
    public interface Second : First
    {
        void second_interface();
    }

    // Class utilizes both First and Second interface methods
    class InterClass : Second
    {
        public void first_interface()
        {
            Console.WriteLine("Implementing first_interface() method.");
        }

        public void second_interface()
        {
            Console.WriteLine("Implementing second_interface() method.");
        }
    }

    class Program
    {
        static void Main(string[] args)
        {
            InterClass IC = new InterClass();
            IC.first_interface();
            IC.second_interface();
        }
    }
}
```

When the above program executed, it will produce the following output

```
Implementing first_interface() method.
Implementing second_interface() method.
Press any key to continue . . .
```

14.9 Explicit Interface Implementation

As we know that C# does not support multiple inheritance, when implementing a member of an interface, it is possible to fully qualify its name with interface name. Let is consider the following example,

```
public interface First
{
    void print_message();
}

public interface Second
{
    void print_message();
}
```

Notice that the two interfaces **First** and **Second** contains a method called **print_message()**. When we call the the method using,

```
First.print_message();
Or
Second.print_message();
```

It produce an ambuguous compiler error for the **print_message()**. Because there is collision happens between the name **print_message()** interface method.

So, to avoid the confusion, use an explicit interface implemention with **print_message()** interface method. For example,

..\CSharp_Book\Chap14\ExplInter

```
using System;
using System.Collections.Generic;
using System.Text;

// Explicit interface implementation
namespace ExplInter
{
    public interface First
    {
        void print_message();
    }

    public interface Second
    {
        void print_message();
    }
```

```
    class ExplicitClass : First, Second
    {
        void First.print_message()
        {
            Console.WriteLine("Implementing First.print_message() method.");
        }

        void Second.print_message()
        {
            Console.WriteLine("Implementing Second.print_message() method.");
        }
    }

    class Program
    {
        static void Main(string[] args)
        {
            ExplicitClass IC = new ExplicitClass();
            First F1 = (First)IC;
            F1.print_message();

            Second S1 = (Second)IC;
            S1.print_message();
        }
    }
}
```

When the above program executed, it will produce the following output

```
Implementing First.print_message() method.
Implementing Second.print_message() method.
Press any key to continue . . .
```

Exercise

1. What are interfaces ?
2. What are the features of interfaces ?
3. Give the syntax of interface declaration ?
4. What is the difference between interface and classes ?
5. Write a simple program to implement an interface ?
6. How properties are declared inside the interface ?
7. What are interface indexers in C# ?
8. How will you inherit an interface ?
9. Can an interface have properties ?

10. What is the difference between abstract class and interface ?
11. What are read-write, read-only, or write-only property ?
12. What is the purpose of accessor in interface property ?
13. Why can't you specify the accessibility modifier for methods inside the interface ?
14. Can you inherit multiple interfaces ?
15. What will happen if interfaces have conflicting method names ?
16. What is the default accessibility for members of an interface ?
17. Can the members of an interface be private ?
18. What is explicit interface implementation ?

Delegates and Events 15

15.1 Introduction

During previous chapter, you learned how to implement reference types using language constructs such as classes and interfaces. These reference types allowed you to create instances of objects and use them in special ways to accomplish your software development goals. Classes allow you to create objects that contained members with attributes or behavior. Interfaces allowed you to declare a set of attributes and behavior that all objects implementing them would publicly expose.

15.2 Delegates

A **delegate** is a C# language element that allows you to reference a method. That is it can work for another. If you were a C or C++ programmer, this would sound familiar because a *delegate* is basically a function pointer. This was even more useful when programming for the Microsoft Windows operating systems because the Win32 library relies on the concept of callback functions. Callback functions are used in Microsoft Windows programming to process messages. For this reason and because of their functionality, callback functions were carried out in the .NET Framework but they were defined with the name of delegate.

A delegate is a special type of user-defined variable that is declared globally, like a class. In fact, a delegate is created like an interface but as a method. Based on this, a delegate provides a template for a method, like an interface provides a template for a class. Like an interface, a delegate is not defined. Its role is to show what a useful method would look like. To support this concept, a delegate can provide all the necessary information that would be used on a method. This includes a return type, no argument or one or more arguments.

15.3 Delegate Declaration

To declare a delegate, the basic formula is:

[attributes] [modifiers] delegate result-type identifier ([formal-parameters]);

Here,

- The *attributes* factor can be a normal C# attribute.
- The modifier can be one or an appropriate combination of the following keywords: **new**, **public**, **private**, **protected**, or **internal**.
- The **delegate** keyword is required.
- The **ReturnType** can be any of the data types we have used so far. It can also be a type **void** or the name of a class.
- **Identifier** is *t*he *Name* must be a valid name for a method.

Because a delegate is some type of a template for a method, you must use parentheses, required for every method. If this method will not take any argument, you can leave the parentheses empty. For example,

```
delegate void StartDelegate();
delegate int MathCalc(int x, int y);
public delegate float calcInterest(float p, int t, float r);
```

As we declare three different delegate examples, it tells that, it uses the **System.Delegate** as the base class. All delegates are classes that are implicitly derived from **System.Delegate**. You do not normally need to use its members directly. After declaring a delegate, remember it only provides a template for a method, not an actual method. In order to use it, you must define a method that would carry an assignment the method is supposed to perform. That method must have the same return type and the same (number of) argument(s), if any.

15.4 Using Delegates

Since it is class type declaration, it can be declared at any place where a class definition is permitted. It can be declared at :

- inside a class
- outside the class
- at the top level object in a namespace.

For example, the above declared delegate is of type **void** and it does not take any argument. You can define a method as follows:

```
using System;

// Delegate outside the class
delegate void SimpleDelegate();
```

```
class DelegateExample
{
    private static void Hello()
    {
        Console.WriteLine("Welcome to C# .NET Programming!");
    }

    static int Main()
    {
        return 0;
    }
}
```

15.4.1 Invoking Delegate

When the delegate is declared, the C# compiler creates a sealed class having the name of the delegate identifier. That is, consider a delegate as :

```
delegate void SimpleDelegate();
```

The class defines a constructor that accepts the name of a method-static or instance-as one of its parameter. It contains method that enable the delegate to maintain a list of target methods. This means that-unlike the callback approach-a single delegate can call multiple event handling methods.

With such a method implemented, you can associate it to the name of the delegate. To do that, where you want to use the method, first declare a variable of the type of the delegate using the new operator. In the parentheses of the constructor, pass the name of the method. Here is an example

..\CSharp_Book\Chap15\DelegateDemo

```
using System;

// Delegate outside the class
delegate void SimpleDelegate();

class DelegateExample
{

    private static void Hello()
    {
        Console.WriteLine("Welcome to C# .NET Programming!");
    }

    static int Main()
    {
        SimpleDelegate Sample = new SimpleDelegate(Hello);
```

```
        Sample();
        return 0;
    }
}
```

When the above program executed, it will produce the following output :

```
Welcome to C# .NET Programming!
Press any key to continue . . .
```

15.4.2 Delegate Returning Value

You can also declare a delegate that returns a value. When defining a method that would be associated with the delegate, remember that that method must return the same type of value. For example;

..\CSharp_Book\Chap15\DelegateRet

```
using System;

delegate void SimpleDelegate();
delegate double Addition();

class DelegateExample
{
    private static void Hello()
    {
        Console.WriteLine("Welcome to C# .NET Programming!");
    }

    private static double Add_Two()
    {
        double a = 440.36, b = 65.87;

        return a + b;
    }

    static int Main()
    {
        SimpleDelegate Sample = new SimpleDelegate(Hello);
        Addition Add = new Addition(Add_Two);

        Sample();
        Console.WriteLine("\n440.36 + 65.87 = {0}", Add());
        return 0;
    }
}
```

When the above program executed, it will produce the following output :

```
Welcome to C# .NET Programming!
440.36 + 65.87 = 5.6.23
Press any key to continue . . .
```

Example. Write a program to do mathematical operations on two integer numbers.

..\CSharp_Book\Chap15\MathDelegate

```
using System;
using System.Collections.Generic;
using System.Text;

namespace MathDelegate
{
    // This delegate can point to any method by taking
    // two integers and returnsing an integer
    public delegate int MathOperation(int x, int y);

    // This class contains methods MathOperation will point to.
    public class SimpleMath
    {

        // Addition
        public static int add(int x, int y)
        {
            return (x + y);
        }

        // Subtraction
        public static int Subtract(int x, int y)
        {
            if (x > y)
                return (x - y);
            else
                return (y - x);
        }

        // Multiplication
        public static int Mult(int x, int y)
        {
            return (x * y);
        }
```

```
        // Division
        public static int Division(int x, int y)
        {
            if (x > y)
                return (int)(x / y);
            else
                return (int)(y / x);
        }
    }

    class Program
    {
        static void Main()
        {
            // Create a MathOperation object that points to class methods.
            MathOperation mo = new MathOperation(SimpleMath.add);
            Console.WriteLine("20 + 30 is : {0}", mo(20, 30));

            MathOperation sb = new MathOperation(SimpleMath.Subtract);
            Console.WriteLine("Difference between 20 and 30 is : {0}", sb(20, 30));

            MathOperation mlt = new MathOperation(SimpleMath.Mult);
            Console.WriteLine("20 x 30 is : {0}", mlt(20, 30));

            MathOperation dv = new MathOperation(SimpleMath.Division);
            Console.WriteLine("30 / 20 is : {0:F2}", dv(20, 30));
        }
    }
}
```

When the above program executed, it will produce the following output as shown in Fig. 15.1.

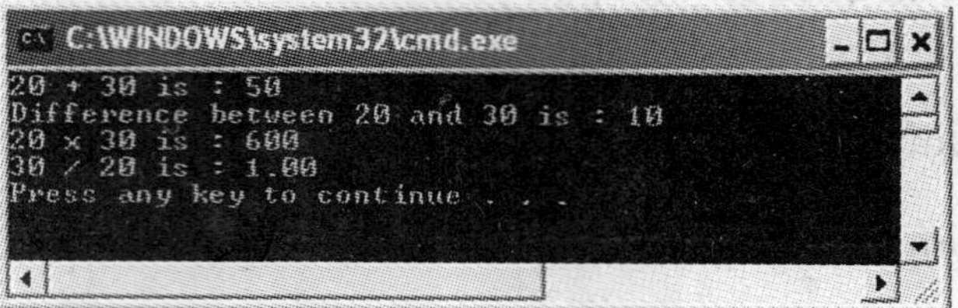

Fig. 15.1 Mathematical operations using delegate.

15.5 Delegates and Classes

In the above sections, we associated delegates with only method of the main class. Because delegates are usually declared globally, that is outside of a class, they can be associated with a method of any class, provided the method has the same return type (and the same (number of) argument(s)) as the delegate. When we created the methods of the main class, we defined them as static, since all methods of the main class must be declared static.

Methods of any class can also be associated to delegates. Here is an example of two methods associated with a common delegate:

..\CSharp_Book\Chap15\DelegateMethod

```
using System;
using System.Collections.Generic;
using System.Text;

namespace DelegateMethod
{
    delegate double Multiplication();

    public class Cube
    {
        private double _side;

        public double Side
        {
            get { return _side; }
            set { _side = value; }
        }
        public Cube()
        {
            _side = 0;
        }

        // Side of the cube
        public Cube(double s)
        {
            _side = s;
        }

        // Calculating are of the cube
        public double Area()
        {
            return 6 * Side * Side;
        }

        // Calculating volume of the cube
        public double Volume()
        {
```

```
            return Side * Side * Side;
        }
        public void CubeDetails()
        {
            Multiplication AreaDefinition = new Multiplication(Area);
            Multiplication VolDefinition = new Multiplication(Volume);

            Console.WriteLine("Cube  Details....");
            Console.WriteLine("Side of the cube :   {0}", Side);
            Console.WriteLine("Area of the cube :   {0}", AreaDefinition());
            Console.WriteLine("Volume of the cube : {0}\n", VolDefinition());
        }
    }

    class Program
    {
        static void Main()
        {
            Cube CubeBox = new Cube(5.5);
            CubeBox.CubeDetails();
        }
    }
}
```

When the above program executed, it will produce the following output as shown in Fig. 15.2.

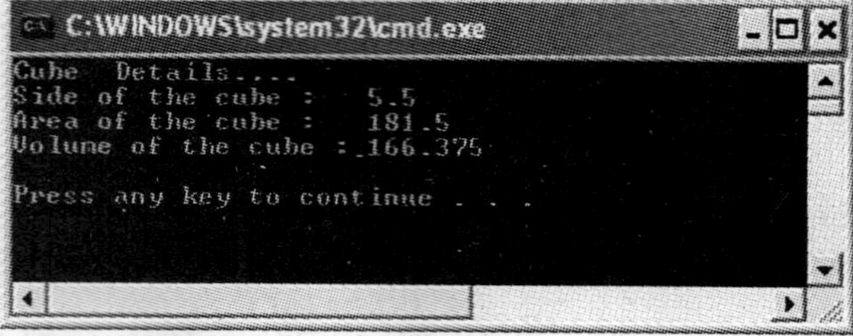

Fig. 15.2 Working with delegate method.

One of the characteristics that set delegates apart from C/C++ function pointers is that one delegate can be added to another using the + operation. This is referred to as composition. This is done by adding one delegate variable to another as in **a = b + c**.

15.6 Delegates and Arguments

If you want to associate a method that takes arguments to a delegate, when declaring the delegate, provide the necessary argument(s) in its parentheses. Here is an example of a delegate that takes two arguments (and returns a value):

```
delegate double Addition(double x, double y);
```

When defining the associated method, besides returning the same type of value if not void, make sure that the method takes the same number of arguments. For example;

```
using System;

delegate void SimpleDelegate();
delegate double Addition(double x, double y);

class DelegateExample
{
    private static void Hello()
    {
        Console.WriteLine("Welcome to C# .NET Programming!");
    }

    private static double Add_Two(double a, double b)
    {
        return a + b;
    }

    static int Main()
    {
        SimpleDelegate Sample = new SimpleDelegate(Hello);

        Sample();
        return 0;
    }
}
```

Once again, to associate the method, declare a variable of the type of delegate and pass the name of the method to the constructor of the delegate. For example;

```
Addition Add = new Addition(Add_Two);
```

Notice that only the name of the method is passed to the delegate. To actually use the delegate, when calling it, in its parentheses, provide a value for the argument(s) conform to the type specified when declaring the delegate. For example,

..\CSharp_Book\Chap15\DelegateArg

```
using System;

delegate void SimpleDelegate();
delegate double Addition(double x, double y);
```

```
class DelegateExample
{
    private static void Hello()
    {
        Console.WriteLine("Welcome to C# .NET Programming!");
    }

    private static double Add_Two(double a, double b)
    {
        return a + b;
    }

    static int Main()
    {
        double Value1 = 440.36, Value2 = 65.87;
        double Result;
        SimpleDelegate Sample = new SimpleDelegate(Hello);
        Addition Add = new Addition(Add_Two);

        Result = Add(Value1, Value2);

        Sample();
        Console.WriteLine("Addition value of {0} and {1} is : {2}",
                Value1, Value2, Result);
        return 0;
    }
}
```

When the above program executed, it will produce the following output as shown in Fig. 15.3.

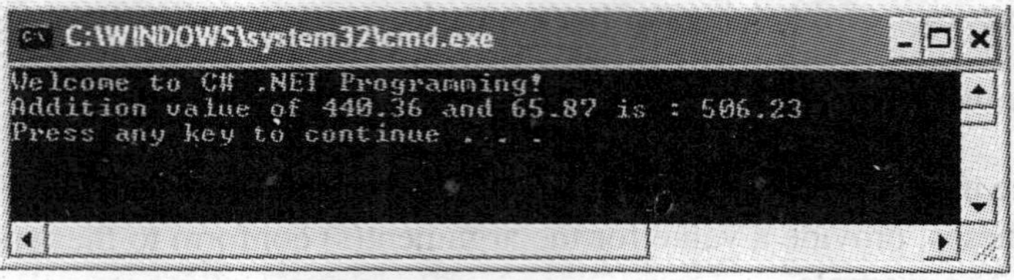

Fig. 15.3 Working with delegate argument.

15.6.1 Delegate as Argument

Using delegates, one method can be indirectly passed as argument to another method. Such an argument would be used as if it were a method itself. This means that, when accessed in the body of the method, the name of the delegate must be accompanied by parentheses and if the delegate takes an argument or argument, the argument(s) must be provided in the parentheses of the called delegate.

For example;

```
public delegate double Squared(double x);
public class Circle
{

    private double _radius;

    public double Radius
    {
        get { return _radius; }
        set{ _radius = value; }
    }

    // Delegate argument
    public double Area(Squared sqd)
    {
        return sqd(_radius) * Math.PI;
    }
}
```

After declaring a delegate, remember to define a method that implements the needed behavior of that delegate. For example,

```
public delegate double Squared(double x);
public class Circle
{
    private double _radius;

    public static double ValueTimesValue(double Value)
    {
        return Value * Value;
    }

    public double Radius
    {
        get { return _radius; }
        set{ _radius = value; }
    }

    // Delegate argument
    public double Area(Squared sqd)
    {
        return sqd(_radius) * Math.PI;
    }
}
```

Once the method that implements the delegate is known, you can use the delegate as you see fit. To do that, you can declare a variable of the type of that delegate and pass the implementing method to its constructor. For example;

```
public delegate double Squared(double x);

public class Circle
{
    private double _radius;

    public static double ValueTimesValue(double Value)
    {
        return Value * Value;
    }

    public double Radius
    {
        get { return _radius; }
        set{ _radius = value; }
    }

    // Delegate argument
    public double Area(Squared sqd)
    {
        return sqd(_radius) * Math.PI;
    }

    public void CircleDetails()
    {
        Squared Sq = new Squared(ValueTimesValue);
    }
}
```

So, the complete example is as :

..\CSharp_Book\Chap15\PassDelegate

```
using System;
using System.Collections.Generic;
using System.Text;

namespace PassDelegate
{
    public delegate double Twice(double x);
    public delegate double Squared(double x);

    public class Circle
    {
```

```
private double _radius;

public Circle()
{
    _radius = 0;
}

public Circle(double r)
{
    _radius = r;
}

public static double TwoTimes(double Value)
{
    return Value * 2;
}

public static double ValueTimesValue(double Value)
{
    return Value * Value;
}

public double Radius
{
    get { return _radius; }
    set { _radius = value; }
}

// Diameter of circle
public double Diameter(double rad)
{
    return rad * 2;
}

// Circumference of circle with parameterized delegate
public double Circumference(Twice FDiam)
{
    double Circf;

    Circf = FDiam(_radius);
    return Circf * Math.PI;
}

// Delegate argument
public double Area(Squared sqd)
```

```
            {
                return sqd(_radius) * Math.PI;
            }

            public void CircleDetails()
            {
                Squared Sq = new Squared(ValueTimesValue);
                Twice Tw = new Twice(TwoTimes);

                Console.WriteLine("Circle  Details....");
                Console.WriteLine("Radius of the circle: {0}", Radius);
                Console.WriteLine("Diameter of the circle: {0}", Diameter(_radius));
                Console.WriteLine("Circumference of the circle: {0:F2}", Circumference(Tw));
                Console.WriteLine("Area of the ciecle: {0:F2}\n", Area(Sq));
            }
        }

        class Program
        {
            static void Main()
            {
                Circle RoundShape = new Circle(5.5);
                RoundShape.CircleDetails();
            }
        }
    }
```

When the above program executed, it will produce the following output as shown in Fig. 15.4.

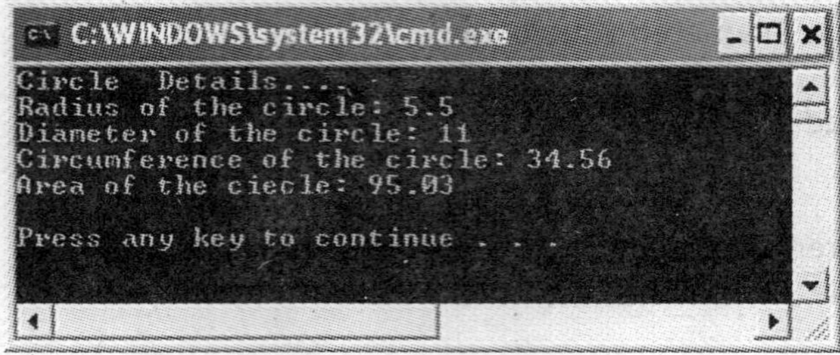

Fig. 15.4 Passing delegate as argument.

15.6.2 Delegates as an Array

Before creating the array, you must first know or have the methods you would be referring to. These methods must have a similar signature. This means that they must return the same type of value, they must have the same number of arguments and they must have the same type(s) of argument(s). Let us look at the following class declaration :

```
class Circle
{
    const double PI = 3.14159;

    static double Diameter(double Radius)
    {
        return Radius * 2;
    }

    static double Circumference(double Radius)
    {
        return Diameter(Radius) * PI;
    }

    static double Area(double Radius)
    {
        return Radius * Radius * PI;
    }
}
```

An array is a normal declaration like C# array. To declare a delegate an array :

```
{
    delegate double Measure(double R);
    . . .
    . . .
    static int Main()
    {
        Measure[] Calc = new Measure[3];

        return 0;
    }
}
```

After creating an array of delegate object we can invoke the methods using C# for loop. For example,

..\CSharp_Book\Chap15\DelegateArray

```
using System;
using System.Collections.Generic;
using System.Text;

namespace DelegateArray
{
    delegate double Measure(double R);
```

```
class Program
{
    const double PI = 3.14159;
    private double _radius;

    static double Diameter(double Radius)
    {
        return Radius * 2;
    }

    static double Circumference(double Radius)
    {
        return Diameter(Radius) * PI;
    }

    static double Area(double Radius)
    {
        return Radius * Radius * PI;
    }

    static void Main()
    {
        double R = 5.5;
        double Result;
        Measure[] Calc = new Measure[3]; // Declaring an array

        Calc[0] = new Measure(Diameter);
        Calc[1] = new Measure(Circumference);
        Calc[2] = new Measure(Area);

        Console.WriteLine("Circle   Details....");
        String[] name = new String[30];
        name[0] = "Diameter of the circle: ";
        name[1] = "Circumference of the circle: ";
        name[2] = "Area of the ciecle: ";

        for (int i = 0; i < 3; i++)
        {
            Console.Write(name[i]);
            Result = Calc[i](R);    // Radius as parameter
            Console.Write("{0:F2}", Result);
            Console.WriteLine();
        }
    }
}
}
```

When the above program executed, it will produce the following output as shown in Fig. 15.5.

```
C:\WINDOWS\system32\cmd.exe
Circle  Details....
Diameter of the circle: 11.00
Circumference of the circle: 34.56
Area of the ciecle: 95.03
Press any key to continue . . .
```

Fig. 15.5 Working delegate as an array.

15.7 Events

Traditional Console applications operate by waiting for a user to press a key or type a command and press the *Enter* key. Then they perform some pre-defined operation and either quit or return to the original prompt that they started from. This works, but is inflexible in that everything is hard-wired and follows a rigid path of execution. In stark contrast, modern GUI programs operate on an event-based model. That is, some event in the system occurs and interested modules are notified so they can react appropriately. With Windows forms, there is not a polling mechanism taking up resources and you don't have to code a loop that sits waiting for input. It is all built into the system with events.

A C# **event** is a class member that is activated whenever the event it was designed for occurs. An event is an action that occurs on an object and affects it in a way that its clients must be made aware of. Events are mostly familiar to those who do graphical (GUI) programming as they are able to "visually" work on Windows controls and as they are able to access the objects on which actions are happening and the objects that must know when these actions occur. Still, because events are dealt with in C#, you should be aware of their functionality.

Events and *delegates* work hand-in-hand to provide a program's functionality. It starts with a class that declares an *event*. Any class, including the same class that the *event* is declared in, may register one of its methods for the *event*. This occurs through a *delegate*, which specifies the signature of the method that is registered for the *event*. The *delegate* may be one of the pre-defined .NET *delegates* or one you declare yourself. Whichever is appropriate, you assign the *delegate* to the *event*, which effectively registers the method that will be called when the *event* fires.

Although events are mostly used in Windows controls programming, they can also be implemented in console applications.

15.7.1 Event Creation

An event is declared like a pseudo-variable but based on a delegate. Therefore, to declare an event, you must have a delegate that would implement it. The syntax for declaring an event is

```
[attributes] [modifiers] event type declarator;
[attributes] [modifiers] event type member-name {accessor-declarations};
```

Here,

- The **attributes** factor can be a normal C# attribute.
- The modifier can be one or a combination of the following keywords: **public**, **private**, **protected**, **internal**, **abstract**, **new**, **override**, **static**, **virtual**, or **extern**.
- The **event** keyword is required. It is followed by the name of the delegate that specifies its behavior. If the event is declared in the main class, it should be made static. Like everything in a program, an event must have a name. This would allow the clients to know what (particular) event occurred.

For example,

```
public event SimpleDelegate EventOK;
public event InterestModify Interest;
```

From above declarations, **SimpleDelegate** and **InterestModify** are the two delegates and **EventOK** and Interest are two events respectively.

For example,

```
delegate void SimpleDelegate();

class EventExample
{
    public static event SimpleDelegate Simply;

    private static void Hello()
    {
        Console.WriteLine("Welcome to C# .NET Programming!");
    }
    ...
    ...
}
```

After declaring the event, you must define a method that calls the event. For example;

```
public static void SayHello()
{
    Simply();
}
```

When the event occurs, its delegate would be invoked. This specification is also referred to as hooking up an event. As the event occurs (or fires), the method that implements the delegate runs. This provides complete functionality for the event and makes the event ready to be used. Before using an event, you must combine it to the method that implements it. This can be done by passing the name of the method to the appropriate delegate, as we learned when studying delegates. You can then assign this variable to the event's name using the += operator. Once this is done, you can call the event. For example;

..\CSharp_Book\Chap15\EventDemo

```
using System;
using System.Collections.Generic;
using System.Text;

namespace EventDemo
{
    delegate void SimpleDelegate();

    class EventExample
    {

        public static event SimpleDelegate Simply;

        private static void Hello()
        {
            Console.WriteLine("Welcome to C# .NET Programming!");
        }

        public static void SayHello()
        {
            Simply();
        }

        static int Main()
        {
            Simply += new SimpleDelegate(Hello);

            SayHello();

            return 0;
        }
    }
}
```

When the above program executed, it will produce the following output :

```
Welcome to C# .NET Programming!
Press any key to continue . . .
```

Exercise

1. What is delegates ?
2. Give an example of using delegates ?
3. Describe the benefits of delegates ?
4. How will you declare and call a delegate ?
5. Describe the features of delegates?
6. What is multicast delegates ?
7. Write some code for multicast delegate
8. What is the difference between delegates and classes ?
9. Give an example of delegate that take two arguments and returns a value ?
10. How delegates and arrays are related ?
11. Is it possible that delegates will return a value ?
12. What is an events ?
13. How will you declare an event ?
14. How delegates and events are related ?
15. Are events synchronous or asynchronous ?

Exception Handling 16

16.1 Introduction

In C# exception is an object created (or thrown) when a particular exceptional error condition occurs. This object contains information that should help track down the problem. During the execution of a program, the computer will face two types of situations: those it is prepared to deal with and those it doesn't like. Imagine you write a program that requests a number from the user:

..\CSharp_Book\Chap16\ExcepDemo

```
using System;
using System.Collections.Generic;
using System.Text;

namespace ExcepDemo
{
    class Program
    {
        static void Main()
        {
            double Number;

            Console.Write("Type any number: ");
            Number = double.Parse(Console.ReadLine());

            Console.WriteLine("\n{0} * 2 = {1}", Number, Number * 2);
        }
    }
}
```

This is a classic easy program. When it comes up, the user is asked to simply type a number. The number would then be multiplied by 2 and display the result.

Imagine that a user types something that is not a valid number, such as some characters. Since this program was expecting a number and it is not prepared to multiply a string to a number, it would not know what to do. The only alternative the compiler would have is to send the problem to the operating system, hoping that the OS would know what to do. What actually happens is that, whenever the compiler is handed a task, it would try to perform the assignment. If it ca not perform the assignment, for any reason it is not prepared for, it would produce an error. As a programmer, if you can anticipate the type(s) of error(s) that could occur in your program, you can deal with it (them) by telling the compiler what to do when this type of error occurs.

Although you can create your own exception class, .NET provides you with many predefined exception classes. The generic exception class, **System.Exception**, is derived from **System.Object**, as you would except for a .NET class. In general, you should not throw generic **System.Exception** objects in your code, because they provide no specifics of error condition. Two important classes in the hierarchy are derived from **System.Exception**:

- **System.SystemExcepiton.** This class is for exceptions that are usually thrown by .NET runtime or that are considered to be of a generic nature and might be thrown by almost any application. For example, **StackOverflowException** will be thrown by the .Net runtime if it detects the stack is full. On the other hand, you might choose to throw **ArgumentException** or its subclasses in your own code. If you detect that a method has been called with inappropriate arguments. Subclassses of **System.SystemException** include classes that represent both fatal and non-fatal errors.
- **System.ApplicationException.** This class is important, because it is the intended base for any class of exception defined by third parties. Hence, if you define any exceptions covering error conditions unique to your application, you should derive these directly or indirectly from **System.ApplicationException**.

Out of these two, other exception classes that might come in handy include the following

- **StackOverflowException.** This exception is thrown when the area of memory allocated to the stack is full. A stack overflow can occur if a method continuously calls itself recursively. This is generally a fatal error, because it prevents your application from doing anything apart from terminating (in which case it is unlikely that event the finally block will execute). Trying to handle errors like this yourself is usually pointless.
- **EndOfStreamException.** The usual cause of an **EndOfStreamException** is an attempt to read past the end of file. A stream represents a flow of data between data sources.

16.2 Exceptional Behaviors

An exception is an unusual situation that could occur in your program. As a programmer, you should anticipate any abnormal behavior that could be caused by the user entering wrong information that could otherwise lead to unpredictable results. The ability to deal with a program's eventual abnormal behavior is called exception handling. C# provides three keywords to handle an exception.

- **Trying the normal flow:** To deal with the expected behavior of a program, use the **try** keyword as in the following syntax:

```
try {Behavior}
```

The **try** keyword is required. It lets the compiler know that you are attempting a normal flow of your program. The actual behavior that needs to be evaluated is included between an opening curly bracket "{" and a closing curly bracket "}". Inside of the brackets, implement the normal flow that the program must follow, at least for this section of the code. For example;

```
using System;
using System.Collections.Generic;
using System.Text;

namespace ExcepDemo
{
    class Program
    {
        static void Main()
        {
            double Number;

            try
            {
                Console.Write("Type any number: ");
                Number = double.Parse(Console.ReadLine());

                Console.WriteLine("\n{0} * 2 = {1}", Number, Number * 2);
            }
        }
    }
}
```

- **Catching Errors:** During the flow of the program as part of the **try** section, if an abnormal behavior occurs, instead of letting the program crash or instead of letting the compiler send the error to the operating system, you can transfer the flow of the program to another section that can deal with it. The syntax used by this section is:

```
catch {WhatToDo}
```

This section always follows the **try** section. There must not be any code between the **try**'s closing bracket and the **catch** section. The **catch** keyword is required and follows the **try** section. Combined with the try block, the syntax of an exception would be:

```
try
{
    // Try the program flow
}

catch
{
    // Catch the exception
}
```

A program that includes a catch section would appear as follows:

```
using System;
using System.Collections.Generic;
using System.Text;

namespace ExcepDemo
{
    class Program
    {
        static void Main()
        {
            double Number;

            try
            {
                Console.Write("Type any number: ");
                Number = double.Parse(Console.ReadLine());

                Console.WriteLine("\n{0} * 2 = {1}", Number, Number * 2);
            }

            catch
            {
            }
        }
    }
}
```

16.3 Exceptions and Custom Messages

As mentioned already, if an error occurs when processing the program in the try section, the compiler transfers the processing to the next catch section. You can then use the catch section to deal with the error. At a minimum, you can display a message to inform the user. For example;

..\CSharp_Book\Chap16\ExcepCatch

```
using System;
using System.Collections.Generic;
using System.Text;

namespace ExcepCatch
{
    class Program
    {
        static void Main()
        {
            double Number;

            try
            {
                Console.Write("Please type any number: ");
                Number = double.Parse(Console.ReadLine());

                Console.WriteLine("\n{0} * 2 = {1}", Number, Number * 2);
            }

            catch
            {
                Console.WriteLine("Hello ! There was a problem with the program.");
            }
        }
    }
}
```

From the above program, if you type any string or character, it will display a message as :

```
Please type any number: s
Hello ! There was a problem with the program.
Press any key to continue . . .
```

16.4 The Exception Class

In traditionally-oriented error dealing languages such as C/C++ or Object Pascal, you could create any exception of your choice, including numeric or strings. To customize exception handling, you could also create your own class(es). Most libraries such as Borland's VCL and Microsoft's MFC also shipped with their own classes to handle exceptions. Event the Win32 library provides its type of mechanism to face errors. To support exception handling, the .NET Framework provides a special class called **Exception**. Once the compiler encounters an error, the **Exception** class allows you to identify the type of error and take an appropriate action.

Normally, **Exception** mostly serves as the general class of exceptions. Anticipating various types of problems that can occur in a program, Microsoft derived various classes from **Exception** to make this issue friendlier. As a result, almost any type of exception you may encounter already has a class created to deal with it. Therefore, when your program faces an exception, you can easily identify the type of error. There are so many exception classes that we cannot study or review them all. The solution we will use is to introduce or review a class when we meet its type of error.

16.4.1 The Exception's Message

In exception handling, errors are dealt with in the **catch** section. To do this, use catch as if it were a method. This means that, on the right side of **catch**, opening a parenthesis, declare a variable of the type of exception you want to deal with. By default, an exception is first of type **Exception**. Based on this, a typical formula to implement exception handling is :

```
try
{
    // Process the normal flow of the program here
}
catch(Exception e)
{
    // Deal with the exception here
}
```

When an exception occurs in the **try** section, code compilation is transferred to the **catch** section. If you declare the exception as an **Exception** type, this class will identify the error. One of the properties of the **Exception** class is called **Message**. This property contains a string that describes the type of error that occurred. You can then use this Exception.Message property to display an error message if you want. For example;

..\CSharp_Book\Chap16\ExcepMessage

```
using System;
using System.Collections.Generic;
using System.Text;

namespace ExcepMessage
{
    class Program
    {
        static void Main()
        {
            double Number;
            try
            {
                Console.Write("Please type any number: ");
```

```
                Number = double.Parse(Console.ReadLine());

                Console.WriteLine("\n{0} * 2 = {1}", Number, Number * 2);
            }

            catch (Exception ex)
            {
                Console.WriteLine(ex.Message);
            }
        }
    }
}
```

When the above program executed, it will produce the following output :

```
Please type any number: s
Input string is not in a correct format.
Press any key to continue . . .
```

16.5 Custom Error Messages

As you can see, one of the strengths of the **Exception.Message** property is that it gives you a good indication of the type of problem that occurred. Sometimes, the message provided by the **Exception** class may not appear explicit enough. In fact, you may not want to show it to the user since, as in this case, the user may not understand what the expression "correct format" in this context means and why it is being used. As an alternative, you can create your own message and display it to the user. For example;

..\CSharp_Book\Chap16\CustomError

```
using System;
using System.Collections.Generic;
using System.Text;

namespace CustomError
{
    class Program
    {
        static void Main()
        {
            double Number;

            try
            {
                Console.Write("Please type any number: ");
```

```
                Number = double.Parse(Console.ReadLine());
                Console.WriteLine("\n{0} * 2 = {1}", Number, Number * 2);
            }
            catch (Exception ex)
            {
                Console.WriteLine("The operation could not be performed because
                    input number is not valid.");
            }
        }
    }
}
```

When the above program executed, it will produce the following output :

```
Please type any number: 100
100 * 2 = 200
Press any key to continue . . .
```

If you execute again and input the an alphanumeric number then it will display the custom error message as :

```
Please type any number: 100e
The operation could not be performed because input number is not valid.
Press any key to continue . . .
```

But in the same previous program, you can also combine the **Exception.Message** message and your own message:

..\CSharp_Book\Chap16\CustomExp

```
using System;
using System.Collections.Generic;
using System.Text;

namespace CustomExp
{
    class Program
    {
        static void Main()
        {
            double Number;

            try
            {
                Console.Write("Pleast type any number: ");
                Number = double.Parse(Console.ReadLine());
```

```
                Console.WriteLine("\n{0} * 2 = {1}", Number, Number * 2);
            }
            catch (Exception ex)
            {
                Console.WriteLine(ex.Message + "\nThe operation could not be performed
                        because input number is not valid.");
            }
        }
    }
}
```

When the above program executed, it will produce the following output :

```
Please type any number: 100
100 * 2 = 200
Press any key to continue . . .
```

If you execute again and input the an alphanumeric number then it will display the custom error message as :

```
Please type any number: 100e
Input string was not in a correct format.
The operation could not be performed because input number is not valid.
Press any key to continue . . .
```

16.6 .NET Exception Classes

The .NET Framework provides various classes to handle almost any type of exception you can think of. There are so many of these classes that we can only mention the few that we regularly use in our application.

There are two main ways you can use one of the classes of the .NET Framework. If you know for sure that a particular exception will be produced, pass its name to the catch() clause. You don't have to name the argument. Then, in the catch() section, display a custom message. The second option you have consists of using the **throw** keyword.

From now on, we will try to always indicate the type of exception that could be thrown if something goes wrong in a program

16.6.1 FormatException

While data formatting in Chapter-5, we saw that everything the user types into an application using the keyboard is primarily a string and that you must convert it to the appropriate type before using it. When you request a specific type of value from the user, after the user has typed it and you decide to convert it to the appropriate type, if your conversion fails, the program produces (in the next lessons, we will use he word "**throw**") an error. The error is of from the **FormatException** class. For example,

..\CSharp_Book\Chap16\FormatExcep

```
using System;
using System.Collections.Generic;
using System.Text;
namespace FormatExcep
{
    class Program
    {
        static void Main()
        {
            double Number;
            try
            {
                Console.Write("Please type any number: ");
                Number = double.Parse(Console.ReadLine());
                Console.WriteLine("\n{0} * 2 = {1}", Number, Number * 2);
            }
            catch(FormatException)
            {
                Console.WriteLine("You typed an invalid number.");
            }
        }
    }
}
```

When the above program executed, it will produce the following output :

```
Please type any number: 100
100 * 2 = 200
Press any key to continue . . .
```

If you execute again and input the an alphanumeric number then it will display the custom error message as :

```
Please type any number: 100e
You typed an invalid number.
Press any key to continue . . .
```

16.6.2 The OverflowException Exception

A computer application receives, processes, and produces values on a regular basis as the program is running. To better manage these values, as we saw when studying variables and data types in Chapter-

3, the compiler uses appropriate amounts of space to store its values. It is not unusual that either you the programmer or a user of your application provides a value that is beyond the allowed range based on the data type. For example, we saw that a byte uses 8 bits to store a value and a combination of 8 bits can store a number no more than 255. If you provide a value higher than 255 to be stored in a byte, you get an error. Consider the following program:

..\CSharp_Book\Chap16\OverFlowExcep

```
using System;
using System.Collections.Generic;
using System.Text;

namespace OverFlowExcep
{
    class Program
    {
        static void Main()
        {
            byte NumberOfPages;

            Console.Write("Enter the number of pages in C# .NET book:");
            NumberOfPages = byte.Parse(Console.ReadLine());

            Console.WriteLine("Number of Pages of the book: {0}\n", NumberOfPages);
        }
    }
}
```

When the above program executed, it will produce the following output as shown in Fig. 16.1.

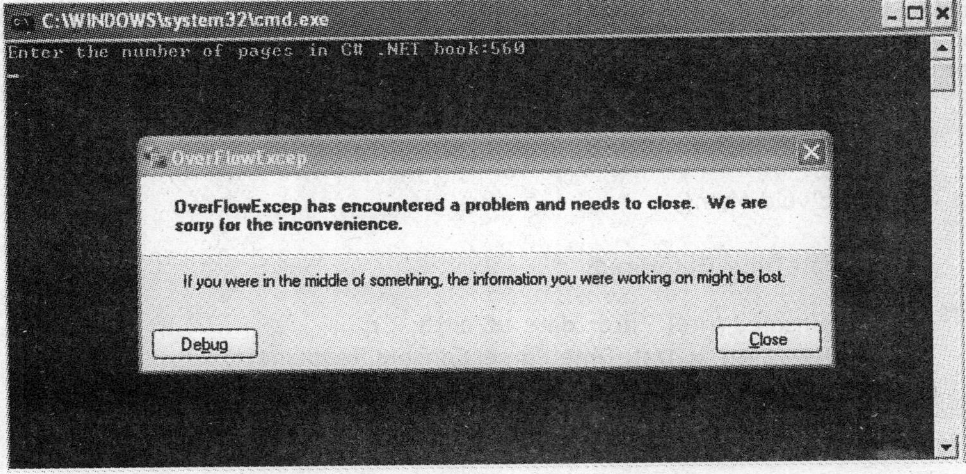

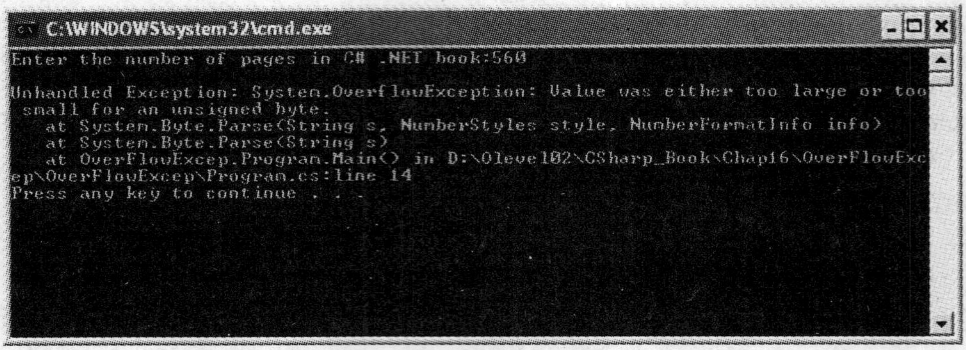

```
C:\WINDOWS\system32\cmd.exe
Enter the number of pages in C# .NET book:560

Unhandled Exception: System.OverflowException: Value was either too large or too
 small for an unsigned byte.
   at System.Byte.Parse(String s, NumberStyles style, NumberFormatInfo info)
   at System.Byte.Parse(String s)
   at OverFlowExcep.Program.Main() in D:\Oleve102\CSharp_Book\Chap16\OverFlowExc
ep\OverFlowExcep\Program.cs:line 14
Press any key to continue . . .
```

Fig. 16.1 Overflow exception error.

16.6.3 ArgumentOutOfRangeException

Once again, when studying the techniques of converting or formatting values in Chapter-5, we saw that a value is passed to the **Parse()** method of its data type for analysis. For a primitive data type, the **Parse()** method scans the string and if the string cannot be converted into a valid character or number, the compiler usually throws a **FormatException** exception as we saw above. Other classes such as **DateTime** also use a **Parse()** method to scan the value submitted to it. For example, if you request a date value from the user, the **DateTime.Parse()** method scans the string to validate it. In US English, **Parse()** expects the user to type a string in the form **m/d/yy** or **mm/dd/yy** or **mm/dd/yyyy**. Consider the following program:

..\CSharp_Book\Chap16\ExcepOut

```
using System;
using System.Collections.Generic;
using System.Text;

namespace ExcepOut
{
    class Program
    {
        static void Main()
        {
            DateTime DateHired;

            Console.Write("Enter date of birth: ");
            DateHired = DateTime.Parse(Console.ReadLine());

            Console.WriteLine("Birth date: {0:d}\n", DateHired);
        }
    }
}
```

From above program if you enter a correct date format entry as :

```
Enter date of birth: 09/27/1997
Birth date: 9/27/1997
Press any key to continue . . .
```

Otherwise, if you enter the date in an invalid format like : 27/09/1997 (i.e., mm/dd/yyyy), then it will produce an exception as shown in Fig. 16.2.

```
C:\WINDOWS\system32\cmd.exe
Enter date of birth: 27/09/1997

Unhandled Exception: System.FormatException: String was not recognized as a vali
d DateTime.
   at System.DateTimeParse.Parse(String s, DateTimeFormatInfo dtfi, DateTimeStyl
es styles)
   at System.DateTime.Parse(String s)
   at ExcepOut.Program.Main() in D:\Olevel02\CSharp_Book\Chap16\ExcepOut\ExcepOu
t\Program.cs:line 14
Press any key to continue . . .
```

Fig. 16.2 Exception on DateTime class.

16.6.4 The DivideByZeroException Exception

Division by zero is an operation to always avoid. It is so important that it is one of the most fundamental exceptions of the computer. It is addressed at the core level even by the Intel and AMD processors. It is also addressed by the operating systems at their level. It is also addressed by most, if not all, compilers. It is also addressed by most, if not, all libraries. This means that this exception is never welcomed anywhere. The .NET Framework also provides it own class to face this operation.

If an attempt to divide a value by 0, the compiler throws a **DivideByZeroException** exception. As mentioned above, the **Exception** class is equipped with a **Message** property that carried a message for the error that occurred. We also mentioned that the message of this property may not be particularly useful to a user. Fortunately, you can create your own message and pass it to the **Exception**. To be able to receive custom messages, the Exception class provides the following constructor:

```
public Exception(string message);
```

To use it, in the section that you are anticipating the error, type the **throw** keyword followed by a **new** instance of the **Exception** class using the constructor that takes a string. For example;

..\CSharp_Book\Chap16\ThrowExcep

```
using System;
using System.Collections.Generic;
using System.Text;
```

```
namespace ThrowExcep
{
    class Program
    {
        static void Main()
        {
            double Operand1, Operand2;
            double Result = 0.00;
            char Operator;

            Console.WriteLine("This program allows you to perform an operation on two
                    numbers.");

            try
            {
                Console.WriteLine("To proceed, enter a number, an operator, and
                    a number:");
                Operand1 = double.Parse(Console.ReadLine());
                Operator = char.Parse(Console.ReadLine());
                Operand2 = double.Parse(Console.ReadLine());

                if (Operator != '+' && Operator != '-' && Operator != '*'
                    && Operator != '/')
                    throw new Exception(Operator.ToString());

                switch (Operator)
                {
                    case '+':
                        Result = Operand1 + Operand2;
                        break;

                    case '-':
                        Result = Operand1 - Operand2;
                        break;

                    case '*':
                        Result = Operand1 * Operand2;
                        break;

                    case '/':
                        Result = Operand1 / Operand2;
                        break;

                    default:
                        Console.WriteLine("Bad Operation");
                        break;
```

```
            }
            Console.WriteLine("\n{0} {1} {2} = {3}", Operand1, Operator,
                                Operand2, Result);
        }

        catch (Exception ex)
        {
            Console.WriteLine("\nOperation Error: {0} is not a valid operator",
                        ex.Message);
        }
    }
  }
}
```

When the above program executed, it will produce the following output :

```
This program allows you to perform an operation on two numbers.
To proceed, enter a number, an operator, and a number:
12
+
32
12 + 32 = 44
Press any key to continue . . .
```

If you execute again and input the different sequence of numbers and operator, then it will produce error as shown in Fig. 16.3.

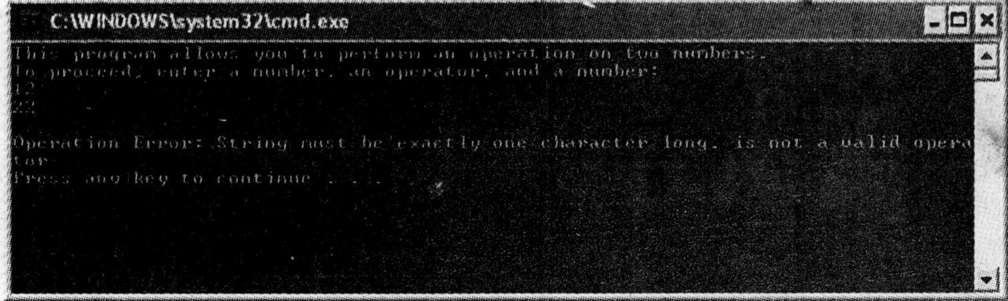

Fig. 16.3 Operation error.

16.7 Catching Exceptions

In the examples above, when we anticipated some type of problem, we instructed the compiler to use our default **catch** section. We left it up to the compiler to find out when there was a problem and we provided a **catch** section to deal with it. A method with numerous or complex operations and requests can also produce different types of errors. With such a type of program, you should be able to face different problems and deal with them individually, each by its own kind. To do this, you can create different **catch** sections, each made for a particular error. The formula used would be:

```
try {
    // Code to Try
}

catch(Arg1)
{
    // One Exception
}

catch(Arg2)
{
    // Another Exception
}
```

The compiler would proceed in a top-down:

1. Following the normal flow of the program, the compiler enters the **try** block
2. If no exception occurs in the **try** block, the rest of the **try** block is executed.

If an exception occurs in the **try** block, the compiler registers the type of error that occurred. If there is a throw line, the compiler registers it also:

- The compiler gets out of the **try** section
- The compiler examines the first **catch**. If the first **catch** matches the thrown error, that catch executes and the exception handling routine may seize. If the first **catch** doesn't match the thrown error, the compiler proceeds with the next **catch**
- The compiler checks the next match, if any and proceeds as in the first match. This continues until the compiler finds a **catch** that matches the thrown error
- If one of the catches matches the thrown error, its body executes. If no **catch** matches the thrown error, the compiler calls the **Exception** class and uses the default message

Multiple catches are written if or when a try block is expected to throw different types of errors. Once again, consider the following program:

..\CSharp_Book\Chap16\CatchMore

```
using System;
using System.Collections.Generic;
using System.Text;

namespace CatchMore
{
```

```
class Program
{
    static void Main()
    {
        double Operand1, Operand2;
        double Result = 0.00;
        char Operator;

        Console.WriteLine("This program allows you to perform an operation on two
                numbers.");

        try
        {
            Console.WriteLine("To proceed, enter a number, an operator, and a
                        number:");
            Operand1 = double.Parse(Console.ReadLine());
            Operator = char.Parse(Console.ReadLine());
            Operand2 = double.Parse(Console.ReadLine());

            switch (Operator)
            {
                case '+':
                    Result = Operand1 + Operand2;
                    break;

                case '-':
                    Result = Operand1 - Operand2;
                    break;

                case '*':
                    Result = Operand1 * Operand2;
                    break;

                case '/':
                    Result = Operand1 / Operand2;
                    break;

                default:
                    Console.WriteLine("Bad Operation");
                    break;
            }
            Console.WriteLine("\n{0} {1} {2} = {3}", Operand1,
                    Operator, Operand2, Result);
        }
```

```
            catch (Exception ex)
            {
                Console.WriteLine("\nOperation Error: {0} is not a valid operator",
                    ex.Message);
            }
        }
    }
}
```

When the above program executed, it will produce the following output :

```
This program allows you to perform an operation on two numbers.
To proceed, enter a number, an operator, and a number:
12
+
32
12 + 32 = 44
Press any key to continue . . .
```

If you execute again and input the different sequence of numbers and operator, then it will produce error as shown in Fig. 16.4.

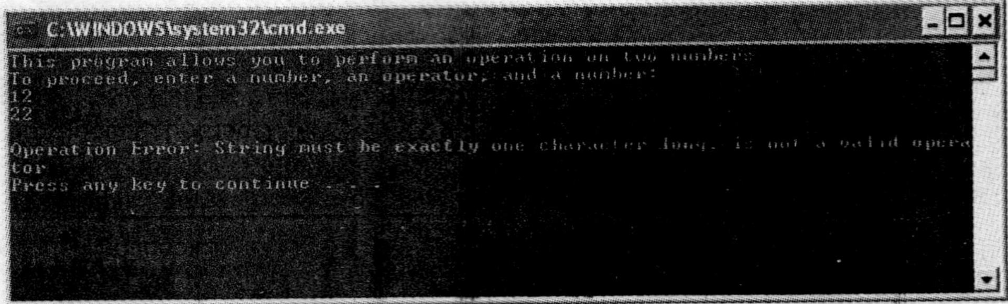

Fig. 16.4 Catching more exception.

This program works fine as long as the user types a valid sequence of values made of a number, a valid arithmetic operator, and a number. Anything else, such an invalid number, an unexpected operator, or a wrong sequence (such as a number then another number instead of an operator), would cause an error to be thrown. Obviously various bad things could happen when this program is running. To handle the exceptions that this program could produce, you can start with the most likely problem that would occur. Trusting that a user is able to provide the two numbers that are requested, it is possible that a user would type an invalid operator. For example, for this program we will perform only the addition (+), the subtraction(-), the multiplication(*), and the division(/). Therefore, we will first validate the operator. This can be done as follows:

..\CSharp_Book\Chap16\CatchOther

```
using System;
using System.Collections.Generic;
using System.Text;

namespace CatchOther
{
    class Program
    {
        static void Main()
        {
            double Operand1, Operand2;
            double Result = 0.00;
            char Operator;
            Console.WriteLine("This program allows you to perform an operation on two
                    numbers");

            try
            {
                Console.WriteLine("To proceed, enter a number, an operator, and a
                        number:");
                Operand1 = double.Parse(Console.ReadLine());
                Operator = char.Parse(Console.ReadLine());
                Operand2 = double.Parse(Console.ReadLine());

                if (Operator != '+' && Operator != '-' && Operator != '*'
                                    && Operator != '/')
                    throw new Exception(Operator.ToString());

                switch (Operator)
                {
                    case '+':
                        Result = Operand1 + Operand2;
                        break;
                    case '-':
                        Result = Operand1 - Operand2;
                        break;
                    case '*':
                        Result = Operand1 * Operand2;
                        break;
                    case '/':
                        Result = Operand1 / Operand2;
                        break;
                    default:
                        Console.WriteLine("Bad Operation");
```

```
                break;
            }
            Console.WriteLine("\n{0} {1} {2} = {3}", Operand1,
                              Operator, Operand2, Result);
        }
        catch (Exception ex)
        {
            Console.WriteLine("\nOperation Error: {0} is not a valid operator",
                              ex.Message);
        }
    }
  }
}
```

When this program runs, if the user provides a valid number followed by a wrong operator, we call the **Exception(string message)** constructor and pass it a string converted from the character that was typed. Then, when the compiler gets out of the **try** block, it looks for and finds a **catch** clause that receives a character value. Therefore, this **catch** is executed.

16.7.1 DivideByZeroException

Imagine that the user wants to perform a division. You need to tell the compiler what to do if the user enters the denominator as 0 (or 0.00). If this happens, the best option, and probably the only one you should consider is to display a message and get out. Fortunately, the .NET Framework provides the **DivideByZeroException** class to deal with an exception caused by division by zero. As done with the message passed to the **Exception** class, you can compose your own message and pass it to the **DivideByZeroException(string message)** constructor.

Exception is the parent of all exception classes. This corresponds to the three periods of a C++' **catch(...)** block. Therefore, if you write various catch blocks, the one that takes the **Exception** as argument must be the last.

Here is an example that catches two types of exceptions

..\CSharp_Book\Chap16\CatchDivide

```
using System;
using System.Collections.Generic;
using System.Text;
namespace CatchDivide
{
    class Program
    {
        static void Main()
        {
            double Operand1, Operand2;
            double Result = 0.00;
```

```
char Operator;
Console.WriteLine("This program allows you to perform an operation on two
                    numbers.");

try
{
    Console.WriteLine("To proceed, enter a number, an operator, and a
                        number:");
    Operand1 = double.Parse(Console.ReadLine());
    Operator = char.Parse(Console.ReadLine());
    Operand2 = double.Parse(Console.ReadLine());
    if (Operator != '+' && Operator != '-' && Operator != '*'
                        && Operator != '/')
        throw new Exception(Operator.ToString());

    if (Operator == '/')
        if (Operand2 == 0)
            throw new DivideByZeroException("Division by zero is not
                    allowed");
    switch (Operator)
    {
        case '+':
            Result = Operand1 + Operand2;
            break;
        case '-':
            Result = Operand1 - Operand2;
            break;
        case '*':
            Result = Operand1 * Operand2;
            break;
        case '/':
            Result = Operand1 / Operand2;
            break;
        default:
            Console.WriteLine("Bad Operation");
            break;
    }
    Console.WriteLine("\n{0} {1} {2} = {3}", Operand1,
                        Operator, Operand2, Result);
}
catch (DivideByZeroException ex)
{
    Console.WriteLine(ex.Message);
}
```

```
                catch (Exception ex)
                {
                    Console.WriteLine("\nOperation Error: {0} is not a valid operator",
                        ex.Message);
                }
            }
        }
    }
```

When the above program executed, it will produce the following output if you enter an invalid operator:

```
This program allows you to perform an operation on two numbers.
To proceed, enter a number, an operator, and a number:
12
^
32
Operation Error: ^ is not a valid operator
Press any key to continue . . .
```

When running this program, if the user types a wrong operator, the compiler gets out the try block and looks for a **catch** that takes an Exception as argument. It finds the second and executes it. If the user enters the right values (a number, an operator, and another number), then the compiler finds out if the operator entered was a forward slash "/" used to perform a division. If the user wants to perform a division, the compiler finds out if the second operand, the denominator, is 0. If it is, we create a **DivideByZeroException** instance and pass our own message to it. Based on this exception, the compiler gets out of the **try** block and starts looking for a **catch** block that takes a **DivideByZeroException** argument. It finds it in the first catch. Therefore, the compiler executes it.

16.7.2 Nesting Exceptions

You can create an exception inside of another. This is referred to as nesting an exception. This is done by applying the same techniques we used to nest conditional statements. This means that you can write an exception that depends on, and is subject to, another exception. To nest an exception, write a **try** block in the body of the parent exception. The nested **try** block must be followed by its own **catch**(es) clause. To effectively handle the exception, make sure you include an appropriate **throw** in the **try** block. For example;

..\CSharp_Book\Chap16\NestExcep

```
using System;
using System.Collections.Generic;
using System.Text;

namespace NestExcep
{
```

```
class Program
{
    static void Main(string[] args)
    {
        double Operand1, Operand2;
        double Result = 0.00;
        char Operator;

        Console.WriteLine("This program allows you to perform an operation on two
                                numbers");

        try
        {
            Console.WriteLine("To proceed, enter a number, an operator, and a
                                number:");
            Operand1 = double.Parse(Console.ReadLine());
            Operator = char.Parse(Console.ReadLine());
            Operand2 = double.Parse(Console.ReadLine());

            if (Operator != '+' && Operator != '-' && Operator != '*'
                                && Operator != '/')
                throw new Exception(Operator.ToString());

            switch (Operator)
            {
                case '+':
                    Result = Operand1 + Operand2;
                    Console.WriteLine("\n{0} + {1} = {2}", Operand1,
                            Operand2, Result);
                    break;
                case '-':
                    Result = Operand1 - Operand2;
                    Console.WriteLine("\n{0} - {1} = {2}", Operand1,
                                Operand2, Result);
                    break;
                case '*':
                    Result = Operand1 * Operand2;
                    Console.WriteLine("\n{0} * {1} = {2}", Operand1,
                                Operand2, Result);
                    break;
                case '/':
                    // The following exception is nested in the previous try
                    try
                    {
                        if (Operand2 == 0)
```

```
                        throw new DivideByZeroException("Division by zero is not
                                allowed");

                    Result = Operand1 / Operand2;
                    Console.WriteLine("\n{0} / {1} = {2}", Operand1,
                            Operand2, Result);
                }
                catch (DivideByZeroException ex)
                {
                    Console.WriteLine(ex.Message);
                }
                break;
            }
        }
        catch (Exception ex)
        {
            Console.WriteLine("\nOperation Error: {0} is not a valid operator",
                ex.Message);
        }
    }
  }
}
```

16.8 Exceptions and Methods

One of the most effective techniques used to deal with code is to isolate assignments. We have learned this when studying methods of classes. For example, the **switch** statement that was performing the operations in the "normal" version of our program can be written as follows:

..\CSharp_Book\Chap16\ExcepMethod

```
using System;
using System.Collections.Generic;
using System.Text;

namespace ExcepMethod
{
    class Program
    {
        static void Main()
        {
            double Number1, Number2;
            double Result = 0.00;
            char Operator;
```

```
Console.WriteLine("This program allows you to perform an operation on two
                    numbers");
try
{
    Console.WriteLine("To proceed, enter");

    Console.Write("First Number: ");
    Number1 = double.Parse(Console.ReadLine());

    Console.Write("An Operator (+, -, * or /): ");
    Operator = char.Parse(Console.ReadLine());
    if (Operator != '+' && Operator != '-' &&
            Operator != '*' && Operator != '/')
        throw new Exception(Operator.ToString());

    Console.Write("Second Number: ");
    Number2 = double.Parse(Console.ReadLine());

    if (Operator == '/')
        if (Number2 == 0)
            throw new DivideByZeroException("Division by zero is not
                        allowed");

    Result = Calculator(Number1, Number2, Operator);

    Console.WriteLine("\n{0} {1} {2} = {3}", Number1, Operator,
                    Number2, Result);
}
catch (FormatException)
{
    Console.WriteLine("The number you typed is not valid");
}
catch (DivideByZeroException ex)
{
    Console.WriteLine(ex.Message);
}
catch (Exception ex)
{
    Console.WriteLine("\nOperation Error: {0} is not a valid operator",
                    ex.Message);
}
}
static double Calculator(double Value1, double Value2, char Symbol)
{
    double Result = 0.00;
```

```
            switch (Symbol)
            {
                case '+':
                    Result = Value1 + Value2;
                    break;
                case '-':
                    Result = Value1 - Value2;
                    break;
                case '*':
                    Result = Value1 * Value2;
                    break;
                case '/':
                    Result = Value1 / Value2;
                    break;
            }
            return Result;
        }
    }
}
```

When the above program executed, it will produce the following output as shown in Fig. 16.5.

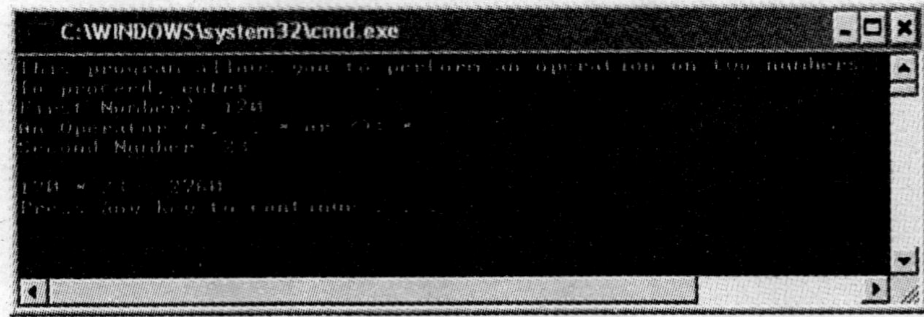

Fig. 16.5 Exceptions working on method.

You can still use regular methods along with methods that handle exceptions. As done in the **Main()** function, any method of a program can take care of its own exceptions that would occur in its body. Here is an example of an exception handled in a function:

..\CSharp_Book\Chap16\ExcepFunction

```
using System;
using System.Collections.Generic;
using System.Text;

namespace ExcepFunction
{
    class Program
    {
```

```
static void Main()
{
    double Number1, Number2;
    double Result = 0.00;
    char Operator;

    Console.WriteLine("This program allows you to perform an operation on two
            numbers");

    try
    {
        Console.WriteLine("To proceed, enter");

        Console.Write("First Number:  ");
        Number1 = double.Parse(Console.ReadLine());

        Console.Write("An Operator (+, -, * or /): ");
        Operator = char.Parse(Console.ReadLine());
        if (Operator != '+' && Operator != '-' &&
                Operator != '*' && Operator != '/')
            throw new Exception(Operator.ToString());

        Console.Write("Second Number: ");
        Number2 = double.Parse(Console.ReadLine());

        Result = Calculator(Number1, Number2, Operator);
    }
    catch (FormatException)
    {
        Console.WriteLine("The number you typed is not valid");
    }
    catch (Exception ex)
    {
        Console.WriteLine("\nOperation Error: {0} is not a valid operator",
                    ex.Message);
    }
}
static double Calculator(double Value1, double Value2, char Symbol)
{
    double Result = 0.00;

    switch (Symbol)
    {
        case '+':
            Result = Value1 + Value2;
            Console.WriteLine("\n{0} + {1} = {2}", Value1, Value2, Result);
            break;
```

```
                case '-':
                    Result = Value1 - Vaiue2;
                    Console.WriteLine("\n{0} - {1} = {2}", Value1, Value2, Result);
                    break;
                case '*':
                    Result = Value1 * Value2;
                    Console.WriteLine("\n{0} * {1} = {2}", Value1, Value2, Result);
                    break;
                case '/':
                    // The following exception is nested in the previous try
                    try
                    {
                        if (Value2 == 0)
                            throw new DivideByZeroException("Division by zero is not
                                allowed");
                        Result = Value1 / Value2;
                        Console.WriteLine("\n{0} / {1} = {2}", Value1, Value2, Result);
                    }
                    catch (DivideByZeroException ex)
                    {
                        Console.WriteLine(ex.Message);
                    }
                    break;
            }
            return Result;
        }
    }
}
```

Isolating assignments and handing them to functions is a complete and important matter in the area of application programming. Consider a program that handles a simple exception such as this one:

..\CSharp_Book\Chap16\DevideByZero

```
using System;
using System.Collections.Generic;
using System.Text;

namespace DevideByZero
{
    class Program
    {
        static void Main()
        {
            double Number1, Number2;
```

```
            double Result = 0.00;
            char Operator = '/';
            Console.WriteLine("This program allows you to perform a division
                    of two numbers");
            try
            {
                Console.WriteLine("To proceed, enter two numbers:");
                Number1 = double.Parse(Console.ReadLine());
                Number2 = double.Parse(Console.ReadLine()); ;
                if (Number2 == 0)
                    throw new DivideByZeroException("Division by zero is not allowed");
                Result = Number1 / Number2;
                Console.WriteLine("\n{0} / {1} = {2}", Number1, Number2, Result);
            }
            catch (DivideByZeroException ex)
            {
                Console.WriteLine(ex.Message);
            }
        }
    }
}
```

One of the ways you can use methods in exception routines is to have a central method that receives variables, and sends them to an external method. The external method tests the value of a variable. If an exception occurs, the external method displays or sends a **throw**. This **throw** can be picked up by the method that sent the error. Observe the following example that implements this scenario:

..\CSharp_Book\Chap16\DevideBy

```
using System;
using System.Collections.Generic;
using System.Text;

namespace DevideBy
{
    class Program
    {
        static void Main()
        {
            double Number1, Number2;
            Console.WriteLine("This program allows you to perform a division
                                of two numbers");
            try
            {
                Console.WriteLine("To proceed, enter two numbers:");
```

```
                Number1 = double.Parse(Console.ReadLine());
                Number2 = double.Parse(Console.ReadLine()); ;
                Division(Number1, Number2);
            }
            catch (DivideByZeroException ex)
            {
                Console.WriteLine(ex.Message);
            }
        }
        static void Division(double a, double b)
        {
            double Result;
            // If an exception occurred,
            if (b == 0) // then throw a string to the function caller
                throw new DivideByZeroException("Division by zero is not allowed");
            Result = a / b;
            Console.WriteLine("\n{0} / {1} = {2}", a, b, Result);
        }
    }
}
```

In this program, the Division method receives two values that it is asked to perform a division with. The Division method analyzes the second argument that represents the denominator. If this argument is zero, an exception is found and the Division method throws a **DivideByZeroException** exception.

A method can also be called to perform more than one test to eventually **throw** more than one exception. Such a method can (and should) be programmed to **throw** different types of exceptions.

Exercise

1. What is an exceptions ?
2. What is an error ?
3. How exceptions are handled in C# ?
4. Write some exceptions thrown in C# ?
5. List the types of errors ?
6. What is the difference between runtime error and compile time error ?
7. How will you throw your own exceptions in C# ?
8. What are nested try blocks ?
9. How will you implement a nested try blocks ?
10. What is try catch finally block ?
11. What does try block do ?
12. What is the purpose of finally block ?
13. What does catch block do ?
14. What is the purpose of throw keyword ?

Operator Overloading 17

17.1 Introduction

Operator overloading is one of the advanced features of C# and it aims to make user-defined data types behave much like built-in data types. In C# there are number of operators works, which included + (plus), - (minus), ^ (exclusive or), and others. Operators are defined for the built-in types, but that's not all. You can add operators to your own types, allowing them to be used much like the operators with the built-in C# types.

17.2 Need of Operator Overloading

To understand the need for operator overloading, imagine that you need to perform matrix math operations in your program. You could instantiate a couple 2-dimensional arrays and do what you need. However, add the requirement for the matrix behavior to be reusable. Because you need to do the same thing in other programs and want to take advantage of the fact that you have already written the code, you will want to create a new type.

17.3 Defining Operator Overloading

To give an additional meaning to an operator, we must specify what it means in relation to the class to which the operator is applied. This is done with the help of a special function, called operator method. The general syntax for overloading operator is :

```
public static ReturnType operator op (argument_list)
{
    Method body defining the task
}
```

Here,

- An operator overloaded method must be defined as **public static**.
- ReturnType is the value which the operator will return by the specified operation.
- Operator is keyword to define an operator method, which defines the action of the operator relative to its class.
- op is substituted by the operator that we are overloading, such as + or /.
- argument_list is the list of arguments passed into the method.

Note. Operator parameters must not use the ref or out modifier.

17.4 When Not to Use Operator Overloading

A very important concept to remember is that although operators are simple, they are not always natural. In the example above it made sense to use operators with the *Matrix* type. This is similar to the reason why operators make sense with the built-in types such as *int* and *float*. However, it is easy to abuse operators and create convoluted implementations that are hard for anyone, including the original author, to understand.

17.5 Rules for Operator Overloading

The following are some rules for operator overloading :

- Only existing operators can be overloaded.
- The overloaded operator must have at least one operand of user-defined data type.
- The overloaded operators follow the syntax rules of the original operators. They cannot be overridden.
- The operators like sizeof, ., .*, :, : and ? cannot be overloaded.
- Unary operators overloaded by means of a member function takes no parameter and return no values.
- Binary operator overloaded by means of a member function takes single parameter and return a value.

17.6 Overloading Binary Operators (+ and -)

When a member operator function overloads a binary operator, the function will have only one parameter. This parameter will receive the object that is on the right side of the operator.

As like a general method, we can add two class objects using binary operators + and -. For example, when we use a method called,

```
public double Addition (num1, num2)
```

Here, like general addition the above method adds two numbers which returns a double type value. Similarly, the binary operators also hold the same concept to use + and -. Let us start with an example that overloads two binary operators, + and -.

..\CSharp_Book\Chap17\BinaryOperator

```
using System;
using System.Collections.Generic;
using System.Text;

namespace UnaryOperator
{
    public class CounterValue
    {
        private int value1, value2;

        public CounterValue() // Default constructor
        {
            value1 = value2 = 0;
        }

        // Overloading of increment operator
        public CounterValue(int num1, int num2)
        {
            value1 = num1;
            value2 = num2;
        }

        // Overloading binary + operator
        public static CounterValue operator +(CounterValue ctr1, CounterValue ctr2)
        {
            CounterValue ctr = new CounterValue();
            // Adding two numbers
            ctr.value1 = ctr1.value1 + ctr2.value1;
            ctr.value2 = ctr1.value2 + ctr2.value2;
            return ctr;
        }

        // Binary operator -
        public static CounterValue operator -(CounterValue ctr1, CounterValue ctr2)
        {
            CounterValue ctr = new CounterValue();
            // subtracting two numbers

            if (ctr1.value1 >= ctr2.value1)
                ctr.value1 = ctr1.value1 - ctr2.value1;
            else
                ctr.value1 = ctr2.value1 - ctr1.value1;

            // subtracting two numbers
            if (ctr1.value2 >= ctr2.value2)
```

```
                ctr.value2 = ctr1.value2 - ctr2.value2;
            else
                ctr.value2 = ctr2.value2 - ctr1.value2;
            return ctr;
        }

        public void display()
        {
            Console.WriteLine(value1 + " and " + value2);
        }
    }

    class Program
    {
        static void Main()
        {
            CounterValue c1 = new CounterValue(10, 20);
            CounterValue c2 = new CounterValue(11, 22);
            CounterValue c3 = new CounterValue();

            Console.Write("The value of c1 : ");
            c1.display();
            Console.Write("The value of c2 : ");
            c2.display();

            c3 = c1 + c2; // Adding c1 and c2
            Console.Write("The sum of corresponding values of c1 and c2 are : ");
            c3.display();

            c3 = c1 - c2; // Adding c1 and c2
            Console.Write("The difference of corresponding values of c1 and c2 are : ");
            c3.display();
        }
    }
}
```

When the above program executed, it will produce the following output as shown in Fig. 17.1.

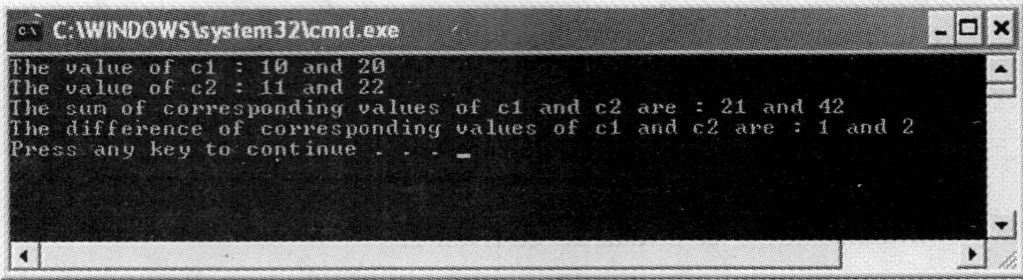

Fig. 17.1 Use of binary operator.

17.7 Overloading Unary Operators (+ and -)

Overloading a unary operator is similar to overloading a binary operator except that there is only one operand to deal with. When you overload a unary operator using a member function, the function has no parameters. Since there is only one operand, it is this operand that generates the call to the operator function. There is no need for another parameter. The following example demonstrates the unary operators ++ and —.

..\CSharp_Book\Chap17\UnaryOperator

```
using System;
using System.Collections.Generic;
using System.Text;

namespace UnaryOperator
{
    public class CounterValue
    {
        private int value1, value2;

        public CounterValue() // Default constructor
        {
            value1 = value2 = 0;
        }

        // Overloading of increment operator
        public CounterValue(int num1, int num2)
        {
            value1 = num1;
            value2 = num2;
        }

        // Overloading binary + operator
        public static CounterValue operator +(CounterValue ctr1, CounterValue ctr2)
        {
            CounterValue ctr = new CounterValue();

            // Adding two numbers
            ctr.value1 = ctr1.value1 + ctr2.value1;
            ctr.value2 = ctr1.value2 + ctr2.value2;
            return ctr;
        }

        public static CounterValue operator -(CounterValue ctr1, CounterValue ctr2)
        {
            CounterValue ctr = new CounterValue();
```

```
        // subtracting two numbers
        if (ctr1.value1 >= ctr2.value1)
            ctr.value1 = ctr1.value1 - ctr2.value1;
        else
            ctr.value1 = ctr2.value1 - ctr1.value1;

        // subtracting two numbers
        if (ctr1.value2 >= ctr2.value2)
            ctr.value2 = ctr1.value2 - ctr2.value2;
        else
            ctr.value2 = ctr2.value2 - ctr1.value2;
        return ctr;
    }

    // Overloading unary ++ operator
    public static CounterValue operator ++(CounterValue ctr1)
    {
        ctr1.value1++;
        ctr1.value2++;
        return ctr1;
    }

    public void display()
    {
        Console.WriteLine(value1 + " and " + value2);
    }
}

class Program
{
    static void Main()
    {
        CounterValue c1 = new CounterValue(10, 20);
        CounterValue c2 = new CounterValue(11, 22);
        CounterValue c3 = new CounterValue();

        Console.Write("The value of c1 : ");
        c1.display();
        Console.Write("The value of c2 : ");
        c2.display();
        c3 = c1 + c2; // Adding c1 and c2
        Console.Write("The sum of corresponding values of c1 and c2 are : ");
        c3.display();

        c3 = c1 - c2; // Adding c1 and c2
        Console.Write("The difference of corresponding values of c1 and c2 are : ");
```

```
            c3.display();

            // Using Unary operator
            c3 = c3++;
            Console.Write("The increment values of c1 and c2 are : ");
            c3.display();
        }
    }
}
```

When the above program executed, it will produce the following output as shown in Fig. 17.2.

```
C:\WINDOWS\system32\cmd.exe
The value of c1  : 10 and 20
The value of c2  : 11 and 22
The sum of corresponding values of c1 and c2 are  : 21 and 42
The difference of corresponding values of c1 and c2 are  : 1 and 2
The increment values of c1 and c2 are : 2 and 3
Press any key to continue . . .
```

Fig. 17.2 Use of Unary operators.

17.8 Overloading Relational Operators

It is possible to overload the relational and logical operators. When you overload the relational and logical operators so that they have in their traditional manner, you will not want the operator functions to return an object of the class for which they are defined. Instead, they will return an integer that indicates either true or false. This not only allows these operator functions to return a true/false value, it also allows the operators to be integrated into larger relational and logical expressions that involve other types of data.

..\CSharp_Book\Chap17\RelationalOperator

```
using System;
using System.Collections.Generic;
using System.Text;

namespace RelationalOperator
{
    public class CounterValue
    {
        private int value1, value2;

        public CounterValue() // Default constructor
        {
            value1 = value2 = 0;
        }
```

```
        // Overloading of increment operator
        public CounterValue(int num1, int num2)
        {
            value1 = num1;
            value2 = num2;
        }

        // Overloading >.
        public static bool operator >(CounterValue ctr1, CounterValue ctr2)
        {
            if ((ctr1.value1 > ctr2.value1) && (ctr1.value2 > ctr2.value2))
                return true;
            else
                return false;
        }

        // Overloading <.
        public static bool operator <(CounterValue ctr1, CounterValue ctr2)
        {
            if ((ctr1.value1 < ctr2.value1) && (ctr1.value2 < ctr2.value2))
                return true;
            else
                return false;
        }
        public void display()
        {
            Console.WriteLine(value1 + " and " + value2);
        }
    }

    class Program
    {
        static void Main()
        {
            CounterValue c1 = new CounterValue(10, 20);
            CounterValue c2 = new CounterValue(11, 22);
            CounterValue c3 = new CounterValue();

            Console.Write("The value of c1 : ");
            c1.display();
            Console.Write("The value of c2 : ");
            c2.display();

            if (c1 > c2)
                Console.WriteLine("c1 > c2 is true");
```

```
            else
                Console.WriteLine("c1 > c2 is false");
            if (c1 < c2)
                Console.WriteLine("c1 < c2 is true");
            else
                Console.WriteLine("c1 < c2 is false");
        }
    }
}
```

When the above program executed, it will produce the following output as shown in Fig. 17.3.

```
C:\WINDOWS\system32\cmd.exe
The value of c1 : 10 and 20
The value of c2 : 11 and 22
c1 > c2 is false
c1 < c2 is true
Press any key to continue . . .
```

Fig. 17.3 Use of relational operators.

17.9 Implementing an Overloaded Operator in Matrix

The syntax required to implement an overloaded operator is much the same as a static method with a couple exceptions. You must use the *operator* keyword and specify the operator symbol being overloaded. Here's a skeleton example of how the dot product operator could be implemented:

```
public static Matrix operator *(Matrix mat1, Matrix mat2)
{
    // dot product implementation
}
```

Notice that the method is static. Use the keyword *operator* after specifying the return type, *Matrix* in this case. Following the *operator* keyword, the actual operator symbol is specified and then there is a set of parameters to be operated on. The following program demonstrates how to implement and use an overloaded operator in a matrix operation.

..\CSharp_Book\Chap17\MatrixOperation

```
using System;

using System;
using System.Collections.Generic;
using System.Text;

namespace MatrixOperation
{
    class Matrix3D
    {
        // its a 3D matrix
        public const int DIMSIZE = 3;
```

```
        private double[,] matrix = new double[DIMSIZE, DIMSIZE];

        // allow callers to initialize
        public double this[int x, int y]
        {
            get { return matrix[x, y]; }
            set { matrix[x, y] = value; }
        }

        // let user add matrices
        public static Matrix3D operator +(Matrix3D mat1, Matrix3D mat2)
        {
            Matrix3D newMatrix = new Matrix3D();

            for (int x = 0; x < DIMSIZE; x++)
                for (int y = 0; y < DIMSIZE; y++)
                        newMatrix[x, y] = mat1[x, y] + mat2[x, y];
            return newMatrix;
        }
    }
    class MatrixTest
    {
        // used in the InitMatrix method.
        public static Random rand = new Random();
        // test Matrix3D
        static void Main()
        {
            Matrix3D mat1 = new Matrix3D();
            Matrix3D mat2 = new Matrix3D();

            // init matrices with random values
            InitMatrix(mat1);
            InitMatrix(mat2);

            // print out matrices
            Console.WriteLine("Matrix 1: ");
            PrintMatrix(mat1);

            Console.WriteLine("Matrix 2: ");
            PrintMatrix(mat2);

            // perform operation and print out results
            Matrix3D mat3 = mat1 + mat2;

            Console.WriteLine();
            Console.WriteLine("Matrix 1 + Matrix 2 = ");
            PrintMatrix(mat3);
```

```
        Console.ReadLine();
    }
    // initialize matrix with random values
    public static void InitMatrix(Matrix3D mat)
    {
        for (int x = 0; x < Matrix3D.DIMSIZE; x++)
            for (int y = 0; y < Matrix3D.DIMSIZE; y++)

                mat[x, y] = rand.NextDouble();
        }

        // print matrix to console
        public static void PrintMatrix(Matrix3D mat)
        {
            Console.WriteLine();

            for (int x = 0; x < Matrix3D.DIMSIZE; x++)
            {
                Console.Write("[ ");
                for (int y = 0; y < Matrix3D.DIMSIZE; y++)
                {
                    // format the output
                    Console.Write("{0,8:#.000000}", mat[x, y]);

                    if ((y + 1 % 2) < 3)
                        Console.Write(", ");
                }
                Console.WriteLine(" ]");
            }
            Console.WriteLine();
        }
    }
}
```

When the above program executed, it will produce the following output as shown in Fig. 17.4.

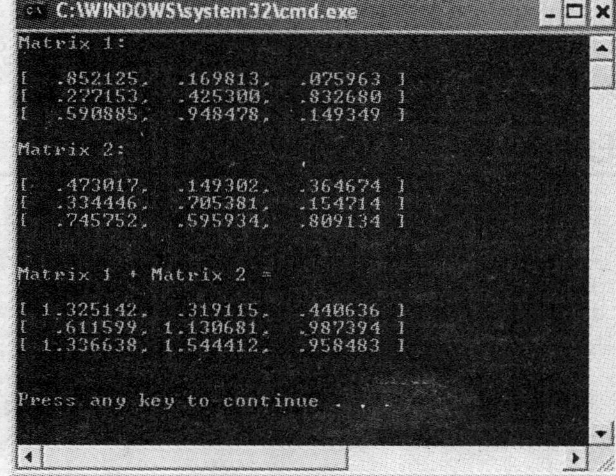

Fig. 17.4 Operator overloading in matrix operation.

From the above program of the dot product operator, the *Matrix* class contains an operator overload for the + operator. For your convenience, I've extracted the pertinent overload implementation in the code below:

```
public static Matrix3D operator +(Matrix3D mat1, Matrix3D mat2)
{
    Matrix3D newMatrix = new Matrix3D();

    for (int x=0; x < DIMSIZE; x++)
        for (int y=0; y < DIMSIZE; y++)
            newMatrix[x, y] = mat1[x, y] + mat2[x, y];
    return newMatrix;
}
```

The operator is *static*, which is the only way it can and should be declared because an operator belongs to the type and not a particular instance. The return type is *Matrix3D* - its enclosing type. What designates this as an operator is the use of the keyword *operator*, followed by the + symbol. The parameter types are both of the enclosing type, *Matrix3D*. The implementation of the operator overload creates a new instance of the return type and performs a matrix add.

Basically, it is that easy. There are just a few rules you have to follow when implementing operator overloads.

17.10 Operator Rules

C# enforces certain rules when you overload operators. One rule is that you must implement the operator overload in the type that will use it. This is sensible because it makes the type self-contained.

Another rule is that you must implement matching operators. For example, if you overload ==, you must also implement !=. The same goes for <= and >=.

When you implement an operator, its compound operator works also. For example, since the + operator for the *Matrix3D* type was implemented, you can also use the += operator on *Matrix3D* types.

Exercise

1. What is operator overloading ? Example with an example.
2. Write few rules about operator overloading.
3. What is binary operator overloading?
4. What is unary operator overloading?
5. How many operands needed for a ++ operator overloading?

18 File Handing in C#

18.1 Introduction

File Handling is an important part of all programs. File handling is as simple as writing in a book, much more easier to modify and find. What is a file? A file is just a bunch of bytes stored on a hard disk. Some have a specific structure others don't. Files are used to save info so that it can be retrieved later for use.

The techniques for file input and output, I/O, in C# are virtually identical to those introduced in earlier lessons for writing and reading to the standard output devices, the screen and keyboard.

Actually there are only two types of files : text files and binary files. In text files data is stored as readable chars and binary file are in machine language. So if you output abc123 to a text file you will see abc123 but in a binary file you may see only a bunch of black blocks if you use notepad. The binary files are smaller in size.

18.2 Types of Files

A file is a series of bytes of data that are arranged in a particular manner to produce a usable document. For easy storage, location, and management, the bytes are stored on a medium such as a hard disc, a floppy disc, a compact disc, or any valid and supported type of storage. When these bytes belong to a single but common entity and hold values that are stored on a medium, the group is referred to as a file.

Based on the way the data is stored, files can be divided into two categories :

- **Text files.** In these files, data is stored in the form of ASCII codes irrespective of the data type, *i.e.*, for character data, their ASCII codes of the individual characters are stored and the numeric data, the ASCII code of individual digits of a number are stored. Text files can be manipulated by any text editor.

- **Binary Files.** In these files, data is stored in the same as it is stored in memory irrespective of the data type i.e. for character data, their ASCII codes of the individual characters are stored and for numeric data, numbers are stored in binary format.

Note

Binary files provide more efficient way of storage but it can be read only through program.

18.3 Files Input and Output

As we know that the file is a collection of logically related records and stream is a data flow from source to destination. We have already studied various input and output streams. These unformatted streams are :

Stream	Meaning
ReadLine	standard input stream
WriteLine	standard output stream

The above stream is useful only when we have to accept the data from keyboard and display the data on screen or printer.

A stream is a sequence of bytes. It can either as a source from which the program takes input data or as a destination to which the program can send output data. The source stream that supplies data to the program is called input stream and the destination stream receives data from the program is called output stream.

18.4 System.IO Namespace

In the framework of .NET, the System.IO namespace is the region of the base class libraries developed to file-based (and memory-based) input and output (I/O) services. System.IO namespace contains the primary classes used to move and process streams of data. To support file processing, the .NET Framework provides the **System.IO** namespace that contains many different classes to handle almost any type of file operation you may need to perform. Therefore, to perform file processing, you can include the **System.IO** namespace in your project. Many of the types within the System.IO namespace focus on the programmatic manipulation of physical directories and files as shown in Fig. 18.1.

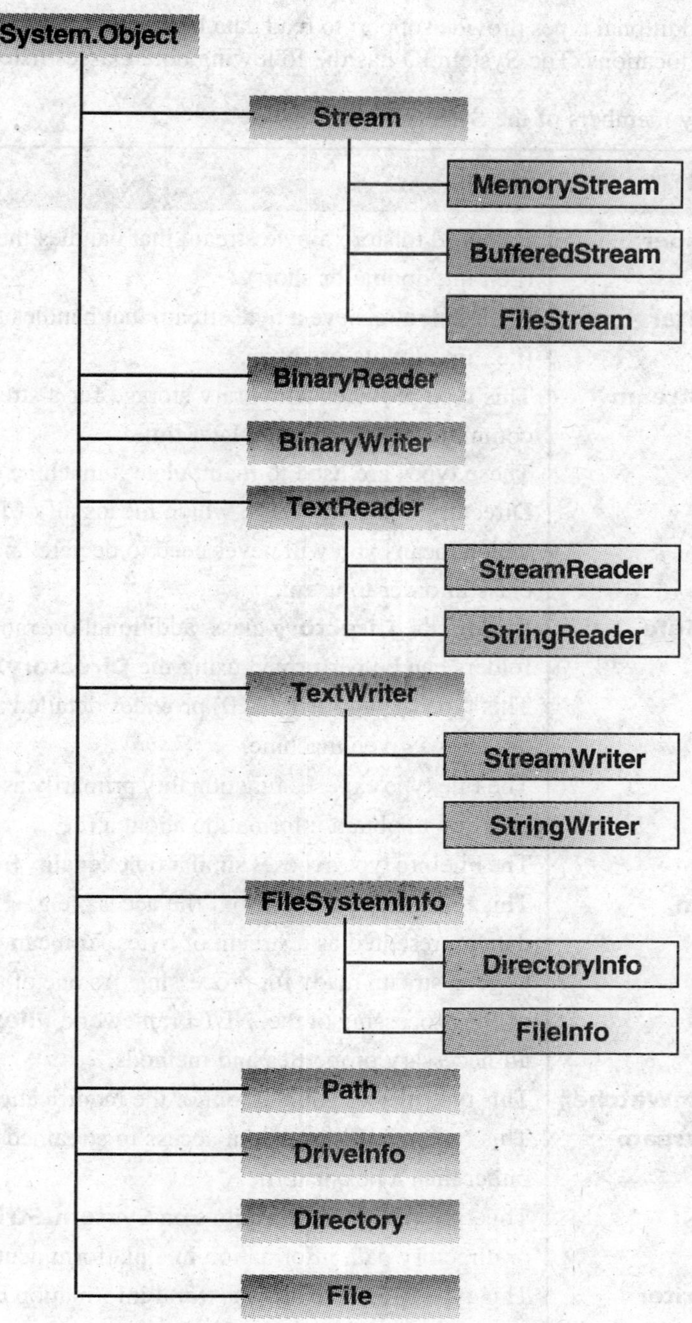

Fig. 18.1 System.IO namespace files and directory hierarcy.

However, additional types provide support to read data from and write data to string buffers as well as raw memory locations. The System.IO has the following core classes listed in Listing 18.1.

Listing 18.1 Key members of the System.IO namespace.

I/O Class Type	Meaning
BinaryReader	It is used to store a byte stream that handles the reading of binary data (i.e., int, double or short).
BinaryWriter	It is used to retrieve a byte stream that handles the writing of binary data (i.e., int, double or short).
BufferedStream	This type provides temporary storage for a stream of bytes that may be committed to storage at a later time.
Directory	These types are used to manipulate a machine's directory structure. Directory is a static class, which means all of its methods are static, which means you will never need to declare an instance of the Directory class in order to use it.
DirectoryInfo	Besides the **Directory** class, additional operations of folders and sub-folders can be performed using the **DirectoryInfo** class.
DriveInfo	This type (new to .NET 2.0) provides detailed information regarding the drive on a given machine.
File	The File type exposes functionality primarily as static methods. It enables program to obtain information about a file.
FileInfo	The FileInfo type exposes similar functionality from a valid object variable.
FileStream	This type allows for random file access (e.g, seeking capabilities) with data represented as a stream of bytes. You can use a **FileStream** object to get a stream ready for processing. As one of the most complete classes of file processing of the .NET Framework, **FileStream** is equipped with all necessary properties and methods.
FileSystemWatcher	This type allows you to monitor the modification of a given external file.
MemoryStream	This type provides random access to streamed data stored in memory rather than a physical file.
Path	This type performs operations on **System.String** types that contain file or directory path information in a platform neutral manner.
StreamWriter	This type is used to store textural information to a file. That is, write characters to a byte stream. This class wraps a byte output stream.
StreamReader	This type is used to retrieve textual information to a file. That is, read characters to a byte stream. This class wraps a byte input stream.

StringWriter	This type write characters to a string.
StringReader	This type read characters to a string.

In addition to these creatable class types, **System.IO** defines a number of enumerations, as well as a set of abstract classes (**Stream**, **TextReader**, **TextWriter** and so forth), that defines a shared polymorphic interface to all descendents.

18.5 Working with Stream

The parent class of file processing is **Stream**. With **Stream**, you can store data to a stream or you can retrieve data from a stream. **Stream** is an abstract class, which means that you cannot use it to declare a variable in your application. As an abstract class, **Stream** is used as the parent of the classes that actually implement the necessary operations. You will usually use a combination of classes to perform a typical operation. For example, some classes are used to create a stream object while some others are used to write data to the created stream.

Its purpose is to abstract data into a stream of bytes independent of any underlying data devices. This frees the programmer on focus on the data stream rather than device characteristics. The class members support three fundamental areas of operations: writing, reading and seeking (identifying the current byte position within a stream). The following Listing 18.2 shows some of important members defined by Stream.

Listing 18.2 Selected Stream members.

Member	Description
bool CanRead	It indicates whether the stream can support reading.
bool CanSeek	It indicates whether the stream can support seeking.
bool CanWrite	It indicates whether the stream can support writing.
long Length	It finds the length of stream in bytes; and return long type.
long position	It gets or sets the position within the current stream; has long type.
void Close()	It closes the current stream and release resources associated with it.
void Flush()	Flushes data in buffers to the underlying devices – for example, a file.
Read(byte array, int offset, SeekOrigin, count)	Read a sequence of bytes (or a single byte) from the current stream.
ReadByte()	It reads in advance the current position in the stream by the number of bytes used.

long SetLength()	Sets the length of the current stream. It can be used to extend or truncate a stream.
long Seek(long offset, SeekOrigin origin)	Sets the position in the current stream to the specified offset from the specified origin.
void Write(byte array, int offset, int numBytes)	Write a sequence of bytes (or a single byte) to the current stream.
void WriteByte(byte b)	It advance the current position in the stream by the number of bytes written.

Remember the stream class, including FileStream, are defined in the System.IO. Thus to process file operation in your application, you will usually include the following line,

```
using System.IO;
```

18.6 Working with FileStream

A **FileStream** object is created to process a stream of bytes associated with blocking store – a term used to refer to any storage medium such as disk or memory. The **FileStream** is the main class which helps to process file into secondary memory.

You can use a **FileStream** object to get a stream ready for processing. As one of the most complete classes of file processing of the .NET Framework, **FileStream** is equipped with all necessary properties and methods. To use it, you must first declare a variable of it. The class is equipped with nine constructors. One of the constructors (the second) of the **FileStream** class has the following syntax:

```
public FileStream(string path, FileMode mode);
```

This constructor takes as its first argument the name or the file or its path. The second argument specifies the type of operation to perform on the file.

Other than this, the **FileStream** class has several constructors. The most useful ones accept the path of the file being associated with the object and optional parameters that define the file mode, access rights and sharing rights. The following Fig. 18.2 shows its possible values with different parameters.

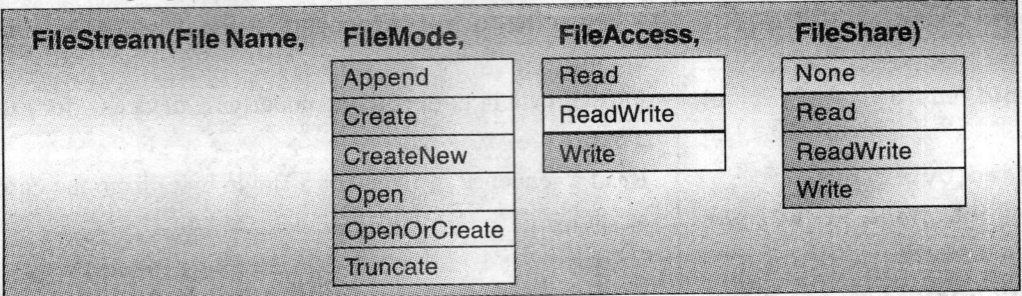

Fig. 18.2 FileMode, FileAccess and FileShare values.

From the Fig. 18.2, we know that a file can only be processed if its **FileStream** satisfies. For example,

```
// Create a FileStream object
FileStream fs = new FileStream("Employees.txt",
                    FileMode.OpenOrCreate, FileAccess.ReadWrite);
```

From the above declaration, if you omit the **FileMode** and **FileAccess** paramters, then, it will automatically take the **FileMode** as **ReadWrite** and **FileShare** as **None**)

The FileStream has four parameters :

- **File Name.** The file you want to access. This is the name of the file which will be storing your input data.

Note

If you are creating a new file, there are certainly some rules you must observe. The name of a file follows the directives of the operating system. On MS DOS and Windows 3.X (that is, prior to Microsoft Windows 9X), the file had to use the 8.3 format. The actual name had to have a maximum of 8 characters with restrictions on the characters that could be used. The user also had to specify three characters after a period. The three characters, known as the file extension, were used by the operating system to classify the file. That was all necessary for those 8-bit and 16-bit operating systems. Various rules have changed. For example, the names of folders and files on Microsoft Windows >= 95 can have up to 255 characters. The extension of the file is mostly left to the judgment of the programmer but the files are still using extensions. Applications can also be configured to save different types of files; that is, files with different extensions.

The file name is given according to your data and application. For example, **Emp.dat**, **Employees.txt**, **Salary.Dat**, etc. In programming, you can name the file as :

```
// Create a FileStream object
FileStream fs = new FileStream("Employees.txt");
```

The **Employees.txt** file will be created inside

```
. . .\CSharp_Book\Chap18\txtFile\txtFile\bin\Debug
```

Or

```
// Create a file Employees.txt in the C:\Temp directory.
FileStream fs = new FileInfo(@"c:\temp\Employees.txt");
```

- **FileMode.** Besides the access to the file, another option you will most likely specify to the operating system is referred to as the mode of a file. It is specified through the **FileMode** enumerator. The members of the **FileMode** Enumerator are listed in Listing 18.3.

Listing 18.3 FileMode Enumeration values.

Value	Description
Append	Open the file for appending (adding to it). That is Open an existing file or creates a new one. Writing begins at the end of the file only.
Create	Open file for writing. That is, it creates a new output file. If there is any preexisting file by the same name, then it will be destroyed.
CreateNew	Create a new file. An existing file is overwritten.
Open	It will open a preexisting file.
OpenOrCreate	Opens a file if it exists; otherwise, creates a new one.
Truncate	Opens an existing file, removes its contents and positions the file pointer to the beginning of the file.

- **FileAccess.** It indicates how you want access to file. The **FileAccess** has three enumeration values. These enumerations define how the current **FileSystem** may access the files. These are :
    - o **Read.** This is a read-only property, where data can only be read.
    - o **Write.** This is a write-only property, where data can only be writing.
    - o **ReadWrite.** This is a read-write property, where data can be read or write.
- **FileShare.** It specifies whether you want exclusive access to the file or are you willing for other streams to be able to access this file simultaneously. In standalone workstations, one person is usually able to access and open a file then perform the necessary operations on it. In networked computers, you may create a file that different people can access at the same time or you may make one file access another file to retrieve information. Based on this, when an operation must be performed on a file, you may have to specify how a file can be shared. This is done through the **FileShare** enumerator. The values of the **FileShare** enumerator are:
    - o **FileShare.Inheritable.** Allows other file handles to inherit from this file
    - o **FileShare.None.** The file cannot be shared
    - o **FileShare.Read**. The file can be opened and read from
    - o **FileShare.Write.** The file can be opened and written to
    - o **FileShare.ReadWrite.** The file can be opened to write to it or read from it

18.7 Working with FileInfo Class

In its high level of support for file processing, the .NET Framework provides the **FileInfo** class. This class is equipped to handle all types of file-related operations including creating, copying, moving, renaming, or deleting a file. **FileInfo** is based on the **FileSystemInfo** class that provides information on characteristics of a file.

The **FileInfo** class is equipped with one constructor whose syntax is:

```
public FileInfo(string fileName);
```

This constructor takes as argument the name of a file or its complete path. If you provide only the name of the file, the compiler would consider the same directory of its project. For example;

```
FileInfo fs = new FileInfo("Test.txt");
```

Alternatively, if you want, you can provide any valid directory you have access to. In this case, you should provide the complete path. That is,

```
FileInfo fs = new FileInfo(@"C:\temp\Test.txt");
```

Other than this, the FileInfo and File classes offer an alternative to creating **FileStream**, **StreamWriter** and **StreamReader** objects directly. The **FileInfo** class contains some important members described in Listing 18.4.

Listing 18.4 FileInfo members for operating a file.

Member	Description
AppendText()	Opens a file in append mode. That is, it creates a StreamWriter which appends text to a file. If the file does not exist, it is created.
CopyTo()	Copy the contents of an existing file to a new file.
Create()	Creates a file and returns a FileStream object.
CreateText()	Opens a file for writing. If the file exists, its contents are overwritten.
Delete()	Deletes the file which a FileInfo instance is bound.
Open()	Open a file with access.
OpenRead()	Creates a read-only FileStream.
OpenWrite()	Creates a write-only FileStream.
OpenText()	Opens the file in read mode.

The **FileInfo.Open** method is the generic and most flexible way to open a file.

```
public FileStream Open(FileMode mode, FileAccess access, FileShare share)
```

From the above listing, **Create**, **OpenRead** and **OpenWrite** are specific cases of **Open** that offer an easy-to-use method that returns a **FileStream** object and requires no parameters. Similarly, the **OpenText**, **AppendText** and **CreateText** method returns a **StreamReader** and **StreamWriter** object. For example,

```
FileInfo f = new FileInfo(@"C:\temp\Test.txt");
```

```
FileSystem fs = f.Create();
```

The **FileInfo.Create()** method returns a **FileStream** object. You can use this returned value to write any type of value into the file, including text. If you want to create a file that contains text, an alternative is to call the **FileInfo.CreateText()** method. Its syntax is:

```
public StreamWriter CreateText();
```

This method directly returns a **StreamWriter** object. You can use this returned object to write text to the file.

18.8 Opening and Closing a File

Before you can create, write to, or read from a disk file, you must open the file. Opening a file is analogous to opening a file cabinet before working with a file stored in the cabinet. After you are done with a cabinet's file, you close the file door. You must also close a disk file when you finish with it.

When you open a disk file, you must inform C# of the file name and what you want to do with it (write to, add to or read from). C# and the operating system work together to make sure that the disk is ready and to create an entry in your file directory (if you are creating a file) for the file name. When you close a file, C# writes any remaining data in the file, releases the file from the program, and updates file directory to reflect the file's new size.

To open a file call the **Open()** member function with one of the file stream objects. To close a file, call the **Close()** member function. The formats of these two member function calls look like this :

```
FileInfo f1 = new FileInfo(@"C:\temp\Test.txt");
FileStream fs = f1.Create();    // Create Test.txt file
```

Here, the **FileInfo.Create()** method returns a **FileStream** type, which exposes synchronous and asynchronous write/read operation to/from the file. Once you create a file, you can close the file using the **Close()** method of the **FileStream** class. That is,

```
fs.Close();
```

18.8.1 File Existence

When you call the **FileInfo.Create()** or the **FileInfo.CreateText()** method, if the file passed as argument, or as the file in the path of the argument, exists already, it would be deleted and a new one would be created with the same name. This can cause the right file to be deleted. Therefore, before creating a file, you may need to check whether it exists already. To do this, you can check the value of the Boolean **FileInfo.Exists** property. This property holds a **true** value if the file exists already and it holds a **false** value if the file doesn't exist or it doesn't exist in the path.

Here is an example of checking the existence of a file:

```
FileInfo fs = new FileInfo(@"C:\Temp\Test.txt");
```

```
fs.Create();

if( fs.Exists == true )
    return;
```

18.9 Working with StreamWriter and StreamReader Classes

These are the two basic classes which helps to both write and read text information into a file. The **StreamWriter** writes text using **Write** and **WriteLine** methods. The method has several constructors like;

```
public StreamWriter(string path)
public StreamWriter(string s)
public StreamWriter(string path, bool append)
public StreamWriter(string path, bool append, Encoding encoding)
```

Here,

- **Path.** The name of the file to be appended.
- **s.** It is FileStream.
- **append.** Set to true to append data to file; false overwrites.
- **encoding.** Specifies how characters are encoded as they are written to a file.

18.9.1 Creating a Text File

Let us consider the following example to write file different names into a text file "Test.txt".

..\CSharp_Book\Chap18\txtFile

```
using System;
using System.IO;

namespace txtFile
{
    class Program
    {
        static int Main()
        {

            FileInfo f1 = new FileInfo(@"C:\Temp\Test.txt");
            FileStream fs = f1.Create();    // Create Test.txt file

            StreamWriter wr = new StreamWriter(fs); // Create a StreamWriter
            wr.WriteLine("Sanjay Mehra");
            wr.WriteLine("Vinod Kapoor");
```

```
            wr.WriteLine("Ravi Mehta");
            wr.WriteLine("Rajat Sharma");
            wr.WriteLine("Monika Ghai");

            // Insert a new line
            wr.Write(wr.NewLine);

            // Closing automatically flushes!
            wr.Close();
            return 0;
        }
    }
}
```

Here, the above example creates StreamWriter object from a FileStream and writes five different names into Test.txt file. The file is created in a C:\Temp folder.

> **Note**
> *Before executing the above program, make sure that the Temp folder is created in C: drive. Programmers can take any other folder according to your need.*

When you explore the above folder, you will notice that the Test.txt file contains all the file names as shown in Fig. 18.3.

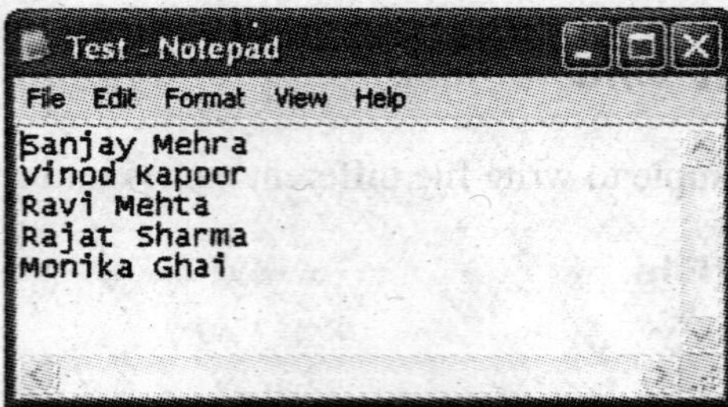

Fig. 18.3 Text file data.

From the above program, instead of writing,

```
FileInfo f1 = new FileInfo(@"C:\Temp\Test.txt");
FileStream fs = f1.Create();    // Create Test.txt file
StreamWriter wr = new StreamWriter(fs); // Create a StreamWriter
```

You can write the **FileInfo**'s **CreateText()** method as

```
FileInfo f1 = new FileInfo(@"C:\Temp\Test.txt");
StreamWriter wr = f1.CreateText();
```

From the aboce code, the **CreateText()** method returns a **StreamWriter** object (**wr**) for writing text information.

Once you write text inormation into a file, you can read the lines of text using **StreamReader** object. A **StreamReader** object is used to read text from a file. It has several methods for reading and viewing character data as shown in Listing 18.5.

Listing 18.5 StreamReader methods.

Member	Description
Peek()	Returns the next available character without moving the position of the reader. Returns an int value of the character or -1 if none exists.
Read()	Reads data from an input stream.
Read(char butt, int ndx, int count)	Reads fix number of characters into a character array beginning from a position.
ReadLine()	Returns a string comprising one line of text.
ReadToEnd()	Reads all characters from the current position to the end of the TextReader.

18.9.2 Reading Data from a Text File

The following programs reads data from Test.txt file.

..\CSharp_Book\Chap18\TFileRead

```
using System;
using System.IO;

namespace txtFileRead
{
    class Program
    {
        static int Main()
        {
            FileInfo f1 = new FileInfo(@"C:\Temp\Test.txt");
            FileStream fs = f1.Open(FileMode.OpenOrCreate, FileAccess.Read);
            StreamReader sr = new StreamReader(fs); // Create a StreamReader

            string input = null;
            while (((input = sr.ReadLine()) != null))
            {
                Console.WriteLine(input);
            }

            sr.Close();
            return 0;
```

```
            }
        }
    }
```

Here, the **FileInfo.Open()** method used to open existing files (here, Text.txt) as well as create new files with far more precision than **FileInfo.Create()**. Once the call to Open completes, you are returned a **FileStream** object (**fs**) . When you execute the above program, it will produce all the five names in your command window as shown in Fig. 18.4.

Fig. 18.4 Reading data from text file.

Also, the above program can use the **FileStream** method as :

```
static int Main()
{
    FileStream fs = new FileStream(@"C:\Temp\Test.txt", FileMode.Open);
    StreamReader sr = new StreamReader(fs); // Create a StreamReader

    string input = null;

    Console.WriteLine("The names are ....");
    while (((input = sr.ReadLine()) != null))
    {
        Console.WriteLine(input);
    }

    sr.Close();
    return 0;
}
```

Which will read all the five names from **Test.txt** file. There is another method which of **FileInfo** type is **OpenText()**. The **OpenText()** method returns an instance of the **StreamReader** which reads the text information from a text file. For example,

..\CSharp_Book\Chap18\TFileRead

```
using System;
```

```
using System.IO;
namespace TFileRead
{
    class Program
    {
        static int Main()
        {
            // Get a StreamReader object
            FileInfo fs = new FileInfo(@"C:\Temp\Test.txt");
            StreamReader sr = fs.OpenText();

            string input = null;

            Console.WriteLine("The names are ....");
            while (((input = sr.ReadLine()) != null))
            {
                Console.WriteLine(input);
            }

            sr.Close();
            return 0;
        }
    }
}
```

18.9.3 Direct use of StreamWriter/StreamReader

So far we use the **StreamWriter** and **StreamReader** through **FileInfo** object class. Every time the **FileInfo** creates an object and use the methods like **CreateText()**, **Create()**, **Open()**, etc. But you can use **StreamWriter** and **StreamReader** directly to manipulate string data. The **StreamWriter** and **StreamReader** create itself the file objects to access string data.

Let us consider the following example to write few numbers into a new text file **Number.txt** and read the data as strings.

..\CSharp_Book\Chap18\Test

```
using System;
using System.IO;

namespace Test
{
    class Program
    {
        static int Main()
```

```
        {
            // Get a StreamWritter and write string data
            StreamWriter wr = new StreamWriter(@"C:\Temp\Number.txt");
            for (int i = 1; i<=10; i++)
                wr.WriteLine(i);

            wr.Close();

            // Get a StreamReader and read string data
            StreamReader sr = new StreamReader(@"C:\Temp\Number.txt");

            string s = null;

            Console.WriteLine("The numbers are ....");
            while (((s = sr.ReadLine()) != null))
            {
                Console.WriteLine(s);
            }

            wr.Close();
            sr.Close();
            return 0;
        }
    }
}
```

The above program will write numbers from 1 to 10 into Number.txt file and simultaneously, it also read the same number and display as shown in Fig. 18.5.

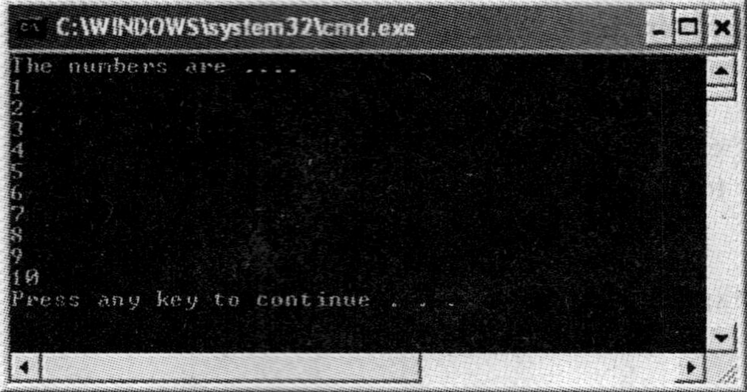

Fig. 18.5 Handling data using StreamWriter and StreamReader.

18.9.4 Appending Data to a Text File

You can easily add data to an existing file or create new files by opening the file in append access mode. Data files in the disk are rarely static; they grow almost daily as business increases. Being able to add to data already on the disk is very useful indeed.

When you open a file for append access (open the file as **AppendText()**), the file does not have to exist already. If the file does exist, C# opens the file such that any data written appends to the end of the file. If the file does not exist, C# simply creates the file (just as when you open a file for write access).

Example The following program adds three more names to the Test.txt file created earlier.

..\CSharp_Book\Chap18\AppendText

```
using System;
using System.IO;

namespace AppendText
{
    class Program
    {
        static int Main()
        {
            // Get a StreamWritter object
            FileInfo f1 = new FileInfo(@"C:\Temp\Test.txt");
            StreamWriter wr = f1.AppendText();
            wr.WriteLine("Amit Vats");
            wr.WriteLine("Priyanka Dev");
            wr.WriteLine("Bharat Bhusan");
            // Insert a new line
            wr.Write(wr.NewLine);
            // Closing automatically flushes!
            wr.Close();
            return 0;
        }
    }
}
```

Here, the **AppendText()** method add the three additional names into **Test.txt** file. When you open the Test.txt file, it will look like Fig. 18.6.

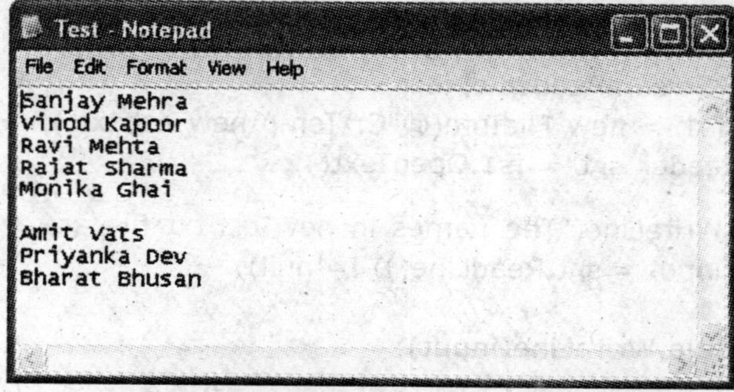

Fig. 18.6 Data appended into text file.

Example You might want to use such a program to back up important data in case the original file gets damaged. The following program reads one file (Test.txt) and copies it to another file (newTest.txt). Also display the contents of newTest.txt file contents.

..\CSharp_Book\Chap18\FileCopy

```
using System;
using System.IO;

namespace FileCopy
{
    class Program
    {
        static int Main()
        {
            // Steps to open an existing file for reading data.
            // Get a StreamReader object
            FileInfo fs = new FileInfo(@"C:\Temp\Test.txt");
            StreamReader sr = fs.OpenText();

            // Get a StreamWritter object
            FileInfo f1 = new FileInfo(@"C:\Temp\newTest.txt");
            StreamWriter wr = f1.AppendText();

            string input = null;

            Console.WriteLine("Copying data....");
            while (((input = sr.ReadLine()) != null))
            {
                wr.WriteLine(input);
            }
            sr.Close();
            wr.Close();

            input = null;

            // Steps to open an existing file for reading data.
            // Get a StreamReader object
            FileInfo fs1 = new FileInfo(@"C:\Temp\newTest.txt");
            StreamReader sr1 = fs1.OpenText();

            Console.WriteLine("The names in newTest.txt file are ....");
            while (((input = sr1.ReadLine()) != null))
            {
                Console.WriteLine(input);
            }
```

```
            sr1.Close();
            return 0;
        }
    }
}
```

When the above program executed, it will produce the following output as shown in Fig. 18.7.

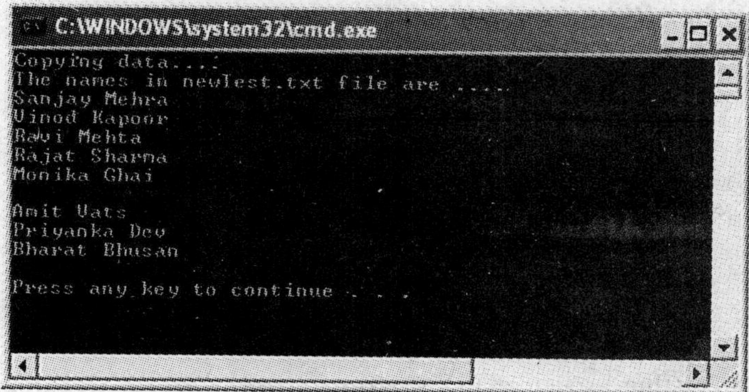

Fig. 18.7 Contenets in new file.

18.10 Working with StringWriters and StringReaders

These two classes **StringWriter** and **StringReader** are so similar in practice to the **StreamWriter** and **StreamReader**. But the main difference is that the streams are stored in memory, rather than a file.

..\CSharp_Book\Chap18\StringOperation

```
using System;
using System.IO;

namespace StringOperation
{
    class Program
    {
        static int Main()
        {
            // Get a StringWritter and write string data
            StringWriter wr = new StringWriter();

            wr.WriteLine("27th September 1997 is my son's birthday.");
            wr.WriteLine("18th May 2004 is my daugher's birthday.");
            wr.WriteLine("It is nice to celebrate a party.");
```

```
            wr.Write(wr.NewLine);
            wr.Close();

            // Read strings just written from memory

            string str = wr.ToString();
            StringReader sr = new StringReader(str);
            string line = null;
            while ((line = sr.ReadLine()) != null)
            {
                Console.WriteLine(line);
            }

            sr.Close();
            return 0;
        }
    }
}
```

The most interesting aspect of the **StringWriter** is that it is implemented underneath as a **StringBuffer** object. In fact, **StringWriter** has a **GetStringBuilder()** method that can be used to retrive it.

18.11 Reading/Writing Binary files

When we want to write few numbers or characters to a disk it is possible with the text files. But when we want to store a large amount of data, the more efficient way of doing the same is using binary I/O also known as block I/O, in which numbers are stored as they are stored in the computer main memory. To read and write binary values of the C# built-in types we will used **BinaryWriter** and **BinaryReader**. Class **BinaryWriter** and **BinaryReader** provide methods for writing and reading bytes to streams, respectively. The **BinaryWriter** and **BinaryReader** constructors receive as arguments references to instances of class **System.IO.Stream**.

These two classes are deriving directly from **System.Object**. When using these streams, it is important to understand that this data is read and written using its internal, binary format, not its human readable text form.

18.11.1 Working with BinaryWriter

A streaming operation is typically used to create a stream. Once the stream is ready, you can write data to it. The writing operation is performing through various classes. One of these classes is **BinaryWriter**. The **BinaryWriter** class can be used to write values of primitive data types (**char, int, float, double,** etc). To use a **BinaryWriter** value, you can first declare its variable. To do this, you would use one of the class' three constructors. One of its constructors has the following syntax:

```
public BinaryWriter(Stream output);
```

Here, output is the stream to which data is written. **BinaryWriter** contains several usable method which are listed in Listing 18.6.

Listing 18.6. BinaryWriter methods.

Method	Description
void Write()	Writes a value to the current stream. The value can be sbyte, byte, short ushort, int uint, long, ulong float, double char, string or an array of bytes and array of characters.
Close()	This method closes the binary stream.
Flush()	This method flushes tbe binary stream.
Seek()	This method sets the position in the current stream.

Let us consider to write certain employee information like employee code, employee name, employee designation and salary into a binary file called **Emp.txt**. So, to write data into using **BinaryWriter**, the program is as :

..\CSharp_Book\Chap18\BinaryWrite

```
using System;
using System.IO;

namespace BinaryWrite
{
    class Program
    {
        static int Main()
        {
            // Creating employee data variables;
            int empcode;
            string empname;
            string empdesig;
            float empsalary;
            char ch = 'Y';

            BinaryWriter bw;
            bw = new BinaryWriter(new FileStream(@"C:\Temp\Emp.txt",
                        FileMode.Create));
            Console.WriteLine("Employee Console");
            Console.WriteLine();

            while ((ch == 'Y') || (ch == 'y'))
            {
```

```
                Console.Write("Employee code = > ");
                empcode = int.Parse(Console.ReadLine());
                Console.Write("Name => ");
                empname = Console.ReadLine();
                Console.Write("Designation => ");
                empdesig = Console.ReadLine();
                Console.Write("Salary => ");
                empsalary = float.Parse(Console.ReadLine());
                bw.Write(empcode);
                bw.Write(empname);
                bw.Write(empdesig);
                bw.Write(empsalary);
                bw.Flush();
                Console.WriteLine();

                Console.Write("Do U want to continue...");
                ch = (char) Console.Read();
                Console.ReadLine();
            }

            bw.Close();
            return 0;
        }
    }
}
```

When the above program executed, it will produce the following output as shown in Fig. 18.8.

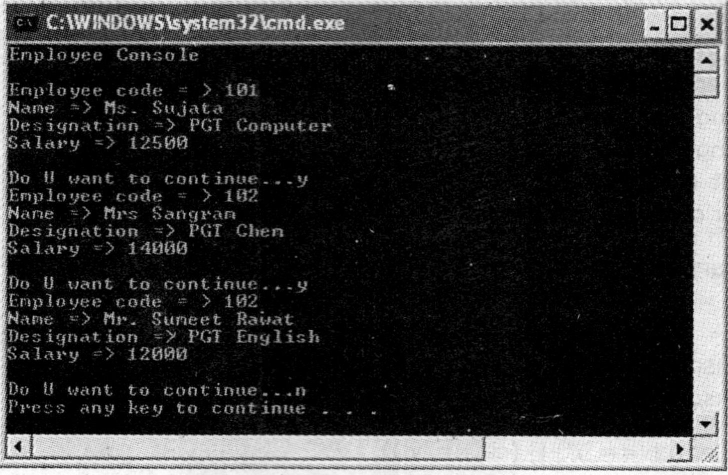

Fig. 18.8 Writing data using BinaryWriter.

If you will open the **Emp.txt** file from **C:\Temp** folder, you will notice that it contains some data in binary format. Here, the method Write of the **BinaryWriter** object used to write the data. Method **Write** is an overloaded method that receives as an argument any primitive data type, and then writes that type to a stream of bytes.

18.11.2 Working with BinaryReader

Once the stream is ready, you can get prepared to read data from it. To support this, you can use the **BinaryReader** class. This class provides two constructors. One of the constructors (the first) has the following syntax:

```
public BinaryReader(Stream input);
```

This constructor takes as argument a **Stream** value, which could be a **FileStream** object. After declaring a **FileStream** variable using this constructor, you can read data from it. To do this, you can call an appropriate method. This class provides an appropriate method for each primitive data type. BinaryReaderr contains several usable method which are listed in Listing 18.7.

Listing 18.7 BinaryReader methods.

Method	Description
Read()	This method r3eads a given set of bytes or characters and stores them in the incomming array.
Close()	This method closes the binary stream.
PeekChar()	This method returns the next available character without actually advancing the position in the stream.
ReadXXXX()	Reads numerous type data from the BinaryReader. For example, sbyte, byte, short ushort, int uint, long, ulong float, double char, string or an array of bytes and array of characters.

Let us consider the previous example which creates a **BinaryWriter** data file. Now, the following program demonstrates to read the data from **Emp.txt** binary data file usieng **BinaryReader** object.

..\CSharp_Book\Chap18\BinaryRead

```
using System;
using System.IO;

namespace BinaryRead
{
    class Program
    {
        static int Main()
        {
```

```
            // Creating employee data variables;
            int empcode;
            string empname;
            string empdesig;
            double empsalary;

            BinaryReader br;
            br = new BinaryReader(new FileStream(@"C:\Temp\Emp.txt", FileMode.Open));
            Console.WriteLine("Employees Information");
            for (int i = 0; i <= 40; i++)
                Console.Write("=");
            Console.WriteLine();

            // Condinue to read information in Emp.txt file
            try
            {
                while (true)
                {
                    empcode = br.ReadInt32();
                    empname = br.ReadString();
                    empdesig = br.ReadString();
                    empsalary = br.ReadDouble();
                    Console.WriteLine("Employee code = > " + empcode);
                    Console.WriteLine("Name => " + empname);
                    Console.WriteLine("Designation => " + empdesig);
                    Console.WriteLine("Salary =>" + empsalary);
                }
            }
            // Continue when End of file occur
            catch (EndOfStreamException)
            {
            }

            // If the file unable to read
            catch (IOException exc)
            {
                Console.WriteLine(exc.Message + "File read error.");
            }

            br.Close();
            return 0;
        }
    }
}
```

```
        bw.Write(emp.empsalary);

        bw.Flush();

        Console.WriteLine();
        Console.Write("Do U want to continue...");
        ch = (char)Console.Read();

        Console.ReadLine();
    }

    // Steps to display Employee information
    Console.WriteLine("Employees Information");
    for (int i = 0; i <= 70; i++)
        Console.Write("=");
    Console.WriteLine();

    // Condinue to read information in Emp.txt file
    Console.WriteLine("Code          Name          Designation       Salary");
    for (int i = 0; i <= 70; i++)
        Console.Write("=");
    Console.WriteLine();

    try
    {
        while (true)
        {
            emp.empcode = br.ReadInt32();
            emp.empname = br.ReadString();
            emp.empdesig = br.ReadString();
            emp.empsalary = br.ReadDouble();
            Console.WriteLine("{0}\t\t{1}\t\t{2}\t\t{3:F2}", emp.empcode,
                        emp.empname, emp.empdesig, emp.empsalary);
        }
    }

    // Continue when End of file occur
    catch (EndOfStreamException)
    {
        for (int i = 0; i <= 70; i++)
        Console.Write("=");
        Console.WriteLine();
    }
```

```
            // If the file unable to read
            catch (IOException exc)
            {
                Console.WriteLine(exc.Message + "File read error.");
            }

            bw.Close();
            br.Close();
            return 0;
        }
    }
}
```

18.11.4 Handling Class Information

The **BinaryWriter** class object can also write the user defined class information. Let us consider the **Employee** class as given :

```
public class Employee
{
    public int empcode;       // Data member
    public string empname;    //..........
    public string empdesig;   //..........
    public double empsalary;  //..........
}
```

Now, using the above class, data members can be writing and read through **BinaryWriter** and **BinaryReader** class object. The program as:

..\CSharp_Book\Chap18\FileClass

```
using System;
using System.IO;

namespace FileClass
{
    public class Employee
    {
        public int empcode;      // Data member
        public string empname;   //..........
        public string empdesig;  //..........
        public double empsalary; //..........
    }
```

Member	Description
Create()	Create a dire
CreateSubdirectory()	Create a
Delete()	Delet
GetDirectories()	Re in th
GetFiles()	Returns
Parent	Retrieves pa

```
class Program
{
    static int Main()
    {
        // Creating Employee structure object;
        Employee emp = new Employee(); // Object of type emp

        char ch = 'Y';

        // For data write
        BinaryWriter bw;
        bw = new BinaryWriter(new FileStream(@"C:\Temp\Emp.txt",
                    FileMode.Create));

        // For data read
        BinaryReader br;
        br = new BinaryReader(new FileStream(@"C:\Temp\Emp.txt", FileMode.Open));

        // Steps to write Employee information
        Console.WriteLine("Employee Console");
        Console.WriteLine();

        while ((ch == 'Y') || (ch == 'y'))
        {
            Console.Write("Employee code = > ");
            emp.empcode = int.Parse(Console.ReadLine());
            Console.Write("Name => ");
            emp.empname = Console.ReadLine();
            Console.Write("Designation => ");
            emp.empdesig = Console.ReadLine();
            Console.Write("Salary => ");
            emp.empsalary = double.Parse(Console.ReadLine());

            bw.Write(emp.empcode);
            bw.Write(emp.empname);
            bw.Write(emp.empdesig);
            bw.Write(emp.empsalary);
            bw.Flush();

            Console.WriteLine();
            Console.Write("Do U want to continue...");
            ch = (char)Console.Read();

            Console.ReadLine();
        }
```

```
        // Steps to display Employee information
        Console.WriteLine("Employees Information");
        for (int i = 0; i <= 70; i++)
            Console.Write("=");

        Console.WriteLine();
        // Condinue to read information in Emp.txt file
        Console.WriteLine("Code          Name          Designation     Salary");
        for (int i = 0; i <= 70; i++)
            Console.Write("=");
        Console.WriteLine();

        try
        {
            while (true)
            {
                emp.empcode = br.ReadInt32();
                emp.empname = br.ReadString();
                emp.empdesig = br.ReadString();
                emp.empsalary = br.ReadDouble();
                Console.WriteLine("{0}\t\t{1}\t\t{2}\t\t{3:F2}", emp.empcode,
                        emp.empname, emp.empdesig, emp.empsalary);
            }
        }

        // Continue when End of file occur
        catch (EndOfStreamException)
        {
            for (int i = 0; i <= 70; i++)
                Console.Write("=");
            Console.WriteLine();
        }

        // If the file unable to read
        catch (IOException exc)
        {
            Console.WriteLine(exc.Message + "File read error.");
        }

        // bw.Close();
        br.Close();
        return 0;
    }
  }
}
```

18.12 Random-Access Files

These files are stored in such a manner that it is possible to move pointer directly to any record in the file and read it without passing through any intervening records. These files can only be stored on discs. These files are preferable if you need to access only a few records in a file. For example, Bank account details.

Most random file records are fixed-length records. That is, each record (usually a row in the file) takes the same amount of disk space. When you are reading or writing sequentially, you have no need for fixed-length records because you input each value one character, word, string, or number at a time, looking for the data you want. With fixed-length records, your computer can better calculate exactly where the search record is located on the disk. Although you waste some disk space with fixed-length records (because of the space that had some of the fields), the advantages of random file access sometimes make up for the "wasted" disk space.

Till now, we have been using sequential files, which are files that accessed from beginning to till end (linear manner), one byte after another. But, C# also allows you to access the contents of a file in random order. C# has a special method **Seek()** defined in **FileStream** class object. This method allows you to set the file position indicator (also called the file pointer) to any point within a file. The method is:

```
long Seek(long position, SeekOrigin origin);
```

Here,

- The **position** is the number of bytes in the file you want to skip, C# then does not read these many bytes but literally skips the data by the number of bytes specified in position. Skipping the bytes on the disk is much faster than reading them. If position is negative, C# skips backward in the file (enabling you to read data several times). Because data files can be large, you must declare position as a long integer to hold a large amount of bytes.
- The **origin** is a value that tells C# where to begin the skipping of bytes specified by position. The origin can be any of the three values shown in Listing 18.8.

Listing 18.8 Position of stream in file.

Value	Description
SeekOrigin.Begin	Seek from the beginning of the file.
SeekOrigin .Current	Seek from the current file position of the file.
vSeekOrigin .End	Seek from the end of the file.

While seeking the record from a file, it may produce two types of exceptions.

- If an error occurs while seeking, an **IOException** is thrown.
- If the underlying stream does not support position requests, a **NotSupportedException** is thrown.

18.12.1 Writing Data Randomly

For random access files, C# does not impose structure on files, so applications that use random-access files must implement the random-access capability. There are a variety of techniques for creating random-access files. Perhaps the simplest involves requiring that all records in a file be a uniform, fixed length. The use of fixed-length records enables a program to calculate (as a function of the record size and the record key) the exact location of any record in relation to the beginning of the file. For example, consider the following **EmployeeRecord** class:

```
public class EmployeeRecord
{
    // Length of employee name and designation
    public const int CHAR_ARRAY_LENGTH = 20;

    public const int SIZE_OF_CHAR = 2;
    public const int SIZE_OF_INT32 = 4;
    public const int SIZE_OF_DOUBLE = 8;

    // Length of record
    public const int SIZE = SIZE_OF_INT32 + 2 * (SIZE_OF_CHAR * CHAR_ARRAY_LENGTH)
                                              + SIZE_OF_DOUBLE;

    public int empcode;    // Data member
    public char[] empname = new char[CHAR_ARRAY_LENGTH];
    public char[] empdesig = new char[CHAR_ARRAY_LENGTH];
    public double empsalary;   // . . . . . . . .
}
```

From above declaration, the **EmployeeRecord** contains public data mebers for storing record information. However, class **EmployeeRecord** does not contain attributes [Serializable] before its class definition. We do not serialize this class, because C# does not provide a means to obtain an object's size at runtime. This means that, if we serialize the class, we cannot guarantee a fixed-length record size.

Instread of serializing the class, we fix the length of the public data members, then write those data as a byte stream to the file. To fix length we use fixed size array for character data and others. The **SIZE** variable hold the total size of a fixed length record. The const **SIZE**, which specifies the record's length.

Thus, the complete program is as :

..\CSharp_Book\Chap18\RandomFile

```
using System;
using System.IO;

namespace RandomFile
```

```
{
    public class EmployeeRecord
    {
        // Length of employee name and designation
        public const int CHAR_ARRAY_LENGTH = 20;

        public const int SIZE_OF_CHAR = 2;
        public const int SIZE_OF_INT32 = 4;
        public const int SIZE_OF_DOUBLE = 8;

        // Length of record
        public const int SIZE = SIZE_OF_INT32 + 2 *
                        (SIZE_OF_CHAR * CHAR_ARRAY_LENGTH) + SIZE_OF_DOUBLE;

        public int empcode;     // Data member
        public char[] empname = new char[CHAR_ARRAY_LENGTH];
        public char[] empdesig = new char[CHAR_ARRAY_LENGTH];
        public double empsalary; // . . . . . . . . .
    }
    class Program
    {
        static int Main()
        {
            // Creating Employee structure object;
            EmployeeRecord emp = new EmployeeRecord(); // Object of type emp

            char ch = 'Y';
            string s1, s2;
            FileStream fs = new FileStream(@"C:\Temp\Emp.txt",
                            FileMode.Create, FileAccess.Write);

            BinaryWriter bw = new BinaryWriter(fs);

            // Steps to write Employee information
            Console.WriteLine("Employee Console");
            Console.WriteLine();

            while ((ch == 'Y') || (ch == 'y'))
            {
                Console.Write("Employee code = > ");
                emp.empcode = int.Parse(Console.ReadLine());
                Console.Write("Name => ");
                s1 = Console.ReadLine();
                s1.CopyTo(0, emp.empname, 0, s1.Length);
```

```
            Console.Write("Designation => ");
            s2 = Console.ReadLine();
            s2.CopyTo(0, emp.empdesig, 0, s2.Length);
            Console.Write("Salary => ");
            emp.empsalary = double.Parse(Console.ReadLine());
            if (emp.empcode > 0)
            {
                bw.Seek((emp.empcode - 1) *
                        EmployeeRecord.SIZE, SeekOrigin.Begin);
                bw.Write(emp.empcode);
                bw.Write(emp.empname);
                bw.Write(emp.empdesig);
                bw.Write(emp.empsalary);
                bw.Flush();
            }
            Console.WriteLine();
            Console.Write("Do U want to continue...");
            ch = (char)Console.Read();
            Console.ReadLine();
        }

        bw.Close();
        return 0;
    }
  }
}
```

From above program, each record contains empcode, empname, empdesig (two 20-element char array) where each car occupies two byttes, resulting in a total of 80 bytes) and an empsalary (8-byte double). Also, each record (i.e., the four public data members that our program will read to and write from files) occupies 92 (4 butes + 80 bytes + 8 bytes) data.

When you execute the above program, the data will write randomly into **Emp.txt** file. Because, each time the **Seek** of the **FileStream** object will locate an extra position (point) in the file. That is, the method Seek sets the position of the file-position pointer for the **FileStream** object to the byte location calculated by **(emp.empcode - 1) * EmployeeRecord.SIZE** or you may take any other method.

```
bw.Seek((emp.empcode - 1) * EmployeeRecord.SIZE, SeekOrigin.Begin);
```

We use const **SeekOrigin.Begin**, because we want the method to seek in relation to the beginning of the file. After the program determines the file location at which to place the record the lines,

```
bw.Write(emp.empcode);
bw.Write(emp.empname);
bw.Write(emp.empdesig);
bw.Write(emp.empsalary);
```

write the record to the file using the method Write of the **BinaryWriter** object to write the data as has discussed earlier.

18.13 Working with Directories and Files

The **System.IO** namespace includes a set of system-related classes are used to manage files and directories. As you have already seen the heirarcy of Directories and Files in Fig. 18.1, some of the classes objects are shown in Fig. 18.10.

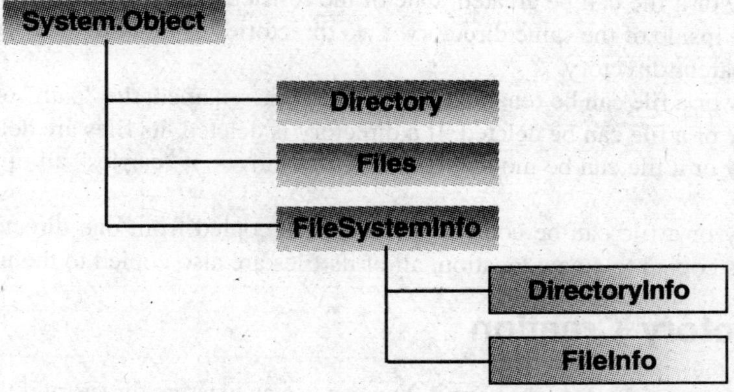

Fig. 18.10 Directory and File classes in the System.IO namespace.

Directory and **DirectoryInfo** contain members to create, delete and query directories. The only significant difference in the two is that you use **Directory** with static methods, whereas a **DirectoryInfo** object must be created to use instance methods. In a parallel manner, **File** and **FileInfo** provide static and instance methods for working with file.

18.13.1 FileSystemInfo Class

The **FileSystemInfo** class is a base class for **DirectoryInfo** and **FileInfo**. It defines a range members that are used primarily to provide information about a file or directory. The abstrack **FileSystemInfo** class takes advantage of the fact that files and directories share common features. Its properties includes **CreationTime**, **LastAccessTime**, **LastWriteTime**, **Name** and **FullName**. It also includes tow ikportant methods: **Delete** to delete a file or directory and **Refresh** that updates the latest file and directory information.

18.14 Working with Directories

A directory is a section of a medium used to delimit a group of files. Because it is a "physical" area, it can handle operations not available on files. In fact, there are many fundamental differences between both:

- A file is used to contain data. A directory doesn't contain data
- A directory can contain one or more files and not vice-versa
- A directory can contain other directories
- A file can be moved from one directory to another. This operation is not possible vice-versa since a file cannot contain a directory

The similarities of both types are:

- A directory or a file can be created. One of the restrictions is that two files cannot have the same name inside of the same directory. Two directories cannot have the same name inside of the same parent directory.
- A directory or a file can be renamed. If a directory is renamed, the "path" of its file(s) changes
- A directory or a file can be deleted. If a directory is deleted, its files are deleted also
- A directory or a file can be moved. If a directory moves, it "carries" all of its files to the new location
- A directory or a file can be copied. A file can be copied from one directory to another. If a directory is copied to a new location, all of its files are also copied to the new location

18.14.1 Directory Creation

Before using a directory, you must first have it. You can use an existing directory if the operating system or someone else had already created one. You can also create a new directory. Directories are created and managed by various classes but the fundamental class is **Directory**. **Directory** is a static class, which means all of its methods are static, which means you will never need to declare an instance of the Directory class in order to use it.

Besides the **Directory** class, additional operations of folders and sub-folders can be performed using the **DirectoryInfo** class. The DirectoryInfo class has the following methods listed in Listing 18.9.

Listing 18.9 DirectoryInfo class member methods.

Member	Description
Create()	Create a directory.
CreateSubdirectory()	Create a subdirectory.
Delete()	Delete a directory.
GetDirectories()	Returns an array of DirectoryInfo type containing all subdirectories in the current directory.
GetFiles()	Returns an array of FileInfo types contains all files in the directory.
Parent	Retrieves parent directory of current path.

Similarly, the **Directory** class contains number of member methods for handling directories as listed in Listing 18.10.

Listing 18.10 Directory class member methods.

Member	Description
CreateDirectory()	Pass the string path to the method. Failure results in an exception.
Delete(string)	Deletes an empty directory.
Delete(string, bool)	Deletes a directory and all subdirectories if Boolean value is true.
GetDirectories(string)	Returns a string array containing the names of directories in the path.
GetParent()	Retrieves parent directory of specified path.
GetLogicalDrives()	Returns string containing logical drives on system.

To create a directory, you can call the **CreateDirectory()** method of the **Directory** class. This method is available in two versions. One of the versions uses the following syntax:

```
public static DirectoryInfo CreateDirectry(string path);
```

The following example shows some of **FileSystemInfo** members using **DirectoryInfo** and **FileInfo** objects. Also helps to create a subdirectory.

..\CSharp_Book\Chap18\DirInfo

```
using System;
using System.IO;
using System.Collections.Generic;
using System.Text;

namespace DirInfo
{
    class Program
    {
        static void Main()
        {
            // DirectoryInfo
            string dirInf = @"C:\Temp";
            DirectoryInfo d = new DirectoryInfo(dirInf);

            d.Refresh();

            DateTime dateCreate = d.CreationTime;
```

```
            Console.WriteLine("{0:d}", dateCreate);

            // FileInfo
            string file = @"c:\temp\emp.txt";
            FileInfo fi = new FileInfo(file);
            if (fi.Exists)
            {
                fi.Refresh();
                dateCreate = fi.CreationTime;
                Console.WriteLine(dateCreate); // Show the date and time
                Console.WriteLine(fi.Name); // Show the name of the file
                Console.WriteLine(fi.Extension); // Show the extension of the file
                Console.WriteLine(fi.Attributes); // Show the file archieve mode
            }

            // Directory static method to create a directory in C:\Temp
            string newPath = @"C:\Temp";
            if (!Directory.Exists(newPath))
                Directory.CreateDirectory(newPath); // Checks the path to create directory

            // DirectoryInfo
            string curPath = @"C:\Temp\ss1";
            d = new DirectoryInfo(curPath);
            if (d.Exists)
                d.CreateSubdirectory(newPath);

        }
    }
}
```

18.14.3 Directories and Files

As like to create directories, we can also list directories and files. The files has also number of characteristics like :

- **The Date and Time a File Was Created.** To keep track of it, after a file has been created, the operating system makes a note of the date and the time the file was created. This information can be valuable in other operations such as search routines. You too are allowed to change this date and time values to those you prefer.

As mentioned already, the OS makes sure to keep track of the date and time a file was created. To find out what those date and time values are, you can access the **FileSystemInfo.get_CreationTime()** property is. This would be done as follows:

```
DateTime dteCreationTime = fleLoan.CreationTime;
MessageBox.Show("Date and Time Created: " + dteCreationTime.ToString());
```

Of course, by entering the appropriate format in the parentheses of the **ToString()** method, you can get only either the date or only the time.

If you don't like the date, the time, or both, that the OS would have set when the file was created, you can change them. To change one or both of these values, you can assign a desired **DateTime** object to the **FileSystemInfo.set_CreationTime()** property.

- **The Date and Time a File Was Last Accessed.** Many applications allow a user to open an existing file and to modify it. When people work in a team or when a particular file is regularly opened, at one particular time, you may want to know the date and time that the file was last accessed. To get this information, you can access the **FileSystemInfo.LastAccessTime** property.

If you are interested in know the last date and time a file was modified, you can get the value of its **FileSystemInfo.LastWriteTime** property. You can also change this value if you want to make sure the file holds your own.

- **The Name of a File.** The operating system requires that each file have a name. In fact, the name must be specified when creating a file. This allows the OS to catalogue the computer files. This also allows you to locate or identify a particular file you need.

When reviewing or opening a file, to get its name, the **FileInfo** class is equipped with the **Name** property. Here is an example:

```
MessageBox.Show("The name of this file is: \" " + fleIn.Name + "\"");
```

- **The Extension of a File.** With the advent of Windows 95 and later, the user doesn't have to specify the extension of a file when creating it. Because of the type of confusions that this can lead to, most applications assist the user with this detail. For example, when we implemented the routines that allow the user to save or open a file, we specified a default extension for the Save Dialog or the Open Dialog objects. This allows the user not to care for the extension. Based on this, some applications allow the user to choose among various extensions. For example, using Notepad, a user can open a text, a PHP, a script, or an HTML file.

When you access a file or when the user opens one, to know the extension of the file, you can access the value of the **FileSystemInfo.Extension** property. Here is an example:

```
MessageBox.Show("File Extension: " + fleIn.Extension);
```

- **The Size of a File.** One of the routine operations the operating system performs consists of calculation the size of files it holds. This information is provided in terms of bits, kilobits, or kilobytes. To get the size of a file, the **FileInfo** class is quipped with the **Length** property. Here is an example of accessing it:

```
MessageBox.Show("File Size: " + fleIn.Length.ToString());
```

- **The Path to a File.** Besides the name of the file, it must be located somewhere. The location of a file is referred to as its path or directory. The **FileInfo** class represents this path as the **DirectoryName** property. Therefore, if a file has already been created, to get its path, you can access the value of the **FileInfo.DirectoryName** property.

Besides the **FileInfo.Directoryname**, to know the full path to a file, you can access its **FileSystemInfo.FullName** property.

- **The Attributes of a File.** Attributes are characteristics that apply to a file, defining what can be done or must be disallowed on it. The Attributes are primarily defined by, and in, the operating system, mostly when a file is created. When the user accessed or open a file, to get its attributes, you can access the value of its **FileSystemInfo.get_Attributes()** property. This property produces a **FileAttributes** object.

When you create or access a file, you can specify or change some of the attributes. To do this, you can a **FileAttributes** object and assign it to the **FileSystemInfo.set_Attributes()** property.

FileAttributes is an enumerator with the following members: **Archive, Compressed, Device, Directory, Encrypted, Hidden, Normal, NotContentIndexed, Offline, ReadOnly, ReparsePoint, SparseFile, System,** and **Temporary**.

Exercise

1. What is text file and binary file?
2. Name two input and output unformatted stream.
3. What is System.IO namespace?
4. What is Stream? Name any two Stream class objects.
5. Differentiate between Stream and FileStream.
6. Explain any two methods of FileStream class.
7. Name the methods to open and close a FileStream.
8. Write the step to check a file existence.
9. Differentiate between StreamWriter and StringWriter.
10. Differentiate between StreamReader and StringReader.
11. What is the use of SeekOrigin method.

Programming

1. Create a text file STUD.TXT containing student rollno, name, class, total marks, percentage and grade.
2. Write a program to read the STUD.TXT contents of Qno. 1.
3. Using StreamWriter and StreamReader, perfrom the operation of Qno. 1 and 2.
4. Using BinaryWriter and BinaryReader, perfrom the operation of Qno. 1 and 2.
5. Create a random file containing the information of Qno. 1.